Teaching Civic Engagement:

From Student to Active Citizen

Alison Rios Millett McCartney

Elizabeth A. Bennion

Dick Simpson

editors

AMERICAN POLITICAL SCIENCE ASSOCIATION

STATE OF THE PROFESSION SERIES

Photo Credits:

Photos courtesy of Alec Hosterman: Cover, pages 1, 7, 99, 105, 124, 406, 447.

Photos courtesy of Stephanie Whitaker, UIC National Student Issues Convention 2011: pages 331 and 335.

Photo courtesy of Caterina Stratakis: page 370.

Photo courtesy of Matthew Kaplan, taken for *LAS ATLAS* magazine, January 2012: page 403.

ISBN 978-1-878147-40-0

For all teacher-scholars seeking to improve
civic engagement education

TABLE OF CONTENTS

Section III: Incorporating Civic Engagement into the Curriculum and Beyond

Section IV: Assessing Civic Engagement Objectives and Outcomes

Conclusion

Tables and Figures

Tables

Figures

FOREWORD

The American Political Science Association (APSA) has had an interest in civic education from its founding, and attention to civic education has cycled in and out throughout the association's history. Association founders were motivated from its earliest days by a sense of purpose to improve the functional workings of government and strengthen the operation of democracy. Neglect of civic learning was thought to have weakened both.

This concern with civic health has stayed with us today with many new dimensions and nuances, but also with a nagging doubt. We know today that the benefits of civic learning extend beyond the effective and efficient workings of government institutions to private and quasi-public organizations as well. We know that the density and character of civil society has advantages that reach beyond individual civic behavior alone. We know that the practice of civic effort through service learning, simulations, and internships can bring lifelong benefits for the development of citizenry. There is broad agreement that civic engagement is a social responsibility, but it has become less certain whether it is a professional or disciplinary responsibility.

The work in this volume represents a rich collection of research and innovative pedagogy that helps reaffirm APSA's voice in civic engagement education and advances and reshapes the commitment with which the association began. This work does not stand alone. In the last 15 years, APSA has redoubled its commitment to civic education and engagement. This volume emerges in tandem with the intellectual laboratory of APSA's annual Teaching and Learning Conference, the work of its committees on teaching and learning and on civic education and engagement, the sponsorship of the Alma Ostrom and Leah Hopkins Awan Civic Education Fund of the APSA Centennial Center, and more. The appearance of this volume parallels other APSA work on the structural issues challenging civic life—major studies and task force reports on the ways in which institutional designs for public life and inequalities in social structures and opportunities can impede civic engagement regardless of how well-educated or informed citizens are.

The relation between public life and political science as a profession and scholarly pursuit is marked by many disputes and challenges. Early emphasis in the discipline looked to a public connection in a variety of ways—whether focused on explicit training for government service or on community formation and neighborhood democracy. At various stages in its history the discipline has withdrawn from these emphases. Some would say that public service morphed into scholasticism, that a neighborhood and civic focus withdrew into academic and public institutionalism, and that learning about how to engage in society retracted into teaching about how to analyze society.

Political scientists have wrestled with the concerns that civic education and civic learning are distractions or digressions from our roles as scholars and teachers—as though being asked to be of service is to diminish scholarship. This is not the only topic on which we have this debate. We puzzle over whether it is warranted to focus scholarship on relevance of public policy or "national needs" rather than on knowing for its own sake. We question how, or even whether, the public sector should fund our work. We wonder whether science can meaningfully ground our scholarship, or whether we should turn as well to other, perhaps more-localized ways of knowing in the interpretation of knowledge. We ask whether scholarship can be, or ought to be, of use. The question of teaching civic engagement in the end is no different from questions of the relation of political or social science to public policy-making or national needs, and each effort to understand the role of the discipline can inform the other.

It is a mistake, however, to see attention to teaching civic engagement or to the scholarship of teaching and learning as being in opposition to academic scholarship or teaching or learning for its own sake. The teacher-scholar speaks with a special voice that is protected and shaped by the principles of academic freedom. This autonomy to speak truthfully comes with accountability to peers and through them to the integrity of research findings and scholarly thinking. Scholarship, teaching, and service strengthen each other. Together, they reinforce the principles that sustain academic freedom—principles that call for scholars to hold themselves accountable and carry out work that is in the end of good use. Teaching civic engagement, grounded in strong scholarship, thus provides full value both to society and to the discipline.

Themes addressed in this volume then are not just about civics and citizenship. They also amplify a rich debate about the character of the scholarly enterprise itself and its place in society and thus illuminate what the discipline of political science itself can become.

We owe a large debt of gratitude to the scholars who contributed to this book for their own acts of civic engagement in offering the time and thoughtfulness to produce this work. Their work revives an old tradition in political science. They put forward tested and principled strategies for civic engagement, and offer us a pathway for an engaged political science.

Michael Brintnall
January 2013

PREFACE

I am excited that APSA is publishing this book, as it marks the culmination of more than a decade of work by political scientists. While not directly sponsored by APSA, one of the initial volumes to be published in the American Association of Higher Education's Service-Learning in the Disciplines series was in political science.[1] In addition, in 2000, under the leadership of Sheilah Mann, APSA launched a "Service-Learning in Political Science" webpage, produced a special issue of *PS: Political Science & Politics* with the same title, and initiated a series of workshops and panels at its annual and regional meetings—part of an effort to involve disciplinary associations in service-learning and civic engagement funded by the Pew Charitable Trusts and Campus Compact. Some of the faculty who participated in these initial activities have written chapters included in this volume.

Although this work is only 15 years old, the effort to link community-based experiences with academic learning has a long history. Political science internships and other experiences outside the classroom connected to the academic curriculum date back to the origins of the discipline more than a century ago. With roots that include thinkers like John Dewey and programs begun during the 1960s and 1970s, a concerted effort has been made by colleges and universities for almost 30 years to engage students in the larger community as part of their learning. In this Preface, I concentrate on this more recent history, dating back to the 1980s, which has been called different things at different times by different people: "community (or national) service," "service-learning" (with and without the hyphen), "community-based learning (or research)," and "civic (or political) engagement."

This movement was certainly aided by the formation of the Campus Outreach Opportunities League (COOL)—a student-run organization—in 1984 and Campus Compact—an organization of college and university presidents—in 1985. With the support of these two organizations, institutions of higher education began to explicitly link experiential pedagogies to the burgeoning student community service movement of the 1980s. Most programming during this period aimed simply to place undergraduate students in community-based service activities—many of these led by students themselves—in the hopes that such community service would stem the documented tide in young people toward civic *dis*engagement and what was perceived as an "excessive individualism."[2] The primary language for these campus efforts was "community service," and campus efforts ranged from providing more service opportunities to adopting service requirements for graduation.

By the end of the 1980s, campuses had become more aware of service-learning as a pedagogy linking service with academic study and the formal curriculum. With a 1989 Wingspread conference sponsored by the Johnson Foundation and the National Society for Experiential Education's subsequent three-volume publication, *Combining Service and Learning*,[3] awareness of service-learning both as a pedagogy and a means of civic education began to spread through both the higher education and K-12 educational communities. By 1992, the federal government's Learn and Serve America program—which lost its funding as part of the 2011 congressional budget deal—was providing funding resources for service-learning initiatives in higher education. Then in 1993, the Corporation for National Service's definition of service-learning was revised to include the goal of "foster[ing] civic responsibility."

Thus began a period of "institutionalization" of service-learning, whereby colleges and universities pumped resources into their service-learning infrastructure, supporting campus-based service or community engagement centers, providing faculty development for the growth of this new pedagogy, and cultivating community partnerships that could sustain growing efforts to link campus and neighborhood resources. Although there was criticism of this institutionalization, both in terms of the reduction of student leadership and the limited impact on communities,[4] the growth of service-learning was spectacular: Campus Compact went from an organization of five presidents in 1985 to more than 900 by the end of the century. By this point, the primary language used to describe this work had shifted from "community service" to "service-learning."

By the end of the 20th century, however, the leaders of this movement to connect campus with community began to call for another change in emphasis. A number of studies in the late 1990s showed that there was a huge disconnect between students actively involved in community service and indicators of political and civic engagement. Data were beginning to suggest that while more and more college-age youth were volunteering, fewer and fewer were voting or getting involved in politics or political issues. In fact, many studies suggested that students were consciously choosing community service *over* political engagement, as volunteering became an alternative to involvement in politics. One study, sponsored by the Kettering Foundation, charged that higher education "appears to leave students without concepts or language to explore what is political about their lives."[5] Harry Boyte concluded that "community service is not a cure for young people's political apathy" because "it teaches little about the arts of participation in public life."[6]

In 1999, Campus Compact issued a document coauthored by Boyte and Elizabeth Hollander. The *Presidents' Declaration on the Civic Responsibility of Higher Education* called on colleges and universities "to renew our role as agents of our democracy, [to] catalyze and lead a national movement to reinvigorate the public purposes and civic mission of higher education."[7] Subsequently, the language used to describe this work shifted again, from "service-learning" to "civic engagement." The new focus was to use service-learning and other community-based experiences to strengthen the civic learning of students and the public problem–solving capacities of institutions of higher education.[8]

There have been problems, however, with this approach. First, the term "civic engagement" is fairly amorphous and has been used to mean many different things. That is one of the reasons why it has been so popular, as it can be used to describe different kinds of activities and can be incorporated into the conceptual framework of most disciplines. Another problem has been that campuses have not changed their practices to align with the concept of civic engagement, as opposed to service-learning or community service. Service-learning most often means limited volunteer work, such as distributing meals at a soup kitchen, whereas civic engagement usually means a longer-term involvement and, often, an attempt to solve the problems that a community faces. Finally, and most importantly for this volume, the language of civic engagement often was used to avoid delving directly into politics, public policy, and political engagement. Political engagement requires involvement in political campaigns or government policy making.

To address this last issue, in 2003 Anne Colby, Thomas Ehrlich, Elizabeth Beaumont, and their colleagues at the Carnegie Foundation for the Advancement of Teaching launched an effort to bridge the "serious gap" between college civic engagement efforts and education for political engagement in a democracy. The Political Engagement Project, discussed in more detail in Chapter 3, brought together practitioners representing 21 different higher education programs aimed at developing the political knowledge, skills, motivation, and identity of college students. Emerging from this initiative were new conceptual frameworks and ongoing projects for thinking about political education, experiential learning, and the role of colleges and universities in developing the political capacities of democratic citizens.[9] One of the projects developed at this time was the American Democracy Project of the American Association of State Colleges and Universities (AASCU).

This volume, which has been a long time coming, owes its existence to a long line of efforts to educate for political engagement. It contains an impressive array of contributors from a discipline that should have, but has not always had, its central focus on the civic and political learning of students. The chapters range from theoretical treatises on the connections between political science as a discipline and civic, or political, engagement as a goal of higher education, to more practical narratives of how to incorporate political engagement into courses from all the subfields of the discipline. The book also includes an assessment toolkit, which provides practical suggestions to assess the outcomes of the efforts to engage students in the political process. Through assessment, teaching and service can be incorporated into a research enterprise that expands the collective knowledge about the best ways to engage students and strengthen democracy.

All of this leaves me quite hopeful. Hopeful that members of the American Political Science Association will read this volume and develop a new understanding of their own work and its connection to the crucial goal of citizen engagement. Hopeful that APSA will continue to see the development of engaged citizens as one of its central missions. And hopeful that political science as a discipline will lead the way in reinvigorating the active participation of American citizens, and with it, the revival of American democracy itself.

Richard Battistoni
Providence College
2013

ACKNOWLEDGEMENTS

The editors would like to thank the many people whose efforts contributed to the completion of this book. Michael Brintnall, APSA Executive Director, provided key support to the project's development. Elizabeth Matto of the Eagleton Institute is graciously serving as online editor of the book's supplemental material, which we hope our readers will consult. Polly Karpowicz, APSA Director of Communications and Publishing, and her staff Betsy Schroeder and Anastasia Fete who guided every aspect of the book. The Civic Education and Engagement Committee of APSA gave us useful feedback at the beginning of the project, and an anonymous reviewer made thoughtful, considered comments that have greatly improved the final manuscript. Our skilled copyeditor, Lorna Notsch, carefully reviewed every page. As with every project of this level, student assistants help with many needs, great and small, and we would like to thank Hannah Dill, Anneliese Johnson, and Missy Zmuda. Jeremy and DeAnna Millett of Millett Indexing provided expert assistance in the final hours.

The editors also would like to thank the University of Illinois at Chicago; the Indiana University South Bend Research and Development Committee; and Towson University's Dean of the College of Liberal Arts office, Political Science Department, International Studies program, and Faculty Research and Development Committee for financial support of the research and writing of this volume. Finally, we want to thank our families for their unending patience, especially in the final months of the project.

SECTION I

Higher Education, Civic Engagement Pedagogy, and Political Science Education

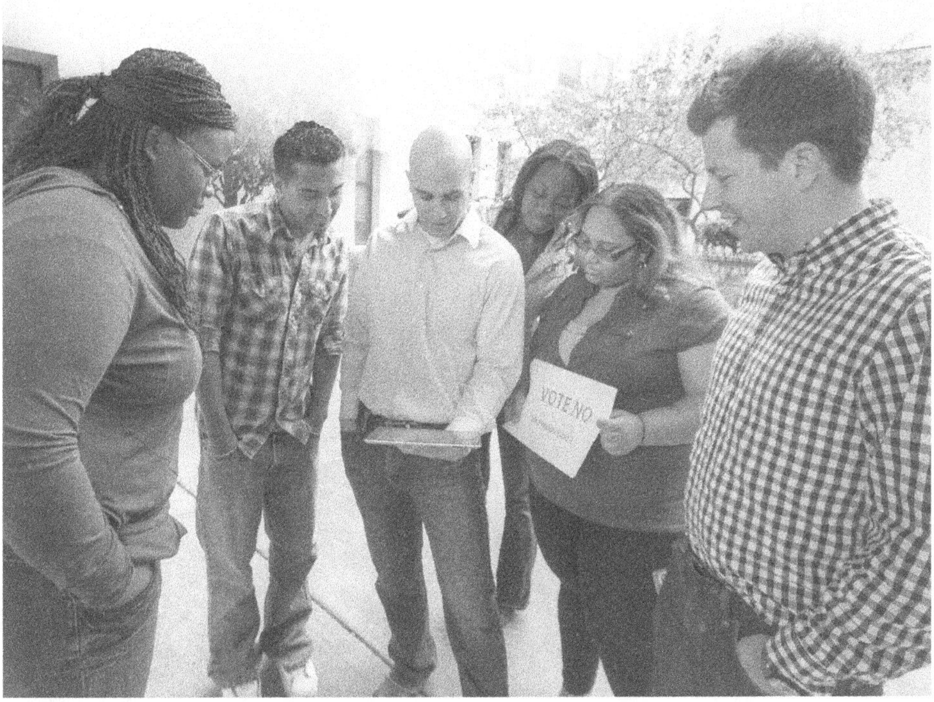

Introduction to Section I

Higher Education, Civic Engagement Pedagogy, and Political Science Education

This section explores civic and political engagement pedagogy for colleges and universities as a whole and for political science as an academic discipline. Each chapter provides a unique link in this chain, moving from theoretical debates to societal actors to roles of teacher-scholars. Overall, the authors argue in favor of a more prominent place for civic engagement education in higher education and demonstrate why political scientists should be more active in fostering students' abilities to be civically engaged citizens.

Alison McCartney reminds political scientists that the debates over the role of higher education institutions and the political science discipline in civic engagement are hardly new. Twenty-first–century education standards, however, and societal expectations have changed. She argues that political scientists should now act upon our pedagogical interest in fostering civically engaged citizens. This goal is described in the report issued in January 2012 by the National Task Force on Civic Learning and Democratic Engagement, a joint project of the US Department of Education and the American Association of Colleges and Universities (AACU). In *A Crucible Moment: College Learning and Democracy's Future*, the AACU argues that higher education institutions must take the following "essential actions":

1. Reclaim and reinvest in the fundamental civic and democratic mission of schools and of all sectors within higher education.

2. Enlarge the current national narrative that erases civic aims and civic literacy as educational priorities contributing to social, intellectual, and economic capital.

3. Advance a contemporary, comprehensive framework for civic learning—embracing US and global interdependence—that includes historic and modern understandings of democratic values, capacities to engage diverse perspectives and people, and commitment to collective civic problem solving.

4. Capitalize upon the interdependent responsibilities of K-12 and higher education to foster progressively higher levels of civic knowledge, skills, examined values, and action as expectations for every student.

5. Expand the number of robust, generative civic partnerships and alliances, locally, nationally, and globally to address common problems, empower people to act, strengthen communities and nations, and generate new frontiers of knowledge.

These actions dovetail with the arguments, evidence, and examples presented in this book and align with its primary goals of fostering civically engaged citizens and providing quality political science instruction.

Support from societal and governmental actors is crucial to the ability of colleges and universities to achieve these goals. However, challenges remain. McCartney argues that to really move civic engagement education forward, the reward and incentive structures in higher education must be changed, starting with the current systems of promotion, tenure, and merit. These systems currently are dominated by a view that traditional scholarship of discovery in a particular subfield is the standard of measurement for one's value to academia, rather than one's understanding of, innovations in, and research on quality teaching. While traditional scholarship should not be displaced in favor of the scholarship of teaching and learning (SoTL), this book seeks a more prominent place for SoTL research as an equally important part of academic inquiry.

To advance SoTL's place in academia, political scientists need to take responsibility for demonstrating what exactly we are doing, how we are doing it, and the outcomes that follow. In Chapter 2, Brian Harward and Dan Shea explain that political scientists need to create learning opportunities that move students beyond what the authors refer to as "drive-by" participation in their communities and the polity. These quick-and-easy forms of participation, such as signing petitions or posting online, are useful, but they are not enough to keep democracy alive and thriving. They do not entail much risk of encountering major disagreement, disappointment, or failure, but the democratic system of the United States was not built upon quick answers, easy debates, and episodic work. It was created with checks on popular passions, balances against tyranny, and hard-won compromise. Harward and Shea propose that political scientists must prepare students for the complicated system of democracy and focus civic engagement education on developing a deeper sense of commitment among students, one that can withstand an election loss or a bill's veto. They provide examples of how to reach this goal by making students take responsibility for their own development through more engaged learning rather than allowing them to pass by on surface knowledge that creates drive-by citizens.

Elizabeth Beaumont continues this theme through her discussion of the Carnegie Foundation's Political Engagement Project (PEP). This project found that some approaches to civic engagement pedagogy increase political understanding, civic engagement skills, and civic and political involvement without politically indoctrinating students to their instructors' political views. This last point is crucial in advancing this pedagogy. The intention is not to brainwash students with any one party's view of what government should or should not do; rather, it is to show them why their diverse voices are necessary in a well-functioning democracy. Political science educators can help students to learn how they can affect change when they do not agree with what their government is doing.

In the Carnegie Foundation study of about 1,000 undergraduates in 21 different political courses and programs, the researchers began with a presurvey of participants so that a baseline was established. This survey explored students' levels of political understanding, including foundational political knowledge and current events knowledge; political motivation, including political interest, political media attention, political identity, political values, and sense of personal and institutional political efficacy; civic and political skills for political influence, action, collaboration, analysis, leadership, and communication; and civic and political involvement. At the end of the courses and programs, the study found in the postsurvey that students made significant gains in knowledge, skills, and sense of political efficacy and exhibited an increased interest in politics. Yet, students did not make major changes in their political ideologies or affiliations as a group. This evidence is important because civic engagement pedagogy does not support any particular political party, although it is certainly in favor of democracy writ large.

Beaumont also addresses how political scientists can most effectively teach civic and political engagement. She discusses how to increase a sense of efficacy—the necessary attribute of civically engaged citizens. The Carnegie Foundation proposes four learning mechanisms to achieve this goal: experiencing a politically active community, acquiring political action skills, engaging in political discourse in an open and respectful atmosphere, and participating in pluralist collaborative contexts. The first mechanism can actually fix the disadvantages experienced by students who were not raised in politically active or aware families and communities by providing an alternative, supportive, and politically active community.

The Carnegie Foundation also found that teaching political action skills was "the single most important factor for shaping development of political efficacy." By learning and practicing how to put their ideas into action, students gained the necessary confidence to become civically engaged. Moreover, political discussions in open and respectful communities not only increased political knowledge, they also taught students how politics is relevant to their lives and how their political opinions and judgments matter in actual political decisions. This component of political socialization is particularly significant in youth development as political discussion and engagement becomes normalized within their communities.

Finally, the Carnegie Foundation found that students in collaborative and racially pluralist contexts learned how to navigate their differences, overcome anxieties and negative predispositions, and thus feel more able to find ways to bring change and solve problems. Overall, the foundation demonstrated that civic engagement education, properly designed and executed, can reduce inequalities in family and community backgrounds that may hinder a student's ability to become an effectively engaged citizen and thus reduce the "democratic achievement gap."

Beaumont's work connects directly to Bobbi Gentry's exploration of youth political identity. Gentry explains how understanding of the self in the political realm, or political ego identity, leads to civic engagement. Steeped in political socialization literature, this discussion of how and why one internalizes identity as a civically engaged person can help political scientists work toward fostering a civic engagement identity among those students still in the identity development stage of life. Gentry argues that once this identity is developed and takes root through experience, knowledge, and practice, students are more likely to engage in behaviors that continually reconfirm that identity. Since the college years are when this political ego identity is most likely to be consolidated within an individual's overall identity, it is also the period when instructors have an opportunity to work within the developmental processes to secure political ego identity. These processes are, according to Gentry, socialization, exploration, judgment of others, self-questioning, and coherence. By considering these processes from a psychological development perspective, she offers an additional dimension of understanding how socialization and identity processes work so that a better understanding of why students do or do not become civically engaged citizens after graduation can be achieved. She invites the use of this information to construct more effective civic engagement pedagogy during students' formative years to help to establish a firm foundation for lifelong democratic engagement.

Most colleges and universities claim a commitment to students' development as citizens, but as Jean Harris shows, they do not always follow through on these declarations. Harris explores how colleges and universities have not always fulfilled their obligations under federal legislation, such as the 1998 Higher Education Act and the 2002 Help Americans Vote Act college program. These federal mandates suggest significant government concern about low voter registration, especially among youth. As political scientists, Harris argues, we should work to dismantle such institutional barriers as voting registration rules, processes, and staff that may prevent or discourage students from becoming registered voters—a basic form of civic engagement.

Paul Frank examines the potential for college instructors to affect their students' civic engagement, first, as role models who practice what they preach and second, as insiders with unique knowledge about political participation to deliver to students. He argues that, overall, instructors should not shy away from being politically engaged themselves or bringing that experience into the classroom. He explores four hypotheses about which factors lead political science instructors to model political engagement for their students. Through survey research, Frank

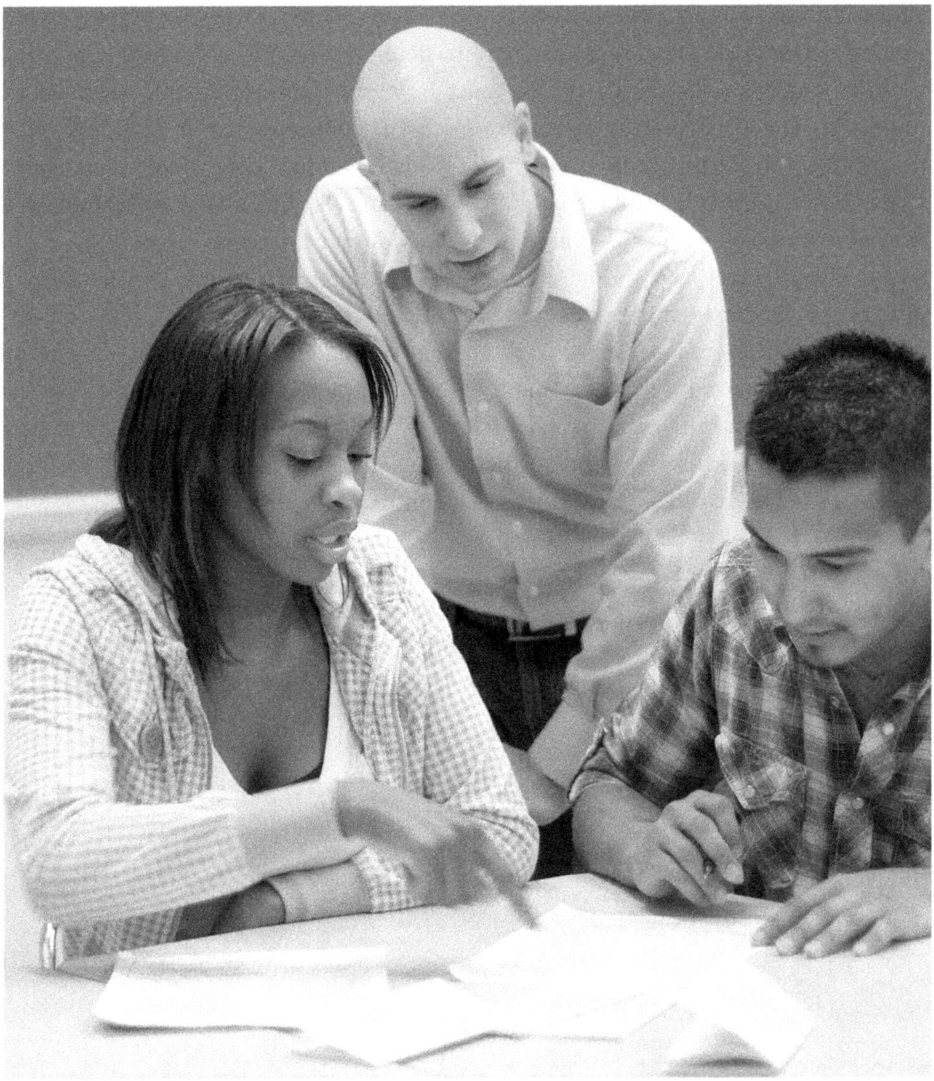

presents evidence that political science instructors are more likely to be politically engaged than other segments of the population, that political science instructors' beliefs in modeling political participation correlate with their actions, and that politically engaged political science instructors are more likely to bring their political actions into the classroom. He also found differences in the prevalence of these modeling practices between faculty at two-year and those at four-year colleges and between new and experienced teachers. Instructors who are themselves politically engaged are most likely to support modeling behavior and incorporate civic engagement exercises, including community-based hands-on learning experiences, into their classes.

Like others in this volume, Frank argues that civic and political engagement activities should be educational options at higher education institutions, both in and outside the classroom. Rather than conceiving of civic or political engagement as a form of volunteerism or limiting it to the realm of internships, civic engagement education can be most effective in creating engaged citizens when combined with properly structured classroom instruction, deliberation, and reflection. Civic and political engagement education also must be more than a one-time event or an unintegrated add-on to existing course material. Only then can it become part of deep or vertical learning and, thus, part of student identities. It cannot be mandated that all students take advantage of these opportunities, but instructors can present well-designed courses and assignments that encourage citizen development.

The chapters that follow present key concepts, challenges, and benefits of pursuing civic engagement pedagogy in political science education. The authors place these issues and debates in the context of contemporary discussions about the role of higher education and political science curriculum. Although political scientists may have different partisan views, we all agree that the development of this generation's skills and interest in civic engagement is crucial to the success of democracy in the United States in the 21st century.

Teaching Civic Engagement: Debates, Definitions, Benefits, and Challenges

1

By Alison Rios Millett McCartney

This chapter sets the foundation for this volume by establishing basic definitions and parameters of the civic engagement education debate. It explores the benefits and best practices of the service-learning method and the challenges faced by those teaching students to be civically and politically engaged. These challenges include a perceived liberal bias, outdated reward and incentive structures, miscategorization of this pedagogy as "mere" service, instructors' limited resources and time, and incomplete institutional support. Despite these challenges, I argue that political scientists can heed the call of key government and societal actors and help direct the evolution of civic engagement pedagogy and research. Otherwise, we will be followers, not leaders, in the development of priorities and goals in political science education and the country's future citizens.

Almost 100 years ago, John Dewey started his landmark *Democracy and Education* with a chapter entitled "Education as a Necessity of Life." In this chapter, he argued that just as humans must physiologically reproduce to survive, we must also reproduce our social structures through communication and education. He wrote that for a democratic society to survive, "[S]uch a society must have a type of education which gives individuals a personal interest in social relationships and control, and the habits of mind which secure social changes without introducing disorder."[1] In this and other works, Dewey proposed to secure democratic society through an educational system that develops democratic citizens. This system should include programs that teach such citizenship skills as free deliberation, openness to alternative viewpoints, and critical thinking and should allow a wide variety of ideas to emerge from a diverse group of people. With such a system, democracy continually renews and sustains itself.

Others, including Robert Maynard Hutchins, president of the University of Chicago in the mid-20th century and an ardent advocate of quality higher education, preferred to preserve democracy in an educational environment unfettered by political conflicts and disagreements. Hutchins argued that education should be centered instead on individual intellectual development through immersion in Western literature and philosophy.[2]

While fully agreeing that the nuts and bolts of political ideas, theories, processes, and structures must be taught and individual contemplation fostered, the authors in this volume clearly side with Dewey. We see teaching students the skills and values of civic and political engagement,[3] in addition to foundational knowledge, as central to the survival and vitality of democracy and the educational mission of colleges and universities in the 21st century.

Powerful national voices concur with this perspective. Commended with a White House reception in January 2012, the National Task Force on Civic Learning and Democratic Engagement, a joint project of US Department of Education and the American Association of Colleges and Universities (AACU), published a report exhorting that,

> [a]s a democracy, the United States depends on a knowledgeable, public-spirited, and engaged population. Education plays a fundamental role in building civic vitality, and in the twenty-first century, higher education has a distinctive role to play in the renewal of US democracy.

Referring to colleges and universities as among the country's "most valuable laboratories for civic learning and democratic engagement," the report recommends civic engagement pedagogy as "an undisputed educational priority for all of higher education, public and private, two-year and four-year." This type of education, it concludes, is central to local, national, and global economic prosperity, the social and political well-being of all people, and citizens' ability to take collective action to address public issues at all political levels.[4]

These statements by the National Task Force on Civic Learning and Democratic Engagement build upon earlier conclusions of the AACU. Its 2004 report, *Taking Responsibility for the Quality of the Baccalaureate Degree*, states that a widespread consensus had been reached among higher education institutions that "civic, social, and personal responsibility" was an accepted and desired learning outcome of a college education.[5]

Since then-president Elinor Ostrom's call to action in 1996, the American Political Science Association (APSA) has renewed its commitment to and search for ways to reinvigorate democracy in the United States through innovative political science education. As Ostrom advocated, "Learning effective skills of citizen involvement and responsibility are critical to a fully representative democracy."[6] She created the APSA Task Force on Civic Education, which noted in 1998 that "current levels of political knowledge, political engagement, and political enthusiasm are so low as to threaten the vitality and stability of democratic politics in the United States." The report continued by positing that it is our responsibility as political science educators to help address this problem.[7]

Many contemporary works agree with this goal of strengthening democracy through political science education.[8] Civic engagement education pioneer Richard Battistoni exhorted in an introduction to a 2000 teaching symposium in the journal *PS: Political Science & Politics* that political science as a discipline has been and should remain at the forefront of the development of effective civic engagement education.

This pedagogy becomes even more important and possible as hundreds of public and private colleges and universities add the goal of increasing students' civic engagement to their mission statements. Many have taken the additional steps of creating offices or centers of civic engagement, starting fellowships for faculty to create civic engagement courses, and creating special award categories for faculty civic engagement.[9] In addition, peer-reviewed publishing venues for articles on civic engagement pedagogy, such as the *Journal of Political Science Education*, are proliferating, and the APSA's own *PS: Political Science & Politics* has regularly included articles in the past 10 years about civic engagement pedagogy.

Responding to increased interest in fostering better teaching in the discipline as a whole, the APSA has created a yearly Teaching and Learning Conference, which has had to add a second civic engagement pedagogy track to accommodate burgeoning interest. Prominent research institutes such as the Carnegie Endowment have created programs to foster quality civic engagement pedagogy. National interdisciplinary organizations such as AACU and Campus Compact have ardently pursued this agenda. In short, academic society and the discipline of political science have begun to incorporate the development of civically engaged citizens as an accepted goal of their programs and course offerings.

One may wonder why, despite past failures, higher education is finally listening to Dewey and other Progressives. I posit four reasons why civic engagement pedagogy is becoming an accepted practice. First, community service is a regular activity for today's college students. For example, the annual freshmen survey conducted by the University of California, Los Angeles's Higher Education Research Institute determined in 2011 that 87.9% of college freshmen had frequently or occasionally participated in community service in the year before entering college, with 57.4% reporting participating as part of a class. This number represents a large increase since volunteerism hit a low of 66% among college freshmen in 1989. A large majority, 69.7%, of the students in the 2011 survey also stated that they considered "helping others in difficulty" as an "essential" or "very important" objective in their lives, and this objective was ranked third behind raising a family and being financially comfortable. This concern for others has been on a steady rise, from 66.7% in 2006 and 61.4% in 2001.[10] Such a snapshot of college freshmen suggests that the rising calls for civic engagement education at the collegiate level are connected to changes in social and personal values among undergraduates and thus may have a stronger foundation upon which political scientists can build.

Second, the student population has changed. No longer are universities and colleges home to only white, mostly upper-middle-class, males between the ages of 18 and 24. More women, more ethnic and racial minorities, and more older students who have started or restarted their studies after age 25 are now entering institutions of higher learning.[11] This expanding student population comes from a wider variety of social and economic backgrounds and educational experiences and thus needs different types of instruction beyond the traditional lecture model. As William Newell writes, this diversity means that multiple tools of communication are needed as a "powerful complement" to traditional educational methods.[12] Older students may be accustomed to more hands-on applications of knowledge because of workplace experience, and many students respond positively to the type of problem-based projects inherent to much civic engagement pedagogy.[13]

This changing population raises a third reason why the incorporation of civic engagement education is more likely to work this time. While the rising rate of student applications for financial aid certainly correlates to rising college costs and declining economic conditions, it also is due to an increase in options in financing a college education for the lower and middle classes. In his 2012 State of the Union address in which he called for increased government aid options, President Barack Obama stated, "Higher education can't be a luxury—it is an economic imperative that every family in America should be able to afford."[14] Yet as the federal government has gotten more involved in financing options for higher education, now ranging in the billions of dollars, it increasingly scrutinizes how that money is spent. Colleges and universities that receive government money—which means almost all of them—have been asked to account for the success of their programs in creating productive citizens.[15] Thus, as Fear and Sandmann predicted in 1995,[16] instructors can only expect more calls to demonstrate how courses and programs are strengthening the American citizenry. Our success now rests not on just teaching specific job skills, but also on American citizens' abilities to maintain a democratic system.

Finally, evidence that a primary method of civic engagement pedagogy—that is, service-learning[17]—works is an additional reason why civic engagement pedagogy can find a place in higher education at this time. Ample assessment evidence now exists to show that well-organized and well-planned service-learning courses can enhance student subject-area learning and move beyond volunteering.[18] Beginning with Battistoni and Hudson's path-breaking volume in 1997,[19] political science educators have begun to demonstrate and research effective service-learning practices in the discipline. Since their volume was released, service-learning and other active-learning approaches have been expanded to all disciplinary subfields, all levels of instruction, and all types of higher education institutions. The selections in this book demonstrate the variety of success.

As noted earlier, a more diverse student population also means that more pedagogical options must be provided. Many more structural and evidentiary foundations support the work of political science instructors than in the past, so our efforts no longer wallow in wishful thinking and result in, as Stephen Leonard suggests, "Pure Futility and Waste."[20] Further, Ehrlich (2000), Dalton (2009), and others cited throughout this book note that concern for one's community has now become a norm among college students, and like the students in the 2011 UCLA survey, most have some significant precollegiate exposure to community-based work. In sum, rising societal and governmental support for student work in communities and innovative teaching approaches has helped political scientists pursue effective civic engagement pedagogy and achieve the goals Ostrom and others have set for us, thereby creating an engaged citizenry.

But what is meant by "engaged citizenship"? How do we reach that goal through our teaching? To answer these and other questions, this discussion now moves to defining the key terms involved in achieving this goal and distinguishing among community service, civic engagement, and political engagement.

Definitions and Parameters in Civic and Political Engagement Pedagogy

One reason the push for civic engagement education failed to bear fruit in the past may be due to a lack of understanding of goals, terms, and effective methods. Clear definitions of the terms involved, such as the distinctions between volunteering and service-learning and among civic, political, and community engagement suggest that political scientists often are arguing very different points. Without recognized theoretical parameters and the linkage of these ideas and theories with pedagogical practices, we will continue to muddle through these debates. The following is not meant to suggest definite resolution can be provided to address all concerns, but only to set a baseline for discussion.

1) Why is civic engagement education ***not*** *the same as volunteering?*

Volunteering has an important place in the building of all types of communities. However, the emphasis is on activity that benefits a recipient, client, or partner. The benefit to the volunteers lies in building this community of which they may be a part or the sense of emotional well-being that comes from knowing that others were helped. A connection to academic learning is not required, though it may help in citizens' personal growth as they become aware of the problems, situations, and difficulties faced by others. It also does not require any examination of political structures, power relationships, or ideas that may be contributing to or preventing resolution of the issue for which one is volunteering. In addition, reflection is not necessarily part of the activity—volunteering can be a one-time event unconnected to the rest of a citizen's life.[21]

2) How is civic engagement education different from an internship?

Internships are now more commonly seen as a way to advance students' career development. A benefit to the community from the work done while a student is engaged in an internship is not required, nor is reflection on how that type of career may benefit the community. The internship should be connected to traditional academic learning, but it need not always have a direct connection to classes taken. While models are presented in this book that bridge this gap, internships do not necessarily entail gaining any knowledge of or connection to the community nor do they necessarily add to one's understanding of the political system or political issues. It is hoped that many internships do more than provide job training, but again, additional educational or community value and connections are not consistently required.

3) What is the difference between civic engagement and political engagement?

Civic engagement can be seen as a larger, more encompassing term, whereas political engagement grows out of civic engagement either directly or indirectly. In essence, civic engagement is a catch-all term that refers to an individual's activities, alone or as part of a group, that focus on developing knowledge about the community and its political system, identifying or seeking solutions to community problems, pursuing goals to benefit the community, and participating in constructive deliberation among community members about the community's political system and community issues, problems, or solutions. It means actively participating in and seeking to influence the life of the community, whether motivations emanate from self-interested reasons, moral principles, altruistic concerns, political viewpoints, or any combination thereof. Civic engagement includes a wide range of activities, such as collecting and disseminating information; voting; working voter registration drives; designing, distributing, or signing petitions; participating in civic and political associations; attending public meetings, rallies, or protests; and entering into public or private discussions of community and political issues via various formats.[22] It also may include coproduction actions, wherein community members collectively deliver services that the political system lacks sufficient will or capacity to provide,[23] or it may become political engagement.

Political engagement refers to explicitly politically oriented activities that seek a direct impact on political issues, systems, relationships, and structures. For example, participating in a community recycling program or working with a local youth group may not necessarily have an explicit political goal, though these may have a community goal and indirect political implications. On the other hand, working to enact community laws regarding recycling or gain government aid for low-income school districts are actions directly connected to changing political structures or decisions.[24] These are examples of *political* engagement. However, voting is an activity that may be included in both the broader civic engagement category and the narrower political engagement category, exemplifying that there can be significant overlap between these two categories.

Regardless of which type of engagement is sought, both civic and political engagement activities are distinct from volunteering in several ways. Civic and political engagement include connection to the political and community components involved and reflection upon the consequences of one's actions. These activities also empower participants to find common means to address common concerns. Third, both require active rather than passive participants; that is, individuals who do more than just watch community or political developments. Democracy cannot thrive as a mere spectator system.[25] Thus, the ultimate goal of this volume is to encourage the development of capable citizens who have the confidence, knowledge, skills, and motivations to maintain a dynamic, vibrant democracy. Political scientists need to advance in this direction now, lest we lose existing momentum much as political scientists in the 1920s and 1930s did.[26] The next section explores proven pedagogical methods to reach this goal.

PEDAGOGICAL METH[...] EXPERIENTIAL LEARNIN[...]

Returning to Dewey, who argued that p[...] edge with actions, many teacher-scholar[...] ture formats[27] to increase student und[...] cesses, relationships, systems, and struct[...] cept of "active learning," in which "lear[...] in the learning process [because it] ena[...] and construct their own understanding."[...] exchange type of teaching, wherein instr[...] dents return that knowledge in exams a[...] of knowledge between students, betwe[...] but not necessarily, between students an[...] ing exchanges broaden student learnin[...] empowered to engage in and find soluti[...] their lives. Evidence has shown that whe[...] environment, students gain deeper leve[...] advance their critical thinking and anal[...] with consequences (see Chapters 11 and[...] the information longer.[29] There are m[...] including experiential education option[...] simulations and problem-based learnin[...] (Chapters 8, 10, 15–17, and 19).

Several examples presented in th[...] learning pedagogy. While there are m[...] this volume defer to Bringle and Hatch[...]

> a credit-bearing, educational exp[...]
> in an organized service activity t[...]
> and reflect on the service activity[...]
> standing of course content, a bro[...]
> an enhanced sense of civic respon[...]

As the authors go on to explain, serv[...] because the service activities are direct[...] within course learning goals, oral an[...] assignments.[31] As Dicklitch (2003) expl[...] weds academic rigor with real civic eng[...] students' understanding of course mater[...] edge as well as to provide a positive exp[...] civic participation, inculcating the value[...] productive civic participation.[33] In short[...] through building the necessary knowle[...] ble, effective, and successful citizens.

[...]litical indoctrination, the academy's overly [...]d lack of investment and training in effective [...]ple inertia may partially encompass the two [...]nd government and societal actors continue [...]ements of effective civic engagement peda- [...]lies all three concerns. Let's take a moment [...]ht be overcome. [...]amed for a perceived liberal political bias. [...]litical science, but a required partisan view- [...]ment pedagogy. The value of participating [...]or even mostly exist in just a left- or right- [...]emocracy as a whole and is inherent to the [...]ocracies are created. Political scientists can [...]e by demonstrating how we encourage and [...]different political viewpoints, as Beaumont [...] mean we will avoid political conflicts. But [...]e instructive in itself, and civic engagement [...]t an advantage in creating environments for [...]gogy demands reflections from students."[38] [...]ded in this book can be used for both class- [...]ogical activities and, as Donahue suggests, [...] facilitate negotiation, transformation, and [...]hout preferential treatment to specific polit- [...]can point to evidence, such as that provided [...]nt courses do not significantly alter political [...]eepen the politically neutral value of being [...]est to increase political motivation than to [...]vard structures must be promoted. A some- [...]rgued that recent efforts to promote civic [...]hose of political scientists for the past cen- [...]ficant structural obstacles to their success. [...]a monumental reconstruction of American [...]n which only a large volume of publications [...]mic's success. In essence, he suggested, as [...]ut valuing civic engagement in its teaching [...]omote civic engagement in its students.[42] It [...]ditional scholarship of discovery guarantees [...]ducation institutions, whereas teaching and [...]respectively. Academics need to heed Boyer's [...]ngle vision of scholarship and definitions of [...]titutions. There needs to be an acceptance [...] is fundamental to the purpose of academic [...]emics to critically examine what we do, how we do it, and whether or not we are really contributing to the collegiate mission of educating students.[43] SoTL skeptics need to consider how intellectually rigorous this scholarship is, and newcomers need to be taught proper techniques of SoTL. The advent of several peer-reviewed interdisciplinary SoTL journals since the 1990s and the creation in 2005 of one in political science, the *Journal of Political Science Education*, demonstrate that sufficient quality scholarship exists and can find critical and rigorous outlets.

Yet political scientists also need to reconsider the place of civic engagement pedagogy in scholarship, teaching, and service and the relative weight of these categories for a higher education institution in the 21st century. Part of this challenge includes advancing the understanding that civic engagement can rightly belong in all three categories, rather than being pigeonholed under service. The recommended changes will differ depending upon the type of institution and the size of its student body, but those in academics can no longer remain wedded to the supremacy of one type of scholarship so high above all else and a rigid division and outdated hierarchy among these three potentially comingling cores of our jobs. Otherwise, we will become trapped in our own inertia (an outcome Leonard suggests is a real possibility)[44] and lose the opportunity to make civic engagement pedagogy an integral part of 21st-century higher education.

Finally, political scientists must work to adapt support structures at our colleges and universities to foster investment in the unique necessities of effective civic engagement pedagogy. Untenured faculty need to have the additional work and time investment inherent to these courses and activities valued for promotion and tenure. All faculty need additional conference and fellowship support to develop their civic engagement pedagogy, test ideas, and get crucial feedback on preliminary drafts of publishable work. Creating, enhancing, and continuing civic engagement courses and activities are more time- and energy-intensive than most other courses in part because few faculty have been trained in how to appropriately choose and use active-learning and service-learning methods to achieve civic engagement outcomes. This type of pedagogy simply was not taught as part of graduate training in the past and in most cases still is not taught.[45] It is also more time-consuming due to the nature of these courses, which require organizing and managing many groups both within and outside the university community at multiple times, a difficult and constant juggling act that is not part of normal course workloads. Further, an educator's continual quest to find resources to support the associated activities siphons off even more time and energy and, again, is not part of traditional course preparation and instruction.

Therefore, the authors in this volume advocate not only for systematically including civic engagement pedagogy in the promotion, merit, and tenure system, but also for colleges and universities to devote significant, reliable resources to faculty as they investigate, develop, implement, and maintain civic engagement pedagogy. These resources must encompass support at all stages of program and course development. Funds are required for conference attendance, research support, service-learning activities, and administrative assistance, possibly through graduate or undergraduate student workers, in addition to reconsidering time and workload allocations.

All of these challenges require political scientists to better inform coworkers, administrators, and key societal and governmental players about exactly what is being done, how it is effective, and why civic engagement education is vital to the country's future. Without a doubt, we do face limitations in addressing these challenges. Among these is that we cannot overstate our claims. As Rimmerman reminds political scientists and McHugh and Mayer (Chapter 22) agree, no one course or activity can create a democratically engaged citizen.[46] Instead, civic engagement pedagogy needs to be part of the larger revision of the mission and corresponding actions of colleges and universities to give students opportunities to go beyond what Harward and Shea in Chapter 2 call horizontal, or episodic, participation. They need to be exposed to these opportunities early, such as in first-year experiences and freshmen seminars, and exposed often through multiple types of engagement networks, including extracurricular activities (see Strachan and Senter, Chapter 24) and construction of formal academic plans of study (see Meinke, Chapter 20).[47] Service-learning and other active-learning methods can advance the goal of creating effective, capable, and engaged citizens, but only if they are a part of larger institutional plans and if faculty and staff continue to receive support from government and societal actors.

A second limitation is that this is a time of stretched resources. Both public and private colleges and universities must do more with less financial support. As such, it is even more imperative that rigorous research on the benefits and limitations of civic engagement pedagogy be developed, as discussed in Section Four of this book. Without demonstrable results in teaching, research, and service, there will be difficulty in getting and maintaining sufficient resources to capitalize on the gains that civic engagement pedagogy has made thus far.

In addition, not every educator and not every student is well-suited to the service-learning method prominent in several chapters in Section Two, and not everyone should be asked to try to adapt to just this one method of active learning. A variety of options are needed to develop civically engaged citizens, including adapting foundational teaching methods, increasing collegiate extracurricular activities that involve civic engagement, and adding web-based learning (See VanVechten and Chadha, Chapter 11). All options should be equally respected, assessed, and rewarded by the academy as they help students become capable and effective citizens by advancing their knowledge and their critical thinking, research, oral presentation, and writing skills. Further, some students work full-time and may not be able to devote the extra time that service-learning courses often require. Political scientists should be wary of mandating only the service-learning method and remember that other activities outside of the classroom may have more flexible scheduling (see Chapters 5 and 24) and can also be part of an active-learning approach. As educators develop both course- and noncourse-based options, we need to ensure that we are creating worthwhile, meaningful, and valuable civic engagement experiences, lest civic engagement become a distasteful chore.[48]

Lastly, political scientists need to remember that we are not alone in this endeavor, and we cannot achieve our goals by operating at the collegiate level only. As Colby et al. remind us, we can look to primary and secondary schools as partners. K-12 education can and should provide youth with a foundation for citizenship by teaching students their fundamental civic and political rights and responsibilities and the basic workings of the American political system. In addition, life experiences, or one's "informal education[,] is critical for an informed and thoughtful electorate." However, Colby et al. also argue that relying on life experiences is inadequate and incomplete and that current evidence suggests that most high school civics programs do not fully achieve their goals.[49] O'Shaughnessy (Chapter 19) and Owen (Chapter 20) explore civic engagement options for high school students, and political scientists must reach out more to K-12 educators as partners in the quest to advance civic engagement education for all the country's youth. We are limited in the extent to which we can impact K-12 education. Nonetheless, we should use our resources and our research capabilities to help educators at these levels and bring them into this conversation.

Conclusion

The structure of the student body at institutions of higher learning has changed. The federal government now asks faculty to be more accountable for our work both financially and in terms of developing citizens capable of fulfilling the country's needs. Communities increasingly look to our institutions as partners in common missions. Given these 21st-century realities, higher education institutions cannot be expected to look as they did in the last century. As understanding politics is our discipline, we are in a unique position to be at the center of these developments on our campuses and in our national and local communities. Political scientists can heed the call of the *Crucible Moment* and help direct the evolution of civic engagement pedagogy and research, or we can be spectators at a game on our own playing field. The following chapters show that political scientists have developed many models for how to pursue this goal and are accumulating the evidence to show what the best teaching practices are and why. Now is the time to capitalize on our achievements and build upon these authors' ideas and examples to assist in the fruitful evolution of our students' education and the country's future.

2

Higher Education and the Multiple Modes of Engagement

By Brian M. Harward and Daniel M. Shea

Following years of anemic turnout by young voters, many observers suggested that the 2008 elections presaged a welcome shift in youth political engagement. However, recent data show that the 2008 phenomenon was likely episodic rather than enduring. In this chapter, we explore the connection between electoral participation and young voters' disinclination to engage deeply with policy disputes. Movement from an episodic form of political engagement to sustained forms of engagement—like the movement from a passive view of student learning to a "deepened" view of the obligation of learners—is a critically important goal to explore. By focusing on these themes, we provide examples of how institutions, departments, and faculty might create contexts that deepen student learning and political engagement. An emphasis on deepening patterns of engagement and learning challenges not only the canonical view of higher education and pedagogy, but also demands more of citizens in a democratic society

It is both common and appropriate to use voter turnout as a means to assess the health of a democracy. Competitive races and high turnout are markers of robust civic institutions. When voters "vanish,"[1] as in the decline in youth participation in the United States in recent decades, it is understood that one of the necessary conditions for democratic government is imperiled. Yet democratic governance requires more than preference aggregation; it demands commitment to the principles of citizenship and responsibility. "Voting," Riker suggests, "is a necessary, but not sufficient condition of democracy."[2]

This chapter explores the connection between broad-scale voter turnout and young voters' disinclination to engage policy disputes. We propose that "flattened," "thin," or "horizontal" patterns of political engagement reward participants and campaigns in limited, immediate ways. Discrete acts of political engagement, like voting or signing petitions, are generally more attractive to new voters because they are less risky activities than sustained, large-scale commitments, such as working to persuade policy makers. In this sense, passing involvement with political phenomena is not inconsistent with college students' passing engagement with ideas. An emphasis on "deep," or "vertical," patterns of engagement and learning challenges not only the canonical view of higher education and pedagogy, but also demands more of citizens in a democratic society. The connection between patterns of political disengagement and intellectual risk aversion is not coincidental. In the following sections, we explore these multiple themes and provide examples of how institutions, departments, and faculty might create contexts that help deepen student learning and political engagement.

The More Things Change...

Meager levels of political engagement among young Americans at the end of the 20th century were stark and, for some, unsettling. Election turnout had dropped precipitously: In 1972, when 18-year-olds were first given the right to vote, 50% of those 30 years old and younger came to the polls. By 1996, participation had dropped to just 32%. As for midterm congressional elections, one in four in this age group was making it to the polls by the end of the century. A 2002 study of younger Americans, commissioned by the Center for Information and Research on Civic Learning and Engagement (CIRCLE), found that only about two-thirds of 18- to 25-year-olds had even registered to vote, and 49% of those 25 years of age and younger said that voting was "a little important" or "not at all important" to them.[3]

The problem ran much deeper than nonvoting, however. According to the American National Election Study (ANES), in the 1960s about 35% of those 30 years old and younger "tried to influence how others voted." By the end of the century that figure had dropped to roughly 20%. The percentage of young citizens "very much interested in campaigns" stood at roughly 30% from the 1950s to the 1980s, but declined to just 6% by the 2000 election. In 2002, 67% of all Americans cared "very much" or "pretty much" about the outcome of congressional elections in their area, but only 47% of those 25 years old or younger felt the same way.[4]

The Higher Education Research Institute (HERI) at the University of California, Los Angeles, conducts an annual survey of college freshmen. In 1966, HERI data found some 58% of respondents agreed that "keeping up to date with political affairs" was very important. That figure dropped to 26% by 1999. Only 14% of freshmen in 1999 said that they frequently discussed politics, compared with a high of 30% in 1968.[5] Further, a poll of Americans in their late teens and early twenties conducted by the Pew Research Center found that fewer than 50% were thinking "a great deal about" elections in 2000. This result compares to roughly 70% in 1992. Roughly 40% suggested that it did not matter who was elected president in 2000, twice as many as in 1992.[6]

The withdrawal of young citizens from politics appeared to be rapid, deep, and broad. Robert Putnam, in *Bowling Alone: The Collapse and Revival of American Community*, summed up the issue this way:

> Very little of the net decline in voting is attributable to individual change, and virtually all of it is generational.... [D]eclining electoral participation is merely the most visible symptom of a broader disengagement from community life. Like a fever, electoral abstention is even more important as a sign of deeper trouble in the body politic than as a malady itself. It is not just from the voting booth that Americans are increasingly AWOL.[7]

One year later, scholar William Galston, one of the founders of CIRCLE, suggested that "the withdrawal of a cohort of citizens from public affairs disturbs the balance of public deliberation—to the detriment of those who withdraw, but of the rest of us as well."[8]

The response to this decline was equally swift and comprehensive. The number of youth-centered political mobilization efforts that either took root or dramatically expanded their efforts by 2004 was truly impressive. A partial list of these includes Rock-the-Vote; Redeem the Vote; Choose or Lose; Head Count; Hip Hop Summit Action Network; Citizen Change; Punk Voter; Your Country, Your Vote; Declare Yourself; and Smackdown Your Vote. Hefty philanthropic initiatives were launched, most notably the Pew Charitable Trust's "New Voters Project," the Youth Coat Coalition, and several programs by the Carnegie Corporation. A number of college and university programs also were created, including the Vanishing Voter Project at Harvard, CIRCLE at the University of Maryland (now at Tufts University), the Center for Political Participation at Allegheny, and the Goldfarb Center at Colby College, and there was an accompanying burst of scholarly studies, reports, and books documenting the decline in participation. Both the Democratic and Republican Parties allocated unprecedented resources to youth engagement efforts, likely due to the shrinking number of persuadable older voters.

Although a direct causal connection to these efforts would be difficult to verify, interest among young citizens clearly swelled in the 2004 and 2008 elections. By the 2008 election, turnout for those 30 years of age or younger had risen to 51%. Many other indicators of political behavior, such as participating in campaign events, talking about politics with friends and family, and paying attention to the news, also suggested greater youth interest between 2000 and 2008. According to ANES data, between 1996 and 2008 the number of young Americans who tried to influence the vote choice of others doubled from roughly 20% to 40%.[9]

Given the role that young voters played in several of the early 2008 presidential nomination contests, it seemed to make sense when *Time* dubbed it the "Year of the Youth Vote."[10] The bearing of this demographic group seemed particularly robust in light of arguments offered by some scholars regarding the root of the so-called decline. McDonald and Popkin, for example, suggested that lower turnout was a myth because most estimates include individuals who are unable to vote, such as prison inmates and convicted felons (that is, the denominator in the turnout calculation was artificially large).[11] As there is little evidence to suggest that the disenfranchised felon and prison populations declined between 2001 and 2008, it seems that either this view missed the mark or that the resurgence of young citizens into politics was quite spectacular.

In the aftermath of the 2008 election, those fretting about the long-term stability of the American democratic system breathed a sigh of relief. It seemed that young citizens had rediscovered the potential of politics and were once again making their voices heard. Proclaiming the impact of its efforts, Rock the Vote asserted: "2008 is the year of the young voter. We're not going to take politics as usual anymore, and we won't be ignored. We're taking the country into our hands.... Today's youth are a political powerhouse."[12] Surely Democratic operatives were pleased with the change, as their presidential candidate netted some 68% of the under-30 vote in 2008. The youth vote was large, progressive, and consequential.

The problem is that the reemergence of young voters may have been a temporary surge rather than a sea change. Or, at the very least, it might be consigned to merely voting in presidential elections. The first indicators of the limited nature of the resurgence were the 2009 gubernatorial elections in New Jersey and Virginia. Young voters stayed home for both contests. Exit polling found that voters age 30 and younger accounted for just 9% of voters in New Jersey compared with 17% in 2008, and 10% in Virginia, down from 21% in 2008. According to one analysis, "Young voters were Obama's biggest supporters [in 2008], but their uncertain turnout makes them a less reliable base."[13] The explanation, at least for Heather Smith of Rock the Vote, lay not with young voters, but instead with neglectful candidates and party operatives: "[T]he engagement of young people does not occur without investment by candidates and campaigns."[14]

Yet young people also stayed home during the critically important special election to fill the Massachusetts Senate seat vacated by the death of Edward (Ted) Kennedy. All eyes were turned to the Bay State because it represented the "60th seat"—the number of seats the Democrats needed to overcome GOP filibusters in the US Senate. By holding that seat, Obama's agenda of change, seemingly so important to young voters one year earlier, could continue. Without that seat, the Obama agenda would grind to a halt. Many watched as money and activists poured into Massachusetts. On Election Day, turnout was high for a special election, a robust 54%. Yet, generational differences were stark; turnout for those older than 30 was nearly 60%, but for younger voters it was a scant 15%.[15] The young voters who did make it to the polling station overwhelmingly supported the Democratic candidate, but with so few going to the polls, an upset was inevitable.

Turnout for those 30 years old and younger reached just 22.8% in the 2010 midterm election, slightly less than in the previous midterm election in 2006. In the wake of the 2010 election, the folks at CIRCLE suggested that "the most reliable conclusion is that youth turnout has stayed between 20 percent and 23 percent in all midterm elections since 1994."[16] So, the heightened turnout for the 2008 presidential election was then followed by a return to rather anemic levels in youth turnout in the next midterm. Yet the level of turnout for all voters in the 2010 midterms actually increased—up to 41%. As noted by McDonald , "[P]articipation in in midterm elections has increased for four consecutive elections, rising from a low of 38.1%

in 1998."[17] Youth participation in 2010 seems to have run the other way, however, suggesting that the gap between younger and older voters is actually growing.

As the 2012 presidential election drew close, many observers noted a rather stark youth-centered enthusiasm gap. A Gallup poll taken in early September of that year, for example, found that 63% of registered voters ages 18 to 29 "definitely" planned to vote. At roughly the same point in 2008 that figure stood at 79%.[18] "Politics has gone back to that thing you don't want to bring up," noted a first-year student at Elmhurst College in the fall of 2012.[19] In the presidential primary elections the youth vote was nearly nonexistent in some states. In Maryland and Louisiana, for instance, just 2% of those 30 years of age and younger came to vote in the primary (those figures were 15% and 7%, respectively, in 2008). In Wisconsin it was just 8% (25% in 2008), and in Michigan it was 7% (14% in 2008).[20]

Actual levels of youth turnout in the 2012 election were similar to 2008. The proportion of young voters in the overall electorate also remained about the same—roughly 19%. A few days after the election CIRCLE reported that a near-identical number of those 30 years of age and younger came to the polls in 2012—about 23 million.[21] Because a large majority of these voters (60%) backed Obama, many on the left proclaimed that this generation had once again come through. Yet one should also keep in mind that as a proportion of the overall population this group is growing.

These numbers suggest that young voters can become engaged during presidential general elections. Young voters always have had less interest in off-year, midterm, and primary elections, but the steep drop in engagement after a surge seems to run counter to a long line of scholarship that argues that once a citizen votes, repeating the act at all levels becomes habitual. It now seems that an initial act of voting in presidential contests may not cut the costs of sustained commitment to politics—an engagement with policy or issues of public moment that extends beyond these exciting, high-profile events.

Millennial Myopia

So what happened? One possibility might be that expectations were too high. Perhaps younger voters are inclined to pay more attention to high-profile contests—that is, presidential contests, particularly with exciting candidates like Barack Obama. Midterm elections, off-year gubernatorial contests, specials elections, and the like are simply off their radars and always have been. Maybe political scientists should be grateful that higher numbers have been paying attention to presidential contests, but not expect much more than that. One might reason that voting falls within the orbit of young citizens, even as expecting them to attend town hall meetings, email the editor, or pay rapt attention to the news is expecting too much.

A second possibility might be that the conduct of politics following the 2008 election turned away many of the new voters. Given that "change" was a central theme in 2008, the incremental pace of policy adjustments since then might seem exceptional to young citizens. As ideological polarization and party cohesion increase, the distance from the majority party median to the filibuster pivot or the veto pivot presumably increases as well.[22] Consequently, activists' reformist goals often are thwarted in favor of incremental policy proposals. Policy shifts of a significant magnitude are less likely to garner sufficient support to defeat threatened filibusters or vetoes. As a consequence, reformers new to the policy-making environment may become quickly dismayed at the lack of responsiveness from their elected officials—even unitary actors like the president. If their discrete acts of political engagement do not generate meaningful policy shifts, one might imagine that the likelihood of further engagement decreases. This effect may be more exaggerated for new voters than for more-seasoned participants. At best, policy making in a democracy is like watching the "strong and slow boring of hard boards," to use Max Weber's famous line, but more often it seems like the "makings of sausage," to paraphrase Otto von Bismarck.

It also may be speculated that the ever-sharper tone of politics since the 2008 election may have pushed young Americans from politics. Even as the scholarly literature on campaigns has demonstrated repeatedly that negative campaigning works and that it may actually mobilize voters,[23] angry protestors at town hall meetings, death threats toward members of Congress, rabid participants to call-in radio shows, diatribes in the blogosphere, and outbursts on the House floor may be disturbing enough to dissuade young voters from staying involved. The United States has witnessed numerous periods of political intensity and partisan acrimony, but many believe the acrimony in recent years (perhaps recent decades[24]) is particularly stark and certainly novel since World War II. Peggy Noonan of the *Wall Street Journal* commented, "It's a mistake not to see something new, something raw and bitter and dangerous, in the particular moment we're in."[25] Brookings Institution scholar Darrell West has suggested Americans are now in an "arms race of incendiary rhetoric [that is] quickly reaching the point of mutually assured destruction."[26] And *New York Times* columnist Thomas Friedman pondered "whether we can seriously discuss serious issues any longer and make decisions on the basis of the national interest."[27]

For instance, an Allegheny College survey on civility and compromise shows that four times as many respondents perceived a decline in levels of civility in politics between 2011 and 2012, and a majority believed the 2010 midterm election was the most negative seen to date.[28] It is not unreasonable to posit that the coarsening of public discourse has a substantial negative effect on sustained political engagement by young citizens. New voters' sense of commitment to policy may be conditioned or limited by their willingness to engage the cacophony of high-demanders. Writing of the irony of a deep youth commitment to community service but limited interest in politics, columnist and author Jane Eisner put it this way:

> [T]he attraction of service for young people is undeniable, and growing. It is propelled by the characteristics of this generation—their tendency toward compassion and their nonjudgmental concern for others, and away from what they see as a political system driven by conflict and ego.[29]

Why engage in large-scale policy disputes when one can have a "make a difference day" free of criticism?

Each of these explanations may contribute to the lackluster levels of political engagement seen in young citizens. None captures the whole story, however. In addition to such contributing factors as the unreasonable expectations of observers, frustrations with policy incrementalism, and the increasing incivility of campaign rhetoric, we believe that something else might be at the core—something a bit more fundamental that connects many of these themes. In short, this disconnect between thin and deep political engagement is an unwillingness on the part of young citizens to expand their commitments, participate beyond an election cycle, and open themselves to criticism and opportunities for failure.

Wither Twitter

In the drive to register and mobilize as many young Americans as possible at the lowest possible costs, campaigns and many (perhaps most) youth engagement organizations employ the quickest, most cost-efficient way to produce big numbers of new voters. Ambitious goals are established, and costs per registrant guidelines are suggested. For example, Politico reported on a new fund-raising tool adopted by several Democratic campaigns that was based on social networking and

> offered a measure of competition among volunteers, via "leaderboards" that reflected the most doors knocked on and calls placed. They also gave far-flung volunteers a way to collaborate and more successful ones a forum for sharing rudimentary canvassing tips, like how long to wait on one door before knocking on the next.[30]

Such incentives and fund-raising platforms push activists to move quickly from one "new voter" to the next. A common technique is also to prompt students to change their voting address from their parents' residence to their school address; subsequently, they are often considered "new" registrants on a program's tally sheet. In addition, if one technique registers 20 new voters per hour and another just 10, the former must surely be "better." The logic of cost-efficient new voter work is explicit in Green and Gerber's oft-cited, *Get Out the Vote: How to Increase Voter Turnout*.[31] The book is a "guide for campaigns and organizations that work to formulate cost-efficient strategies for mobilizing voters."[32] The authors admit that their volume is focused on short-term considerations and *not* on "how voter turnout relates to broader features of society,"[33] and it seems quite clear that much of their data come from partisan campaign operations. Nonetheless, the logic is clear: some voter mobilization techniques are more cost-efficient than others.

The Obama net-root campaign likely paid close attention to these sorts of cost-benefit calculations in 2008. As noted by one observer, "The architects and builders of the Obama field campaign have undogmatically mixed timeless traditions and discipline of good organizing with new technologies of decentralization and self-organization."[34] Their reach was massive, including an email list that boasted some 13 million addresses, 7,000 different email messages sent during the course of the campaign, and one billion emails sent overall. On Election Day, everyone who signed up for alerts received *three* text reminders to vote. Some three million phone calls were made during the final days of the race using MyBo's virtual phone-banking system, and more than five million people signed up as supporters of Obama on social network sites. More than five million individuals also clicked the "I Voted!" button on Facebook.[35]

Many youth engagement programs, both partisan and nonpartisan, are guided by the idea that once young citizens are brought into the system, their engagement will continue. Registration and voting are considered "gateway activities" that lead to continued voting and other political activities. There is, however, a qualitative difference between involvement designed to change the outcome of an election and engagement directed toward shifting the course of government. Malcolm Gladwell makes an analogous argument regarding the relationship between social networking sites and democratic engagement.[36] Contrary to the hopes of the "evangelists of social media," he suggests that new modes of communication have *not* drawn young citizens into the political fray in significant ways. He writes, "Social networks are effective at increasing participation—by lessening the level of motivation that participation requires." For example, the Save Darfur Coalition Facebook page boasts some 1,282,339 members, but the average donation is just nine cents. People surely care about what happens in Darfur, but little is expected of them beyond linking to the site. Social media are designed to allow access to information, Gladwell argues, but do little to forge connections to other political actors or to the larger political system. He continues, "It makes it easier for activists to express themselves, and harder for that expression to have an impact."[37]

We suggest that at the heart of truncated, episodic youth engagement is an important distinction between horizontal and vertical behaviors.[38] In our view, it may be helpful to consider the axes as reflecting divergent ways of thinking about change. Registering to vote, heading to the polls, signing a candidate's Facebook page, and tweeting about a policy dispute are horizontal modes of engagement. They broaden involvement, but do so in limited ways and for a short period of time. Each of these behaviors requires a modest level of commitment. Little risk is involved and scant reflection is required. The significance of that involvement for future choices and actions are also rarely explored.[39] As such, there are no regrets or sense of irony in turning out to help elect a president with an agenda of change, but not joining the fray to defend his top policy priorities or coming back to the polls two years later to help keep members of his party in the majority in Congress.

Horizontal, "drive-by" participation is risk averse, insulates individuals from dismay, and limits the resources that must be brought to create change. Individuals get the t-shirt or the bumper sticker that conveys their sensibilities without deepening their commitment in a way that involves risking their resources (time, reputation, or well-being, for example). In the language of positive political theory, horizontal participation does involve collective action problems, but certainly not the free-riding difficulties faced by vertical engagement.

Vertical participation involves a deeper understanding of the obligations and opportunities for substantial, prolonged engagement to alter the course of government. It builds upon the cultivation of information by calling upon participants to apply information in strategic ways and merge with like-minded citizens in concerted, specific activities. Verticality also demands a level of commitment that overcomes the costs associated with bearing the burden of fully taking on an issue. In this sense, depth of commitment is sufficient to overcome the free-riding that normally attends any collaborative endeavor for a public good. The risk, then, is in bearing these costs of commitment. One assumes a position of heightened responsibility, visibility, and scrutiny. Thus, as commitment deepens, so too does one's risk. It is this willingness to engage vertically that invites a level of risk to which many young persons are unaccustomed. Disappointment itself may be a risk, and a deeper commitment may lead to deeper dismay when anticipated results do not emerge. Like the tide, the higher the commitment rises, the further it ebbs. Citizen vertical engagement in what is often a zero-sum game invites significant disillusionment when preferred positions or candidates do not prevail. Even when a preferred outcome is hard-won, the institutional contexts and policy-making processes of federal, state, and local governments impede rapid change.

Perhaps this problem can help explain the preference for volunteerism over political engagement. Volunteerism or community service may have a direct effect on individuals (provider and recipient), but it does not typically give rise to broad political change. Service activity typically provides private goods (either positive or negative payoffs) and as a result may be more appealing to both providers and recipients who have immediate, time-sensitive gains in mind. The diffuse benefits of large-scale political change may serve only the interests of the reformist (vertically engaged) citizen.

On a pragmatic level, vertical engagement is essential in a democracy because significant policy change does not happen quickly or without sustained effort. Elections may change the personnel of government, but not public policy. In a classic work on power and politics, V.O. Key explained that in the American setting, "constitutional obstruction"—the various checks, balances, and sharing of powers—creates a slow, laborious policy process. There is a "widespread dispersion of power, [in which] actual authority tends to be exercised not solely by governmental officials, but also by private individuals."[40] Indeed, even a cursory look at policy change in the United States at both the national and local levels underscores the essential character of prolonged individual engagement. More recently, scholar Stephen Frantzich, in his collection of essays on the effectiveness of individual political action, wrote, "Contemporary political policy decisions are still strongly dominated by individuals who work with the system as opposed to those who stand outside it.... Democracy is a participatory game of contact and blocking, not a spectator sport."[41]

Higher Education and Vertical Political Engagement

Historically, two of the most important institutions for deepening the involvement of new generations to the political process have been political parties and schools. Local political parties, in particular, have been at the frontlines of drawing new citizens into the political process in broad, meaningful ways for since the 19th century. Their likelihood of affording a viable avenue for continued greater youth engagement in the 21st century is discussed elsewhere.[42] Here, our focus is, as Colby et al. propose, on how institutions of higher learning can play a lead role in helping young Americans develop an understanding of the importance of the broad range, depth, and efficacy of democratic activities.[43] Newman explains further,

> If there is a crisis in education in the United States today, it is less that test scores have declined than it is that we have failed to provide the education for citizenship that is still the most important responsibility of the nation's schools and colleges.[44]

In introducing the vertical/horizontal dynamic, it is clear that we are privileging the vertical dimension. We do so to make the point that the educative value of deep engagement, or high-impact opportunities, is achieved only in the context of vertical engagement. That is not to say that a robust horizontal dimension is not a necessary condition for change as well. Our concern, however, is that the depth of student commitment to political phenomena does not match the horizontal connectedness generated by campaigns and various targeted drives. The shallow, or thin, form of participation might include passing association with multiple areas of interest. In this way, environments can be controlled by orchestrating and limiting exposure to critical counterpoints to the commitments held, however thinly. Individuals prefer to create a "Daily Me" as Cass Sunstein called it—a narrow world of influences tailored to specific tastes and views—rather than expose themselves to the serendipity of multiple experiences and perspectives.[45]

Just as deep, vertical political engagement involves substantial risk, so too does students' intellectual emancipation. Freedom from prejudice and presupposition is a risk-bearing enterprise. Skill development, rote memorization, information transfer, and emphases on pre-professional training do not typically carry with them elements of intellectual, pedagogical, or institutional risk. Too often, the rejection of such canonical conceptions of learning brings with it substantial risk for an institution from benefactors, employers, and prospective students and their families.

Consider the recent calls for accountability within the academy. Faculty are asked to justify themselves with measurable outcomes. They are told to cut costs, generate revenue, and produce a better "product." While meaningful assessment of teaching and learning are justifiable expectations, the form taken by most calls for accountability mischaracterizes the purpose of higher education by construing it almost exclusively as an enterprise that serves a private good for individual participants and their families.

Higher education, and a liberal arts education in particular, is ultimately about providing a public good. Conceiving of higher education as a private gain has predictably led to its commodification. In many cases, institutions of higher education themselves have been complicit, whether it is the corporate sponsorship of programs, technology transfers, corporate-funded research, or financial arrangements with credit card companies that deepen student debt. Each might have a particular compelling justification, but together they contribute to a view of the undergraduate enterprise as one in which consumers pay a high price for a service.

These are familiar critiques. Beyond institutions of higher learning, however, we also believe that this issue is of particular salience to political scientists. Political scientists understand the fragility of democracy and the importance of both horizontal and vertical participation from a broad spectrum of citizens. A generation turned off from politics or a particular dimension of politics is a problem because it mutes the democratic character of the system and distorts the outcome of the policy process.

Conceptualizing College-Level Instruction

Most instructors confront an array of challenges, including large classes, a wide range of student abilities, numerous important topics to cover, and cynical, unprepared students. Thankfully, interest in finding ways of breaking the cycle of indifference has grown, as evidenced by the burgeoning attendance at the APSA Teaching and Learning Conference; efforts by many national organizations, including Project Pericles, Bringing Theory to Practice, and Campus Compact; and mounting interest in "The Teacher" section of *PS: Political Science & Politics*. College textbook publishers also have turned their attention to pedagogical innovations to meet market demands. Numerous studies[46] have documented the importance of quality instruction in the promotion of civic and political skills and an understanding of how the democratic process works.

Nevertheless, for many instructors dramatic shifts are both costly and risky. One beginning point may be to reconceptualize the roles of both the instructor and the student. The traditional approach rests upon the idea of information transfer and that the quality of instruction is assessed by the amount and quality of information given students. Students are passive recipients of knowledge, given the job to receive the instructor's wisdom, process this new material, and recall it as necessary. When this process breaks down, it often is deemed the fault of the unmotivated student. Most also assume that learning is an isolated activity, best done in quiet settings. Students should work independently and only consult their instructors when there is confusion regarding information that was passed on to the student at an earlier date.[47] In brief, "[t]he old paradigm of teaching is based on John Locke's assumption that the untrained student mind is a blank sheet of paper waiting for the instructor to write on it," noted a team of researchers. "Student minds are viewed as empty vessels into which instructors pour their wisdom."[48]

An alternative approach turns many time-honored assumptions on their heads.[49] For example, one might consider that knowledge is best constructed, discovered, transformed, and extended *by* students. Rather than simply providing new information to students, faculty can help students discern the meaning and nuance of complex material. Stated a bit differently, students are provided information by the faculty member, but then activate their existing cognitive structures or construct new ones to process the new material. As such, there is an important distinction between new information given by the instructor and new knowledge created by the student. Faculty efforts should be aimed at developing student competencies and talents, not simply emphasizing the retention of new information. Instead of sorting students into static categories ("she gets it," "he's missing the boat," etc.), efforts should be made to broaden dynamic competencies. "Within colleges and universities, a 'cultivate and develop' philosophy must replace a 'select and weed out' philosophy."[50] Instructors might also see learning as a cooperative effort, and instead of information moving in one direction, from instructor to student, enhanced learning happens when the flow of information runs in both directions.[51]

Critiques of the traditional model are not new, and many instructors understand the limits of this old paradigm. Powerful forces still propel its dominance despite myriad technological advances that offer alternative approaches. For one, behaviors are perpetuated through modeling. New instructors often teach the way in which they learned as undergraduates or observed as teaching assistants in doctoral programs. Preparing for each class session or new course can be a difficult, time-consuming, anxiety-driven process. Not wanting to be caught short without enough material or by a tough question, many new instructors retreat to a risk-avoidance strategy of reliance upon hefty, carefully prepared lecture notes. Students are accustomed to this paradigm, so why risk embarrassment by trying something different? New instructors also must receive positive peer assessments, the nod of approval from senior members of the department. Wanting to fit in and keep their jobs, most young faculty members conform to the dominant teaching culture. Peer assessment of teaching is also generally centered more on the breadth of information given to students and not the extent to which students are engaged in their own learning.

Even more disheartening, many young instructors at research institutions are reluctant to develop innovative teaching techniques, not wanting to be perceived as excessively student-focused. As McKeachie and Svinicki explain, "In many universities, for example, formal definitions of the criteria for promotion give research and teaching equal weight, but it is not uncommon to find that research is 'more equal.'"[52]

Finally, as the college population grows and resources shrink, many instructors are being called upon to teach larger classes and more offerings. While true innovation is possible in larger class settings, the safest route is often perceived to be the traditional approach. As Shea wrote, "Certainly, the 300 students assembled in a massive lecture hall would expect little more than robust lectures, a few PowerPoint slides, and a few well-timed video clips."[53]

Bain and Zimmerman have a particularly helpful way of framing the difficulties faced by faculty concerned about deepening student engagement with ideas.[54] They distinguish between "surface learners," who are stymied by risk and would prefer to keep objects of their understanding at a distance, and "strategic learners," who are particularly concerned with requirements and what is on the exam. Further, the authors suggest that strategic learners are just as disengaged as surface learners, in that "they will often fail to understand conceptually, and their learning will have little sustained or substantial influence on the way that they subsequently think, act, or feel."[55] In comparison,

> deep learners are primarily concerned with understanding, with how to apply their ideas to consequential problems, with implications, and with ideas and concepts. Only they are likely to theorize and make connections with other ideas and problems. Only they are likely to become adaptive experts who both recognize and even relish the opportunity and necessity of breaking with traditional approaches and inventing new ones.[56]

It is the challenge not only of faculty, but institutions and departments as well, to see that student opportunities to become deep learners are heightened.

A Few Examples of Engaged Forms of Learning

In this final section, we provide three illustrations of how instructors, departments, and institutions can help students become engaged learners and thereby deepen their connections to the broader political process.

The operational definition of "engaged forms of learning" refers to those pedagogies and academic structures that require active student involvement and critical reflection. Engaged forms of learning often use contexts beyond the classroom and involve the application of inquiry, typically (though not exclusively) in collaboration with the larger community. Service-learning, community-based research, collaborative laboratory, or performance studies can be engaged forms of learning. Quite distinct from volunteerism, each demands greater commitment from students, and they generally push students beyond the receipt of information to the connection between theory and action in an academically rigorous way. Each obliges students to claim greater responsibility for learning and its connection to their individual development and their civic or community lives. As such, engaged learning carries with it at least four common characteristics:

1. The learner is called upon to take an active role in the academic enterprise, to take responsibility for "knowing."
2. A premium is placed upon self-reflection, which is only possible through consideration of that which stands "outside" the learner.
3. A claim is placed upon the learner—a recognition of the learner's responsibility to the objects of his or her understanding. This leads to the realization that the civic, the community, stands in an interdependent relationship with the learner.
4. There is a reconsideration of the resistance to change among the categories of analyses, including *inter*disciplinarity, *intra*disciplinarity, methodological pluralism, etc., as it also involves a reconsideration of how, where, and what one may learn—and from whom.

Understandably, such a radical shift in emphases and pedagogies may not fit neatly into every disciplinary context or every instructor's focus, nor will it fit every institutional context. It may be more helpful to consider these four common characteristics of engaged learning as contributors to a progression of emphases. Many political scientists are already reshaping the conceptual geography of the discipline, and some institutions are actively encouraging, supporting, and rewarding such efforts. Political scientists are, however, generally and often rightly suspicious of such a realignment of the emphases of scholarship and teaching. They recognize the historical connection of the discipline to Jeffersonian notions of training leaders and citizens in the arts of liberty and often understand that obligation in the limited context of contemporary special responsibilities to explain the apparatus of governance and how it works. How might a progression of emphases regarding engaged learning change the view of these obligations? How could educating students in political science come to include encouraging students to become engaged learners in a way that fits the expertise of political scientists and exemplifies the necessary conditions for deep, vertical commitment? Perhaps a few examples are helpful.

Mastery Learning. Taking students seriously and providing opportunities for them to engage vertically demands that political science instructors provide a context in which they can choose to free themselves from prejudice and presupposition. Learners enter into a relationship with the object of their knowing and are affected by it. They might learn about US foreign policy in Latin America, but mechanisms that challenge them by removing them from the familiar, including study abroad and other high-impact learning opportunities like service-learning, problem-based research, or senior projects, are particularly suited to helping students engage deeply with the larger world. Yet to propose institutional change or even class-based change, the empirically demonstrable proposition that all students are capable of deep learning must be accepted as a precondition.[57]

In a very compelling essay demonstrating the importance of "mastery learning" as a necessary condition for deepening student engagement, Miller argues that "[m]astery learning"—in which students focus on a limited set of topics until a high level of achievement is attained, then move to subsequent material—coupled with frequent assessment and feedback, generates profound improvements in student learning relative to conventional approaches.[58] This finding reflects similar results from Kuh's 2008 NSSE study, in which high-impact learning opportunities, such as learning communities, study abroad opportunities, internships, and senior seminars, benefited all students, but were particularly powerful for low-achieving students.

Miller's view is that formative assessments—as opposed to summative, or end of project, assessments—provide students critical feedback while they are in the process of completing the learning activities. These formative assessments are ongoing assessments (e.g., revisions) of student work that allow the students to self-assess. The improvement in their understanding is "visible to both teachers and students" during the course of a discrete assignment.[59]

Developing and articulating essential learning outcomes in the areas of knowledge, intellectual and practical skills, personal and social responsibility, and integrative learning are helpful only if those goals are shared with and understood by the students, Miller argues.[60] "When teachers communicate expectations to students—whether high or low—students tend to meet those expectations."[61] He continues,

> It is especially important for both teachers and students to believe that all students can learn at high levels, because—from setting expectations and goals, to choosing and responding to assignments, to shaping assessments—believing otherwise will trigger decisions and actions that result in lower achievement.[62]

Consequently, expecting students to engage deeply in the classroom and in the political community requires taking all students seriously and developing course-based opportunities for students to take responsibility for coming to know something.

Notice and Comment Project. While students are quick to point out many of the opportunities to become involved with government and policy making, the bureaucracy is rarely mentioned as an avenue for engagement. Students often criticize the bureaucracy for its undemocratic nature, insularity, and perceived inefficiency. While those claims may be justifiable in some sense, this type of project can expose students to the democratic responsiveness of bureaucratic agencies, the oversight function of Congress, interest group representation, and bureaucratic motivations through a semester-long bureaucratic rule-making project.

Early in a semester, students are expected to review the *Federal Register* for Notices of Proposed Rulemaking (NOPRs) that are of interest to them. Students then are required to research the issues involved in the proposed rule and develop an argument in support or in opposition to it. In addition to an in-depth research paper, each student is asked to write a letter to the agency responsible for the rule in accordance with the Administrative Procedure Act's Notice and Comment provisions. One copy of the letter is submitted to the instructor for a grade, while the original may be sent to the agency. Since the agencies are required to consider each comment submitted during the notice and comment period and incorporate reasonable comments into the final rule, students are able to watch to see if their participation was influential.

Study of the bureaucracy is also an occasion to introduce students to the discipline. The class is provided with a scholarly article that examines the role of interest groups and citizens in the notice and comment period. The students often are surprised with the results in the article, which suggest extremely low levels of citizen involvement in rule making. Students then provide methodological critiques, analyze the assumptions of the author, and offer normative arguments regarding changes that they would make in the rule-making process.

This NOPR project requires students to connect thought to action, actually participate in the exercise of collective power, and reflect upon that exercise. Often, their arguments are public—posted on a particular agency's website for consideration by others. When that happens, students often are overwhelmed by the idea that others take their arguments and perspectives seriously. By the end of the term, the students have engaged their federal government in a way they had probably not thought possible just months earlier. In a limited way, the project is an example of a progression of emphases aimed at fostering deep learning and promoting vertical political engagement.

An additional approach that could heighten student engagement and deepen understanding of and involvement in politics could emphasize state and local government.[63] There is some attention given to state and local politics in many introductory courses, and most institutions of higher learning offer stand-alone upper-division state and local classes; many instructors, however, give only passing consideration to those chapters of introductory texts. Only a few states, including Texas and Georgia, require courses on state and local politics, but what a wonderful opportunity to engage students more deeply in their immediate contexts—where an individual's sustained and substantial commitment can really make a difference. It could be expected that sustained engagement may more likely result in increased efficacy at the local level. Political science instructors might further speculate that the inattentiveness observed among young voters in state and local politics is simply a reflection of their own inattention to those issues in their teaching.

Curricular Structure and the Senior Project. Kuh demonstrates the importance of high-impact learning opportunities to the maximization of student learning outcomes.[64] First-year seminars, study abroad opportunities, academically rigorous service-learning programs, learning communities, and substantial senior projects like theses or portfolios are typical high-impact learning opportunities and can be found at many institutions in recent years.

Just as high-impact learning activities may be crucibles for student transformation, the opportunity for faculty to reflect upon the quality of their programs may be similarly transformative. The process of reviewing departmental curricula demands that political science faculty explore exactly what it is they want students to learn and how they want them to interact with the world. Specifically, departments might address two broad questions: First, what are the desired outcomes of a quality political science curriculum, aside from basic informational goals? Second, how can the positive outcomes currently being generated be reinforced and the other desired outcomes be cultivated?

Most departments are likely interested in graduates exhibiting familiarity with the multiple methodological approaches of the discipline; an understanding of the core topics in the multiple fields of inquiry; an appreciation of the world's diversity; analytical and critical thinking abilities; effective oral and written communication skills; and the ability to apply disciplinary approaches to real-world situations, among other skills, values, habits, and sensibilities. In addition to these goals, departments might also consider a few not so immediately apparent objectives—ones that might tend toward a deepened engagement with disciplinary themes as well as deepened political engagement.

Letting go of what faculty take to be control over courses, course material, and student learning can been unsettling. Instructors come to these discussions well trained by their graduate programs and with years of research and teaching in their particular areas within the discipline. The coin of their realm has not been interdisciplinary or even *intra*disciplinary—it has been depth within a rather limited subfield. This narrow focus is perhaps reflective of graduate training in departments in which the conceptual boundaries are well marked. The transformative conversations may begin to chip away at those boundaries, however, making the limits to inquiries and subfields more porous.

Another option might be the development of a "keystone" experience—rather than a "capstone" experience. This experience is foundational—not a culminating, disconnected end-result of a series of isolated academic and cocurricular experiences. Rather, it reflects integrative and collaborative learning, which depends upon and buttresses the student experience. It is contingent upon and connected to student learning, not an ex-post assignment.

The centerpiece of the keystone experience might be a set of "Fellows"—local, national, and international scholars and practitioners—who comprise a pool of talent from which students may select a specific person with whom they want to work during this intensive academic study. Each Fellow would have expertise in a particular thematic track within a major (e.g., Poverty and Inequality; Law and Society; Sustainability; Globalization; War and Peace; Citizenship; or Representation). Participating students then contract with departmental advisers and Fellows to a general course of study within (and perhaps outside) the department that reflects the multiple perspectives that different fields within the discipline can bring to bear on the student's chosen theme. The Fellow and adviser guide the student throughout the student's career, culminating in a senior project as a fully integrative capstone experience.

The keystone approach would be immensely helpful to deepening student engagement and understanding on a number of dimensions. A student connects with a prominent figure in an area of great importance, develops intellectual independence, exhibits facility with the methods of the discipline, and achieves results in something close to a conference paper that could be presented at a professional meeting or submitted to a graduate admissions committee as evidence of independent research. Even if something akin to the keystone program is not appropriate or desirable in a particular department, consideration of the core issues presented by keystone-like options may bring about a rethinking of the major curriculum in political science in a way that privileges vertical engagement with the discipline and the community.

Conclusion

A colleague of ours is less sanguine than we are about the ability of institutions of higher education to generate the kind of sustained patterns of engagement political scientists would prefer to see among young people. In a recent conversation, he noted that the divestiture movement of the 1980s or the civil rights movements of the 1950s and 1960s involved young people, but not because institutions of higher education provided contexts for those students to engage deeply. In fact, in many cases those institutions reflected status quo positions and only later came to divest, desegregate, or diversify as a consequence of student action. The impetus for student engagement, he argued, came not from courses or curricular faddishness, but instead from models of critical consciousness among faculty and others at the institutions. That is, faculty as models of behavior and conscience[65] rather than pedagogues generated deep, vertical commitment among students.

We agree. By modeling behavior, faculty, staff, and administrators can accentuate the importance of numerous forms of engagement and affect the habits and dispositions of students. However, we are not aware of evidence to suggest that our colleagues have retreated from such behaviors in recent years. It seems instead that other changes are at work—and modeling behavior might be insufficient in the decades to come. Deep political and intellectual engagement implicates curricula as well.

There has been a steady increase in the number of Americans attending college, yet levels of political engagement have moved in an inverse direction. This trend contradicts what is known about education and political participation—that increasing levels of education lower the cost of engagement.[66] In 1972, some 26% of Americans had attended college, and turnout in that year's presidential election for those 30 years of age and younger was 50%. In 2000, 55% had attended college, but the turnout for that same age group had dropped to 35%.[67] Thus, the decline in engagement occurred despite what Colby and her colleagues call the "selection effect." That is, in the past, the students most likely to be politically engaged were also the ones most likely to attend college. Also, college-bound young people were much more likely to come from politically active families than their peers who chose not to attend college.[68]

One explanation for this paradox may be that the "type" of student attending college has changed. Babcock and Marks found that 73% of students "defy the stereotype of an undergrad that earns a high school diploma, enrolls in college full-time directly afterwards, depends on their parents for financial support, and doesn't work more than part-time."[69] Might the pressures of work, child-rearing, and untold additional obligations less common of students a generation ago have an effect on the willingness to move beyond horizontal political commitments? We suspect that they might.

The dramatic change in modes of communication, particularly among young citizens, has likely played a role as well. On the one hand, the volume of "contacts" made by a traditional college student in any given day is vastly larger than in the past. Students move quickly and with ease from email, Twitter, Facebook, blogs, and web pages. Yet the nature of these connections is much different—a great deal shorter and arguably less substantive than previous means of maintaining connectedness. One of the many studies commissioned by the Pew Internet and American Life Project found that text messaging has become the primary way that teens reach their friends, surpassing face-to-face contact, email, instant messaging, and voice calling.[70] In what ways might this change affect modes of political connectedness? In meta-analysis, based upon data from 14,000 students over a 30-year period, Konrath and O'Brien found that college students today are vastly less compassionate than those in the 1980s and 1990s.[71] In an interview, O'Brien suggested that "[c]ollege students today may be so busy worrying about themselves and their own issues that they don't have time to spend empathizing with others, or at least perceive such time to be limited."[72] Linking this change to possible effects of social media, the authors note, "The ease of having 'friends' online might make people more likely to just tune out when they don't feel like responding to others' problems, a behavior that could carry over offline."[73]

The proliferation of vocational and community college campuses, commuter campuses, for-profit colleges and universities, and distance-learning classes also may have transformed the nature of coursework for a significant portion of students. We might add that the decline in percentages of full-time, tenure-track faculty lines and the accompanying growth of adjunct faculty may underscore the transitory nature of college work. For better or worse, it is quite plausible that these changes have heightened the importance of a particular type of study, one in which moving quickly through a broad range of topics is essential. New ideas are encountered, but not engaged. Just as contacts with friends and family are numerous and brief, perhaps members of this generation has come to expect that their studies should come in byte-sized chunks.

There has clearly been a shift toward career-centered learning. According to a 2010 HERI study of college freshmen, the importance of finding a good job after graduation has reached its highest level since the question was first introduced in 1983. Some of this movement might relate to current economic conditions, but the focus on the "value" of particular institutions, certain majors, and even higher education more generally extend back several decades. Howe and Strauss, in their oft-cited work, *Millennials Go to College*, write,

> In the early 1980s, a new breed of college freshman arrived on campuses, focusing less on moral and cultural agendas, and more on the bottom lines of higher education. Where a decade earlier, college kids were (in Charlie Reich's term) "greening" their inner lives, students were now more intent on greening their wallets.[74]

Writing of the most recent generation of students the authors note, "With their pragmatic mindset, they tend to feel less at home with the heavily theoretical and ideological atmosphere of academe."[75]

All of these and untold other changes underscore important challenges to higher-learning institutions and political science instructors. Ambiguity, subtlety, curiosity, and responsibility may not be deeply valued or appreciated by students or faculty if a degree is viewed as a chit to be pursued in the interest of financial security. This thin and perhaps prevailing view of higher education reflects a fundamental misunderstanding regarding the relationship between the knower and the known. The myth of objectivity holds the objects of knowing at arm's length and thereby serves risk aversion well. It allows individuals to keep the other at a distance, limiting its ability to make a claim, and it reduces risk by not displacing preconceptions, not challenging assumptions, or implicating a way of behaving. As Parker Palmer writes, "In the popular imagination, knowing is seen as the act of a solitary individual" but "scholars now understand that knowing is a profoundly communal act. Nothing could possibly be known by the solitary self, since the self is inherently communal in nature."[76] So long as classes, assignments, or other significant experiences students have reflect the myth of objectivity, the likelihood of deepening engagement is limited.

Colleges and universities are places where individuals find the encouragement to free themselves from the generalizations, received wisdom, or presuppositions that shape much of the public discussion, action, and inquiry. As liberating institutions, they must be contrarian. They must, at some level, be critical of the prevailing assumptions regarding the accepted paradigms of public understanding. The public good of critical thought and analysis provided in part by these institutions is a necessary condition or precondition for a more robust democracy.

As institutions that critique the norms of acceptance and consumption, it follows that they should similarly critique the notion that higher education is the cost born for an auspicious entrance into the marketplace. Many of the skills, qualities, and habits necessary for success on the job are developed in higher education institutions, but the value of education extends beyond this role. Students gain much more than a skill that may be brought to bear in a particular place or profession. Students are not simply trained; they are offered an education.

In part, then, education is about intellectual emancipation. Colleges and universities must encourage students to extend themselves, deepen commitments to important ideas, become self-reliant, and take responsibility for knowing. To achieve these goals, students and faculty must overcome a deep, understandable, aversion to risk. Such a reconceptualization of the purpose of higher education demands a great deal more from both faculty and students than a model of higher education premised upon the notion of information transfer. It requires that students accept a level of risk that involves exposure to criticism, the rejection of fundamental assumptions that run counter to new evidence and new arguments, and the opportunity for greater failure.

The same holds true for political engagement. The greater the commitment, the greater the exposure to criticism and risk. Movement from an episodic form of political engagement to sustained forms of engagement—like the movement from a passive view of student learning to a deepened view of the obligation of learners—is a critically important goal for political scientists to explore. As teachers they must remove students from the familiar and provide the contexts in which students can deepen their engagement with ideas and their consequences. This is education's emancipatory value, and it is a principle that would go a long way toward encouraging patterns of political behavior that sustain and deepen youth commitment to civic engagement.

Political Learning and Democratic Capacities: Some Challenges and Evidence of Promising Approaches

3

By Elizabeth Beaumont

This chapter shares empirical research demonstrating that well-designed, well-taught courses and programs can contribute to three important goals involved in educating for democracy. First, they can help many different kinds of students move significantly toward a number of important democratic capacities related to political knowledge, skills, motivations, and action. Second, they can promote more informed and active political involvement without producing ideological political indoctrination. Third, they can be effective for undergraduates with little initial interest in politics and can help close the "democratic achievement gap" between students who possess greater and fewer political advantages. In describing findings from the Political Engagement Project (PEP) at the Carnegie Foundation, I argue that while educating undergraduates for democracy is not a panacea for the serious and pervasive problems of modern politics, it can provide vital opportunities for students to develop into more informed and engaged citizens.

In 2012, the National Task Force on Civic Learning and Democratic Engagement made a highly publicized call to renew the civic mission of higher education, calling this a "crucible moment" to focus on educating for democracy.[1] Such calls are neither new nor isolated, but rather overlap with an array of ongoing arguments that colleges should play a role in promoting students' democratic capacities, or what Amy Gutmann calls "cultivation of the virtues, knowledge, and skills necessary for political participation."[2] There are many serious misgivings and misperceptions about civic education, however, including concerns that it is doomed to be ineffective at best, dangerous at worst.[3] Taking seriously the idea of educating for democracy requires recognizing that not all goals or approaches are legitimate or appropriate in academic arenas, not all are viable for faculty, and not all are likely to be equally effective. This chapter sheds light on some of these issues by describing findings from the Political Engagement Project (PEP), I undertook with my colleagues Anne Colby and Thomas Ehrlich at the Carnegie Foundation with input from other researchers and a group of campus partners.[4] This study helps demonstrate that high-quality, legitimate forms of political learning—that is, forms that emphasize open inquiry and critical thinking and are consistent with reasonable pluralism—can contribute to the goals of educating for democracy by fostering political understanding, skills, motivations, and involvement in a broad range of undergraduates. Findings from this project assist in responding to three sets of important challenges related to effectiveness, indoctrination, and political inequality:

1. Ineffectiveness—concerns that civic education efforts are likely to be ineffective
2. Indoctrination—concerns that these efforts involve inappropriate political indoctrination
3. Political Inequality—concerns that these efforts tend to preach to the converted, or will help students who are already "political haves" come out even further ahead.[5]

An Overview of the Political Engagement Project

In recent studies of civic learning in higher education, there is strong emphasis on service-learning and volunteering, with far less concern with politics, even when broadly defined. The Political Engagement Project my team undertook placed a primary focus on political learning as a core aspect of educating for democratic citizenship through a multimethod study of nearly 1,000 undergraduates participating in 21 different political courses and programs at a range of colleges across the country from 2001 to 2005.[6] The project began with a set of basic premises: that fostering robust civic learning in young people involves teaching for a combination of political understanding, skill, motivation, and involvement, and that any such efforts must reflect overarching concerns for open inquiry, critical thinking, and students' intellectual development. The focus was to understand how courses and programs might help students become more knowledgeable and engaged participants in many arenas of public life, as well as understand how such teaching might be smart, effective, and unbiased.

All students and the courses and programs in the study were invited to participate in a preintervention survey upon enrollment, generally from fall to summer of the 2000–2001 academic year, and a postintervention survey upon completion (hereafter referred to as pre- or postsurvey), with the duration ranging from a college quarter to two academic years.[7] In selecting interventions to study, the research team purposefully selected those that featured:

1. Some degree of focus on promoting political engagement (political understanding, skill, motivation, and involvement).
2. At least one key "pedagogy of engagement," or one active experience that prior research suggests may promote political engagement, including extensive political discussion; opportunities to interact with political leaders or activists; participation in politically related internships, community

placements, or service-learning projects; initiation of political action projects or undertaking political activities on campuses or in the community; and engaging in political simulations or role-playing, such as Model UN.[8]

3. Examples of common types and topics of political learning already occurring on many campuses: summer political institutes; a semester in Washington, DC; extracurricular programs; political internships; and multiyear living-learning programs, as well as single-term academic courses offered in political science and other departments. Topics ranged over aspects of local, state, national, and international politics.
4. Some degree of stability, meaning that the course or program had taken place at least once before and was very likely to continue in the future.

We also sought variations in size, duration, level of intensity, institutional context, and student population. Choosing courses and programs that diverged in many respects not only allowed us to ensure the generalizability of our findings, but also allowed us to study variations in the effects that different approaches may have on different types of students. The interventions also diverged in the extent of students' self-selection. Some courses and programs involved a high degree of self-selection on the part of students, such that most students who enroll in them are already quite interested in politics and choose to participate because of that interest. Some basic single-term academic courses also were included that were much less likely to involve students' self-selection related to political interest, including two introductory American government courses.

We know from a question that asked students to rate the importance of various reasons for enrolling in the interventions that about half of the group was strongly motivated to participate because they were interested in politics. The remaining half said that political interest had little or no influence on their enrollment; they were motivated by other things. A quarter of the students, for example, were strongly motivated by the fact that the intervention met a college requirement.

The survey data were supplemented by several other qualitative research instruments, including faculty interviews and a faculty survey, in-depth telephone interviews with a subset of students, and examinations of students' work. In combination, these instruments and data sources yielded quite detailed pictures of political engagement in these students. In general, our other research instruments, particularly the student interviews, provided evidence that the increases reflected in pre- and postsurveys were not simply the result of students responding in a socially desirable way, since students were able to provide concrete and compelling examples of changes in their understanding, attitudes, and behaviors. Several key findings from the project shed light on some of the challenges facing efforts to educate for democracy.

Challenge 1: Can Political Learning Contribute Measurably to Students' Democratic Capacities?

One challenge examines concerns about effectiveness, particularly for the college population of young adults and returning students. This challenge actually involves two components: How can political scientists try to measure important democratic outcomes related to college-level political learning experiences, and what is learned when they are measured?

Developing a New Survey for Studying Political Engagement Outcomes

There are limits to the types of democratic outcomes that can be measured through surveys, but we worked with faculty and program leaders to develop a new survey that could provide a basic snapshot of some common aims loosely shared across different efforts.[9] The survey is not equally useful for all types of civic education efforts, but it represents an attempt to develop an instrument that can tap into aspects of what we took to be several clusters of interconnected developmental outcomes: political knowledge and understanding; political skill, or know-how; several aspects of motivation crucial to political development and engagement; and some important forms of political action and democratic involvement. Following are short descriptions of the major categories of items included in the survey, summarized in Table 3-1.[10]

Political Understanding. Political knowledge—particularly memorable, usable, contextualized knowledge, not just facts—is vital for democratic citizenship. To examine political understanding in the survey, we included both what might be considered foundational political knowledge (knowledge of political theories, institutions, and organizations) and knowledge of current events (knowledge of current political and economic issues at the local, state, national, and international levels). Increasing both types of political knowledge was an explicit aim of all the project's interventions. Because of vast differences in academic content across the programs, it was necessary to measure political knowledge indirectly through self-reports rather than using direct measures involving questions with right and wrong answers.

Table 3-1: Survey Scales and Items, Questions, and Response Options
CLUSTER 1. POLITICAL UNDERSTANDING
Foundational Political Knowledge
Q: ***Please rate your knowledge of the following topics: (6 pt. Likert scale, No knowledge to In-depth knowledge)***
1. Organizations that work on social and political problems
2. Theories about politics and democracy
3. Political institutions and how they work
Current Events Knowledge
1. Current national or international political issues, such as those on the front page of major newspapers
2. Current local or state political issues, such as those dealt with by city councils or state agencies
3. Political leaders and their roles
4. Current economic issues

CLUSTER 2. POLITICAL MOTIVATION

POLITICAL INTEREST & MEDIA ATTENTION

Interest in Politics — single item

Q: ***Some people seem to follow what's going on in government and public affairs most of the time... How often would you say you follow what's going on in government and public affairs? (6 pt. Likert scale, Never to Most of the time)***

Newspaper Attention — single item

Q: ***Listed below are some ways that people get news and information. In a typical week, how often do you… (7 pt. Likert scale, 0 to 7 days per week)***

1. Read about public affairs and politics in a newspaper (print version or online)

POLITICAL IDENTITY & VALUES

Party Identification — single item

Q: ***Generally speaking, do you think of yourself as a…Republican, Independent, Democrat, or other (specified)***

Political Ideology Continuum — single item

Q: ***We hear a lot of talk about conservatives and liberals these days. Here is a scale on which the political views that people hold are arranged from extremely liberal to extremely conservative. Where would you place yourself on this scale? (6 pt. Likert scale, "extremely liberal" to "extremely conservative")***

Politically Engaged Identity Scale

Q: ***How important to your sense of who you are is each of the following characteristics? (6 pt. Likert scale, "Not central to my sense of self" to "Very central to my sense of self")***

1. Concerned about international issues
2. Politically involved
3. Concerned about government decisions and policies

POLITICAL EFFICACY

Internal Political Efficacy

Q: ***Please use the following scale to respond to the statements…: (6 pt. Likert scale, Very strongly disagree to Very strongly agree)***

1. I feel that I have a pretty good understanding of the political issues facing this country
2. I believe I have a role to play in the political process.
3. When policy issues are being discussed, I usually have something to say.
4. I think I am better informed about politics and government than most people.
5. I consider myself well qualified to participate in the political process.

Efficacy in Political Institution Contexts

Q: ***Working with others, how hard would it be for you to accomplish these goals? (6 pt. Likert scale, Impossible to get this done to Easy to get this done)***

1. Getting the town government to build an addition to the local senior center
2. Influencing a state policy or budget decision
3. Influencing the outcome of a local election

Efficacy in Community Contexts

1. Organizing an event to benefit a charity
2. Starting an after-school program for children whose parents work
3. Organizing an annual clean-up program for a city park

Efficacy in Campus Contexts

1. Solving problems on your campus
2. Changing academic offerings or requirements on your campus
3. Influencing decisions about who teaches on your campus

CLUSTER 3. CIVIC & POLITICAL SKILLS

Skills of Political Influence & Action

Q: Listed below are some skills that people use in various situations. Please rate how well you can do each. (6 pt. Likert scale, Cannot do this to Can do this very well)

1. Know whom to contact to get something done about a social or political problem
2. Develop strategies for political action
3. Organize people for political action

Skills of Collaboration

1. Reach a compromise
2. Help diverse groups work together
3. Deal with conflict when it comes up
4. Talk about social barriers such as race

Skills of Political Analysis

1. Recognize conflicting political interests
2. Write well about political topics
3. Weigh the pros and cons of different political positions

Skills of Leadership & Communication

1. Articulate my ideas and beliefs to others
2. Assume the leadership of a group
3. Make a statement at a public meeting

CLUSTER 4. CIVIC & POLITICAL INVOLVEMENT

Expected Conventional Electoral Activities

Q: Below is a list of items...In the future, what do you expect that you will do? (6 pt. Likert scale, Will certainly not do this to Will certainly do this)

1. Vote in future national and local elections
2. Work with a political group or for a campaign or political official
3. Wear a campaign button, put a sticker on your car, or place a sign in front of your house.

Expected Conventional Electoral Activities

Q: Below is a list of items...In the future, what do you expect that you will do? (6 pt. Likert scale, Will certainly not do this to Will certainly do this)

1. Vote in future national and local elections
2. Work with a political group or for a campaign or political official
3. Wear a campaign button, put a sticker on your car, or place a sign in front of your house.
4. Give money to a political candidate or cause

Expected Political Voice Activities

1. Contact or visit a public official—at any level of government—to ask for assistance or express your opinion
2. Contact a newspaper or magazine to express your opinion on an issue
3. Call in to a radio or television talk show to express your opinion on a political issue, even if you didn't get on the air
4. Take part in a protest, march, or demonstration
5. Sign a written or email petition about a political or social issue
6. Buy a certain product or service because you like the company's social or political values OR NOT buy something or boycott it because of the conditions under which it is made, or because you dislike the conduct of the company (avg of 2 items)
7. Work as a canvasser going door to door for a political candidate or cause

Expected Political Discussion — single item

1. Discuss political problems with friends

Expected Community Involvement — single item

1. Work together with others to solve a problem in the community where you live

Political Motivations. Political motivation plays a crucial role in providing energy for and commitment to democratic learning and participation. Such motivations can include increasing students' interest and excitement to help them see the relevance of political issues for their lives, support their sense that what they think and do politically matters, and develop a sense of themselves as active citizens. We were particularly concerned with examining students' political interest, as well as two aspects of political motivation widely believed to be key elements of long-term commitment to democratic participation: politically engaged identity and political efficacy.

By a sense of politically engaged identity, we mean the extent to which being politically engaged is experienced as central to one's sense of self—the perception that being politically informed and acting on one's political beliefs is very important to one's identity or who one is as a person.[11] We included a construct of politically engaged identity adapted from Mary Lou Arnold (1993) because we believe that dominant surveys, such as the National Election Studies (NES), too often focus narrowly on party identification, political ideology or attitudes, or national or ethnic identity while overlooking the key role of other dispositions included in political identity, such as a sense of responsibility to a particular community.

Civic and Political Skills. Both psychologists and political scientists have described skills relevant for civic participation, especially those relating to influence and action.[12] Some argue that one reason why membership in groups and organizations during pre-adult years is related to greater future political engagement is that this kind of involvement helps young people acquire such relevant civic skills as public speaking. Many college experiences beyond the classroom have the potential to contribute to these skills, and fostering civic and political skills was an explicit aim of most of the project's programs, whether curricular or extracurricular.

The PEP survey assessed an array of skill types suggested by several sources, again through self-report (for pragmatic reasons).[13] Two groups of questions focused on some general interpersonal skills: general skills of teamwork and collaboration and general leadership and communication skills. Two others focused on more specific political skills related to various types of political involvement: skills of political analysis and judgment and skills of influence and action.

Civic and Political Involvement. Many consider the expected likelihood of participation in various types of political activities as the most important outcome for political engagement. The measure of expected political involvement was adapted from those used in a national sample by Scott Keeter and his colleagues in their 2002 Pew Foundation study. One of the measures examined conventional electoral activities (voting, working with a political group, or giving money to a candidate). The other examined seven activities related to political voice or expressing political opinions, such as contacting an official, protesting, signing an email petition, or boycotting a product.

Evidence from the Survey: Overall Significant Gains in Key Dimensions of Democratic Learning

Analyses of the student survey data provide evidence that the courses and programs studied did contribute to students' political learning. On average, students experienced statistically significant increases on scales representing key dimensions of political engagement, including political understanding, civic and political skills, and political motivations.[14] As noted in Table 3-2, these increases included students' overall gains in foundational political knowledge and current events knowledge,

TABLE 3-2: Results from Repeated Measures Analysis of Variance Showing Gains in Democratic Outcome Scales

A series of 2x2 repeated measures analyses of variance showed significant main effects for a number of scales measuring different democratic outcome variables, all of which were $p < .05$, and most were more highly significant. This included the following results:

1. ***Sense of Politically Engaged Identity Scale***

The ANOVA yielded a significant pre- to postsurvey main effect, Pillai's Trace = .060, $F(1, 462) = 29.504$, $p < .001$, and a significant interaction between the pre-post measures and the initial level of political interest, Pillai's Trace = .081, $F(1, 462) = 40.472$, $p < .001$.

2. ***Foundational Political Knowledge Scale***

The ANOVA yielded a significant pre- to postsurvey main effect, Pillai's Trace = .161, $F(1, 461) = 88.258$, $p < .001$, and a significant interaction between the pre-post measures and the initial level of political interest, Pillai's Trace = .094, $F(1, 461) = 48.047$, $p < .001$.

3. ***Skills of Political Influence and Action Scale***

The ANOVA yielded a significant pre- to postsurvey main effect, Pillai's Trace = .134, $F(1, 463) = 71.490$, $p < .001$, and a significant interaction between the pre-post measures and the initial level of political interest, Pillai's Trace = .042, $F(1, 463) = 20.322$, $p < .001$.

4. ***Expected Participation in Conventional Electoral Activities Scale***

The ANOVA yielded a significant pre- to postsurvey main effect, Pillai's Trace = .027, $F(1, 450) = 12.669$, $p < .001$, and a significant interaction between the pre-post measures and the initial level of political interest, Pillai's Trace = .021, $F(1, 450) = 9.653$, $p < .003$.

5. ***Expected Participation in Political Voice Activities Scale***

The ANOVA yielded a significant pre- to postsurvey main effect, Pillai's Trace = .023, $F(1, 442) = 10.323$, $p < .002$, and a significant interaction between the pre-post measures and the initial level of political interest, Pillai's Trace = .017, $F(1, 442) = 7.666$, $p < .007$[a].
Within subjects pre- to postsurvey effect: n.s. Pillai's Trace p = .964; Paired sample t-tests conducted by group found no significant pre-post differences for either group). In addition, a chi-square test of independence indicated that students' party identifications did not differ markedly from pre- to postsurvey, $X^2(16, N=473) = 744$, $p<.001$)[b].

Note:
[a] These included the Americorps/Corporation for National Service Assessment (see Aguirre International 2000); the Walt Whitman Center's Measuring Citizenship Project (see Barber, Smith, Ballou, Higgens, Dedrick, and Downing 1997); Rutgers' colleagues, the IEA international survey, and the Pew Foundations' Project 540.
[b] See Beaumont et al 2006.

skills of political influence and action, and sense of political efficacy. Moreover, students who entered this set of courses and programs with lower initial political interest experienced significant gains on an even larger number of survey scales, as well as generally experiencing larger gains overall.

Challenge 2: Concerns about Political Indoctrination

A second challenge for political engagement efforts is the fear that because college faculty and staff have their own political views, these efforts could have the effect of steering students into particular political ideologies or parties. Such outcomes would raise serious concerns about whether educating for democracy could be done in a legitimate way. Instead, the survey analysis showed no significant directional changes in students' political ideology or party identification during the courses and programs. For political ideology, analysis of variance showed that students did not shift significantly in any single direction along the liberal-conservative spectrum from pre- to postsurvey, regardless of whether they began with little initial political interest or higher political interest.[15]

Students entered these courses and programs with a broad spectrum of political beliefs, and the overall distribution of party identification and ideology did not change as a result of participation, even though some individuals shifted in one direction or another. This lack of change provides crucial support for these types of political engagement efforts by demonstrating that they do not seem to guide students to a particular political party or ideology.

Interviews with the project's faculty and program leaders supported these findings by revealing that many took active steps to create an open atmosphere and expose students to a range of political views and values; for instance, inviting individuals representing various political commitments and activities to speak in class. This type of conscious effort for open inquiry is a key issue for those working to promote political engagement. This is not simply because political bias is a sensitive topic on many campuses, but also because the validity of civic education vis-à-vis norms of pluralist democracy and academic integrity rest on demonstrating that this work can support or encourage intellectual diversity and open-minded, critical inquiry at the same time that students learn to develop their own political views, values, and identities and find like-minded political communities.[16]

Challenge 3: Concerns that Civic Education Only Preaches to the Converted and May Even Worsen the Democratic Divide

A third set of challenges stems from fears that political learning may only "preach to the choir" or, even worse, exacerbate existing political inequalities among students. Those concerned about promoting democratic equality—more equal opportunities for involvement and influence across all members of society—sometimes fear that civic education efforts tend to draw in and benefit students who are already more advantaged.[17] There are also related concerns that teaching for democracy may actually exacerbate existing "democratic achievement" gaps between students who are "political haves"—possessing high socioeconomic status and other important civic resources, such as having grown up with politically involved parents—and political "have nots."

The research suggests that well-designed civic engagement efforts do not necessarily reinforce political inequalities tied to background and can help mitigate some of these. First, survey results show that more typical students may experience greater benefits, at least in terms of some of the democratic capacities studied. When we compared students who entered with lower initial political interest with those who entered with higher initial political interest, we found that the low-interest group experienced consistently larger gains (see Table 3-2). In addition, the low-interest group experienced significant increases on a larger number of survey scales, including the likelihood to engage in conventional electoral actions and activities related to political voice.

As Figure 3-1 illustrates, the group that began the interventions with lower levels of political interest can be seen as largely politically disengaged at entry. At the first survey administration, students in this group had not yet developed strong elements of responsible political engagement, nor did they intend to be very politically active. The effect of the courses and program interventions on this group was to help move these students significantly along several dimensions of political engagement. By the time of the posttest survey, their political understandings, skills, and motivations had developed, and they were significantly more likely to anticipate involvement in a range of political activities.

Looking at students who entered the PEP interventions with more political interest shows that they already possessed fairly high levels of many dimensions of political engagement at the outset. The effect of the courses and programs on these students was to boost their political knowledge and skills still higher. In addition, in-depth interviews with a subset of high-interest students revealed that some experienced increases in political engagement through avenues that were not part of the survey, such as commitments to other forms of political activism and leadership.

Figure 3-1: The Multidimensional Nature of Responsible Political Engagement

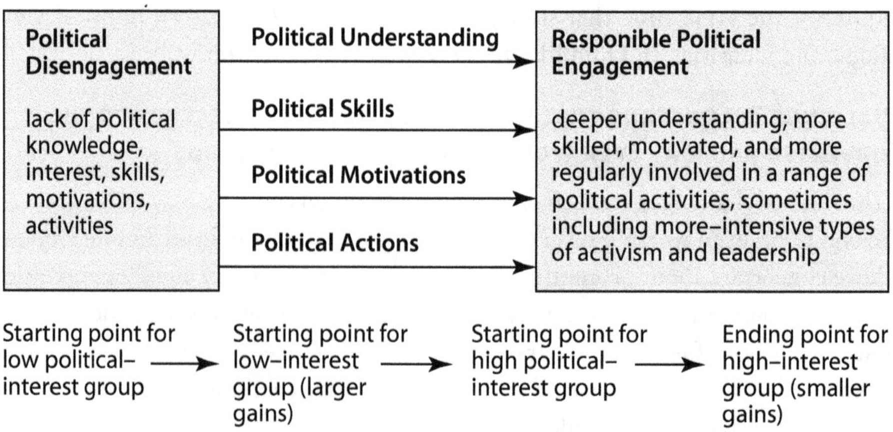

Focusing on Political Efficacy and Agency: What Kinds of Learning Experiences and Processes Can Promote Efficacy and Reduce Gaps between Political Haves and Have Nots?

Recent survey analysis identifies four particular learning mechanisms that may help promote greater overall political efficacy, or students' sense of political confidence and agency, while also closing the efficacy gap.[18] What does a more robust sense of political efficacy look like among study participants? As one student put it, her program:

> made me more confident about my abilities to contribute. Part of the empowerment was that I can do something about the political situation in the country—even if I'm in the minority, I'm still a voice. And that there should be a place for all voices in this country, and not all voices get listened to right now. And part of my responsibility is making that known . . . . And I think all of those things are important parts of the process and they're parts of the process that I feel enough tied to that I can do something about.[19]

Space limitations prevent a thorough discussion of how courses and programs in the program use specific approaches to foster a greater sense of agency, but the broad outlines can be considered here.[20]

Experiences in a Politically Active Community. One important mechanism involves learning within a politically active group or community—people consciously engaging in politics and trying to get things done around some shared political concern. This mechanism relates to the experiential learning that democratic theorists and educators emphasize: learning-by-doing and problem solving.[21] It is also linked to psychologists' studies of self-efficacy; that is, engaging in political experiences through mentoring and opportunities to see others with whom individuals identify and navigating the political realm engenders feelings of political competence.[22] Such experiences can generate feelings of political inclusion, commitment, solidarity, and integrity that foster a sense of political confidence not tied to the rewards of success alone.

Acquiring Skills for Political Action. A second political learning mechanism overlaps with experiential learning but focuses on one key element: opportunities to acquire and practice active political skills, such as organizing people to work on an issue. While intellectual skills like critical thinking can make individuals more sophisticated political analysts, they may contribute less to a sense of competence for political action than do skills that tend to be learned and applied in real-life contexts.[23] Focusing on the nuts and bolts of political action also reveals how individuals and groups can take effective incremental steps toward larger goals, yielding a sense of competence.

Engaging in Political Discourse. A third mechanism that may promote efficacy involves engaging in political discourse. Talking about politics in settings that encourage open inquiry and basic respect for persons not only fosters political development through knowledge and communication skills, it also encourages individuals to see politics as relevant to their own lives and concerns and as something about which their judgments matter.[24] Because discussing current events involves issues that are unfolding and unsettled, it invokes the actual complexity and contingency of politics. Such real-time discussions are particularly likely to generate different opinions, test political views, and encourage individuals to be more attuned to politics and varieties of belief and action. In addition, talking about politics regularly with the same group creates a politically engaged community in which such discussions—and both the political attentiveness and conflicts they entail—come to be seen as normal and valuable.

Inclusion in Collaborative Pluralist Contexts. A fourth important mechanism involves learning in collaborative, racially pluralist contexts. Differences and conflict arising from many other aspects of pluralism—partisanship, class, religion, and so on—can shape personal development by creating dissonance and disequilibrium that can disrupt an individual's worldviews and political status quo.[25] Political experiences in racially pluralist environments, however, are particularly likely to move people out of their comfort zones and open them to political change because racial differences are highly visible and uncomfortable in American politics.

Interracial contexts can be politically motivating or debilitating, depending upon how they are interpreted.[26] While racial contexts influence political behavior, most people lack positive political interactions across racial lines in schools, workplaces, and communities.[27] When racially pluralist contexts are perceived as supportive and collaborative and provide opportunities to form relationships and negotiate tensions, they can contribute to positive political growth.[28] Political learning in contexts that are *both* collaborative and racially pluralist can foster political efficacy by disrupting the stubbornness of early political dispositions. They may help individuals feel more capable of navigating political complexity and difference and reduce anxiety over racial conflict, thus avoiding the negative effects that cross-cutting exposure may have in other environments.

Creating New and More Equitable Pathways to Political Efficacy through Political Learning: Promoting Political Efficacy and Mitigating Political Inequalities

Multilevel regression demonstrates that development of efficacy is significantly, but differently, shaped by these four types of political learning even when other important influences, including socioeconomic status and preexisting civic resources, are taken into account (See Table 3-3). At the most general level, students' development of political efficacy during these courses and programs is strongly influenced by pre-intervention, or baseline, levels of efficacy and by having grown up in a politically active home. However, experiences in a politically active community,

TABLE 3-3: A Multilevel Model of Political Efficacy Achievement (Posttest Efficacy)[a]

Effect of Independent Variable	HLM Standardized Coefficients	
	MODEL	Sig.
On Individual Political Efficacy Achievement		
Gender (1=male)	.01(.01)	.34
SES	.01(.02)	.65
White	-.01(.01)	.24
Politics major	.02(.01)	.03
Past community volunteering	.01(.01)	.37
College selectivity	.01(.03)	.78
On Differentiation in Program Mean for Political Efficacy Achievement		
Average program mean for political efficacy achievement	.66(.04)	<.001
Program emphasis on political action skills	.13(.06)	.03
On Differentiation in Influence of Initial Efficacy on Political Efficacy Achievement		
Average influence of initial political efficacy on efficacy achievement	.64(.26)	.02
Program political experience in community	-.19(.06)	.004
Program emphasis on discussing current events	-.10(.18)	.58
Program emphasis on political action skills	-.39(.21)	.08
Program racial composition (% non-white)	.45(.13)	.002
Program size	.18(.05)	.001
On Differentiation in Influence of Home Political Discussion on Political Efficacy Achievement		
Average influence of home political discussion on efficacy achievement	.56(.14)	<.001
Program political experience in community	-.09(.04)	.02
Program emphasis on discussing current events	-.33(.10)	.001
Program emphasis on political action skills	-.35(.14)	.01
Program racial composition (% white)	04(.10)	.67
Program size	-.10(.04)	.01

	Reliability	Between-program Variance Component	SD	Chi-square
Program mean achievement of political efficacy (program intercept)	.466	.001	.04	65.49
Initial political efficacy	.054	.001	.04	22.16

Level 1 N=595; Level 2 N= 27. 2-level HLM model predicting Intercepts-and-Slopes as Outcomes. Home political discussion slope is fixed because it does not vary significantly by program. Since Model 1 showed that initial efficacy slope varied significantly among programs, it is allowed to vary or is treated as random. This slope no longer varies significantly once level-2 variables are included and could be modeled as fixed; running such a model yields only very slight differences in figures for beta coefficients, standard errors, and p-values without changing substantive interpretation of the model.

Note:

[a]Similar to multiple regression, HLM models estimate intercepts and slopes. The multilevel model can be conceived in terms of an individual-level (within-group) and contextual-level (between-group) equation, but the two equations are estimated simultaneously through maximum likelihood, allowing us to assess individual- and contextual-level effects together. Traditional multiple regression analysis must pool variance or assume that the means (intercepts) would be approximately equal for all groups or programs, often leading to violations of assumptions and biased regression coefficients and standard errors (Raudenbush and Bryk 2002). HLM allows intercepts and slopes to vary over programs as a function of contextual-level predictors.

acquiring skills for political action, engaging in political discourse, and inclusion in collaborative pluralist contexts can all contribute positively to students' development of political efficacy, either by boosting efficacy overall or by closing gaps in efficacy.

Importantly, some aspects of political learning seem to *reduce* the role of some preexisting political advantages reported on the presurvey. One way of interpreting this result is that some processes or experiences of political learning connected to civic education seem to help create alternative—and more equitable—avenues to political resources. These methods of teaching for democracy have the potential to compensate for political disadvantages tied to lower socioeconomic status and low levels of other civic resources. Providing these kinds of robust political learning experiences, particularly to those less likely to have such opportunities, can be critical for both political efficacy and equality.

In the analysis, the measure for political action skills was the single most important factor for shaping development of political efficacy. Finding ways to emphasize political skills that help students work collaboratively and incrementally toward concrete political goals—organizing a group, running a meeting, getting publicity, lobbying political institutions—seem to offer the greatest potential for enhancing greater political efficacy overall as well as political equality by making efficacy achievement less dependent upon background assets.

Three other measures of sociopolitical learning helped close political efficacy gaps among students participating in the PEP study. First, learning related to inclusion in politically engaged communities, such as providing students with opportunities to work with local political groups, appears particularly valuable in this regard, playing the most consistent role in reducing the effects of background inequalities. Second, current events discussions and inclusion in collaborative racial contexts played an important, though less consistent, role in reducing the influence of background political inequalities. Each of these two types of political learning can mitigate the weight that some preexisting political resources exert upon development of political efficacy. Third, courses and programs featuring racial diversity can promote political equality when they strive for cross-cutting collaboration. Additionally, these analyses suggest that course size, in and of itself, does not determine the power of political learning, but rather that actual learning processes, experiences, and contexts involved in courses play the leading role.

Conclusion

The Political Engagement Project research does not end debates over how or whether to educate undergraduates for democratic citizenship. However, this work does help demonstrate that the types of well-designed, well-taught courses and programs studied can help many different kinds of students move significantly toward a number of important democratic outcomes. Such courses can promote more-informed and active political involvement without shifting students' political ideologies in any particular direction. In addition, some of the learning mechanisms used in these courses and programs can help close the democratic achievement gap or help reduce some forms of political inequality between students who possess greater and fewer political advantages. Efforts to promote political engagement are not panaceas for the serious and pervasive problems of modern politics. They can, however, provide vital opportunities for students from many backgrounds to develop more-informed political perspectives, gain valuable civic skills, and generate a greater sense of political agency. Looking to the future, some faculty and campuses are creatively developing ideas from the Political Engagement Project into a "next generation" of efforts to educate for democracy as part of a partnership with the American Association of State Colleges and Universities.[29]

Bridging Adolescent Engagement and Adult Engagement: A Theory of Political Identity

4

By Bobbi Gentry

How do young people see the political world and their place in it? What encourages young people to participate civically and politically? This chapter uses political psychology literature to propose a theory of political identity status that considers how young people answer the question: Who am I politically?

The 2008 primary season saw young people participate at higher rates in presidential primaries and caucuses across the United States than they had for the past several decades. The same was true in 2012, with 50% of young people voting.[1] Youth turnout in the primaries increased by nine percentage points over 2000, resulting in more than 6.5 million youth voters going to the polls.[2] For the first time since 18-year-olds gained the right to vote, rates of young voter turnout rose in three consecutive election cycles.[3] The question is: why? Older models of voting behavior, such as rational choice, fail to explain these changes in youth participation. Youth voting has come into particular focus since the 1971 passage of the 26th Amendment; however, youth voting was on the decline through the 1996 presidential election.

The problem of misrepresenting youth participation lies in how youth are perceived as voters and participants in civic life. Traditionally, most youths fall into the category of nonvoters, with rates of registration and voting of less than 50%. This categorization has labeled youth in such a way that studies of youth voting focus on the negative—that is, why young people do not vote—rather than on the positive focus of what factors encourage youth to vote. For civic engagement, the assessment is that youth are instead volunteering in their communities, signing petitions, boycotting, and buycotting.[4] While the civic engagement literature[5] focuses on the development of a participatory citizenry and what a society can do to encourage participation, the voting behavior literature[6] focuses solely on one aspect of participation—the vote.

The assumption on both fronts is that today's youth are different. The civic engagement literature argues that youth are finding new and different ways of participating in civic life than older generations and that they will continue to participate once they vote (see Harward and Shea, Chapter 2). This assumption that youth will continue to vote once they are registered to do so inadequately considers how this process happens psychologically or politically. Both the civic engagement and political participation literatures are missing a critical piece of the puzzle that explains how to encourage both voting and nonvoting forms of participation in youth.

I address this issue by introducing a new variable—political ego identity. This concept is distinct from focusing on students' sense of efficacy in political actions and civic duty because political ego identity is an understanding of self. While there can be a clear positive relationship between efficacy and identity, having a political identity differs from either the feeling that as an individual one can have an effect on politics (internal efficacy) or the feeling that one needs to participate (civic duty).

Political ego identity combines an individual's self-awareness of political attitudes, feelings, and views with the specific practicing behaviors (discussing politics, considering pros and cons of social or political options) that one engages in to express one's identity. In addition, I adapt Marcia's original four identity statuses of achievement, moratorium, foreclosure, and diffusion,[7] which are explained below, into my own political identity statuses of fully developed, somewhat developed, explorers, and diffuse. I expect young people with a fully developed political ego identity status to engage more in the civic and political process by voting and encouraging others to do so, in addition to other types of participation. Those in the somewhat developed status are expected to participate if their parents or influential others do, but are not expected to participate if these influential others do not. Conversely, those who are either diffuse or in the explorer status will not participate. Diffusion-status individuals want nothing to do with politics, have explored few political alternatives, and have made no commitments in the civic or political realm. This approach is especially applicable to young voters as they go through the process of developing an identity. While this variable may be applied to older citizens, it is especially significant for young participants in the malleable period of identity development.

To bridge the gaps between the voting behavior, civic engagement, and the identity literatures, I put forward a theory that takes into account the unique aspect of youth and their differences from older counterparts based upon where they are in the process of political ego identity development. Looking within the youth participant, I expect to find that an incomplete political ego identity is an obstacle to civic and political engagement. Lack of a cohesive, overarching self-identity occurs frequently with this age group and may correlate with lack of a cohesive political ego identity. Civic engagement is part of the discovery process of an identity, in which young people engage in different aspects of social life within their communities. Youth who know who they are politically or who are actively exploring the civic and political realms are more likely to engage in behaviors that confirm or further develop their identity. Identity may be the key to disentangling the differences between participants and nonparticipants in the youth population and could bridge the gap between civic engagement and voting behavior by offering an explanation as to how civic engagement aids development of a young person's identity and involves young people in their environments, which leads to later involvement in the political process.

Beginning with the gaps in the literature, this work will use the theory of identity development to explain the connections between civic engagement and political participation (see Chapter 1 for definitions). An overview of both literatures and an explanation of what makes political identity development different are followed by the process of political ego identity development, along with examples of each status. In the final section, the application of the theory of political identity development is put within the context of civic and political engagement.

The Gap in the Literatures

Civic Engagement

Where the voting behavior literature focuses on end-product behavior and characteristics of voters and nonvoters, the civic engagement literature discusses the process of becoming a citizen and comes closest to a developmental approach to political identity. Civic engagement authors argue that cultivating democratic principles, allowing for participation within communities, and having environments that are politically stimulating increase youth participation across the board.[8] Gimpel et al. argue that socialization within a democratic community plays a major role in whether young people participate. Communities that have a competitive political environment, open political discussions, and ethnic diversity are more likely to produce citizens who participate. On the other hand, communities with one major party, little political discussion, and ethnic homogeneity are more likely to have young people who believe politics is already decided, the discussion is closed, and everyone has similar political beliefs.[9]

Primary agents of socialization, meaning those elements of an individual's environment that impact socialization, are also particularly influential in how that individual becomes unique (see Beaumont, Chapter 3). These agents include parents, parental circumstances (economic status, citizenship status, etc.) and education.[10] Flanagan also argues for the importance of youth involvement in community organizations and emphasizes how youth come to understand the social order.[11] Values that young people learn in community organizations include connecting and identifying with others, interacting with institutions within communities, and learning how their actions, thoughts, and words can make a difference.[12]

The value of youth involvement is felt both by the community and the individual who participates in it. Yates and Youniss argue that reflection is a valuable aspect of encouraging thoughts about how the world works, individual responsibility, and connections to others.[13] Their assessment of identity and community participation ties in very closely with developing a political identity; however, they fail to connect service-learning and civic engagement to political behaviors in adulthood.

The value of their research is to point to the connections between general identity development and how civic engagement offers opportunities for political awareness.

Though the civic engagement research comes from a developmental perspective, its emphasis is placed on environmental circumstances that encourage development of citizens, not on individuals or their internal development of an identity. The focus on youth civic engagement fails to see development throughout an individual's life and does not accurately connect civic behaviors developed in youth to political behaviors of adults.

Socialization through education, community service, and other social institutions encourages youth to participate in their communities, their societies, and, as they reach voting age, the electoral process. Where the civic engagement literature focuses on the society, what it provides to the individual, and the process of acquiring and sustaining many different civic and political behaviors, including volunteering, petitioning, and holding leadership positions within the community, the voting behavior literature is centered around the individual and the final product of voting behavior.

Voting Behavior

The Michigan model suggests that higher turnout of certain groups is based upon such demographic characteristics as age, race, education level, and gender. Social characteristics also come into play, such as political party affiliation, level of political interest, and internal and external political efficacy.[14] Stability attributes have been added that include marital status, recent change of residence, feelings of connection to the community, and home ownership. For young people, the voting behavior literature argues that they have not yet achieved those stability characteristics that result in political participation.[15] Even though this literature looks at the individual, it focuses on circumstances outside the individual and not the individual's political development in a particular political context.

Plutzer examines voting behavior as gaining inertia and resources as one develops a habit of voting.[16] Arguing within the traditional voting behavior model, which takes into account resources of partisanship, socioeconomic status, education, knowledge, and interest, he finds that voting is a habit youth voters have not yet acquired, and therefore in their first election, they must overcome many costs:

> As young citizens confront their first election all of the costs of voting are magnified: They have never gone through the process of registration, may not know the location of their polling place, and may not have yet developed an understanding of party differences on key issues.[17]

How individuals understand voting, especially voting for the first time, needs to be revised to take into account all of these factors that contribute to low voter turnout. However, Plutzer discusses voter turnout in terms of the traditional forms of resources and learning to vote rather than the aspects of self-reflection or identity.

In discussing youth political behavior, Bogard, Sheinheit, and Clarke consider the issue of social capital in acquiring political information. Some of the most frequently cited reasons why youth do not participate is "lack of knowledge about political issues, lack of understanding about how to get involved, and lack of enjoyment in the political process."[18] Due to the lack of trust both in politicians and the media, youth seem to have nowhere to turn for reliable information about politics. The authors' research introduces different alternatives on university campuses that involve youth in creating forums for discussion, hosting events with multiple perspectives, and offering basic political knowledge about how to register and voting rights. They point out that key elements to voter participation are reflection and multiple perspectives that encourage dialogue. Their discussion is similar to the aspect of self-reflection discussed in the civic engagement literature. This aspect of reflection is one that is taken into account for the political identity variable.

Bridging the Gaps

While both the civic engagement and voting behavior literatures evaluate the behaviors of youth, they choose different scopes, including differences of focus on outcome versus process and different types of participation. Scholars of both fields suggest that they would like to encourage youth participation in democracy, yet they see participation in two different lights. Civic participation scholars focus on adolescent youth as important in developing future citizens and do not limit themselves to studying only political interactions, but also examine civic participation of all types. Voting behavior scholars tend to focus on the average voter and note that turnout among youth tends to be small due to lack of experience, interest, and information. Scholars of voting behavior tend not to look at voting as a process, but instead choose to focus on the outcome of voter turnout and what influences the vote decision rather than looking at the process for developing a political identity.

Gibson notes that the biggest problem is that the civic engagement and voter participation scholars are talking past each other.[19] In explaining why youth do not vote, she argues that youth participants have a deep distrust of the system and are cynical, becoming more so with age. Gibson criticizes the civic engagement literature for scholars' focus on the individual rather than on the effects of institutions or communities.[20] She notes that there is a field of civic engagement research called youth development that makes the link to society and political institutions. However, she believes that the youth development research is focused on the problem of knowledge rather than on "investigating ways in which [young people] come to understand how politics works and how they, as individuals, come to define themselves as political agents."[21]

My work attempts to answer Gibson's criticism of the youth development field as it connects to both civic engagement and voting behavior through development of a political identity. While both fields of study look at individuals, they seem to miss the key variable of how individuals think of themselves politically. The major criticism of youth in both the civic engagement and the voting behavior literature is that youth often are not active in civic and political life. While this observation may be accurate, an explanation is needed to better understand what encourages active participation. I argue that one of the most important tools is knowledge about one's identity; this knowledge affects behavior in all aspects of one's life, including political and civic engagement.

Political ego identity is a way to study and discuss what scholars in both fields hint at but never articulate as a major variable in the study of participatory behavior. The bridge between civic engagement and voting behavior is political identity, which takes into account self-reflection, self-knowledge, and identity confrontation. Civic engagement scholars attempt to develop a citizenry that knows how communities and institutions work and provides practical knowledge and opportunities to youth through service. The self-reflective part of service is a key component to understanding how civic engagement can encourage sustained participation. Bridging the knowledge and experiences of service-learning in particular offers an opportunity for identity development, as Yates and Youniss argue. However, the individual needs to be encouraged to take these experiences and attempt to define oneself as a political being. The lessons learned through civic participation facilitated through schools and communities can be carried over to specific instances of political participation such as voting, but the connection needs to be made between these two types of participation.

The opportunities for reflection about engaging in civic life can be carried over to participating in political life when one reaches adulthood. Learning to reflect upon one's world and one's place in it is a key component of developing an identity. I argue that having an identity makes one more likely to engage in behaviors that confirm that identity. If one is exposed to aspects of civic engagement at an earlier age and takes these behaviors into account when defining who one is, then it is likely that an individual will continue to participate in civic and political life later. The individual internalizing these activities as a part of oneself is the crucial component that explains sustained civic and political behavior. The behaviors of participation become ingrained because they continue to define the person's identity.

This political identity can help bridge the gap between civic engagement of youth and political engagement of young adults by explaining the process of transitioning and defining who one is civically and politically. Political identity also can explain why some young people choose not to engage in political life even though they were previously exposed to opportunities to engage in civic and community endeavors. In addition, political identity can explain the difference that young people see in civic engagement versus political engagement.

Political Ego Identity as a Psychological Approach

In adult psychological development, one of the major issues in transitioning between adolescence and adulthood is the ability to define oneself. Erikson's early work on psychosocial development discusses a pivotal time for the individual, the identity crisis phase,[22] in which one defines one's own "sense of inner identity" and develops the "style of one's individuality"[23]:

> The young person, in order to experience [identity] wholeness, must feel a progressive continuity between that which he has come to be during the long years of childhood and that which he promises to become in the anticipated future; between that which he conceives himself to be and that which he perceives others to see in him and to expect of him.[24]

Emphasizing the importance of the individual within an environment that has particular historical, cultural, and social connections, Erikson argues that identity is not just about individuals, but also about the interaction of individuals with their social environment.

From the developmental psychology literature, Marcia builds on Erikson's original theory and discusses how individuals go through different statuses to form a positive self-identity, meaning that individuals create their own identity and the choices of identity are not made for them.[25] Arguing that the effects of identity are enormous, Marcia notes, "Identity is said to be structural in that, once formed, it affects the ways in which one perceives the world, organizes those perceptions, and subsequently behaves."[26] In Marcia's original framework,[27] the political identity variable is just one component of overall identity development. Individuals are classified into four different statuses: achievement, moratorium, foreclosure, and diffusion. Individuals who possess a cohesive psychological identity, meaning those who know who they are and what they stand for, are in the identity achievement status. Those experimenting with their identity and exploring different aspects of their identity but who have not yet decided upon a cohesive identity are in the moratorium status. An identity in the foreclosure status occurs when an individual did not decide upon an identity but instead bases her or his identity on what others, such as parents or mentors, perceive it to be. Diffusion status exists when individuals have no idea who they are and are making no effort to define their identity. The adult development literature proposes that as individuals move from adolescence to adulthood, they form a more cohesive, achieved political identity. As the cohort ages, therefore, more and more people should have successfully achieved an identity.

Ego identity continues to be a field of research in which psychologists link the individual to the larger world. Adaptation has occurred. For example, relatively recent measures of ego-identity[28] use survey analysis instead of in-depth interviews to assess identity status. Marcia's adaptation of Erikson's original work is to suggest different aspects of the overarching identity of an individual. In Marcia's work he suggested political/religious identity as one of three central aspects. However, Marcia's research on different levels of development often found political identity as the least developed. I create a model of how a person develops a political identity by drawing on Marcia's work. Political scientists can benefit from the ego identity literature as they attempt to understand a larger literature of political identity.[29]

However, neither the political science nor the psychology literature has taken up the development of a political ego identity as a variable to explain civic engagement and voting behavior. Identity can explain voting behavior, as those who have internalized a political identity are more likely to vote, whereas those who have not internalized an identity are much less likely to vote. Identity could explain civic engagement, in that those individuals who have internalized civic aspects of their identity are more likely to participate in their communities, whereas those who have not are less likely to do so.

The psychological literature treats identity as an interaction between the self and society. Identity is in many ways a creation of the individual and society. As the individual presents him- or herself to the outside world, there is a reflection; not only are individuals presenting themselves, but these individuals are also reacting to society's perceptions of them. In this way, society can limit the possibilities of what is deemed acceptable.[30] When encouraging civic engagement, positive reinforcement plays a role, as others are confirming positive perceptions of the individual. If there are competing positive reinforcements, however, from other behaviors of the individual, such as academics or athletics, individuals can choose to define themselves differently and prioritize some identities over others.

Political Ego Identity

Unlike the social identity literature within psychology, the psychological identity literature refers to the individual. Psychological identity is formed from experiences of the individual and constructed by the individual but is not a socially constructed meaning created and imposed by society. Whereas a psychological identity is created by the individual, that individual can adapt his or her identity based on interactions with society. In this way, the individual is the original constructor, who receives information about what is socially acceptable and may choose to alter his or her identity or not as a reaction to society. Even though a psychological identity is developed throughout one's life, the consolidation of an individual's identity usually occurs in very late adolescence and early adulthood.[31] As noted earlier, the literature on identity development places a political identity as one of many aspects of the individual, which makes it so difficult to study. However, I am attempting to create a political identity variable that measures only the aspects of one's identity that are political, whereas Marcia's original measure attempted to capture occupational, religious, and political aspects of identity. I define political ego identity as knowing and caring about a set of political issues, having a set of organized beliefs about the political system, and engaging in practicing behaviors that support those beliefs.

Political identity is one of many identities of an individual. Consider identities as hats. One's political identity hat may be in the closet during off-election years, though some, such as political scientists, may continuously wear that hat. Within the identity literature, typically different forms of identity such as occupational, religious, social, ethnic and racial, and political are discussed. These identities often are overlapping as layers of the individual. Within these layers are placed different identities at the core of who one is. These identities are the aspects of oneself that are considered central and important. Many of the outside layers are considered peripheral. Individuals are often more highly developed in areas in which their identity is central and important to who they are and are less developed in peripheral areas of identity.

Aspects of Psychological Identity

An identity initially begins to take shape in the formation process in which one becomes more committed to that identity. Often, the more committed a person becomes to that identity, the higher a value (salience) the individual places on it. Identity is a complex mixture of different identities; consider a young woman and the number of identities that she may have as a student, employee, citizen, sister, daughter, friend, and significant other. Each identity provides an element of role expectations and fulfillments in addition to the internalization of beliefs about her identity.[32] Identity formation is the process by which one acquires an identity, presents that identity to the social world, and adapts to the reactions. The formation process takes into account childhood interests, future orientation, and present context.[33] For aspects of civic engagement and political participation, identity formation is vital as a series of times in one's life during which one is exploring alternative identities, having confrontations with others, and making commitments.

For youth who are participating in civic activities, exploring options such as working for nonprofits allows them to experience other ways of looking at the world and seeing the situations of others. The civic opportunity and later classroom discussions of engagement opportunities offer students and their peers the chance to confront different beliefs about the world. Periods of self-reflection allow individuals to commit to what they think is important, consider how they think about a social or political situation, and process how they define themselves in context.

Explaining the Process of Development

I argue that the steps of the developmental process of a political identity are socialization, exploration, judgment of others' politics, self-questioning, and coherence. Socialization, illustrated in Figure 4-1, is the first element of the process during which external forces shape a young person's identity. Where people grow up, their economic and social circumstances, parents and families, school situation, and friends all contribute to the formation of the political being. As the first building block of the entire developmental process, socialization—specifically, the amount of political socialization by external forces—provides a foundation for the future of the political identity.

Socialization can be extensive or minimal and, as a consequence, can lead to different levels of identity development. For higher levels of identity in young adulthood, many developed individuals are socialized to be interested in, engaged in, and a part of politics. Focus groups of young people[34] suggest that parental encouragement to have knowledge about politics played a major role in the successful early development of an identity by people in their young adult years. Parents, however, were not the only force of socialization that mattered; schools also played a role, including whether social studies teachers discussed politics and whether schools held mock elections in the early years of education.

From the focus groups, those in the lower statuses often noted that they did not discuss politics in their homes, schools, or communities; for them, socialization of other factors such as vocation or social status were more important than political development. After the socialization stage, individuals who have little to no political socialization often end up in the diffusion status because they have not been socialized to think that politics is important or because other aspects of their overarching identity are more important than their political identity.

Individuals who have been extensively politically socialized in their environment tend to progress to the next stage—exploration. One's exploration of alternative ideas from parents, teachers, and peers is a key component to developing a cohesive and highly developed identity.[35]A portion of the exploration process is discovering how the political system works and what the major issues of debate are. Such exploration can be extensive, minimal, or nonexistent. Individuals with diffuse identities have not explored the political possibilities and, therefore, are not interested or engaged in continuing to find out who they are politically. For individuals who are somewhat developed, the exploration element of the development process can be extremely limited—to the point where their exploration led them to discern what other people's ideas were rather than develop their own ideas.

As the following flowchart suggests, three possibilities happen in the exploration stage. Individuals may explore what their political environment has to offer and may be disappointed to the point that they do not want to interact with any aspect of politics. Through negative interactions with the environment, they become uninterested or disappointed and never continue to the other stages. Another pathway as a consequence of exploration is to find interest in continuing to search within the political environment; individuals then are in the status of explorers. The explorer status may be momentary or ongoing; a person may choose to continually explore what the political environment has to offer without ever deciding how he or she feels about others' politics and without ever deciding on his or her own political identity. Scholars in psychology expect that exploration is a transition status in which one will eventually achieve further development.[36] However, in the context of elections, an individual may explore during every election cycle and see what the political environment has to offer, such as candidates, issue positions, or different political ideologies, without ever deciding what he or she believes. The decision to vote becomes particularly difficult because both candidates offer a believable option, and these individuals cannot decide which candidate to support because they have not judged the value of others' politics or determined their own.

A third alternative is to move on to the judgment stage after one has discovered what the political environment has to offer and feels confident that there is enough information available to judge others' politics. In the judgment stage, young people tend to develop a political identity either through struggle or acceptance. After exploring available options in the political environment, individuals begin to make decisions about what others believe based on whether or not they agree or disagree. At this point in development, there can be an enormous amount of struggle with others or an absence of struggle altogether because the individual accepts others' beliefs. What makes this stage different from exploration is that exploration is about knowledge and facts, whereas the judgment stage deals directly with how the individual reacts to the information found in the exploration phase. During this phase, the individual continues to gather information that is not necessarily factual knowledge, but instead may be opinions about what other people believe, such as those who were important socializers in the past or experts of the present. Two pathways of judgment are doubt and acceptance, where doubt leads to the next level of development and acceptance leads to the somewhat developed status.

From the information gathered in focus groups, individuals who accept what their parents or friends tell them about politics do have an identity and are likely to vote because others tell them to, but they have little individuation—meaning they are unclear where their identity ends and where others begin, and they are unable to differentiate their identity from others' political identity that they have accepted. The practice of doubting what others believe and disagreeing with what others believe is a part of distinguishing one's own identity from others and allows for the individual to differentiate between them.[37] While there is a possibility that an individual can accept the viewpoints of parents or other influential figures after doubting them, the acceptance must be on the individual's own terms. Usually, individuals may agree with their parents, but agree based on different reasoning, meaning that the outcome may be the same, but the process is different. In the focus groups, fully developed individuals often doubt socializers and experts, which leads them to the next level of development. Participants who were fully developed often discussed the judgment stage as a difficult period in which they disagreed with parents and peers, which at best led to an agreement to disagree and at worst led to shunning the topic of politics as the individual attempted to attain an identity.

Where exploration was the discovery of facts about the political environment and judgment was about the discovery of interpersonal information and beliefs, self-questioning is the element of the process that distinguishes somewhat developed from fully developed individuals. At this point in the process, individuals must look inward to figure out what they believe, which is often seen as an inner turmoil. Where judgment was about the external struggle with others who may disagree, self-questioning is the struggle with oneself about who one is and what one cares about. This point is where people individualize themselves from their predecessors and begin to articulate who they are to the outside world. The person is questioning what he or she actually believes in and cares about in politics. In this stage, the importance of politics (salience) becomes personalized—politics is not just important for politics' sake, but politics becomes personally important and relevant to the individual.

The two pathways that result from the period of self-questioning are indecision about what one believes and conclusions about what one believes. Indecision over what one believes leads to the somewhat developed status; even though one has gone through all of the other stages of development, identity can consistently be updated based upon new information. Still not knowing what one believes, stands

Figure 4-1: The Process of Political Identity Development

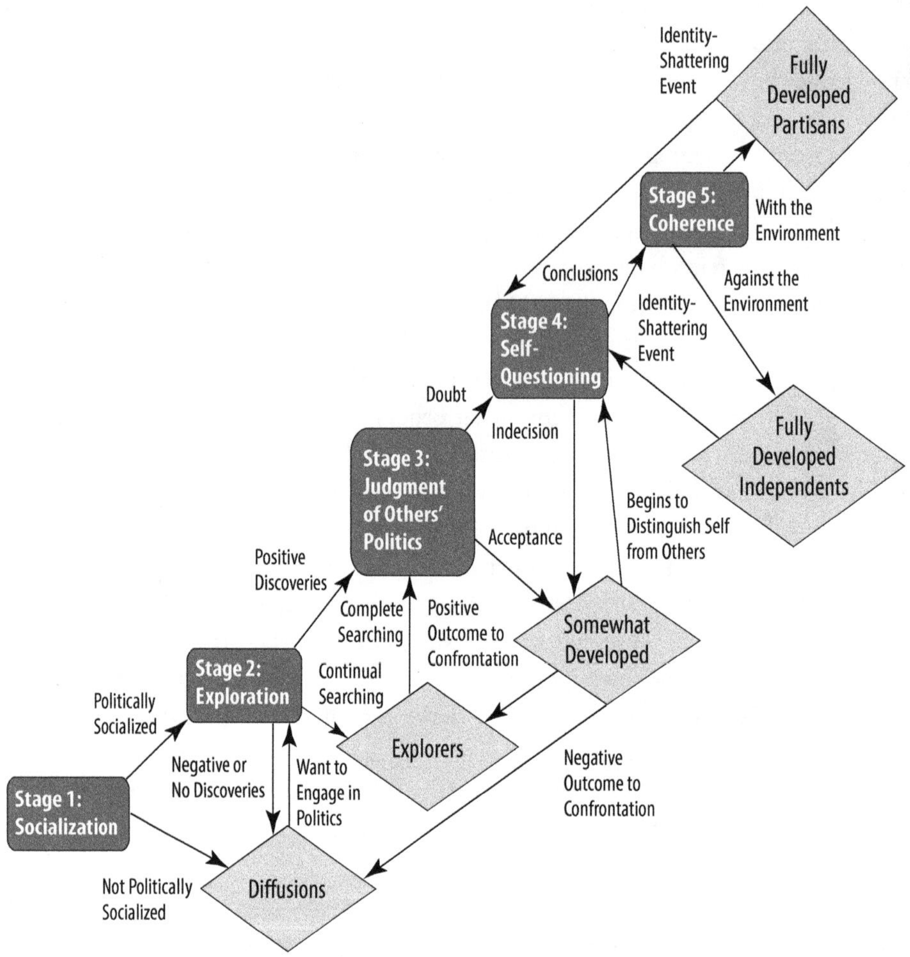

for, and identifies as leads to a somewhat developed status. While individuals may have conclusions about what they believe, who they are, and how they identify themselves, these conclusions are disparate pieces to the identity puzzle.

Conclusions to the internal struggle of what one believes then lead the individual to consolidate the different aspects of a political identity into a coherent whole.

For those individuals in the higher levels of identity development, there is evidence of cohesion, meaning that people are comfortable in their own political skin and are willing to hold opinions that differ from others even though disagreement may be uncomfortable. The process of development is not just finding out who they are, but also defending their beliefs. As the fifth step in the process, political persons begin to merge the parts of themselves that were the foundation, who they were after self-questioning, and the political person they will be. Coherence of a political identity does not suggest that individuals are rigid in their beliefs, but instead means that when new information comes along it does not create a crisis of character; rather, these individuals take the information in and process it against their current knowledge of themselves. In essence, the fully developed stage allows for individuals who have a coherent whole of an identity to continually reevaluate their world. For politics, this reevaluation may be only every four years, but highly developed individuals are open to new information because they are secure in their political identity. Rigidity often occurs when individuals are insecure about their beliefs, and they feel that they must protect their identity from outside factors that might cause them to question their identity or point out inconsistencies. In their minds, people in the fully developed stage see how all of the disparate parts of their political beliefs fit together as a complete whole. This stage can also be understood as the consolidation of the self, in which the malleable elements from self-questioning become firmer.

The final outcomes of coherence are connected with interactions with the political environment. Though development is not dependent upon how well the environment fits the individual, how the individual eventually fits into the environment does matter. Individuals who not only have coherence with their identity but whose identity also fits into the political environment reasonably become partisans. Individuals whose identity does not fit with the environment or who do not feel represented by the partisan options tend to become fully developed Independents. While the final stage may be coherence, the outcome greatly depends upon how these individuals are able to relate with and accommodate their beliefs into the electoral choices available.

These development stages are not necessarily static. When somewhat-developed individuals come into confrontation with their accepted beliefs, they have two reactions to different types of confrontation. They reconsider their position of acceptance and begin to explore again, thus taking on the status of explorers. Somewhat-developed individuals may also progress to the stage of self-questioning when they begin to see distinctions between what they believe and what others believe. In this way, the somewhat-developed person slowly undergoes the process of individuation. When the confrontation of one's accepted beliefs completely destroys one's identity to the point where the individual no longer knows who he or she is and is not pursuing ways to figure out who his or her political self is, then such an individual becomes diffuse. Diffusers may leave their status if they become interested in politics or want to begin engaging with the political world, which leads them to the exploration stage. Explorers may eventually feel as though they have completed their investigation of politics and, based on that decision, can move on to the third stage—judgment. There are also times during which fully developed individuals can undergo an identity crisis and begin to question themselves about their beliefs. In everyday terms, many middle-age people go through some sort of mid-life crisis during which they question their own existence. In terms of a political identity, identity-shattering events can be wars, economic crises, or political scandals that make the person question his or her identity and affiliations.

Contextual Nature of Identity

As a person develops his or her identity, he or she is not doing so without some environmental contexts. Certainly, there can be times during which certain political and social environments either encourage young people to develop an identity or discourage them. Take, for example, the 2008 presidential campaign. Young people may have developed their political identity as a result of the political environment that was focused on the campaign. The particular environment can be conducive to political identity development or can hinder development. An environment that might hinder one's ability to develop a political identity could be a household in which political and social issues are not discussed or are disparaged. Considering political identity as contextual is particularly meaningful to civic engagement, since offering more opportunities for identity development in civic education programs can make higher levels of identity development more likely.

Linking Civic Engagement and Voting Behavior

Political identity links civic engagement and voting behavior through different aspects of reinforced participation. The foundations of civic engagement and political engagement are similar. An individual must internalize the values and have beliefs about civic and political life to sustain engagement in either realm. Civic engagement—focusing on linking an individual's actions to those of the community—can enhance one's interest in interacting with the political system. The biggest link between civic engagement and voting behavior is the connection of the individual with the social and political system. Civic engagement offers more of a hands-on approach to encourage people of all ages, but especially young people, to become active in their communities, whereas political behavior (and especially voting) may be a more infrequent task with no clear consequences from a single person's actions. The link between these two activities is the individual. If, through civic participation, an individual learns how the political system works, who makes the decisions, what he or she believes in, and what he or she thinks society should be like, then the individual is not only getting information about the political system, he or she is also learning information about him- or herself and his or her views about the world—which is the exploration of an identity.

Civic engagement opportunities in college provide concrete knowledge about the political system and examples of how the individual fits into the system, in addition to moments of confrontation about previous beliefs. Part of forming a cohesive political identity is that the identity must come into confrontation with alternative viewpoints. For example, as Yates and Youniss note, students who participate in community service at a soup kitchen are confronted with their opinions on poverty and its causes, but this opportunity occurs because the engagement was structured and put the civic work into a larger political context.[38] Confronting previous beliefs about the world and how individuals define themselves and the political order are valuable stimuli for a more cohesive identity. Confrontation is needed for young individuals to acknowledge their beliefs about themselves and the political world and to know that there may be differences in what they believe and what others believe.

Forming a political identity requires moments of transitioning and defining oneself. Civic engagement in adolescence offers moments of focus on the identity of civic and political life, an identity that can lay stagnant if it is not cultivated. Participation at a younger age offers situations in which individuals define themselves, and this civic engagement gives a reflective element to illuminate the relationship between an individual and his or her world. Participation becomes a crucial aspect to developing an identity, as young people find what they believe in, gain more knowledge about how the world works, and engage in behaviors that address larger social and political issues. Civic engagement allows youth to look beyond themselves and see a larger world to connect with, but civic engagement is also one of many different opportunities available to define oneself. Good programs in civic engagement can foster identity development through readings and the presentation of key theories and concepts, reflective analytical writing, class discussions, and before and after reactions. Those who support civic engagement should find opportunities in which self-definition and transcendence beyond an old identity are possible to encourage young people to evaluate, question, doubt, and analyze who they are.

Political identity also can help to explain why an individual would choose not to engage in civic or political life later. Negative experiences during civic activities may make an individual not want to continue participating. Reinforcement is important in identity. If the experience or the reaction to one's participation is negative, then the individual is less likely to incorporate this value into his or her identity and engage in the future. For example, if a student works in the community at an outreach center and has a negative experience with the director or patrons, then he or she will be less likely to want to go back into that environment, which can affect further civic engagement and have a negative impact on later political engagement because of a lack of positive reinforcement. Careful criticism of civic engagement programs should take into account the costs of turning some students off to civic and political life altogether versus the rewards of exposing students to community and political experiences.

Centrality is another reason why some might choose not to engage in civic life later on; if civic and political identity are not central to the individual, then his or her identity may be formed from other aspects of his or her life, with politics becoming peripheral. If a civic or political identity is not a central part of one's life, other priorities will displace it. Influences to centrality in a person's life include how individuals meet the expectations of their identity and certain consequences to psychological well-being that certain identities have.[39]

Another component to identity development within political and civic contexts is the idea of concrete versus abstract. Civic engagement is often more concrete, meaning that young people can directly see that their involvement has some type of influence, which makes them more likely to participate in the future.[40] Political engagement, on the other hand, tends to be more abstract because involvement by the young person may not result in immediate or direct influence on complex political problems that tend to be more difficult to relate to and therefore personalize. These may seem more daunting, with fewer returns on investments of time, energy, and self. These investments may seem higher than the perceived change in governmental institutions, policies, or procedures. In the end, a developed identity continues to play a role in sustaining participation, whether civic or political, throughout an individual's life because the individual knows who she or he is politically and therefore is less likely to avoid participation.

Conclusion

The value of this exploration was to lay out a theory for building a bridge between civic engagement in adolescence that becomes encouragement for later political engagement, especially voting behavior. The connection of this concept to voting behavior may help political scientists come to understand another element of voting behavior and civic and political engagement levels that is deeper than current measures and takes into account differences based on youth, since a political identity becomes more cohesive as one ages. Identity measures can promote civic and political engagement through conscious pursuit of ways to develop young people's political identity. Political ego identity also can be studied under changes in political contexts that may affect a generation of young people (developed or not) and that generation's development as political beings.

In sum, civic engagement research and implementation could benefit from more emphasis on political identity. Educational programs geared toward civic and political engagement should take into account more than just self-reflection by encouraging youth to be clear about what they believe and what they think and spurring them to understand why they hold certain political views. Self-definition, self-reflection, and positive feedback about the civic and political behaviors that individuals pursue are major components in studying a new variable that not only bridges civic engagement and future political engagement, but also illuminates the peculiarities of what it means to be young and transitioning toward becoming politically active individuals.

Fostering Political Participation: A Call to Action for Higher Education Institutions

5

By Jean Wahl Harris

After establishing political participation as a learning objective of higher education institutions, this chapter discusses the Higher Education Act voter registration mandate, the federal mandate for Constitution and Citizenship Day programming, and the Help Americans Vote Act College Program grant opportunities as means by which colleges and universities can foster political participation in their students and graduates. The chapter ends with a call to action for faculty members and the American Political Science Association.

Political scientists and others in the higher education community have been discussing the benefits of service-learning, civic engagement, and community engagement for decades. Although numerous higher education professionals and political scientists argue that college students' experiences with these forms of experiential learning will foster good citizenship postgraduation, there is an ongoing debate over their effectiveness in fostering political participation.[1] In addition, not all scholars agree on the proper place for actual political participation in these college-supported or mandated activities. Although some believe that experiences devoid of interactions with political institutions or politics—electoral or nonelectoral—are not truly preparing students to be effective, politically engaged citizens,[2] others note that colleges and universities often are reluctant to promote political engagement.[3] Still others fear ideological indoctrination by liberally biased academics. Therefore, some believe that efforts to engage students in civic and political participation threaten students' rights as well as the goal of higher education, which is to teach students how to think, not what to think.[4]

However, the 1998 Higher Education Act mandates and the 2002 Help Americans Vote Act College Program offer opportunities for higher education institutions to provide students with nonpartisan, political participation experiences in the context of learning about public policy processes and electoral politics. With federal mandates and grant opportunities as building blocks, combined with the growing consensus that higher education institutions should foster civic, or community, engagement, and, specifically, political participation, as a learning objective, this chapter calls on political science faculty to take the lead in fostering political participation among undergraduate students.

First, this chapter explores the status of civic engagement and political participation as learning outcomes of higher education. Then, it discusses means by which the federal government supports political participation as a learning outcome for institutions of higher education. Next, barriers to college student electoral participation are highlighted. The chapter then presents some concerns over colleges and universities' knowledge of and compliance with federal mandates relevant to fostering political participation. Lastly, the chapter concludes with a call to action for political science faculty to use the issues raised in this chapter to establish coursework and experiential opportunities that will engage students in policy evaluation, planning, and implementation to foster postgraduation political participation. In the language of Harward and Shea (Chapter 2), this chapter calls on faculty to engage with their students in high-impact learning activities that focus on the study of horizontal participation, to foster vertical participation.

Civic Engagement: A Higher Education Learning Objective

Evidence exists to support the notion that civic engagement should be a learning outcome for undergraduate education.[5] Building upon its 2004 report, which argued that higher education institutions had reached a consensus that "civic, social, and personal responsibility" were accepted learning outcomes,[6] the Association of American Colleges and Universities (AACU) launched its Liberal Education and America's Promise (LEAP) campaign in 2005. Calling for the "most powerful preparation for work, life, and citizenship," LEAP promotes four essential learning outcomes: 1) knowledge of human cultures and the physical natural world, 2) intellectual and practical skills, 3) integrative and applied learning, and 4) personal and social responsibility, including civic knowledge and engagement.[7]

Recognizing the developing consensus on civic engagement as a learning outcome for higher education, the Carnegie Foundation for the Advancement of Teaching established a voluntary Community Engagement Elective Classification for higher education institutions in 2006. The Carnegie Foundation defines community engagement as "the collaboration between institutions of higher education and their larger communities (local, regional/state, national, global) for the mutually beneficial exchange of knowledge and resources in a context of partnership and reciprocity." More specifically, institutions earning the Community Engagement Classification must show that they meet the expectations for two categories of community engagement:

1. **Curricular Engagement** includes institutions where teaching, learning, and scholarship engage faculty, students, and community in mutually beneficial and respectful collaboration. Their interactions address

community-identified needs, deepen students' civic and academic learning, enhance community well-being, and enrich the scholarship of an institution.

2. **Outreach & Partnerships** includes institutions that provide compelling evidence of one or both of two approaches to community engagement:

   A. **Outreach** focuses on the application and provision of institutional resources for community use with benefits to both campus and community.

   B. **Partnerships** focuses on collaborative interactions with the community and related scholarship for the mutually beneficial exchange, exploration, and application of knowledge, information, and resources, such as research, capacity building, and economic development.[8]

By 2010, 311 institutions of higher education had earned Carnegie Community Engagement classifications.[9]

In their review of learning goals in mission statements for 312 of the institutions listed in the Princeton Review's 2002 edition of *The Best 331 Colleges*, Jack Meacham and Jerry G. Gaff found "little consensus among this national sample regarding what should be the primary goals of undergraduate education."[10] However, the most commonly stated learning outcome (discussed by 157, or 50%, of the schools) was a liberal learning or liberal arts education. Several learning outcomes relevant to an education for civic engagement were mentioned by the schools. For example, "contributing to the community" was a learning outcome stated in the mission statements of 121 schools, or about 39%. Close to 29%, or 89, of the schools discussed "social responsibility" in their mission statements. In addition, 53 schools, about 17%, put forth "engaged, responsible citizenship in a democratic society" as a learning outcome.[11] Therefore, some agreement appears among the "best colleges" that civic engagement should be a learning outcome of undergraduate institutions.

It is important to note that the Princeton Review and most national rankings of colleges and universities do not give much, if any, attention to community colleges. Their exclusion is problematic for the study of the prevalence of civic engagement as a learning outcome because almost 30% of higher education institutions are two-year colleges,[12] and during the last decade community colleges enrolled an average of 43% of all postsecondary students each academic year.[13] Moreover, the mission statements of community colleges typically include a commitment to the community, which may include fostering civic engagement as a learning outcome. For example, the California Community Colleges system, which includes 109 colleges with a student body of 2.5 million students during an academic year, states in its strategic plan that one of its framework values is that "an educated citizenry is the basis for democracy."[14]

Support for civic engagement as a learning objective is also evident among political science faculty through the actions of the American Political Science Association (APSA). In 1996, the APSA established the Task Force on Civic Education for the Next Century "in order to initiate a civic education program in political science."[15] Today, APSA has a standing Committee on Civic Education and Engagement. In addition, each of APSA's annual Teaching and Learning Conferences has included one or more tracks on civic engagement and education since their inception in 2004.

Does the growing consensus on civic engagement as a higher education learning outcome include fostering political participation? In *The Good Citizen: How a Younger Generation Is Reshaping American Politics*, Russell J. Dalton argues that citizenship norms are evolving from a traditional image of citizen duty—which is strongly connected to the responsibility to vote—to a newer image of the engaged citizen—which includes a broader notion of participation in civil society, with an emphasis on nonelectoral activities and inclusive of newer technology-based means of communication.[16] Dalton maintains that today's younger citizens are more comfortable with the engaged citizen image, although Barack Obama was successful in moving them from their nonelectoral activities to voting by conducting a campaign that explicitly invited them to vote and mobilized them to vote by talking to them about their concerns using new media.[17] However, according to Dalton, older generations are more inclined to define good citizens as those who fulfill certain traditional duties, such as voting. With this generational difference in understandings of citizenship in mind, I maintain that a college mission statement developed by older generations that puts forth "responsible citizenship in a democratic society" or "civic engagement" as a learning outcome includes fostering political participation—specifically voting—as a learning outcome. The voter registration activities of and calls for changes in voter registration laws from national college student groups and the activities of higher education organizations support the notion that there is a growing consensus in the higher education community that fostering political participation should be a learning outcome for colleges and universities.

Political Participation as a Learning Objective

College students perceive the fostering of political participation as a goal of higher education institutions. For example, the Student Association for Voter Empowerment (SAVE),[18] the United States Student Association,[19] and the Student PIRGs' (Public Interest Research Groups) Voters Project[20] coauthored a Commitment to Civic Engagement pledge—which is really a commitment to foster political participation—that they are calling on all college presidents to sign and implement.[21] While these student organizations have members in the hundreds of colleges across the country, presidents and chancellors at only 11 institutions had signed the commitment by January 2011,[22] which includes the following:

> We, the undersigned presidents and chancellors of colleges and universities, are deeply committed to the civic engagement of students on our campuses. We recognize that voting is the cornerstone of our democracy, the means of representative government. As leaders in the field of

> higher education, we recognize the vital role we can play in supporting youth civic engagement. We believe colleges and universities must exercise leadership in order to equip their students for a lifetime of civic participation. Colleges and universities that successfully support voter education, registration and turnout efforts on campus will both better serve their students and play an active role in creating a vibrant civil society and functioning democracy in America and around the world.[23]

In addition to committing their institutions to make good-faith efforts to distribute voter registration forms, the signatories also commit their institutions to take at least five of the following additional steps to further political engagement:

1. Send a letter to all faculty and staff encouraging them to support voter registration and Get-Out-the-Vote efforts.
2. Provide important voter notifications on the university or college website.
3. Send campus-wide letters and/or emails with information on the importance of voting, voter registration deadlines, nonpartisan voter guides, polling sites, and other vital information to voters.
4. Register first-year students to vote during orientation.
5. Work with local election officials to secure one or more centralized polling sites on or directly adjacent to campus.
6. Take actions to make civic engagement a part of the curriculum and other educational experiences for all students.
7. Encourage other college and university presidents to join this effort and become signatories to this commitment.[24]

Another indication that college students are interested in enhancing their political participation is the Student Association for Voter Empowerment's (SAVE's) work with members of the US House and Senate to develop and introduce into Congress the Student Voter Opportunity to Encourage Registration (VOTER) Act. First introduced into the 110th Congress in 2008, the Student VOTER Act was reintroduced in the 111th Congress. Representatives Jan Schakowsky (D-IL) and Steven La Tourette (R-OH) introduced the bill in the House, and Sen. Dick Durbin (D-IL) introduced it in the Senate.

The Student VOTER Act would amend the 1993 National Voter Registration Act by adding colleges and universities as designated voter registration agencies. As voter registration agencies, colleges and universities receiving federal funds would be required to offer voter registration to students "during enrollment for a course of study." SAVE and the bill's supporters argue that the act will "aid the 32% of non-voting young people (18- to 29-year-olds) who cite problems with the voter registration process as the reason why they did not participate."[25] If enacted, the Student VOTER Act would ameliorate some of the barriers to registering, and thereby voting, experienced by college students. The Student VOTER Act would make it easier for college students to fulfill a traditional duty of citizenship—voting.

In addition to the focus of college student organizations on political participation, the Washington Higher Education Secretariat (WHES) sponsors a student voter registration project. WHES is a voluntary forum of chief executive officers from approximately 50 national higher education associations. Responding to the increased voter participation of college students in the 2008 election, the co-chairs of the WHES Voter Registration Project—the presidents of the National Association of Independent Colleges and Universities (NAICU), the American Association of State Colleges and Universities (AASCU), and the Council of Independent Colleges (CIC)—stated that the increased college student voter turnout reflected "the success of our colleges and universities in meeting one of their most basic responsibilities: to encourage and facilitate widespread participation in the electoral process."[26] Clearly, there is a growing consensus among higher education institutions and college students that fostering civic engagement, including duty-based citizenship forms of political participation such as voting, should be a learning outcome of higher education institutions. Federal mandates also support this learning outcome.

Political Participation: Federal Mandates and Grant Opportunities

Whether or not institutions of higher education claim civic engagement or political engagement as a learning outcome, the federal government mandates that educational institutions receiving federal funds provide at least one program each year pertaining to the US Constitution. In addition, through the 1998 Higher Education Act (HEA), the federal government mandates that institutions of higher education receiving federal funds make good-faith efforts to offer each student enrolled in a degree or certificate program and physically attending classes at the institution a voter registration form or the opportunity to receive such a form from the institution. Moreover, the federal government offers grants through the Help Americans Vote Act (HAVA) to encourage college students to assist state and local governments in the administration of elections, another form of nonpartisan political participation. These laws indicate that the federal government perceives the fostering of political participation as a legitimate outcome of higher education.

Constitution and Citizenship Day

In the 2005 Consolidated Appropriations Act, Congress approved a new statutory requirement for educational institutions. As a result, all educational institutions currently receiving federal funds must implement an educational program pertaining to the US Constitution on Constitution and Citizenship Day, which is September 17 of each year. Albeit a minimal level of mandated civic education, research shows that such civic education relates to voting behavior. More specifically, the Intercollegiate Studies Institute's report, *Failing Our Students, Failing America*, reported, "[A] student's overall civic knowledge had no relationship to his likelihood to vote. What mattered was how much the student's civic knowledge *increased* during college."[27] Moreover, the report claimed that the number and quality of civic education courses—the study defined history, political science, and economic courses as civic education courses—that students take during their college career positively correlates with their civic knowledge.[28] Therefore, if fostering political engagement is a learning outcome of higher education institutions, these institutions need to pay attention to the number of civic education courses required and the quality of these courses.[29] At a minimum, as already noted, given the federal mandate regarding Constitution and Citizenship Day, institutions must offer one program on the Constitution each academic year. For those interested in increasing civic engagement, including political participation, increasing civic knowledge is an important means to achieve that goal.

APSA has resources to assist faculty in fulfilling the federal mandate to offer Constitution Day programs and teach about the US Constitution.[30] In addition, APSA, in collaboration with the Leonore Annenberg Institute for Civics of the Annenberg Public Policy Center at the University of Pennsylvania, invites political scientists to participate in an outreach program with secondary schools for their Constitution Day programs.[31]

The Higher Education Act

While the 1998 Higher Education Act (HEA) requires higher education institutions that receive federal funds to provide students with voter registration information, it is important to note that a school must only provide registration forms for the state in which the school is located, not forms for all states from which its students are drawn. Excluded from this mandate are schools located in states that do not require voters to register to vote—North Dakota—and states with Election Day registration—Idaho, Iowa, Maine, Minnesota, Montana, New Hampshire, North Carolina, Wisconsin, and Wyoming.

The 1998 HEA required institutions to request voter registration forms from the state government 120 days prior to the voter registration deadline for every federal and gubernatorial election. The 2008 Higher Education Reauthorization Act (HERA) makes it easier for institutions to comply with the HEA mandate. This act deems an institution in compliance with the mandate if it electronically transmits to students a message devoted exclusively to voter registration that contains a voter registration form acceptable for use in the state in which the institution is located or an Internet address where students can download such a form.[32] This component of the HEA Reauthorization Act went into effect on August 14, 2008.

The Help Americans Vote Act: College Program

The Help Americans Vote Act of 2002 (HAVA) established the HAVA College Program, which offers competitive grants that have ranged in value from $10,000 to $130,000 for the development of programs that:

1. Encourage students enrolled at institutions of higher education, including community colleges, to assist state and local governments in the administration of elections by serving as nonpartisan poll workers or assistants.

2. Encourage college students to become cognizant of the election process and civic education and assist in the smooth administration of elections in their community.
3. Encourage state and local governments to use the services of the students participating in the College Program.[33]

From 2004 through 2010, HAVA College Program grants were available for the years in which national elections were held (even-numbered years). Grants were also available in 2009 (a non-national election year). State-controlled and private institutions of higher education, community colleges, nonpartisan student organizations, and other nonprofit organizations all were eligible applicants for these grants.

The US Election Assistance Commission (EAC), the federal agency administering the HAVA College Program, awarded the first grants in 2004. The EAC awarded 15 grants that year, worth a total of $627,000, with 12 higher education institutions receiving $427,000. In 2006, the EAC awarded 19 grants, of which 15 went to institutions of higher education (two to community colleges); of the $300,000 awarded, $237,250 went to institutions of higher education. The EAC awarded 27 grants, worth a total of $692,000, in 2008. Twenty-one of these awards went to higher education institutions (six to community colleges), for a total of $502,115. In 2009, 13 institutions received a total of $749,000. Of this amount, $600,071 went to institutions of higher education, including one community college. Fifteen institutions, including 13 institutions of higher education, won $750,000 in HAVA College Program grant money in 2010. Fourteen colleges and universities received grants totaling $666,000.[34]

Barriers to College Student Electoral Participation

Despite these laws and programs, the ability of colleges and universities to fulfill the learning outcome of fostering political participation is limited by barriers created by state and local governments that restrict student voter registration and qualifications to work the polls on Election Day. In addition, the level of funding for the HAVA College Program limits how many institutions can take advantage of this program to prepare college students to work the polls.

Barriers to Student Voting

No matter how committed higher education institutions are to implementing the Higher Education Act's voter registration mandate, college students frequently hit barriers when they attempt to register to vote in their college communities. Although federal and state courts have ruled that students have the right to vote where they attend college,[35] state residency laws for voter registration purposes and local election officials' administrative practices often create undue burdens on students trying to register to vote at their college address as opposed to their address of permanent residence.[36]

In their study of residency laws and administrative practices regarding student voter registration, O'Loughlin and Unangst identified 38 states that "either through explicit statutory language or administrative practice" allow college students to determine their own residency for voter registration purposes.[37] The District of Columbia also allows students to determine their own residency for voter registration. For many of these states, it is the local election officials' administrative practice of accepting a student's college ID as sufficient proof of residency that allows the students to choose to register to vote in their college community.[38]

In the remaining states, state law or local administrative practices prevent students from registering to vote in their college community. In some of these states, state law either declares or implies that a temporary college residence is not a student's official residence, and so a student cannot register to vote in his or her college community. In addition, in some of these states administrative practice requires multiple sources of identification to prove local residency, including forms of ID that college students do not normally possess, such as a photo ID with a local or in-state address or an in-state tax return.[39] Moreover, some local election officials require college students to fill out long questionnaires that other registrants do not have to complete or state that they are committed to becoming long-term residents of the community, which is a commitment that nonstudents are not required to make to register to vote. However, courts have ruled that local election procedures that subject students or any subset of voters to questions or criteria beyond those posed to any other citizens for voter registration purposes violate the equal protection clause of the 14th Amendment to the US Constitution.[40] Moreover, the US Supreme Court ruled in 1979 that students can register to vote where they attend college.[41]

New state voter ID requirements enacted since 2006 also create barriers. For example, Indiana now requires a government-issued photo ID with a current address. Most out-of-state students attending schools in Indiana do not have such an ID. In general, college IDs do not include a local address. Moreover, while election officials may deem a college ID from a state or community college a government-issued ID, college IDs from private institutions of higher education are not government-issued.

Even where state and local governments allow students to determine their residence for voter registration purposes, misinformation about the negative impacts of registering to vote where they attend college have deterred many students from registering to vote in their college community. For example, in the fall of 2008, the local registrar of elections erroneously informed Virginia Tech students that they could lose scholarships if they registered to vote in Blacksburg.[42] A county clerk in Colorado Springs erroneously told Colorado College students that they could not register to vote in the county if their parents claimed them as dependents on tax returns.[43]

College students can, of course, register to vote based on their address of permanent residence and then vote by absentee ballot. However, the Higher Education Act does not encourage this process, because it mandates that colleges and universities distribute registration forms only for the state in which the institution is located. They need not distribute forms from all the states from which they draw students nor must they provide absentee ballot information. Yet according to a study of a voter registration drive at Northwestern University in the fall of 2008, "more than 1.7 million students attend out-of-state colleges," and most of the students at the university who were offered the opportunity to register to vote locally in Illinois or in their home states preferred registering and voting by absentee ballot in their home states. The researchers noted that in the past the burden of providing state-by-state registration and absentee ballot request materials made out-of-state voter registration drives and absentee ballot drives very difficult. However, they also noted that today most state and county materials are available online, and there are websites that have "compiled materials and guides across all states, making drives like the one at Northwestern achievable in a way that they have not been in the past."[44] Therefore, not requiring institutions to provide voter registration forms for each student's home state is no longer as great a barrier to college-student voter registration as in the past.

Barriers to Student Poll Workers

Another way for students to become involved in voting and increase their political participation is by serving as poll workers on Election Day. The US EAC's *Compendium of State Poll Worker Requirements* contains the election laws and administrative regulations that govern poll worker eligibility for each of the 50 states, the District of Columbia, and each US territory.[45] The HAVA College Program grant announcement notes that state laws establish the eligibility requirements for poll workers and that these requirements vary from state to state. The EAC summarizes poll worker eligibility by stating, "Typically, poll workers are required to be registered voters in the precinct or county where they are serving. *State and local voter registration rules vary on allowing college students who live at school to register to vote using their school address* [italics added].[46] Some states have recently changed their rules to allow college students to work the polls near their schools even if they are not registered to vote in that jurisdiction."[47] Ultimately, the HAVA College Program's usefulness can be limited by state election laws and administrative regulations.

The HAVA College Program's impact on fostering college student political engagement is limited by its level of funding as well as by the number of quality applications received. Between 2004 and 2010, only 74 institutions of higher education (of the approximately 4,000 that exist) received HAVA College Program grants, worth a total of $2,432,436.[48]

In summary, the federal mandate regarding at least one annual program pertaining to the US Constitution and the HEA's mandate that institutions of higher education make good-faith efforts to distribute voter registration forms to their students present opportunities for higher education institutions to foster political engagement. However, residency laws in numerous states and local election officials' administrative practices limit the Higher Education Act's positive impact on student political engagement. The Help Americans Vote Act presents another opportunity for institutions of higher education to foster student political engagement. The proposed Student VOTER Act may eliminate some of the barriers that limit the positive impacts the HEA and HAVA College Programs could have on college student political engagement and voting.

Higher Education Institutions' Compliance with HEA and Constitution Day Mandates

Higher education institutions' compliance with HEA and Constitution Day mandates is hard to assess because federal law does not include a reporting requirement for these mandates. Financial aid offices at institutions of higher education should be documenting what is being done to comply with these federal mandates, but they usually report these activities to the Department of Education only when it conducts a formal program review.

There is a dearth of research on how well higher education institutions are complying with the federal mandates regarding Constitution Day and efforts to offer students voter registration forms. A search of university websites, using the search terms "voter registration" and "Constitution Day" suggests that the responsibility for complying with these mandates falls on a variety of divisions or offices: student affairs divisions, library staff, political science departments, provosts, registrars, presidents, or chancellors. For many institutions, the website search garnered no results.

In the "HR 1729: The Student VOTER Act" YouTube video, SAVE's executive director, Matthew Segal, and Rep. Jan Schakowsky (D-IL) claim that 40% of colleges are not in compliance with the Higher Education Act's voter registration mandate. According to a 2004 *Chronicle* and Institute of Politics at Harvard University survey report, "a majority of colleges and universities [were] not in strict compliance" with the federal mandate to make a good-faith effort to provide students with voter registration forms. Forty-eight percent of the 249 institutions that responded to the email survey maintained that they had procedures in place for requesting voter registration forms from their state or local elections offices. Yet only 42 of these 119 schools had made a request to their election offices at least 120 days prior to their state's voter registration deadline, as required by the HEA. In addition, 33% of the institutions reported having no procedures for requesting voter registration forms from their election officials, and 19% indicated that they did not know if they had procedures in place to comply with the mandate.

Certainly, the HEA 2008 Reauthorization Act makes it easier for higher education institutions to comply with the mandate for good-faith efforts to provide students with voter registration forms. However, even with compliance made easier by the Internet, will it improve? Compliance assumes that institutions are aware of the mandate. Is it possible that lackluster implementation of the HEA mandate has been due to a lack of knowledge about it? Are higher education institutions aware of the 2008 change to the mandate, which makes it easier to comply by sending students an email with a link to voter registration forms online? What about compliance with the Constitution Day programming mandate? In higher education institutions, who is responsible for complying with this mandate?

I did not know of the HEA mandate until I came across it by accident five years ago, which was during my 20th year of teaching political science! Am I an aberrant case, or are most political science faculty not familiar with the HEA mandate? Which higher education administrators should be aware of it? How do faculty, students, staff, or administrators become aware of it? How does an institution determine who is responsible for fulfilling it? One can ask the same questions about the Constitution Day mandate. In sum, these mandates lack visibility, clear lines of accountability, and a reporting requirement, which collectively limits their capabilities to effectively foster political participation.

A Call to Action

An action agenda for political science faculty interested in fostering political participation of undergraduate graduates is evident. Supported by the consensus in the higher education community that political participation is a valid learning objective for colleges and universities and by federal laws, faculty can foster political participation in their students by working with them on any of the following projects, as either course requirements or extracurricular activities. These projects will provide students with experiential learning opportunities in the context of political institutions and policy processes. They can work to gain clout over decision makers within an institution of higher education and possibly within state and local governments.

- Develop and implement an assessment plan to determine how well one's college or university is complying with the HEA mandate for a good-faith effort to offer each student enrolled in a degree or certificate program and physically attending classes at the institution a voter registration form.
- Develop and implement an assessment plan to determine how well one's college or university is complying with the federal mandate for an educational program pertaining to the US Constitution on September 17 of each year.
- Develop and implement a voter education plan for in-state and out-of-state students that includes information on registration, polling place locations, and absentee ballot applications.
- Apply for a HAVA College Program grant to encourage students to assist state and local governments in the administration of elections by serving as poll workers; urge state and local governments to use the services of students on Election Day; or inspire college students to become cognizant of the election process and civic education.
- Assess the success of a HAVA College Program grant.

- Propose a plan that will institutionalize a sustainable program to implement the actions called for in the Commitment to Civic Engagement put forth by the Student Association for Voter Empowerment, the United States Student Association, and the Student PIRGs' Voters Project at one's college or university.
- Propose a plan that will institutionalize a sustainable program to implement the Constitution Day educational program mandate at one's college or university.
- Study one's state election laws and local administrative regulations with regard to college student voter registration and poll worker qualifications. If deemed necessary, develop a plan for students to lobby for changes in the laws or regulations.
- Develop a plan to lobby for more HAVA College Program funds.
- Propose a plan that will institutionalize a sustainable program that educates students on their voting rights and how to take advantage of them at one's college or university.

Lastly, APSA should publicize the mandates for the Higher Education Act's requirement for higher education institutions to make a good-faith effort to offer each student a voter registration form, and the Help Americans Vote Act College program grant opportunities. In addition, an APSA committee should monitor how well colleges and universities are complying with these laws, using an online survey of department heads through the regular department heads' email newsletter to do so. APSA should also determine to what extent political science faculty and colleges and universities are implementing the programs proposed in the action agenda. Collectively, all of these actions can effectively foster more civic and political engagement among college students at all types of higher education institutions.

Political Science Faculty as Models of Political Engagement

6

By Paul E. Frank

Political scientists are generally categorized as having research and teaching expertise, but not necessarily real-life political experience. This chapter evaluates whether this categorization is accurate and whether political science instructors who are politically engaged have a greater influence in motivating the political engagement of students. This first-of-its-kind study hopes to bring to light the various political activities of instructors, as well as whether these experiences are imparted to students. Using a survey sample of 1,293 full-time political science educators at two- and four-year American institutions, it seeks to shed light on the link between instructor engagement and student engagement.

College instructors, whether in the classroom, during office hours, or on informal occasions, have perhaps the best opportunity to shape the civic and political engagement potential of college students. One obvious way to shape student engagement is to include elements of participation in a course's design. Just as a coach who has played the sport has greater legitimacy with players, a college instructor who is or has been politically engaged may have greater legitimacy when motivating students to become participatory citizens. Conversely, an instructor with weak engagement credentials may find it more difficult to motivate students. In other words, instructors who practice what they preach may add more value to the classroom experience. The practical knowledge gained by a politically engaged instructor is also invaluable. For example, the first-hand lessons learned by an instructor who has run for political office, including working with the media, walking neighborhoods, communicating a message, raising money, motivating volunteers, and adhering to election rules, can be shared with students in the classroom.

The following study brings to light the various political activities of political science instructors, as well as whether these experiences are imparted to students. Four key questions were asked: 1) Are political science instructors politically engaged compared to the larger population? 2) Do instructors believe they *should* model political participation in the classroom? 3) Do instructors *actually* model political participation in the classroom? and 4) What factors affect the modeling of political engagement by political science instructors for their students?

This study takes an important first step in determining a link between instructor civic and political engagement and student civic and political engagement. The study begins with a review of the literature on this subject, followed by a discussion of the study's methodology, case study reflections, results, conclusions, and recommendations.

Instructors in the Civic Engagement Literature

Existing literature argues that college students' civic and political engagement can be influenced by their learning environments. According to Colby et al., "[W]hen undergraduates have the understanding and skills to be politically engaged, many are motivated to do so," and colleges are "well positioned to promote democratic competencies and participation" among students.[1] Attendance at a two- or four-year college,[2] taking classes that encourage civic engagement,[3] adhering to class requirements that keep up with politics and national affairs,[4] completing a political science course,[5] and other variables have been studied as specific factors that foster civic and political engagement.

The current literature on civic and political engagement also suggests a need to better understand why students are or are not engaged. A more-focused interest is brewing to understand why students may be more civically engaged at the expense of political engagement. Colby et al. observe that political engagement is the least attended–to aspect of civic engagement in higher education, "even among schools with strong commitments to moral and civic learning."[6] Longo describes a "scissor effect," whereby political participation among students has been declining while community involvement and volunteering have been growing. He also refers to general agreement in the literature that colleges must better educate and provide opportunities for student political participation.[7]

The literature looks broadly at colleges and universities as institutional engines to promote engagement and sometimes looks more specifically at instructors across disciplines as parts of that engine. For example, in *Educating Citizens*, the authors suggest that faculty are important to the civic engagement movement insomuch as they participate in curriculum reform, act as advisers and partners to administrative leaders, and establish systems for cross-campus integration.[8] In other words, instructors are important within the context of institutional moves toward civic engagement, but not necessarily where instructors have the most impact on students—in the classroom.

For direct influence, students can "learn positive moral lessons" when they see faculty practicing certain behaviors, such as integrity, honesty, fairness, respect, and commitment.[9] While the current study does not look at broader moral lessons, the message outlined in *Educating Citizens* of modeling morality by faculty is equally applicable to modeling political behavior by faculty, which *is* the focus of this study.

In their follow-up book, *Educating for Democracy*, Colby et al. suggest that "[p]olitical science or government departments may seem to be the obvious home for programs addressing students' political development." However, they add, the political science discipline has generally ignored the normative and applied aspects of politics in favor of the objective and mathematical study of institutions and behavior.[10]

The cases used in their Carnegie Political Engagement Project (PEP) study do focus on normative/applied aspects and offer clues on how faculty can develop student political engagement. Of the five pedagogical strategies that the authors found to be most important to developing political engagement—political discussion and deliberation, political research and action projects, structured reflection, invited speakers and program-affiliated mentors, and external placements[11]—the latter two may be influenced most by instructors who have a degree of political experience and personal contacts themselves. According to the authors, four dimensions of political engagement must be emphasized in the classroom—knowledge, skill, motivation, and participation. When it comes to providing political knowledge in the classroom, *Educating for Democracy* suggests that the way to achieve this pedagogical goal is still the lecture format. In terms of teaching political skills, feedback from a "coach," or in this case, a faculty member is vital. The authors found that a primary way to instill political identity (a key aspect of political motivation) among students is to connect them with political role models. Finally, *Educating for Democracy* found that students' participation in internships and service-learning programs develops civic and political engagement. The authors observed "that hands-on political experiences yield specific learning contributing to political understanding, motivation, and skills."[12]

One aspect of understanding the connection between faculty roles and youth civic engagement is to understand how "instructors *perceive* [emphasis added] the issue of youth engagement."[13] For example, in a nationally representative sample, Shea shows overwhelmingly that political science instructors perceive that they should be on the front lines of engaging students in the political process. However, it is less clear from the survey respondents which innovations should be used to motivate students (such as role-modeling), and the political engagement of faculty as a motivating factor was not addressed in Shea's research.

Some studies of civic engagement refer to the political activism experiences of the authors, who also teach political science themselves,[14] but do not make the connection of that experience as a tool to teach political engagement. Instead, these studies focus on traditional tools of teaching participation (textbooks, video clips, service-learning, technology, etc.). Likewise, surveys that ask instructors "from what sources do you draw" information about civic participation generally include only traditional response choices.[15] They leave out the choice of "instructor's own experience with participation" as a potential survey response.

One study that indirectly makes the connection between the real world of political engagement and the academic world of political science instructors is Jason Scorza's "Social Entrepreneurship and Undergraduate Learning: Challenges and

Opportunities for Political Science." According to Scorza, social entrepreneurship is defined as "the creation of enterprises drawing on the principles of conventional entrepreneurship to promote social welfare and meet social needs."[16] He suggests that "[s]ocial entrepreneurship may gradually become not just something that academics, including political scientists, want to study and teach, but also something that faculty across the disciplines actually want to *do*."[17] Although Scorza's focus is on social entrepreneurship, the argument he makes applies equally to political engagement. He advocates that academics be "citizen-scholars."

However, this point is where Scorza's advocacy of the scholar entrepreneur and the current study's focus on political engagement of political science faculty depart. His argument is that political science scholars can use their knowledge and skills to improve society. This study, however, looks at how scholars who practice politics can use their experiences and skills to improve learning and civic engagement among students. Both place citizen-scholars at the center; however, Scorza pulls them toward social entrepreneurship, whereas this study pulls them toward teaching civic and political engagement.

Most studies have not looked specifically at the engagement of students' college professors as a possible factor of civic and political engagement among young people. This current study attempts to examine whether a link exists and analyze the factors that lead political science instructors to model political engagement for their students.

Methodology

This study begins with four primary hypotheses:

1. Political science instructors are more politically engaged than the larger general population.
2. Political science faculty who *believe* in modeling political participation in the classroom *actually* do model it.
3. Political science instructors who are very politically engaged are more likely to model political engagement in the classroom than instructors who are not engaged or only somewhat engaged.
4. Other factors, such as length of teaching experience, whether instructors teach at a two-year or four-year colleges or universities, and whether instructors use civic engagement exercises in the classroom, will not determine the degree of modeling in the classroom.

The survey tool used to test these hypotheses consisted of 26 multiple-choice and open-ended questions.[18] It was distributed by paper questionnaire at the APSA Teaching and Learning Conference in February 2008 and by electronic questionnaire using Surveymonkey.com between March and April 2008. The anonymous and confidential survey was distributed to 1,273 members of the APSA. The participants were randomly selected from among approximately 10,078 APSA members and are representative of those members who teach political science courses full-time at two-year colleges, four-year colleges or universities, and four-year graduate degree–granting colleges or universities in the United States. Four hundred and ninety-three respondents completed the survey, for a 38.73% response rate.[19] Categories of "Very Engaged" (six or more activities), "Somewhat Engaged" (two to five activities), and "Not Engaged" (one or fewer activities) were used to describe the degree, or level, of faculty political engagement.

The survey instrument for this study was modeled in part on the instrument used in Verba, Schlozman, and Brady's *Voice and Equality*. However, liberty was taken with the exact language of the *Voice and Equality* survey to reflect the scope and resources of this study. Nevertheless, the broad indicators of "political activity" were generally the same (with the exception of adding "running for office," "publicly displaying a political message," and "paid activities" as indicators) and focused on "doing" politics, rather than on "being attentive to politics." Response scales also were meant to reveal respondents' "volume of activity" (how much they participate), rather than just whether or not they participate, as is done in *Voice and Equality*. Additional questions were used in this survey to indicate whether political science professors do or do not model their own political engagement in the classroom. Demographic questions for this study were also narrower than in *Voice and Equality*, given the focus on political science faculty. Because this study examined "whether" instructors are politically engaged, rather than "why" they become politically engaged, it excluded reference to nonpolitical activity, unlike *Voice and Equality*, which includes it.

The time frame of political participation relative to when the survey questions were asked is important to understand. The use of participatory experiences by political science professors need not be recent for them to have an impact on modeling engagement to students. Therefore, for the purposes of this study, it was important to look at a much larger time frame of activity. While the questions in this survey were generally reflective of the language used in the *Voice and Equality* survey,[20] they were purposefully written to include a much broader time frame of political participation relative to when survey questions were asked.

Cases

In addition to the survey, several case studies were evaluated to help determine political science faculty civic and political engagement. The Carnegie Political Engagement Project (PEP) identified 21 civic engagement programs at institutions of higher education in the United States. At least two of the programs relied heavily on the political experiences of the instructors to bring home the idea of political engagement to students.

One of the programs, The Politics of San Francisco, at San Francisco State University is a one-semester course team taught by a former deputy mayor of the city, three long-time community activists, and a university instructor.[21] According to the Campus Compact website,

> The course offers students an opportunity to combine academic study with practical experience. SFSU students are joined in the course by non-profit staff, who attend the course through the university's extension program. The course is unique in that many of the issues under study directly involved persons teaching the course. Indeed, three of the instructors were major participants in the land use and development struggles of the past twenty years, often sharply at odds with one another. The course thus allows students to revisit these debates through the eyes and analyses of the actual participants.[22]

Another program reviewed by PEP is The Future of Chicago at the University of Illinois at Chicago. This one-semester course is taught by Dick Simpson, himself heavily involved in Chicago politics and former holder of elected office. Simpson also brings in past Illinois governors, Chicago mayors, members of Congress, political activists, and heads of local nonprofit groups[23] as models of political participation. According to Simpson, the course allows him to structure student papers as an evaluation of local government agencies, which gives students an additional experience with "real politics and government."[24]

The 2008 APSA Teaching and Learning Conference included several papers and presenters that illuminated the fact that political science faculty are politically engaged. For example, professors Michael Cain and Zach Messitte described the Maryland Professors at the Polls Initiative.[25] The authors developed this pilot program to get faculty to serve as nonpartisan poll workers in the 2006 elections. The goal of the initiative was not only to fill a need at the polls, but also to encourage faculty and students to be politically engaged. It ultimately "allowed political science professors to see firsthand the gratification of the voting process." Approximately 20 political science professors participated in the training and poll work. The program developers, in addition to their poll work, were integrally involved in legislation that would make the initiative a statewide program. Both Cain and Messitte confirmed that they talk about their experiences as poll workers with students in the classroom. Several other presenters had served as a poll worker, a media analyst in the Iowa caucuses, and as an elected official; these individuals briefly discussed their own political engagement to conference attendees as well as to students in the classroom.

Survey Results

As stated earlier, the four questions asked were: 1) Are political science instructors politically engaged compared to the larger population? 2) Do instructors believe they *should* model political participation in the classroom? 3) Do instructors *actually* model political participation in the classroom? and 4) What factors affect the modeling of political engagement by political science instructors to their students?

On the first question, the survey indicated that political science instructors are, overall, *more engaged* than the population surveyed in *Voice and Equality*[26] and other studies (see Table 6-1). None of the 12 indicators of political activity were lower among political science instructors than among the larger general popula-

Table 6-1: Comparison Results of Political Science Faculty Surveys

	This Study (n=493)	Voice & Equality (n= 2,517)	Other Studies
Voting[a]	78.4% (all presidential)	71% (1988)	62.2% (1988) 63.8% (2004) 77.4% (advanced degree) 51.8% (all presidential)
Political Organization	58.8% (political party) 58.3% (interest groups)	48% (all political orgs)	n/a
Campaign Contributions[b]	55.2%	24%	12%
Contacting Elected Officials[c]	52.9%	34%	11%
Display Political Messages	39.6%	n/a	n/a
Campaign Work[d]	39.3%	8%	n/a
Protest[e]	30.8%	6%	5.5%
Board Member[f]	29.3%	3%	12%
Attend Board Meeting[g]	26.3%	14%	n/a
Run for Office[h]	9.1%	n/a	> 1%

a. The "This Study" percentage reflects respondents who answered that they voted in "all" presidential elections since they were old enough to vote, the Voice & Equality percentage reflects eligible voter respondents who voted in the 1988 presidential election, the "Other Studies" percentage reflects eligible voter respondents who voted in the 2004 presidential election according to the US Census and all elections according to CIRCLE, 2006, 41.
b. The "This Study" percentage reflects respondents who answered "often" and "sometimes." Percentages from "Other Studies" is from Nelson, Candice, 35.
c. The "This Study" percentage reflects respondents who answered "often" and "sometimes." Percentages from "Other Studies" is from Putnam, Robert, 44.
d. The "This Study" percentage reflects respondents who answered "often" and "sometimes."
e. Percentages from "Other Studies" is from Putnam, Robert, 41.
f. Percentages from "Other Studies" is from Putnam, Robert, 43.
g. The "This Study" percentage reflects respondents who answered "often" and "sometimes."
h. Percentages from "Other Studies" is from Putnam, Robert, 41.

tion. Furthermore, on all indicators but two, political science faculty participation was higher than the larger general population by a range of 12 to 43 percentage points. On the two other indicators—membership in political party/interest group and running for office—faculty participation was still higher, but only by eight to 10 percentage points. Campaign contributions as a form of participation showed the highest gap (43 percentage points) between political science faculty and the larger general population (see Figure 6-1 and Table 6-1).

On the second and third questions, it was observed that the rate of actual modeling of political participation in the classroom was higher than the belief that it should be modeled. The survey indicates that 48% of all respondents feel that it is important to discuss their personal political activities or inactivity with students

Figure 6-1: Political Activity of Faculty Compared to Larger Population

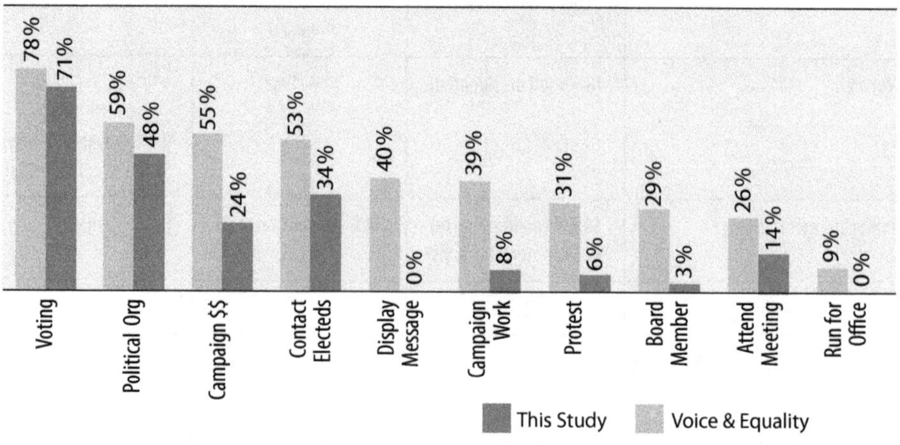

in the classroom. Overall, 64.7% of the respondents *actually* discuss their personal political experience(s) with students "often" or "sometimes." Of all respondents, 44.3% answered that they both believe that political participation should be modeled and actually model it. Of the 317 respondents who actually model political participation, 215 of them (67.8%) also believe that they should model it.

On the fourth question, this study found that two-year college professors, faculty who teach civic or political engagement in the classroom, and those who have taught 20-plus years are more inclined to support by both belief and action the modeling of engagement to their students. Among two year college professors, 72.9% feel that modeling engagement is important, whereas among four-year college and university professors only 44.4% believe it is important (Pearson Chi-Square=16.777, df=1, p< .001). Similarly, the 64.8% of faculty who use actual civic

Figure 6-2: "Do you feel it is important to discuss your personal political activities (or inactivity) with students in the classroom?" Yes answers

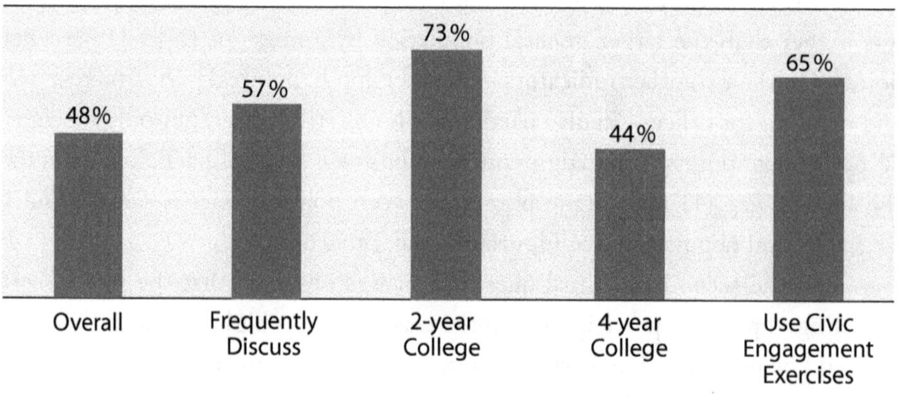

Figure 6-3: "How would you describe your frequency discussing your personal experience(s) in political activities in class with your students?" Often/Sometimes

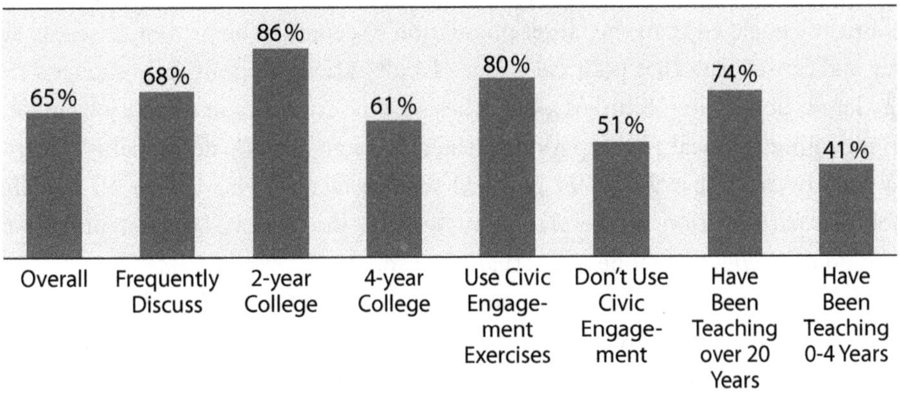

or political engagement exercises in their classrooms had significantly higher rates (Pearson Chi-Square= 48.083, df=1, p< .001) of feeling it is important than those who feel it is not (see Figure 6-2). There were no significant differences among other categories when answering this question.

In actually modeling political participation, two-year faculty outpaced four-year faculty, 81.47% to 62.6% (Pearson Chi-Square=10.754, df=3, p< .013), faculty who teach civic or political engagement surpassed those who do not, 80.1% to 51.5% (Pearson Chi-Square=55.075, df=3, p< .001). Also, professors who have been teaching more than 20 years were more likely to actually discuss their political experiences in the classroom, 73.6% compared to 41.5% for those teaching 0 to four years (Pearson Ch-Square=36.019, df=9, p< .001) (see Figure 6-3). There were no significant differences among other categories when answering this question.

A content analysis of the written comments in the survey indicated that some faculty members (13 out of 42) expressed unease about discussing their political experiences because that might reveal their political views to students. For example, some respondents wrote:

> "I think it is very problematic to discuss one's own political activity in the classroom setting."
>
> "A faculty member's political positions should not intrude in the classroom."
>
> "The classroom is not normally a place to discuss one's personal political activities."

On the other hand, only five of the 42 written comments felt that it was appropriate, even necessary, for political science faculty to discuss their political experiences with students in the classroom. Based upon their responses, none of these five professors seemed concerned with biasing their students with their own political views.

Survey Results

Based on the survey results, there were mixed conclusions on the proving of the four hypotheses. For example, hypotheses 1 ("political science instructors are more politically engaged than the larger population") seemed to be proven, based on survey and census data that political science faculty are more politically engaged than the larger population. Similarly, hypothesis 2 ("political science faculty who *believe* in modeling political participation in the classroom *actually* do model it") seemed to be proven in that 92.6% of political science faculty who believe in modeling political participation in the classroom actually modeled it, whereas only 38.6% who do not believe in modeling actually did so.

Hypothesis 3 ("political science instructors that are politically engaged are more likely to model this in the classroom than instructors who are not") also seemed to be proven. Not only did 80.3% of "very engaged" political science faculty actually model participation in the classroom, compared to 53.4% of "somewhat engaged" and 30.7% of "not engaged," but 58% of faculty who actually modeled were themselves very engaged, compared to 39.4% who were somewhat engaged and 2.5% who were not engaged (Pearson Chi-Square= 65.499, df=6, p< .001) (see Figure 6-4). So, there seemed to be a correlation between political engagement and modeling in the classroom, at least among political science faculty.

On the other hand, hypothesis 4 could not be proven. Indeed, variables such as length of teaching experience, whether the instructor teaches at a two-year or four-year college or university, and whether the instructor uses civic engagement exercises in the classroom factored into a higher degree of modeling in the classroom.

On length of teaching experience, these results might be explained by two factors: 1) in general, faculty with more experience teaching are likely to be older and therefore have had more time to become politically engaged and have some-

Figure 6-4: Degree of Political Engagement and Modeling by Faculty

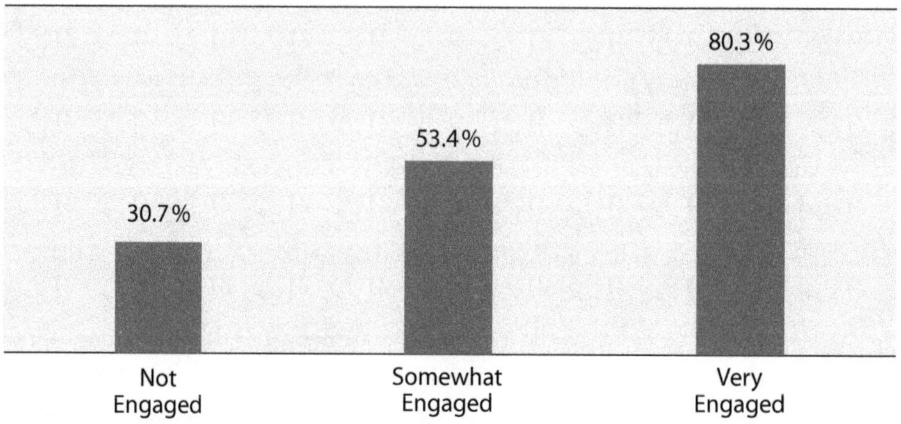

thing to model in the classroom; and 2) perhaps longer-tenured faculty have had more time see the value of modeling in the classroom. On differences between two-year or four-year college or university faculty, these results might be explained by the fact that publishing requirements at two-year institutions are generally less demanding than at four-year colleges and universities, and therefore two-year faculty have more time to be engaged politically. Lastly, it is reasonable to assume that if faculty use civic or political engagement exercises in the classroom, they are more enthusiastic about civic and political engagement in general and therefore more likely to model civic and political engagement for their students.

Recommendations

There should be continued support for colleges and universities to educate for political participation, including the modeling of political participation by faculty, as long as it does not compromise other important goals of academic learning. Educating for civic and political engagement actually supports and contributes to the outcomes of critical thinking, communication skills, problem solving, and knowledge acquisition.[27] Faculty modeling of political participation should be considered as one method to reach these outcomes. The people who faculty connect with as participants in politics can greatly improve their ability as instructors to connect students with the real world of politics. Their experiences and connections can 1) provide realistic information and feedback to students (knowledge and skills), 2) bring in guest speakers (motivation), or 3) direct students toward internship and volunteer opportunities (participation).

Advocacy of faculty modeling in the classroom treads a thin line, however, between the impartiality of the instructor and the need to demonstrate political engagement. Rightfully, there is some concern in the academic field that by discussing their own political activities and experiences, faculty members might inappropriately bias the political views of students in the classroom. However, according to Goff "a demonstrated engagement in political affairs on the part of the professor has an important pedagogical point—it shows that there are a variety of ways that they [students] can be involved in issues that they find important and meaningful regardless of the ideological content of those issues."[28] He continues, "[F]ar from being indoctrination, teaching students how to be fully engaged in their world increases their ability to participate in the issues that they find important."[29] Faculty who model for political engagement may find students involved in political organizations or causes opposite to a faculty member's own views, which would be a healthy pedagogical outcome.

Modeling political participation is a legitimate tool that can be used by instructors in the classroom. In the literature, terms such as "modeling,"[30] "coaching,"[31] and "mentoring"[32] are used to describe the important role of educational institutions in encouraging civic engagement. "Mobilizing" is also used in the context of why students become civically engaged.[33] The premise of this study has been that individual college instructors are in a position to personally model, coach, mentor, and mobilize for civic engagement. An argument can be made that not only are instructors capable of modeling political engagement, but indeed they *should* model such behavior.

For example, at Aquinas College in Grand Rapids, Michigan, the civic and political engagement of political science faculty is not only promoted, it is used as a marketing tool for new students. According to the Aquinas College Political Science Department website,

> The political science faculty study, teach, and do politics. They maintain active relationships with local, state, and national elected and appointed officials. They have worked on campaigns, run for office, and consulted on the problems of governing at all levels.... Students are strongly encouraged to participate as well.[34]

Taking it a step further, the National Association of Social Workers (NASW), recommends in its "Code of Ethics" that its members "engage in social and political action" and "be aware of the impact of the political arena on practice and should advocate for changes in policy and legislation to improve social conditions in order to meet basic human needs and promote social justice."[35] Results from the present study discussed in this chapter and other studies suggest that the American Political Science Association (APSA) should consider language in a code of ethics for faculty that recognizes the benefits and limitations of faculty civic engagement. Like the NASW language, anything from APSA should not require faculty to be civically or politically engaged, nor should it require that faculty share their political experiences, positions, or ideologies with students.

Political science needs further research into the subject of faculty political engagement and its effects on students. Comparisons of faculty in different disciplines would broaden understanding of modeling political participation. Also, studies of the direct relationship between faculty participation and levels of student political engagement would be fruitful. Lastly, a framework should be developed that allows faculty the opportunity to consider ways to model their political participation in the classroom. This book takes an important step in providing a series of examples and case studies highlight different ways of effectively modeling and teaching political engagement that can advance goal of fostering students' lifelong civic and political engagement.

SECTION II

Implementing Civic Engagement in the Classroom

Introduction to Section II

Implementing Civic Engagement in the Classroom

There is no one best way to implement civic engagement pedagogy. Instead, political science educators need a wide range of options and tools to fit diverse teaching styles, course subjects, intellectual interests, students, and institutions. This section provides political science educators with many intriguing, tested models that can spark development of more course-based means to foster civic and political engagement among students at various levels of college and high school instruction.

One of the first questions educators often ask is: "How can I implement something like this at my institution?" That is a loaded question. Many factors must be considered before educators can explore specific tools, assignments, courses, and partnerships. First, educators must discern what their home institutions want to do in the community and the resources they are willing to commit to a civic engagement project. These resources include workload, assistants, space, and technical and financial support. Part of this discussion also includes clarifying a definition of the "community" the project will serve and finding an appropriate community partner. The following chapters provide a range of examples: some educators such as Lorenzini found their community partners through a mutually evolving conversation about interests and needs; others such as McLauchlan and Sanders sought out community partners that could fit with preconceived pedagogical goals; still others such as McCartney were approached by a community partner seeking help in fulfilling an unmet need. These methods of selecting partners often defined the "community."

Some contributors, including Allen, Parker, and DeLorenzo, defined community based on close geographic proximity, whereas Dicklitch demonstrates that small geographic distances, such as her students' 30-minute drive to York County prisons, can be overcome. What to do , however, in a rural setting that does not offer a lot of options? VanVechten and Chadha and Perry provide excellent examples of how to create a "community" in which students can practice civic and political engagement. VanVechten and Chadha created a national community utilizing online techniques; Perry's communities are both state and local. Geographic location, though sometimes a limitation, can often become an opportunity for innovation.

Civic engagement projects will reflect the intellectual interests and disciplinary subfields of their creators. The most prominent subfields of political science, absent research methods, are included in this section. In particular, while the development of civic engagement pedagogy has been ongoing in national, state, local, urban, and public policy courses for some time, political theory, comparative politics, and international relations often have been left out of these conversations. McKinlay reminds us that civic engagement is actually a core part of political philosophy, going back to its roots in ancient Greece, and argues that educators should encourage students to do more than just ponder these great philosophers' teachings. Indeed, as they sought to transform ideas into action, so can the political scientists of today.

Dicklitch and McCartney fill an important niche in having created courses in non-American subfields, yet unlike most existing civic engagement pedagogy in comparative politics and international relations, students never need to leave their institutions. Once again, these teacher-scholars have found innovative ways to overcome geographic limitations. As increasing numbers of nontraditional students seek college degrees, international civic engagement options should be made available for students who cannot travel. Indeed, studying homelessness in, say, Jakarta or Rio de Janiero is an exciting and informative experience, but educators need more-inclusive options for students whose interests lie beyond the borders of this country.

One complaint sometimes voiced about higher education in general, and civic engagement pedagogy in particular, is that it has an inherent liberal bias. This section provides examples from courses at public and private, faith-based and public, red state and blue state institutions. The courses also cover a wide variety of issues. For example, neither Republicans nor Democrats have a monopoly on caring about effective solutions for poverty, homelessness, or human rights violations. Both major parties are interested in whether international institutions are doing their jobs. Members of both are engaged in debates about free speech versus privacy rights, gay marriage, protests at funerals of members of the armed forces, and locating a mosque near Ground Zero. Further, both parties are clearly (self-) interested in getting students to work for their campaigns, at polling places, and in other political capacities.

The teacher-scholars represented here have constructed several means of ensuring that political bias is absent from these classes by constructing assignments and activities expressly designed to invite students to develop their own sense of political identity. For example, in Perry's student issues conventions and VanVechten and Chadha's online deliberation forums, students devise their own questions and decide which issues are most important to debate. In Dicklitch's course, students must first assess whether an asylum seeker's claims are even valid, and several have discovered that this was not the case, resulting in an adverse outcome for the applicant. Courses such as those led by Sanders and McLauchlan even invite candidates from both parties to help students choose with whom they will work during the semester. All courses include in-class discussions of experiences and their relation to course materials, as well as written reflection assignments that prod students to consider the link between their classroom-based learning and their civic engagement activities and the impacts, if any, of this combination on their ideas about what it means to be a "good" citizen. After all, the common goal is to create civically engaged citizens, with the skills, confidence, and knowledge needed to put their ideas into action in the political system and their communities.

The American-based examples in this section provide an exciting mix of innovative approaches to achieving these goals. They vary greatly in terms of the type of schools, level of study, and subfields they represent, as well as the assignments and community partners chosen. Sylvester, Allen et al., Jenkins, and Lorenzini work in public policy and public law for underserved populations in upper-level courses. Allen et al. explicitly engage in legal training as part of their service-learning activity, whereas Sylvester, Jenkins, and Lorenzini focus more on public policy, asking students to work directly on identifying and addressing public policy issues in their communities. In all four cases, the authors show how students learn that they can have a positive impact on their communities, while also advancing their academic skills and knowledge. These achievements increase students' confidence in their capacities to be civically engaged citizens, a key component of lifelong citizenship.

VanVechten and Chadha and Perry use introductory American government courses to get students politically engaged. Utilizing an innovative Internet-based format, VanVechten and Chadha teach respectful deliberation on a variety of contentious issues, and that format enables them to promote the benefits of political involvement while allaying fears of unconstructive negative feedback. Perry achieves the same goal, but through a student convention that requires students to grapple with the difficult decisions of politics and offer proposed policy solutions to actual political leaders. Sanders's chapter follows, with an example of how to get students involved in local caucuses. While not all states have this option, he suggests the use of political campaigns in American government courses as a way to bring the material alive and facilitate students' understanding of how politics actually works.

McKinlay helps readers contemplate how even a theory-based class can include a service-learning component that expands students' understanding of civic and political engagement. This course is an excellent example of how theory, praxis, and self-reflection can be combined to heighten students' comprehension of the course material and develop their sense of themselves as civic actors. Dicklitch and McCartney go into comparative government and international relations courses, which, like political theory, are often neglected in the civic engagement literature. It is often assumed that service-learning in these subfields must include study abroad, yet Dicklitch and McCartney demonstrate that this is not the case. Dicklitch teaches her students how to evaluate and, as warranted, help asylum seekers held in a local correctional facility. As part of this project, students must learn about human rights conditions in other countries and discern whether those cases fit US law. McCartney's political science students are involved in a university-sponsored Model United Nations conference for local high school students. Her students work with the high schoolers in preparation for the conference in a variety of ways. They also prepare research projects that evaluate the effectiveness (or lack thereof) of United Nations' agencies and explore these agencies' connections to local groups and issues. McCartney ends with a preliminary set of evidence to gauge whether or not these activities parlay into continued civic engagement after students graduate.

Internships often are seen as gateways to jobs after graduation, and McLauchlan seeks to use them for this purpose as well as a gateway to lifelong civic and political engagement. Utilizing four different courses at various levels of study, she explores how and where internships can best advance students' understanding of and interest in civic engagement, especially in a state (Florida) that currently ranks relatively low in measures of citizen civic engagement, such as voter turnout, volunteering, and attendance at public meetings. She concludes that internships can be an effective service-learning tool to create engaged citizens.

O'Shaughnessy and Owen argue that educators should not wait until the collegiate years to start working on creating civically engaged citizens. They present two models of how the discipline can effectively engage high school students. As just over 50% of the population will never attend college, it is imperative that educators not limit themselves to working with college students. Instead, as several authors argue, educators need to share these lessons with students early and often to embed them in their identities and regular practices.

Collectively, the chapters in this section also demonstrate that civic engagement can be taught by political scientists to both political science majors and nonmajors. We need not just preach to the politically interested, civically engaged choir. Some of these chapters do work on furthering the civic engagement skills of those already interested, whereas others are focused on the preliminary step of sparking interest in politics. In introductory-level courses that serve broad student populations, McKinlay and VanVechten and Chadha demonstrate that students do not need to be previously committed political science majors to develop an interest in and key skills for civic engagement. Indeed, the goal should be to reach nonmajors whose citizenship skills and knowledge can be fostered.

Bennion and Nickerson present evidence that political science educators can promote students' civic engagement without even requiring an active-learning or service-learning component to a course. Their large-scale, multicampus field experiment demonstrates that even a brief (15-minute) classroom intervention can have a demonstrable effect on the likelihood that students will register to vote. Further, as Lorenzini and McCartney show, even upper-level courses can be appropriate for related majors, such as international studies and sociology.

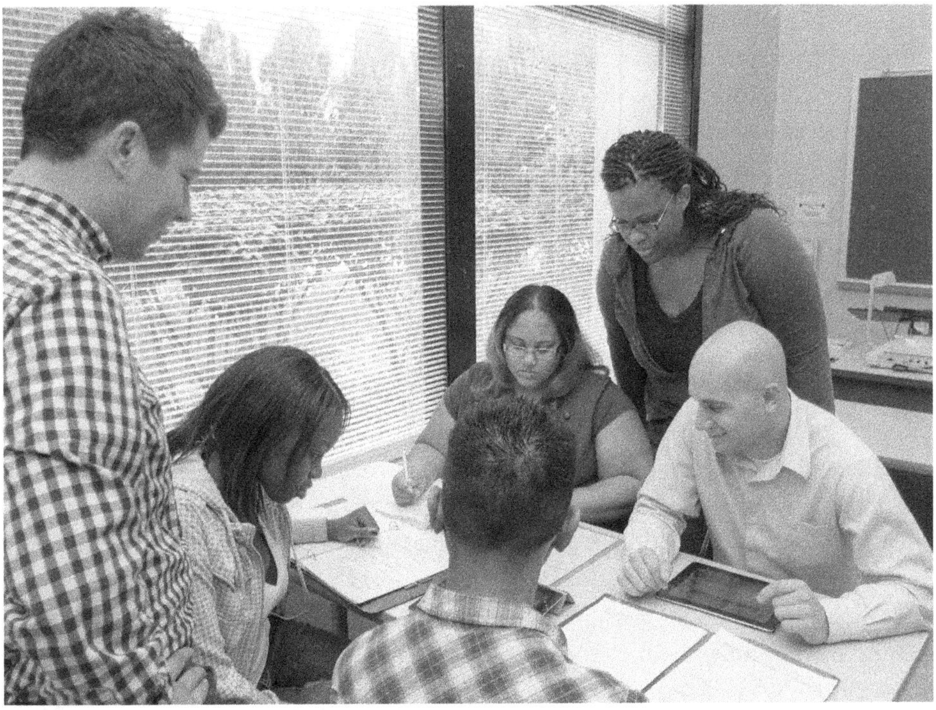

While many in this section, such as Jenkins, Sylvester, and Sanders, provide more specialized courses suited to committed majors, political science educators need not feel wedded to that approach. Indeed, as Section 3 suggests, the discipline needs a variety of options and continual opportunities for students to learn about and experience civic engagement. One class cannot be expected to complete the job of developing citizens and teaching all required citizenship skills.

Finally, these chapters overcome many of the early criticisms of civic engagement and service-learning courses. Some early courses lacked key components that foster deep learning, such as reflection exercises following the activity. The courses discussed here all contain various modes of reflection. In 2002, Mary Kirlin found that "little evidence supports expectations that service-learning encourages civic behaviors such as voting, contacting elected officials, and being active in community affairs." Kirlin argued that one reason for this failure is that "many service and volunteer programs have failed to sufficiently address development of fundamental civic skills such as expressing opinions and working collectively to achieve common interests."[1] The chapters included in this section of the book provide many options for fostering deliberation and developing specific citizenship skills. Some have narrower common interests as an explicit goal, such as Dicklitch's work on determining valid versus invalid asylum seeker claims or Sanders and McLauchlan's goals of working with political campaigns. Others have the more general goal of learning how to effectively participate in citizenship activities, such as voting (see Bennion and Nickerson and O'Shaughnessy) or respectful debate of political issues (see VanVechten and Chadha and Perry). All have some component of practicing being active in community affairs, and Sylvester and McCartney even begin to test whether or not students remain active after graduation. In sum, while Kirlin's concerns may have represented valid claims for a previous generation of civic engagement education, these authors have built more comprehensive foundations for lifelong citizenship.

Overall, these chapters show how political science educators can effectively get students engaged with political processes and politics—warts and all—while also providing important foundational knowledge and advancing key skills. The chapters demonstrate how we can deepen students' civic and political knowledge through active engagement with other students, community partners, politicians, and political systems. Rather than becoming discouraged by the complexities of politics, students can learn how to appreciate, work with, or overcome them and in doing so gain a sense of efficacy and self-confidence that makes them good citizens. The book presents a wide variety of assignments and activities so that teacher-scholars across the discipline will have many options to choose from in creating their own civic engagement courses. Some activities require intensive involvement that is more like training for a job in politics. Others provide more foundational—broader—civic knowledge and skills. In addition, the authors offer several models for assessing courses and service-learning activities to better gauge what works, what does not, and what can be improved. As several authors note, further research into both the short- and long-term effects of this pedagogy on students and their future roles as citizens is needed, but these chapters present important steps forward for the future of political science education including the development of robust educational models for civic and political engagement.

Using Best Practices Research and Experience with Local Governments to Increase Political Engagement

7

By Shannon Jenkins

Community-based projects have consistently demonstrated positive impacts on student development and civic engagement; however, many of these projects have limited results because they do not explicitly focus on politics or political engagement. I argue that if students are to become more politically involved as a result of their community-engaged projects, then these projects must be focused explicitly on fostering political involvement. One way to achieve this goal is by working with local government. Local governments often have many problems but few resources with which to solve them. This chapter describes a community-based research project that focuses on identifying best practices in local governments, examines the results and impact of this project, and discusses how such a project might be implemented in other classes.

The benefits of service-learning and community-based research projects are well documented. These projects have been found to lead to increased retention of students in their college or university, higher academic performance, and continued community engagement, even after graduation.[1] However, the impact of community-based projects on political engagement—defined either as knowledge and beliefs about the political system or participating in political activities—is less clear.[2] Some research has found that these projects lead to increased political engagement; other studies have found that community-based projects generally have little impact on political engagement.[3] For political science, this outcome is particularly troubling because fostering political engagement is one of the key goals of the discipline, as evidenced by the goals of the APSA Task Force on Civic Engagement.[4] However, the lack of connection between projects and political engagement may be because many, if not most, community-based projects are not specifically focused on fostering political engagement. As Saltmarsh, Hartley, and Clayton note, the civic engagement movement largely sidestepped the political dimension of civic engagement.[5] Research has shown that the key is to focus projects specifically around explicitly political activities, because then they can have a positive impact on political as well as civic engagement.[6]

One way to directly engage students in political activity is to have them work with local governments. Many colleges and universities are located in municipalities with nonpartisan governments, and many of these local communities are faced with a wide range of problems but possess few resources to effectively deal with them, especially during the economic downturn that began for most in 2008. These local governments offer an opportunity to create community-based projects that have students directly interact with political actors and the political system.

In this chapter, I first review the research on community-based projects and how these projects influence civic and political engagement. Next, I describe a community-based project that was offered as part of a senior-level political science seminar. Finally, I examine the benefits and problems associated with this project through analysis of student evaluations, critical reflection papers, and discussion. I also offer suggestions about how such projects can be offered in other political science courses. I conclude that if political science as a discipline seeks to foster increased political engagement, then community-based projects must focus more explicitly on this goal.

Community-Engaged Projects in Local Governments

Both service-learning and community-based research have been found to have positive effects on a variety of educational outcomes. For example, Eyler et al. found that service-learning projects have a positive impact on students' relations with their institutions of higher learning; students engaged in such projects report stronger relations with faculty and are more likely to graduate.[7] In addition, research also shows that students engaged in these projects perform better academically, with higher grade point averages and improved critical thinking and writing skills.[8]

Similar to service-learning, community-based research also has been found to improve academic performance and persistence.[9] These projects have a positive impact on students' personal outcomes, such as efficacy, moral development, and the ability to work with others, as well as social outcomes, such as facilitating racial and cultural understanding, citizenship skills, and continued community involvement.[10] The latter outcome is particularly noteworthy—students who participate in community-based projects are more likely to continue to be involved in their communities.[11] Yet while definitions of civic engagement typically include dimensions that focus both on political and nonpolitical involvement, as previously noted, research shows that community-based projects have the clearest positive impact on nonpolitical involvement.[12]

The effect of these projects on political engagement is less clear,[13] and the research that does exist focuses on one of two key dimensions of political engagement. More research has looked at students' knowledge of and beliefs about the political system. As Delli Carpini and Keeter argue, knowledge about politics is critical to becoming an engaged citizen.[14] In political science classes, several studies have shown that service-learning projects have a positive impact on students' learning about politics, which leads to a more-sophisticated understanding of the political process, more-positive beliefs about the importance of politics, and an increase in issue identification and political participation skills.[15] As Ball notes, however, "[W]hile participation in community service and volunteerism clearly has a positive impact on the propensity of young people to dedicate themselves to further service, the evidence of the effects of service on political engagement is, at best, mixed."[16] He cites his own survey as well as the work of Hunter and Brisbin as evidence of this disconnect between service and political engagement, which the authors all measure as knowledge of and beliefs about the political system.[17]

The second area of political engagement that has been researched involves participating in such political activities as voting and contacting elected officials. As noted earlier, very little research examines the impact of community-engaged projects on later political activity. In the case of voting behavior, Perry and Katula's review of the literature on citizen service finds little evidence that service-learning leads to any positive effects on voting.[18]

In sum, little is known about the impact of community-based projects on political engagement, due to the fact that few projects focus on politics and political engagement, and little mention is made of the political implications of the community work.[19] This is problematic. If community volunteerism only leads to increased political engagement with sustained community participation over extended periods of time, then class-based practices to foster community volunteerism will do little to solve the problem of decreased political engagement among youth while they still fit this demographic. In addition, if students see community volunteering as an alternative to political engagement, then community-based projects may never lead to increased political engagement. In fact, there is some evidence that students turn to volunteering as a way of rejecting political action, which they see as corrupt and distasteful.[20]

The remedy to these perceptions is to design projects that focus on explicitly political outcomes, such as increasing political knowledge, raising students' valuation of engaging in political activity as a means of fostering change, and engaging students directly in political activity.[21] As Walker finds, students involved in community-based projects understand how to perform service, but they do not necessarily understand how to effect political change. Therefore, it is wrong to assume that teaching students about service will lead them to clearly see the connections between community participation and political engagement.[22] Rather, these connections need to be made explicit by concentrating attention on students' understanding of government and their ability to use political tools to influence government.[23]

So, how can one design community-based projects that explicitly focus on fostering political engagement? The literature suggests at least three ways. First, both Walker and Ball offer several examples of community-based projects with nonprofit organizations that focus on public policy.[24] The key difference here between this traditional community-based project and one centered on fostering political engagement is that instructors must take time in the classroom to explicitly connect the service work to political issues and activities.[25] As an example, Walker had students write a research paper and develop a public advocacy campaign on a policy issue related to their community service placements, although the efficacy of this project in increasing political engagement was questionable.[26]

Alternatively, students could be placed directly with political organizations, such as political campaigns, political parties, or interest groups. Markus, Howard, and King argue that when students engage in service-learning with political organizations, they are performing public-oriented service, "an appellation that should not be bestowed solely upon work with 'needy' groups."[27] This option may be difficult in communities or regions dominated by a specific party, leaving few options for students who do not adhere to the dominant political beliefs of the area. Even in areas with two-party competition, there may be few options for students who are Independents or who identify with a minor political party. Further, universities in more remote locations may not be able to offer a wide variety of such placements.

A third way to accomplish the goal of increasing student political involvement is to design community-based projects with local governments themselves. As Jenkins notes, working for government can be seen as service since it, like nonprofits, often relies on volunteers to solve public problems.[28] Furthermore, such service is explicitly political as students are interacting regularly with political actors and the political system. In fact, contacting public officials is often used as a standard measure of political participation, such as in the General Social Survey.[29] In interacting with public officials and local government, students can see how government action can help alleviate public problems, whether through creating programs or reducing red tape to allow for private solutions to problems to emerge. This option also helps students make connections to individuals who can actually produce political change at the local level.

One fruitful way to engage students in community-based projects with and for local governments is to have them utilize best practices research. Once a problem has been identified, best practices research involves looking for solutions that have been tried and appear to work well in other municipalities.[30] This type of research has several benefits. First, while local governments often have numerous problems, resources for this type of research are typically scarce, particularly in smaller communities. There is often little free time or resources to engage in exchanges with other communities about what sorts of innovative solutions they are pursuing. Thus, local governments often reinvent the wheel, so to speak, as they develop solutions to problems. Best practices research conducted by student researchers can help local communities identify alternative solutions that have been proven to work elsewhere.

Second, best practices research is appropriately matched to the skill sets of most undergraduate students. Good policy analysis involves data collection and statistical analysis, skills that are often beyond the capacity of many undergraduate students, even those who may have research methods training. Searching the web, however, and contacting local communities for information about innovative solutions is not beyond the skill set of undergraduates, and with help from the instructor and local government officials, students can carefully craft questions designed to analyze whether the potential solutions that they uncover can be appropriately applied in the local community in which the students are working.

Third, such projects directly connect students with the public officials dealing with public issues. As Walker found, students who engage in community service alone understood how to serve, but they did not know how to effect political change.[31] By connecting students with local public officials, the students develop relationships with the people they need to target to effect political change in the local community in which they reside while at college. Furthermore, through their research, they seek to convince public officials to make changes in how they do things, an explicitly political activity. So when students identify best practices and advocate for their adoption, they are directly engaging with the political system.

Thus, best practices research offers opportunities to craft a community-based research project that 1) is useful to local municipalities, 2) is appropriately targeted to the skill set of undergraduates, and 3) directly engages students with politics and government. In the following sections, I describe just such a project offered in a senior-level political science class and analyze its benefits and problems.

Best Practices Research in State and Local Policy

State and Local Policy (PSC 401) was a senior-level seminar in the Department of Political Science at the University of Massachusetts, Dartmouth; the course was also cross-listed in the interdisciplinary Sustainability Program.[32] It was a small course of 12 students that met once a week for two and a half hours. Of the 12 students, eight were political science majors, two were political science minors, and two were sustainability minors. Class readings and discussions were focused on teaching students about the structure of state and local governments, the policy-making process (few students had taken courses on these topics), and the nature of public policy in a number of substantive policy areas. In addition, course materials focused on analyzing and evaluating policy outputs produced by these two levels of government. The class's goals were for students to understand how to analyze public policies and the actions of government and how to work to produce policy change, a goal that explicitly focuses on political engagement.

To meet these goals, the course was divided into three main sections. The first section focused on creating a common knowledge foundation for all class members. Because students had varying levels of background preparation, the first three weeks of class provided them with information on state government, local government, and the policy process. Students were each assigned a chapter to read about the topic for the week and were responsible for teaching other students about their topics. For example, during the class on state government, the chapters focused on socioeconomic and political context, parties and elections, interest groups, direct democracy, legislative politics, governors, and the courts.[33] Two students were assigned to each chapter; students then wrote summaries of their assigned chapters and gave copies to their fellow students. The pairs of students later gave a brief oral summary of their chapters, further ensuring that all students had the same background knowledge. A similar plan was followed for the course meetings on local government and public policy.[34]

The second section of the course focused on policy analysis, and all students read Bardach's *A Practical Guide for Policy Analysis: The Eightfold Path for More Effective Problem Solving.*[35] The book gave students clear, concrete guidance on how to conduct a policy analysis. Included in this book was a section on what Bardach calls "Smart (Best) Practices." The three classes devoted to policy analysis focused on discussing what policy analysis entails and how the information students read could be applied to their community-based research projects. The final section of the class, which encompassed five meetings, focused on specific policy areas for which state and local governments have substantial responsibility. These included economic development, education, social welfare policy, environmental policy, and crime and criminal justice policy. For this section, each student was assigned a *CQ Researcher* reading; several students for each class identified a "best practice" implemented by a state or local government related to the topic at hand and presented information on that best practice to the rest of the class.

In addition to these in-class presentations and reading summaries, the other key methods of assessment were three exams (one for each section of the course) and a group community-based research project with the town of Dartmouth. Dartmouth is a moderately sized community of approximately 35,000, with a representative town meeting form of government. Town meetings are typically held twice a year; in between these town meetings, the town is governed by an elected Select Board, which hires a town administrator to run the town government. While many local communities are experiencing financial difficulties, Dartmouth's financial problems predated the 2008 economic crisis by several years. In each of these years, cuts were made to town services and staff; an override in 2008 eliminated the need for cuts but did not restore services to previous levels. Thus, the town was faced with numerous challenges but had greatly reduced resources to deal with these challenges.

The instructor worked with two town administrators prior to the start of the semester to identify two potential projects: one focused on sustainability and one focused on information transparency.[36] The goal of the first project was to make the town more sustainable while at the same time saving money. There was much interest in promoting environmental practices; the community already had an alternative energy committee as well as a conservation commission. There was perhaps even more interest in saving money given the town's financial status. Thus, the sustainability team was charged with identifying green solutions implemented in other municipalities that had the potential to save money.

The goal of the second project was to increase information transparency. The town already had created an ad-hoc committee to review the Dartmouth town website and determine how to better provide information to citizens. However, all of the members had full-time jobs and volunteered for the committee in their spare time. In addition, the town only had one information technology staffperson, who was responsible for all IT needs in every town department except for the police and school departments. As a result, none of these people could devote themselves to this project for more than a few hours every other week. The information transparency team was charged with identifying ways to better provide information to residents at a low cost and to report back to the ad-hoc committee.

At the beginning of the semester, the class was given readings about sustainability and information transparency; these terms were discussed, including what they meant and how to go about promoting them at the local level. The class also hosted guest speakers from the local newspaper (to give students the "dirt" about local politics), a representative from the town website committee (also a UMass Dartmouth librarian), and the chair of the Dartmouth Select Board.

Students were charged with three key tasks on which their group would be assessed. First, each team was required to identify articles and research about their subject area. For example, the transparency team needed to define transparency and find information about how to promote information transparency in local governments. Each team member was charged with identifying and summarizing at least two relevant articles on the class website; the team then had to synthesize these into a cohesive summary of what the literature suggests is good practice in their area.[37]

Second, students were charged with interviewing important actors in the community in their issue area. The goal was for these interviewees to give students some insights into problems for which potential solutions could be identified. Students on the sustainability project team were connected with the director of the Department of Public Works, a Select Board member, the financial director of the school department, the director of the UMass Dartmouth Sustainability Institute, and an employee of the Southeast Regional Planning and Economic Development District. Students on the transparency team were connected with the town's information technology employee, the town's director of budget and finance, a member of the Select Board, a local political activist, and members of the town's website committee. Each team member was responsible for interviewing one person and summarizing that interview on the class website. Students were given complete latitude in determining how long these interviews should be; the key was that they were expected to get the information they needed to move forward with their project. The teams were then responsible for identifying common themes in these individual interviews and producing a group summary of the findings. Thus, students from each team interacted with official government actors; in all, 10 of the 12 students had some direct contact with a local public official.

Lastly, each team was charged with identifying best practices in other communities to recommend to the town. Based on the interviews, the teams picked several key problems on which to focus. Then, each team member was responsible for finding at least two potential solutions that had been successfully implemented elsewhere. These best practices could come from articles, interviews, or primary research (for example, examining another town's website for the transparency team). Each team member summarized this best practice on the class website; the summary described the practice, why it was a best practice, and how it might be adopted in Dartmouth.

From these best practices identified by individual members, the teams picked at least five best practices to recommend to the town for adoption. On the last day of class, each team turned in a literature summary, an interview summary, and a set of recommendations. There was no required length for this project, but the final projects from these teams were 17 and 18 pages in length. Each team also gave a group presentation to the class about what its members had learned. The final grade for the group project was a joint grade, but each student was also required to submit an evaluation of the other team members' work. Some students received very low scores from their peers; based on this feedback, I gave these students a lower final report grade. Participation was a required portion of the class grade as well, and the progress of the projects was frequently discussed as well as what students were learning from these projects during class sessions. Finally, students were required to produce a critical analysis of the Bardach book as part of the final exam, reflecting on whether the process he described in the book was useful in their projects.

Discussion

As with the first run of any community-engaged project, there were several positive outcomes of this project along with several areas in which improvement was clearly needed. While both teams identified several suggestions that were of use to the town, it was clear at the end that they should not have been given as much latitude in designing their workload as they were. As described above, the expectations for what the groups needed to submit were clearly defined; however, students were also told that they would be allowed to amend the division of labor, so long as they turned in their required work. The thought was that this structure would give students ownership of their project. Additionally, almost any sort of political activity will require the coordination of multiple actors; the thought was that learning to coordinate and manage the efforts of individual team members would be a useful skill for students to learn.

The sustainability team kept with the original plan, and in the end, its project was more complete than that of the transparency team. The transparency team, rather than giving each student some responsibility for each portion of the project, gave pairs of students complete responsibility for a portion of the project. So, two students were responsible for summarizing the literature, two were responsible for interviews, and two were responsible for identifying the best practices. Unfortunately for this team, the two students who had responsibility for the interviews did little work, and the team did not do a good job of monitoring their progress or working with me as the course instructor to deal with this issue. Interestingly though, the two students responsible for identifying best practices did a very good job, with in-depth research about the web practices of other communities. Other students had identified some towns as examples of best practices; these students went out and interviewed the person responsible for the website in each of these communities and then assembled a visual presentation of what these town websites looked like, how they were financed, and why the students considered them to be best practices.

While the sustainability team worked together better, its recommendations were not as useful as those of the transparency team. This outcome is probably due to the fact that the team was less clearly focused on specific problems. Team members had different interests in the area of sustainability—land use, energy consumption, etc.—so each focused on his or her preferred problem. In the end, the key lesson was that students need more concrete guidelines and milestones for turning in work. It is clear that more careful monitoring and guidance is needed.

Nonetheless, there were several positive benefits that stemmed from this project. The suggestions in the final reports from these teams were submitted to the town website committee (for the transparency team) and to the Select Board (for the sustainability team). The town revamped its website, so the ultimate goal of providing more information to the public in a timely fashion was met. Additionally, the town of Dartmouth moved to engage in several projects related to sustainability. One of the suggestions from the sustainability team related to lighting had already been implemented on a limited scale in the schools and will be rolled out on a larger scale, but because the school department had not communicated this plan to other town departments, this option had been considered in other areas until the best practices suggestion was shared. Thus, the project provided some use to the town. However, in future offerings of this course, I plan to work more closely with the teams to provide useful suggestions. This microlevel guidance will mean that teams will have less latitude in designing their projects, but I hope the end result will be more specific and useful suggestions for the town.

Students did feel engaged in the class and the work they were doing. Anonymous class evaluations were very positive: out of a scale of one (most optimal) to five (least optimal), the average student rating across nine questions was 1.12.[38] Several students commented positively about the community-based research project in their end-of-semester evaluations, stating that they learned a lot from the project and that it was the most worthwhile part of the class. The end of semester presentations included a wide array of best practices and suggestions for the town, indicating that students had been exposed to quite a few examples of the innovative practices of local governments. Too often, news and information focus on what governments are doing wrong, so for students to learn about some of the things that governments are doing right was a pleasant surprise for many of them. In fact, given this experience with local government, one of the students pursued an internship with the town of Dartmouth and now has plans to pursue a master's in public administration and work in local government, and another student is pursuing a law degree with a focus on public law and sustainability.

Next, as noted, 10 of the 12 students enrolled in the class directly contacted local public officials. If this contact is taken as a measure of political engagement like those used in the General Social Survey (GSS), more than 80% of the students would score affirmatively. Many of these students also noted that they had never before contacted a public official. Whether this level of political engagement continues is difficult to assess as most of these students have graduated, but research shows that early political participation can have a lasting impact on future political participation, suggesting that this project may increase the future political engagement of these students.[39]

In addition, students got to see how their work led to a change in the actions of town government, whether it was through the adoption of green practices or the implementation of a new and improved town website. Their best practices project gave them exposure to the full range of activities necessary to produce policy change, from identifying a problem to locating solutions and then convincing political actors to adopt those solutions. In the future, I plan to emphasize the latter portion of the project even more, by scheduling a formal presentation of the project's results at a public Select Board meeting.[40]

In sum, while there were clear lessons to be learned from the implementation of this best practices community-based research project, the project increased the short-term political engagement of the students by having them directly contact public officials and may also increase their long-term political engagement. I do plan on offering this seminar course again, as I felt that the students gained from interacting with local government officials and I enjoyed watching what they learned. However, I would more closely track changes in knowledge about the political system and measures of political engagement to specifically measure the impact of the project on these attitudes and beliefs. It is difficult to analyze questions like these given the small number of students taking the class and its infrequent offering, but it would be worthwhile to do so. Other political scientists who offer a similar project in a larger class might be able to do so more effectively.

Conclusion

While service-learning and community-based research projects have numerous positive impacts, the effect of these projects on political engagement has been less clear. However, research suggests that community-based projects explicitly focused on politics can lead to increased political engagement, and the results of this project, albeit limited, seem to confirm this conclusion, at least within the limited timeframe of the course. This project shows that working with local government can be one fruitful way to directly engage students in nonpartisan political activity, as is evidenced by the fact that more than 80% of the students in the class had direct contact with a local government official, a rate that far exceeds the levels reported in the General Social Survey.

Furthermore, it has been demonstrated that best practices research can be a method of community-based research that is useful both to students and the community and could be utilized in a variety of courses. This project was applied in a course on state and local policy, but it also could be applied in classes on local government, urban government, and public policy. Additionally, best practices research can be done for other types of governmental agencies, such as local environmental protection or police departments, allowing for inclusion in environmental policy or criminal justice courses. In addition, this project could be expanded for use in larger classes, either by creating more groups focusing on different problems or simply requiring the larger groups to identify more best practices.

This type of research also can be pursued with nonprofit agencies, which face similar difficulties. Working with nonprofits may not lead to increased political engagement, but students would still benefit from the other positive impacts that accrue from community-based work, such as increased civic engagement and academic performance. Overall, while it was only one course with a small number of students, this example suggests that more effective ways can be pursued to move students from community service to political engagement and meaningfully contribute to their development as knowledgeable and capable citizens.

From Active Service to Civic and Political Engagement: Fighting the Problem of Poverty

8

By Michelle Lorenzini

Civic engagement programs across college campuses tend to devote minimal attention to political engagement and instead emphasize volunteer service activities at the individual level. As political scientists, this lack of connection to our classrooms should be a cause for concern, but we can build upon and use service to foster civic and political engagement. This chapter provides an example of a course designed to move beyond traditional service-learning to political engagement by connecting students in a community-based research project with a local community partner. The goal is to harness students' commitment to community service to promote local, national, and global civic and political engagement.

For many years, political scientists expressed concern over the future strength of democracy in the United States as we witnessed declining civic engagement, especially among younger generations of Americans.[1] However, in recent years, US colleges and universities have taken a renewed interest in advancing civic engagement. Have the voices of political scientists been heard in this initiative?

While the discipline of political science has been at the forefront of civic engagement initiatives, these initiatives often fall short of expectations when implemented at the institutional level.[2] Civic engagement programs across college campuses tend to devote minimal attention to political engagement and instead emphasize volunteer service activities at the individual level.[3] As political scientists, should this lack of connection to our classrooms be a cause for concern, or can we build upon and use service to foster civic and political engagement?

The discipline of political science can reclaim civic engagement initiatives and take this opportunity to foster political engagement at the local, national, and global levels. To help students move beyond service to political engagement, Saint Louis University (SLU) developed an interdisciplinary, service-learning course—the Structure of Poverty, Globally and Locally. As a private Jesuit university, the school's mission is to educate its students to be fully prepared to contribute to society and to be effective leaders of social change.[4] This mission and tradition of social justice attracts students who want to serve the local community and encourages faculty to incorporate service-learning opportunities into the curriculum.[5] However, these activities largely focus on volunteering at local charitable organizations.[6] The Structure of Poverty, Globally and Locally course is designed to move beyond traditional service-learning courses at SLU by engaging students in a community-based research project with a local community partner. It seeks to harness students' commitment to community service to promote local, national, and global civic and political engagement.[7]

If political scientists truly want to educate students to be responsible citizens, then students must acquire the skills and knowledge to successfully navigate and engage the American political system, but they also must understand how global political, economic, and social structures affect their lives and how their decisions impact the lives of others at home and abroad. The course examines the structural causes of poverty at the local, national, and global levels and how these structures intersect. The objective is for students to understand how local poverty is related to political, economic, and social structures in their community; how similar structures in other countries manifest themselves in distinctive ways in specific local contexts; and how global structures and processes impact poverty at these local levels. The ultimate goal is to provide students with the knowledge and skills necessary to become competent and engaged global citizens.

This chapter describes the development of this course and analyzes its progress in promoting civic and political engagement. First, it locates the course in the context of recent research on civic and political engagement that suggests changing trends and provides new insights into why college students are politically disengaged. Second, it describes how and why this course was developed. As two students initiated the development of this course, the "why" provides important insights into what students need to move beyond volunteering to civic and political engagement. Finally, it assesses the course and its progress toward informing student activism and outlines subsequent course revisions based on these assessments. Qualitative assessments of the course were conducted after each offering of the course in the fall of 2007, 2008, and 2009.[8]

Whereas civic engagement programs across US college campuses have been successful in engaging students in service, they have been less successful in promoting political engagement. The goal of this course is to move students from volunteered service to political engagement. Interestingly, it succeeded not only in encouraging students to become politically engaged at the local level, but also encouraged the partner agency to engage in its own policy advocacy.

Political Disengagement, but Increased Volunteerism

Numerous studies uncovered what seemed to be an apparent paradox across college campuses in the 1990s. On one hand, they revealed a continuous decline in political engagement since the 1970s, as indicated by both declining electoral participation and decreased knowledge and interest in political affairs. On the other hand, they found a significant increase in community service among college students beginning in the 1990s.[9] Longo and Meyer term this situation the "scissor effect," as the trends in voting and volunteering split apart like the blades of a pair of scissors[10].

Survey data indicate that political apathy and civic disengagement has increased for all age groups since the 1970s, but has been especially pronounced among younger generations of Americans.[11] According to the National Association of Secretaries of State's New Millennium Project, since 18-year-olds first voted in 1972, electoral turnout among voters ages 18 to 24 has been the lowest of any age group and has continued to decline over time, dropping from 50% in 1972 to 32% in 1996.[12] In a survey conducted by Pryor et al., there were substantial declines in the proportion of college students who discussed politics and considered it important to keep up with current affairs[13]. Scholars advanced explanations for this declining civic engagement, including alienation from the political system—"a catchall term combining cynicism, distrust, low efficacy, and apathy"[14]—and the excessive individualism of contemporary American culture.[15]

Although scholars continued to find declining political engagement in the 1990s, they also found an increase in community service work and volunteerism among younger generations.[16] Sax offers one explanation for this contradiction in which a growth in service activities has not led to a parallel increase in political engagement: "It is quite possible that students are simply placing their energies where they feel they can make a difference ... students simply may not perceive politics as an effective vehicle for positive change."[17] Several scholars argue that the increase in community service can actually lead to political disengagement. Walker argues, "Educators cannot simply assume that service contributes to political engagement. Rather, I fear, service has been positioned as a morally superior alternative."[18] Lawry et al. speculate, "It may be that the significant increase in volunteerism in the college years and beyond is actually a *detriment* to the kind of full civic engagement many believe is necessary for a democratic society."[19]

Numerous studies have documented continued declining political engagement throughout the 1990s; however, other research indicates that political engagement among college students is on the upswing in recent years.[20] In a study conducted by the Center for Information and Research on Civic Learning and Engagement (CIRCLE), Kiesa et al. reported that the gap between voting and volunteering began to narrow in 2004 as students became more politically engaged.[21] This change was most evident in the increased youth voter turnout in the 2004, 2008, and 2012 general elections.[22]

Two other findings in the CIRCLE study are particularly relevant for this project as they are consistent with my interactions with students in and outside of the classroom at SLU. On one hand, many college students of the millennial generation see community service as "alternative politics," as an effective way for them to make a difference in the world.[23] On the other hand, many want to be politically engaged, but they do not feel adequately informed or knowledgeable about the political system to be effectively engaged.[24]

Engaged Service

Like many other US institutions of higher education, SLU has been very successful in engaging students in service. In a 2005 survey, 96% of SLU students reported completing some service hours during the previous year. The vice president for student development emphasized this commitment to service: "Our students come to campus on the first day ready to serve. Through numerous programs and efforts, we turn their enthusiasm for service into a lifelong passion." Each year, SLU reports the number of service hours conducted by the SLU community and actively works to increase this number annually. In 2009, SLU students completed more than 855,000 service hours. A service-learning project at SLU also has been instrumental in engaging students. Its mission is to promote a sense of "calling," or vocation, in the campus community by promoting engaged service, that is, "living a life of solidarity in service to the world."[25]

The 2007 CIRCLE study also found that many SLU students clearly view service as alternative politics, meaning, they see service as another way for them to make a difference in the world.[26] As one student stated, "We are not [politically] apathetic. We prefer to create social change by joining community service organizations."[27] This echoes the concern of Eliasoph that students see service as a more desirable alternative to political engagement. In precourse surveys in the Structure of Poverty course, students described service as "fulfilling," "enriching," and "rewarding" because they could personally see how they could make a difference through their volunteer activities. Lacking this sense of efficacy in the political arena, they described politics as "complex," "divisive," and even, "pointless." Some students implicitly posited service as the "morally superior alternative," describing it as "self-less" and involving "self-sacrifice," whereas politics was "selfish," involving "self-interest."[28]

Some SLU students see service as a more desirable alternative to political engagement; others recognize that political engagement can be a more effective way to achieve social change. Two students who proposed the development of this course explained why they wanted to move beyond service and learn how to become politically engaged:

> Many SLU students have been serving community needs for several years now. However, they have been expressing discontent and frustration with the walls they have run into. They want to understand why the community service is necessary to begin with. They want to understand and alleviate the causes of injustice. Students were getting frustrated with the idea of charity, which more often than not takes the form of community service.[29]

They no longer wanted to just help people meet their immediate needs, but instead, they wanted to redress the structural injustices of society. As they simply concluded, "the more just a society is, the less service it needs."

Even though these SLU students were inspired to act to address global and local injustices, they felt they lacked the tools and knowledge to facilitate change effectively. As they commented:

> Many of us are already involved in activism for things such as anti-war protests and workers' rights. However, we are disillusioned with this type of common blind activist attitude of fervent protesting, without careful thought of the result or other smarter alternatives. Many [students] believe that fervent protesting is no longer the answer and neither is community service or merely sitting in a classroom only learning about the issues.

As was evident in the 2007 CIRCLE study,[30] many SLU students wanted to be politically engaged, and they wanted their political activism to be effective. However, they lacked a sense of political efficacy. As political scientists, it is our duty to provide students with the knowledge and appropriate skills necessary to empower them to become civically and politically engaged citizens.

Informed Advocacy

The two student leaders who provided the impetus for the development of this course were members of OneWorld, a student social justice organization. The mission of OneWorld is to raise awareness of global and local injustices and to respond individually and collectively. The two students proposed bringing that mission into the classroom and formally institutionalizing it as part of the social science curriculum.

Whereas OneWorld has been successful as a student organization, the students recognized the need for social science faculty expertise to guide their work. They wanted to not only raise awareness of issues of social injustice and serve those in need, but also to examine and understand the factors that underlie injustice. They recognized that achieving these goals requires knowledge of local, national, and global political, social, and economic structures and how these structures shape the possibilities for individual and collective social justice initiatives.

As the student leaders of OneWorld stated in their course proposal:

> Students were beginning to reveal for themselves that much of the walls they were running into in the community were built and supported by some of the very structures our society is based on. They began to realize that most of the world's greatest problems stem from structural injustices.... Students were eager to draw on faculty knowledge to become fully educated about the systemic nature of the injustice before they advocated for it—as a result, the activism would be focused, direct, and, therefore, effective.

If students are to effectively apply what they learn in the classroom and heed their call to action to address global and local injustices, then the social sciences, and political science in particular, must teach them how to increase the efficacy of their actions. Students and instructors need to move beyond volunteerism and community service to the idea of informed advocacy. Informed advocacy includes both raising awareness of issues of public concern and responding collectively to address these

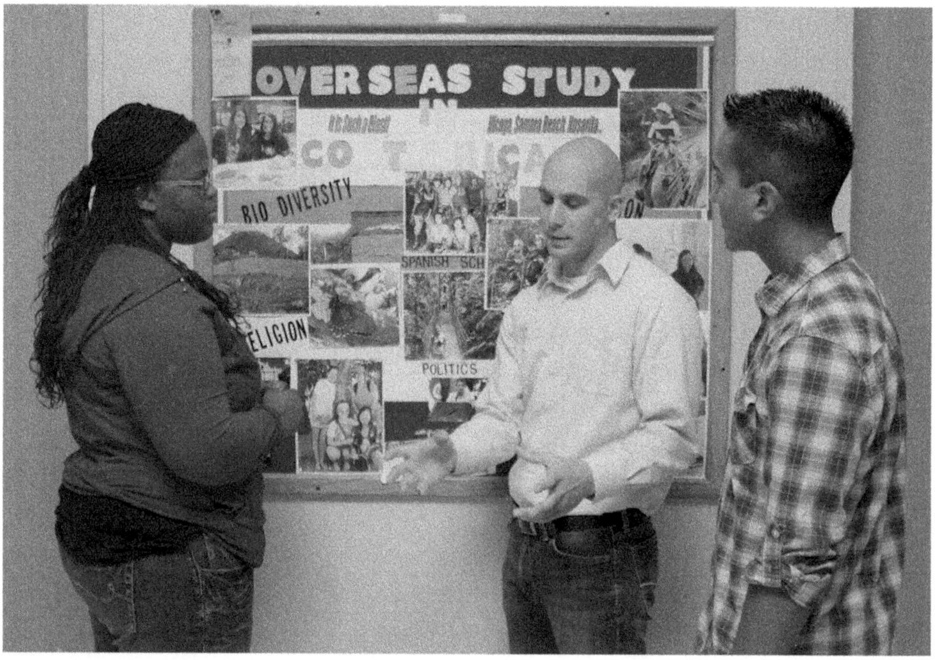

issues by advocating for policy change. It requires informed and active engagement with the political system. Some scholars are rightly concerned that increased student volunteerism may lead to political disengagement;[31] however, political scientists must use students' commitment to service to promote political engagement.

The problem is that students lack political literacy—the knowledge to participate meaningfully in the process of governance. Informed advocacy is a way for them to make connections between their community service and political engagement. By combining the two, they can become informed advocates and effective leaders of social change. Their community service becomes a vehicle for connecting with the political system, adds a personal dimension to an abstract policy problem, and allows students to see firsthand which public policies are ineffective, are insufficient, or are even creating the very problems they seek to address. However, instructors also must provide students with the skills necessary to navigate the political system and understand the process of governance. A service-learning course can become the tool to make this connection.[32]

Development of the Course—The Structure of Poverty, Globally and Locally

To help students make the connections between community service and political engagement, SLU created a course entitled, The Structure of Poverty, Globally and Locally. The theoretical component of the course focuses on the structural causes of poverty and how these structures hinder or propel antipoverty efforts. To see how these structures are actualized in St. Louis, the service-learning component of the course focuses on engaging students in a community-based research project aimed at local poverty alleviation. The goal is for students to use the theoretical knowledge they gain in the classroom to become informed advocates in their service activities.

The initial development of this course involved collaboration among social science faculty from the Departments of Political Science, Sociology and Criminal Justice, and Public Policy Studies; undergraduate and graduate students; and a nonprofit community organization, Queen of Peace Center (QOPC).[33] Since its initiation, the collaboration has expanded to include the School of Social Work.[34] The development of this course was generously funded by the VOICES Project at SLU.

The community partner agency, Queen of Peace Center (QOPC), provides substance abuse treatment services for women and their children living in the St. Louis metropolitan area.[35] An overwhelming majority of QOPC clients are low-income, unemployed, homeless, single mothers with poor social support.[36] In 2009, QOPC provided comprehensive family-based treatment services for nearly 1,100 women.[37]

Course Content and Service-Learning Research Project

In the Structure of Poverty course, students examine the theoretical and empirical literature on the structural causes of poverty at the global and local level from a multidisciplinary perspective. Other variables are not discounted, but the course focuses on the social, political, and economic structures that produce and perpetuate cycles of poverty. The global dimension of the course focuses primarily on developing countries. The local dimension focuses on policies in the United States, with some emphasis placed on research conducted in the St. Louis metropolitan area.[38] The course begins at the local level and builds to the global level. Its underlying premise is that one needs to examine global, national, and local structures to understand the underlying causes of poverty and engage in successful antipoverty alleviation efforts.

The course is organized around the following questions:

1. What is poverty? How should poverty be measured? Locally? Globally?
2. How do we view poverty? Political Ideologies and the Role of Values
3. What are the attributes of poverty? Who is more likely to be poor?
4. What are the structural causes of poverty? Global and Local Perspectives
5. What are the solutions? Global and Local Approaches
6. Why should we care? What can we do? How do we become informed advocates?

Course Material

While the poverty discourse in the United States is largely apolitical and focuses on individual rather than structural causes, the primary goal of this course is for students to understand that poverty is a political concept because it involves the exercise of power and resource distribution.[39] As such, the first third of the course focuses specifically on the relationship between politics and poverty. Who gets what in society reflects a country's political values and who has power in the political competition over the distribution of societal resources. This section covers the following areas: (a) a comparison of Western welfare states, their underlying ideologies, and their different conceptions of citizenship;[40] (b) non-Western views of justice, social welfare, and poverty and differences within the Christian tradition; (c) the legacy of New Deal reforms on US social welfare policy and the politics behind these policies; (d) the evolution of a social welfare policy in the United States and how public policy changes reflect shifting political values; and (e) the 2008 presidential campaign and the candidates' global and national poverty alleviation strategies. Also incorporated into the class was an abbreviated version of the Oxfam America Hunger Banquet® event to emphasize the vast difference in degree between global and local poverty; that is, how resources are distributed throughout the world.[41]

The second section of the course addresses the economic, political, and structural causes of poverty in the United States and around the globe. The section also focuses on how these same structures shape the possibilities for poverty alleviation initiatives. At the national level, the following causal factors are examined: global economic transformations and the resulting structural dislocations, gender inequality and the feminization of poverty, racial inequality and the wealth gap, and the intersection of social class and lack of human capital. To connect the readings more with students' research projects, the structural causes of poverty in the United States are specifically related to the problems experienced by the clients of QOPC. An attempt is also made to put a human face on poverty by including readings about poverty in the local St. Louis metropolitan area—stories with personal relevance for students. The theoretical arguments that focus on the globalization of the international economy, the role of international economic institutions, and the impact of domestic political institutions are examined to link the poverty discussion to the global community.

The final section of the course explores poverty alleviation strategies and the role that active, engaged citizens can play. Topics include the role of foreign aid, microfinancing programs, asset-building approaches, the role of multinational corporations, and the increased relevance of transnational advocacy networks in an increasingly global world. As the student projects research local poverty, this section places greater emphasis on macro- and microlevel approaches to address poverty alleviation in the developing world.

Guest Lectures and Interactions with the Community Partner

Several guest lecturers involved in poverty alleviation programs were invited to speak to the class. These speakers instructed students on alternative poverty alleviation strategies, as well as sharing their stories of how they got involved in this issue area and imparting how they became informed advocates. The goal was to provide role models working at the local, national, and global levels to inspire students to get involved and to demonstrate the different ways in which they could also engage in policy advocacy.

Sr. Tony Temporiti, founder of Microfinancing Partners in Africa (MPA), spoke about the collaboration of MPA with Jamii Bora, a microfinance organization in Kenya which provides services similar to Grameen Bank in Bangladesh. Two faculty members from the School of Social Work, Julie Birkenmaier and Jami Curley, spoke about their work with and research on asset-building programs, particularly individual development accounts (IDAs), at the local, national, and global levels, such as the SEED Foundation in Uganda. Lastly, QOPC invited the director and three other organizers from the Rebecca Project to speak to the class. The Rebecca Project, headquartered in Washington, DC, is a national policy advocacy organization for families struggling with poverty, substance abuse, and the criminal justice system. It trains low-income mothers in recovery who have also interacted with the criminal justice and child welfare systems to become community leaders and policy advocates.

The course also included several opportunities for the students to interact with the administrators and clients of QOPC. The class visited QOPC during the second class session for a tour of the center and an orientation from the administrators. The orientation covered the services offered by QOPC, how the problems faced by its clients intersect with poverty,[42] and an overview of the research project requirements. The students then returned to the center to meet with a client and conduct a one-on-one interview. Students were provided with suggested questions in advance that were designed to allow QOPC clients to share their personal experiences with the students. Later in the semester, the class again visited QOPC and joined its clients in viewing a performance by a local organization called Let's Start. This organization assists women in transition from prison life to society. It is run by women who themselves have been through the criminal justice system and now help others through advocacy, education, and sharing their personal experiences. This event was included to provide both QOPC clients and the students with models of successful advocates giving back to their local community. It was also intended to foster a sense of community between the class and the center.

Lastly, two clients from QOPC came to speak to the class about how chemical addiction and poverty intersected in their lives. Students also were given the opportunity to serve at QOPC or visit the center outside of these structured activities. The goal was to use these personal interactions to inspire students to become engaged in their local community and to encourage a sense of community and solidarity between the class (students and faculty) and the center (clients and administrators) by working together rather than on behalf of the organization.

Service-Learning Component

To ensure that the course was a mutually beneficial learning experience, the development of the service component of the class was also a collaborative effort between the administrators of QOPC and myself as the instructor. The intent was to create a research project to accomplish several goals:

- Help students understand the structural causes of poverty by seeing the connections between problems in their own local communities and local and far-reaching global structures.
- Provide personal experiences for the students to interact with the clients of QOPC, so they can experience firsthand how the problems faced by clients intersect with poverty and how existing public policies affect these individuals.
- Enable students to become informed advocates working on behalf of the agency.
- Serve the needs of QOPC by enabling it to expand the services it currently offers to its clients toward poverty alleviation.

Students conducted individual research projects on one of five issue areas in which QOPC seeks to further expand the services offered to its clients: housing, mental health, domestic violence, child welfare, or the criminal justice system. Within their issue area, students focused on a specific policy issue related to poverty in the United States. The project's requirements were specifically designed to engage students with the political system at the local and national levels. These included conducting a needs assessment, evaluating current public policy, and formulating a policy response that reflects an understanding of the policy process.

As part of the project, students were required to conduct interviews with a client of QOPC, a local community provider (St. Louis Housing Commission or a local homeless shelter), and a local stakeholder (state representative or policy advocacy group).[43] The first was designed to provide personal interaction with a client of QOPC and help students delineate their research issue area based on the client's personal needs and experiences. The provider interview was intended to help students identify existing services offered in the St. Louis metropolitan area. Finally, the stakeholder interview was meant to assist students in evaluating current public policies, learning of alternative policy recommendations, and identifying key stakeholders related to their policy issues. Students were also required to attend two designated field educational experiences outside of class related to their topics; for example, if housing was the topic, they should attend a Shelter Plus Care (SPC) hearing.[44] The field experiences were designed to allow students to experience the clients' trials and tribulations when they engage with a disconnected and inadequate social services network. The primary goal of the research projects was for students to conduct research and collect data that QOPC could use in future grant applications. The administrators at QOPC encouraged students to meet with them to discuss their research topics and made themselves available throughout the semester to offer assistance and discuss any problems students encountered. This assistance primarily focused on narrowing their research topics and identifying community agencies and stakeholders for their required interviews.

Evaluating the Course

Preliminary assessment of the course is based on student course evaluations and an analysis of their written work.[45] While somewhat different conclusions can be drawn from the two qualitative assessment tools, both provide valuable insights into the student learning experience and its success in promoting political engagement. Below, I detail the successes, followed by several weaknesses.

1. *The course material and assignments greatly increased student knowledge of the structural causes of poverty at both the global and local levels.*

Through evaluation of midterm and final essay exams to determine student knowledge and understanding of the course material, it was found that the students greatly increased their knowledge of the issue area, were able to critically evaluate alternative theories, and developed sufficient knowledge and skills to devise their own policy proposals. In final reflection papers, many students admitted that prior to the course, they had little to no knowledge of the structural causes of poverty. By the end of the semester, they not only felt informed, but also believed they had sufficient knowledge to inform others regarding the issue area. According to one student evaluation:

> I almost feel as if it is my duty to inform others in the areas they don't know.... Sometimes I even shock myself by the passion that I have been overcome with. I do believe that I have the knowledge and skills to truly make a difference regarding this issue area if even at the most basic level I simply talk to people and continue to inform as many people as possible about these issues.

Another stated:

> [Now], I can speak with intelligence and authority from the readings and first-hand experience. I feel like I am much more credible in my position, Lmuch more clear.... Facts are very powerful when making a position for a social cause and since taking this course I believe I have the necessary facts to make a strong argument for the fight against poverty.

2. *The service-learning component enhanced student learning by increasing their substantive knowledge of the issue area and allowing them to apply their knowledge outside of the classroom.*

A student wrote, "The experience helped me see how the structures we learned about are actualized in the St. Louis community." Still another stated, "It is really important to have hands-on activity that lets students use the information they have learned in a real-world setting." Through their experiences at QOPC, students also gained first-hand knowledge of how public policies affect individuals. As one claimed, "Experiencing testimonials of victims who have suffered from poverty while learning about the structural causes of poverty made the subject matter more concrete." Most significantly, they experienced how disconnected the US social welfare system is and the obstacles people face in trying to access the system.

3. *The service-learning component also helped students connect their academic coursework with their future career paths.*

One student wrote, "The service that we did through our research had a bigger impact. I found a way to help others by using the skills that I have developed over the past few years I've spent at SLU; it gave me an idea as to how I can focus my career to help others." Another student reinforced this career connection by stating, "In the future, I anticipate entering the urban planning field. Knowing the structural causes of poverty and how they can be addressed will help me focus on poverty alleviation in future professional work."

4. *The service-learning component of the class inspired students to become engaged by adding a personal dimension to an abstract policy problem.*

One student noted, "Hearing their stories gives motivation and also greater insight." Another, "Never underestimate the power of personal testimony." Another reiterated, "Putting a face to an idea as abstract as poverty is a huge step to promote student involvement in the local community." It also helped students move beyond service to informed advocacy. As one student stated,

> The most valuable thing I learned in the course is the idea that the people you are trying to assist are the experts in their field. I learned that to effectively make a difference on poverty, you must consult the people you are helping and listen to their needs.

5. *The course encouraged civic engagement and helped students develop the skills necessary to become engaged citizens.*

As one student commented, "This Service Learning experience has prepared me for the responsibility of living in a democratic society, exposure to different cultures, and encourages critical thinking, researching and problem solving." Another wrote, "By completing the project my research skills were improved as was my ability to communicate effectively with representatives and top officials of various organizations."

6. *The course showed students how to channel their energies into political engagement.*

The research project helped students see that they had an alternative to volunteerism if they wanted to make a difference in the world. They could actually try to advocate for policy change. As one stated, "The most important aspect of the class is the advocacy it promoted.... [It] encouraged students to take what they learned in the classroom into the real world." To some, it came as a surprise to think about trying to actually engage the political system. One student explained:

> The most impressive thing, to me, is that this course actually forces students to not just look at the causes of poverty and the flaws in the system, but to also think of a way to change it. It forces us to step outside of the comfort zone of learning and understanding an issue and pushes us into a realm where we have to think about changing it. The

> course is almost empowering in that way, in that students have to be more than just students. They have to be political actors. They have to give an effort to make changes.

It appears that the collective activities of the class also enhanced the learning experience—as students learned about civic and political engagement as part of a group rather than as individuals, they experienced the power of collective action. As one student explained,

> The overall strengths of this course was that it brought together a lot of committed people learning not just to better ourselves, but to improve the world and people around us. You created a community among the class of like-minded students who genuinely want to make a difference.

In working with their fellow students and QOPC, they could see how they could personally join with others to make a difference in the world. As a student commented, "I think the project really opened my eyes to the many ways in which the greater community is involved in working to combat poverty, and how I could join them."

One of the most interesting outcomes of the course was that it encouraged the community partner to become politically engaged. QOPC administrators realized that they needed to engage in the political process and advocate on behalf of the agency, especially if they were to be more effective in securing federal, state, and local funding. This collaboration marked the beginning of their policy advocacy activities.[46]

PROBLEMS EXPERIENCED

Course evaluations, student discussions, and assessment of written work also revealed three primary weaknesses in the course.

1. *The research project was too large of an assignment for individual students.*

Many of the students found the research project to be overwhelming. At the same time, they believed it was a great learning experience, and the majority of students believed they had completed solid research projects. According to one student, "I can safely say the research project has been the most challenging, yet most rewarding, project I have done at SLU." While I agree that it was a great learning experience, as course instructor I was disappointed in the quality of their projects. QOPC will benefit from their research; however, additional data will need to be gathered by the center before it can utilize the student-supplied information in grant applications.

The most significant obstacle students faced was narrowing down their research questions, given their lack of initial knowledge of their particular research topic; for example, housing. They experienced difficulties gathering the necessary data for the needs assessment component of their projects, which demonstrated significant weaknesses in their methodological skills. Students also were challenged to identify and arrange interviews with local providers and stakeholders.

Student suggestions for improvement included designing group projects as opposed to individual projects and providing students with a list of community agencies and stakeholders who have agreed in advance to be interviewed. The university is also considering linking the course with a research methodology course to address students' inadequate skills in this area.

2. *Insufficient interaction with the clients of QOPC.*

The students requested more one-on-one interaction with the clients of QOPC. Suggestions included pure volunteerism at the organization, follow-up client interviews, shadowing the administrators at QOPC for a day, and a final meeting with the administrators of QOPC to discuss students' completed assignments.

3. *Insufficient attention to the global dimension of the course.*

Many students were more interested in the issue of global poverty than poverty in the United States. These students felt that the service-learning component shifted the emphasis to poverty in the United States and suggested also partnering with an agency that focuses on global poverty alleviation; dividing the course into two courses, one that focuses on global poverty and the other on poverty in the United States; or some combination of these. However, two students who were primarily interested in global poverty stated that the course did motivate them to become involved in local poverty alleviation efforts. As one of these students commented, "I've always thought I would work on international poverty ... but now, maybe I'll work here at home!" At the same time, those most interested in local poverty "deeply appreciated the global poverty dynamic."

Course Revisions

After assessing the course and preparing to offer it a second time, I worked with QOPC to address the problems and develop a new research project. We designed the projects to be more manageable for students while also building upon the collaborative learning experience that occurred in the previous course. The two-part projects still focused on asset-building approaches to poverty alleviation.

Part I was a group project in which students gathered information on four agencies in the St. Louis metropolitan area that offer individual development accounts (IDAs) and other financial education services to low-income households.[47] As part of their projects, students were required to visit the agencies and conduct interviews to understand the services offered. The goal was to develop a resource manual for QOPC. QOPC wants to refer its clients to these agencies in an effort to expand the services it offers to alleviate poverty.

Part II included individual projects designed to focus on the policy process and policy advocacy. The students identified and analyzed national and state policies that promote or inhibit asset-building activities. They could focus on one of four issue areas: savings and investment, postsecondary education, homeownership, or entrepreneurship. Based on their analysis, they were required to recommend best policy proposals and suggest policy changes. For this part, students also conducted stakeholder interviews with local politicians or advocacy organizations to gain insights into existing federal and state policies and proposals. Students were provided with a list of stakeholders who had agreed to be interviewed in advance to address the difficulty students experienced arranging interviews in a timely fashion during the previous offering of the course.

To increase student interaction with the clients of QOPC, the field experiences and service-learning activities were revised. After an initial orientation at QOPC, students visited St. Philippine Home, QOPC's transitional housing program, to conduct client interviews. Clients from QOPC also visited and spoke to the class.

Two new experiences were also created that were attended by the students and clients and administrators of QOPC. Both events were designed not only to teach the students how they could become politically engaged, but also to advance the newly engaged policy advocacy efforts of QOPC. The first was a legislative roundtable held at QOPC on the "Structures of Poverty in Missouri," which eight Missouri state senators and representatives attended and shared their views on how to combat poverty in the state. The roundtable was designed as a vehicle to help students connect with the political system as they queried politicians about alternative poverty alleviation strategies and the most effective ways for students to become politically engaged. For QOPC, it presented a lobbying opportunity to familiarize state legislators with its successful work and the policy and financial obstacles it faces. The second new experience was an advocacy training session for the students and the clients of QOPC, conducted by the Rebecca Project.[48] These two events helped students see how they could become informed advocates at the local, state, and national levels as they directly interacted with elected state officials and received policy advocacy training.

Second Course Assessment

After teaching the course a second time, I again assessed the success of the course in achieving its objectives. The quality of the student research projects increased substantially—particularly in their policy analyses. Students successfully identified and analyzed policies that promoted or inhibited asset-building activities and developed proposals of their own. They also recognized the importance of understanding how to navigate the political system to successfully advocate for policy change. This research has been used by QOPC to familiarize itself with federal and local legislation and assist in the group's advocacy efforts. The resource manual provided valuable information to QOPC, which is currently taking initial steps in working with one of the agencies.

In many ways, the course surveys echoed the successful outcomes of the previous course. As one student stated, the service-learning component made the course "three-dimensional." However, several new insights also emerged:

1. *The course encouraged students to become "responsible" and "informed" citizens.*

Students not only felt inspired and motivated to address poverty, they also felt that they had a responsibility to do so. As one student stated, "Citizenship holds each of us individually responsible for the welfare not only of ourselves, but also our fellow citizens." Another student revealed that the class showed her "how it is our job as citizens to affect these changes." One student, expressing his desire to become "more civically engaged," noted, "I have become very informed about effective policies and I will be a much 'better' citizen because of this."

2. *The service-learning activities increased students' level of political efficacy.*

Students gained confidence in their abilities to engage the political system and their abilities to achieve results. In precourse surveys, the two words most often used by students to describe politics were "complicated" and "confusing." When the same survey was administered at the end of the course, students used the words "feasible," "attainable," and "comfortable" to describe their abilities to engage the political system. As one student elaborated,

> I used to think that politics simply could not work and that the only way to work toward poverty alleviations was through social service organizations, but I now realize that as long as individuals work to make their voices heard in the political process that change can be achieved.

Many also stated that they now believed they could achieve greater success working inside of the political realm than outside. According to student evaluations, the legislative roundtable, stakeholder interviews, and advocacy training session with the Rebecca Project were key in making this transition. One student stated, "Becoming an advocate is much easier than I expected, and does make a difference. Meeting and speaking with legislators was both exciting and make the task seem more attainable, a little less scary." Another agreed, "I was really worried at first for the interviews, but afterwards, I felt more confident in myself and my abilities." As students engaged key stakeholders, their levels and senses of political efficacy increased.

3. *The collaborative activities of the class enhanced the learning experience.*

Students learned from each other, and the service-learning activities created "class unity through shared experience." As one student wrote,

> I think one of the most valuable things I learned in this course was that I have an invaluable resource in my peer.... I am extremely confident about future efforts to alleviate poverty after being in class with people that know what they are talking about." The shared learning experience also empowered students to move from volunteerism to advocacy. Students gained personal confidence working together to achieve a group goal. As foreshadowed in the previous class, students also learned the power of collective action. As one explained, "I learned that while an

> individual can make a difference, collective efforts are more substantial.... We are definitely an individualist nation,... but we would be able to affect more change as a whole if we worked together.

Many of the students still felt that the course covered too much material; however, none of them wanted to eliminate anything. Instead, many again suggested dividing the course into two separate, sequential courses, one covering the global dimension, the other the local. They also felt there needed to be a closer connection between the local project and the global dimension of the course. Like the students in the first course, they suggested working with two partner agencies for the student research projects—one that focuses on global poverty and one that focuses on local poverty.

As I am very hesitant to divide the course into two separate courses for theoretical reasons, I do believe that a greater effort can be made to connect the local project with the global dimension of the course, perhaps by including the successful application of asset-building approaches around the globe. I am also exploring the possibility of joining with Microfinancing Partners for Africa as a second partner agency.

Conclusion

Many students at Saint Louis University want to be engaged in the world in which they live. True to the university's mission statement, they want to become "effective leaders of social change." As a former student and the founder of OneWorld wrote:

> The democratic nature of the US relies on the decisions of its citizens to determine the outcome of our political choices.... Especially, at a Jesuit university that strives to be "men and women for others," we not only have the capacity, we have the moral responsibility to take advantage of our democratic power to be the voice for the voiceless.[49]

Civic engagement programs across US college campuses have been successful in getting students into volunteering; however, they have been less successful in promoting civic and political engagement. Service-learning grounded in traditional classroom instruction and assignments can lead to political engagement, but it is our job as political scientists to help students make connections between the two. By providing students with the knowledge, skills, and tools needed to become informed and able advocates, students understand how they can engage the political system to increase the efficacy of their actions. At the end of the SLU course, students had a clearer understanding of the structural causes of poverty—they were "informed." Moreover, they wanted to engage the political system to make policy changes and work toward alleviating poverty—they had become the advocates the university seeks to encourage and the responsible citizens the political science discipline seeks to cultivate.

From Policy to Political Efficacy and Engagement: Using Government in Action to Promote Understanding of Public Policy

9

By Dari E. Sylvester

This chapter outlines the integration of a service-learning component into a required course for undergraduate political science majors entitled Government in Action: Public Policy. It measures the effectiveness of service-learning in creating more positive attitudes toward civic participation in the immediate aftermath of the semester and three years later and highlights methods for improving understanding of course content and increasing students' political efficacy through service-learning.

As a political science professor at a liberal arts school, I am committed to teaching students in ways that maximize their learning. Many students (including myself) learn best by doing. An experiential learning course is intended to increase learning by enabling students to engage subject matter outside the classroom. One particular form of experiential learning—service-learning—requires that students "give back" to partners outside the classroom in the form of volunteerism or community service and reflect upon that service. As a citizen and educator who believes that good democratic government depends upon active engagement by its people, I feel an additional obligation to educate my students about the importance of and skills for political engagement.

This chapter outlines the integration of a service-learning component into a required course for undergraduate political science majors entitled Government in Action: Public Policy, and measures the effectiveness of service-learning in creating more positive attitudes toward civic participation in the immediately following the semester and three years later.[1] It seeks to shed light on the following questions: Can service-learning in a public policy course enable students to feel empowered and motivated to become politically active? To what extent will that sense of empowerment last once the semester is completed?

Through teaching this class, I have determined that a service-learning component can increase students' sense of political efficacy, increase their understandingsof course content, and, ultimately, affect students' levels of political engagement. This study contributes to the literature on the impact of service-learning for political engagement in three ways. First, while more studies are still needed to assess the long-term impact of service-learning, this research analyzes both short-term and long-term effects on attitudes toward political engagement. Second, this research examines student survey data collected in both service-learning and nonservice-learning versions of the course, allowing for a careful comparison of student attitudes across otherwise identical courses. Finally, I employ a mixed methodological approach that combines quantitative and qualitative analysis of student data to paint a comprehensive portrait of the impact of service-learning on political attitudes.

The chapter proceeds as follows: first, I explain why I have chosen the service-learning method to increase student political engagement. Next, I describe the course design in detail, including the course and service requirements. Subsequently, I review results of both quantitative and qualitative analysis and outline final conclusions.

Choosing the Service-Learning Method

The millennial generation of students that most faculty teach tends to be "disillusioned, distrustful, [and] often downright disgusted about politics." Research abounds that demonstrates young people's preference for volunteerism and underperformance in the political process, especially in voting.[2]

Some scholars have looked to the incorporation of service-learning (SL) as one way to attempt to understand and ultimately reverse the low engagement levels among young people. The evidence regarding the success of such attempts has been mixed. A variety of studies have found support for the notion that service-learning courses increase civic participation. For instance, among community college students, engaging in SL increased civic engagement (broadly defined) compared to non-SL courses,[3] though one author cautioned about the possibility of a selection effect.[4] Alternatively, other studies have found little evidence for SL affecting civic engagement levels. For example, in a study of graduate-level MPA courses, SL did not increase levels of civic engagement,[5] though that may have been a function of small sample size, high levels of civic engagement among students at the pretest level, or some combination of both. Similarly, sociology courses incorporating various models of SL did not significantly affect civic outcomes.[6]

Other authors have focused on the design of SL courses to ensure maximum impact. Reviewing a number of important studies, Galston concluded that SL course effectiveness was contingent upon the link between discussion and reflection on the service-learning experience.[7] In addition, Hepburn et al. highlighted the need to ensure that SL goals are explicit and tied to course content and that the length of the SL component was sufficient to allow for "working relationships" with community partners to flourish.[8] Indeed, several studies have emphasized the need for a significant SL time commitment to achieve outcomes, such as the development of more racially tolerant attitudes[9] and knowledge gains.[10] To the extent that the ultimate goals are improved learning of course material and the development of prosocial attitudes, research consistently demonstrates the need for lengthier service commitments.

Keeping this research in mind, I embarked upon the creation of an SL course that incorporates best practices for achieving the goal of improving students' sense of the political process and their role in it. In the spring of 2007, I was selected as a fellow in the California Campus Compact–Carnegie Foundation Faculty Fellows: Service Learning for Political Engagement Program. The program was developed to help professors construct service-learning courses aimed at increasing student political activity. I employed my fellowship in the development of a service-learning course for the existing Government in Action: Public Policy course at the University of the Pacific, a private institution located in Stockton, California.[11]

In previous nonservice-learning versions of the course, I had observed that certain public policy content areas proved more challenging for students fairly consistently across semesters. For example, I had found that most students developed a stronger understanding of the roles of federalism and various policy actors within the policy-making sphere, but struggled to analyze and articulate policy problems. I sought to promote a deeper understanding of the policy cycle to give students a firmer grip on politics overall, thereby allowing them to better negotiate their place within the system. Thus, an effective SL approach would need to continually reinforce the link between external service and the material students learned in class by validating that the course content was enacted daily in the real world. This service-learning project was developed to foster undergraduate students' understanding of the policy process and facilitate growth in their sense of political efficacy by combining guided student reflection and service in the nonprofit sector with a strong foundation in public policy theory.

Service-Learning Course Design

My fellowship entailed the redesign of the public policy course required for political science majors, but the course also attracted nonmajors interested in learning more about the policy process or considering a policy-oriented career.[12] Traditionally, POLS 119: Government in Action: Public Policy is an upper-level course that examines the theoretical literature on policy making, including the role of multiple actors such as Congress and interest groups; policy analysis; and the nature of policy change. The course is typically offered once per year in the spring. The service-learning version of the course was offered in spring 2008 and consisted of two major parts: a conceptual and theoretical classroom-based course[13] and the new service-learning segment.

The new service-learning segment required a substantial time commitment: seven to 10 additional hours per week outside class working onsite with a nonprofit community partner, the Community Partnership for Families of San Joaquin County (CPF). This time commitment was far more than any other that I had seen in the literature.[14]

At CPF, students worked on local policy issues and assisted families navigating the local social services labyrinth. CPF's mission is to aid marginalized families in locating the services and information they need to be successful. It provides consultation and information on a variety of issues, including obtaining social services, job assistance, financial advice/planning, housing assistance, and health care.[15] The nonprofit's location only three miles from campus was also an asset, given the time commitment students made to the organization.

In the service-learning segment, students worked directly on policy issues that ranged from education to health care for the underserved members of the Stockton community. At the beginning of the course, students chose from four different projects offered by CPF. Prior to the start of the semester, students were emailed on several occasions in an effort to help set expectations about the nature of the service-learning, particularly with regard to the time commitment. On the first day of class, representatives from CPF visited to introduce students to the mission of the nonprofit and the four projects from which they would choose to do their service.

By early January 2008, student enrollment in the course had nearly reached the maximum, with 24 students. Once the first week of the semester had been completed, representatives from CPF had visited the class, and course expectations and service-learning obligations had been explained, however, only 14 students remained enrolled.[16] Interestingly, most of the students who made the decision to drop the course in the first week contacted me to let me know they were sorry to be doing so. The majority of these students expressed eagerness to do the service-learning but were not in a position to make the necessary time commitment. Descriptive statistics of the remaining students are listed in Tables 9-1, 9-2, and 9-3.

Given that the course is a major requirement as well as a mandatory course for prelaw minors, it is not surprising that 94% of the students were either majors or prelaw minors. Furthermore, with the exception of one student, enrolled students were juniors and seniors.

As one of the course requirements, students were told to keep weekly journals with free-form and structured responses to prompts.[17] All of the writing assignments were specifically geared toward strengthening the students' abilities to link their experiential learning to the traditional learning of the classroom. Students were instructed to reflect upon their experiences and link them to theory in an effort to continually practice bridging abstract, conceptual knowledge to the real-world practical challenges of policy process. Structured prompts helped students synthesize classroom learning with their service-learning experiences. I adapted the prompts as the semester proceeded to increase their relevancy and timeliness. Written responses were due approximately every other week.

Oral communication skills were also used frequently throughout the course. Class sessions were based heavily on discussion and required frequent student reflection, with my primary role being that of a presenter of questions and stimulator of thoughtful discussion. Outside the classroom, students further honed these skills by directly interfacing with the community nonprofit and its clients. This

Table 9-1: Student Majors

Major	Number of Students Enrolled in SL Semester	Number of Students Enrolled in Both Non-SL Semesters
Political Science	9	34
English	1	0
Visual Arts	1	0
Self-Designed	1	0
Double Major: POLS and Spanish	2	0
History	0	1
Communications	0	1
Double Major: POLS and Philosophy	0	1
Total	14	37

Table 9-2: Sex Ratios of Students

Sex	Number of Students Enrolled in SL Semester	Number of Students Enrolled in Both Non-SL Semesters
Female	10	23
Male	4	14
Total	14	37

Table 9-3: Class Rank

Class Rank	Number of Students Enrolled in SL Semester	Number of Students Enrolled in Both Non-SL Semesters
Freshman	1	0
Sophomore	5	7
Junior	7	11
Senior	1	19
Total	14	37

time presented a distinctive opportunity for professional interaction with the community partner, given that college students are mostly accustomed to practicing communication at a student level.

In the final part of the semester, as critical thinking and problem-solving skills were sharpened, students submitted a final research report to CPF and me and presented their findings in class. Members of CPF were invited to attend one of the presentation sessions. The final report was a culmination of the theoretical and practical knowledge obtained throughout the course. Its intention was to solve a local policy problem of importance through research and analysis, including an extensive literature review. The level of political participation this project required far surpassed that found in a traditional class setting, in part because witnessing an entire policy cycle is a unique experience for most students.

In the two consecutive semesters after the service-learning version was taught (spring 2009; spring 2010), a nonservice-learning traditional version of Public Policy was offered. The non-SL semesters essentially offered a very similar classroom experience whereby the same content was covered, but no outside work or journaling was required. These courses were meant to serve as control groups to the experimental service-learning group.

Quantitative Assessment

On the first full day of class, students in all three semesters (SL and non-SL) took a pretest consisting of a standard inventory of internal and external political efficacy.[18] At the conclusion of the semester, students took a posttest intended to gauge any changes or improvements in their sense of political efficacy. On the posttest, after completing a political efficacy survey, students were asked to reflect upon changes they observed in their answers over the course of the semester. Scores were coded from a low score of 0 to a high score of 1. The mean scores of the pre- and postsurveys for all three semesters are shown in Figures 9-1 through 9-7.[19] Items in the scale

Figure 9-1: Pre- and Postsemester Mean Scores for Informed about Government

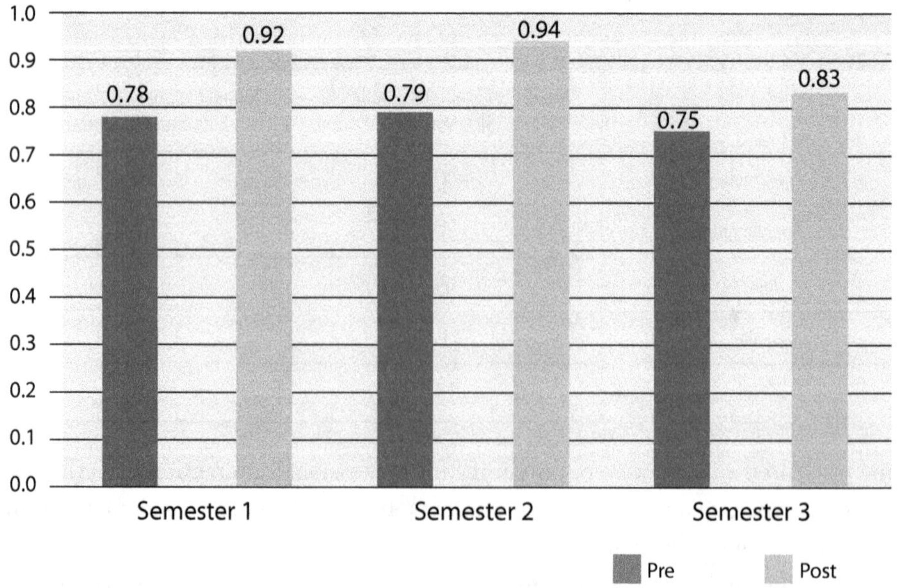

Note: Semester 1 (SL): n=9; Semester 2: n=17; Semester 3: n=20

Figure 9-2: Pre- and Postsemester Mean Scores for People Have No Say[a]

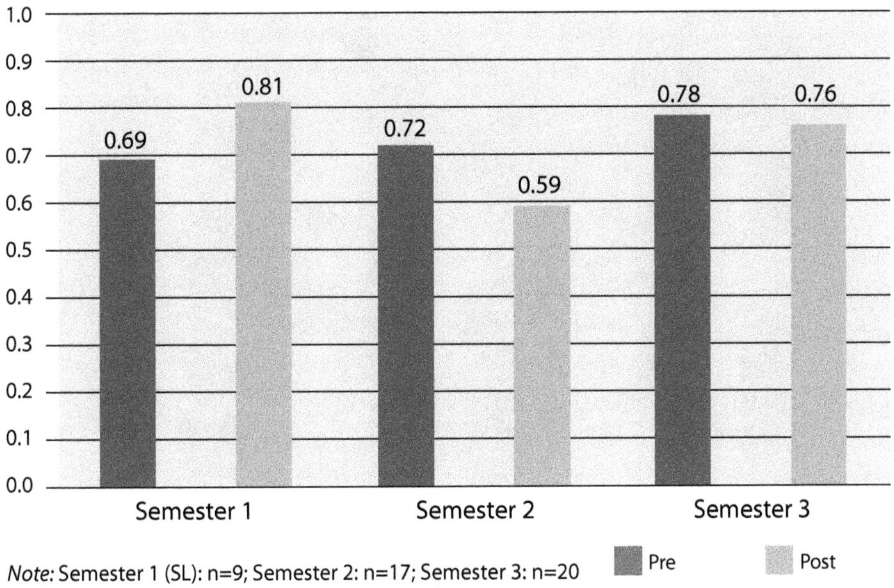

Note: Semester 1 (SL): n=9; Semester 2: n=17; Semester 3: n=20
[a]Note that this item is reverse-coded such that higher scores indicate higher political efficacy.

that reflected *less* political efficacy (e.g., "Public officials don't care…"; "People like me don't have any say"; "Sometimes politics and government seem so complicated") were reverse-coded such that higher scores across all items reflect *more* political

Figure 9-3: Pre- and Postsemester Mean Scores for Public Officials Don't Care[a]

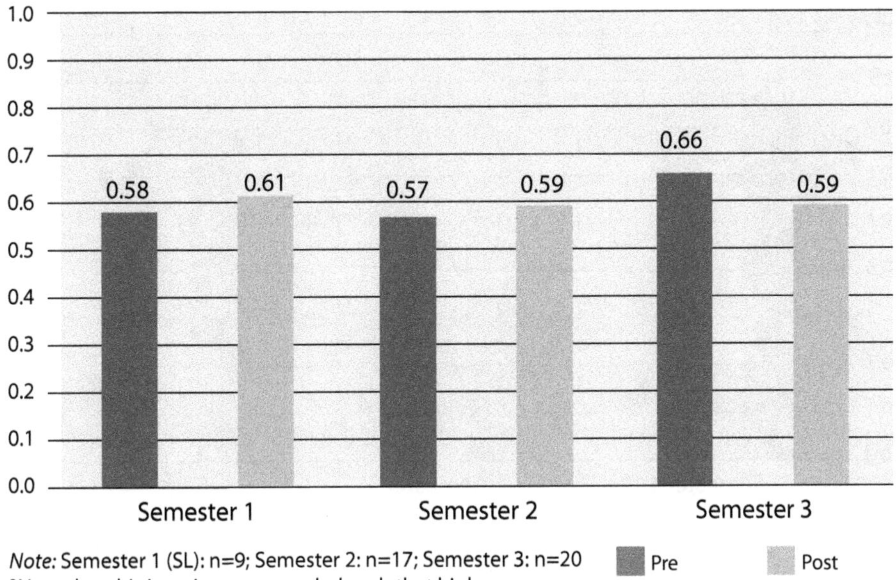

Note: Semester 1 (SL): n=9; Semester 2: n=17; Semester 3: n=20
[a]Note that this item is reverse-coded such that higher scores indicate higher political efficacy.

Figure 9-4: Pre- and Postsemester Mean Scores for Politics Is Complicated[a]

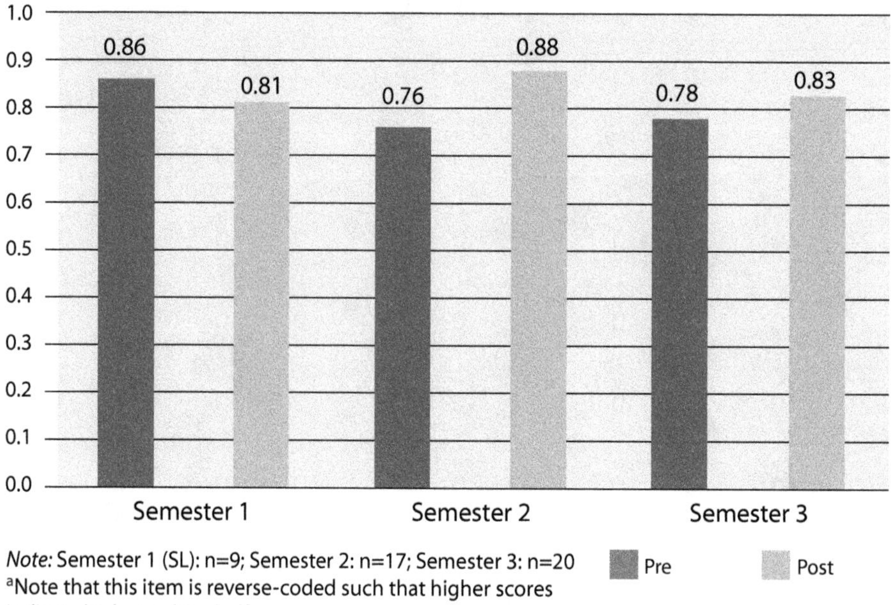

Note: Semester 1 (SL): n=9; Semester 2: n=17; Semester 3: n=20
[a]Note that this item is reverse-coded such that higher scores indicate higher political efficacy.

efficacy. In the service-learning semester, scores across most items of the political efficacy scale increased or stayed the same, indicating increased (or stable) political efficacy. The notable exceptions were "Politics is so complicated" and "I consider

Figure 9-5: Pre- and Postsemester Mean Scores for Good Job in Public Office

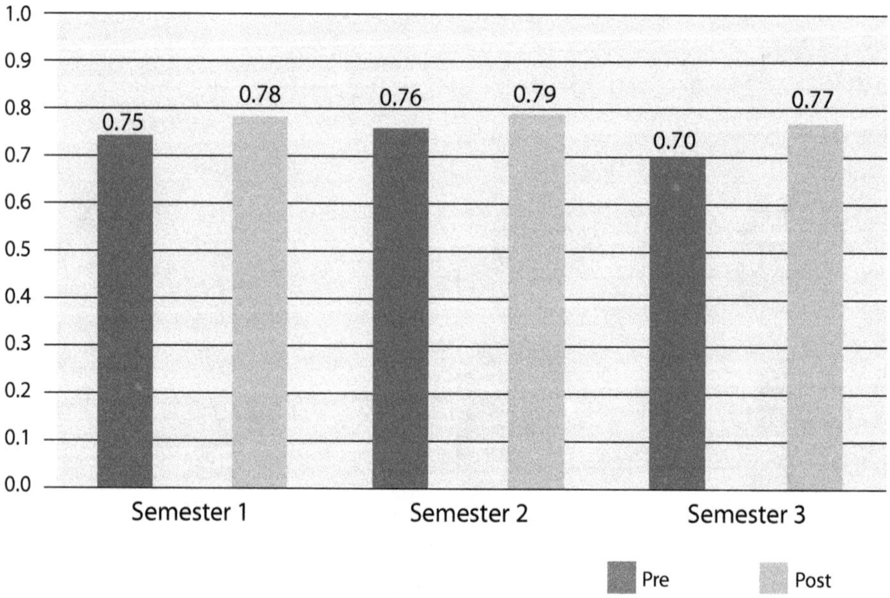

Note: Semester 1 (SL): n=9; Semester 2: n=17; Semester 3: n=20

Figure 9-6: Pre- and Postsemester Mean Scores for Well-Qualified to Participate

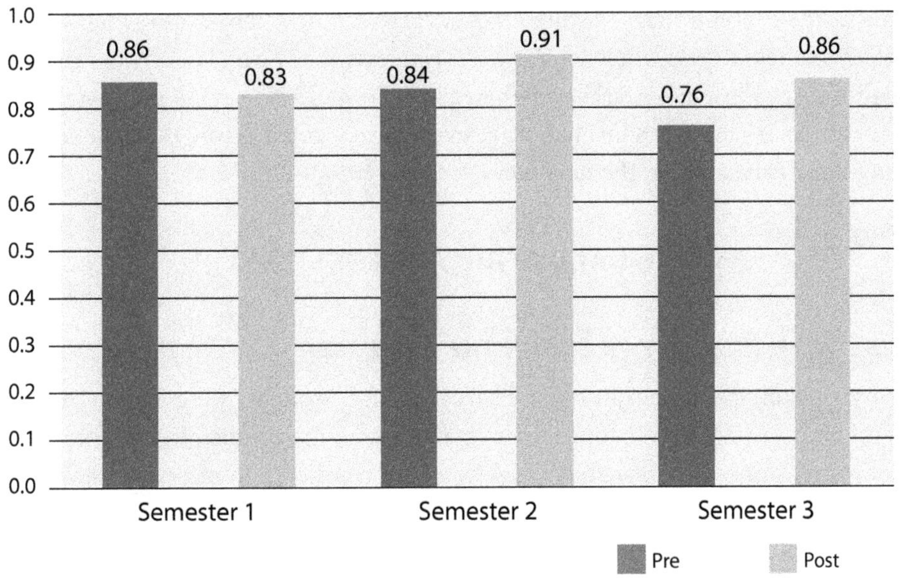

Note: Semester 1 (SL): n=9; Semester 2: n=17; Semester 3: n=20

myself to be well-qualified," in which scores decreased by a small amount.

Given the hands-on nature of service-learning, students came to appreciate just how complex navigation of the political system is and often expressed a degree

Figure 9-7: Pre- and Postsemester Mean Scores for Understand Issues

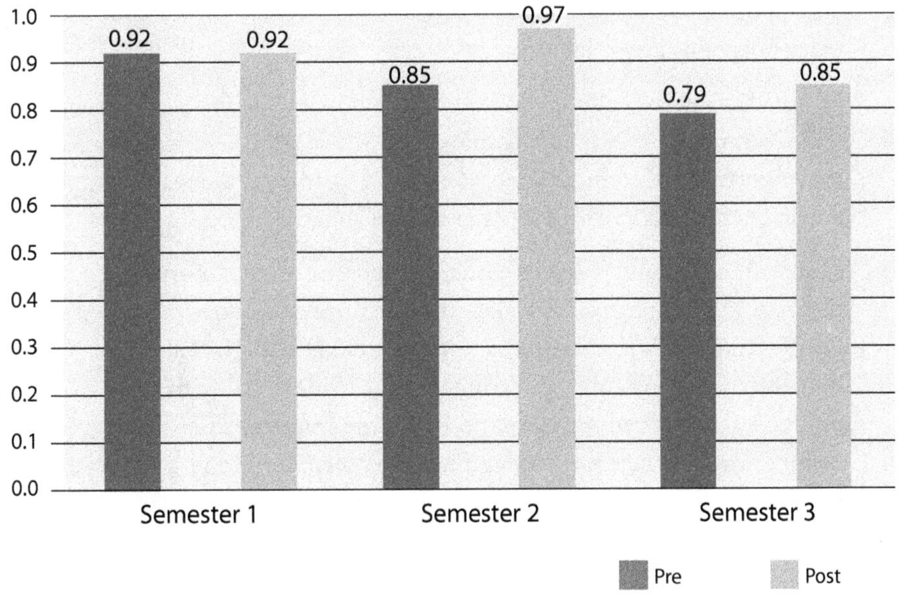

Note: Semester 1 (SL): n=9; Semester 2: n=17; Semester 3: n=20

of feeling overwhelmed by the process. Although a small sample size precludes the possibility of the promising results reaching standard levels of statistical significance, these preliminary results are instructive. First, across most items of the political efficacy scale, students in the SL semester made gains in efficacy from the beginning to the end of the semester. Second, the general trend of increasing political efficacy is reinforced by qualitative evidence collected throughout the semester and after, as reported in the next section.

Qualitative Assessment

Less than Halfway through the Semester

Approximately five weeks into the 15-week course, students were given the choice to fill out a questionnaire about their service-learning experiences for extra credit. They were instructed that their answers would neither help nor hurt their grade, but that extra credit would be given simply for answering the questions. Responses were fairly illuminating, despite the early time frame.[20]

First, students had generally positive reactions to the service-learning experience. There was early indication that learning had taken place. Some examples of responses follow.

In answer to the question, *"What, if anything, has the service-learning portion of the course taught you about public policy that you did not know before?"*

> Through the service-learning, it has become extremely clear how important funding is to all programs that CPF is running. Every individual program must keep records of the amount of people that they help in order to receive more funding and demonstrate how important these programs are to local people.

> So far I have been really surprised by the amount of action that a group that is not involved in politics can make. Specifically I have seen firsthand the importance of community organizing. Organizing to create change is a monumental ability that I had not known about.

> I learned that public policy is easier to become a part of than I did before. For example, our first day we were informed about the op-ed pieces. All it takes is initiative. I learned how the CPF was able to influence our community government to provide funding to build new offices. I also learned the extent to which organizations like these are communities in their own right. They may seem large and detached, but, if you really wanted to, you could get involved and you would be welcomed with open arms.

Certain students also seemed able to start making connections between theory and service-learning, whereas others had not yet reached that point. Response samples follow.

In answer to the question, *"What connections, if any, have you seen between our readings and experiences with CPF?"*

> It is required for a program to have a demand by people, otherwise the funders and leaders of the organization will shut programs down. This was seen in Munger with supply and demand, but applied in real life to a public policy organization it can determine something's existence. It also involves politics, and experts. Through my time I have seen the demand, and I have seen the politics in "helping their community" and the experts in how things should be accomplished.
>
> In class, we read about policies regarding charter schools. The day before this particular reading had been assigned, I was given the opportunity to facilitate a presentation at a nearby charter school. This charter school had a class committed to environmental needs. As a long-term assignment, they had been challenged to create their own garden on school grounds. I thought it was fascinating that the students really took initiative to make it a successful project. The reading by Christopher Lubienski explained how charter schools had become popular and what they were seeking to accomplish. It was a great experience to witness how these policies affect students attending charter schools.
>
> We discussed public policy having to do with taxes and some of the terms used in class I wasn't familiar with. Since taking my position with VITA [the civic organization], I've learned a lot about taxes. Therefore, when it comes to public policy having to do with taxes, or even just discussion about the topic, I feel I could be more actively engaged. Other connections I've made also are the extent to which bureaucracy is a reality, but it's something that is for the good and protection of the people. I've always known that, but now I'm able to understand what this means from the perspective of the government worker.

Earlier in this chapter I indicated that one of the major motivations behind the Carnegie Fellowship was to get students to become more politically involved. I had hoped that by designing a course that engaged students in policy-oriented service, students' awareness of the necessity of political involvement would naturally evolve, increasing the probability of political participation. Early indications of motivation for political participation were mostly positive, with a couple of mixed responses. Examples of student responses follow.

In answer, *"Does working with CPF make you feel more or less likely to get involved in politics (e.g., volunteering), or has it had no effect?"* and *"Please explain your answer."*

> More likely. Currently, we are planning a Youth Conference with the goal of enabling students to see the alternative to jail, which is school. I am slowly trying to convince the student leaders involved that it would be a good idea to invite local political leaders. Unfortunately, many seem to be discouraged at the idea of politicians involved in their

> work. I try to explain that if politicians know the problems that their young constituents face, solutions can be created. I hope to further my involvement with politics.
>
> Has had no effect. Working in the community has shown me some of the more negative aspects of politics. In particular, the lack of interest shown in south Stockton is disheartening. Though working with CPF has thus far had no effect in making me feel more or less likely to get involved in politics, it has made me more skeptical of political players.
>
> Has had no effect. Politics has always been an ambition of mine. This program gave me the opportunity to experience what I've always known that I wanted to experience. I just didn't expect the experience to come as soon. This project is actually a pleasant surprise. I had no idea I was going to be a part until after the semester began.
>
> I am in between (a) and (b). I usually work in the political field, and I am pretty politically involved, but I do think I will look more deeply into public policy areas after this experience. It is nice to feel like you have made a positive change in peoples' lives and it is worth the extra effort to make sure a positive change is there for anyone who needs it.
>
> More likely. As the trend seems to be for students seeking to go to law school, I have gained an appreciation for those working in the public sector (such as the site directors that I have had the pleasure to meet). This is definitely something I would definitely like to pursue later on [in] life once I am able to make ends meet in my own life. There are a lot of issues that need to be brought to the public eye that just need that one person to print article or run news report on.

End-of-Semester Comments

At the conclusion of the SL semester, students discussed the impact of the course in changing their political attitudes.

In answer to the question, "*When you look at how you answered this survey today compared to the first day of class, do you attribute any changes in your responses to anything that happened in class this semester?*"

> I changed my response to question F [People like me don't have any say about what the government does.] to disagree strongly with the statement based solely on what I have learned in this class.
>
> The overall idea that there are countless cases of unreported spending and actions that fly below the radar opened my eyes.
> I have learned not to simply take the information given but rather question it if it may be beneficial.

> I feel now that I am better equipped to have a political career. I understand that politicians do care about people's opinions.

In a separate survey administered only at the end of the semester, students were asked to answer a variety of questions pertaining strictly to the service-learning portion of the course and the community partner. Student responses provided strong evidence indicating that not only had students learned first-hand about the scarcity of resources against the backdrop of great need in the nonprofit sector, but also that they had learned personal lessons in the face of such challenges.

In response to the question, "*What were the three biggest lessons/skills/experiences you took from your experience at CPF?*"

> 1) The ability to be patient. I'm horrible at this. 2) To be flexible—I did something different every day. 3) To realize that there are a lot of services out there, but no one knows about them.
>
> Time management/balancing work/school/interning. Applying classroom lessons to CPF training/connections. Patience. ☺
>
> Leadership is good but sometimes overbearing; there are a lot of people that are involved in the decision making command part of CPF.... There are people that REALLY need help. What I mean is that before this I heard about the literacy rate in Stockton but I had never actually met someone who couldn't read, this really made the experience fulfilling because there are people who need our help that we may ignore (not on purpose) because we don't see them. Ideas are key to involvement. Because I am helping setting up an event I have learned that we always need ideas.
>
> It's difficult to get things done. People really want to make things better for others. Tasks can be complicated and burdened by paperwork ... [it] takes a lot of self-initiative and flexibility.
>
> Helping others help themselves is much more rewarding than just helping others. The world is not an equal or fair place, but we as indiv. [sic] can choose to act as though it is. I can make a difference in the community.
>
> Community centers ... are pretty disorganized, though they do provide some good to the community. Initiative takes a LOT of work to start and continue. Community organizing is important and can lead to real progress.

In general, students expressed much initial frustration in getting acclimated to their volunteer work and figuring out the dimensions of their roles. However, a majority reported that they were able to turn their frustrations into valuable learning moments that helped them achieve greater amounts of patience, flexibility, and appreciation for the work of community nonprofits.

Three Years Post-Semester

To date, very few studies have been able to track the longevity of the effects of a service-learning course. In January 2011, I sent electronic follow-up surveys to students from the 2008 semester through email and Facebook. After some investigation, I was able to find contact information for 12 of the 14 students who had been enrolled. I was fortunate enough to receive completed surveys from five of the 12 students at the time of this writing. Admittedly, while I am not able to draw any generalizable conclusions from this sample, insights proved informative and suggest that the attitudes developed during the service-learning course seem to be enduring.

In answer to the question, *"Did the service-learning course have an impact on the way in which you viewed the political system? If so, how?"*

> The service-learning course gave me a better understanding of bureaucracy in the political system. I never realized the amount of government involvement in everyday life, and the services that are made available through the government. It was a very eye-opening experience.

> I don't think it changed the way I view the political system. Our system is flawed and we are working to improve it.

> The service-learning course had a great impact on the way in which I view the political system. Interning for the nonprofit organization made me realize that "politics" are important; who you know and who you build relationships with, is important to push your agenda through.

In answer to the question, *"Did the service-learning course have an impact on the way in which you viewed your involvement and stake in the political system? If so, how?"*

> I believe it did. It made me realize that every little bit that you do counts. I participated in Youth Conferences, from an intern point of view; it seemed almost not feasible that a small organization in Stockton could mobilize a whole community. I think that's the same way it works in real life. It takes only an idea to initiate change and people are capable of effecting change.

> The service-learning course did have an impact on how I view political and civil involvement, as I find it important for citizens. My lack of current involvement has less to do with the impact the course, or Pacific, made on me, and more to do with the fact that
> I am currently in a "transitional" phase, and unsure about career and personal moves I am to make, to make me a successful (self-sufficient) adult.

> Yes. I learned of the difference one person can make in a public service organization on many peoples' lives.

> I don't think my views have changed. The system should change and we need to work for it.

> The service-learning course showed me how easy it is to become civically engaged in my community. [It] also showed me just how much of a need there is for members of our society to become educated about the issues that surround us, both on a global and city level.

CONCLUSION

I attempted to design a course to accomplish several goals through the addition of a very intensive service-learning portion that would provide extensive exposure to the connections between nonprofit and political realms and between theory and practice in politics. First, by offering a course that organically created the conditions for political involvement through a link to service, I hoped to augment students' sense of political efficacy. Second, the course sought to teach students not only the basics of policy making, but also provide a deeper knowledge and appreciation for the complexity of the policy process. Based on analysis of the data I collected across semesters at various time points, I have evidence that I was relatively successful on both fronts.

Several students expressed some early motivation to get politically involved; others, however, expressed a distressing cynicism about the political field that was seemingly enhanced by their experiences in the field. Postsemester data in the SL course showed that most indicators of students' political efficacy increased; nevertheless, students were more likely to find politics/government complicated to understand by the conclusion of the semester. At first blush, this result struck me as problematic—I had hoped that students would feel like they understood the political system better at the conclusion of their service. However, I have come to interpret this result as a possible success—students came away with a more nuanced, less black-or-white view of the political system. This view is decidedly more complicated, but it also is a more accurate portrayal of political reality. Furthermore, taking this result with SL postsemester increases in the conviction that one can have a say in politics (a result that showed a marked decrease over the span of non-SL semesters), I propose that students achieved a sense that they could make a difference in the political world. This conviction was still apparent in all but one of the three-year postsurvey responses I received, particularly with regard to how students viewed the impact of the SL on their attitudes toward involvement. Four students expressed a positive attitude toward service, though interestingly, the fifth (who claimed that the SL had no impact) is currently working as an outreach leader for a nationally prominent nonprofit organization.

Pertaining to the second goal of students' increased content knowledge, two facets of knowledge gain are apparent. Students in the SL semester demonstrated an ability to connect theoretical content with practical knowledge. This ability was evidenced in a variety of responses to prompts they were given throughout the semester. Furthermore, as previously described, I contend that students' increased characterization of the complexity of politics reflects a more nuanced view of the political system.

Despite the significant time commitment that teaching a service-learning course poses, I hope to teach an SL version of the course again. My own teaching practice benefitted in a number of ways. For example, I was able to better identify areas of content that were more difficult for students to understand and use their service as an example for helping to explain these areas. Second, I learned how building flexibility into the syllabus could provide for powerful teaching moments. Specifically, reflective class sessions—which students likely viewed as "fluff" at first blush—tended to be some of the most profound moments of student insight in class. For these reasons, I deem the service-learning course to have been a success.

Civic Engagement in the Community: Undergraduate Clinical Legal Education

10

By Mahalley D. Allen, Sally A. Parker, and Teodora C. DeLorenzo

The Community Legal Information Center (CLIC) of California State University, Chico, provides a unique civic engagement program designed to address the legal service needs of Northern California. Founded in 1969, CLIC is now a 12-program, on-campus law clinic staffed by up to 125 undergraduate students each semester and is perhaps the most extensive undergraduate legal clinic in the country. Although free legal clinics are not unusual at law schools, they are very rare at the undergraduate level. In this chapter, we discuss how CLIC successfully provides students with the opportunity to serve the legal needs of their community, while also applying what they have learned through traditional classroom learning. We explore how CLIC serves as a framework upon which other academic programs can model their own civic engagement programs, such that they integrate traditional academic exercises with service-learning.[1]

Although clinical legal education is common at America's law schools, it is very rare at the undergraduate level.[2] At the law school level, clinical education integrates civic engagement with traditional academic teaching. Law school clinics have been praised for providing students with first-hand knowledge about how the legal system works. Additionally, clinical programs at law schools provide free or low-cost legal services to underrepresented and underserved populations.[3] The Community Legal Information Center (CLIC), a program of the Department of Political Science at California State University, Chico (CSU, Chico), provides these same benefits at the undergraduate level. CLIC offers a unique civic engagement program for undergraduate students and is designed to serve the legal service needs of Northern California. Originally founded in 1969, CLIC is now a 12-program, on-campus law clinic staffed by 100 to 125 undergraduate students each semester. It is the most extensive undergraduate program of its kind in California, likely in the entire country, and has received national recognition based on the service that CLIC provides to the Northern California community.[4]

In this chapter, we discuss how CLIC has become a successful example of undergraduate clinical legal education and offer insights into how colleges and universities can provide undergraduate civic engagement opportunities by combining community service with traditional academic teaching. In the first section, we discuss the benefits to both students and the community that come from running an educational legal clinic. Although the operation of a legal clinic like CLIC is admittedly more intensive than most traditional undergraduate political science courses, the benefits to students and the community are immeasurable. In the second section, we discuss how to organize and structure an undergraduate legal clinic. Ultimately, our chapter serves as a guide for other colleges and universities interested in incorporating clinical legal education into their undergraduate political science programs and advances our understanding of effective civic engagement pedagogy.

Benefits to Students and Community

Law clinics such as CLIC provide significant benefits to both the participating students and the community.[5] Past research has shown that good practice in undergraduate education incorporates active learning, whereby students physically participate in educational projects rather than passively reading or listening to lectures.[6] CLIC internships provide undergraduate students with the chance to start actively learning the profession of paralegal or attorney.[7] The legal clinic helps students to "see firsthand how the legal system works, and gain the tools, experience and insight to discover in themselves how to advocate for their clients."[8]

As noted, another incentive for student participation is the opportunity to gain work experience as a paralegal, a growing field. According to the US Department of Labor, Bureau of Labor Statistics, employment for paralegals is expected to rise much faster than average for all occupations through 2018.[9] In particular, paralegal employment opportunities are expected to rapidly grow as "an expanding population increasingly requires legal services, especially in areas such as intellectual property, health care, international law, elder issues, criminal law, and environmental law."[10] Further, the US Department of Labor projects that government agencies as well as the private sector will continue to hire increasing numbers of paralegals.[11] Given demographic and economic changes, CLIC positions are particularly valuable to undergraduate students because those who have been formally educated in the legal field have the best employment opportunities.[12]

By combining community service with traditional academic teaching, CLIC gives students the chance to apply what they have learned in the classroom to real-world situations. Political science faculty who teach in CLIC relate many valuable skills and techniques that students have learned in the classroom to the applied activities in the service-learning positions. For example, in the Political Science Department's Legal Research and Writing course, students learn legal research techniques, legal analysis and writing, issue spotting, and use of electronic legal databases such as Lexis-Nexis and Westlaw. Students learn direct and cross-examination techniques in the department's moot court course, as well as how to prepare witnesses and perform opening and closing arguments. These skills are then used by CLIC students when they represent clients in administrative hearings. In the department's constitutional law courses, students learn how to read and analyze court cases and are taught to understand how facts relate to the US Constitution and various statutes. CLIC students use these skills when researching clients' legal questions.

In addition to supplying the occasion for students to apply what they have learned in the classroom to experiences in the field, clinical legal education can often supply "many sobering lessons" about careers in the law and about the situations of actual people in real need of legal assistance.[13] Because CLIC students work directly with clients from the community, they learn how to maintain professional client-counsel relationships.[14] CLIC experiences often introduce students to the many different types of clients they may someday face in their future law or paralegal careers. This active-learning opportunity allows the students to work with a diverse group of people, including individuals whom they might not otherwise encounter during their college experience.

CLIC service-learning experiences also can satisfy students' academic requirements for graduation. Within the Political Science Department, there are four undergraduate majors as well as a paralegal certificate program, each of which has its own learning opportunities and requirements.[15] Students completing a degree within the department's political science major with an option of a concentration in legal studies or completing the paralegal certificate are required to gain practical experience through internships by completing two three-unit law-related internships. The majority of these students complete their internship requirements by working at CLIC, where students can intern in one of the 12 programs (see Table 10-1 for descriptions of each of CLIC's programs). Students completing degrees in several of the other majors within the department also often complete their internship requirements through CLIC. Because the department's paralegal certificate program meets the educational criteria set forth by state law for working as a paralegal within California, students wanting to enter careers as paralegals in the state have another incentive to complete their internship requirements through service-learning at CLIC.[16]

In addition to students majoring in political science, students from other majors, such as journalism, English, criminal justice, philosophy, multicultural and gender studies, business, and economics, also work at CLIC each semester. Because CLIC provides a glimpse of what it is like to work in the legal field, many students interested in eventually applying to law school often serve in one of CLIC's programs.

CLIC positions frequently lead to close professional relationships between the students and their supervising faculty members, which is a significant advantage for those beginning to think about their future careers as legal assistants, paralegals, or attorneys. As members of the state bar and active alumni of their own law schools, CLIC faculty can often be instrumental in assisting students with law school applications or job searches as legal assistants or paralegals. Faculty work closely with students during their CLIC positions, so they are able to assist students

Table 10-1: Community Legal Information Center Programs

Program Titles	Program Descriptions
Consumer Protection Agency	Aid consumers with complaints against businesses and legal issues dealing with fraud, identity theft, credit debt, and bankruptcy.
County Jail Law Project	Assist inmates at the county jail with criminal law issues.
Disabled and the Law	Advocate for disabled individuals in disability determination and other types of Social Security cases.
Environmental Advocates	Provide information on issues regarding city planning, endangered species protection, and sustainable management practices.
Family Law Project	Help clients with issues such as marriage dissolutions, child custody, and child support.
Housing Law Program	Furnish information on such issues as the return of rental security deposits, lease terminations and evictions, and housing repairs and maintenance.
Misdemeanors, Tickets, and Traffic	Assist clients with issues dealing with parking and speeding tickets, driving under the influence offenses, and noise violations.
Penal Law Project	Help incarcerated individuals with issues ranging from correctional injustices and probation and parole to rehabilitation and appeals.
Public Benefits Advocacy Program	Aid clients eligible for public assistance programs.
Student Legal Services/Juvenile Rights	Advocate for students' rights within the university grievance and disciplinary process; assist minors with such issues as guardianships and emancipation.
Women's Law Project	Provide support to individuals who are victims of domestic and workplace violence or harassment.
Workers' Rights Program	Offer legal information on issues surrounding worker discharge, wage and hour disputes, working conditions, and employment discrimination.

with their law school applications by writing detailed letters of recommendation and perhaps providing valuable introductions to law school faculty, admissions representatives, and deans.

Not only does CLIC provide significant educational benefits and opportunities for active learning to undergraduate students, it also provides significant benefits to the Northern California community and has done so since 1969, when the clinic first opened. CLIC's service to indigent and underserved populations is especially important given the "sharp disparity in our society between those who can afford legal services and those who can't."[17] As legal service organizations that aid indigent and low-income clients have faced budget cuts and been forced to scale back their operations, educational legal clinics such as CLIC have become even more important.[18] In California alone, "two-thirds of the legal needs of the poverty community go unmet."[19] Low-income Californians often do not have the financial resources to secure legal assistance for common legal situations involving such problems as "divorce, child support, child custody, domestic violence, loss of housing and employment, education and discrimination."[20] In Northern California, CLIC is able to assist clients with all of these legal matters, as well as others. Today, CLIC primarily serves clients from rural Butte and Glenn Counties. Through this educational partnership, CLIC students served 11,342 clients and worked a total of 8,213 hours during the 2009–2010 academic year.[21] Of the 193 clients who completed a questionnaire during this period, 47% reported an average yearly household income of less than $10,000 and 20% reported that they were disabled. Thus CLIC students are generally assisting a typically underserved socioeconomic part of the community.[22]

Organizing and Structuring an Undergraduate Legal Clinic

At CSU, Chico, four political science faculty, who are also licensed members of the California Bar, oversee CLIC students as a part of their regular teaching load. The average student to faculty ratio within CLIC is 27:1, depending on how many students are admitted into each of program. Just as with any traditional academic course, the faculty prepare detailed syllabi for CLIC programs so that students are able to keep up with required readings, quizzes, and written assignments. Faculty often use traditional evaluative methods, such as a grading rubric, to assess student interns and directors in CLIC. The goal is for the students to have a traditional classroom experience while also participating in service-learning–based civic engagement.

Student Training and Legal Ethics Education

The preparation and training for each CLIC program starts with a mandatory Mass Intern Meeting, which takes place at the beginning of every semester. During this training session, faculty instruct CLIC's students regarding legal professional responsibility requirements, such as client confidentiality issues and avoiding client conflicts of interest. Detailed intern manuals are distributed to students during this initial training meeting and are the students' resource guide on legal responsibility and professionalism as well as the limitations of what they are allowed to do in their positions. For example, the manual clearly outlines that CLIC interns are not allowed to provide legal advice, which is the role of licensed attorneys and constitutes the practice of law, but are instead limited to providing their clients with the most current legal information. After the semester's Mass Intern Meeting, each student is required to sign a contract agreeing to abide by the contents of the intern manual before performing CLIC work.

Each of CLIC's 12 programs has an academic syllabus for interns to follow throughout the semester. This syllabus includes a weekly topic of study in a relevant area of law and lessons regarding legal ethics. Students work a total of 60–120 hours per semester, depending on the number of units they are completing; for example, if a student is earning three units, the total required 120 units are divided into the

17-week semester so that the student works at the clinic seven to eight hours each week. After the initial Mass Intern Meeting, most of CLIC's student training is completed at each individual program's weekly one-hour meetings that follow the topics of the program syllabus. During these program meetings, interns receive direct feedback from faculty regarding specific cases, discuss assigned weekly readings or topics of study, and are provided additional guidance regarding legal ethics. It is also during these weekly program meetings that CLIC's faculty train the interns in that program's area of law. In addition to instruction from faculty, student directors instruct interns during these meetings on office policies, including attendance requirements, office dress codes, and the professionalism required in CLIC offices. Along with these training sessions, interns are also taught through field trips, guest speakers, and program trainings by attorney specialists, commissioners, and judges in a specific field of law. Interns working in one of CLIC's advocacy programs are given additional intensive training and direction by their instructors to prepare them to represent clients at administrative hearings.

With the purpose of encouraging CLIC interns to gain confidence in their paralegal abilities, as well as protecting CLIC clients, many protections are put into place so that students know what to expect and how to deal with a number of variable client situations. For example, written statements are placed near each CLIC telephone so that students can use them as prompts if they feel unsure about how to properly answer the phone in a professional manner. These telephone prompts, along with specific office procedures, letter templates, email confidentiality statements, and student director authorization requirements before client contact is made, help guide students in the educational environment of CLIC yet also protect clients and the larger public from any miscommunication or incorrect legal information.

Lastly, interns are trained in legal research and writing each semester by the faculty member primarily responsible for teaching the university's Legal Research and Writing course. All students have access to the two primary legal research databases, Lexis-Nexis and Westlaw, both of which are available in academic versions through the campus library, along with other legal reference books and practice guides that also help them complete their tasks.

Students often come to CLIC as juniors or seniors.[23] Thus, they frequently have already completed some courses in the political science major, which provides them with a good background in the process of legal research and analysis. Many times they have also taken classes that focus on the substantive law of their programs, such as criminal law. The legal studies courses in the Political Science Department provide students with a theoretical framework for many of the tasks and activities they will undertake as paralegal interns at CLIC.

To focus on teamwork and leadership skills, all student program directors, administrative directors, and faculty members meet once a week to discuss issues the students are dealing with in their individual programs. At these weekly director meetings, students are encouraged to help each other with problem-solving skills and ideas for program projects and events.

Student Program and Administrative Directors

Within CLIC, students serve as paralegal interns, program directors, and administrative directors.[24] Each of CLIC's 12 legal programs is directed by one or two student program directors. Working between eight and 16 hours in the clinic each week throughout the semester, program directors are responsible for helping to recruit, train, and supervise each program's student interns. They are also responsible for assisting faculty in overseeing the daily operations of the programs by maintaining and reporting client and case statistics and meeting weekly with student interns. Although political science faculty have the final authority and responsibility for supervising CLIC students and programs and assigning student grades, the program directors are given the day-to-day task of ensuring that the programs run smoothly.

Program directors not only learn about the substantive and procedural law of their individual programs, they also have the unique experience of learning how to manage people. CLIC's faculty allow the program directors the latitude to set some of the semester's goals, which are assessed at the end of the semester in determining the program director's grade. Therefore, the program directors have a vested interest in leaving their mark on the program so that future program directors can build upon their work.

Once CLIC students have spent time working as paralegal interns and then program directors, they may apply to work as one of two administrative directors, the highest and most prestigious CLIC student positions. The student administrative directors are responsible for overseeing the daily operations of the entire legal clinic. They also assist the faculty in managing CLIC's annual budget, applying for various grants, handling a range of personnel issues, and gathering and reporting statistics for the clinic's annual client contacts and internship hours. Because of the hours that CLIC's program and administrative directors work through the year, they can receive up to 16 graded academic units over the course of one calendar year.

Student Paralegal Interns

Each semester between 100 and 125 students earn academic credit at CLIC by working as paralegal interns, and these students comprise the largest share of CLIC's student staff. CLIC student interns receive from one to three upper-division political science units graded on a credit/no credit basis each semester. Over the course of a 17-week semester, students must complete 60 hours for a one-unit internship, 90 hours for a two-unit internship, and 120 hours for a three-unit internship. The amount of hours that students work each week at CLIC varies with the number of units they are earning over the course of the semester.

Most of the students' weekly internship hours are spent working on client issues in the CLIC offices. Interns often work one-on-one with clients and assist them with legal paperwork and research on particular issues of the law. The specific job duties of CLIC interns depend upon the individual program in which the interns work. For example, interns working in the Family Law program assist clients in navigating their family law cases (e.g., divorce, paternity, and child custody cases) through the court system by providing information about the filing of legal paperwork. Interns working in the Disabled and the Law program frequently assist clients in filing appeal paperwork related to claims for Social Security disability benefits and then represent those clients in related administrative hearings, during which they are often responsible for writing hearing memorandums and directing the oral examination of witnesses.

Although most of the CLIC students' internship hours are spent working on client issues, students also spend time in the community performing outreach by informing the local population of CLIC services, conducting fund-raising, and advocating for clients in administrative hearings. In addition to the requirement that students spend a minimum number of hours working in the CLIC offices and the community, CLIC students must also meet various other requirements. For example, students may be required to complete weekly readings relevant to the area of the law they are working in and complete semester projects based on their course readings and CLIC experiences, such as research papers or community presentations about various legal issues.

Assessing Clinical Internships: Student Responses, Community Reaction, and Future Research

Research on the value of civic engagement exercises and active learning routinely points out the benefits to students in terms of acquiring skills and knowledge through nontraditional methods of instruction.[25] To evaluate whether CLIC's nontraditional methods of instruction enhance students' academic skills, such as their research aptitude and writing abilities, the chapter authors assessed students across three semesters by asking them to respond to a questionnaire concerning their experiences in CLIC. In our Intern Learning Outcomes questionnaire, students were asked a variety of questions related to the skills they used during their CLIC internships and how their CLIC experiences enhanced their classroom learning. Although our assessment methods are limited because we do not have control groups like other research with similar evaluation methods, our self-assessment data nonetheless are relevant to basic questions about the effects of clinical legal education experiences on student learning.[26]

The most significant question in terms of the assessment is the effect of the students' clinical experiences on their classroom learning. Students overwhelmingly reported that their clinical internships positively enhanced their classroom experience. As reported in Table 10-2, of the 88 respondents in spring 2010, 91% reported that they agreed that their CLIC experiences strongly or moderately enhanced their classroom learning. Although not quite as high as the data from spring 2010, students in spring 2009 (84%) and fall 2008 (77%) also reported that their CLIC experiences enhanced their classroom learning.

In addition to assessing whether their CLIC experiences improved the overall quality of their classroom learning, we also wanted to evaluate whether the

Table 10-2: Impact of Clinical Internships on Classroom Learning

	Percentage of Students Indicating in Spring 2010	Percentage of Students Indicating in Spring 2009	Percentage of Students Indicating in Fall 2008
Strongly Agree	60%	52%	22%
Moderately Agree	31%	32%	55%
Neither Agree nor Disagree	9%	10%	15%
Moderately Disagree	0%	4%	1%
Strongly Disagree	0%	3%	6%
N	88	79	67

Note: The question read: "Please indicate your level of agreement with the following statement: My internship experience enhanced classroom learning." Percentages may vary because of rounding.

students' internships taught them specific skills and knowledge. In the questionnaire, students were asked to evaluate whether their internships taught them how to recognize and appropriately handle potential ethical conflicts, an important skill for interns working in a legal clinic and planning careers in the legal profession. In terms of learning about potential ethical conflicts and how to handle them, students once again reported positive experiences in their internships (see Table 10-3). In both spring 2010 and spring 2009, 75% of students strongly or moderately agreed that their CLIC internships helped them learn about potential ethical conflicts in the legal field and gain skills about how to handle those conflicts. In fall 2008, 71% of respondents reported the same.

Table 10-3: Impact of Clinical Internships on Ethical Conflict Knowledge and Skills

	Percentage of Students Indicating in Spring 2010	Percentage of Students Indicating in Spring 2009	Percentage of Students Indicating in Fall 2008
Strongly Agree	47%	48%	34%
Moderately Agree	28%	27%	37%
Neither Agree nor Disagree	5%	9%	16%
Moderately Disagree	0%	1%	1%
Strongly Disagree	0%	1%	3%
Not applicable	20%	14%	7%
N	88	79	67

Note: The question read: "Please indicate your level of agreement with the following statement: My internship helped me learn how to recognize potential ethical conflicts and take appropriate measures to handle them." Percentages may vary because of rounding.

Table 10-4: Impact of Clinical Internships on Client Interviewing Skills

	Percentage of Students Indicating Skill in Spring 2010 (N)	Percentage of Students Indicating Skill in Spring 2009 (N)	Percentage of Students Indicating Skill in Fall 2008 (N)
Assessing legal questions raised in interviews	88% (77)	94% (69)	96% (54)
Researching answers to client questions	92% (73)	96% (69)	94% (53)
Reporting results of research and analysis to client	92% (72)	95% (65)	94% (54)

Note: The question read: "Over the course of your internship, what did you learn about interviewing a client in terms of... assessing the legal questions raised by the facts communicated in the interview, researching answers to client questions, reporting results of research and analysis to client."

To further access which legal skills students acquired during their CLIC internships, students were asked to expand upon specific client interview skills they learned during their clinical experiences, another significant responsibility for students serving in a legal clinic. Students were presented with three possible skill sets related to client interviewing: assessing the legal questions raised in client interviews, researching answers to client questions, and reporting the results of their research and analysis to clients. Table 10-4 shows the percentage of students reporting that they learned each of the three skills sets related to client interviewing. Over the course of the three semesters assessed, 88% to 96% of students reported learning each of the presented client interviewing skills.

Finally, in an effort to understand which general legal skills students learned during their CLIC experiences, students were asked to evaluate the broad categories of legal skills they used in their internships. As shown in Table 10-5, students reported that their CLIC internships gave them the opportunity to employ several legal skills. Ninety-four percent or more of students in all three semesters assessed indicated that they employed legal research skills during their service-learning. Although only 39% to 44% of students reported that they were given the opportunity to practice their legal writing skills, 87% to 90% of students indicated that their internships gave them the occasion to learn how to identify legal issues through client interviews. These data, along with the data presented in Table 10-4, suggest that students are able to practice and learn several sets of skills from their experiences in legal clinic service-learning internships.

For instructors who incorporate active learning in their courses, our data provide some initial observations about the effect that legal clinic service-learning internships can have on student learning and skill acquisition. The assessment results clearly illustrate that clinical internships successfully provide students with the opportunity to serve the legal needs of their community while also giving students the chance to apply what they have learned through traditional classroom learning. For example, students who have taken the Legal Research and Writing course learn to identify the issues presented by fact patterns, what law governs those issues, and

Table 10-5: Impact of Clinical Internships on Students' Legal Skills

Legal Skill	Percentage of Students Indicating Use in Spring 2010	Percentage of Students Indicating Use in Spring 2009	Percentage of Students Indicating Use in Fall 2008
Legal Research	94%	95%	96%
Legal Analysis	72%	67%	54%
Identifying Client Issues	97%	89%	86%
Legal Writing	44%	41%	39%
Client Interviews	87%	90%	90%
Other	16%	9%	14%
N	87	81	71

Note: The question read: "Which of the following skills did you make use of in your internship: legal research, legal analysis, identifying clients' issues, legal drafting or writing, fact gathering/client interviews, other?"

how the law applies to the facts of cases, knowledge which students in CLIC apply in assisting their clients. Students interning at the Community Legal Information Center consistently report that their clinical internships positively enhance their classroom experiences. Students also report that their CLIC internships taught them how to use various specific legal skills appropriate to their positions as paralegal interns.

In addition to assessing student experiences in CLIC, we were also interested in client feedback about the quality and usefulness of the services the students provide. During the 2009–2010 academic year, CLIC clients were asked to respond to a questionnaire concerning their experiences at CLIC. Table 10-6 shows that 76% to 86% of client respondents reported that CLIC provided excellent services, with another 14% to 22% reporting that they found CLIC services to be good. This data

Table 10-6: Community Evaluation of CLIC Services

	Percentage of Respondents Indicating in Spring 2010	Percentage of Respondents Indicating in Fall 2009
Excellent	86%	76%
Good	14%	22%
Average	0%	2%
Below Average	0%	0%
Poor	0%	0%
N	90	103

Note: The question read: "Overall, how would you rate the services provided to you by CLIC?"

indicate that not only are students receiving very positive experiences at CLIC, but so are the clients.

Although the initial findings from the assessment methods are overwhelmingly positive, more sophisticated methods are appropriate for future research. For example, more comparative analysis is needed of how much legal knowledge students gain in clinical experiences compared to students in traditional classroom environments. Surveys of control groups of students not participating in clinical internships would help to provide these data. More objective measures of student skill acquisition also would be beneficial to future research on clinical learning environments. Because the standard student course evaluations used at CSU, Chico do not ask specific questions about student learning in courses with clinical settings as compared to courses with no clinical components, it has not been possible to use these course evaluations to assess students' service-learning experiences, as other scholars have.[27]

Adapting CLIC's Model to Other Institutions

CLIC's model of an undergraduate legal clinic that offers important service-learning experiences to students while also providing critical legal information to the underserved legal needs of the community can be adapted to other educational institutions in several different ways.

Partnering with Legal Services or Legal Aid Offices

Many communities already have existing legal services programs that are often funded through the federal Legal Services Corporation. Because most of these agencies are underfunded or have limitations on the kinds of services they can offer, student interns offer an option for filling in some of these service gaps. Within each agency's federal funding restrictions, undergraduate students can be housed and cosupervised by the agency's staff attorneys and by faculty from the local university. One of CLIC's programs, the Public Benefits Advocacy program, is housed in a local Legal Services office and provides assistance to that agency by representing clients in administrative hearings and negotiating with social service agencies on behalf of clients. This program's faculty member works closely with the attorneys and paralegal staff at the Legal Services office to supervise and train interns. This partnering provides additional paraprofessional staff for the legal services office and is an existing office within which students can be placed. This partnering also cuts some of the overhead costs that exist when a college or university creates a separate legal clinic.

Creating a Separate Clinic

A stand-alone undergraduate law clinic offers several advantages, such as independence and control over service areas, clients, staff, and practices. A stand-alone clinic, however, also offers several challenges. Institutional acceptance is key to the success of a program such as CLIC. To be an accepted part of a college or university's civic engagement and internship offerings, this kind of program should be tied to academic coursework. Institutionally, the faculty's department, division, or unit must accept that this work will be valued and counted as part of a student's instruction, professional growth, or service duties for this type of internship supervision to be worth their substantial commitment to developing and sustaining the program. At CSU, Chico, CLIC is a mere 10-minute walk from campus and thus offers a convenient location for students majoring in political science as well as many other disciplines on campus to undertake their service-learning internships under the supervision of university faculty.

How a Program such as CLIC Might Be Adapted to a Small Liberal Arts College

A number of activities are needed to create a program such as CLIC, but this chapter offers a guide to begin implementation. Faculty support is critical, so a key faculty member or administrator must spearhead the effort, along with a body of dedicated students willing to commit at least one or two semesters to start the program. Faculty in political science or any discipline in which there are law-related courses usually have an interest in this area and can be approached to help. These faculty will have to commit to supervising students and assigning grades either as part of their teaching load or as service. Administrators working in student services have contact with students and can often recognize in what areas students have legal needs. Developing a survey to determine what legal assistance students need, what legal assistance community members most need, and the legal areas students are most interested in pursuing would identify what subjects are most relevant to the legal clinic and potential student workers.

Identifying funding sources for operating expenses, such as facilities and overhead, will allow the program to open its doors and continue to operate. Part of this cost is faculty time, so administration will need to agree to allow faculty to use their supervision as part of their course load. Developing relationships with campus student government leaders who might be potential sources of funding and programmatic support also could be a solution to finding operating funds. Establishing a legal clinic that offers a single subject, such as landlord/tenant law or student legal information, is more manageable for campuses with limited faculty support and funding yet can still offer students a clinical service-learning experience and the community useful legal information. If funding and faculty resources allow, one program aimed at on-campus students and one program directed toward community concerns satisfies the two main goals of a program like CLIC—provide an experience for students in the field and provide a service to the community.

Conclusion

In this chapter, we discussed how the Community Legal Information Center at California State University, Chico, is a flourishing example of undergraduate clinical legal education. If civic engagement is generally defined as making a difference in the "civic life of our communities and developing the combination of knowledge, skills, values and motivation to make that difference," then the skills that students learn in the classroom are further refined and the value of making contributions to their community is developed in service-learning internships like those available at CLIC, during which students get to make a difference in the lives of clients who are often underserved by the legal profession.[28] As rigorous internship experiences, legal clinics like CLIC are valuable not only because of the benefits they bring to their communities, but also because these types of intensive undergraduate experiences help participating students explore more fully the types of career paths they hope to pursue upon graduation and advance their development as effective citizens after "graduation".

How Students Talk to Each Other: An Academic Social Networking Project

11

By Renée Bukovchik VanVechten and Anita Chadha

Academic websites built to complement traditional political science courses create virtual spaces in which students from more than one institution can dialogue and learn from each other on a continuous basis. However, because online academic communities based on social networking are a relatively new development, there is little research demonstrating their value as a learning tool. Guided by research showing that discussion and dialogue promote critical reflection through an active-learning process, this study investigates the use of an academic website as a means to educate and prime students for civic and political participation. Focusing on our fall 2010 website project, which included 328 students from six Introduction to American Politics courses across the United States, we performed content analysis on a subset of 4,879 discussion forum postings and on open-ended responses to survey questions about the nature of students' online interactions. We found that, as an extension of the traditional classroom, a carefully designed website can promote learning that prepares students for active civic engagement.

Researchers are beginning to uncover the efficacy of web-based applications that are carefully designed to promote specific learning outcomes. Common web-based social networking such as Facebook and Internet chat areas, however, or course management tools such as Blackboard that limit access to members of only one institution are ill-equipped to deliver the educational goals of a team of college instructors. That said, social networking sites specifically designed to function as bounded academic spaces allow students to exchange ideas by questioning themselves and each other, test knowledge gained in the classroom, reexamine their views, deepen their understanding of theoretical concepts and current issues, practice being deliberative, and develop or deepen their sense of belonging to a larger political community. In sum, social networking sites can function as virtual civic communities that promote deliberative forms of civic engagement.

This chapter adds to the growing literature on innovative teaching technologies by examining how an online community creates opportunities for students to practice those skills that enable active political engagement. Our website (or more accurately, series of websites[1]), was designed for undergraduates as a "virtual civic square," in which participants could think further and more deeply about what they had heard in their own classes, voice their opinions in a less pressure–filled environment, exchange ideas on current topics with peers, hold each other accountable for their views, participate in live chats that included many participants at once, and practice low-stakes writing. One of its main purposes was to provide a space in which students studying the same topics could learn from others possessing different work-life experiences and diverse racial, ethnic, geographic, social, and economic backgrounds.

Initiated in 2008, the American Politics Project represents a collective pedagogical effort to provide an online complement to traditional political science classes: a virtual meeting space for undergraduates enrolled in Introduction to American Politics and American government courses on different campuses.[2] The ongoing project has grown to include six professors whose students participate in a semester-long endeavor that includes discussion forums, live chats, and student-to-student interviews. In fall 2010, more than 330 students and their professors participated.[3]

The bulk of activity on the American Politics Project website occurs in the open discussion forums, with a new question posed each week by a professor and at will by students. As we discuss, the site provides participants with ongoing opportunities to deepen their understanding of democratic practices, reinforce conceptual or theoretical lessons, expand their sense of belonging to a larger political community, and enhance their interest in political affairs. These outcomes are tied directly to our pedagogical aim of creating "high-impact participation" among students, which involves active learning through critical reflection that is both inward- and outward-looking. We also endeavor to give students opportunities to practice critical thinking, writing, and deliberative skills. Our hypothesis is that iterative discussions about common and often challenging issues with a diverse collection of peers will deepen students' sense of citizenship and interconnectedness not only as members of a larger class, but also as part of a larger civic community.

The following sections briefly discuss how communication channeled through an academic website can promote critical reflection and dialogue, activities that both promote and prepare students to become civically engaged. After characterizing the six classes that participated in fall 2010, we describe our approach to analyzing two separate data sets: students' responses to discussion questions posted on the website and open-ended responses to questions contained in an end-of-semester survey. Through content analysis of both data sets, we explore how website activities can engender and even constitute meaningful forms of civic engagement.

What do we mean by civic engagement in this context? Adding to the definitions provided in Chapter 1, Jacoby and Associates (2009) present multidimensional intellectual and behavioral aspects of civic engagement, noting that the concept involves one or more of the following:[4]

1. Learning from others, self, and environment to develop informed perspectives on social issues
2. Valuing diversity and building bridges across differences
3. Behaving, and working through controversy, with civility
4. Taking an active role in the political process
5. Participating actively in public life, public problem solving, and community service
6. Assuming leadership and membership roles in organizations
7. Developing empathy, ethics, values, and a sense of social responsibility
8. Promoting social justice locally and globally

We believe that an academic website creates opportunities to fulfill criteria 1, 2, 3, and 7 in particular and that these help educate and prepare students to fulfill the citizenship, community service, or activist roles traditionally associated with civic engagement captured in the remaining criteria. However, as Jacoby and others point out,[5] each of the practices listed constitutes singular forms of civic engagement. Not merely preparatory, each represents a personal capacity that meaningfully connects individuals to larger communities—in the case of our website, a wider and more diverse circle of peers, but also others with whom they interact or discuss politics—through the layering of new sensitivities, skills, and awareness that should endure beyond a given semester.[6]

Active, Reflective Learning: The Importance of Critical Reflection

Being knowledgeable about political issues, feeling confident about discussing these issues, and feeling qualified to act upon them are dimensions of political efficacy, or a sense of agency considered a precursor to civic engagement.[7] Though political efficacy is conditioned by many internal and external forces,[8] it can develop through a learning process that includes regular, purposeful opportunities to read, talk, and think about political affairs in personal rather than abstract ways.[9]

Talking politics or deliberating with others is an important act focused upon in this project because it links learning, developing a sense of efficacy, and civic engagement. As a basic form of civic participation, conversing about politics can help students develop a deeper comfort level with theoretical concepts and contemporary issues, especially those they might have otherwise disregarded, and also might help them pay closer attention to those issues when encountered later in conversation, the media, or class. When discussants seek new information, explain or justify their positions, and hold others accountable for their views, they engage in a learning process—an active-learning process that allows them to reach deeper levels of understanding. The volley of ideas that occurs through dialogue helps students create meaning out of a "purposeful combination of experiences and academic materials."[10]

As Pollock, Hamann, and Wilson (2005) have shown, online discussion forums permit the kind of active learning that enables higher-order reasoning, such as when peers help each other puzzle through problems. Through composing their own responses and responding to others' statements in asynchronous exchanges, students are driven to critically reexamine evidence, value and weigh other perspectives and experiences, dissect reasoning, and challenge conclusions, all of which may help them refine their positions.[11] In an online environment that includes a highly diverse membership, the chances that one's own perspectives will be challenged increase immensely.

Blount (2006) explains that when thoughtfully considering and questioning their own or each other's views, students are engaging in a process of critical reflection that leads to deeper levels of understanding. Though not all political actors will take time to reflect upon themselves, their reasoning, their positions, or their behaviors, the process of critical reflection is an important component of learning, becoming a participatory member of a political community, and also being a leader of it. As Blount continues, critical reflection occurs when students examine their relationships to their community experiences, consider how their own statements or actions intertwine with or influence others, and contemplate the roles they can play in a community. Critical reflection also involves placing issues into a context, synthesizing information and distilling concepts from complex interactions, developing viewpoints about issues in light of evidence presented by others, personalizing issues, and "learning to communicate one's viewpoint to others—including questions, concerns, and insights—in a public setting."[12]

Blount draws his conclusions about active learning from an undergraduate student internship project, yet the central element—that of thinking about an issue and writing about it in the context of shared experiences—is a core feature of the American Politics Project. Precisely because students build the project's website through their contributions to open discussion threads begun by professors or those they initiate themselves, we consider it a place in which active learning may occur through student-to-student interactions and individual reflection—and less so through professor-to-student interactions, which occur infrequently on the site. Students connect in a crosscultural environment filled with people and ideas that may be radically different from their own. In addition, the online medium allows participants to express "well-thought-out ideas that are often of higher quality than are the more spontaneous contributions in face-to-face classroom settings."[13] With more time to assemble a statement that will become semipublic, students can simultaneously prepare themselves for in-class discussions and address lingering questions after class. In other words, opportunities for critical reflection—an exercise that begets a sense of political efficacy, promotes information retention, and prepares students for active civic involvement—are wide open on the American Politics Project website.

Furthermore, by interacting with a widely diverse group, students can develop an awareness of alternative points of view that can lead to their developing "a more nuanced understanding" of collective problems, a deeper appreciation of minority rights, and an empathy for others,[14] as well as refine their conceptions of the common good.[15] Exposure to and experience with diversity also can help students develop skills to handle and resolve disagreements arising from conflicting perspectives.[16] Finally, by exploring extra source materials to help them bolster their positions and posing questions that could provoke further deliberation and discussion with peers, students can exercise—if not improve—communication skills necessary for civic engagement.

Not all students will avail themselves of these opportunities, even when their grades depend upon it. As Pollock, Hamann, and Wilson (2005) rightly point out, "not all students behave similarly in an online environment. Just as student behavior varies in 'traditional' classrooms, so can differences in behavior be expected in an online context."[17] Students' level of personal investment in the site will vary widely, from abstention and withdrawal to complete immersion. In the latter case, more frequent, critical, thoughtful, and deliberative contributions to the website should yield larger payoffs with longer endurance. We expect that students will carry over what they have learned into their civic lives; however, substantiating lasting effects lies beyond the scope of this study.

Overview of the Project

Prior to fall 2010, the project collaborators agreed to a common set of assignments. They distributed and discussed a standardized list of instructions on the first day of class and reminded students of these ground rules when necessary.

The project was built around three categories of website assignments. All students were required to create a profile, or avatar; upload a distinguishing photo or image; and participate in weekly discussions organized around a question posed by an instructor. To build dialogue, students also had to reply to others' posts, although the frequency and total requisite number varied among classes (see the sample course material in the online supplement to the book).[18] Second, all students were required to participate in at least one "Virtual Town Hall" meeting, or live chats that included members of all six classes; a variety of times and topics were offered to accommodate students' varying schedules.[19] Lastly, students from different campuses were paired so that they could interview each other, thus furthering the opportunities to build a sense of community through personal interaction and investment in the site.[20] While the array of activities was the same across participating classes, each professor maintained control over his or her syllabus by basing a different percentage of the course grade on website assignments (these ranged from 10% to 15%; see Table 11-1).

In all, 328 students participated in the website, beginning the last week of August 2010 and ending the third week of December 2010.[21] The professors administered an online anonymous survey during the first week of class in August and September and a follow-up survey at the end of the semester in December.[22]

The Settings: Six Campuses, Six Classes

Six campuses were linked through the American Politics Project 2010 website, a private site accessible by invitation only.[23] Besides the rich ethnic and racial diversity

Table 11-1: Summary of Class Statistics

	Univ. of Redlands (U of R)	Univ. of Maryland, Baltimore County (UMBC)	Adirondack Community College (ACC)	SUNY York College (York)	Carroll Univ. (CU)	Univ. of Houston, Downtown (UHD)
Location/Setting	Redlands, California *Suburban WEST*	Baltimore, Maryland *Suburban MID-ATLANTIC*	Adirondack, New York *Rural NORTHEAST*	Queens, New York *Urban NORTHEAST*	Waukesha, Wisconsin *Suburban UPPER MID-WEST*	Houston, Texas *Urban SOUTHWEST*
Students on Website[a]	29	42	64	81	23	89
Class Demographics	Mostly white, mostly on-campus residents, good academic skills	Very diverse, generally well-prepared academically	White, commuter, wide range of skills	Nonwhite, immigrant, employed, young parents, wide range of skills	Mostly white, mostly on-campus residents, good academic skills	Very diverse ethnically/racially; commuter students
Student Status	Full-time	Full-time	Mostly part-time	Full-time	Full-time	Full- and part-time
Percentage of Grade based on Website Activity	14%	15%	10%	10%	15%	10%
Overall Usage[b]	Heavy	Medium	Medium	Low	Low	Heavy
Course	American Politics	Introduction to American Government & Politics	American National Government	American Politics	Introduction to American Politics	US Government I

[a] Numbers are based on those who created a profile.
[b] Overall usage is based on the average number of posts by November 30, 2010, as well as the total number of days students visited the site.

among students, there was a great deal of other variation among the campus populations. They included public and private universities; four-year-degree universities, PhD-granting institutions, and a community college; geographic dispersion across four time zones; full- and part-time students; and smaller classes (23) to large classes (89).

Individual activity levels varied widely over the semester and across campuses. Some students posted long messages, whereas others kept their comments brief. Some students created more elaborate profile pages than others. Some never posted to the site, whereas others made it a weekly habit. One student set a record for activity on the site, posting a total of 216 times, plus 41 blogs. Summary statistics for each class are presented in Table 11-1, followed by an overview of the website "class."

Overall Demographics. For the most part, students did not know the geographic location of the other participating students because the profile pictures and names did not contain those identifiers. However, students likely gleaned some demographic information from photos, names, and information provided by the students themselves in their posts, and, if curious, participants could visit each other's profile pages, where a student's hometown was listed. Overall demographics presented here for the 2010 website class of 328 were obtained from the survey given at the beginning of the semester.

Sophomores comprised the largest group on the site, at 42.9%. Freshmen came in second, at 27.2%; 22% were juniors, and 8% were seniors (four or more years). Forty-four and a half percent of the participants were male to 54.5% female. The group was ethnically and racially diverse as well—no ethnic group or race represented a majority on the site. Whites comprised 42.5% of the participants; African Americans and Hispanics/Latinos totaled 17.8% each; Asian Americans equaled 8%, and 12.5% indicated "Other."

Students' overall political preference was for the Democratic Party, with 62.4% identifying as or leaning toward the left. Republicans comprised 19.3% of participants. Including those who leaned toward either party, 35.4% considered themselves politically independent. Just over 9% of students identified with a third party. However, this political distribution did not seem to overtly prejudice any website discussion.

Measuring Critical Reflection and Learning: Methods and Hypotheses

All of the participating professors required their students to respond to a certain number of instructor-initiated weekly discussion questions, which resulted in long threads that ran to many pages. In general, the professors neither coached nor closely instructed their students about how to respond. Printed guidelines directed the students to write a minimum of 50 words (approximately four lines) and to be respectful of differing opinions, prohibited the use of "IM" (instant-messaging) acronyms and obscene language, and prompted them to support statements with reasoning (see the online supplement to this book for guidelines). In class several professors further suggested that students avoid one-line replies and simply agreeing with each other. Apart from encouraging participants to "make the site theirs," little other guidance was provided.

Professors created a total of 14 Weekly Discussion forums, attracting 4,283 total replies.[24] The questions covered current events and theoretical concepts introduced in class. The most popular question asked students to consider the controversy in New York over the building of a mosque near Ground Zero (413 posts). Professors monitored conversations for signs that students were abiding by the general rules of respect, decency, and civility, but generally refrained from participating in the discussion forums. On average, 305 students replied to each question.

Some students began their own discussion threads, resulting in 71 separate student-initiated discussion forums that attracted 596 total responses. One professor did require his students to establish a discussion forum; however, the majority of the forums (44 of 71, or 62%) were initiated solely by students.[25] The most popular questions related to voting ("Should voting be mandatory?" with 41 responses), marijuana (40 responses to "Why Not Weed?"), and the military's "Don't Ask, Don't Tell" policy (39 responses, plus two similar forums that included 21 more). Student usage of the site—that is, the frequency and volume of posts—varied significantly.[26]

The Reflectiveness Index

The instructors wanted to understand if and how students were learning through their online activity. Was there evidence that they were learning from each other? Were they genuinely being reflective, or were they merely fulfilling their course requirements without much thought? Were they thinking critically through these exchanges or not?

Several discussion question forums were analyzed for evidence. Referring to the Jacoby and Associates (2009) index of civic engagement previously detailed, the authors of this chapter wondered if students were developing informed perspectives about civic issues, learning from each other, and interacting in a civil way. Were they being deliberative, or were they reacting emotionally, making broad and unsupported generalizations, and providing knee-jerk, or "automatic," reactions to a question or post?

Content analysis was performed on the statements by coding whether they were generally thoughtful, deliberative, or reflective; whether they referred to a civic issue; referenced their class texts or professors; provided links or references to related material; or posed honest questions rather than rhetorical ones (see Table 11-2 for coding scheme). First, the students' posts were rated for overall reflectiveness or deliberativeness, assigning a "1" for high levels of these and "0" for low. When posts were not deliberative overall, they were coded as knee-jerk, that is, automatic, based on emotion and lacking evidence. Some students did both and were double-coded, but the majority of responses were determined to be either reflective or not. By developing the rubric together over a period of several days and consulting frequently over questionable codings throughout the research process, a high degree of intercoder agreement was achieved.[27]

Based on this coding scheme, a composite index was developed to measure the reflectiveness of postings. To capture the multidimensional nature of "critical reflection," we developed a seven-point scale of reflectiveness, where a score of zero was the least reflective. Posts that were deliberative (nominally reflective), discussed civic roles, referred to a class text, provided a link to outside media, posed an honest question, and were longer than four lines (the minimum) were considered the most reflective. Thus, our composite index was computed using these variables:

> reflective/deliberative + civic roles + referred to class or text + provided media link + posed an honest question + length of post (+1 for medium length, +2 for long)

Table 11-2: Coding Scheme Used to Evaluate Discussion Questions (Basis for Reflectiveness Index)
Reflective/Deliberative: Did the students reflect, deliberate, or reconsider their own views when they responded to a question or when they commented to student posts? Did they puzzle through problems or issues, further question others, challenge others or hold them accountable for their views in a positive way: *"I disagree with you… have you considered…?"* Did they think about the question and respond with reflective, deliberate comments? A score of "1" is a general judgment about the overall quality of the post. (1=yes, 0 =no)
Direct Address: Did the student directly address someone when responding, or address comments to other participants on the site? *"Hey guys"; "I agree with Patty…"* (No points given for posts that could "stand-alone.") (1=yes, 0 =no)
Knee-Jerk: Did the student respond in a manner that was reactive and not reflective? Was it a response that was emotional, opinionated, and not well-reasoned? (1=yes, 0 =no)
Civic Roles: Was the student a thoughtful citizen? Did he or she think about the question posed and respond in a way that reflected a theoretical or practical application of American politics? Did he or she discuss a civic issue, such as First Amendment or voting issues, rather just mention it? Did they engage each other, not just agree or disagree with each other but challenge or push each other to think in a civil way? (1=yes, 0 =no)
Personal Experience/History: Did they directly state or imply that they had some vested interest in the topic at hand? Did they have personal experience taking on the role in the discussions. For instance, "*…I have experienced this before as a Muslim…*" Or "*…as a military man…*" (1=yes, 0 =no)
Classroom Ideas or Texts: In their responses did they refer to ideas they had heard in class or mention their professors or discussions in class. "*…I learned this in class…*" Or "*…the text says…*" (1=yes, 0 =no)
References or Outside Links: Did the student post or cite links to external sites when responding to a question, or did he or she refer to a (court) case in a specific manner that one could look it up? Did they cite current events or media-related stories that could be looked up or located by another student? Did they provide an actual link to another related source? (No points for stand-alone quotes by famous individuals.) (1=yes, 0 =no)
Unsupported Generalizations: Were the comments made by the student wrong or unsupported, "sweeping generalizations"? (1=yes, 0 =no)
Derogatory Comments: Did students comment directly about an individual or group in a hostile and judgmental way? "*You are stupid…*" (1=yes, 0 =no)
Negative Tone: A five-point scale for this category: 1=clearly irritated, annoyed; strident, abrasive tone; 2=more exclamation, some bolded letters were used or words were capitalized to "shout" or "yell"; 3=beginning to use strong language or cuss words; 4=strong language, direct accusations, ad hominem attacks; 5=most hostile, with comments directed at a student or group directly; uncivil. This category measures a person's level of anger, rather than merely strong feelings about an issue.
The Prescriptive/Normative "Should": Made at least one normative statement that includes a "should" as in, "*…the US should get out of that war…,*" or "*…the US should not send prisoners to war…*" (1=yes, 0 =no)
Poses Honest Question: The student actually asks a question (one or more) that enlarges the scope of the discussion, not a rhetorical one that assumes an answer. "Who decides what is proper and appropriate?" (1=yes, 0 =no)
Length: A scale of 1–3 was used: 1= a short response of usually 75 words or fewer, or up to 4 full lines of text; 2=a medium response, between 5–9 lines of text, or about 80–200 words; and 3=a long response, longer than 10 lines, or more than 200 words.
Revisited: Did the students revisit the questions they initiated, or did they revisit another student's question and respond? (= number of revisits)
Geography: Did they mention where they lived, or a place to which they have travelled or lived? "*I am from NY*" (1=yes, 0 =no)

We interpreted a score of four or more as robustly reflective and did not expect students to easily reach seven because of the many separate elements that needed to be present. A score of three was moderately reflective, two was somewhat reflective, and a score of one was considered shallow. A score of zero indicated that a student contributed very little to the discussion and appeared to put forth little effort in constructing a response.

Results: The Instructor-Initiated Questions

We focused on three instructor-initiated questions, two of which address classic tensions in American politics: "Should the mosque be built near Ground Zero?" and "Free speech versus privacy rights: where is the balance?" and a third that prompted students to consider the 2010 midterm election results, which left the number of women in Congress unchanged at 17% ("What does this mean for the future of women in politics?"). We refer to these as "DQ" 1, 2, and 3, respectively, and indexed the coded responses to create a measure of reflectiveness, presented in Figure 11-1.

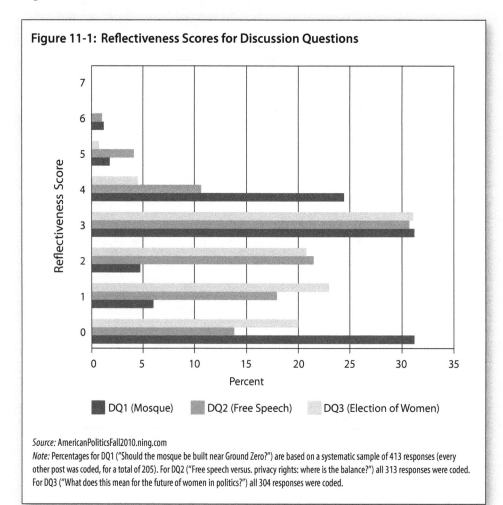

Figure 11-1: Reflectiveness Scores for Discussion Questions

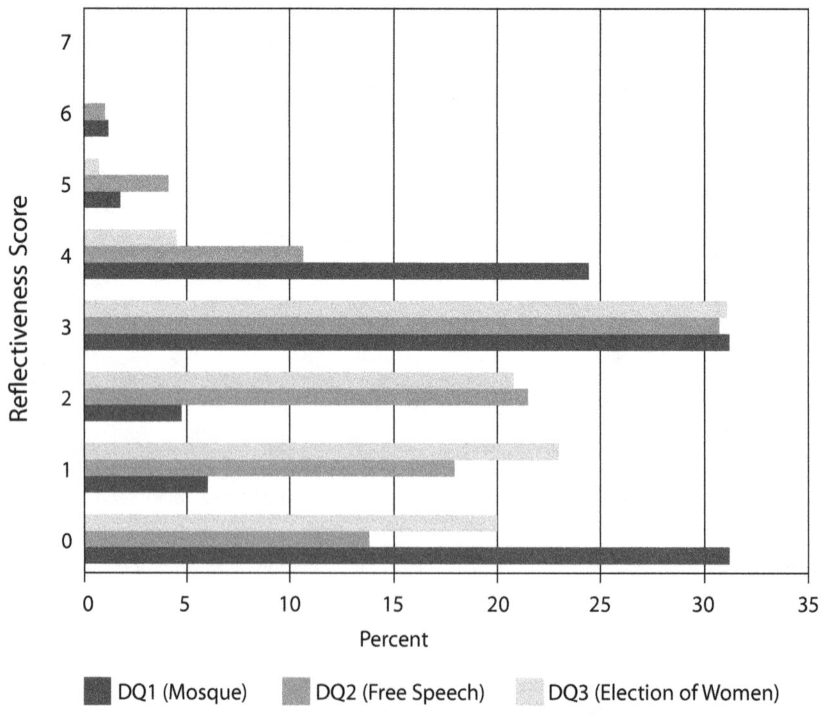

Source: AmericanPoliticsFall2010.ning.com
Note: Percentages for DQ1 ("Should the mosque be built near Ground Zero?") are based on a systematic sample of 413 responses (every other post was coded, for a total of 205). For DQ2 ("Free speech versus. privacy rights: where is the balance?") all 313 responses were coded. For DQ3 ("What does this mean for the future of women in politics?") all 304 responses were coded.

As this figure illustrates, depth and quality varied across the response sets, which included students from all classes. Given the lack of instruction about the content of posts or what would constitute a "reflective" response, we attribute this variability in part to the nature and phrasing of the questions. Questions that challenged deeply held values or beliefs, such as those asking students to weigh the relative importance of civil rights and liberties (e.g., "Should a fringe church be allowed to protest gay rights at a fallen soldier's funeral?"), tended to provoke far more emotional reactions than those asking students to think about a political trend or theoretical concept (e.g., "What does the election mean for the future of women in politics?"). However, regardless of students' interest levels, personal values, or prior exposure to issues, each discussion question represented an open invitation to reflect and deliberate.

Results presented for DQ1 (the mosque question) indicate that students on the whole were neither extremely shallow nor extremely reflective. Approximately a third (31%) fell into the "shallowest" category with a score of zero; these responses tended to be short, knee-jerk, "hit-and-run" emotional posts, editorial or normative in nature, often devoid of fact-based evidence, and argued from a moral standpoint. When responding to their peers' posts, students often just agreed with a previous statement and repeated points already made. A typical unreflective response to the question about the mosque was: "I agree ... there seems to be some type of hidden agenda. Why even attempt to build there? I'm sure they can find another location some where[sic] in the country."

For DQ2 (privacy vs. free speech), almost a third (31.7%) of the responses scored a zero or one, another 21.4% scored two points, and almost a third (30.6%) scored three points. Only 15.9% scored four points or more. DQ3 (women in politics) encouraged the least amount of considered thought: 43.2% scored a zero or one, and virtually all (94.7%) scored less than four. Common themes were echoed in the following post (which scored three points):

> I think that these statistics only mirror the outcome of the entire election. It['s] no secret women are more democratic and the democrats lost a lot of seats in this election. Voters seemed to have swept the GOP in and in doing that voted more women out of office then[sic] ever before. I do not believe that this is a trend however, during the 2012 election things will more than likely even back out between the two parties and more women will gain seats back.

Gauging reflectiveness provided different results. A substantial percentage of DQ1 responses fell into the upper tiers of reflectiveness: 27.4% scored four points or more, meaning that the entries were five lines or more in length; were generally reflective; referred to a civic issue; contained references to ideas discussed in the classroom, textbook, outside media; contained actual links to other articles or materials; or posed an honest question that furthered the discussion. For example, in this lengthy posting a student[28] addresses the constitutional issues, considers both sides, and references an idea from class:

> 10/12/10, Stephanie: I think it is necessary, like you pointed out, to make it clear that the reason for protest is "legitimate" in the perspective of the Westboro Baptists. They were properly protected by their First Amendment right, and they were not in any of the "buffer" zones mentioned in the first link/article. However, I do agree that it was the wrong time, and wrong place to be making a protest. Like we discuss in our political science class, preferences, times, and institutions all result in the final outcome. If the Westboro Baptists are the only ones who "prefer" to make this somewhat contradictory argument that their God is punishing America by killing soldiers who are homosexuals, it will not factor into the outcome much if the strong majority thinks that it is the wrong time and place for it to be protested.... Though they are entitled to their freedom of speech, and of religious beliefs, it almost seems paradoxical that they are pushing their beliefs on one issue (sexuality) by going against what most citizens would think is typical christian [sic] behavior.... A funeral is a place where any citizen—especially a member of the Marines—should be respected by all....[29]

Numerous examples of critical reflection also can be found in the exchanges students had with each other: dialogues built around questioning an issue together, questioning each other, or holding each other accountable for their positions. It is worth highlighting the fact that students agreed with each other far more often—*10 times* more often—and it seemed far easier for students to agree and supply their reasoning for doing so. These tended to be among the least reflective posts, as they repeated ideas already expressed without adding materially to the discussion. However, the mere presence of disagreement and dialogue (an original post plus direct replies), despite their comparatively low frequency, can be instructive to students who shy away from engaging in controversy themselves.

Dialogues provide good examples of critical reflection and intellectual civic engagement that prepare one for active political participation, namely, developing informed perspectives; valuing diversity; behaving, or working through, controversy with civility; and developing empathy, values, and social responsibility (i.e., criteria 1–3 and 7 of the Civic Engagement Index). The following excerpt captures all of these qualities of civic engagement and is lifted from an exchange involving 32 direct, secondary, or tertiary responses:

> 9/19/10: Shaya: The thing is not all of us know the pain and suffering that many families experienced in the attacks of 9/11 and, in reality, we will never completely understand, we can only empathize. I believe that since these extremists only represent a few of the Muslim community and the others of the Muslim community believe that what happened was wrong, that they would understand the sensitivity of the subject and understand why it would be more practical to build their mosque maybe in a different location. However, I also believe we have the freedom of

> religion and the Muslims do have the right to put their place of worship anywhere they desire to. It's completely up to them.
>
> 9/20, Rita: I agree with Shaya, a very thoughtful response. Honestly, I'm on both sides of the fence.... I regret that I don't have a more concrete stance regarding this issue. They have a right to build their place of worship wherever they please, but it is hard to let go of what happened.
>
> 9/20, Graycen: I agree with Rita completely. I too, am stuck in the middle. I feel that the events that took place on September 11th have a huge impact on people and this would draw them away from wanting to allow the building of the mosque. But, on the other hand, should we not let the place of worship for the Muslims to be built? I can't honeslty [sic] say that I am for or against.

As this particular exchange illustrates, students were reading and responding in ways that furthered the discussions and their own understandings. Yet as the forums ran to as many as 35 webpages, students appeared to read selectively, focusing on the first and most recent postings, for example, thereby missing some very insightful writing because it was difficult to move through them quickly (for students in the "middle" of a long forum, it was rather like being on the ninth page of a Google search).

At times students puzzled through issues together; most frequently they agreed with each other. Sometimes the posts assumed a more strident tone:

> 9/3/10, Adam: I believe that the Muslims have the right to pursue their religion, but not that close to ground zero. I shed a lot of sweat blood and tears in Iraq. I also lost a lot of my friends that died because some people are too much of a coward to fight us face to face. Instead they have got to shoot at us when we are not looking. Biggest cowards in the history of mankind!
>
> 9/18, Robert: I have also served in Iraq and certainly understand where you are coming from. What we must look at are the people we were fighting which were the extremists. They are a small percentage of the population unfortunately giving a bad reputation to all Muslims in the eyes of the American. I have met, as well as you I'm sure, many friendly Muslims overseas that love what we do and would never intend to bring harm to us. Why they are choosing the site near Ground Zero I am not entirely sure but if we single Muslims out and try to prevent the center from being built nothing good will come of it.

Deliberately offensive comments or derogatory posts infrequently appeared, but they were usually either ignored (students did not reply to them) or were softened with a diplomatic response such as the one above. Overwhelmingly the posts were respectful, and when they crossed the line, students usually declined to take the bait or brought these comments to the instructors' attention for further discussion in class.[30]

The preceding exchange also demonstrates that students' own experiences and backgrounds provided important talking points and thinking points. In every discussion forum at least a few students justified their positions by bringing up their own experiences or unique identifying characteristics, such as religion (Christianity, Islam), location (New York, Texas, etc.), and other personal indicators (married to a Marine, a parent). It was apparent that each mention of a critical difference had the power to influence opinions. In fact, open-ended responses to the end-of-the-semester survey indicated that students overwhelmingly appreciated the opportunity to discuss political issues "with professors and students from other institutions" and "people from all the way across the states."[31]

Students appeared to read through the posts with varying degrees of attentiveness. A few revisited the site to modify their original positions, and some admitted having changed their minds based on what they read. Few students posted a third time to an instructor-initiated question; however, it is likely that students revisited the threads but chose not to respond further. In effect, it was possible that they monitored the discussions, but because the site lacked a built-in visit counter, we could only count the posts made rather than the number of times students logged on to the site. It is likely that the total number of site visits was underestimated.

We found many instances of students listening and responding to each other, and their choice of words signaled their involvement in an ongoing, collective discussion. About half of the posts contained direct addresses to previous responders ("As Jani said...") or used an inclusive second-person address ("you," "you all," "we students"). Numerous instances also were found of students reformulating their own positions in light of information or ideas presented by others.

Many of the posts exceeded the required length of 50 words (about four lines), a sign that students were behaving deliberatively and taking time and space to flesh out their ideas. For the freedom of speech discussion question, 53% exceeded the minimum post requirements, and 14.3% were about three times as a long as they needed to be (at least 10 lines, about 200 words or longer). Across the board, the average long post was rationally argued and thoughtfully written, and not merely a "rant." Some were equivalent to mini-essays, at 700 to 1,000 words.

Overall, it is clear that students on the site behaved much as they do in class or when completing other types of assignments: some did the minimum required without much thought, whereas others took the assignments seriously and went far beyond what was expected.

Results: The Student-Initiated Questions

Seventy-one questions were initiated by students themselves, attracting 596 replies. We wondered how the students interacted and learned from each other apart from the instructor-initiated forums. Would students approach those questions differently because they were not required to answer them? Would students revisit more frequently? We suspected that students would feel freer to converse with each other in forums that they or their peers had established, perhaps because they felt more ownership of them. We evaluated their postings to determine whether students were showing the same levels of engagement and reflectiveness evidenced in the instructor-initiated forums.

A subset of users tended to frequent the student forums fairly regularly. Of 328 individuals on the site, only 142 (43.3%) responded to a student-initiated question, and 100 of these students posted to these forums an average of 4.1 times (SD=5.5). That 11.9% of this group revisited the same forum two or more times suggests that they were actively following the unfolding conversations, a rare occurrence in the instructor-initiated posts. Most likely the higher number of revisits was prompted by students' personal investment in the questions they had written themselves; in fact, some students thanked others for their participation with comments, such as "You had a great point that stood out to me.... All the points were great and I'm glad for your feedback."

Shorter forums were easier to navigate, and greater interest in the subject matter also may have been a factor.[32] Compared to the professor-initiated discussion questions analyzed, a higher percentage of students asked honest questions of each other (14.6% compared to 6.8% of professor-initiated posts), 10.1% referenced outside materials or provided links (found in only 2.8% of professor-initiated posts overall), and several more made references to class or the text in the student forums.

The reflectiveness index also was used in the content analysis of all 596 responses to students' discussion questions. As shown in Figure 11-2, about a third (34.7%) fell into the "shallowest" category: these tended to be short posts, often normative or emotional in nature, and not particularly argumentative. These could have been either responses to other students or original posts; for example, in a question regarding scanners at airports:

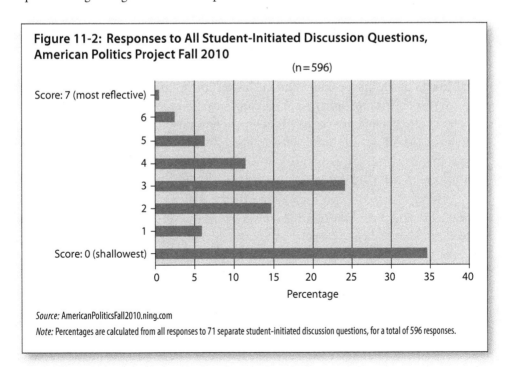

Figure 11-2: Responses to All Student-Initiated Discussion Questions, American Politics Project Fall 2010

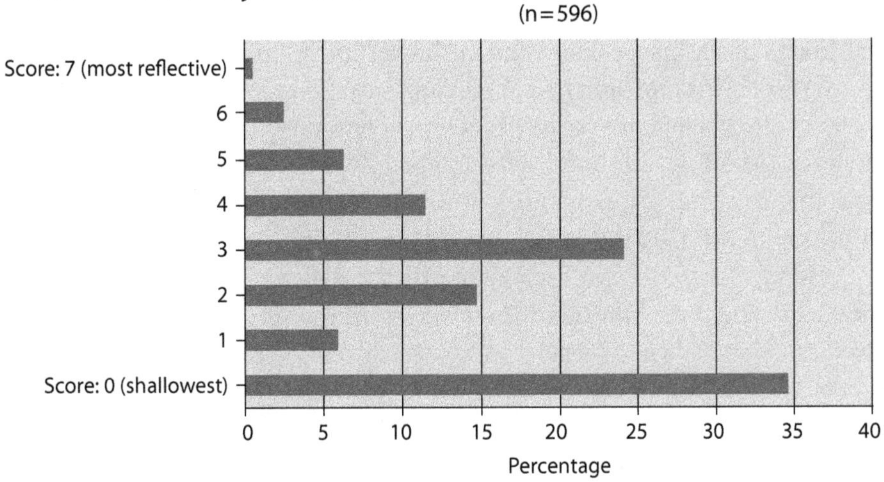

Source: AmericanPoliticsFall2010.ning.com

Note: Percentages are calculated from all responses to 71 separate student-initiated discussion questions, for a total of 596 responses.

Table 11-3. Statistical Comparison of Responses to Instructor-Initiated and Student-Initiated Discussion Questions

	Instructor-Initiated ("DQs") N=822	Student-Initiated ("DSQs") N=596
Length:		
Short (1-4 lines; up to 75 words)	40.0%	34.8%
Medium (5-9 lines; ~ 80-200 words)	43.3%	46.1%
Long (10+ lines; 200+ words)	16.8%	19.1%
Reflectiveness Score:		
0–1 (Shallow)	37.3%	40.6%
2 (Mildly reflective)	15.7%	14.8%
3 (Moderately reflective)	30.9%	24.2%
4–7 (Most reflective)	16.2%	20.5%

> I agree with this also because i [sic] would rather feel safe walking into an airport knowing nothing bad is going to happen to me. Then again, I think that these people are looking at you and you should be able to say why you think this is so or not. Like you said, it is harder to get on a plane without getting searched. It's not like you can just get on without getting searched.

About one in five (20.8%) scored four points or more on the reflectiveness scale.

However, there were long threads containing between 20 and 30 responses on some substantial topics that contained few to no knee-jerk responses, such as one thread about sending prisoners into combat and others addressing the "Don't Ask, Don't Tell" policy. The majority of students' posts were thoughtful and argued from a defensible position, and in this respect were not much different from responses to instructor-initiated discussion questions. As shown in Table 11-3, they were also comparable in length, with about a third of students posting short statements (34.8% at four lines or fewer, about 75 words apiece), 46.1% at medium length (five to nine lines, or between 80 and 200 words), and 19.1% at or exceeding 10 lines (more than 200 words).

Overall, we found that the way in which questions were asked and the "curb appeal" of questions influenced appreciably how students initially responded. Questions that touched them personally, such as civil rights and liberties, tended to provoke the liveliest exchanges, though not the most consistently reflective posts. Levels of reflectiveness fluctuated in both instructor-initiated and student-initiated forums, yet we observed that a fairly high percentage across the site were reflective and deliberative, tied in ideas from texts and outside materials, and asked honest questions as opposed to rhetorical ones. As already mentioned, students appeared more eager to revisit their own discussion forums to see how others had responded to them. In summary, discussion in these online spaces provides evidence of active and engaged student learning, which we also uncovered in our analysis of end-of-semester surveys.

Survey Evaluations: Additional Evidence of Learning

Evidence of active learning, critical reflection, and priming for active civic engagement is contained in the responses to open-ended questions on the end-of-semester survey as well. Those response sets provide a wealth of information about how the students valued their online experience. Focusing on one of these, we asked students to relate what they learned, and then we performed content analysis on the 183 statements provided by 146 respondents. Building on the criteria for civic engagement outlined previously, Table 11-4 summarizes students' responses.

As these open-ended statements show, the website functioned as a virtual extension of the classroom. Students could be civically engaged by learning from and about others and themselves in an educational community structured around diversity, intellectual challenge, and deliberation that enabled the development of more informed citizens. At least 30% of all statements volunteered could easily be placed in category one (learning from others, self, and environment to develop informed perspectives on social issues).[33] Self-improvement is the underlying assumption of an educational setting, and we believe that it also applies to the educational website. This goal sets it critically apart from other types of social networking sites, on which the rules regulating interaction are ill-defined and individuals are generally not expected to reflect deeply on public policy issues or engage in critical self-examination.

Developing informed perspectives on social issues also was possible because students could relate to each other. Students were asked about this factor in the end-of-semester survey. Among 144 respondents, 64.6%—almost two-thirds—agreed or strongly agreed with the statement: "I feel I could relate to others who participated in the website." We regard this result as an indication that students made interpersonal connections that helped to create a sense of community, however short-lived or shallow. This online, academic community allowed them to explore issues with what appeared to be a general sense of responsibility to and for each other.

It also mattered that students' sense of connectedness depended somewhat on whether others responded to, acknowledged, or ignored their posts. When asked, "Did you feel as if you were a valuable member of this online community?" it was clear that interaction made all the difference. Two very different statements illustrate the point: "Not really. I participated but almost no one replied or discussed with me," said one. Stated another: "Yes, definitely. It was kind of exciting, to come back to the dorm and wait to see who agreed with what you said and who tried to cut you down." We did not see much evidence of students "cutting each other down" in the sense of personal attacks, which in any case was actively discouraged.

Table 11-4: Coded Responses to Open-ended Survey Question: "What did you learn by participating in the American Politics Fall 2010 Website?"

Civic Engagement Criteria	Percentage/ Number of Mentions	Examples of Statements Made (N=183)
1. Learning from others, self, and environment to develop informed perspectives on social issues	29% (53)	"I learned . . . that many individuals REALLY have different opinions, which is why it is so hard for the government to satisfy everyone's needs and its own." "It was a way for me to see others views on current political topics. It made me think about the reasons that I had the view that I did, sometimes softening my views, and some times [sic] firming my views."
2. Valuing diversity and building bridges across difference	9.3% (17)	"[I]t was quite interesting and educational to hear the various voices." "People as a whole are different with different opinions and means of expressing themselves"
3. Behaving, and working through controversy, with civility	6.6% (12)	". . . to always have secure facts before disputing someone's argument ... respectfully, of course" "That everyone has diverse views that one may not agree with but one has to be tolerant"
4. Taking an active role in the political process (includes SKILLS acquired)	8.2% 15	"I also learned new words to help me understand political language better." "I learned how to express my opinion about specific topics and to think a little more in depth about topics that I had not thought about prior to the American Politics website"
7. Developing empathy, ethics, values, and sense of social responsibility	7.1% (13)	"I learned that people all around the country are dealing with the same issues no matter where they reside. Suburbs, cities, and etc. We are all people of America and need to work together to make change." "I learned that many people have different opinions but still the same goal seems to be everyone wants to try to better America"
Other/Additional Comments:		
Learned about politics/ government/a topic/current issues/knowledge	25.7% (47)	"I learned about topics that I normally would have never paid attention to." "I learned a lot more about the government and how it works."
Referenced larger community, or national or state context (double-counted in Categories 1 & 2)	6.0% (17)	"That people from all the way across the states could have opinions almost exactly like mine even if their beliefs are completely different" "I also learned that things that may be important and of a big issue in my state, may have little importance in another state."

Source: American Politics Project Fall 2010 Posttest (December 2010).
Note: Categories do not add up to 100%; general comments about different aspects of the website experience (Town Hall meetings, "great experience," "didn't learn much by participating," etc.) are not reported here. It is also interesting to note that among the 149 students who responded to this question, only 10 (6.7%) commented that they "didn't learn much by participating" or "nothing," or made a similar remark.

In summary, the extended, back-and-forth dialogue that occurred on so many different issues and on so many occasions could not have been replicated in a traditional classroom. Overall response to the website was overwhelmingly positive, although not universal: 79% of survey respondents recommended that future classes participate in this kind of website; 21% did not.[34] Considered together, students' self-reported learning and perceptions, in addition to the types, depth of (many) posts, volume of insights, quality of responses, inclusiveness of the dialogue, and diversity of perspectives voiced on the website provide clear indications of the added benefits that a carefully designed social networking site can promote.

Conclusions and Lessons Learned

The central purpose of the collaborative website was to provide an educational space in which undergraduates studying the same topics could learn from others with different racial and ethnic backgrounds, ideological viewpoints, and social, geographic, and economic experiences. Through our analysis of discussion-based activities, we found that a carefully designed website can function as a virtual national classroom, replete with opportunities for students to learn from each other. Enlarging the space through their own involvement, students can critically reflect on classic and contemporary issues in American politics; practice skills such as critical thinking, argumentation, and communication; and become more aware and engaged citizens who are better prepared to participate in public life. It is important to note that these outcomes are neither universal nor automatic, because they depend on the students' own level of commitment; however, the medium encourages various forms of civic participation that can simultaneously enhance the learning process, from discussing and disagreeing with civility to developing more informed perspectives based on interaction with a diverse set of peers. These observations were based on careful analysis of students' posts and their online behavior, conclusions echoed in students' self-assessments.

Built around discussion forums, the website drew students into a learning process that emphasized creative expression, self-exploration, deliberation, and critical reflectiveness, all of which are components of high-impact learning that can lead to effective civic engagement.[35] The practice of critical reflection involves assessing evidence, articulating viewpoints, weighing other perspectives, examining conclusions, and refining positions. Through their contributions to discussion forums, students engaged this process when they commented thoughtfully on others' posts, defended their stances, integrated links to outside materials, and asked questions that furthered the discussion by challenging their peers to think differently. These effects were plainly evident across the discussion question forums in short replies as well as in mini-essays.

The virtual classroom supplemented traditional instruction by creating an uninterrupted, all-inclusive learning space that students could access at any time. Ideas could be tested on the website and brought back to the classroom for further discussion. Every student had an opportunity to prepare statements and contribute to ongoing discussions on a wide range of subjects that instructors would be unable to cover in-depth in class. More important, without classroom walls, the boundaries presented by geographic region, class size, and institution type became permeable. Community college students talked with their peers at private and public four-year universities, returning students interacted frequently with traditional college-age students, and commuters deliberated with full-time students from across the country. Unlike traditional classrooms in which students may refrain from actively participating in discussions,[36] and unlike many on-campus organizations in which students tend to seek out others like themselves,[37] this online community compelled students to mingle with an enlarged group that may have been more representative of the body politic than that of their own campus or community.

As such, participation in online dialogues also has implications for building civic community beyond the boundaries of a defined academic space. Though online exchanges may be a less-than-perfect substitute for face-to-face interaction, students can develop a sense of interconnectedness and belonging to a larger community that is enlivened by common issues. By talking to each other about controversial subjects, students can learn to bridge differences, practice civility, develop empathy, and cultivate a deeper sense of social responsibility and shared purposes. Based on theories about learning previously discussed, we believe that these lessons may not entirely dissipate after online communities scatter. Therefore, what students learned from their website experiences could motivate them to participate more fully in other political settings, though further study is needed to confirm that these outcomes persist beyond semester's end. In other words, this study suggests spillover and longitudinal effects that a well-funded, multistage, longitudinal research project could definitively test.

It is important to note that the outcomes of a collaborative website project depend upon instructors' efforts to help students invest in the site. Their thoughtfulness in creating challenging discussion questions will be mirrored in the depth of students' responses, and the incentives that they set will condition students' willingness to contribute regularly. In addition to making expectations clear, orienting their students to open discussion questions, and addressing website content in class, instructors may require students to create their own discussion forums, require links to relevant sources, or offer rewards for habitual participation. Tapping into newsworthy national events and tying them to enduring theoretical debates help to not only capture students' imaginations but also reinforce key lessons.[38]

At a time when social scientists continue to document significant declines in civic engagement among college students[39] and many educational institutions have renewed their advocacy of civic education, pedagogical tools with the power to deliver both are worth implementing. Despite the generally cool reception among educators of social networking and other online forms of interaction to date, this study shows that academic social networking innovations, especially cross-institutional projects such as this one, have the demonstrated ability to complement traditional modes of teaching and learning without sacrificing substance. By enlarging and diversifying the learning community through cross-institutional collaboration, academic websites can invigorate educational experiences of discovering, generating, deepening, and sharing knowledge, while also creating interpersonal experiences that can enhance democratic civic participation. The promise of academic social networking lies not just in its ability to harness students' growing proclivities for online communication, but also in its ability to prime students for different forms of engaged democratic citizenship.

Practicing Politics: The National Student Issues Conventions

12

By Anthony Perry

The National Student Political Issues Convention provides a venue for students to create a unified issues agenda that they promote in person to elected officials. Students learn how to develop a consensus and work together in coalitions to promote general concerns. As either a semester-long or single event, the National Student Political Issues Convention includes effective tools to engage students for learning about politics and public policy and helps students develop such skills as careful listening, responding to critiques in their positions, managing their emotional reactions, and engaging others in political conversations with civility. Overall, the convention links politics, public policy, and democratic citizenship to foster a greater appreciation for course learning objectives and the workings of American government.

Many political science instructors have likely found themselves teaching an introductory American government course in which the students were generally disinterested and not engaged. Indeed, this situation may be the norm in many introductory courses. Educators often point to the students as the problem, because while the class as a whole is disengaged, there are students who are participating and learning. If some students can excel, then success is achievable if only the other students cared more about their education and were more disciplined.

Although these perceptions may be correct, most political scientists are good educators who want to help *all* of their students understand and learn the importance of government and politics. They hope students will become engaged in their classes and in public affairs. They want to provide ways to encourage participation both in and outside the classroom.

Many active-learning methods are being developed to inspire more students to participate in their learning environment. Textbook publishers are developing multimedia tools aimed at engaging students, including clickers, video clips, and online games. Some faculty have found these tools to be successful; however, as tools they have their limitations. Anecdotal evidence exists of cases in which students were more engaged in the classroom when active-learning models were used, compared with engagement in more traditional classroom environments, yet there is no evidence that this engagement correlates to students viewing political science as more relevant to their lives.[1]

Historically, college faculty lectured, students took notes, and either learned the information or not. Success in learning often was a factor of time spent on task, wherein one absorbed the information, synthesized it, and showed the professor that one knew what was expected. If the course material was not relevant to students, however, even when they were very successful, their long-term memory of the information was quite limited. Many introductory political science classes used this method as the faculty sought to give the students an overview of the discipline's essentials and set a foundation for future political science majors. The memorization of details was emphasized, with little attention to how to motivate students to learn about American government, politics, and the policy making that affects them directly.

Since the beginning of the 21st century, there has been an emphasis placed upon modifying teaching pedagogy to improve learning outcomes. The fact remains that motivating students to learn the information for end-of-term assessments is not the same as engaging students to learn for long-term retention. If students do not perceive the information being taught as relevant to their lives, then long-term retention may not follow.

In the example that follows, I show how participating educators modified their pedagogy using the concept of agenda setting to refocus lessons so that students discovered the personal relevancy of the civic knowledge and skills being taught. The integration of agenda-setting activities into the learning process allowed students to develop a personal interest in public policy and a stake in the process by which a National Student Issues Agenda is created and shared with elected officials. This process, in turn, may promote long-term retention of key concepts and the development of skills that can be applied outside the classroom.

The National Student Issues Agenda is brought to the attention of elected officials at city- or statewide National Student Political Issues Conventions. These conventions and the active-learning model associated with them require students to build their own political agenda and then learn how to promote their chosen issues. The agenda-building activities in which students participate have been shown to provide an effective mechanism to make political science courses more relevant to students.[2] Courses that have students develop a political agenda, research policy concerns, and engage in the political process can inspire them to learn political science, encourage greater retention of information, and help foster higher-order critical thinking as students develop strategies to build effective coalitions for promoting their concerns. This chapter first explains the agenda-setting model and then reviews the phases involved in creating a well-functioning model that can be applied to any size course or institution. The discussion focuses on how this model was used in Michigan and Illinois at different types of institutions and explores the successes gained.

The Agenda-Setting Model

The agenda-setting model can be implemented in various ways. In many cases, students are randomly selected to first meet in small groups to select their own leaders and through persuasion convince each other which issues should be on any student-issues agenda. A later stage—perhaps initiated after further research, discussion, and study—is to adopt a common agenda in a larger convention of several hundred students. The final step is to present these student issues to elected officials and candidates for public office to compel them to respond. So, the agenda-setting model has three core areas:

1. The development of a list of concerns, limited in number, that pushes students to engage each other through direct dialogue in class and indirect discourse on electronic discussion boards.
2. Definition of issue(s) and the building of evidence to support a concern's legitimacy; this can be used in advocacy activities.
3. The development of a strategic plan for pushing the issue(s) onto the political agenda.

The methods used to help students develop a political agenda do not require an omission of the traditional lectures, discussion groups, or exercises that are standard in most introductory courses. Agenda-building activities are integrated alongside the traditional pedagogy to engage students in the learning process and focus their attention on the personal and societal significance of the principal lessons of American government. These methods also help to place course materials in a context of civic responsibility and citizen power.[3]

This approach contrasts with the course design that emphasizes a grand overview of American government and politics to prepare the future political science major. It also differs from courses that offer a predetermined theme or niche area that may or may not appeal to students in any given semester. Instead, the agenda-setting model allows the focus to be more organically developed by the students themselves. Students discuss and debate the issues that they see as most important to their communities, states, countries, or the world. The process leads them to champion a single issue that they feel requires more attention. Learning how to champion their own concerns is the hook that draws them toward seeing the personal relevance of political science. Note that having the students decide upon and focus on a concern and not on a select solution reduces conflict and increases cooperation, as the goal is to get the concern on the political agenda rather than approving or disapproving a solution. Thus, the hope is to create higher profiles to the problems identified by students so that legislative bodies might consider solutions. Most important, all of this gives students the opportunity to learn about democracy by practicing it rather than by just reading about it.[4]

The agenda-setting model used to develop discourse around issues and subsequent public policy has an exponential capability—it can be used to increase participation from a small group of students to larger and larger groups as they move toward a consensus political agenda. Therefore, it can be used with small classes of fewer than 30 students or larger lecture classes of 500 or more students. The following section details how this process works.

The Agenda-Building Process

Phase I: Building a Consensus Agenda (Class Level)

This section illustrates how to implement the model throughout a course and an institution. The suggestions here are not the only methods for implementation. Faculty can easily add or subtract from the activities. However, the following description illustrates how the model can be used in an individual class, a school, or a group of schools or classes. Many faculty have incorporated this model more extensively, with an entire class devoted to issue championing and political empowerment, whereas others have had their classes participate on a much smaller scale.

In the first two weeks of class, students brainstorm. They are asked to discuss what they think are the most pressing concerns facing their communities, their country, and the world. At first, this discussion is allowed to develop without any parameters. The students can talk about a wide range of issues; for example, from issues affecting their cities that may only require individuals engaging their city council or school board to those so global in scope that no single country could solve them unilaterally, such as global climate change. The conversation can begin in class or online; however, at some point in this process students should meet face-to-face in small groups of three to five students to discuss and debate what they perceive as the most important concern.

The initial phase serves two functions. The first is to get students to learn about each other, but, more important, it's to get students to engage in and begin to take ownership of the activities that drive the lessons for the class. Since some students may begin to overpower the discussion, procedures and voting rules are decided upon to ensure that all students have a voice. Each group selects one person as a secretary to take notes and another as the group reporter to either put the issues on the board or to speak before the class in a semiformal process.[5]

Initial classroom groups are randomly determined to prevent cliques and improve overall discussion. One simple way of dividing students is to give each student a number that corresponds to a group placement, keeping workability in mind. For instance, in a class that has 20 students, an instructor will want to keep the groups small enough for discussion but large enough to allow sharing of diverse viewpoints. These initial groups are given limited time in class to meet and begin discussing which issues they think are the most important.

Students are asked during this phase to determine the most pressing concern facing their communities (students determine their own definition of community), the United States, and the world. Each group is allowed to choose no more than three issues from each category during this first phase. The initial classroom time allotted for this first discussion can be as little as 15 minutes and rarely exceeds 30 minutes. The time given usually depends upon the instructor's goals for the semester and whether or not the project is a major or minor component of the course.[6]

Next, the list from each group is put on the board, and duplicates are eliminated. With large lecture classes or classes with more than 40 students, faculty can modify the number of issues allowed for each group as well as the reporting method. For example, if each group has up to nine issues, the board could easily be filled with more than 30 different issues. However, depending on the nature of the political times, there are usually certain issues that most groups have on their list. For instance, in hard economic times, jobs and employment are top concerns in almost every group. Overall, the issues initially developed represent the students' concerns and the challenges they face. Students from high crime areas see crime and drugs as critical concerns, whereas students who do not have health care or whose parents do not have health care see this issue as a top concern.

The instructor asks students to write down what they see at this point as the most pressing issue; that is, their first choice of an issue to solve, which would be their first choice to champion. Next, students are asked on the count of three to shout their concerns. Everyone shouts simultaneously. Then, the instructor asks the students, "What was that?" If no one answers with "noise," the instructor announces, "That was noise." The instructor follows this exercise by picking one of the issues on the board and asking the students on the count of three to say the issue aloud. "What was that?" the instructor asks again, and the answer is, "Voice!" The point is that if political elites are hearing a unified message as to what is most important, then they can act accordingly. If political elites are hearing that everything is important, then they may not take up a given concern. The difference between "noise" and "voice" is explained as the reason to narrow the students' agenda to the most pressing concerns so that the students have a more effective political voice. Students take this simple lesson with them as they are given the assignment of exploring the issues perceived in their communities as "most pressing."

The first basic homework assignment is for students to talk to their families, friends, and neighbors about issues they feel are the most pressing. This allows students to narrow their focus based on what they see around them. Students are encouraged to perform some basic research by finding an article or two that speaks to the one concern they think they might want to champion. The issue that the students begin with may or may not become their "champion" issue.[7] However, it is among the concerns for which they want to see effective public policy solutions developed. If the course is using an online discussion board, students can continue their discussion between classes and begin to articulate which issue(s) they think should be on the class agenda. The point here is to teach students the importance of having an effective argument when championing an issue. Students who have a compelling argument with a narrative, data, or both can be more effective in persuading other students to support their concern.[8]

The following week,[9] students are again randomly divided into groups. However, this time they work from a stronger foundation in that they have explored their concerns with their families, friends, and neighbors and have possibly found information and data that highlight a particular concern they think they may want to champion. If the class is using a course management system, such as Blackboard™, Moodle™, or Educator™, then the instructor can require students to post their comments and sources in the discussion board area. This encourages the discussion to become more focused as the process continues.[10] In class, students are given another 15 minutes or so in the new group to discuss, debate, and decide the issue(s) they feel should be on the agenda. This time each group is asked to narrow its lists to no more than three issues. The reporter puts the issues on the board and, after the duplicates are eliminated, the class voting commences.

The Class Vote. The number of issues placed on the agenda and the voting rules (how many votes each student can cast for the class agenda) are established at this time. Students can decide how many votes each student gets; however, each student should get no more votes than the number of issues the class decides to include on its overall class agenda. Since the final National Student Political Issues Agenda is limited to 10 issues, the recommendation for a given class is to have fewer than seven issues. The limited number allows students to work in groups and focus on demand mechanisms that can promote their issues either on the political agenda or raise them higher on the list of important issues already being discussed. A quick way of deciding the number of issues on the class agenda is to start the voting with seven and go down to one. The number that receives the most votes becomes the limit for the class. Issues that clearly are related should be combined.[11] For instance, students might have two separate issues—one general, like crime, and another more specific, like gun violence. If the issues are combined, there might be enough votes for this issue to make it onto the class agenda. The use of parliamentary procedure for combination of issues and voting is advised.

Phase II: Issue Groups, Coalition Building, and Issue Championing

Once the final class agenda is decided, the students break into groups based on the issue they wish to champion. In some cases, students do not want to work on any of the issues on the class agenda, and they decide to either continue with their preferred issue alone or join with other students on an issue that did not receive enough votes to make it onto the class agenda. Although this occurrence is rare, students should be allowed to champion "their" issue, as this option gives them a greater stake in the process. Further, even though their class does not have this issue on the agenda, other classes might. There also may be additional opportunities throughout the semester to get their issues onto the final school, state, or national student issues agenda, depending on the extent to which faculty have incorporated the model into the course. Alternatively, students can work on promoting their concerns to the public through various mechanisms such as social media, letter writing campaigns, or letters to the editor.[12]

These issue-based groups become the permanent groups that students work in throughout the semester, which is why students are encouraged to join one of the groups. If they do not, the students working autonomously from a class group will have more independent research or asynchronous group activity with members who not part of their particular class. Even though the class groups are important, they are not essential.[13]

The job of the issue groups is to clearly and effectively define the issue (problem) and develop a strategy that builds a coalition beyond the class. The skills of issue definition and coalition building can provide students with the ability to effectively articulate a concern and build a political coalition around it. These two items should be discussed briefly on the day on which the issue groups are created so that students immediately know their goals and can act strategically when working in the group.

Note that smaller groups usually can work more quickly than a large group or an entire class. If a group or groups are too large, students can break into subareas. For instance, on an agenda in the fall 2008 semester, several classes placed the economy at the top of their lists of concerns. One class put the economy as its only concern. However, after trying to work collaboratively as a class, a number of items appeared as logical subdivisions. Thus, to champion their concern and best articulate its various nuances, the class broke into four subgroups: job creation, financial reform, outsourcing of jobs, and creating a climate of innovation. The four groups each then defined the overarching concern of the economy from a more specific perspective. The groups worked in synergy to affect the political agenda, but they also each made their own decisions on the specific language used to articulate their aspect of the issue as well as which activities they would use to champion the concern.[14]

The class groups are an effective means to get the students to work together. They also provide students with instant study groups that can snowball beyond their issue-champion strategies into activities that affect the political agenda. Students can receive course credit or extra credit for activities that champion their issue. Instructors can define which activities are acceptable and how many points are available. Activities can range from traditional mechanisms of voice such as letters to the editor and petitions drives to the development of online videos, blogs, or Facebook groups. Some instructors may require several such assignments; others may not require any.

As with nearly any class project, there will likely be some students who attempt to take advantage of their fellow group members and free ride on the work of more diligent individuals. This problem can be easily checked with written reports about each student's engagement around his or her issue and the specific political action activities personally accomplished to champion the group issue. These reports can act as a set-up, with a series of questions that drive student responses. If the class is using a course management system and instructors require groups to post among their members on a weekly basis, then the in-class discussion is supplemented, and there is a record for the instructor to review participation. If the faculty decide to use an online discussion board, then they may wish to have some specific questions that are provided weekly to drive the discussion.[15]

PHASE III: THE CONVENTION

Faculty can have their students participate in the National Student Political Issues Conventions independent of other agenda-building activities, or they may decide to develop their classes around the agenda-building activities and have the convention as a pivotal crescendo[16] to illustrate the capacity of engagement in the political process and provide lessons on how to build a stronger coalition beyond class or school. The National Student Political Issues Convention was originally designed to provide the experience of a real political convention for students who had never directly participated in the dynamics of a political process. The conventions focus on determining a political issue agenda, presenting concerns through formal workshops, and attaining a response from political elites to the students' concerns.

If students have been developing an agenda in their classes, the goal by the time of the convention is to allow them to take their newly learned political tools to the convention and enable them to relate their concerns to strangers who may or may not be sympathetic to their issues. If the students are experiencing their first political engagement at the convention, then it acts as a kick-off to their learning and can be reflected upon as a singular active-learning experience that relates to the course. These conventions as presently designed are flexible instruments that can be used for many purposes, but, ultimately, they are meant to show students that they have political power and can be heard.

The basic elements of the National Student Political Issues Conventions are: 1) to provide a venue for students to articulate their concerns and get their concerns on the political issues agenda and 2) to have elected officials and candidates for public office present who will engage the students and take the student agenda as a priority for considering public policy solutions to these concerns. Elected officials are asked to place these issues on their policy agendas or raise them higher on their lists of concerns. They are also asked to articulate these concerns as their policy priorities when they meet with other elites capable of shaping the political agenda and the policy formulation process. In the process, candidates and elected officials are asked what they have done or will do about these issues.[17]

Opening Plenary. The structure of the Michigan Political Agenda begins with an opening plenary, which ranges from 30 minutes to an hour. Participating students convene in an auditorium to agree to the voting rules, hear from their fellow students who will promote issues that were voted on[18] at the class level, and possibly hear a keynote address[19] from either an elected official or some other political elite who can speak to the importance of political engagement. Previous keynote speakers have included members of the US House of Representatives, such as John Dingell and John Conyers; Michigan secretary of state Terri Lynn

Land; Dearborn mayors Michael Guido and John O'Reilly; Dearborn Heights mayor Daniel Paletko; and the Reverend Jesse Jackson. Most keynotes are generally brief—roughly 10 to 20 minutes.

Since 2006, students who present their concerns formally in a series of issue workshops have provided a brief 30-second pitch at the end of the opening general session. The goals of these brief pitches are to encourage students to attend their issue workshops and to promote a specific concern. Some of these pitches include short video clips that try to appeal to students; others are statements read by students. After these presentations, students break into student-led issue workshops around issues of general concern that have been highlighted by the students prior to the convention.[20]

Easels are set up, and space is provided in the convention registration area for issue poster boards. Students are encouraged to champion their concerns through the development of these poster boards, which both inform and lobby fellow students to vote for a particular concern. Students also can bring these into the general sessions, workshops, and caucuses, or they can leave them in the registration area for other students to view during the breaks.

Issue Workshops. Students can work together or independently to develop a workshop devoted to the issue they are championing. The goals of the workshops are to educate those in attendance about the concern, discuss the various aspects of the concern, and organize those students who agree that it is a champion concern to lobby their friends and others to vote for it during the caucus sessions. The issue voting occurs after the concurrent workshops in the voting caucus sessions. There are usually two to three sets of concurrent workshops, followed by voting caucus sessions. This system allows students to attend multiple issue workshops or one in addition to the workshop in which they are presenting.

Workshops are usually designed to be flexible because some draw little attention, whereas others are so well attended that the rooms overflow. Faculty often can predict which workshop themes are likely draws and make sure that they are held in rooms with adequate space. Students should be prepared to address audiences of various sizes so that a workshop's goals are achieved. Smaller attendance does not necessarily mean that a workshop is less effective, as smaller groups can be managed more easily to get the students in attendance to champion the concern during the voting. Generally the time devoted to each set of workshops ranges from 40 minutes to an hour.[21]

Voting Caucus.[22] Students are arbitrarily assigned to a voting caucus room when they register before the opening session.[23] The voting caucus is where the initial convention agenda is formed.[24] Each has up to 30 students in attendance and a caucus facilitator and a recorder/reporter. The students chosen for these positions run the voting caucus. Although faculty and graduate students have participated as caucus facilitators, the goal is to make as much of the convention student-led and coordinated as possible. Therefore, training a group of students to run the caucus voting is the norm.

An issue must receive one nomination and two seconds from students in a particular caucus to be placed on the board for voting consideration. Each student can make only one nomination for an issue; however, students can second as many issues as they want. Once an issue is nominated and seconded twice, it is added to the list for consideration. Students have three votes that they can cast for an issue(s); plural voting is usually accepted at the opening plenary. A recorder writes down and makes two copies of the list of issues and the number of votes that each student casts for the issue(s). The recorder presents one of the two copies to the tally person[25] at the final convention, and the other list goes to the caucus reporter for the reading of the Report of Caucus Vote in the final plenary session.

Final Plenary Session: Report of Caucus Vote, Vote of Final Agenda, and Elected Official Response to Agenda. The final plenary session generally lasts between 45 minutes and an hour. The students reconvene in the auditorium for the report of the voting, the final vote on the convention agenda, and the response from invited elected officials to the agenda. The student reporter from each voting caucus takes the stage and reports the list of issues and the votes for his or her caucus. The tally person simultaneously counts the caucus votes in a manner that allows all convention participants to see them. Once the list of all the issues that received votes in the caucuses is presented by the student reporters, the issues are sorted from the highest to lowest vote total. The convention chair[26] reads the top seven issues.[27]

The chair next asks for a motion and a second to accept the top seven issues as the convention agenda. Once the motion is made and seconded, discussion can begin. Students use parliamentary procedure to make recommendations on whether to keep the list as it is or modify it. For instance, the chair may have two issues that are directly related, such as combining the two issues of global warming and climate change, but a recommendation and a vote is required to combine them into a single issue, "global warming and climate change." Combining issues can allow for another issue that was not in the top seven votes to make it onto the convention agenda. Similarly, the same parliamentary procedures can be used to modify issue language, possibly for clarification or just for style, such as changing "jobs" to "employment."

After all modifications are made, the convention agenda is voted on formally by the entire plenary. This agenda concludes the convention voting. The chair then invites participating elected officials to address the convention by responding to the student issues agenda, commenting on the convention generally, and making other pertinent comments about political participation.

Political elites who represent the electoral areas that the students are from and the college hosting the convention are invited to participate. Often a mix of elected officials from various elected bodies is invited to ensure that the agenda is heard by those various levels of government.

Convention Models

National Student Political Issues Conventions are designed to engage students politically, inspire their continued civic involvement, and help them to relate actual political engagement with their curriculum. To achieve these goals, educators need a degree of flexibility to meet various conditions, including regional political differences, the election calendar, and overall political climates.

Flexibility in the structure of the conventions is illustrated with the diversity of Student Conventions in Michigan and Illinois. Michigan Student Political Issues Conventions have incorporated several variations to help keep the activity relevant to the political conditions and the election calendar. For instance, during presidential and gubernatorial election years, the convention focuses heavily on the campaigns. These conventions have been held earlier in the semester, either in late September or early October, to also use them for both voter registration and to inspire students to become involved for the remainder of the campaign season.[28]

One drawback to the earlier date, however, is that time for students to develop issue workshops is limited to about four to six weeks from the start of a course. Therefore, fewer students are ready for the challenge of organizing workshops. To accommodate fewer workshops while keeping the issue discussion vibrant, there is often a substitution of one of the two workshop sessions with a panel discussion of elected officials. The panel discussion focuses on an important and timely political or public policy issue. For instance, the 2010 convention had a panel that focused on the impact of the housing crises on regional and local budgets. Representatives from the state, county, and local municipalities were included, with a particular focus on the impact of both property tax revenue losses and a decrease in state revenue sharing. The officials discussed mechanisms to cut costs, maintain services, and stabilize budgets.

Careful selection of the keynote speaker ensures that the conventions respond to the political climate. In the fall of 2011, acrimony was prevalent in the political discourse at every level. The tensions of partisan politics had escalated, and focusing on the utility of political participation for civil society required setting a tone of civility from the beginning. To emphasize civility, the convention chair opened the Veterans Day Convention by noting the importance of honoring the country's veterans for their service as a reminder that service in a democracy comes in many forms and that even though many may not have been called to military service, all are called to participate in strengthening civil society. Former US representative Bart Stupak (D-MI) added an inspirational keynote that emphasized the role that students could play in civil society, the importance of civil discourse, and a reminder that leadership is not about taking sides, but about working together to develop solutions that serve society.

In Chicago, issue conventions have been timed to occur on the same day or in the same week as the Michigan convention so that something like a true National Student Issues Agenda could be developed over time, as more universities and colleges join the convention effort. Chicago conventions have included students from the University of Illinois at Chicago's (UIC) American government and Chicago politics classes, who are required to attend. However, the conventions also are open to students in other political science classes and other students in the university who wish to attend. Between 200 and 400 students participate.

Unlike the longer Michigan process, the Chicago conventions are held for only a half-day and do not involve separate issue workshops or study. They begin with students divided randomly into separate discussion groups for about an hour. Students then reconvene in a general plenary to vote on five key issues to present to public officials and candidates for office. Each convention ends in a session in which a variety of public officials and candidates from both parties respond to the Issues Agenda students present to them.

Participation in the National Student Political Issues Convention requires the faculty and teaching assistants assigned to selected courses to coordinate the convention and take attendance. In Chicago, the UIC Department of Political Science provides logistical support in reserving the room and getting the political officials to attend. The political science faculty at Henry Ford Community College (HFCC) tally the national agenda and report the outcomes to everyone who participates. Regardless of whether the Chicago or Michigan model is used, it is hoped that students get to practice democracy in a way that classroom lectures cannot achieve.

Participating in and Using the Agenda Setting Model with Any Class at Any Institution

Each fall semester, one week is designated as National Student Political Issues Week.[29] Any class or school wishing to develop a student political agenda can do so and send the results to Henry Ford Community College for inclusion in the tally for the National Student Issues Agenda. The results are based on the number of votes received for each issue. Individual classes, colleges, or multiple colleges and universities can develop their own agendas through either a convention or any other process that allows students to vote in a fair and transparent manner. Each fall the Civic Action Project at HFCC provides recommended rules for voting and procedures for submitting results.[30]

If faculty wish to participate in the National Student Political Issues Week or one of the regional conventions, there are several options.[31] If a regional convention is being held nearby, then one may send one's students to this convention. HFCC and UIC regularly welcome students from multiple institutions to their regional conventions.

However, if no convention is being held nearby, then an instructor can develop a class agenda, a college agenda, or a regional convention and submit the results directly to HFCC's Civic Action Project.[32] This option allows students to be a part of something larger than their own classes and institutions and can be a means of motivating students.

Conclusion

The Carnegie Foundation's Political Engagement study concluded that the face-to-face interaction that students experience in active-learning programs can provide a rich learning opportunity and teach skills and a sense of empowerment and efficacy often not emphasized in a traditional learning environment, such as having to articulate their positions on the spot. This Carnegie study was conducted using a preintervention-postintervention survey of students participating in various civic engagement projects, and included qualitative materials from randomly chosen and faculty-selected student interviews and further qualitative materials gathered through faculty interviews and two faculty focus group sessions. This study pointed out numerous noteworthy results, including that nearly 95% of the students surveyed felt involved in their projects and that "these courses or programs have significant effects on political engagement: knowledge, skill, motivation, and participation."[33] The students appreciated interacting on issues with each other as opposed to always having the professor serve as the moderator for the discourse.

The evaluation research of the conventions and the agenda-setting model thus far have consistently indicated increases in engagement and the likelihood for future participation among students who have used the model and participated in the conventions. One evaluation study was a random survey of 75 of the 403 students who participated in the 2004 Michigan Student Political Issues Convention, compared with a control group of 30 students who were also enrolled in the fall 2004 semester in an introductory American government course that did not participate in the convention. This study indicated that students who participated in the 2004 convention reported increased levels of voting to 86.5%, which is approximately 10% higher than the national results of college students ages 18 to 24, as reported by Niemi and Hanmer.[34]

Furthermore, there was a statistically significant difference in the positive responses to the statement: "I think I will be active in politics in the future"[35] between students who participated in the convention and the American government students in the nonparticipating control group. Responses from the 2010 Michigan Convention participant self-evaluations indicated that 83.3% of participants strongly agree or agree with the statement: "I feel a part of the American political process while attending this Convention." Another 56.7% strongly agreed, and 39.7% agreed with the statement: "I think that participating in politics is something that is important." In addition, 83.2% strongly agreed or agreed with the statement: "I am excited about the upcoming election."

The National Student Issues Conventions add a level of relevancy to political science courses. As students in Dick Simpson's Chicago's Future course indicated, this active-learning model provided a real experience not seen in his other political science courses.[36] This mechanism builds student self-confidence and a sense of efficacy. It empowers them to act effectively in their own self-interest and in the community interest in the future, which is facilitated by the inclusion of interaction with policy makers who can address their concerns and enact changes.

Moreover, the faculty surveyed and the focus group evaluations indicated that faculty have noticed observable behavioral responses to the civic action activities. Students tend to be more attentive, engaged, and eager to find solutions to their own concerns. The postconvention student self-evaluations consistently reflect that students have found that their courses exceed their expectations and that the convention and the agenda-building activities provide them with a useful context for learning the information presented in their textbooks. They also help them to understand their role as citizens in a democratic society.

Overall, the number of faculty and students participating in the Michigan and Chicago conventions continues to grow. The 2010 and 2011 Michigan Student Political Issues Convention included 685 and 697 student participants, respectively, from 10 higher education institutions throughout southeast Michigan. The Chicago Student Political Issues Convention has grown from fewer than 200 attendees to conventions with more than 400 student participants. Likewise, the number of faculty who consistently decide to have their classes participate in the Michigan Convention continues to grow, and these faculty indicate that these conventions are a valuable tool to motivate their students. It is hoped that this model can be expanded to more states and more higher education institutions as a way to foster the next generation of citizens who want to be civically engaged and who have the skills and confidence to effectively participate in American democracy.

Documenting the Success of Classroom-Based Voter Registration Efforts: Classroom Presentations Trump Technology

13

By Elizabeth A. Bennion and David W. Nickerson

This chapter reports the results of a series of field experiments carried out on 37 college campuses and designed to assess the effectiveness of various approaches to voter registration. The authors of this chapter randomly assigned students to different voter registration treatments. By using a nationwide voter file to compare the registration rates of the randomly assigned treatment and control groups, the authors were able to determine the most efficient and effective ways for colleges to register students to vote. Classroom-based registration is proven effective at both registering and mobilizing voters.

Political scientists have uncovered a number of factors that correspond with low rates of voter turnout. Those who are young,[1] move frequently,[2] and—perhaps not surprisingly—have no past history of turnout[3] and are disinterested in politics[4] are less likely to vote. College students fit these categories more closely than other demographic groups. Several related factors may contribute to young people's relative lack of political engagement. Young people are less likely than older individuals to follow political news stories, read a daily newspaper, or watch the news.[5] In addition, although many young people turn to the Internet for information, they often do not read online newspapers or news magazines. As a result, they are less likely than older individuals to demonstrate a strong knowledge of public affairs. Young people also are less likely to vote or to believe that voting is a civic duty.[6]

Members of Congress have increasingly argued that colleges and universities should be preparing students for lives as active citizens, and they have legislated accordingly. A 1998 amendment to the Higher Education Act requires colleges and universities to celebrate Constitution Day each September. It also requires institutions of higher learning to obtain voter registration forms before the local registration deadline and distribute them to students enrolled in all degree or certificate programs.[7] Those institutions that fail to comply with the provision could jeopardize their federal student aid funding.

Many universities and teacher-scholars have decided to turn this federal mandate into an opportunity. Scholars with the Carnegie Foundation for the Advancement of Teaching, for example, have promoted civic engagement on college campuses by publishing such books as *Educating for Citizenship: Preparing Undergraduate for Lives of Moral and Civic Responsibility*[8] and *Educating for Democracy: Preparing Undergraduates for Responsible Political Engagement.*[9] Professional associations also have taken up this mission. The American Political Science Association (APSA) created the Standing Committee on Civic Education and Engagement to "articulate a political science of citizenship." The committee's September 2004 report, "Democracy at Risk: Renewing a Political Science of Citizenship,"[10] targeted a broad audience of citizens, public officials, journalists, policy makers, and social scientists—in short, "everyone interested in democracy." Other associations have reached across the disciplines to promote civic knowledge, skills, and participation among US college students. The American Association of State Colleges and Universities (AASCU) partnered with the *New York Times* and AASCU member campuses to create the American Democracy Project in 2003.[11] The goal was to follow the advice presented in *Educating for Citizenship* while creating a national movement designed to promote civic and political engagement among students enrolled in public colleges and universities.

In the United States, even the most minimal level of political participation, voting, requires that citizens add themselves to the voter rolls by learning how, when, and where to register, and they must take the time to complete a registration form each time they relocate. Political scientists have a great deal to learn about the best way to get people to take this critical step. The difficulty is blending theory and practice in applying the methodology of social science to the practice of voter registration. Most academics have little experience in actually organizing voter registration campaigns. Meanwhile, colleges and universities engage in a broad range of activities to register students to vote, yet there is little effort to rigorously evaluate these efforts and no consensus on which techniques are most effective. This study moves the evaluation of such efforts from hearsay and anecdotes to scientific assessment. It serves as a model assessment project that can be replicated to test a wide range of civic engagement efforts at colleges and universities both nationally and internationally.

This study explores several research questions: What is the most effective way for colleges and universities to register their students to vote? What is the most cost-effective way to register students to vote? Should administrators and faculty register students themselves or train students to register their peers? College campuses provide excellent testing grounds to measure the effectiveness of different approaches to voter registration among low-turnout demographics. AASCU campuses provide particularly appropriate settings for this research because they generally are affordable and noncompetitive, catering to first-generation college students, historically disenfranchised groups, and students from middle- and low-income families. Unlike Research 1, Ivy League, and private liberal arts colleges, students at AASCU institutions reflect a broad range of demographics, including those most associated with low levels of political participation.

This chapter reports the findings of randomized field experiments on 37 college campuses (see Table 13-1 for a complete list) and demonstrates that face-to-face registration in college classrooms is an effective way to get students registered to vote, whereas campus mail, direct mail, and email are ineffective. The person making the registration appeal is less important than the registration technique employed. Face-to-face registration efforts in the classroom are highly effective, whether delivered by a faculty member or a fellow student. Unlike other chapters in this section of the book, the conclusions do not rely on a specific class, but rather demonstrate another way in which a classroom-based activity can increase students' civic and political engagement.

Previous Field Experiments on Civic Engagement

The number of academic studies of voter mobilization campaigns has grown significantly since 2002; however, there is very little published about voter registration campaigns. The topic is important because meaningful information about the best way to mobilize voters cannot be provided if it is not known how to get them to take the first step of adding themselves to the voter rolls. Prior work provides a great deal of information about how to get registered voters to the polls, but there is less information on how to get people registered in the first place.

Recent academic field experiments have used random assignment to test the effectiveness of different voter mobilization strategies by measuring the relative effectiveness of direct mail versus phone calls versus door-to-door canvassing.[12] The voter mobilization literature has grown increasingly sophisticated, and several scholars have tested the effect of delivering different types of get-out-the-vote messages.[13] Most recently, scholars have studied the effects of social pressure, including researcher surveillance and publicizing neighborhood voting records.[14]

Another line of studies has explored the effect of the message and the messenger on the success of voter mobilization campaigns. David Nickerson tested the relative effectiveness of professional versus volunteer phone banks.[15] Melissa Michelson tested the relative effectiveness of Latino versus non-Latino canvassers in Hispanic neighborhoods.[16] Other scholars have tested to see if specific messages and techniques work differently for different populations, including Latinos,[17] Asian Americans,[18] and Indian Americans.[19] There even has been some attention given to the degree to which canvassing effects are passed on to other voters living in the same household.[20]

Despite this growth in the field experiment literature studying the effects of various strategies to mobilize registered voters, there is still very little known about the best way to get people on the registration rolls. Recent studies have demonstrated that voting is a habit.[21] Voters who have voted regularly in the past are more likely to vote in the future. However, in most states, citizens cannot vote on Election Day if they are not already on the voter rolls. For this reason, scholars concerned with voting behavior, activists concerned with civic engagement, and politicians concerned with maximizing the participation of would-be supporters must do more to understand which techniques are most effective in getting prospective voters registered. A handful of scholars have begun to study this question using field experiments.[22] By randomly assigning students to specific treatments, field experiments allow scholars to test the actual effects of specific approaches under real-world conditions. Unlike most of the work published in the emerging literature on civic engagement pedagogy, this approach avoids the pitfalls of self-reporting (including inaccurate recall and misrepresentation) that challenge survey research.[23] In addition, it allows scholars to measure the behavioral effects of the intervention directly, rather than relying on students' self-reports about future behavior.

The Experimental Approach

People have different underlying propensities to vote.[24] Those who are more interested in politics or feel a stronger sense of civic duty are more likely to register and vote than people who are disengaged from the political process. This dynamic leads to a situation in which most of the people interested in voting are already registered;[25] that is, people who have selected to register are not comparable to people who have chosen not to register. This self-selection process forces observational studies of civic participation to make unverifiable assumptions that limit the inferences that can be drawn.

When feasible, experiments offer a solution to selection effects by randomly assigning the treatment of interest. Experiments generally require a well-defined subject population that can be tracked, a treatment that can be randomized and administered to the correct person, and the ability to measure the outcome of interest for both the treatment and control groups. Voter mobilization experiments fit these requirements by focusing on registered voters, of whom there is an official list that can be randomized and later updated with turnout. Unfortunately, an official list of unregistered persons does not exist. Even if one used consumer or municipal address lists of all residents, residential mobility is much higher among unregistered persons, and the reliability of such a list would be suspect.

Faced with this problem, many civic organizations evaluate their voter registration drives by the number of cards collected over the course of a campaign. For instance, ACORN touted registering 1.3 million new voters in 2008.[26] However, reports such as these overstate the effect of registration efforts for three primary reasons. First, not all of the cards collected will appear on voter rolls. Second, many of the people who completed cards were previously registered and merely updated address information.[27] Third, and most important, there is no way of knowing how many of these people would have registered another way. Many of the people approaching voter registration tables at supermarkets are likely to be politically motivated and would have found alternative means of registering. A randomly assigned control group would provide a baseline estimate of how many people would register on their own, but it is not obvious how such a control group could be constructed.

Conducting the experiments on college campuses solved the problem of defining a subject population through the use of student directories. A student directory had several notable advantages for the purposes of studying voter registration. First, the addresses should have been accurate because students registered for classes and paid tuition only a month prior to the experiment, and the administration needed correct addresses to mail grades and future bills. Second, where applicable, schools provided both home and local, or school, addresses. Since young people often maintain their parents' address as well as a school address, having both allowed subjects to be tracked more accurately. Third, 84% of the schools in the experiment provided date of birth information to facilitate an accurate match in the voter file, even if the address(es) happened to be outdated. Fourth, directories also contain accurate email addresses, which allowed for the administration of the email treatment. Finally, the directories defined the list of every subject in the experiment.

Campuses were recruited by the AASCU and its American Democracy Project (ADP) through email solicitations to member campuses. Upper-level administrators agreed in principle to participate in the experiments and appointed someone as chief contact and coordinator.[28] This coordinator was paid a small stipend, which most used to hire a student assistant. Researchers followed up with all campus contacts by email and telephone, answering questions, confirming participation, completing institutional review board (IRB) forms, and mapping out campus registration plans. Each coordinator also participated in a five-hour training session at the national ADP meeting in Utah. Coordinators who were unable to attend the training session participated in scheduled make-up sessions that used a combination of telephone and computer technology for interactive teleconferencing.

The campuses in the experiment are all public, do not have competitive enrollment processes, and generally cater to area residents. The participating students came from higher socioeconomic strata than noncollege youth, and were from diverse racial, economic, and social backgrounds. Information about the participating schools is provided in Table 13-1.

On campus, schools could opt to experiment with email, direct mail, or classroom- based registration strategies. In the end, 11 schools tested mail, 28 schools tested email, and 19 schools tested classroombased registration. Administrators presumably opted for strategies that they felt best fit the needs and capacity of their campuses. Thus, it is expected that the treatment effects reported in this study might not be the same on all college campuses.

In all the experiments, registration was ascertained by matching student directories to a nationwide voter file maintained by Catalist. Matches were made to both school and home addresses, but relied primarily on name and date of birth, which were unique identifiers in nearly all instances. As a result, the key dependent variable was measured accurately for both the treatment and control groups regardless of the county of residence.

The design of the mail and email experiments was straightforward. In the mail experiment, students in a directory were randomly assigned to the treatment or control groups. On most campuses, the treatment consisted of a packet containing

Table 13-1: Participating Universities

School	Classroom	Email	Mail	Trained	State	Enrollment	Locale
Ball State University	X	X	X	X	IN	20507	Mid–size city
Bloomsburg University	X	X	X	X	PA	8304	Urban fringe of mid–size city
California State University – Long Beach		X		X	CA	33479	Large city
California University of Pennsylvania	X				PA	6640	Urban fringe of large city
Castleton University	X			X	VT	1971	Rural
Central Missouri State University	X			X	MO	10051	Small town
College of Charleston	X	X	X		SC	11607	Mid–size city
East Central Oklahoma University	X			X	OK	4651	Small town
Eastern Kentucky University	X	X	X	X	KY	16183	Urban fringe of mid–size city
Emporia University		X		X	KS	6194	Large town
Georgia College and State University	X	X		X	GA	5531	Small town
Illinois State University		X	X		IL	20757	Mid–size city
Indiana University – Northwest	X	X		X	IN	5138	Mid–size city
Indiana – Purdue Fort Wayne		X		X	IN	11810	Mid–size city
Indiana University – Purdue University – Indianapolis			X		IN	29953	Large city
Indiana University – South Bend	X	X		X	IN	7501	Mid–size city
Middle Tennessee State University		X		X	TN	22322	Mid–size city
Millersville University		X		X	PA	7998	Urban fringe of mid–size city
Morehead State University	X	X		X	KY	9278	Small town
Pennsylvania State University – Altoona		X		X	PA	3766	Mid–size city
Salisbury University		X		X	MD	6942	Small town
State University of New York – Cortland	X	X		X	NY	7350	Small town
State University of New York – Geneseo		X		X	NY	5573	Urban fringe of mid–size city
University of Illinois – Springfield	X	X		X	IL	4396	Mid–size city
University of Memphis	X	X		X	TN	20668	Large city
University of Tennessee – Martin		X	X	X	TN	6098	Small town
University of Wisconsin – Oshkosh	X	X	X	X	WI	11532	Mid–size city
University of Wisconsin – River Falls	X	X	X	X	WI	5950	Urban fringe of large city
Washburn University			X	X	KS	7251	Mid–size city
Western Carolina University	X			X	NC	8396	Small town
Western Kentucky University		X			KY	18485	Large town

a letter of encouragement and registration card.[29] Ultimately, the mail experiment involved eight campuses and 62,028 students. The email study was similar, but students were randomly assigned to one of three conditions: a) control (no email); b) receive three emails from an administrator, such as the university president or dean of students; or c) receive three emails from a student leader—usually the student body president. The emails were brief, explaining why registration is important and providing a link to the Rock the Vote online registration tool.[30] Administrators were very eager to test the effectiveness of email for boosting voter registration, because this method is highly cost effective. As a result, the experiment involved 26 campuses and 249,384 students. In both experiments, the student was the unit of randomization and analysis.[31]

The classroom-based registration experiment was more difficult to implement and required several steps. Professors first had to be recruited to participate in the experiment, and most did not respond to requests to take part.[32] Several did not agree to participate because they objected to the control group. The set of professors who ultimately signed up covered a broad range of disciplines and levels of classes. It is unlikely that the participating classrooms were wholly representative of classes on the campus, but there was no obvious pattern regarding participation.

Second, the classes needed to be randomly assigned to one of three conditions: a) control, which received no registration outreach; b) registered by the professor, in which an assistant delivered registration cards to professors at the beginning of class and returned at the end of the session to collect the completed cards; or c) registered by a student, in which the professor typically allowed the student assistant to come in at the end or beginning of class to give a brief presentation and pass around registration cards to be completed. Professors had a great deal of latitude as to what they said surrounding registration. A sample script was provided to project coordinators on each campus,[33] but each campus, peer, and professor customized these presentations.[34]

Third, a solution to strictures imposed by the Family Educational Rights and Privacy Act (FERPA) had to be found. FERPA forbids universities from disclosing the courses in which a student is currently enrolled. Working with the legal department of many universities, it was agreed that courses would be provided a meaningless code associated with treatment assignments. These codes were then appended to an institution's student directory. This strategy allowed the researcher to know the assignment and unit of randomization without knowing the specific class taken by a student. In the end, 14 of the 19 schools provided such codes. The remaining five schools appended the treatment assignment but provided no course code.

Knowing the unit of randomization is important because it is possible that students taking a particular course share similar civic participation propensities. For instance, early morning courses may be more appealing to people with afternoon jobs, or students taking political science courses may receive other pressures to register to vote. As a result, the analysis needed to cluster the standard errors on the classroom—the unit of randomization.[35] On average, the clustered standard errors were 24% larger than in a naïve analysis that treated all students as independent observations. For the five schools that did not provide course codes, the standard errors provided by a naïve analysis that treated all students as independent observations were multiplied by 130% to conservatively adjust the standard errors. The next section reports the results from each experiment.

Results

Tables 13-2 through 13-4 report the results of the mail, email, and classroom registration experiments, respectively. The first columns report the effect of each treatment and its associated standard error. The column named "Constant" reports the baseline registration rate among the control group.

Before analyzing the experiments, it is interesting to consider the range of registration rates across schools. The average school had 59% of the control group register. Most of the schools fell narrowly within those parameters (10th percentile = 51% and 90th percentile = 68%).[36] According to the 2006 Current Population Survey (CPS), 78% of citizens 18 years of age or older in the United States were registered to vote, so these figures are below the national average. Only 62% of the eligible students in the 2006 CPS sample reported being registered to vote, so the schools involved in the experiment are fairly representative of the broader student body.

Table 13-2 reports the results from the direct mail experiment. In total, nine campuses participated in this experiment. The University of Wisconsin, River Falls, split its sample into three separate experiments. Students who lived on campus were mailed on campus. Students without a campus address were mailed registration forms to their home address. Since voting laws are slightly different in Minnesota and Wisconsin (the River Falls campus is near the Minnesota border and a number of its students are Minnesota residents), the particular forms mailed depended on the state of residence. The precise point estimate differs from school to school, but none of the mailing efforts at any of the schools significantly boosted registration. Each individual experiment is not very informative, but pooling across the experiments allowed for gains in precision. The ultimate estimate was that mailing decreased registration rates by -0.1 percentage points (s.e. = 0.4). That is, registration did not appear to increase at all when schools delivered letters with registration materials to students at their campus or home addresses. With 62,028 subjects, the experiments are sufficiently precise to claim that any increase in registration from these mail-based registration efforts is unlikely to be larger than 0.7 percentage points (i.e., seven registrants per 1,000 cards).

The picture was very similar for email encouraging registration (see Table 13-3). At the typical school, 4% of the students who were sent an email clicked through to the registration website, so there is good reason to believe that the email was read and acted upon. However, this activity does not appear to have increased voter registration rates. Focusing on emails sent by university administrators, only one of the 25 schools approached a statistically significant increase in voter regis-

Table 13-2: Results from Mail Registration Experiments

School	Mail Effect	Constant	Observations	Type
Ball State University	0.011 0.013	0.336 0.009	5656	Campus
Bloomsburg University of Pennsylvania	-0.02 0.018	0.618 0.012	3064	Campus
College of Charleston	-0.009 0.019	0.574 0.014	2593	Campus
Eastern Kentucky University	0.022 0.015	0.674 0.01	3970	Campus
Illinois State University	-0.013 0.011	0.327 0.008	6860	Campus
Indiana University–Purdue University, Indianapolis	0.004 0.006	0.637 0.004	25694	Home
University of Tennessee, Martin	0.004 0.023	0.668 0.016	1637	Campus
University of Wisconsin, Oshkosh	-0.009 0.009	0.638 0.007	10813	Home
University of Wisconsin, River Falls	0.021 0.034	0.565 0.023	861	Campus
University of Wisconsin, River Falls	-0.039 0.053	0.566 0.038	361	Home MN
University of Wisconsin, River Falls	-0.05 0.044	0.599 0.03	519	Home WI
Pooled	-0.001 0.004		62028	

Note: Top number reports the coefficient, bottom number the associated standard error. Constant reports registration rates among the control group. Pooled results calculated using random effects estimator.

tration rates. This result was likely due to sampling, since another school appears to have decreased voter registration by an equal amount and the other schools range around zero. Pooling all of the results from the administrative emails, the estimate is that receiving the three emails from an administrator lowered registration rates by 0.1 percentage point (s.e. = 0.2). The result was similar for the emails sent by peers. Two of the 20 schools appear to be success stories, but the uncertainty surrounding each estimate never approaches statistical significance. Pooled, the estimate was that receiving an email from a student leader decreased registration rates by 0.4 percentage points (s.e. = 0.2). The estimate did not quite achieve statistical significance, but it was extremely close. At the very least, these results suggest that email is not an effective tool for registering college students to vote—even with well-designed online voter registration tools.

If mail and email appear ineffective at increasing rates of voter registration, classroom presentations were a stark contrast. Table 13-4 presents the results from

Table 13-3: Results from Email Registration Experiments

School	Administrator	Peer	Constant	Observations	Emails Sent
Ball State University	0 0.008		0.531 0.005	17343	3 / 0
Bloomsburg University	-0.015 0.013	-0.01 0.013	0.653 0.008	8043	1 / 2
California State University, Long Beach	0.003 0.006	-0.007 0.006	0.785 0.003	32660	3/3
College of Charleston	-0.024 0.012	-0.022 0.012	0.635 0.007	9612	3 / 2
Eastern Kentucky University	-0.005 0.009	-0.012 0.009	0.735 0.005	15504	2/2
Emporia University	-0.023 0.014	-0.025 0.014	0.742 0.008	6102	3 / 3
Georgia College and State University	0.005 0.015	0.005 0.015	0.704 0.008	5895	3/3
Illinois State University	0.015 0.008	-0.004 0.008	0.384 0.005	20049	3 / 3
Indiana University– Purdue University, Fort Wayne	0 0.028		0.389 0.016	1754	3 / 0
Indiana University, Northwest	-0.007 0.017		0.635 0.01	4836	2 / 0
Indiana University, South Bend	0.004 0.015		0.637 0.009	6379	3 / 0
University of Memphis	-0.005 0.008	-0.004 0.008	0.626 0.005	19885	2 / 0
Millersville University	0.012 0.014	-0.005 0.014	0.628 0.008	7023	3 / 3
Morehead State University	-0.004 0.012		0.722 0.007	8043	1 / 0
Middle Tennessee State University	-0.001 0.008	0.002 0.008	0.642 0.005	22248	1 / 1
Pennsylvania State University, Altoona	-0.007 0.019	0.006 0.019	0.509 0.011	4070	1 / 1
Salisbury University	0.007 0.013	0.013 0.013	0.684 0.008	7190	1 / 2
State University of New York, Cortland	-0.026 0.031	-0.021 0.031	0.647 0.018	1484	3 / 3
State University of New York, Geneseo	0.003 0.015	-0.016 0.015	0.789 0.009	4236	3 / 3
University of Illinois, Springfield	-0.003 0.02	0.01 0.02	0.637 0.011	3572	2 / 2

University of Tennessee, Martin	-0.015 0.014	-0.004 0.014	0.642 0.008	6863	1 / 1
University of Wisconsin, Oshkosh	0.001 0.011	0.005 0.011	0.63 0.006	11026	1 / 2
University of Wisconsin, River Falls	0.02 0.029	0.053 0.029	0.549 0.017	1762	3 / 3
Washburn University	0.009 0.014	0.023 0.014	0.645 0.008	7326	2 / 2
Western Kentucky University	0.004 0.009	-0.007 0.009	0.701 0.005	16479	3 / 3
Pooled	-0.001 0.002	-0.004 0.002		249384	

Note: Top number reports the coefficient, bottom number the associated standard error. Constant reports registration rates among the control group. The number of emails sent first report emails from administrators and then emails from student leaders. Pooled results calculated using random effects estimator.

the classroom mobilization experiments for both professor and student-led presentations. In all, 12 of 17 professor-led presentations resulted in positive coefficients, and eight of these experiments cross traditional thresholds for statistical significance. Pooling all of the experiments, the estimate is that presentations by professors increased the rate of voter registration by 6.3 percentage points (s.e. = 1.3). Since the rate of voter registration in the control group was around 60%, registration rates therefore rose by 10% due to the presentation. Thus, nearly half the difference between registration rates in the general populace and among students could be addressed by classroom presentations by professors.

The picture is nearly as rosy for student-led presentations. Of the 15 schools conducting experiments on student-led classroom presentations, 11 were positive, and three experiments crossed traditional thresholds for statistical significance. Pooling the results, it was estimated that student presentations encouraging voter registration increased registration by 4.0 percentage points (s.e. = 2.0); that is, registration rates increased by 6% in treatment classrooms. Mobilization by students is only two-thirds as large as the effect from professors, but these estimates are statistically indistinguishable.

Conclusion

Democratic theorists, voting behavior scholars, US legislators, campaign professionals, civic organizations, and institutions of higher education are seeking answers about the best way to engage young people in the electoral process. Recent field experiments have shed light on the best ways to mobilize those voters who are already registered, but they largely ignore the question of how to get people on the registration rolls in the first place. People cannot vote if they are not registered to do so.

Table 13-4: Results from Classroom Registration Experiment

School	Professor	Student	Constant	Observations	Clusters
Ball State University		0.021 0.038	0.514 0.026	3020	122
Bloomsburg University	-0.045 0.108	-0.009 0.107	0.624 0.085	377	11
Castleton University	-0.052 0.047		0.55 0.032	478	37
Central Missouri State University	-0.017 0.039	-0.116 0.041	0.719 0.028	1191	45
College of Charleston	0.055 0.027	0.051 0.027	0.616 0.019	3090	209
California University of Pennsylvania	0.112 0.044		0.531 0.032	1263	60
East Central Oklahoma University	0.098 0.037	0.08 0.038	0.583 0.025	1217	97
Eastern Kentucky University	0.083 0.0689	0.032 0.0364	0.673 0.022	1280	N/A
Georgia College and State University		0.119 0.056	0.676 0.044	273	13
Indiana University, Northwest	0.049 0.052		0.585 0.029	702	N/A
Indiana University, South Bend	0.081 0.033	0.056 0.032	0.628 0.023	2160	108
University of Memphis	0.098 0.02		0.596 0.014	3643	107
Morehead State University	0.117 0.039	0.174 0.038	0.584 0.028	1101	65
State University of New York, Cortland	0.131 0.047	0.082 0.045	0.612 0.028	1328	74
University of Illinois - Springfield	0.009 0.0754	-0.046 0.0806	0.534 0.043	424	N/A
University of Wisconsin, Oshkosh	0.086 0.0351	0.057 0.0351	0.476 0.033	2069	N/A
University of Wisconsin, River Falls	-0.02 0.065	0.013 0.0468	0.559 0.025	1424	N/A
Washburn University	0.084 0.057	0.008 0.096	0.593 0.03	1434	89
Western Carolina University	-0.163 0.113	-0.233 0.145	0.545 0.075	94	4
Pooled	0.063 0.013	0.040 0.020		26568	104

Note: Top number reports the coefficient, bottom number the associated standard error. Constant reports registration rates among the control group. Pooled results calculated using random effects estimator.

This study overcame the problems of observational studies and registration card counts by working with college administrators on 37 US college campuses to randomly assign students to different voter registration treatments. In this way, this research is able to answer specific questions about the most effective and cost-effective ways for colleges to register their students to vote. The results suggest that the most effective way of accomplishing this is through face-to-face contacts, such as classroom registration campaigns.

Classroom registration is also more cost-effective than mail and email campaigns. Mail campaigns are more expensive, but much less effective. Attempts to reduce the monetary costs of postage by stuffing campus mailboxes proved ineffective. On campuses where specific boxes were provided to return these registration forms, only a handful of students took advantage of this opportunity to register to vote. Indeed, this study found no consistent results for either campus mail or home mail registration efforts.

Email is virtually free, but also completely ineffective. In fact, when combined with the results of a previous study,[37] there is reason to believe that email may actually demobilize students because it causes them to pass up more immediate and effective registration opportunities such as registration tables and classroom-based registration. Only the classroom registration campaign produced a statistically significant boost in registration rates when comparing the treatment and control groups. A follow-up study suggested that online voter registration systems can be used to increase the effectiveness of email outreach, but only slightly.[38] Face-to-face approaches should be used by colleges and universities wishing to meet legal requirements, conserve resources, and increase the student turnout on Election Day.

Should administrators and faculty register students themselves or train students to register their peers? This study found no evidence that the speaker matters. In some cases, trusted sources may affect political attitudes,[39] and demographic similarity may be sufficient to constitute a trusted source.[40] However, students at AASCU's largely commuter campuses may trust authority figures more than unfamiliar peers. Although peers were slightly more effective on some campuses, and professors more effective on others, there was no statistically significant difference in registration rates based on the identity of the person collecting the registration forms.

Public, noncompetitive, college campuses provide excellent testing grounds to measure the effectiveness of different approaches to voter registration among low-turnout youth. AASCU campuses provide particularly appropriate settings for this research because they are generally affordable and noncompetitive, catering to first-generation college students, historically disenfranchised groups, and students from middle- and low-income families. Because income and educational attainment are strong predictors of voter participation, it is important not to limit mobilization efforts to students in the most selective universities. College instructors committed to civic education and engagement should devote a few minutes of class time to voter registration. It is a prerequisite for electoral engagement, and the data are clear: classroom-based registration works.

Connecting Theory and Practice: The Iowa Caucus 14

By Arthur Sanders

As part of Drake University's commitment to encouraging "responsible global citizenship," a six-credit class was offered in the fall of 2007 in which students combined a full-time internship in an Iowa caucus organization of their choosing with a traditional class on the presidential nomination process. This was done to provide a richer class experience and enhanced internship experience and to deepen students' understanding of and commitment to the democratic process. This chapter discusses how the class worked, providing evidence for the effect that it had on students and concluding with an examination of how this class (or similar classes) might be improved. Overall, the class was largely successful in achieving its goals, serving as a blueprint for creating student experiences that enhance democratic engagement.

Colleges and universities increasingly are coming to the conclusion that part of their mission should be to promote and strengthen civil society. Civic engagement pedagogy, in this view, is designed to help students become active, informed, and empowered democratic citizens.[1] Its goal is "the development of students' civic capacities for democratic participation and responsible engagement in community life."[2] Much of the development in these areas has been shaped by efforts at service-learning, a pedagogical method that combines volunteer activity with coursework and critical reflection, which allows students to connect their volunteer activity to broader social, political, professional or ethical issues.[3] In addition, such efforts can involve other active-learning techniques, such as involvement in internships or participation in cocurricular activities.

Drake University is among the institutions of higher learning placing greater emphasis on civic engagement. In April 2006, the Faculty Senate voted to enhance the university's commitment to, in the words of its mission statement, "engaged global citizenship." Part of this increased commitment included strengthening the academic component of engaged citizenship by changing the required coursework in this part of the general education curriculum of the university from one that relied on large introductory-level classes to one that required completion of an upper-level class. In addition, each year the university has a theme around which classes, cocurricular events, and extracurricular activities are structured in the hopes of encouraging a campus-wide dialogue on the topic. For example, in the first year of the program, the 2007–2008 academic year, the theme was "Democracy and Dissent." In response to these requirements changes and with a belief in the importance of helping students to become empowered democratic citizens, I created a new class designed to encourage civic engagement.[4] The hope was that the class could help each student more effectively "function as a citizen in a democratic society."[5] In this chapter, I describe how the class was structured, explain how and why certain pedagogical tools were used, summarize what worked and what did not, and examine how effective the class was in achieving its primary objective of deepening student understanding and commitment to the democratic process.

POLS115/193: The Presidential Nomination Process/Caucus Internship

In most presidential election years since I came to Drake University in 1990, I have taught the Presidential Nomination Process.[6] The class examines the rules that structure the nominating process, the voters who decide, the role of money and media, and how candidates respond to this environment in an attempt to win their party's nomination. In recent elections, this nominating process has been affected by a phenomenon called "front-loading," which has resulted in states moving up the timing of their primaries and caucuses. Iowa and New Hampshire, the traditional first caucus and primary states, have responded by moving up the dates of their contests as well. In fact, New Hampshire has a law requiring that its date be set prior to any other presidential primary.[7] Thus, the original date of the Iowa caucus in 2008 was set for January 14, and the New Hampshire primary was scheduled eight days later, on January 22. This meant that the bulk of the campaigning would occur, if past experience was a guide, from mid-November through mid-December, with a break for the holidays and then a push in early January.

For anyone who has not experienced the Iowa caucus or the New Hampshire primary, it is hard to fully understand the intensity and breadth of the grassroots campaigning that occurs. Candidates spend enormous amounts of time campaigning everywhere in these two states. They appear in forums of various sizes, from large arenas to living rooms and small restaurants. The best symbol of the time and commitment that this type of campaign takes can be seen in the fact that in the fall of 2007, Democratic candidate Sen. Chris Dodd actually rented a house, moved his family to Des Moines, and enrolled his children in school there.[8] Therefore, by the time votes are cast, a large percentage of citizens have actually met at least one of the candidates. Furthermore, the nature of the caucuses makes having an effective on-the-ground organization crucial.

Turnout, by primary election standards, is relatively low, and all of a candidate's supporters must be at their precincts at the same time on a cold evening in

January. Thus, candidates tend to set up extensive and widespread organizations that rely on large numbers of volunteers. I knew that in 2008 there would be major contests in both parties, which would provide opportunities for students inclined to either the right or the left. So I decided to take advantage of this unique environment to create a learning experience that combined a study of the way in which presidential nominees are chosen in the United States with hands-on experience working in some capacity related to the Iowa caucus.

To turn this opportunity into an in-depth learning experience, I wanted students to do more than occasionally volunteer some time. Rather, I wanted them to have a full-time internship, so the course was set up as a six-credit class, with three credits allocated for the traditional Presidential Nomination Process class and three credits for the internship. As with any three-credit internship in the Political Science Department at Drake, I could expect the students to work 10 to 20 hours per week on their internship and hand in written assignments[9] related to that internship.[10]

The caucus was scheduled after the end of the semester. Because of this timing, students were told that they would receive an In Progress (IP) grade at the end of December when grades were submitted and that the final paper was not due until one week after the caucus. With the original caucus schedule, this due date would have been one day before the beginning of the spring semester. During the fall, however, when Florida moved up its primary, South Carolina responded by moving up its primary, which caused New Hampshire to move up its primary, leading Iowa to reschedule its caucus to January 3, 2008. Despite these changes, I kept the original due date for final paper.[11] A forum also was scheduled, in which students discussed their experiences in the caucus with the wider community as part of the engaged citizen programming on campus.[12]

The class met on Monday, Wednesday, and Friday mornings from 8:30 until 9:45. Most 75-minute classes meet only twice a week, but I scheduled the third meeting in part to allow more class time to discuss the internship experiences and partly to allow me to schedule guest speakers. Unfortunately, guest speakers were available for only three classes. When I approached campaign workers who served in various roles (field director, media relations, fund-raising, etc.) the initial response was almost always positive. Once it was made clear that all of the students in the class were already working for candidates, however, and that speaking to the class would not likely lead to votes for a particular candidate, they usually declined.[13] The class itself, then, was much like a traditional class, with assigned readings, discussion of the material, and written essays. In addition, a class blog was created using Blackboard™ Blog. Every couple of weeks, I would post a question about some aspect of the students' internships that was usually, though not always, tied to the topics being discussed in class at the time. Students were required to make at least one response to my query that reflected their internship experiences. As with any blog, comments about what others wrote and dialogue were encouraged. In addition, the more interesting comments posted were, with permission of the student authors, transferred to a page on Drake's Iowa Caucus website so that a larger potential audience could read about the students' activities.[14]

Students were responsible for arranging their own internships, as I knew that it would be easy to find such opportunities. I did provide contact information for all of the campaigns that the university's Iowa Caucus Project had received, and the information was available at that website as well. In addition, I invited representatives from all of the campaigns, both political parties, and a couple of groups with active caucus efforts to the second class of the semester. I made it clear that there were likely to only be a handful of students who did not already have internships. There were only 20 students in the class, which was the limit. Twelve of the 20 had been involved in previous campaigns, and all were interested enough in politics, elections, and the caucus to sign up for a six-credit experience. This meant that many already knew for whom they wanted to work.[15] Nevertheless, I told the campaigns that if they brought any material to give the students, it would be distributed in other classes. Potential guest speakers also knew that even if they only gained one or two interns from the class, that student would be an intern committed to 10 to 20 hours per week for the duration of the campaign. So, the turnout by campaign representatives for that class was quite good, especially on the Democratic side, which, for a variety of factors beyond the scope of this paper, was a more intense and extensive campaign than was the Republican contest.[16] All six of the major Democratic candidates sent representatives (Clinton, Obama, Edwards, Biden, Richardson, and Dodd). On the Republican side, only one candidate (Giuliani) was represented, though the Republican Party of Iowa also sent someone. One other group, Iowans for Sensible Priorities, also was represented.

The 20 students in the class ended up working in a variety of internships.[17] Initially, 18 of the 20 were working for campaigns. Eleven of these were on the Democratic side (four each for Obama and Richardson, two for Biden, and one for Edwards), and seven were on the Republican side (two each for Romney and Paul, one each for Brownbeck, Thompson, and Giuliani). When Senator Brownbeck dropped out of the race, that student moved over to an internship with the Republican Party of Iowa. One student did his internship with Drake's Iowa Caucus Project, and the other student worked for an online media organization, IowaPolitics.com, helping with its campaign coverage.

The goals of mixing these full-time internships with a traditional class on the nomination process were: 1) to enhance the class experience by bringing the practical side of campaigns into the discussion more easily; 2) to enhance the internship experience by using the class to provide a broader perspective on the campaign; and 3) to provide an opportunity for enhanced civic engagement by the students and help prepare them for a lifetime of engaged global citizenship. Now I turn to how well the experience met these goals.

Results

The students clearly felt that the internship experience enhanced the class. In the class evaluation survey, 71% (12 of the 17 who responded) of the students said that the internship aided in their understanding of the material covered in class. At one level, it was disappointing that all of the students did not feel this way, particularly with a group so deeply engaged in the campaign. On the other hand, it is not clear that reaching every student is a realistic goal, and the fact that almost three-quarters of the class was able to see these connections certainly made a difference in the class discussions and blog entries.[18] In the survey, students made comments such as:

> I was able to see things I had only read about
>
> I gained a greater respect for the complexities of the whole process, especially for a lesser known candidate.
>
> I saw in action the effort to implement theoretical tools for good campaigning.
>
> It helped me discover what tools campaigns actually utilize and how their decisions shape the outcomes of the race.

Similarly, most of the writing assignments asked the students to reflect upon the readings and other class material in light of their internships, and students consistently applied lessons from the campaign to the theories and ideas found in the readings.

The students were more divided over whether or not the class materials enhanced their internship experiences, with 53% (9) saying it did, and 47% (8) saying it did not. On the positive side, students commented:

> They put things into some perspective. They helped me identify what kind of voters we were trying to attract.
>
> It helped me understand what campaign staffers were talking about when planning strategy meetings.
>
> Some of the readings significantly enhanced my ability to understand the actions of the campaign especially ones concerning campaign finance.

On the negative side, they stated:

> It did not. The internship stands alone as a learning experience.
>
> I found it hard to relate what we were doing in class to what was going on at my internship.
>
> I didn't see very much connection between the two.

I was satisfied with the 71% who said that the internship helped the class, but this result was nonetheless disappointing. As noted later in this chapter, I believe there are changes that could have improved these student perceptions, and class discussion and blog entries did seem to highlight connections between class materials and internship experiences. Still, the fact that half of the students did not see these connections in their final reflections does raise concerns.

Two members of the class made it clear that they did not like the "class," finding all of the reading and paper writing to be "too time consuming," and they were not particularly engaged in the traditional class. In fact, each of them skipped half of the class sessions over the course of the semester (18 of 36 sessions). They were, however, very engaged in their internships and trying to help their candidates do well. For example, one of them, who worked for the Obama campaign, wrote a long final blog entry that ended by noting:

> We fought hard and we earned victory and the moment we silenced those who said we could not win was the greatest moment we will ever experience.

This immersion in the campaign at the expense of the class might account for some of the disconnect that seemed to exist in response to this question. The class discussions did seem to reflect student recognition of these connections, but these students often did not participate in the discussions, which would have made the connections less clear to them. For others, immersion in aspects of the campaign process might have had the tendency to pull them away from the class, particularly as the actual date of the caucus approached and the campaign frenzy increased. A future iteration of this class needs to pay more attention to keeping this broader context and connection clear.

All of this is not to say that students did not make these connections in class discussions, because they often did, noting how some aspect of their campaign seemed to fit the focus of the reading or noting why it did not and allowing the students to probe why that might be. In addition, their blog entries about what was happening in the campaign often reflected these broader perspectives. To give just two examples of this dialogue between readings and the campaign in the blogs, one student wrote, in the blog on campaign finance and the role of money:

> Many [of the authors] believe that campaigns like Romney's target larger donors. This is true, however they also devote considerable resources to targeting smaller fundraisers as well. This is because fundraising on the individual and grass roots level is often very effective even for more heavily financed campaigns like Romney's. The campaign uses private dinners and banquets as a way to draw in large contributors but also depends on smaller scale events to raise a portion of their funding.

In the blog on media coverage, another student wrote:

> Even with the valiant efforts of staff to organize and plan events, without media coverage the battle is lost already. At this point in time, even a bad story still gives name recognition, that maybe people will pay attention to a certain candidate in a debate or speech and suddenly see that mistake highlighted by the media was an isolated event, and that perhaps the candidate deserves a second look. (As a side note, those candidates who are already nationally known would seem to be more hurt by bad news coverage over none at all, as the populous tends to expect more from them.)

In retrospect, one way in which I might have improved the ability of the students to see these connections would have been to change the order of the readings. I should have started the class with the book on voters, *How Voters Decide*, by

Richard Lau and David Redlawsk.[19] Since most of the internship activity involved voter contact, beginning with this book would have helped students to see why campaigns behave as they do. It was during this section of the class that a number of students in the class discussion and in their papers began to make very clear connections between their internships and the rest of the class. For the rest of the semester, in fact, students referred back to the insights from this book concerning the voters with whom they were interacting. Making those connections right at the beginning of the class might have made the link between political science and campaign behavior more visible and evident as students thought about the entire class experience. In any case, it did seem clear from the blogs and the papers that the insights provided in the literature were enhancing students' insights of what went on in their internships, even if only slightly more than half of the students at the end of the semester responded that this was the case.

Finally, there is the issue of engaged citizenship, and here the evidence is again quite clear. This experience did promote the students' capacities for "democratic participation and responsible engagement in community life."[20] In the class survey, 47% of the students (8 out of 17 responses) said that the experience made them more likely to be involved in a political campaign in the future. Another 18% (3 students) said that it made no difference in terms of their likely involvement because they were involved before and were planning on staying involved. The other 35% (6 students) said the experience made them less likely to be involved, but only two of those students expressed concern about the process itself. The others felt that they would be less involved because they did not enjoy the particular ways in which campaigns employ their volunteers. Most promising, 72% of respondents said that they would recommend the class to others if it were offered again in four years. The 28% who would not recommend it were primarily students who felt that the required internship took too much time for too little benefit, though two students clearly did not like anything about the class.

The strongest evidence for the effectiveness of the class in encouraging students to become more engaged in the democratic process and develop a commitment to maintain that engagement in the future came from the final papers the students wrote, which reflected on both the caucus and their experience. Sixteen of the 20 papers expressed satisfaction with the class and the experience provided. Most reflected a basic satisfaction with democratic participation. Some examples include:

> This year, working on the Richardson campaign by making persuasive phone calls, canvassing door-to-door to motivate voters and working with the campaign office made me feel more a part of the process; that what I was doing could make the difference.

> There was never any question in my mind that I would be involved in politics in some way, and this experience lived up to my expectations and surpassed them. I don't think that I would say that I am more or less likely than I was before I joined a caucus campaign to seek out involve-

> ment in a similar capacity, but I think it would be safe to say that I will be found working in campaign politics for at least a few years to come.
>
> Reflecting on the course of my internship, I truly began to understand how a caucus is actually conducted. Attending and participating in the caucus allowed me to tie all the lose strings together and I was finally able to understand the importance of what I had been working so hard for during the past several months. More importantly I felt rewarded.
>
> I can honestly say that participating in the 2008 Iowa Caucuses has been an extremely rewarding experience that I will never forget. Even though my candidate has dropped out of the race, the insight I gained into the Iowa Caucuses was great.

For some, the transformation was even more significant, reflecting a new appreciation for American democracy and the feelings of empowerment that emerged from their engagement in the process. For example:

> This whole experience is something that I will never let go of, and I'm glad that I was able to take part in such a momentous moment in history. What I've learned and how I understand the political process has grown exponentially. And to be perfectly honest, I think it has changed me in a way that I can now see more clearly what course my own life will take from college here on out.
>
> I felt the excitement and the enthusiasm really run through me and this made me want to get even more politically involved. My bookshelf was restocked over break and I continue to read books that analyze the election, the truths and the lies. I can also not go more than two hours without checking CNN and getting the latest information on the election.
>
> In reflection on this class, I had no idea what to expect. I was assuming I would be able to skim by with the minimum and pick up a side job along with it. However, after meeting with the staff and getting a feel of the job, I know that this is what I wanted to do. After many years of confusion of what I want to do in life, I am satisfied now knowing that I have at least a few more years of my life planned.

Each of these quotes came from the papers of students who worked on losing campaigns. Not surprisingly, the students who worked on the Obama campaign also were likely to claim almost life-altering experiences. Two examples:

> In my opinion, this last semester was a stroke of luck to be part of such an historical time in history. I have loved soaking up politics and am proud that I now actually know what I am talking about. With what I have learned this semester and insistent on keeping up with, I can't imagine not caring about politics in the future. I am sure that because of this class, I will always have an interest in my country's government and encourage others to become informed as well. So many people don't

> take the time to learn about the candidates and vote, or possibly vote for looks or party affiliation alone. I am so grateful to be informed and have the tools to stay informed wherever it is I end up.
>
> and
>
> Suddenly everything snapped into place. I was absolutely thrilled to work on the campaign. I was so grateful to be a part of the wonderful environment that I did any job that was asked of me and more; I was happy to, but I never realized how wonderful it felt to really be a part of something so much larger than myself. I know now more than ever that this is what I want to do for the rest of my life. As disappointing as things can be, and as hard as things get, every moment is worth it. Working for Barack Obama has helped me to realize that the disappointments will never stop unless I stick with this and work them out myself.

These reflections indicate that many of the students developed a deeper appreciation for the democratic process, one of the goals of the class. The quotes do come from a graded assignment, so it is possible that some of the students were writing what they thought that I would want to read; however, the prompt for the paper would have limited such responses. Part of the goal of the paper was for the students to provide "critical reflection on their internship experience." This aspect, however, was only worth 20% of the paper grade.[21] Furthermore, the instructions said nothing about that reflection beyond that general statement. There was no mention of the specific issue of engagement in, or appreciation of, the democratic process, but instead only critical reflections on their experiences. Thus, these comments more likely reflect development of that appreciation, not a desire to please the instructor.

Conclusion: Successes and Future Changes

For many of the students involved, this class was a very positive experience. In fact, four of the students in the class ended up with full-time (paid) jobs during the general election campaign. Two (one with the Polk County Republican Party and one with the Obama campaign) remained in Des Moines and juggled school and work. The two other students were placed by the Obama campaign in other locations, one in Maine and the other at headquarters in Chicago. Independent study and internship experiences were arranged for those students so that they could maintain full-time status and not jeopardize their financial aid or progress toward their degrees.

By mixing the theoretical and the practical, the class helped the students to better understand the US political system and how it operates. It created an experience that allowed them to be engaged citizens and prepare for a lifetime of such citizenship. The class was far from perfect, however. If I taught it again, there are some things that I would do differently. I would, as previously noted, put the unit on voters at the very beginning of the class. I also would set aside more time to talk specifically about students' internships. Some of the best conversations that the class had started with the question, "So how are things going in your internships?" In retrospect, I was too concerned with having students see specific connections between their campaigns and the materials in the class right from the start. It might have been better to allow those connections to emerge from less-structured discussions, guiding students to them. Learning can sometimes be enhanced when the students themselves make the connections.[22]

I also would like more campaign professionals to attend the class. The three sessions in which there were guest speakers—the early class with representatives from various campaigns trying to recruit interns, a session with Hillary Clinton's Iowa press coordinator, and a session with a journalist who used to work at CNN but was at the time in charge of online news production for *Newsweek*—were all very well received by the students and provided additional insights into various aspects of the caucus process. One possibility is to coordinate such visitors with other classes.[23] Another is to give extra credit for or replace class with visits to other events on campus revolving around the caucus. Despite these difficulties, however, the class was largely successful in achieving its desired outcomes. Students did develop a clearer understanding of the presidential nomination process and the role of the Iowa caucus, and they did become engaged in the democratic process and more appreciative of its potential.

Still, the Iowa caucus is an opportunity available only once every four years. So if this model of learning and action is effective, it is advantageous to figure out ways of incorporating it into other classes. I asked the students about this model, and nearly all thought it was a good idea. As Des Moines is also the state capitol, a number of them suggested classes on state government in which students could do internships in the legislature.[24] Others suggested classes on the executive branch and bureaucracy, in which students could work as interns in various government agencies. One student suggested a class on interest groups, in which students could work for various groups that had active PACs or lobbying programs. Others suggested a fall semester election class in which students could intern in federal, state, and local elections. All of these might make good experiences; I have enrolled students in standalone internships in all of these types of organizations. Setting up such a program in these organizations, however, would probably take more work than doing so in the Iowa caucus, in which campaigns were continually attempting to increase their number of volunteers. These classes are more labor intensive for faculty than a traditional class, and finding ways to provide administrative support to ease that burden is essential if these opportunities are to be expanded.[25]

The final activity for the class, as noted, was a forum held on a Thursday evening at the end of January during which my students discussed their experiences in the caucus. I gave a very brief welcome and introduction to the audience, which consisted of about 40 people not including the students in my class who were present either on the panel or in the audience. I then turned the discussion over to the student who had interned with the Iowa Caucus Project and whose last official responsibility was to moderate the discussion. The students were honest in their feelings about what they liked and disliked about working on campaigns. That said, their passion for what they had done and their excitement in being involved in "democracy as it should be practiced" (as one of them put it) was clear. That was exciting for me. I hope that some of the other students in the audience were inspired by the excitement expressed by my students to become more engaged over the democratic process themselves.

The current political science literature in the area of political engagement is dominated by a concern with the lack of engagement in the political process by American citizens in general and young people in particular.[26] This class, or others like it, provides ways to reignite a spirit of democratic engagement and participation among students. That made teaching this class a remarkably satisfying experience.

Political Hermeneutics as Pedagogy: Service-Learning, Political Reflection, and Action

15

By Patrick F. McKinlay

Amid the debates surrounding competing notions of citizenship, social capital, and political critique, political theory confronts the question: Does citizenship matter? This chapter proposes that students be invited to construct their own politics of engagement that reflect their values, commitments, and sense of citizenship. I argue that student propensity for thinking about civic responsibility can be encouraged through interlaced practices of active learning, service-learning, and focused reflective writing as part of a political theory course.

An objective for teaching political theory is to develop characteristics of reflective citizenship among one's students.[1] Amid the debates surrounding competing notions of citizenship, social capital, and political critique, political theory confronts the practical conditions of the age: profound cynicism about civic and political engagement. Does citizenship matter? Discussions of political participation yield manifold expressions of apathy that verge on despair of the significance of the political. Even as students are encouraged to consider a critical theory of citizenship, their own experiences and observations of the political realm suggest not so much the irrelevance of political theory as much as suspicion of political thought itself.

This project examines potential avenues for the challenge of teaching the political theory of citizenship against the current political malaise that militates against and disempowers students and their efforts to imagine any form of authentic political action. How can possibilities be cultivated for students to imagine their own engaged citizenship, such as the country witnessed in the 2008 campaign for Sen. Barack Obama or, more recently, during the Arab Spring in 2011? Can students be invited to construct their own politics of engagement that reflects their values, commitments, and sense of citizenship?

The starting point for this inquiry is the Janus-faced dilemma of responsibility and apathy. There is no need to dwell on the myriad indicators of a broad societal disengagement from the political realm. Current national political leaders are locked in both deep ideological conflict and surface-level partisan gaming that conspire to depress and disconnect the population from an active role in their own governance. Many writers are struggling to find the sources of this dynamic in the American political system,[2] and students are not alone in feeling a sense of disenchantment with the political. My goal in this chapter is not to overcome those specific dynamics, but rather to consider how students' college experiences might mitigate these trends and even equip them with tools for sifting through the drama that is not politics to grasp some more elemental forms of political engagement and active citizenship, or what John Adams called "public happiness."

The current generation of students provides some provocative challenges regarding the dilemma of responsibility and apathy. As evidenced in previous chapters, students are increasingly interested in community volunteerism, yet their interest in civic and political engagement appears slight.[3] I have found little evidence of any specific political commitment on the part of current students regarding specific issues, other than perhaps some general environmental concerns. Even with two wars to support or to protest, a global recession dimming future job prospects, skyrocketing college costs, a health care crisis that has brought anxiety to many American families, and a variety of other issues that could agitate the political passions of young minds, there seems to be mostly silence in response.

Still, many students come to college with résumés of activities in local school groups, churches, community groups, and other community activities. College essays relate experiences of helping the poor, saving the Amazon, and improving the lives of others. Yet students appear to make no connection between these issues and political engagement. What is the nature of this disconnect? Russell Dalton's research suggests that this disconnect may reflect two competing conceptions of citizenship: duty-based citizenship and engaged citizenship.[4] Part of Dalton's analysis is that a generation change may be taking place; that is, that conceptions of citizenship are in flux and the new generation is constructing an alternative and perhaps even more empowered form of citizenship.

I find much of Dalton's analysis to be very instructive regarding the current generation of college students; however, I am, like many teacher-scholars in this volume, still left wondering how they will manage to make the connection between their own personalized sets of values and a broader understanding of political and economic structures. Many students are, for example, full of moral indignation toward illegal immigration; however, they appear uninspired to grasp the current political-economic system that perpetuates the status quo (let alone ponder one that imagines an alternative). Without question, these are complex issues; nonetheless, I offer a simple assertion that I may be a component of their political apathy. Do students know how to think about the political? More specifically, have political science instructors prepared them to think critically as citizens about the political realm?[5] In this chapter, I present and analyze some pedagogical practices designed to invite students to thought, critical reflection, moral introspection, and a listening for the call of vocation and service.

Thinking does not stand alone in this context. Political reflection here is defined by the nature of its object, the *civitas*, or the city. Political thinking asks the fundamental question: What is the nature of individual responsibility to the *civitas*?

My course design then flows from an objective to encourage students to connect thinking and responsibility, principally regarding the object of the political. After noting the problem of apathy and lack of engagement, I offer a proposition for addressing this educational puzzle. I argue that student propensity for thinking about civic responsibility can be encouraged through interlaced practices of active learning, service-learning, and focused reflective writing. I go on to outline the literature informing my conception of civic responsibility. Then I briefly describe the specific pedagogies employed to provide students experiences of civic responsibility. Finally, I present some preliminary assessment data that support my thesis and pedagogy. My conclusion suggests some provisional analysis of the pedagogy's shortcomings and considers prospects for longitudinal research to consider its effectiveness regarding civic dispositions and behaviors.

A Note about Content and Pedagogy

Educators are confronted with an awesome responsibility when they design a new course. Much attention is focused on course content, assessment of student learning outcomes, and training students with practical skills. Instructors consider how much emphasis to place on knowledge content and dispositions. Some scholars have suggested reasonable challenges regarding the impact of service-learning pedagogy in addressing the disconnect among volunteer service, civic engagement, and genuine cognitive development.[6] One argument is that knowledge as such is passé; students, properly trained, will learn all new knowledge for themselves. In moral and political theory, ample evidence suggests that this approach is appropriate because it equips students with critical thinking skills for analyzing the political.

Course design is discussed further later in this chapter, but I assert that the content of the course remains vital, especially when the task is to stimulate both reflection and action, indeed, to cultivate judgment. What individuals think about when they think about the political very much shapes how they approach it. The educator must be phenomenologically sensitive to *what* the political is.[7] As Hannah Arendt notes, the political realm is the space in which citizens appear to one another in their plurality (if not also in their difference).[8] The content of practical applications and examples is as important as the seminal texts that inform the conversation.

For these reasons then, I began the class on citizenship with the question of prejudice. Following Hans Georg Gadamer's philosophical hermeneutics, knowledge is always already understood through language as interpretation.[9] Understanding is a happening, an experience, which requires a dialogue between "I and Thou." Thou in this context can be tradition, a text, an event, a person, or the "Other." This means that individuals are always bringing to their understanding their prejudgments embedded in their preunderstanding. Everyone has some "baggage," regardless of the topic. Hermeneutics states that this baggage can be overcome through the process of interpretation, translation, the to-and-fro play of understanding. Individuals emancipate themselves from their prejudices through the process of reflection and interpretation.

Needless to say, I do not require my students to read the fundamental texts of the Habermas-Gadamer debate, but the issue of prejudice is central to my pedagogy. How can the educational experience as interpretation empower students to disclose their own prejudgments so that their political and moral perspective is situated in a conscious posture toward critical reflection? I endeavor to help them ask themselves: Why do I hold this view of this problem or phenomenon? What do I bring to this condition that already shapes how I conceive it? What new evidence should I pursue to enhance my understanding of the problem?

If developing hermeneutic skills for interpretation and overcoming prejudice, then content is embedded in the pedagogical puzzle. Arendt's conception of the political as a public space of appearances serves as a useful starting point for a collective investigation of citizenship generally and civic responsibility specifically. Students are introduced to the concept of the public realm as a place where human plurality can be *seen*.[10] The pedagogy then offers a phenomenological experience for entering the public realm as such. Each step in the process requires a return to the task of reflection and pondering: Why do I perceive the problem in this way? What do I learn about myself through this experience? What is the nature of my relationship to this phenomenon or problem?

Ingredients for a Pedagogy of Civic Responsibility

Recently, there has been a resurgence in theoretical considerations of the classical question of citizenship.[11] Many contemporary political debates surround immigration and population flows that result from globalization and intrastate political, social, economic, and ecological crises, but Western political theory tends to remain fixated on the citizen as subject and author of legitimate authority in a republican form of government. In my courses, I introduce students to some of these other dimensions of citizenship, but mostly as they inform student efforts to construct personal conceptions of their own citizenship. Much work also has focused on the evolving accumulation of social capital in various societies.

Among these perspectives, I find Arendt's examination of the self-concept of citizens as those who can rule and can also be ruled as the most elegant approach to introduce to students. For her, the goal appears to be the creation of a consciousness on the part of citizens in that they are both the authors as well as the subjects of the laws. Citizens are in-terested and inter-ested in the matters of the *polis*. That is, citizens have personal self-defined interests, the basic political assumption of liberal pluralism. What is more, citizens also have a civic republican interest in the common good of the *polis*. The dual quality of this definition captures both liberal and classical civic republican conceptions of citizenship. I also rely heavily upon Derek Heater's valuable contributions to both tracking the historical evolution of citizenship as well as its more contemporary manifestations in diverse political systems.[12]

Taking this broad view of citizenship for the purpose of my pedagogy leaves open many doors for students to find their own pathways for experience and reflection. Given that so many bring experiences in community service, students immediately depart from these experiences as foundational to their conceptions of political citizenship. Nonetheless, their respective conceptions of their political citizenship remain under-thematized and pre-reflective. Most often there is virtually no self-concept of agency or voice.[13]

In a sense, this discussion invokes the old Marxist concept of false consciousness. Instead of employing traditional class consciousness as a spark to ignite political action, the issue is consciousness of citizenship itself: What does it mean for *me* to be a citizen? I am reminded also of Jean-Jacques Rousseau's categories of citizenship and the laws in *The Social Contract*; that is, how am "I" both a citizen and a subject?

Learning Outcomes

Morningside College is a small liberal arts college in Sioux City, Iowa.[14] The faculty conducted a thorough review of the curriculum and developed an outcomes-based curriculum inspired by the college's mission and vision statements. The curriculum intends that students will demonstrate the college's outcomes through their performance in their majors and clusters and completion of general education courses associated with several core competencies. The mission statement indicates several of these outcomes with profound clarity: The Morningside College experience cultivates a passion for lifelong learning and a dedication to ethical leadership and civic responsibility.[15]

As the Political Science Department considered its response to the challenge of delivering an outcomes-based curriculum, faculty also considered what their appropriate role was in delivering several of the general education curriculum courses—called "rubrics," as these were intended to be staffed by diverse departments using courses with a broad spectrum of content but common major learning outcomes. Furthermore, the faculty included a graduation requirement that each student complete a course that utilized service-learning as a substantial pedagogy within the course. Many political science majors planned on taking an upper-level course within their major that would fulfill this requirement; however, many other students looked for opportunities to get this requirement "out of the way" early in their collegiate careers.

The curriculum also has a specific rubric focused on "Ethics and Personal Values."[16] I have long had a concern with the issue of civic responsibility and the question as to whether the faculty at Morningside were cultivating it. Indeed, I agree with Nesteruk that faculty must endeavor to "ennoble" rather than "enable" their students to consider what they value and why.[17] Such a process requires a hybrid of pedagogies, especially since service-learning is a key ingredient in the process. I therefore volunteered to create POLS 182: Citizenship, largely for the purpose of general education students rather than strictly for political science majors. Deciding to create a 100-level course for nonmajors relieves one disciplinary constraint, but imposes limitations on content selection and course design.

The course was required to meet the conditions for two areas:

1. *Ethics and Personal Values.* The course was required to introduce students to at least two or more ethical approaches. Students were expected to demonstrate understanding of at least two approaches and be able to apply them to cases appropriately. Furthermore, students should demonstrate specific reflection on their personal beliefs and values in light of these ethical approaches.
2. *Service-Learning.* Students were required to complete a substantial service-learning project that met a community-defined need through 10 or more hours of direct service to the community. The project requires oral and written reflection.

I determined the following course objectives:

1. To appropriately apply different ethical theories to problems confronting citizens and communities
2. To identify different models of citizenship
3. To define and apply a personal conception of civic responsibility and citizenship
4. To improve communication skills, particularly critical writing and oral presentation skills

These objectives were designed to meet the criteria specified by Morningside's curriculum and monitored by the Curriculum Policies Committee. The process was designed to encourage maximum experimentation on the part of faculty while retaining a commitment to student learning outcomes. The evidence of success is to be determined through assessment. This concern returns the discussion to the dilemma of content. Full disclosure requires that I admit that in the four iterations of this course, I have varied substantial elements of the specific content, while remaining faithful to the course outcomes. Before describing those changes, let me first explain how my pedagogy and content were intimately related.

Toward Political Hermeneutics as Pedagogy

As I have already indicated, my philosophical perspective is hermeneutic in character, giving special attention to context, historical conditions, and individual perspective among the students. As I chose readings for the course, I was concerned that even the many great theoretical resources available to students regarding the nature of citizenship would be too abstract for introductory-level students to grasp and engage for the purposes of critical reflection. It struck me that I needed to commit to a particular concrete theme around which reading, reflection, and action could crystallize. In the following sections, I discuss how I achieved this goal without prejudging the students' own discoveries of their respective ethical perspectives and values.

A Preferential Option for the Poor

Borrowing a page from liberation theology, I opted for the topic of poverty. Over years of teaching American government courses, I have found that this topic is one of the most interesting categories in American political discourse, especially for young people. The reality is that students rarely have a clear appreciation for the social science of poverty, and yet, class is a pervasive theme in contemporary society. Students tend to respond to many of its cues, albeit for a myriad of often competing and contradicting reasons. In other words, class has baggage. This issue is a perfect point of departure for a hermeneutic pedagogy.

Poverty is obviously a great issue around which to discuss citizenship, since that concept's origins are linked precisely to status, property, and often, gender and race. Poverty raises the question of a set of individuals who might very well be even less politically conscious, less politically engaged, and more politically disenfranchised than students. Also, poverty introduces the prospect of coalition-building and service with agencies and programs aimed at alleviating the costs and challenges of poverty. Students can find many opportunities to serve and respond to community-identified needs and challenges.

In addition to providing a specific social challenge through which to test and examine prejudgments and opening the stage for a whole variety of service activities, poverty also opens itself to a litany of ethical and ethical-political debates regarding responses based on individual responsibility; collective, or social, responsibility; and universal ethical principles. At its root, poverty invites individuals to consider "Am I my brother's/sister's keeper?" That is, how is my civic responsibility tied in any way to the substantive conditions of another human being?

The raw materials for the course included readings and resources on ethical theories, the concept of citizenship, and the question of poverty in the United States. In the course design, I considered the following question: Which pedagogies lend themselves to not only meeting the prescribed learning outcomes, but also contribute to the students' formation of some kind of reflective and even critical notion of citizenship?

Reading, Simulation, Reflection, Action: An Integrated Service-Learning Approach

The goal, as described in the following sections, was to create the proper conditions through which students could apprehend vestiges of their own prejudgments and consider resources that might agitate the process of critical thinking and positive action, that is, active critical citizenship. To that end, I briefly review readings, classroom activities, writing assignments, and finally, the service-learning project itself.

Some might consider introducing largely first-year students to abstract conceptions of citizenship as an educationally flawed strategy. Note that each iteration of the course was offered in the spring semester—on the hope that first-year students might be more receptive and prepared for abstract content. Given concerns about the difficulty of abstract readings and substantial evidence that political apathy was a present variable, I broke my reading selections into three categories:

1. Basic readings in the concept of citizenship
2. Elementary readings in ethical theory
3. Concrete readings tied to the topic of poverty in the United States

Choosing a text on citizenship proved one of the greatest challenges. In all three iterations of the class, I used different resources, including a first-year writing textbook that blended basic college writing and research with the topic of citizenship. If this class had been explicitly focused on formal writing, I would have continued using this text; however, an overemphasis on formal writing would have precluded student focus on ethics and citizenship itself.[18] For the spring 2006 semester, I adopted Bloustein's *Education for Democracy*, a marvelous collection of resources linked to the civic engagement literature.[19] It contained many great readings that linked well with my overall approach. Ultimately, however, its cost and lack of a new edition encouraged me to try another source. I have been reading Derek Heater's work on citizenship for some time and decided to give students a more formal introduction to citizenship through his *A Brief History of Citizenship*.[20] I found this resource useful for giving a concrete historical foundation for the concept of citizenship; however, the text remained dry and somewhat unapproachable for the students. Regardless, as I selected texts, I found that I tend to return to a few resources in all iterations of the class. Let me briefly discuss several specific texts that fulfilled specific roles in the classroom discussion.

Ralph Ellison, *The Invisible Man*[21]

This classic text provided an outstanding opportunity to discuss the operation of the public realm. Students were encouraged to think about the problem of invisibility through an array of social issues that are unseen and therefore absent from public discourse. This text also set the stage for classroom discussion of the poverty simulation, which further displaced the student's self-conception and introduced the possibility of thinking about conditions different from one's own. It captured issues of prejudice, apathy, voicelessness, and action in one place. It provided no concrete answers, but did spur many questions. Indeed, class discussion often turned to issues of class and gender as well as race, from which students' own experiences of invisibility could be shared.

Hannah Arendt, *The Human Condition*[22]

This selection both introduced some elements of civic republican conceptions of citizenship and provided a textual reference for my own pedagogy. The short reading introduced the public-private distinction I later problematized and critiqued in readings, discussions, and experiences. I built linkages through discussion between Ellison and Arendt, so that students developed a shared conception of the public realm as the space of appearance. Arendt argues that as citizens appear to each other in their diversity and plurality, through speech and action, they create a common world. It is in this public realm that individuals take up the responsibilities of citizenship. I argue that this model provided a relatively simple foundation for students to understand the political realm.

Martin Luther King, Jr., *Letter from the Birmingham Jail*

This text provided many themes for discussion. Each group took different lessons from this text, making it always fresh. It opened an opportunity to approach questions of prejudice, enfranchisement, and justice all in the same dialogue. Furthermore, it allowed another resonance with Arendt's concept of the public realm as a space for *agon*, contestation, and struggle. Students were quite alarmed when they read that King was advocating tension to bring about change. This discussion also opened the question of civic disagreement—how do individuals construct practices of citizenship that permit them to express their own beliefs, values, and moral-political arguments while at the same time listening to those of others?

Robert Putnam, *Bowling Alone*

This text has become a contemporary classic in the civic engagement literature. The overall argument regarding recent trends in social capital is hotly debated, but the text was an accessible articulation of the current political malaise and apathy that society and students confront. It also provided a different conception of civic engagement from strict partisan political activism, which is distasteful to so many undergraduate students and citizens in general. As students participated in a variety of community activities, they began to appreciate their own relevance to and indeed vitality in serving the creation and animation of the public realm.

Readings in Ethics and Personal Values: The Value of Formal Ethics versus Personal Beliefs

This course fulfilled the requirements for the Ethics and Personal Values rubric at Morningside College. As such, my course was required to integrate student learning outcomes that demonstrate a foundational understanding of two or more ethical approaches, an ability to apply those approaches to appropriate cases, and, finally, the opportunity for students to reflect on their own personal beliefs and values. For the purposes of reading, I again moved among several texts. In each iteration of the class, I used a combination of theorists' original texts as well as contemporary readings on these primary sources. I introduced the students to at least five different ethical approaches, often blending them with associated theories of civic comportment. These approaches included virtue ethics (Aristotle and MacIntyre), deonotological ethics, utilitarianism, contractarianism, and feminism. Frankly, it was a difficult set of issues to discuss; however, Peter Wenz's *Political Philosophy in Moral Conflict* was an outstanding source to introduce these classic ethical approaches within contemporary public policy choices and debates.[23] Indeed, the students were often scandalized by some of the implications of these approaches. In a similar vein of current controversy and classic debates, Michael Sandel has introduced a new resource based on his popular Harvard course, *Justice: What's the Right Thing to Do?*

In all iterations of the course, I focused on engaging the students with two or more approaches in depth, following either scripted assignments or through self-selecting preferences. To not only meet but exceed the criteria of the Ethics and Personal Values rubric, I felt compelled to make this content relatively important in the class readings and discussion. Both my own preferences and the rubric encouraged me to focus my course-embedded assessments to concentrate on these criteria.

David Shipler, *The Working Poor: Invisible in America*

For most of the classes, I used David Shipler's outstanding study of the conditions confronting the working poor throughout America. In the same vein as Barbara Ehrenreich's *Nickeled and Dimed*,[24] Shipler introduces readers to the diverse faces of America's working poor. His emphasis on the working poor presented a strategy to confront many students' prejudgments regarding the face of poverty. More often than not, students articulated a greater sense of solidarity as they reviewed the many issues that confront working persons who fall through the cracks of the social welfare system.

On one occasion, I turned to a collection of essays from the *New York Times* called *Class Matters* to make class itself more visible for student reflection. Since this text covered upper, middle, and lower classes, it served well to get students to think critically about a variety of issues confronting middle-class Americans, especially access to education and health care and the difficulties they face in their daily lives.[25] The text gave some insight into my central theme of poverty, but it was more muted and required more lecture than I would otherwise prefer to keep a theme in place for purposes of the overall pedagogy.

Developmental Reflection Pedagogies

As previously described, a central desired learning outcome of Morningside's curriculum is critical thinking, especially as it can be applied through citizenship skills. The course utilized a variety of developmental writing assignments to demonstrate these outcomes.

Presurvey and the Good Life

For purposes of assessment as well as to better understand my students' respective vantage points, I collected data from a survey on attitudes and experiences regarding volunteerism and service-learning. I also asked students to write two brief essays. The first was assigned before the class had started reading the ethical literature. I asked students to describe the "good life" for themselves. Through lecture and discussion, I had already tipped my hat regarding the Aristotelian origins of this question, but most students answered it with some variation on a middle-class, American dream model of living well, having a family, and building a successful career. I gave credit for completing the assignment, but I did not actually evaluate the content of the assignment.

As the semester progressed, students returned to this fundamental question as they considered different applications of the ethical approaches they studied. These exercises provided ample evidence of demonstrated student learning of the approaches themselves, but I was more interested in how students applied them to specific examples drawn from other readings or other experiences in their service projects.

What Is Poverty?

In this brief assignment, students shared their own first experience of poverty. Again, with credit but without evaluation, I encouraged students to share a personal definition of poverty. Following the hermeneutic approach, these first activities allowed the students to present their first preunderstandings of the central content areas. Because poverty is so value-laden, the assignment allowed them to disclose their own preconceptions of poverty and class. Students often also expressed their own personal locations on the socioeconomic spectrum. I believe this to be a positive moment for self-reflection.

Throughout the remainder of the semester, I returned to themes taken from this early writing to reinforce student understandings of the ethical, public policy, and political implications of poverty and class in American society. For instance, essay questions during exams might challenge students to apply one of the ethical approaches to a public policy solution regarding a particular issue related to poverty. When the students read Shipler, I frequently encouraged them to make explicit connections to topics, lessons, and dilemmas he developed that were raised in their readings, class discussions and activities, or during their service projects.

The Poverty Simulation

A challenge with the form of thinking encouraged by Arendt in her lectures on Kant's political philosophy is actually representing oneself in the position of another, or what Kant calls an "enlarged mentality." With the assistance of the local branch of the Iowa State Extension Service, a civic engagement group has sponsored a Poverty Simulation on Morningside's campus for seven years.[26] The main participants in this exercise are my students in POLS 182: Citizenship, as well as advanced nursing students.[27] The simulation has included from 40 to 60 student participants. The college civic engagement group, the Morningside Civic Union, provides 10–15 student workers, who help staff the simulation. A role is assigned to each person who enters the simulation, and he or she is placed into families with other participants. Families are given varying resources to begin the simulation. Their challenge is to fulfill the daily obligations of getting kids to school, finding and maintaining employment, and paying the bills. The simulation takes place over four "weeks" that are about 12 minutes long. The goal is to genuinely simulate the need to accommodate for all of the aspects of household management with limited time and resources. As the "month" progresses, families encounter financial and even personal crises. Usually by the third or fourth week, chairs are overturned to indicate that a family has been evicted from their home.

As a collective experience, students reported that it was one of the most formative components of the semester. It gave them pause about a whole variety of basic everyday assumptions. Since the simulation takes place in late January, it occurs before many students have spent much time in the community doing service. It is a simulation, so it provides a blend of activity and discussion that is generally fruitful for reflection and application to new cases.

Service-Learning Project

Another general education curriculum requirement at Morningside is the service-learning component. Not unlike a research paper or a comprehensive exam, the service project provided an opportunity for students to demonstrate a range of learning that touched on every dimension of my course objectives. The assignment requirements were pretty simple.[28] Since the class was not designed around a pre-existing competency (such as a marketing class developing a plan for a nonprofit), I encouraged students to participate in a range of service activities. My intent was to train them to reflect appropriately on whatever activities they chose. I was fortunate to be assisted by excellent VISTA Americorps volunteers, who served as service-learning coordinators during each semester. They created and stewarded many of the community agency relationships and coordinated the service-learning activities for the entire campus. The first assignment usually consisted of students developing a plan for the activities in which they wanted to engage to meet the minimum number of hours for the project (usually 15 hours, 10 of which had to be direct service). One of their first tasks was to meet either with me or the VISTA volunteer to develop their plans. I asked them to write a paragraph outlining what they hoped to learn about the class content and about themselves so that they might make more careful, thoughtful selections of agencies and activities that fit their own learning goals.

Students sometimes were permitted to count hours attending various campus or community events, such as visits by political notables, against the total number of hours required. They also could accrue hours by attending at least two required formal government meetings, for example, city council or school board meetings. Sometimes students needed to have something spark their interest before they decided to commit more serious time to a specific activity. They were encouraged to complete a few different activities, but some of the best experiences were drawn from sustained experiences with a particular agency. I also required the students to identify an agency staff person they could interview for their final projects. Students had to turn in a spreadsheet that outlined their hours and activities at regular intervals through the semester. This tool helped both the student and the instructor manage the process better and gave students tangible means for making oral and written reports prior to writing the final reflective essay. Each report contained cells designed to allow a student to journal regarding how an experience connected directly to the readings and classroom activities. A second cell asked them to reflect upon their personal observations regarding the service. Both writing tasks directed the student to reflect upon connections across the different components of the course. It may not always have incited critical reflection, but it gave me enough information to prompt the student to dig deeper for possible connections and insights.

At the end of the semester, students were required to write a five-to-seven-page reflective paper that demonstrated critical reflection on their service experiences and how they helped students to consider their own citizenship and their own beliefs and values. Students were instructed to integrate references to the reading materials as well as to gather additional information about the particular issues or problems they confronted during their service (e.g., someone working in an after-school program might find articles pertaining to its future state or federal funding). Students were asked to submit a rough draft and receive feedback before turning in a final version of the paper. I expand upon the effectiveness of this pedagogy in the next section.

Eulogy

The Eulogy assignment was one key element of the final exam each semester. Students were asked to write their own eulogy describing a long life. I required them to cite influential readings, discuss at least two ethical approaches that may have influenced how they lived their life, and describe their life's accomplishments. It was an appropriate bookend activity to contrast with the Good Life essay. This assignment was designed as both an evaluative instrument and an assessment tool for the course and for my interest in examining student critical reflection and their attitudes toward the public realm. Combined with the service-learning reflection paper, it served as a closure to the hermeneutic circle to see if horizons had been expanded, if students' capacities to think with enlarged mentality were evidenced, and whether they had demonstrated an understanding of critical citizenship.

Evaluating Thinking, Assessing Action

Students progress through this course in their own ways. Some were very excited by the service activities at the outset of the semester. It was sometimes a challenge to harness that enthusiasm for service, so that students adequately reflected upon the meaning of their service. Others slowly acquired a commitment to their service-learning projects. While their progress may have seemed slow, it did appear to be steady, and it generally appeared in an ever-more reflective appreciation for the ethical and political questions raised in readings and class discussions. I do not know that it is necessary to provide any typology of these learning styles; it goes without saying that political hermeneutics allowed students to think about their actions, their values, and broader political questions following their own particular learning style. Another conclusion is also plausible: if students did not engage in service, they did not succeed in the course. Therefore, this pedagogy holds no special solution for the stubbornly disengaged student. I explained to students at the outset of the course and reinforced this point as the semester progressed—that engaging in a service project was a requirement—and success in the course was not possible without their participation. As the following data show, the students who did not participate were scored "not proficient" in any of the course outcomes, as they provided no evidence of their learning on course outcomes. It is a minimal test of civic responsibility: Can a student complete a service project?

Table 15-1: POLS 182: Citizenship, Service-Learning Flag Aggregate Outcomes, 2005–2007[a]

Outcome	Exceeds Expectations	Meets Expectations	Does Not Meet Expectations	
	Advanced	Proficient	Partially Proficient	Not Proficient
1. At a foundational level, Morningside students are able to identify connections between course objectives/content and their student service.	43	32	8	10
	46.24%	34.41%	8.60%	10.75%
2. At a foundational level, Morningside students are able to identify how their ethical and active participation contributes to the community.	39	36	8	10
	41.94%	38.71%	8.60%	10.75%
3. At a foundational level, Morningside students are able to identify knowledge they gain about themselves, their strengths and limitations, through their service in the community.	40	37	7	9
	43.01%	39.78%	7.53%	9.68%

Note:

[a] The traditional model of assessment at Morningside rests on faculty self-reporting of data, but the Service Learning Work Group, the Ethics and Personal Values faculty, and the Political Science faculty provide a means of informal validity testing through workshops in which rubrics and random examples of student work have been examined by multiple reviewers. These practices provide some greater reliability for these measures, but more important, they have given everyone a chance to gain feedback on their rubrics and assignments, and to develop shared standards for student learning in a collaborative nonthreatening format.

The service project reflection paper was only one of the artifacts utilized to assess student learning. For the purposes of the service-learning assessment (see Table 15-1), I used a combination of measures taken from the Eulogy, the service-learning logs, and the reflection paper. I also took data from select final exam essay questions. Table 15-1 reports the data for the service-learning flag for POLS 182 for four terms from 2005 to 2010.[29] The four courses enrolled a total of 93 students. With respect to collegewide outcomes (see Appendix 15-1 in the online material for this book),[30] the faculty looked specifically to the service-learning flag to promote progress toward Outcomes 3, 6, and 7. In tandem with the Ethics and Values rubric, the course was designed to highlight Outcomes 1 and 8. Since the course required a five-to-seven-page reflection paper that specifically focused on identifying links between key ethical approaches and the political issues and challenges explored during their service projects, the course also contributed to the development of Outcome 2. The course was not intended to demonstrate all of these outcomes in student work, but its design reflected attention to multiple General Education concerns.

Fully 80% of students met or exceeded all course outcomes. The remaining 20% may have only partially demonstrated the appropriate outcomes. In most cases, those failing to meet outcomes generally failed to complete the assignment.

The Morningside model of service-learning emphasizes the learning component. Since 2005, instructors have emphasized more projects and opportunities in the community to enhance the likelihood of student civic engagement with under-represented communities, especially youth. For example, more than 50% of students in the Sioux City Community Schools receive free or reduced-cost lunch. After-school programs, Big Brothers–Big Sisters, and Head Start are several of the many organizations through which students interact with members of the broader Siouxland community. These opportunities afford students opportunities to hear and experience diverse minority perspectives on contemporary social and political challenges in the community.

As students reflect upon these experiences, opportunities arise to reconstruct some of their previous thoughts of basic self-understanding. Reflection regarding originally held prejudgments often gives way to what Kant called an enlarged mentality, whereby they grasp these ethical and political issues from another perspective than their own. It affords them an opportunity to reflect upon and reevaluate their initial values statements, as well as to critically evaluate their own personal strengths and weaknesses. In the case of my course, it was generally at the end of the semester that the combined experience of the Poverty Simulation with their service activities moved students to think more carefully about their own circumstances, strengths, and opportunities for personal growth and values clarifications.

The service-learning assessment identified some significant progress with respect to students' self-perceptions and a consciousness of their relationship to the community, but I argue that it was the nexus of these activities alongside students' progress toward learning outcomes associated with the Ethics and Personal Values rubric that signified student progress toward engaged civic responsibility. The assessment data for the aggregate of POLS 182: Citizenship are reported in Table 15-2.[31]

Table 15-2: POLS 182: Citizenship, Ethics and Personal Values Aggregate Outcomes, 2005–2010

Outcome	Exceeds Expectations	Meets Expectations	Does Not Meet Expectations	
	Advanced	Proficient	Partially Proficient	Not Proficient
1. At a foundational level, Morningside students are able to understand and apply basic ethical distinctions and terminology.	34	36	12	11
	36.56%	38.71%	12.90%	11.83%
2. At a foundational level, Morningside students are able to identify and reflect upon their personal beliefs and values.	43	37	4	9
	46.24%	39.78%	4.30%	9.68%
3. At a foundational level, Morningside students are able to critically evaluate and apply at least two major ethical theories to particular situations.	33	35	14	11
	35.48%	37.63%	15.05%	11.83%

The student work utilized to make these assessments was drawn from a variety of sources, including essay exam questions, essays reflecting on the *Working Poor* (or other readings), the Eulogy, and the service-learning reflection paper. As a theorist interested in assessing student progress on learning one of several ethical approaches covered during the semester, many of these evaluations concentrated on students demonstrating an understanding of these key ethical approaches and demonstrations of appropriate applications of these approaches to everyday ethical-political examples.[32] One of the principal advantages of the Eulogy project was that it required students to not only apply appropriate ethical analysis, but also to do it with respect to their own values and their own future inclinations toward citizenship and service. What kind of citizen will they want to have been? What values will their life's accomplishments reflect? It is a speculative activity, but many of the students reflected on logical extensions of their previous service activities. Though some of their stories were somewhat grandiose, often these stories reflected an appreciation of the transformative possibilities that their own ethical-political actions could create.

More important, these speculative ventures, when tied to their service praxis, suggested that students might actually have been engaging in active reflection. Displacing their experiences from their everyday experiences, the service projects, the disruptive readings, and the relatively firm criteria of the various ethical approaches explored in class provided a setting for students to engage in actual critical reflection. Was it necessarily authentic "thinking"? Perhaps. What is more intriguing is whether the students acquired a mode of learning that will travel with them into other courses and experiences. I cannot claim to have established a monitoring system that will tell me with any accuracy whether this particular learning experience will shape their future learning or action. Nonetheless, I believe that the relative success of so many students with respect to the specific learning outcomes crafted for this course indicates that they at least once engaged in a political hermeneutics of self-reflection.

One conclusion I draw from this analysis is that a pedagogy of political hermeneutics would best be experienced in multiple contexts. Indeed, the service-learning faculty at Morningside have formed a Service-Learning Working Group committed to supporting individual efforts in utilizing these pedagogies. What may yet be possible is to measure the combined effect of such multiple experiences for students in a variety of disciplines. Already, a small but not insignificant number of students are seeking out service-learning courses in several disciplines. It is possible that faculty can coordinate efforts to make this learning cumulative.

From Civic Engagement to Civic and Political Responsibility: Prospects for Political Hermeneutics

While I am reluctant to derive too many hard conclusions from the assessment data, I do believe that this hybrid pedagogy offers something for the instructor interested in addressing the disconnect between civic engagement and civic duty and responsibility. If students come to classrooms with an openness to volunteerism and an interest in taking direct action,[33] how can their learning experiences be crafted to help them challenge their own dispositions and confront any lack of political fervor and political knowledge? How concerned ought political scientists be regarding students' future political and ethical comportments after graduation? Political hermeneutics suggests that students cannot and should not be pushed toward a specific, single conception of citizenship or ideal of political reflection. Rather, the pedagogy is interested in providing students with an approach to political reflection and political action that encourages them to continue engaging in the political play of interpretation and understanding of their own political worlds. How they choose to appear in their respective public realms reflects their own expressions of political freedom. More important, have they experienced a setting in which they can reflect upon prejudgments—an awareness of new and different circumstances experienced by an Other—and have an opportunity for shared service and learning about themselves in the process? Political hermeneutics encourages students to develop skills as well as dispositions that invite opportunities to think about what they are doing when they enter the public realm or confront life's mysteries and challenges in their own personal private ones.

Future research will require longitudinal capacity to permit a developmental picture of this learning strategy. Further, a more comprehensive and cross-disciplinary conversation on campuses can facilitate reinforcement of elements of this pedagogy that may yield more conclusive and sustained student learning. Finally, political scientists should consider new opportunities for studying not only styles of citizenship but also the effectiveness of these models. Perhaps political scientists can only hope that they have created opportunities that encourage their own development (*Bildung*) for the practice of engaged and responsible citizenship and service.

Blending Cognitive, Affective, and Effective Learning in Civic Engagement Courses: The Case of Human Rights–Human Wrongs

16

By Susan Dicklitch

Service-learning courses are still outside of mainstream political science departmental offerings, and the academy as a whole has yet to fully embrace service-learning courses as a valid pedagogy.[1] *This chapter focuses on a service-learning course, Human Rights–Human Wrongs, as an example of how cognitive, affective, and effective learning objectives can coexist and thrive to bring students an exceptional learning opportunity while providing an important service to communities. I argue that there are three core elements of successful service-learning courses: high-level cognitive learning, high-level affective learning, and effective community service.*

It often is difficult to create a real-world, meaningful service-learning experience for students in international or comparative politics courses, unless there is a travel component to the course. Travel, however, frequently is not a viable option given economic limitations and the increasing enrollment of nontraditional students. Yet students need to be exposed to real-world political science issues, and through high-quality service-learning courses that bridge theory with practice, they can have a discernible impact on the real world and learn early on the effect of civic engagement.

They also learn that the global is local. I offer my Human Rights–Human Wrongs (HR-HW) course—a senior-level, international/comparative political science seminar—as an example of a service-learning course that combines hands-on, in-the-field work with theoretical, academic inquiry on human rights yet does not require study abroad. I propose that this model could be used to create capstone courses in all majors to help develop a level of professional commitment in students; that is, help to make them more likely to seek careers in political science–related fields by showing them that they can help people by doing so.[2]

Courses like HR-HW are still outside of mainstream political science courses. One of the key impediments to the acceptance of courses like HR-HW and other service-learning courses[3] as a mainstream academic pedagogy is the persistent misperception that service-learning focuses mainly on affective learning to the exclusion of cognitive learning.[4] In other words, many academics believe that service-learning practitioners are mainly interested in the touchy-feely stuff—not in cognitive, or thinking, skills. Furthermore, many in academia still believe that affective learning objectives like being sensitive to the values of others, becoming aware of one's own talents and abilities, and developing an appreciation for lifelong learning are not valid academic pursuits—at least not in the college classroom. Yet service-learning, if done well, can simultaneously bridge these gaps and address these concerns by blending cognitive and affective learning, providing effective community service, and connecting students to their communities.[5]

In this chapter, I present HR-HW as an example of how cognitive, affective, and effective learning objectives can coexist and thrive. The class provides students with an exceptional learning opportunity while helping and improving the community through an important service.[6] I argue that there are three core elements of successful service-learning courses: high-level cognitive learning, high-level affective learning, and effective community service. After reviewing these learning types, this chapter outlines the course components and analyzes the cognitive and affective learning objectives associated with HR-HW and the impact that this service-learning course has on students.

Learning Types and Course Development

One of the most widely respected scholars on education, Benjamin Bloom, offers a taxonomy of educational objectives that focuses on cognitive, affective, and psychomotor objectives.[7] Cognitive objectives generally refer to thinking skills and include knowledge, comprehension, application, analysis, synthesis, and evaluation. As noted in the previous paragraph, affective objectives generally refer to attitudes and values and include being sensitive to the values of others, becoming aware of one's own talents and abilities, and developing an appreciation for lifelong learning. Psychomotor objectives are usually skill-based and more vocational in their desired outcome; examples include physical movement, coordination, and the use of the motor skill areas.[8]

HR-HW incorporates both cognitive and affective learning objectives as well as an effective service to the community by requiring students to learn the intricacies of asylum law, pairing students with current asylum seekers, and having students (working under attorney supervision) interview asylum seekers to learn their stories. Students also are instructed in how to compile evidentiary packets based on the persecution experienced by the asylum seekers and how to submit these packets to immigration court; and students write a legal memo outlining the strengths and weaknesses of each case. They learn about international human rights, specifically, asylum law, and then apply this knowledge to actual ongoing cases. In addition, HR-HW provides students with an opportunity to learn about another culture, learn about the human rights issues in other countries, and have a significant effect on another person's life.

Seventy percent of the each student's grade in HR-HW is based upon the asylum/withholding of removal/convention against torture case. Students are evaluated not on whether they win cases, but instead on the quality of research conducted, the comprehensive nature of the affidavits, and the legal research and writing of the legal briefs and memos. In a mock court, students present their cases to the rest of the class, and class members get an opportunity to evaluate their peers.[9] Team members share the same grade, so teams have an added incentive to work together. The remaining 30% of the grade is based upon individual performance, which includes: in-class participation, posting and commenting on the HR-HW class blog,[10] and a reflection journal. The reflection journal is especially important because it gives the student a vehicle to connect in-class learning with out-of-class experience.

Asylum seekers fleeing persecution in their home countries often arrive at a US port of entry with very little. If an asylum seeker does not have a valid passport or visa, he or she is most likely arrested, shackled, and sent to a detention facility to wait for an adversarial hearing in front of an immigration judge and an Immigration and Customs Enforcement (ICE) attorney. Asylum seekers often are suffering from post-traumatic stress disorder (PTSD), and they may be further traumatized by their incarceration with criminals in the maximum-security prisons that sometimes serve as ICE detention facilities.[11] Detainees are not provided with an attorney unless they are able to afford to hire an immigration attorney or are fortunate enough to get pro bono help from a law firm or organization. Meanwhile, studies have shown that legal representation is crucial to winning asylum.[12]

Before discussing the details of the course, it is important to note that students in HR-HW are not law students, nor do they "practice" law in this class. Many are senior political science majors or major in another social science or the humanities. They are trained on the basics of asylum law by attorneys from a community partner—the Pennsylvania Immigration Resource Center (PIRC)—in a five-hour legal seminar early in the semester. The course relies heavily on PIRC to provide specific legal training and supervision.[13] The class meets weekly in a formal three-hour seminar, although I also meet with each team weekly to discuss the progression of its cases.

The course begins with a general introduction to international human rights law and then moves on to intensive training in US asylum law, appropriate techniques for interviewing survivors of torture, and legal research and writing. Several specialists are brought in to speak to the class, including a clinical psychologist who specializes in working with survivors of torture, an immigration judge, and an asylee (someone who has won asylum). In addition, I organize a prison tour and have students attend an asylum hearing. Usually one class period is devoted to each of these activities. Students are required to sign a confidentiality agreement as well as a Memorandum of Understanding (vetted by the college's attorney) with the community partners. Students essentially serve as paralegals to these community partners and always work under the direct supervision of an attorney. This course is thus dependent upon a true academic-community partnership.

I taught HR-HW for the first time in 2002. The course was created as an outgrowth of my own work as an expert witness in asylum cases. Realizing the life-changing effect that helping another person win asylum had on me, I wanted to create an opportunity for students to experience it as well. Although students do not serve as expert witnesses, they do help address a crucial need in the local community. (York County Prison [YCP] is about 30 minutes away and houses many unrepresented asylum seekers.[14]) The course is usually taught once a year.[15]

The course is capped at 16 students, and these students are divided into teams of two to work on safe-haven relief—meaning asylum,[16] withholding of removal,[17] and Convention Against Torture[18] cases—with PIRC and other local attorneys.[19] Since many detained immigrants[20] do not have legal representation, they rely on pro bono counsel or go in front of an immigration judge pro se (on their own). Students in the course help structure their detainees' affidavits of persecution, compile relevant country-specific human rights–conditions research, and write legal briefs or memos. PIRC and the other local attorneys with whom the students work represent the asylum seekers in court based on the information that the students compile, although some asylum seekers still appear pro se.

As they compile documentation, students learn about not only the law of asylum and international human rights, but also about the application of asylum law and international human rights on individuals. They learn first-hand about the human rights conditions in other countries and what effects these conditions have on people in those countries. They learn to discern a strong case from a weak case; think critically about the evidence; hone their skills in knowledge, comprehension, application, analysis, synthesis, and evaluation; become able to receive and respond to phenomena; and organize and internalize values.

Since 2002, students in the class have worked on 66 asylum cases from more than 35 countries, winning asylum for 26 individuals fleeing from persecution in Angola, Botswana, Cameroon, China, Cote D'Ivoire, Cuba, Dominican Republic, El Salvador, Guyana, Haiti, Honduras, Jamaica, Kenya, Liberia, Mali, Mauritania, Mongolia, Morocco, Niger, Nigeria, Russia, Serbia-Montenegro, Sierra Leone, Somalia, The Gambia, Togo, Turkey, and Uganda. As previously noted, most of the asylum seekers that the students work with are detained in the YCP without representation while waiting to appear before an immigration judge.[21]

Cognitive Learning Objectives

As outlined in Bloom's taxonomy of learning objectives, there are five key learning objectives that build upon one another: knowledge, comprehension, application, analysis, synthesis, and evaluation. I address each of these objectives and illustrate how HR-HW incorporates them into the student learning objectives.

Knowledge and Comprehension

One of the central goals of HR-HW is to teach students about human rights, and more specifically, about human rights abuses that occur in different countries.

Students explore the key international conventions on human rights, including the Universal Declaration of Human Rights; the International Covenants on Civil and Political Rights (ICPR); the Social, Economic and Cultural Rights (ICSECR); the Convention Against Torture (CAT); and the Convention on Refugees. The domestic interpretation of international law is translated into federal statute in the Immigration and Nationality Act (INA) and is based on case law. Consequently, students must become familiar with not only the federal regulations but also with the precedent-setting case law as it relates to their detainees' cases. Students then apply their knowledge and understanding of this information to actual cases. However, the course is not just about asylum law—it is not a law school course, after all. Finally, HR-HW requires students to understand the concept of human rights and why states violate their citizens' human rights.

Application and Analysis

Most faculty are unwilling to admit that students often forget facts and figures—no matter how interesting—they memorize for a test shortly after that test is taken. However, information retention is much more likely if students must apply that knowledge to a problem.[22] As one student in the HR-HW class explained in a weekly reflection paper,

> Something I really loved about this course is the hands-on involvement (service learning). There is no better way to learn about something than to be directly involved in it. I couldn't imagine learning about the asylum process from lectures and textbooks only. There is nothing like going to prison to meet a real asylum seeker, to hear her/him talk about her/his story, to see the court hearings, to strategize with the attorney, to have to research real conditions in a real country, to hear the judge render his/her decision ... it really makes it a special learning experience (Student "A", HR-HW 2004).[23]

Students in HR-HW apply their knowledge of US asylum law and international human rights law to their particular asylum, withholding of removal, or convention against torture cases—an involved process. There are three key components to a complete safe haven relief application: a detainee's affidavit documenting the basis for his or her "well-founded fear" of future persecution and his or her past persecution (the subjective basis for relief); documentary evidence of human rights abuses within the detainee's country of origin (objective basis for relief); and a legal brief.[24]

The detainee's affidavit documents his or her story of persecution. To qualify for asylum, the detainee must show that he or she has suffered past persecution, has a well-founded fear of future persecution, or provide proof of both. The problem is that persecution is not clearly defined in American immigration law. Persecution implies that a person or group will impose harm or suffering on the applicant. Whether the harm or suffering rises to the level of persecution is a case-by-case determination and fact-specific. Courts look at such things as:

- severity of harm
- frequency of events
- cumulative effects of the mistreatment
- arbitrary interference with a person's privacy, family, home, or correspondence
- relegation to substandard dwellings
- exclusion from institutions of higher learning
- enforced social or civil inactivity
- passport denial
- constant surveillance
- pressure to become an informer
- a combination of these

The key—or in legal terms, the nexus—is that the persecution is either by the government or a group that the government cannot or will not control. Thus, students must outline how each detainee's story of persecution relates to these conditions.[25]

Furthermore, the asylum applicant needs to show a reasonable probability that she or he will be persecuted. The US Supreme Court's basis for establishing a well-founded fear of persecution includes "having a fear of an event happening when there is even less than a 50% chance that it will take place, establishing a 10% chance of being shot, tortured, or [being] otherwise persecuted."[26] Elements of a "well-founded fear of persecution" include:

- the applicant possesses a belief or characteristic that persecutors seek to overcome by punishment
- the persecutor is aware, or could easily become aware, of the belief or characteristic
- the persecutor has the capability to punish the applicant
- the persecutor has the inclination to persecute the applicant[27]

Given these limitations, students are challenged to document detainees' stories to accurately reflect how each detainee's persecution qualifies for asylum, withholding of removal, or convention against torture relief. Navigating these challenges is often the most difficult aspect of the class because listening to someone's story of torture, rape, female genital mutilation, or detention can be traumatizing.[28] However, it is very educative in that it gives students first-person accounts of some of the human rights abuses that happen throughout the world and insight into other cultures. Students also have to hone their interpersonal skills to try to relate to the detainees and help them trust enough to tell their stories.

In addition to the affidavit, students must submit documentary evidence to support the objective basis for relief. Acceptable documentation includes reports from the US State Department Country Conditions on Human Rights, Amnesty International, and Human Rights Watch; reports by other international nongovernmental organizations; expert witness affidavits; family member affidavits; and local newspaper reports (available through Lexis-Nexis) on relevant issues related to the detainee's case. Each student team must then analyze and summarize the relevant material in a table of contents, with legal tabs identifying all of the material and showing how it relates to a detainee's case. The evidentiary packets that the student teams assemble are often 200–300 pages or more. These packets are submitted to the immigration court on behalf of the detainee. Students therefore apply their research and critical thinking skills to find relevant corroborating evidence for their detainees' stories. They become mini-experts on the human rights conditions within their detainees' countries and on the detainees' cases.[29]

Synthesis and Evaluation

How do the students provide evidence and convincing arguments that their detainees qualify for asylum, withholding of removal, or convention against torture relief? In addition to the affidavit and country conditions research, each student team must write a legal brief or memo.[30] This brief or memo must be a persuasive document that ties an applicant's story of persecution to the objective human rights country conditions and legal case law, synthesizing and applying these different sources of information. As part of this process, students must evaluate their detainees' cases and anticipate problems within each detainee's story. They also must be able to argue what a detainee qualifies for—that is, for asylum, for withholding of removal, or for convention against torture relief. Therefore students must be familiar with the statutory barriers to asylum,[31] the narrow definition of what constitutes torture,[32] and the difference between withholding of removal under the INA and withholding of removal under the CAT. They also must learn to evaluate the available evidence (objective and subjective) and transform it into a persuasive argument. As one student opined in her reflection journal,

> Last week, while preparing for the mock court, KL's story came back to me. Earlier, while actually preparing all the materials for the case, I was so caught up in doing a good job and meeting deadlines that I was almost removed from the reality that surrounded me—that this was a true story about a real person. However, when my partner and I were going over our mock court questions, KL's story became all the more real to me. I think this is the advantage of a class such as Human Rights/Human Wrongs. One is truly able to take knowledge from the classroom and apply it meaningfully to the real world (Student "B", HR-HW 2007).

Students are often amazed by the final product that they produce—comprehensive, logical, and court-ready documents, full of supportive evidence.

To a certain extent, the course does have a built-in safety net—since the stakes are so high, I prescreen each student before admittance into the course, discussing requirements and expectations.[33] It is a class that is useful for students interested in studying international politics and human rights because they learn first-hand how to conduct primary research on the human rights abuses within countries outside the United States while learning about international humanitarian organizations and the US interpretation of international obligations. In other words, this course brings the local and global closer together.

Affective Learning Objectives

Without a doubt, students in HR-HW are affected by what they witness, read, and do in the course. But what does that really mean? The affective domain focuses on how the students deal with things emotionally, including receiving phenomena; responding to phenomena; valuing, organizing, and internalizing values; and characterization.[34] Linking cognitive learning objectives with affective learning objectives creates a powerful and lasting imprint on students.

Receiving and Responding to Phenomena

Receiving phenomena refers to students' awareness of or willingness to listen to others. Responding to phenomena requires that students become active and motivated participants in their learning. To help complete affidavits, students in their teams of two (with their supervising attorney present) must meet with their asylum seekers multiple times for two to three hours to get the complete details of their stories of persecution. Sitting across from someone from another country, another culture, and another reality, students come face-to-face (perhaps uncomfortably so) with another human being's struggles and suffering.

Students do not always think that their asylum seekers are telling the truth. Teams have worked on several cases in which students find a story to be inconsistent or unbelievable based on a country's conditions. It is up to the supervising attorney, however, to determine whether a case moves forward.

Simply being a witness or receiving information about someone's trauma can have an emotional effect on the students. As one student reflected,

> At the end of this process, I have to say that perhaps this has been one of my most rewarding educational experiences, not simply because of the amount of work that a class such as this one demands, but also because of how emotionally challenging it can get. I think it really tests us out as human beings, and truly takes knowledge outside the classroom (Student "B", HR-HW 2007).

In addition, a strong bond often develops between a detainee and the students. Students become passionate and totally invested in helping their asylum seekers.[35] This connection leads to students not simply receiving phenomena, but responding to phenomena as well. As Student "B" commented,

> Yesterday, I went to meet KL at York County Prison. It was one of the most visceral experiences of my life. She is 21 years old and already has two children. She is only two years older than me. As I heard her

> story, the harsh reality of what goes on during war became clear to me. I have never had to experience war first hand. I have seen it on television, read about it in books, but I have never sat face to face with someone who had witnessed the wrath of war like KL has (Student "B", HR-HW 2007).

Students cannot be passive recipients of phenomena in this class—they have to become active participants in their learning. They are given the tools and opportunity to understand and interpret legal documents and develop skills to interview an individual from another culture suffering from PTSD. They do not regurgitate these rules or processes; rather, they apply them to real-life situations with real-life outcomes. Even when students have lost their cases, the experiences have been worthwhile—both intellectually and personally. As one student reflected,

> It has taken me some time to get over the loss (of the case) but I am glad for every minute of it. This project not only tested my logical skills but my emotional strength. I now know what it takes to be a lawyer and what it takes to lose a case as well. This has given me more insight into law then any book will ever give me (Student "C", HR-HW 2007).

Thus, regardless of the case outcomes, students appreciate the intellectual and personal gains they have made.

Valuing, Organizing, and Internalizing Values

Valuing refers to the worth that a person attaches to a particular object, phenomenon, or behavior. For example, it may refer to how sensitive one is toward individual and cultural differences. Organization refers to comparing, relating, and synthesizing values. Examples include accepting professional ethical standards and prioritizing time effectively to meet the needs of an organization, family, or self. Internalizing values suggests that students show self-reliance when working independently and that they revise judgment and change behavior in light of new evidence.[36]

Students in HR-HW are empowered to make a real difference in someone's life. With this role comes responsibility. Therefore, their commitment to their asylum seekers often takes on a life of its own:

> I don't think I have ever worried about a class this much. It's a very different kind of worry. I don't even think about grades. I think we are all beyond that point now. It has never happened to me before. I have always worked to get a good grade. Never to give the best I have to help someone else. Grades become such trivial stuff in the real world and I'm just glad I got the opportunity to do something that made me realize that there were things we can do even as students that are FAR more important than an A in your transcript! (Student "D", HR-HW 2003).

In fact, students frequently become so committed to their cases that I have to remind them that they have other classes that require their attention.

As noted, students learn important skills like collaboration, effective communication, organization, presentation, and debating. They would be unable to complete the asylum application (affidavit, documentary evidence, and legal brief/memo) if they did not work collaboratively with their partners. The workload is just too great. Students therefore have to learn to divide up the workload of interviewing the detainees, conducting Internet and other research on country-specific current and past human rights conditions, researching relevant case law, and writing the legal briefs or memos. In addition, students have to become effective communicators with their detainees, PIRC, their professor, and their teammate.

This real-life experience, combined with their formal training on immigration law and human rights research, helps provide the seeds for lifelong engagement. Most students crave a real learning experience in which they can make a real impact:

> This course has taught me so much about myself and my inner feelings and it is very strange to know that it is about to end in just a few short weeks. This course has put up front and "hot button" issues onto my doorstep. It was very difficult to get outside of my shell and make judgments or take a position on subjects that I didn't even have a definitive opinion on. This class has really enabled me to take a stance, even if it is very controversial, and stand by it, and defend it. By putting real issues at the forefront of our class, we have learned from each other that various opinions are present and that not everyone should be so closed minded to their own opinions on every subject (Student "E", HR-HW 2007).

It is very gratifying to see the personal growth that many students develop in HR-HW. As another student reflected:

> At the beginning of this course, I did not know much about immigration law. I did not know anything about asylum or withholding of removal. At the beginning of this course, I did not think I was interested in being a lawyer or that there were careers in law that could really make such a positive impact on the lives of the suffering. I did not think that working on the case and listening to my client's story would [make] me feel physically ill and would keep me up at night. But, then again, I did not know that I would feel this passionate about a cause and that the overwhelming feeling of work combined with the pressure to put together a good case would actually produce one of the most rewarding feelings that I've ever felt from a class. At the beginning of this course, I did not know what this course would actually mean to me.
>
> Now, I realize that it means first-hand knowledge and experience in an issue that I will never forget because I lived through it. It means a greater understanding of what is happening around the globe along with how that affects what is happening in the United States. It means understanding of the asylum law process, its shortfalls, its strengths and potentially how it could be reformed. And it means seeing judges and ICE attorneys as people instead of as the heartless robots that they can sometimes appear to be from the applicants' perspective. All of this

together means that I am more of a global citizen than ever with knowledge of how we are all interrelated (Student "G", HR-HW 2009).

Once students are exposed to the complexity of the asylum process and, more important, the role that they can play in positively affecting the outcome of a case, they become truly engaged in and committed to making a difference—at the very least—in the lives of the asylum seekers with whom they are working. The global boundaries are torn down as students realize that the person sitting across the table is more like them than not and that their common humanity binds them. As one student in HR-HW noted, "The most empowering moment in my life was when I realized that my ability to conduct research and analyze data had helped to grant someone safe haven in the United States."[37] It is my hope that this commitment to civic engagement and making a difference will last a lifetime.[38]

Effective Service to the Community

Reciprocity and sustainability are two key attributes of high-quality service-learning courses. Rigor is another. In other words, not only should students benefit from their community engagement, but they also should provide a valuable service to the community. Institutions of higher education are perfectly poised to make a difference in their communities and should do so if they wish to avoid continued criticism and produce graduates who have developed important civic engagement and citizenship skills. If reciprocity between the community and the college or university is not present and consistent in its presence, then the course is not sustainable. Similarly, the course must be rigorous and not regarded as "fluff."[39] Thus far, HR-HW students clearly have provided an incredible service to the community.[40] In their 66 cases, they have a 39.3% grant rate, higher than the national average for detained asylum seekers.

As demonstrated, students do not have to win their asylum, withholding of removal, or CAT cases to reach an effective learning outcome. Some of the cases that students worked on were not very strong, and no matter how much time or effort students put into them, they could not win because of the limitations of the cases themselves—for example, if a case did not meet any of the five enumerated grounds for winning asylum or if the asylum seeker was not credible. I work with the students to ensure that they can critically assess the validity of a case, and if they do work on a case that is not credible, I work with them to understand the context and reason why some individuals file fraudulent asylum claims. An effective learning outcome occurs if the students gained knowledge and skills in the process of providing a valuable service to the community. The immediate beneficiaries of the students' work are the individual detained immigrants, but the larger community also benefits. From the perspective of taxpayers, the service that these students provide allows for greater clarity and evidence for the cases, which helps expedite them through the immigration court process and lowers detention costs.

Conclusion

Service-learning is not for the faint of heart. It can be time-consuming, stressful, and logistically challenging.[41] If done correctly, however—with rigor, reflection, and reciprocity—it can be one of the most professionally rewarding pedagogical methods. It is especially gratifying to engage students in a meaningful service activity such as winning asylum for another human being and at the same time bring to light the connections between the local and the global. Students who have taken HR-HW have been profoundly transformed by the experience, as evidenced by some of their anecdotal comments included here.[42]

Perhaps equally important, those who teach service-learning courses like HR-HW are also profoundly transformed by the experience. My research and scholarly interests have benefited from an infusion of passion that comes from recognizing that one teacher can actually make a difference. In sum, this course has brought a new level of productivity to my teaching, scholarship, and service while also actively engaging students in the learning process, in original research, and in service to the community. If instructors are excited and passionate about what they teach, it is difficult to keep it from spreading. And who couldn't benefit from an infusion of passion and excitement about what we teach?

Bringing the World Home: Effectively Connecting Civic Engagement and International Relations

17

By Alison Rios Millett McCartney
with Sivan Chaban

Most existing civic engagement courses in political science are focused on national, state, or local politics. This chapter shows that civic engagement pedagogy that utilizes the service-learning method can be effectively practiced in international relations courses. It also presents some beginning efforts at gathering data on postgraduate outcomes. We ask: Do students from these courses remain civically engaged after the classes end, especially after graduation? We argue that, overall, this combination can be effective in developing knowledge about and sustained interest in international relations and civic engagement both during and after college.

The final question in civic engagement pedagogy is often whether a particular class will make a difference in students' knowledge and practice of civic engagement once the class has ended. Some scholars have already begun to evaluate the civic engagement of college students,[1] both during and after college, and multiple chapters in this volume present excellent examples of how to pursue this goal. The project discussed in this chapter aims to build upon these and other studies by including the subfield of international relations (IR) and taking a first step toward assessing the postgraduate effects of civic engagement pedagogy in an IR classroom.

The connection between learning about international relations and teaching the skills, knowledge, and values of civic engagement has not been pursued nearly as vigorously in international relations as in subfields such as state and local government, American government, and public policy. This gap is significant when considering that more than 200,000 undergraduates enrolled as political science majors in 2007–2008, another 44,000 enrolled as international studies majors in 2007–2008, and almost 20% of APSA's members consider their primary subfield as international relations.[2] At my home institution alone, 35% of enrollment since 2010 has been in international relations and comparative politics courses.[3] When an international relations course in the discipline does contain a civic engagement component, the course is usually part of a study abroad program. Such study abroad opportunities should continue to be strongly encouraged and can be a valuable way to foster civic engagement; however, this option is out of reach for students who lack the economic resources required for such programs and for an increasing number of nontraditional students with significant domestic responsibilities. Students also may encounter civic engagement literature and opportunities in other political science courses, but these may not be tied to their area of greatest academic interest and therefore not necessarily subject to their most thoughtful inquiry and investigation. In short, they may never enroll in civic engagement courses if the subject matter does not engage them. Further, if Zivi is correct that the service experience involved in some civic engagement courses can enrich learning and help students "live, test, and challenge academic theories,"[4] then instructors are missing an important learning option in international relations pedagogy.

Another reason to use civic engagement pedagogy in the international relations subfield is:

> Americans tend to perceive globalization as a unidirectional process in which American culture, goods, and ideas flow out into the world without recognizing how exogenous influences from other countries are reciprocally incorporated into the American fabric.[5]

Americans and others often assume that globalization means Americanization, without analyzing the interconnectedness inherent to globalization, the local effects of globalizing influences, or even the accuracy of such perceptions.[6]

A civic engagement service-learning component of an international relations course can go a step further than nonexperiential learning courses in several ways. First, such a component can push students to recognize the interconnectedness inherent in globalization and require them to gain the extra knowledge about actual global-local connections. Second, it can compel the students to disseminate this knowledge and meet an unmet (and perhaps unknown) need to improve a local community's collective knowledge of its role and place in the world community, in effect bringing home global connections. In addition, these courses can help address the call for greater internationalization of the curriculum.[7]

If the benefits are so potentially great, then why haven't more such courses been created in this subfield? There are many potential reasons,[8] including:

- lack of knowledge of how to make connections between local civic engagement and international problems and issues
- lack of awareness of how to incorporate service-learning tools in international relations classes
- lack of emphasis on this type of education in graduate programs
- a perceived lack of opportunity to practice combining the two learning areas of international relations and civic engagement through service-learning tools

This chapter demonstrates that civic engagement service-learning pedagogy can be effectively practiced in international relations courses. It argues that this combination can develop knowledge about and sustained interest in international relations and civic engagement both during and after college.

After a brief review of methodology, this chapter reviews the structure of the civic engagement options that I currently provide at Towson University (TU) and the connection to and activities with the course's community partner. I then present qualitative data on the beliefs, discoveries, transformations, challenges, and gaps between students' expectations of the difficulty or ineffectiveness of civic engagement and their actual experiences with efficacy, as reported by class members. I hope to uncover what students gained the most from the two classes and where changes in attitudes and understandings of both civic engagement and international issues occurred.[9] I also provide quantitative data gathered from course evaluations and qualitative data derived from reflection essays and course evaluations to determine the overall strengths and weaknesses of the civic engagement courses featured in the chapter. Lastly, I provide preliminary survey data on postgraduation activities and attitudes toward civic engagement, continued learning about international relations, and use of skills developed in the classes. I argue that the data demonstrate sufficient benefits to students' learning and development as citizens to warrant further exploration and creation of civic engagement–themed international relations courses in political science.

Methodology: Student and Alumni Feedback Mechanisms

This chapter adds to previous work about Civic Engagement and International Affairs[10] and that course's second semester counterpart, Independent Study: Civic Engagement and International Affairs Research, at Towson University[11] by providing new qualitative and quantitative data. The qualitative data collected during students' college careers were extracted from reflective essays students were required to write for a grade at the end of each semester. As these essays were graded, it is expected that some answers may not be completely honest. However, reliability increases when the same answers to the same questions (see the following sections) are repeated over different semesters, and with a certain number of similar responses. Another common concern is that researchers (as course instructors) will interpret students' comments based upon their own a priori assumptions about what students are learning in class. To address this, three years of data were coded independently by two separate researchers, with a high degree of intercoder reliability.[12]

The quantitative data set seeks to determine if measurable or perceived effects on civic engagement, interest in international relations, or both can be tracked for graduated students who took at least one of the two classes. The postgraduate survey represents a relatively small sample of students over five academic years from fall 2004 to spring 2009, but it demonstrates the importance of gathering useful postgraduate data and indicates where the class has or has not been successful in reaching its stated pedagogical goals. These goals include:

- facilitating collegiate and postgraduate civic engagement
- gaining an understanding of connections between civic engagement and international issues
- developing a long-term interest in and attention to international issues
- creating or affirming one's efficacy in being civically engaged
- building useful skills for civic engagement and a variety of postgraduate careers, such as constructive deliberation, research, organizational abilities, leadership, advanced writing, and oral presentation to diverse groups

Collecting both postcourse and alumni data has helped to determine where and how these classes can be improved and better survey instruments can be designed. Ultimately, the data presented in this chapter will be used to (1) provide a preliminary analysis of the effects of the civic engagement international relations courses on students' long-term knowledge, skills, and practice of engagement; (2) present a preliminary model for other teacher-scholars in international relations to consider adding civic engagement components to their courses; and (3) spur disciplinewide discussion about best practices in promoting and analyzing the effectiveness of civic engagement pedagogy within and across disciplinary subfields.

Context: Meeting the Needs of a Community Partner

In the fall semester, I teach the upper-level class Civic Engagement and International Affairs. As a full discussion of the structure and rationale for the creation of the class has been presented elsewhere,[13] only some of that article's key points follow, as is relevant to this stage of research. After being approached in the summer of 2002 by Hugh Kearney, then a teacher in the poorest school district in the Baltimore County Public Schools (BCPS) system, he and I created a Model United Nations Conference to be held at Towson University[14] for Baltimore County 10th graders.[15] Kearney came to TU because of its mission of active involvement in the community and its identity as a metropolitan university, a label which includes dedication to community issues and problems.[16]

As other scholars have documented, partnerships between a university and community partners are more productive for both sides when the partnership is created for mutual gains rather than as a form of charity by one toward the other.[17] Lisman (1998) elucidates a number of key guidelines to follow in creating these partnerships. For example, he cites the importance of mutual respect of individual goals and agreement upon mutual goals, benefits, and values in a long-term, sustained commitment to achieve concrete successes for both partners. Kearney and I started with several research and brainstorming meetings between the conference cofounders, followed by meetings that included our supervisors to ensure this compatibility and sharing of institutional goals, benefits, values, and costs.[18]

Unlike large, national Model UN conferences, this model was created with two distinguishing goals. First, we sought to make the conference free for all participants. This provided learning opportunities to middle- and lower-income high schools in the county whose socioeconomic status prohibits utilizing existing national or regional options.[19] Second, we wanted to include academically based interaction with college professors to expose the students to college-level educational practices, expectations, and instructors. A third component, meaningful interaction with current college students, was later added as an additional means to encourage college aspirations, provide contacts for learning about college life, and present potential role models.

After the first year, it was clear that participating high school students needed more instruction in several areas, including: (1) researching issues, (2) writing policy proposals and other documents, (3) oral presentation and negotiation, and (4) techniques of international negotiation. Instruction before the two-day conference was necessary to allow students to take full advantage of this learning opportunity. To address the needs of BCPS, Kearney and I created a November Model UN Training Day to prepare the high school students for the March conference. Activities for the day include:

- an introductory lecture on the United Nations
- a group activity on the UN's priority issues, which my students and I facilitate
- a review of the major political, economic, and social issues, led by a TU professor who is an expert in the region that each group of students was assigned to represent
- lunch with TU students
- small-group negotiation and diplomacy workshops with TU students
- a review of conference procedures by Mr. Kearney

Yearly conference evaluations submitted by high school teachers and participants have shown that this opening event ensures that the partnership of BCPS and TU is better able to achieve its goals of helping lower- and middle-income students participate in academic activities that can increase their college opportunities, advance their academic knowledge and skills, and provide meaningful interaction with college professors and students. The hope is that this last goal includes gaining familiarity with college life and expectations and encouraging college aspirations, though more research is needed to provide evidence for this outcome.

To make this community endeavor work, many TU student volunteers were needed to run the March conference. At an informal gathering after the first conference in March 2003, the TU students asked me—unprompted—if there were more ways in which they could get involved with the program. After the second year of the conference and the first Training Day in November 2003, my students again pressed me to turn their work into something more than mere volunteering. After consulting with my department chair and dean, I developed a civic engagement service-learning course to run in conjunction with the November Training Day.[20]

Course 1: Civic Engagement and International Affairs

The first class, Civic Engagement and International Affairs, runs on a discussion-based model.[21] It is an upper-level elective class that counts for both political science and international studies majors and minors, but it is open to other students if they have taken an introductory international relations course. The pedagogical goals include advancing students' understanding of:

1. the purposes, complexities, difficulties, and rewards of civic engagement, including the need for open deliberation that demonstrates respect for diverse viewpoints
2. contemporary international issues
3. the role of the United Nations in the world
4. the connection between local and global issues
5. the ways in which students' own civic engagement can be connected to both local and global affairs
6. a personal sense of efficacy as a civically engaged citizen
7. an understanding of the service-learning method

Additional goals include the growth of writing, research, critical thinking, oral presentation, and leadership skills. The course begins with three to four weeks of readings and discussion on the concept of civic engagement in a democracy, the role of citizens in a democracy, and the role of colleges and universities in fostering (or not) students' civic engagement. In the following six weeks, students read about and discuss the major issues on the UN General Assembly's agenda for that fall. In the past several years, the focus has been mostly on the Millennium Development Goals—whether progress has been made in achieving those goals and whether the UN is playing positive role in any of these achievements. One week in November is spent preparing for the Training Day events. On the Training Day, the students run two activities entirely on their own—the UN activity and the diplomacy and negotiation workshops—in addition to performing such functional duties as staffing the registration table.

The remainder of the semester is spent reviewing students' presentations of their research projects and exploring the most effective ways to communicate their findings.[22] These projects require them to choose one organ or associated agency of the UN (e.g., UNICEF, World Health Organization), evaluate its success in pursuing its mission in the world, and explain its connection back to the Greater Baltimore Metropolitan Area (Washington, DC, is purposefully excluded). In December, they must present their research to one of the BCPS high school social studies classes involved with the conference and include learning activities based on their presentations.[23] Thus they learn about research, civic engagement, and international relations issues and then must disseminate their knowledge of the UN, global issues, and connections between the community and these global issues to the community both in the university setting and the community partner's setting.[24] Through these presentations and the Training Day events, students are providing a service to the community that would otherwise remain unmet. Creating activities that enrich student learning while meeting a previously unmet community need places this project within the framework of service-learning.

Course 2: Independent Study: Civic Engagement and International Affairs Research

Students who participated in the high school outreach project as part of the first civic engagement course wanted to keep working with the conference to see how their work with the high schoolers came to fruition, and some were interested in working further on their research projects. In determining what the students wanted, what would advance their learning and skill development, and what would help the community partner, I decided to create a second semester research course open only to those who get a grade of B or higher in the first class, thereby demonstrating the skills, capabilities, and personal maturity necessary to satisfactorily complete the more advanced work required.[25] My pedagogical goals in this second class include:

- advancing students' civic engagement skills by giving them the opportunity to practice working with community members on a common project
- enhancing students' leadership skills as they direct high schoolers' conference preparation
- furthering students' writing, research, and oral presentation skills
- developing students' critical thinking skills through exposure to advanced research
- deepening students' knowledge of international issues
- increasing students' understanding of the importance of and confidence in being civically engaged citizens who connect global and local issues.

Following upon the previous semester's work, Towson students continue helping high school participants prepare for the Model UN Conference and run the conference in March. In addition, they assist BCPS teachers by running after-school meetings to prepare for the Model UN event.

The resulting class has four components: a civic engagement "internship" with the Model UN program, an advanced research paper, a reflective essay, and at least one application to present advanced research at a local, regional, or national undergraduate research conference. Students can pursue two of these four options. For three credits, students:

- serve as "school coaches" (approximately 10–12 contact hours, see the following description) for the UN Conference

- consult with me regularly regarding this activity (about two hours)
- help prepare materials for and work the two-day March conference (about 16–18 hours)
- continue to develop their research projects from the previous semester into a work presentable at a national, regional, or local undergraduate research conference
- practice presentations and critique any practice research presentations of those taking three-credits (about four hours)
- attend debriefing meetings after the Model UN Conference and after research conferences (about two hours)
- write another five-page reflection paper

For one credit, students must do all of these except develop their research project and present it at a conference. In either case, they serve as school coaches and conference interns for a minimum of 30 hours, with most working 40–50 hours in addition to independent research, writing, and preparation as relevant to their amount of credits. This course is also an upper-level elective class that counts for both the political science and international studies majors and minors.

Serving as a school coach means helping at least one high school's team prepare for all components of the conference in several after-school meetings and online. In the meetings, coaches prepare information about the conference and the countries the high school student teams will represent. They also are expected to help the high school students prepare their own research, write conference communication materials, and practice conference presentations. They must keep a record of these meetings and the research they compile in a portfolio and discuss them in their reflection papers.

For the research component, students must substantially revise their papers from the previous semester by providing a greater quantity and quality of research (for example, through additional case studies). They also must refine their writing skills through a continual revision process. Finally, they apply critical thinking by consulting materials and evaluating various arguments on their agencies' abilities and successes (or lack thereof) in achieving their goals. This structure is similar to what is traditionally done in an independent study course with a professor and includes the regular research consultations with the instructor inherent to these courses.

The research component requires students to apply to present their research at a local, regional, or national undergraduate research conference. By the end of first semester, I have reviewed their work and can gauge which level is best for each student. Students complete their own applications in consultation with the instructor, though they are graded only on the application, not their acceptances. To date, I have not had a student denied a spot in at least one venue, though I have had two who did not apply.[26] Such conferences present an excellent opportunity to promote the value of disseminating research, prepare advanced work for an audience beyond their immediate peers, practice fielding comments and criticism from strangers, and evaluate the work of others. For those students intending to attend graduate school, this experience can show them the level of work expected, help them decide if they really want to pursue advanced academic work, and enhance their applications to graduate school. As of the end of the spring 2011 semester, six student presentations had been made at the national level, six at the regional level, and nine at the local level.[27]

DATA ANALYSIS: ACHIEVING PEDAGOGICAL GOALS

From 2004 to 2011, 86 undergraduates and two graduate students took the first class, Civic Engagement and International Affairs. The demographics of undergraduate enrollees are shown in Table 17-1:

TABLE 17-1: Undergraduate Demographics, 2004–2009[a]

Gender	Race	International	Year	Major
Male: 43%	White: 87.2%	7%	Freshman: 3.5%	Political Science: 48%
Female: 57%	Black: 7.0%		Sophomore: 21%	International Studies: 22%
	Asian: 3.5%		Junior: 37.2%	Political Science/International Studies (combined): 9.3%
	Hispanic: 2.3%		Senior: 37.2%	Social Science: 2.3%
			Nondegree: .1%	Business: 2.3%
				Other: 10.5%
N= 86 (always)				Unknown: 5.8%

Note:
[a] All percentages are rounded to nearest tenth, and thus at times the total does not equal 100%. International students also were counted in an additional category as the subject of democracy was not confined to just American-style democracy. These demographics are largely in line with the overall student body, except for the overrepresentation of males (overall, 62% female and 32% male) and a slight underrepresentation of blacks (12%) See Towson University Center for Diversity, "Diversity Profile," accessed on August 26, 2011, at http://www.towson.edu/diversity/profile.asp.

For the second semester class, Independent Study: Civic Engagement and International Affairs Research, 33.3% of the undergraduates were ineligible to continue because they had graduated or transferred or had not received a grade of B or higher in the first class. An additional 2.3% of students were ineligible because they studied abroad in the spring semester. Of the 56 students eligible to continue, 51.8% chose to take the second class.[28] Another 32.1% of the students who completed the first course and were eligible to continue chose to volunteer for some or all of the one-credit duties assigned to students who enrolled in the second-semester course.[29] These volunteers were unable to take the second independent study class for credit for several reasons, including lack of space in a final semester schedule due

Figure 17-1: Student Enrollment, Second Semester, of 56 Total

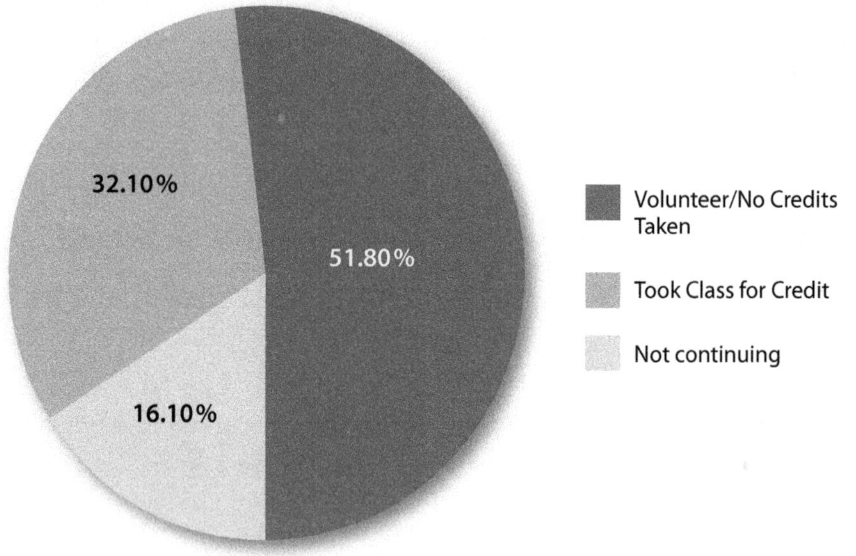

to requirements toward a major or minor, work obligations, sports team conflicts, or lack of funds to pay for the credits. Nonetheless, many students continue to volunteer in later semesters when they can no longer earn credit. In sum, 83.9% of eligible undergraduate students have chosen to continue working at some level with the conference (see Figure 17-1). Both graduate students volunteered in the second semester,[30] as their program does not allow them to pursue the second semester course credit option.

These results suggest that a clear majority of the students enjoy the civic engagement experience, and an overwhelming majority continues to participate when given the option. Comments from the most recent reflection essays highlight why they make this choice. One student noted,

> I learned that I am passionate about teaching others and helping encourage understanding regarding international issues.... This is a new realization, as I always knew I loved international affairs but I was uncertain as to how to pursue this venture in the future. Now I have a new area of focus for my life.

Another commented,

> While in class I was still ruminating on my frustration because of the thought that nothing I did could make a big enough difference.... Presenting at a school changed my thinking about my role in a democracy. An idea can become a norm, and I now think that I can make a difference.

Yet another reflected,

> Adding the civic engagement portion of the class emphasized the larger importance of why I am majoring in political science—to understand the way society works, and to hopefully make a difference in it.... Being in this class made me reevaluate my priorities and realize that civic engagement is something that has to remain a part of my life because it really does make me happy.[31]

Further, university-administered, anonymous teaching evaluations demonstrate that the pedagogical foundations of the first class, Civic Engagement and International Affairs—its organization, learning objectives, and explanation of requirements and expectations—are solid, with 85–98% of students from 2004 to 2011 rating the clarity of these components as good or excellent.[32] Written comments from these evaluations improved from the first time the fall class was offered, with fewer students asking for more clarity over time.

Requests to shorten the paper length and assigned readings appear every semester, but these are not unique requests of students in any class. As one student[33] stated in 2005, "It was challenging, but I expected that and would have been disappointed if it wasn't." Most students also comment favorably on the discussion format in an open-ended question, "What did you like about the way the teacher taught the course?" One student in 2005 responded that it "was very interactive and made learning fun. I always wanted to go to class." Another student that same year stated, "The discussions could go wherever we wanted to take them," suggesting that the student felt some ownership of the learning experience. In 2010, one offered that this format was "a great way to learn of different perspectives and bring up interesting topics," with many students over the years commenting that they felt free to express a variety of opinions. These comments also suggest some success in achieving the pedagogical goal of understanding the need to respect openness and diverse viewpoints as part of civic engagement.

Reflection essays also suggest that pedagogical goals are achieved. Most students' essays have echoed several goals. For example, on the goal of understanding the complexities, difficulties, and rewards of civic engagement and the development of critical thinking skills, one student noted:

> Having the opportunity to develop real perspectives and ideas is something I have not always had the chance to do in other courses ... I felt that even just our class discussions were a great example of civic engagement because it was a group of people genuinely working together to understand and to try to make a difference.... I think I can speak for a lot of people in our class who left the room on one day or another feeling compelled to continue to consider a problem with a hope to find viable solutions. To me this is an essential part of civic engagement—actually getting personally invested in learning.

To illustrate the goals of understanding connections between global and local issues and students' own engagement as part of that connection, one student commented in 2010: "I found out that participation does not only address domestic issues but the UN is a case study on how a citizen's role can grow to a global scale." Another student added: "Civic engagement makes politics, even on the international level, real and not just a spectator event." The tie between the personal empowerment of being civically engaged and the development of leadership skills was expressed by this same student in stating that "helping with the conference increased my leadership experience, because the students listened to me, which was very exhilarating." Again, I accept that some comments may be skewed by the lack of anonymity and the fact that it is a graded exercise. Instructor statements regarding course learning objectives also can shape students' responses. However, students received no specific prompts as part of the assignments, therefore, reflective exercises can help measure conscious learning and development, particularly by coding for common phrases and words that denote values and benefits gained.

To begin to discern where and how the class has made an impact on students, reflective statements over three years were content coded for the following types of statements: discovery, beliefs, evaluative, transformative, skill development, challenges, expectations versus outcomes, and, solely as a check on intercoder reliability, discussions of assigned readings.[34] These categories were chosen in conjunction with questions given on the Carnegie Foundation Political Engagement Survey (pre- and postcourse), which was administered at the beginning and end of the course, and specific course goals.[35]

Discovery statements, such as an introduction to new international issues and concepts, increased understanding of the United Nations, learning the satisfaction and enjoyment of civic engagement, a new understanding of what civic engagement is, and a new feeling of the personal ability to bring change, were among those included most frequently.[36] These correspond with the course learning objectives of understanding contemporary international issues, the role of the UN in the world, and the purposes and rewards of civic engagement. Second were belief statements, with the highest ranking being the importance of citizen participation, the importance of civic engagement overall to a healthy democracy, and the importance of remaining informed to effect citizen participation; these correspond to course learning objectives involving increasing understanding of all aspects of civic engagement.[37] The third biggest category was transformative statements, which included increased awareness of global issues and their impacts, a new sense of accomplishment or achievement, and a deeper understanding of civic engagement.[38] Statements in this category correspond to the goals of understanding the connection between global and local issues and ways in which students' own civic engagement can tap into this connection, as well as the goal of understanding the complexities and difficulties of civic engagement. The top placement of these three types of statements and the content of the most numerous statements correspond to the learning objectives of the class related to civic engagement and international issues.

The next most often-mentioned category is expectation versus outcome statements, a focus of many of the Carnegie survey questions and students' questions on the first day of the fall class. These are interesting because the category is almost exclusively filled with positive comments regarding the gap between the college students' anticipation of low levels of participation quality by the high school students and the actual performance of the high school students in the UN Conference activities and in-class exercises that students generated as part of their presentations at the high schools.[39] This better-than-expected performance by the high school students likely added to Towson students' positive perceptions of civic engagement and their efficacy in civic engagement, a clear goal of the college classes.[40] Finally, the challenges that students most expected were the high school presentation and public speaking; students were nervous about their ability to communicate clearly and effectively with high school audiences. I do not have data to explain students' fears and concerns about public speaking, but I speculate that residual feelings about their high school experiences may be an important factor.[41]

The data presented here support the conclusion that the civic engagement courses described in this chapter provide a useful model for others who wish to incorporate service-learning and civic engagement into their international relations courses. As with any course, clear learning objectives, a supportive environment, and challenging[42] assignments that require both knowledge acquisition and application will strengthen learning outcomes. Indeed, rooting learning in the classroom while providing experience in the community is key to moving students beyond volunteering to civic engagement. Connecting theory to application helps students more fully understand the duties and capabilities of citizens in a democracy and provides a starting point to build social capital for a community's future.[43]

Because the ultimate goal of any civic learning course is long-term, transformative change, I now turn to some preliminary evidence on whether the civic engagement classes described in this chapter have fueled ongoing interest in civic engagement and international relations; provided students' with the skills, motivation, and sense of efficacy needed to pursue civic engagement activities after graduation; or resulted in some combination of these. Knowing what students do when their teachers are no longer there to prompt their actions can provide insight into whether or not long-term pedagogical goals are being reached—in other words, whether or not the development of civically engaged and politically aware citizens is being fostered.

Where Are They Now? Postgraduate Civic Engagement Attitudes and Activities

To begin to assess whether or not these classes have a positive effect on former students' civic engagement attitudes and practices and interest in international issues, my research assistant, Sivan Chaban, and I developed a survey in the fall of 2010 of those who had taken at least one of the classes from 2004 to 2009. We did not include the most recent 2010–2011 classes because so few of the students had graduated when the data were collected. The surveys were emailed from December 2010 to April 2011, after contact with about three-quarters of the former students via Facebook to get current contact information and alert them to the forthcoming survey. Of the

FIGURE 17-2: Comparative Voter Turnout 2004 and 2008[a]

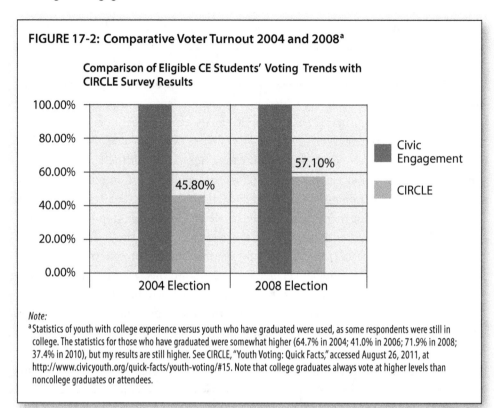

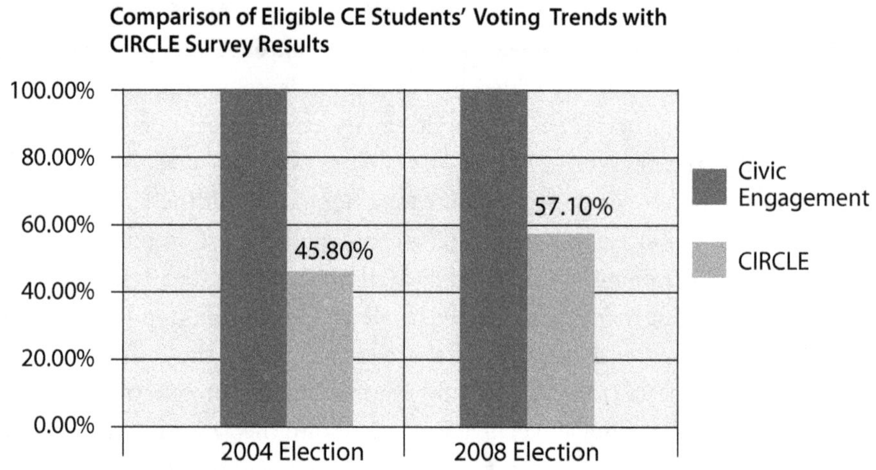

Note:
[a] Statistics of youth with college experience versus youth who have graduated were used, as some respondents were still in college. The statistics for those who have graduated were somewhat higher (64.7% in 2004; 41.0% in 2006; 71.9% in 2008; 37.4% in 2010), but my results are still higher. See CIRCLE, "Youth Voting: Quick Facts," accessed August 26, 2011, at http://www.civicyouth.org/quick-facts/youth-voting/#15. Note that college graduates always vote at higher levels than noncollege graduates or attendees.

74 people in this category, 25 responses (33.7% response rate) were received. These were sent directly to my student assistant, who has kept all responses anonymous, and survey responders knew that the answers and the list of who did or did not respond would remain anonymous; this information was not even shared with me.[44]

The survey included basic demographic, political and religious affiliation, and voter turnout questions.[45] Most significant in this question grouping was the finding that voter turnout was very high among these former students when they were eligible. In the midterm elections, all but three voted in 2006 (two ineligible) and 17 voted in 2010 (one ineligible), giving this group turnout rates of 86.9% in 2006 and 70.8% in 2010. CIRCLE reports that 28.7% of youth with some college experience voted in 2006, with 27.4% voting in 2010. In presidential election years, all former students who were eligible reported voting in both 2004 and 2008. In contrast, 45.8% of youth with college experience voted in 2004, rising to 57.1% in 2008 (see Figure 17-2).

The importance and role of regular voting in a successful democracy was a regular subject of class discussion, so higher voting outcomes among this group were anticipated. While these preliminary data provide only correlation rather than causation, they nonetheless suggest that there is reason to explore this connection further and continue research on the connection between students who take a civic engagement class in college and their postgraduation voting practices.

In the questions specifically geared toward the courses' learning objectives, two-thirds of the respondents were found to watch, read, or listen to international

FIGURE 17-3: Long-Term Effects of Civic Engagement Experiences on Former Students

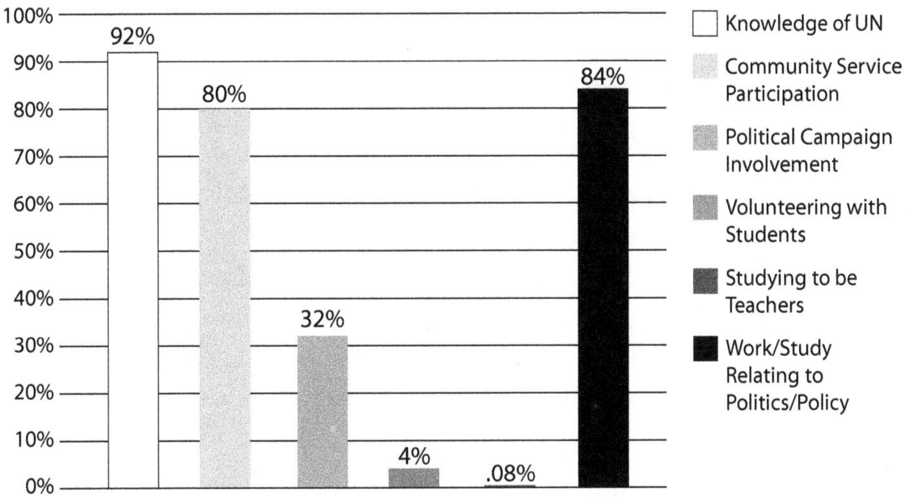

news stories daily and one-third do so weekly. All but two of the 25 students responding were still able to accurately name at least five UN agencies and their main goals, which supports the findings on continued attention to international issues and whether specific knowledge from the class remained. Twenty students have volunteered for community service in the past five years, 18 currently volunteer, and eight have worked on political campaigns. Twenty-three ranked the importance of their civic engagement classes to their educations between 8 and 10 on a 10-point scale, with 10 being of greatest importance (see Figure 17-3).

When asked an open-ended question about whether or not the class(es) changed the way that the respondents perceive their roles as citizens, 78% said yes, and most of those who said no added that it deepened or strengthened their pre-existing ideas about the importance of participation. In another open-ended question about the most important things they took from the class into their daily lives, the most common responses were:

- their research, writing, and editing skills improved
- they learned how to develop and defend political and social views
- the experience made them more confident speaking in public
- they learned how to become more proactive as citizens
- they better understand the importance and long-term effects of proactive involvement in their communities

Other respondents commented that they learned the importance of and skills for peer and self-evaluation, advanced their personal growth and development, and gained skills for and interest in working with high school and middle school students.

Ten respondents reported volunteering to work with middle or high school students in the past five years, with two of these individuals working with simulations like the Model UN while at their graduate institutions. Two respondents are studying to be high school teachers, and a third already is a high school social studies teacher. From a prompted question, seven other respondents noted that the classes affected their specific civic engagement activity choices, such as engaging in areas (for example, working with AIDS patients after studying the UNAIDS agency) that they had not previously considered.

Comments from these open-ended questions shed further light on the benefits of civic engagement pedagogy. Sample quotes include:

> I think that the most important thing that I took away is that I am not helpless in my community or even in the world community. Civic Engagement too[k] something (politics) that seemed out of reach and confusing and put it all in my hands and made it seem easy. I learned that I am a lot more capable than I realized.

> More so than any other course, I feel that Civic Engagement prepared me to be an active citizen, comfortable to discuss local, state, national, and international issues with a global view.

> Civic Engagement was one of the most fulfilling classes I ever participated in.

> The class made me see the need for a more collaborative form of engagement…, not just by individual action.

> Too often, as Americans, we become complacent because we think that, as one person, we cannot affect[sic] change, but it only takes one person to get other involved and engaged.

> Civic Engagement class taught me that sometimes, voting isn't enough. As responsible citizens, we must justify our vote through our words and actions—and live our vote. Otherwise, we will never see change in this world.

Most students who took these courses in civic engagement and international relations have gone on to or are developing careers in public service or international relations or are attending graduate school. The knowledge and practice they gained in these courses have affected their career choices as well as their future citizen engagement. Of those not in graduate school at the time of the survey, one was an AmeriCorps teacher, another was a high school social studies teacher, one is in active service in the US military, and one is a program assistant at an international women's rights nongovernmental organization. When asked a question about the most important things from these classes that resonate with them or help them in their daily lives, this last student responded, "Well, the class literally changed my life. It introduced me to human rights and their importance, and made me realize that I want to work in this field." Eleven students are currently in related master's programs (one of whom also serves in the military), two have master's degrees and are in related doctoral programs, two have completed related master's degrees, and three were in the process of applying to related master's programs; that is, 60% are attending or have completed a master's degree, with the potential for that percentage to increase once admissions decisions were made. While in graduate school, one respondent was a campaign manager, and another is a research macroeconomist for an international organization.

Respondents were not explicitly asked if the civic engagement courses affected their career choices; however, six stated in open-ended questions that the classes did move their career choices toward something connected to politics or public policy. Three more added that the class(es) did affect some significant aspect of how they pursued goals at their jobs, such as assigning particular types of tasks to subordinates based on how they learned to work with others in the classes. Overall, 21 of 25 respondents are engaged in study or work in jobs directly connected to politics or public policy (see Table 17-2).

TABLE 17-2: Postgraduate Careers[a]

Postgraduate study, related field	13	Campaign manager	1
Applying to postgraduate program, related field	3	Related NGO	1
Completed postgraduate program, in job market	2	Related IGO	1
Teacher, Secondary	2	Active military	1

Note:
[a] Note that there are three overlaps: one was both in graduate school and working; one had just finished one graduate program and was applying to another in a related field; and one was a teacher also applying to a postgraduate program.

More long-term studies are needed, especially given that so many of the individuals who took the courses are still in graduate school, and comparative data with other classes will be needed. These data, however, suggest a definite connection exists among civic engagement, service-learning classes in political science, and career choices.

Limitations of This Study

The data presented in this chapter provide preliminary evidence to suggest that these classes have succeeded in their pedagogical goals of fostering informed, engaged citizens who remain aware of international issues after graduation. In the current first course, questions are now being asked about student attitudes toward civic engagement at the beginning of the class to better determine before and after effects. There may be a self-select bias of students taking this class who are already positively predisposed toward civic engagement and interest in politics as political science and international studies majors, though as a state institution, there is no inherent self-select bias of school selection wherein students agree to a service mission upon enrollment. Pointed questions specifically about the effects of both classes may provide the opportunity to find further links between perceived cause and effect outcomes. Further research is also needed to disentangle if service-leaning experiences are, like internships, gateways to employment opportunities because of the skills, knowledge, and connections gained or if students' self-selection into civic engagement, service-learning classes is an indicator of existing characteristics, such as high self-motivation, that make these individuals inherently more attractive job candidates.

Application to Nonresearch I College and Universities

Civic engagement courses are currently available at several universities. However, Research I–classified colleges and universities have substantial resources that allow them to more easily expand offerings; provide extra staff to compensate for a tenured or tenure-track instructor's work in more labor-intensive classes, including, but not limited to, graduate students; provide extra funding for civic engagement projects; or some combination of these. While applicable to Research I universities, this chapter provides a feasible model for schools at which the teaching load of instructors is higher and the available resources are lower.

In terms of financial costs, the civic engagement project described here currently costs the university approximately $3,000, which includes the venue, technology, and all supporting material. In addition, the university pays to hire an adjunct to teach one class per semester that I no longer teach so that I may teach these courses. The county school system pays for bus transportation to and from the university. Each high school currently pays a fee of about $225 per year for activities and the cost of substitute teachers for days teachers come with their students to the Model UN conference ($150 per teacher, total). In sum, the financial costs are not prohibitive for either the university or the high schools involved in this project.[46]

Like all courses with embedded civic engagement projects, this course requires additional time, energy, and intellectual investment by the instructor. However, it is possible to teach such courses without having to create a civic engagement project. Instructors could send their students to already-existing campus-sponsored projects, such as those discussed in this book, and still pursue this model. Finally, once colleagues are convinced of the usefulness of such projects for political science education, they may be more willing to count organizing the civic engagement projects and teaching the courses as the equivalent of a two-course load, which would facilitate the hiring of an adjunct to teach other courses.

One critical aspect is that this course combines civic engagement and international relations in a format that does not require study abroad or travel. Thus, it is open to a wider variety of students currently enrolled at a college or university. Most study abroad programs that offer a civic engagement option in an international community are available only to those with economic resources or personal circumstances that allow them to spend a significant amount of time away from their home institutions. The civic engagement and international affairs courses described in this chapter require neither leaving the home institution nor any additional expense to the student, a significant point for widespread campus adoption.

Ways Forward in Research and Teaching

These courses present another means for students to learn that politics does not stop at the waters' edge. Students are required to delve into how issues beyond national borders affect local communities, rather than just perceiving an American impact upon the world. Coupled with their work as interns, they become connected to their community on both an intellectual and a practical application level. The assessment of these courses is necessarily limited, and thus my claims are minimal. This study, though preliminary, illuminates possibilities for researchers to demonstrate the effects of civic engagement pedagogy. Larger studies across multiple colleges and universities would provide greater confidence in the results while accounting for different local circumstances. Longitudinal studies conducted in the future, after students move into the working world, also will help determine the long-term effects of the courses. Lastly, utilizing control groups of students who did not take civic engagement classes, but instead took similar courses without a service-learning project, would help researchers untangle the effects of course content from the effects of experiential learning methods such as service-learning.

These assessment challenges are not insurmountable. One key purpose of the larger book in which this chapter appears is to develop networks of teacher-scholars interested in pursuing collaborative research projects. Here we present a well-developed, well-received model that can be used by other teachers to further both college and high school students' understanding of international and local political affairs and their desire and ability to think globally and act locally to make a difference in the world. We invite others to consider these options and adapt them to their institutions so that more students can have opportunities to become civically engaged in a global context.

Learning Citizenship by Doing: Integrating Political Campaign Internships into Political Science Coursework[1]

18

By Judithanne Scourfield McLauchlan

In considering whether and how incorporating internships into the political science curriculum could increase students' civic and political engagement, this chapter analyzes data from two courses, American National Government and Practical Politics, taught since 2004. As the author, I discuss course design and implementation, as well as course outcomes. I conclude that the political campaign internship component had a dramatic impact on the students' understanding of and appreciation for the subject matter, interest in participating in government, and willingness to take an active role as citizens.

> *Overall, I feel that working on this campaign made me feel more like a "citizen."*[2]
>
> *My interest in politics has grown tremendously over the past few months, and I think I can attribute this to the time spent interning at the Bush/Cheney headquarters.*[3]
>
> *Working on this campaign has affected my life in ways I never imagined. I am now more driven than ever to get involved and make a difference.*[4]

The Corporation for National and Community Service assesses trends in civic engagement across the United States by looking at five key areas: service, participating in a group, staying informed about current events, social connectedness, and political action.[5] Its 2010 study found that 62 million Americans volunteered with an organization (26.2% of adults), 20.8 million Americans worked with neighbors to fix a community problem (7.2% of adults), and almost half of adults (49.4%) donated money, assets, or property with a value of $25 or more to charitable or religious organizations.[6] Yet nationwide, whereas 64.9% of eligible adult citizens were registered to vote in 2008, only 58.2% of them actually voted in the 2008 presidential election.[7]

If a democracy is to flourish, the society needs well-informed, capable, engaged, and public-spirited citizens. The Florida Civic Health Index report found that Florida ranks 34th in average voter turnout, 49th in the percentage of citizens who volunteer, 48th in the percentage of citizens who attended a public meeting, and 37th in the percentage of citizens who worked with others to address a community issue.[8] Because of this poor level of participation and because I am a political science professor teaching at a state university in Florida,[9] I wondered how the university, and, more specifically, the political science curriculum, could help reverse these low rankings of citizens' political engagement by preparing students to be active and engaged citizens.

In this chapter, I argue that one way to achieve this goal is to incorporate political campaign internships into the curriculum. I teach several courses that include an internship component, including POS 4941: Field Work, POS 3931: The Road to the White House,[10] POS 3273: Practical Politics, and POS 2041: American National Government. These courses represent a broad range of internship requirements and variation in the degree to which the internships are integrated into the courses.

Field Work is a stand-alone internship for which students can receive academic credit, but it is not part of a traditional course. Students are required to work at least one day a week at their placements during the semester (a minimum of 120 hours).[11] The Road to the White House is an upper-level course about the history and politics of presidential campaigns that includes a 10-day internship on a presidential campaign in New Hampshire leading up to the state's primary.[12] Practical Politics is a course about political campaigns and how to win elections, and the internship is the centerpiece of the course (a minimum of 80 hours). American National Government is a standard introductory course about US politics and government, and the campaign internship requirement is a more modest 25 hours, total.

In considering the question of whether and how incorporating internships into the political science curriculum could increase students' civic and political engagement, I have focused on the American National Government course. For many students it is a required course, and it is usually filled with freshmen who are not political science majors. Therefore, it has the greatest potential to increase civic engagement among students not already interested in politics. However, since data from the semesters in which I taught American National Government with an internship component were from even-numbered years—when students were working on presidential, US Senate, and gubernatorial races—I also include data from the Practical Politics course, in which all students interned in a municipal race in St. Petersburg, Florida. The data from the two courses are analyzed separately to allow for comparisons between the students' predispositions and learning experiences.

This chapter reviews course logistics and the results of adding a civic engagement component to these two courses. I conclude that this component had a dramatic effect upon students' understanding of and appreciation for the subject matter as well on their interest in participating in government and willingness to take an active role as citizens.

POS 2041: American National Government

At the University of South Florida, St. Petersburg (USFSP), American National Government is an introductory-level, required course, not only for political science majors, but also for a variety of other majors on campus. In the fall 2004 semester, I decided to add a political campaign internship requirement to the course for the first time.[13]

Students were unaware of this civic engagement requirement when they registered. The requirement was quite an unpleasant surprise for some when they learned about it during the course syllabus review on the first day of class. Indeed, I learned after a review of the preinternship surveys, journal entries, and internship papers that many students considered dropping the class when they learned of the internship requirement. As one student confessed,

> I have to admit that upon hearing that we would be completing an internship for a grade in our American National Government class, I was hesitant. Politicians? Three hours a week? Did I really want to devote my time to a cause I wasn't sure I supported?[14]

The internship component was worth 20% of each student's final course grade. The requirements included working 25 hours on a political campaign, keeping a journal detailing internship experiences and lessons learned, writing a five-page paper about the internship experience, keeping a log of hours worked at the placement (and having the supervisor initial the hours), and returning an evaluation of student performance completed by the internship supervisor.[15]

The preinternship surveys revealed that very few students had previous campaign experience. Most found the prospect of working on a campaign to be daunting, and they had no idea of how to go about getting involved in such an activity. During the third week of the semester, I invited representatives from every campaign to come and speak to the class as part of a "Campaign Internship Job Fair."[16] The candidates or their campaign staff spoke to the class, and at the conclusion of all of the presentations, they met with interested students one-on-one. This individual time with the campaign staffers prior to final selection of their internship placements allowed the students to ask their potential supervisors questions and get a sense of the kinds of projects on which they would be working and helped ease anxieties.

Students selected their candidates or campaigns, but I arranged all of the internships. I created an internship application and other paperwork, including a liability waiver and supervisor evaluation form, to facilitate this process.[17] This process created extra paperwork for me; however, it increased the students' comfort level toward their internships because of the additional information these documents provided. It also allowed me to develop a working relationship with their supervisors, something that was useful when I needed to troubleshoot as issues arose during the semester and to evaluate student performance at the conclusion of the campaigns.

It turned out that the process of selecting a candidate or campaign to work for was a learning process in and of itself. Students were compelled to think about their party identification and political values. Many students found themselves asking: "Am I a Democrat? Am I a Republican?"[18] One student noted: "If not for this internship assignment, I wouldn't have given a second thought about who was running for what, or which party I sided with the most."[19] In the end, the classes were closely divided between Republicans and Democrats. Students interned on a variety of campaigns throughout Tampa Bay. Depending on the election cycle, students worked for candidates running for president, US Senate, US House of Representatives, governor, Florida Senate, Florida House of Representatives, or various 527s, or to defeat/support constitutional amendments.

The Tampa Bay region is not only the bellwether for Florida, but it is also the anchor of the I-4 Corridor, the battleground region of the state. During the 2004 presidential and 2006 gubernatorial campaigns, both major parties fought hard in Hillsborough (Tampa) and Pinellas (St. Petersburg) Counties. As a result, all participating students had the opportunity to meet their candidates at multiple events, and they had the choice of several local field offices in each county. As one student pointed out in her journal: "We are spoiled here in Florida. We get plenty of opportunities to see the candidates speak."[20]

In addition to the campaign internships, I also sponsored other election-related activities for the class, such as presidential and gubernatorial debate watch parties. These debate watch parties provided another forum in which students could watch the candidates and discuss the campaigns.[21] These debate watch parties were opened to the campus community, and I was pleased with the large turnout. During post-debate discussions, the American National Government students frequently drew on their internship experiences and newfound expertise while discussing their reactions to the presidential candidates with others on campus. Further, the internship experience was integrated into the course material and class discussions during the course of the semester.[22]

Pre- and Postinternship Survey Results

Surveys administered in class before and after the internships[23] attempted to measure the students' attitudes toward campaigns, politicians, elections, politics, and American government. I wanted to learn whether the internship experiences changed students' views of politics and whether the internships enhanced their understanding of political campaigns.[24]

Overall, the preinternship survey results painted a grim picture of what students thought about American government. Students displayed little confidence in the political system or politicians and very little confidence that participation in campaigns—or even voting—would make a difference. After reading through the students' surveys and compiling the results, I doubted that 25 hours of work on a campaign would be able to move students to reconsider their firmly held cynical beliefs. Still, I hoped that they would learn about campaigns and the issues dominating the election cycle. Much to my surprise, not only did students learn a great deal about campaigns, but they also were inspired by their experiences.

Sample Comments from the Preinternship Surveys

When asked about their attitudes toward American campaigns, students focused on the importance of fund-raising, the influence of special interests, and their disgust with negative television advertisements. Students tended to look at elections as providing a "lesser of two evils" choice. The 2000 presidential election in Florida increased students' apathy and cynicism; several students mentioned this election as proof that their votes would not be counted and as evidence that elections are "not valid." One student commented about feelings toward campaigns gleaned from other political science courses: "The classes I have taken before make it very difficult to believe that individuals can make a difference."

When asked about their attitudes toward politicians and elected officials, students responded that they are "shady," "favor wealthy corporations," are "corrupted by lobbies and corporate interests," are "very removed from the general population, not very plausible to get your voice heard," are "overpaid and underworked," and that "even though a candidate has a position on a topic, that doesn't mean that he/she will be able to change it." One student lamented, "There are too few great thinkers in government today. The brilliant minds stay away because of muckraking and corruption." Overall, the answers in the survey provided a less-than-positive picture of student perceptions of their public servants. In regard to their expectations for the internships, most students said that they hoped to learn about campaigns first-hand, but they also confessed that they had no idea what to expect from the experience and admitted that they were nervous about the prospect of working on a political campaign.

Sample Comments from the Postinternship Surveys

Despite their initial doubts about the internship experience, students provided very positive responses in their postinternship surveys. In answer to the question, "Do you feel elections make the government pay attention to what people think?" twice as many students responded "4" or "5" on the postinternship survey (on a scale of 1 to 5, with 1 being "not much" and 5 being "a great deal"). In terms of percentage of the respondents, during the fall 2004 semester, 32% of the students responded "4" or "5" in the preinternship survey; 57% responded "4" or "5" in the postinternship survey. During the fall 2006 semester, 39% responded "4" or "5" in the preinternship survey; 65% responded "4" or "5" in the postinternship survey. During the fall 2004 semester, twice as many students responded "yes" in the postinternship survey to the question, "Do you think you can make a difference in changing the direction of this country by becoming involved in the 2004 presidential campaign?" than had in the preinternship survey (see Figure 18-1).

The research design for this study did not include a control group of students who took American National Government without the internship component,[25] but in the short answer section of the anonymous surveys (as well as in the internship

Figure 18-1: Fall 2004 Pre- and Postinternship

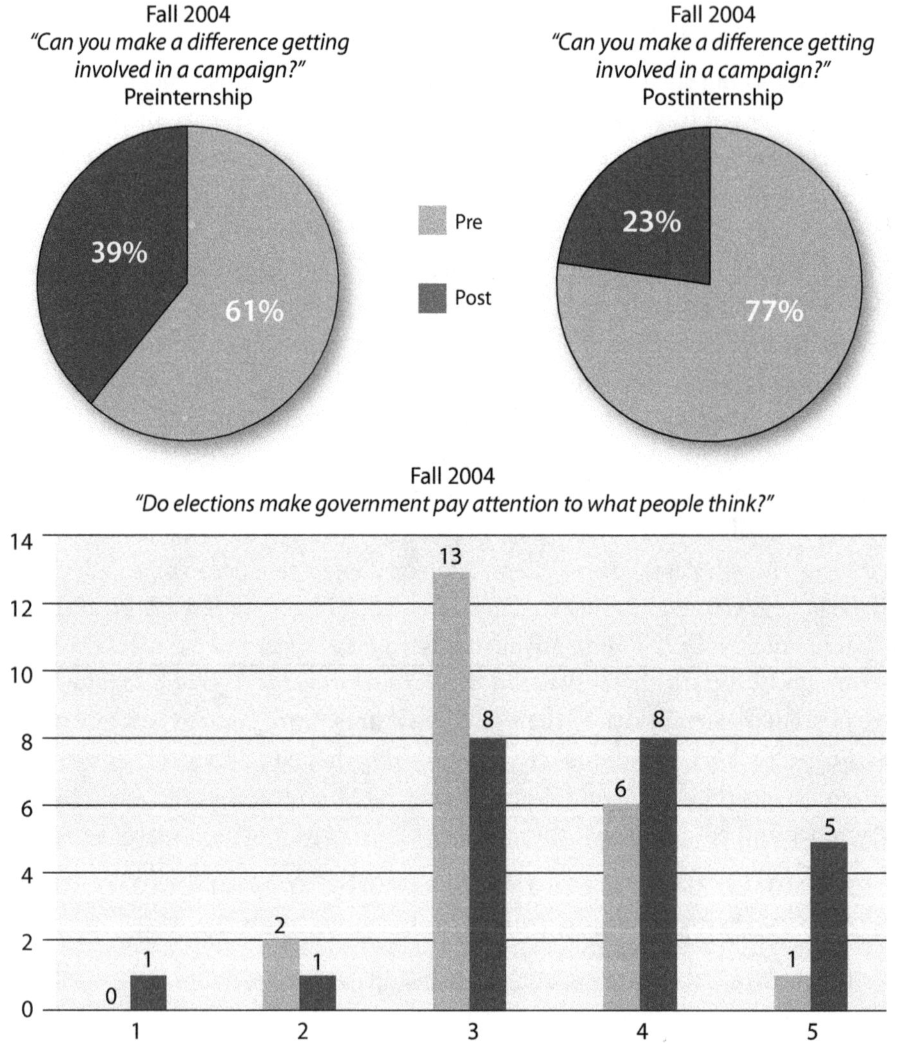

papers and journals) students pointed to the importance of their campaign experiences. For example, students explained that they learned that they could make a difference in their communities by becoming involved in politics. Students felt that they learned what "a campaign was all about, what it means to be involved and the importance of people to a candidate's success."

Students also expressed a change in attitude in regard to whether the internship assignments were worthwhile endeavors. Students talked about the benefits of their first-hand experiences and their greater appreciation for the subject matter. They stated that the internships were enjoyable educational experiences. One student thought that the internship component was "essential to this course." Following are some representative answers to the question of whether students would recommend including an internship in future American National Government classes.

> It is definitely a unique experience and will make you want to keep getting involved in politics.
>
> Yes, I think it was helpful to get a better idea of what campaigns do and you get direct experience which you can't learn about in a classroom.
>
> Yes. It was a great, insightful experience that I had never had the chance to do. I believe that from here on forward I will volunteer for presidential elections every cycle. Great learning tool for American Government and also meet a great group of people.

In response to the question of whether the internships met their expectations, the overwhelming response was that they surpassed them:

> I thought it would be boring—but—the internship was one of the best things I have done since I have been in college.
>
> At first I thought it would be boring, because I was told it would be mainly phonebanking[sic]—but it was great.
>
> I expected to learn what goes on behind-the-scenes and to get a feel for what my candidate stood for. Yes [it met my expectations], I had an enjoyable time and got a great deal out of the experience and learned how a campaign works.

Students also talked specifically about what they learned from their internships: campaign tactics, voter contact activities, and different methods of voting (absentee, early vote, and Election Day). One student remarked, "The campaign internship met all of my expectations. I learned the importance of teamwork, about campaign finance, PACs, FEC reports, canvassing, voter turnout, etc."

Excerpts from Students' Internship Journals and Papers

In addition to completing the anonymous pre- and postinternship surveys, students were required to keep journals of their internship experiences and write a paper about what they learned about campaigns and elections as a result of their campaign work. Mirroring their preinternship comments, students expressed trepidation about their internships early in their journals. One student wrote, "This is the first campaign that I had ever been involved with, as well as my first time voting, so to me the entire experience was like walking into some odd dream." After these initial entries, students wrote about the various candidate events that they attended and the rallies and fund-raising events they planned and attended. They included entries about going to lunch with campaign staff and how they used those opportunities to learn more about life on the campaign trail. Students' journal entries also indicated that they had increased access to the candidates due to their internship experiences (e.g., "rope line" tickets to events when they were attendees).

Throughout their internships, students engaged in a variety of voter contact activities, including absentee ballot and early vote recruitment, phone banking, data entry, visibility,[26] training and recruiting volunteers, canvassing, and Get Out the Vote activities on Election Day. They described their training for and participation in these various activities, and they explained what they learned about grassroots organizing in the process. In addition to traditional field activities, students wrote of learning about fund-raising techniques, Federal Election Commission reports, campaign finance laws (including more about 527s than was discussed in class), press (most students reported that there were television cameras and reporters in their offices every day), website development, mailings, and general office work.

As noted, the classes were almost evenly split between Republicans and Democrats, so many of the students worked on losing campaigns. I was interested to learn how the students, who by Election Day had become invested in their respective campaigns, dealt with losing. Ultimately, while those on the losing side were not pleased with the outcome, they were not discouraged from future participation, as seen in these representative comments:

> I was disappointed that the candidate I supported lost the county, state, and country I worked in. But this disappointment drives me to do more during the next election cycle, on both the local and federal level. I've learned a great deal about how it is to work on a federal campaign and also how difficult and time-consuming it is. But even in defeat, it is still worth it to work for a cause that one believes in.[27]

> This is when I realized that even though they had lost, they [the campaign staff] would still fight for what they believed in. This is one of the greatest freedoms that we have: the ability to speak out against what we believe is wrong, and then to be able to fight for change.[28]

Students reported that the internships increased their interest in politics. One student explained in his internship paper: "My interest in politics has grown tremendously over the past few months, and I think I can attribute this to the time I spent interning at the Bush/Cheney headquarters."

Further, students were more positive about politics, politicians, and campaigns in general in their postinternship reflection pieces. One student explained,

> I came to the assignment with a very pessimistic outlook on politicians and government as a whole. I came out with a new understanding of the political arena and the realization that the benefits of government far outweigh the negative undertones that so many associate with the politics of America.[29]

Students also felt they had become more knowledgeable about politics, and reading through the papers, it was evident that they did learn a great deal about campaigns and elections as a result of their internships. One student described herself as a more educated voter this election cycle: "Without my internship experience, I would have voted based on likes and dislikes versus real political issues, but because I got involved I was educated in all aspects."

This increased understanding led to a corresponding rise in comfort levels with talking about politics and the presidential election. As one student explained in her internship paper:

> Overall, I feel that working on this campaign made me feel more like a "citizen." I found myself paying more attention to politics on the news, and I even watched the debates. I also feel I became more outspoken about my candidate of choice. . . . I really just enjoyed the feeling that I was in some way making a difference by interning on this campaign.

Students also were much more talkative in class discussions than they were prior to becoming involved in politics themselves. According to their responses in the preinternship surveys, most students in the class were taking American National Government because it was a required course, and they had little or no interest in American government. That changed over the course of the semester, as students' participation in the internships heightened their interest in and willingness to talk about politics.

Despite the overwhelmingly negative response to the preinternship survey question, "Do you think you can make a difference in changing the direction of this country by becoming involved in the campaign?" many students later reported that they believed that they did make a difference by becoming involved in the elections:

> I think we all learned something from this election about the strength each and every one of our voices holds. . . . I learned a great deal about how the whole election process works. For a first-time voter like me, being involved helped me understand just how important it was for me and people my age to get out and vote. I am proud of the support and effort that I put into this election year.[30]

> I learned that one person really can make a difference. When I think of all the people I visited and how encouraged they were and how some of them changed their vote, and to know I had a part in making that happen makes me feel good to be a Republican and great to be an American. For me this was a life-changing event because I feel that not only have I had an impact on history but I was able to exercise the rights that were paid for by millions of men and women who have served in our armed forces over the past 250 years. Working on this campaign taught me how elections run and how each person is needed for the common goal of the group. I learned where all the money goes, who does what, and I learned that the American public is not as apathetic as politicians would like to think they are, and, finally, I learned that I could make a difference.[31]

Students once reluctant to get involved in politics declared that they were inspired to take part in future campaigns:

> This was the first opportunity I had to work for a political campaign. I learned many things during my time as an intern. Most importantly,

> I learned how much work, both paid and unpaid, goes into a political campaign. It was a wonderful opportunity, and I cannot imagine another campaign going by that I don't volunteer for.[32]

> For once I as a citizen was able to make a difference. . . . This was an experience I will never forget, and I plan to continue to volunteer in every election for as long as I am physically able. Even though working on the campaign was very hard work, it was very rewarding and it taught me a great deal about federal elections at the same time.[33]

After reading about how reluctant students initially were to participate in the internship component of the course, I was also surprised to read that, in the end, they were grateful for their campaign work experiences:

> Working on this campaign has affected my life in ways I never imagined. I am now more driven than ever to get involved and make a difference. I have come out of this experience with a tremendous amount of respect for those who work on campaigns and for those who run for office. The dedication and commitment is commendable. They came in as individuals and left as a family. I was privileged enough to be a small part of that family. It was with a heavy heart that I said goodbye to the campaign and all the staff. I have come away from this with new friends, contacts, and a knowledge I had never expected.[34]

> When this internship project was first announced I was not looking forward to it. Now that it's over, I am glad I did it because it opened my eyes to how important it is to be involved in politics.[35]

In addition, students mentioned the variety of skills they developed during their internship experiences. Many believed they developed their communication, teamwork, and leadership skills over the course of the semester. They discussed the benefits of the experiential learning component of the course, not only in terms of the skills they developed and the connections they made, but also in terms of the knowledge they gained about the course material. For example,

> While it is certainly possible to learn all the facts of the election process in a classroom context, I now believe that the only way to truly understand the process is to become involved in a campaign itself. . . . That is more meaningful and memorable than any textbook or article could be.[36]

One of the questions I asked on the preinternship survey was "What does it mean to be a 'citizen'?" The answers presented a rights-based view of citizenship, with the citizen's only obligation that of voting in elections. However, students developed a deeper notion of citizenship during the course of the semester. One concluded in his internship paper that "Democracy is a job."[37] Even those who retained a rights-based notion of citizen defined in terms of suffrage became more enthusiastic about the importance of exercising the franchise. As one student commented, "I gained a new, more optimistic outlook on the world of politics. No longer will I overlook my right to vote. I will take full advantage of the gift the Constitution protects."[38]

Reflections on Adding Required Campaign Internships in American National Government

Students indicated in their anonymous preinternship surveys that they were largely disinterested in the study of American government. They were taking the American National Government class because it was required to graduate. (Few of the students enrolled in the class were political science majors.) Students also indicated that they were reluctant to participate in a campaign internship. Most were disinterested in politics and had extremely negative views toward politics, politicians, elections, and campaigns. Getting involved in an election seemed the furthest thing from their minds. Yet, despite their initial hesitations, students found the experiences rewarding, enjoyable, and educational.

There was a profound difference during lectures as the semester progressed—especially as the election drew near. Students were much more engaged with the subject matter, and they were more active participants in class discussions. They followed current events, paid more attention to the news, and raised relevant issues during lectures. The class discussions were much more robust, and students once shy about participation found the confidence to speak. After being trained to go door-to-door and phone bank complete strangers, suddenly the classroom was not as intimidating. This transformation made the class so much more enjoyable for me as the instructor, as I saw the interest level rise and knew that the students were engaging with the material.[39] Reading through the postinternship surveys, internship papers, and journals, I was amazed at the transformation. Students claimed they felt like "citizens," believed that they had made a difference in their communities, and were inspired to participate in future elections.

POS 3273: Practical Politics

After delivering a conference presentation regarding the campaign internships that were a part of my American National Government and Road to the White House courses, I was asked whether I thought that the students would have been so transformed if they were working on local rather than presidential campaigns, or if they were working in a less-targeted region of the country. It is true that USFSP is situated in the battleground region of a battleground state and that it benefits from this location a great deal in terms of the time and resources national and statewide candidates spend in this area. I certainly hoped that the students would have been similarly engaged, but whether they would be remained an open question. Therefore, I am including my Practical Politics course as another opportunity to assess the effects of incorporating campaign internships into the curriculum. When I taught this course in the summer of 2009, all of the students interned in one of the municipal races in St. Petersburg.

This was quite possibly the most fun course I have had the privilege to teach. It also was the first time I could use my many years of campaign experience (prior to entering academia) in an academic setting. In the past, I had drafted numerous campaign plans, hired and managed hundreds of campaign staff, and managed budgets in the millions of dollars. Now I was able to take this practical knowledge, and, in conjunction with the scholarly literature on campaigns and elections, develop a course that gave undergraduate students all of the tools they needed to be successful in the field.

The logistics were similar to those described in the previous American National Government section. I organized a campaign internship job fair and invited all of the candidates and campaigns to make a presentation to the class, after which the speakers met with the students one-on-one.[40] I also created a Field Work Packet that included an internship application, log of hours form, liability waiver, supervisor evaluation, and information about all of the candidates on the ballot, some of which were similar to the previous course. As with the previous course, I arranged all of the internships on behalf of the students. As outlined in the syllabus, the course objectives were as follows:

> Practical Politics is a course about political campaigns and how to win elections. The objective of this course is to combine lectures, readings assignments, and guest speakers with the student's "real world" experience on a political campaign.
>
> One of the highlights of this course is the required internship component. The Instructor will organize a Campaign Internship Job Fair and Candidate Forum on the first day of class. After having the opportunity to meet all of the candidates and their campaign staff—and doing additional research on your own—you will select your internship placement. Students are expected to intern at least eight (8) hours a week during the 10-week summer session, for a total of eighty (80) hours. More information about this assignment will be distributed in the Field Work Packet on the first day of class.
>
> We are fortunate to be studying political campaigns during the summer of 2009, when there is an open seat for the Mayor of St. Petersburg: the fourth largest city in Florida in the 12th largest media market in the country. There is a large, diverse field of candidates for the St. Petersburg primary election, which will take place on 1 September 2009. As a result, this summer will be an active, exciting time for the campaigns. Through your internship experience, <u>you</u> can have an impact on the future direction of our city!

It was rewarding for me to put my practical campaign experience to use in designing this course, but I do not believe it is essential for instructors to have similar experience. I incorporated many guest speakers into the seminars, who could share their expertise about fund-raising, polling, media buys, and so forth. While I have extensive contacts within my party, I had to develop contacts and working relationships on the other side. I am confident that colleagues interested in designing such a course would be able to make contacts on both sides, especially while organizing the campaign internships that are a part of the course, and tap into the expertise of local political campaign consultants and party operatives.

PRE- AND POSTINTERNSHIP SURVEYS

I administered pre- and postinternship surveys similar to the ones described in the American National Government class. The preinternship survey responses for Practical Politics were significantly less negative and cynical than those in American National Government. This result is likely due in large part to the fact that all of the students who enrolled in this course did so knowing that a campaign internship was the centerpiece of the course and, therefore, they probably had an interest in politics before registering. This course also came on the heels of the historic election of Barack Obama to the presidency, so it may be that there was also a decrease in youth cynicism from that previously reported by my students on the surveys in 2004 and 2006.[41]

The students in Practical Politics provided more robust definitions of citizenship on both the preinternship and the postinternship surveys than those presented by the American National Government students. Only one response in the Practical Politics preinternship survey responded to the question, "To you, what does it mean to be a citizen?" with the one word answer "VOTE!" The following are two other preinternship responses:

> I have never really stepped back and thought about the question what it means to be a citizen. We all have responsibilities as citizens to improve and maintain the communities we live in. Citizens are the extension of government and they ultimately reflect the image of the community. So the job of the citizen is to keep and uphold the standards of the community.

> To be a part of a community and an asset to society. Every citizen does his/her part in developing a positive, active community.

In the postinternship surveys, there was a similar emphasis on community, but there was more of an emphasis on local politics and government. One student commented: "To be actively engaged with your community, and with local, state, and national politics. On a personal level, to be honest, open, compassionate, and to follow through on what you say you will do."

To the survey question, "How much attention does the government give to what people think before it decides what to do?" with responses on a five-point scale, with 1 being "not much" and 5 being "a great deal," 59% of the students on the preinternship survey responded with a 4 or a 5; on the postinternship survey, 71% responded with a 4 or a 5. To the survey question, "Do you feel elections make the government pay attention to what people think?" using the same five-point scale, 75% of the students responded with a 4 or a 5 on the preinternship surveys; on the postinternship survey, *100%* of the students responded with a 4 or a 5.

Figure 18-2: Representation of student responses to the question "What are your expectations going into the campaign internship this semester?"

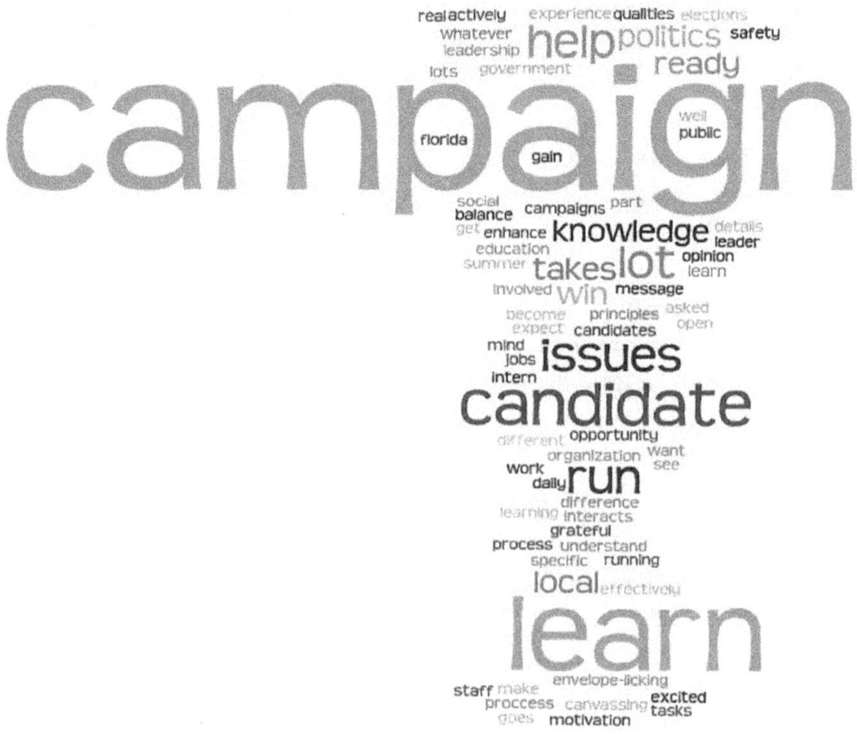

After the municipal campaign internship experience, 100% of the students also answered "Yes" to the question, "Do you think you can make a difference in changing the direction of the city of St. Petersburg by becoming involved in a 2009 municipal campaign?" (The sample size was the same for the pre- and postinternship surveys; no students dropped this summer course.)

See the "word cloud" (Figure 18-2) for a graphic representation of student responses to the question on the preinternship survey, "What are your expectations going into the campaign internship this semester?"[42] Their responses clearly were dominated by their eagerness to learn about campaigns. On the postinternship survey, I asked the question again this way, "What were your expectations going in to the campaign internship this semester?" Responses included:

> To do a lot of grunt work, but I am glad that was not the case! I honestly felt part of the team and that my opinions mattered to the campaign staff.
>
> I did not think I would have such a big role on the campaign, but I am very happy I do.
>
> My expectations were to learn about local government, and I have learned a lot.

When asked, "Did the campaign internship meet your expectations?" 100% of the students responded that the internships met or exceeded their expectations.

Students' responses to the postinternship survey question, "What did you learn about campaigns and elections and about American government through your participation in this internship?" were very positive as to the lessons that they learned about the value of civic participation. For example, one student wrote: "If you really want to change your community, you have to get involved with your local elected officials." Another stated, "I learned that every person—young, old, rich or poor—can make a change in the community." Students also provided specific examples of lessons learned about campaigns and elections in the United States.

In response to the postinternship survey question, "What have you learned about Florida and St. Petersburg politics as a result of the internship experience?" students provided specific public policy answers. For example, one student explained, "I've learned the details of the issues surrounding our city ... such as we have less police officers per capita than Tampa and the average of other cities and if we wanted to be on target we would have to add about 200 more police officers."

To the postinternship survey question, "What do you think is the most important skill (or skills) that you learned as a result of your campaign internship?" students answered that they gained leadership and communication skills as well as lessons on how to work as part of a team. Students also believed that these campaign internships prepared them to be hired on future campaigns. For example, one student reported learning "How to effectively run a field grassroots operations. From what I learned in class and from what I saw in the field, I feel pretty confident that I could land a job directly underneath a field coordinator or running it myself in a small election."

Perhaps the most telling question about whether students appreciated the campaign internship component of the course was, "Would you recommend to future students that they should participate in a similar 'Practical Politics' internship experience? Why or why not?" All students recommended this internship requirement. Sample responses included:

> Yes! It's an experience of a lifetime, especially if you get involved in a small local race.
>
> YES! Even if you're not interested in politics, the hands-on learning will teach you about local government and policy-making and give you insight into all aspects of law and politics.

The most interesting aspect of the post-internship surveys across the many questions is the emphasis on local politics and government. The answers demonstrate that the students definitely left this course with an enhanced understanding of and appreciation for municipal government.

Internship Papers and Journals

It was clear from reading the students' internship papers and journals that the internship experience strengthened the knowledge they gained in class regarding campaign strategy and tactics. Students provided many examples of what they learned about campaign strategy, fund-raising, targeting, grassroots organizing, phone banking, canvassing, absentee ballots/vote-by-mail, media strategy (paid and earned, including their involvement in producing television ads). Students also learned a great deal about the city of St. Petersburg, politics in St. Petersburg, and how the city government works. In addition, they participated in a variety of community events while interning on their campaigns that they would not otherwise have attended.

In all of my courses that require campaign internships, students have reported that the experiences were "life-changing." In some cases, as in Practical Politics during the summer of 2009, the campaign internships were life-changing experiences of a particularly personal nature,[43] as described in one of the internship papers:

> [my openly gay candidate's] courage has taught me about myself, and not hiding from the person I am. With the courage he has given me, I have finally come out to my friends. Even in the face of adversity and strife, I hold strong to the person I am. That lesson cannot be taught in a book, or studied in a case log, or seen in a video. That lesson comes from hard work, dedication and perseverance for what you believe is right.

Reflections on Including a Campaign Internship Component in Practical Politics

The survey data and the students' reflections in their journals and internship papers provide strong evidence of the value of the experiential learning component of the course. Certainly, many courses about campaigns and elections do not include a field component, but it provides a much richer learning experience for those students who have the opportunity to combine theory with practice. In Practical Politics, the internship was an integral part of the course, and students unanimously agreed that it was an essential part of their learning experience. They described the internship as "amazing" and "priceless" and stressed the importance of "physically performing the tasks you learn about in class."

When reading through the surveys, papers, and journals, I was reminded of House Speaker Tip O'Neill's adage that "all politics is local." My students certainly had an interest in national politics and elections before this course, and they registered for the course wanting to learn more about campaigns. Perhaps the most noticeable change from the pre- and postinternship surveys was the emphasis on and appreciation for local government after working on a municipal campaign.

The campaign internship provided students with the skills they needed to become active citizens in St. Petersburg. They left the course with increased knowledge about how city government works and what they need to do to seek public policy changes. Through the campaign experience, students also became more integrated within the community—for example, they attended neighborhood association meetings and community events—and generally increased their knowledge about the community in which they live. USFSP is a metropolitan university, and these types of experiences allow the students to leave the proverbial ivory tower, get to know their neighbors, and learn how to work together to address community needs.

Conclusion

Integrating a campaign internship component into political science coursework can have extraordinary results. Certainly, adding this civic engagement requirement demands a great deal of extra effort on the part of the instructor and the students. My extra work included arranging the internships, monitoring the students' progress, intervening when issues arose, and working with supervisors from numerous campaigns. Students at USFSP, many of whom are nontraditional students, had to balance work, family, and school responsibilities with the campaign internship requirement. In the end, all of the extra effort was rewarded.

Students were enriched by their experiences in ways that they never expected. For me, as a professor, to see the students engaged in the material and energized and inspired to get involved in politics—described in the American National Government preinternship surveys as completely unappealing—was truly rewarding. The American National Government preinternship surveys also painted a rather bleak picture of what students thought about American government, politicians, politics, campaigns, and elections. When reading the postinternship surveys, journals, and internship papers, I was overwhelmed by their transformations. Students found that they could make a difference by getting involved in the election as campaign volunteers and as voters. They reported that they felt as if "for the first time in their lives" they were "citizens." Even those students whose candidates or campaigns lost (about half the class) were not discouraged from future participation.

A dramatic difference existed between teaching American National Government with and without the internship component. The difference between teaching American government in the fall of 2003 (no internship requirement) versus the fall of 2004 (with the internship requirement) was like the proverbial difference between night and day. During the fall 2003 semester, it was a struggle for me to convince the students that the study of American government was relevant to them. The fall 2004 semester started the same way, but students ended up in a very different place by the end of the semester.

The Practical Politics example demonstrates that this phenomenon holds even when students' internship opportunities are on municipal campaigns. In addition to the enhanced understanding of campaign strategy and tactics, students left with a better understanding of city government and politics and with the skills needed to seek public policy changes. Through their campaign experiences, students also became more integrated into the St. Petersburg community.

I conclude with two student quotes that encapsulate why I believe that incorporating a civic engagement component into political science coursework can have a profound effect on the students' civic education and future civic and political engagement:

> Thanks for introducing the class to the campaign life. I think by incorporating an experience like this into a grade, allowed some of us to be a part of something that makes history and something some of us wouldn't have done on our own. Most of us in the beginning didn't understand why a teacher would want their class to do something like this. The point came to me on my first day. Campaigning is fun, and it connects you to this country by giving you a voice and a chance to stand your ground. Thanks.[44]

> This experience was very influential to me. I feel like this internship and the course has opened a new chapter in my life. I am not saying this will be a new career path. I am saying that every election going forward, I will take more seriously and try to get involved in any way that I can. I think my understanding of American Government has definitely increased. It was a great learning experience. I wish more of my classes were like this one. It was great having the opportunity to be involved in an experience like this.[45]

In sum, incorporating an internship within core political science courses can have a dramatic influence on students' educational experiences and their future citizenship potential. As these examples demonstrate, students became engaged and interested in the material as a result of their internship experiences. All course learning objectives were achieved, as they left the course having learned more about American government, having cultivated a desire to become active citizens, and having realized the value of *their* participation in American constitutional democracy.

High School Students as Election Judges and Campaign Workers: Does the Experience Stick?

19

By Betty O'Shaughnessy

Do election activities—either working for a political campaign or serving as an election judge—socialize high school students to increase their political engagement? A colleague and I asked high school students to either work for a candidate's campaign or serve as election judges during the 2004–2010 election activities. Based upon their reports and surveys assessing their experiences, we found that high school students who served as election judges or worked in political campaigns were more willing to serve in the same capacity again or become politically involved, more so than those who did not work in a political election. I also surveyed alumni from the same school to see if those who had worked elections in high school were more politically active than those who did not. The findings confirmed that civic engagement pedagogy that included practical political experience in high school, if presented in tandem with classroom learning, can increase later political involvement.

Studies have found that 18- to 29-year-olds vote at a much lower rate than other age groups,[1] and while there has been much attention paid to the importance of getting students involved and interested in politics at an early age,[2] students do not show much interest in politics during high school without initiation through school- or community-sponsored activities. Civics is no longer taught in many high schools, and when it is taught, the classes often focus only on structural aspects or the facts necessary to pass a state Constitution test.[3]

What if high school students were given the opportunity to do election work while they were learning about the political process in a civics or social studies class? I argue that students who become politically active in high school through serving as election judges or working for political campaigns continue to be active as young adults. After presenting concepts found in the fields of political science and education as well as pedagogical models on student involvement, this chapter describes an election assignment in which social studies students in one suburban high school were given the opportunity to do election work. To determine the success of this project, I surveyed these students immediately after their election experience and asked them to write reflections. I also surveyed alumni from the same school to see if those who had worked elections in high school were more politically active than those who had not. More comparative studies are needed, but these findings suggest that teaching civic engagement in high school wherein practical political experience is combined with classroom learning can increase later political involvement.

What We Know about Teaching Civic Engagement

In *Bowling Alone*, Robert Putnam argued that many Americans have lost their sense of community and that there is a need to develop new structures and policies to develop civic engagement.[4] The American Political Science Association's Standing Committee on Civic Education's report, *Democracy at Risk*;[5] the Center for Information and Research on Civic Learning and Engagement (CIRCLE);[6] several authors in this volume; and other political scientists stress the importance of teaching civic engagement at all educational levels to maintain a vibrant democracy.[7] Bernstein, Hardt, Meinke, Mello, and Davis and others have developed various programs in higher education for teaching political skills to nonpolitical science majors through civic involvement.[8] In addition, primary and secondary educational programs are increasingly developing hands-on ways of teaching civic engagement, as explained by Islam et al.[9]

In the field of education, research on student-centered learning, experiential learning, and noncognitive learning has found that learning about any subject, including politics or civic engagement, is enhanced by practical experience. Such studies include David Kolb's learning styles inventory (concrete experience, reflective observation, abstract conceptualization, and active experimentation)[10] and the Center for Collaborative Education's ATLAS Communities Dimensions of Learning that involve habits of mind, heart, and work and their later programs.[11] Robert J. Marzano's work on learning-centered instruction likewise emphasizes making knowledge acquisition meaningful through application. He presents five dimensions of teaching and learning: fostering positive attitudes about learning, acquiring and integrating knowledge, extending and refining knowledge, using knowledge meaningfully, and developing productive habits of mind. These dimensions provide a template for teaching both the knowledge and practical components of civic engagement—especially his fourth dimension, in which students are provided opportunities to apply knowledge in meaningful ways.[12] Marzano also finds that cooperative learning, in which students work with others on noncognitive learning goals, can greatly enhance academic learning.[13] In such a manner, working in campaigns and as poll judges encourages students to work with others and makes what is learned in the classroom more meaningful, especially if these experiences are shared with others. Findings of political scientists who research civic engagement seem to be in agreement with education studies.[14]

Some researchers find civic engagement to be related to generational links. Eric Plutzer has found that parental influence on voting or nonvoting is great in youth but diminishes gradually as young voters' individual identities and achievements become noticeable.[15] Laura Stoker and Kent Jennings have shown that citizens who develop habits such as voting or working on campaigns early on are expected to be politically involved as adults.[16] Gentry (Chapter 4) has found that civic engagement provides the direct relationship between the individual and society needed for early identity development.[17]

The concentration on active learning found in all these studies and models provides a solid rationale for teaching civic engagement in secondary schools, but Macedo et al. have shown that public high schools have cut back on civics and government courses and that most civics classes teach *about* government rather than getting students involved *in* governmental processes.[18] Colby et al. have found that such required civics courses often do not produce enough political understanding for students to participate responsibly should they care to do so[19] and rarely contain an active component. Yet a high school political science class—or any social studies class with a solid unit on the political process—can address this issue by combining the study of politics with concrete action, such as working for a campaign. Fine has studied college students serving as election judges,20 but to date no studies have been done on the effects of high school students performing this task. In addition, no investigations have been done on whether working an election as a poll judge or campaign worker in high school might be related to a later inclination to become politically involved.[21]

The School, the Course, and the Assignment

Loyola Academy is a Catholic Jesuit college preparatory high school located in Wilmette, Illinois, an upper middle–class suburb north of Chicago. Its student body comes mostly from the northern suburbs in Cook and Lake Counties and Chicago's north and northwest sides. The Ignatian Pedagogical Paradigm (IPP) used by the school contains five stages of learning: context, experience, reflection, action, and evaluation. Metts found similarities between the IPP and several educational paradigms, such as John Gardiner's multiple intelligences and the ATLAS Communities Dimensions of Learning.[22]

Loyola students are expected to fulfill requirements toward "the profile of graduate at graduation (grad at grad)," in which they are expected to show development of the following qualities: being open to growth, intellectually competent, religious, loving, and committed to doing justice during their years at the school.[23] The school's curriculum includes both a political science seminar and an advanced-placement US Political Science and Government course. Both are electives open to juniors and seniors. The IPP teaching model and the "grad at grad" requirement—particularly the components of being committed to doing justice and open to growth—encourage activities epitomized by working in an election. The mission of the school thus provides a most favorable atmosphere for encouraging public service, making Loyola an ideal location for giving students some practical experience with elections.

From 2004 to 2010 my colleague, Mike Barry, and I asked political science students to either work for a political campaign or serve as election judges whenever either a general or primary election was held. After the elections, students were assigned a one-page reflection report on their experiences. This assignment has evolved over the years. In 1996, students in the political science seminar had the option of working in a political campaign of their choice. By 2000, the project was required for all students in the political science seminar, but not in the advanced-placement course.

Beginning with the 2004 election, the state of Illinois allowed high school seniors in good standing to serve as paid election judges, provided they attend a county-run election judge training program. Since then we have given students the option of working as judges or for campaigns.[24] There were two sets of requirements for serving as a judge: those of the election boards and the class requirements needed to complete the assignment. The election boards involved were those of the Cook County Clerk, the Lake County Clerk, and the City of Chicago Board of Election Commissioners through the Mikva Challenge, a civic education program that promotes the participation of student election judges.[25] The three election boards had similar requirements for serving. Students had to:

- be juniors or seniors in good standing at their school
- complete an application form
- get signed permission from their parents and the principal
- take a three-hour training course[26]

For the 2010 general election, suburban Cook County and the City of Chicago continued their student election judge programs, but suburban Lake County discontinued its student judge program. Fortunately, this change affected only the four political science students from Lake County. The 2010 pay for getting trained and serving as an election judge was $170 in Cook County.

Some students preferred working for political campaigns because they either liked or needed the more flexible time requirements or they wanted to get more involved in politics. Students could work for any candidate on the ballot in any part of the Chicago area. They could find a candidate on their own, although the teachers provided names of campaigns from both major parties that needed help. They were to perform whatever legitimate campaign duties were needed. Most students did not get paid.

Students received instructions on how to approach their work and were told that they had to complete certain course requirements to get credit for what they did. Teachers began providing these general instructions in 2004 (the first year in which Loyola students served as judges) to serve as guidelines for behavior and appearance, a sort of "politics etiquette." Students needed to realize the importance of what they were doing and not to treat their activities casually. As representatives of both their school as well as their candidates (campaign workers) or the government (student judges), they were to be polite and respectful in all circumstances and dress appropriately (in collared shirts and slacks or skirts). Campaign workers were to return to campaign headquarters after completing a task and then ask for another assignment. As a result, many students worked nonstop whenever they went to campaign headquarters, working commuter railroad stations in the morning and finishing up as poll watchers before the polls closed on Election Day. Judges were to be mindful that even though they might be more skillful at running the computerized scanners or touch screens, they could learn a lot from the other judges by listening to their stories. Postelection student reports showed that many students found this to be true. Students were also asked to share their "war stories" in class after the elections, which proved beneficial to the students and provided an extended learning experience for the entire class. As a result of their respect for others and their willingness to work, Loyola Academy students were welcomed as workers in subsequent elections and often given higher-level responsibilities in campaigns.

Assessments

Assessing this activity was simple: political science students were graded on a pass-fail basis, provided they fulfilled their commitments to either serve as judges or work for a campaign. They also were required to hand in one-to-three-page reflection reports on their experiences—relating what they did, discussing their interactions with others, and evaluating their overall experiences. Students who worked in election campaigns had to hand in letters (on campaign letterhead whenever possible) from their supervisors, such as the campaign manager or intern supervisor, verifying that a student worked at least 10 hours for the campaign.[27] The value of the entire project was worth between 10% and to 15% of their semester grade. Students who both worked in political campaigns and served as judges were given up to two extra points on their final grade.

What did the students do? The election judges reviewed applications, verified voters' signatures, issued ballots, and supervised the optical scanners and touch screens.[28] Often, students served as polling place "go-fers," telling people to move campaign signs that were too near the polling place or getting lunch for the other judges. Some senior students who had served as judges in their junior year were trained by their election commissions to serve as higher-paid equipment manager judges. Some students volunteered to serve as supply judges and returned the ballot results to the county clerk's office after the polls closed. All judges had to be at their polling place at 5:30 a.m. and generally did not leave until 8:30 p.m.

The campaign workers' duties were more varied. They canvassed door-to-door, phone banked, did crowd control for rallies and meet-and-greets, delivered yard signs, distributed literature at commuter stations and supermarkets, and poll watched on Election Day. Two of the candidates were graduates of the academy and took students with them on their canvasses; one of these candidates let the students help write his campaign publicity; the other hired some students to work in his legislative office as interns after the election.

The Survey and the Reflections

During the several elections from 2004 through 2010, we tried to keep some record of what students related about their experiences immediately after the elections, but only anecdotal evidence of student experiences and subsequent involvement in politics was available. After attending several APSA Teaching and Learning Conferences, I decided to examine the long-term effects of the election worker assignment and consequently began tracking student reactions. Thus, beginning in 2008 and with the permission of the school and parents, students who had served as judges were asked to complete a survey based on that constructed by the Center for the Study of Elections and Democracy,[29] with questions added about motives for serving, duties as judges, evaluations of their experiences in the preliminary training and on Election Day, and evaluations of how these affected their views of the political process. Since the students were in high school, surveys were distributed only to those students who had written parental permission to participate, resulting in 58 surveys for the 2008 primary elections (47% of all 125 student judges from the school), 74 surveys for the 2008 general elections (43% of the 172 total student judges); and 42 surveys for the 2010 general election, (45% of the 93 judges).

There were limitations. This case study covered students from only one Catholic college preparatory high school with a middle- to upper middle–class population. All participants were self-selectors, since the students involved were either those interested enough in politics to take a political science elective or US history students who volunteered. The school's mission for service also predisposes students to get involved in the community.[30] Nonetheless, treated as a case study, this research can provide information on whether providing high school students with practical political experience can develop attitudinal changes toward politics.

The survey contained questions about training and their experiences on Election Day, but the study focused on responses to the following:

1. Overall, how satisfied are you with your job as an election judge?
2. How likely are you to work as an election judge in the next election?
3. Serving made me more willing to become involved in the political process. (strongly agree / agree / neither agree nor disagree / disagree / strongly disagree).

The first part of this study dealt with the initial reactions of high school students who had worked in election campaigns or served as election judges. The first hypothesis was that high school students who were satisfied with their jobs as election judges were likely to want to serve as judges for the next election or otherwise become involved in the political process. We expected a positive and strong correlation between satisfaction serving as an election judge and the likelihood of serving as a judge in the next election, and satisfaction serving as an election judge and an increased willingness to become involved in the political process.

Since the campaign workers did not participate in the survey, we compared the comments in their reflections with those made by the election judges to evaluate whether they had more satisfactory experiences. For the 2008 elections, students received general writing directions 'to the students', asking them to relate whether they had a positive or negative experience and whether they would do it again, to evaluate the assignment in light of the course, and to explain if the work changed their views about getting involved in politics. For the 2010 election, the guidelines were more specific, still asking them to reflect upon their overall experiences, but also asking them to respond to the following:

1. How did you participate in the election?
2. Would you served as a judge again? (only for election judges)
3. Would you work in a campaign again? (only for campaign workers)
4. Mentions of desires for future political involvement.

Since all of the students had the same instructions for their reflection reports, it was possible to compare the responses of campaign workers and election judges. However, instructions for the reflection report, while similar, varied by election and teacher, and categorizing student responses was based upon a subjective evaluation of written reports. Despite these reservations and based upon such general estimates, we hypothesized that high school students who worked in political campaigns were more willing to become involved in the political process than those who worked as election judges. Anecdotal evidence showed that students generally found campaign work rewarding and many judges found their jobs serving on Election Day tedious, so it was expected that campaign workers would be more willing to become politically involved later in life than the election judges.

Findings from the High School Student Responses[31]

Table 19-1 of this study shows that over three elections held in the state of Illinois, 95% of the students were satisfied or somewhat satisfied with serving as election judges. Table 19-2 compares the frequency of responses to the question, "How likely are you to work as an election judge in the next election?" as asked on the survey given to the student election judges. Omitting students who found going away to college a hindrance to serving as a judge in the future, 78% of the 2008 primary judges, 84% of the 2008 general election judges, and 74% of the 2010 general election judges said that they were either "very likely" or "somewhat likely" to serve again—an average of nearly 80% overall who were likely to work in future elections.

Table 19-3 shows a correlation of responses to the survey questions, "Overall, how satisfied were you with your job as a judge?" and "How likely are you to serve as a judge in the next election?" For all three elections, the Spearman's correlation coefficients indicate significant and positive correlations. Table 19-3 also shows a significant correlation between the relationship between satisfaction with their jobs

Table 19-1: Frequencies—Satisfied with Job as a Judge, 2008 Primary and General Elections and 2010 General Election

		2008 Primary Election			2008 General Election			2010 General Election			Overall		
		N	Valid Percentage	Cumulative Percentage	N	Valid Percentage	Cumulative Percentage	N	Valid Percentage	Cumulative Percentage	N	Valid Percentage	Cumulative Percentage
Valid	Very Satisfied	31	53.4	53.4	41	56.2	56.2	17	40.5	40.5	89	51.4	51.4
	Somewhat Satisfied	24	41.4	94.8	30	41.1	97.3	22	52.4	92.9	76	43.9	95.3
	Somewhat Dissatisfied	2	3.4	98.3	1	1.4	98.6	2	4.8	97.6	5	2.9	98.2
	Very Dissatisfied	1	1.7	100	1	1.4	100	1	2.4	100	3	1.7	99.9
	Total	58	100	100	73	100	100	42	100	100	173	100	100
Missing	No Answer				1						1		
Total		58			74			42			174		100

Table 19-2: Frequencies—How Likely to Serve as Judge Next Election, 2008 Primary and General Elections and 2010 General Election

		2008 Primary Election			2008 General Election			2010 General Election			Overall		
		N	Valid Percentage	Cumulative Percentage	N	Valid Percentage	Cumulative Percentage	N	Valid Percentage	Cumulative Percentage	N	Valid Percentage	Cumulative Percentage
Valid	Very likely	25	49.0	49.0	16	25.0	25.0	8	22.9	22.9	49	32.7	32.7
	Somewhat Likely	15	29.4	78.4	38	59.4	84.4	18	51.4	74.4	71	47.3	80.0
	Not Very Likely	7	13.7	92.2	8	12.5	96.9	5	14.3	88.6	20	13.3	93.3
	Not at all likely	4	7.8	100.0	2	3.1	100.0	4	11.4	100.0	10	6.7	100.0
	Total	51	100		64	100		35	100		150	100.0	
Missing	Would like to, away at college	8			9			6			23		
	No Answer				1			1			2		
	Total	8			10			7			25		
Total		59			74			42			175		

Table 19-3: Correlations between Satisfaction Serving as Election Judges and the Likelihood of Serving as Judges in Next Election and Willingness to Become More Involved in Political Process		
	Likely to Serve as Judge in Next Election	Willingness to Become More Involved in Political Process
Satisfied Serving in 2008 Primary Election	.410[a]	.527[a]
Satisfied Serving in 2008 General Election	.488[a]	.505[a]
Satisfied Serving in 2010 General Election	.496[a]	.389[b]

Note:
[a]Significant at .01 level (2 tailed) Spearman's rho
[b]Significant at .05 level (2 tailed)

as judges and students' willingness to be more involved in the political process. Thus, we can assert with confidence that, at least in this study, high school students satisfied with their jobs as election judges were likely to want to serve as judges for the next election or otherwise become involved in the political process.

Table 19-4 shows the results found in the reflections of the students from all three elections. Students who served as judges or worked in campaigns were asked if they would be open to working in an election in the same capacity again. Almost 50% of students serving as judges in the 2008 primary election said they would serve again, as opposed to 40% of campaign workers, and almost 79% of the student judges said that they would serve again in the 2008 general election, as opposed to 69% of the campaign workers. It was only in the 2010 election that a higher percentage of campaign workers (83%) than judges (76%) said that they would serve again. These findings do not show that campaign workers are more willing to work again as campaign workers than judges are willing to serve as election judges, but the overall reflection findings do show that the majority of the high school students who worked in political campaigns and as election judges were willing to become involved in politics again in the same capacity.

Table 19-4: Cross-tabulation Findings from Reflection Responses, All Elections			
	Percentage of Students Saying They Would Serve Again in an Election		
	2008 Primary Election	2008 General Election	2010 General Election
Served as Judge	50.9 (29)	78.7 (37)	76.0 (19)
Worked in Campaign	40.0 (4)	69.2 (9)	83.3 (10)
Served as Judge and Worked in Campaign	25.0 (1)	25.0 (2)	50.0 (1)
Total Percentage Who Would Serve Again (N)	47.9 (34)	70.6 (48)	76.9 (30)

Did the Students Stay Involved? The Alumni Study

Regardless of how the students responded in the postelection surveys and reflection reports, it remained unknown as to whether working an election in high school had longer-lasting effects. Anecdotal evidence existed that several former students had stayed involved in politics since taking the political science course, but a record had never been kept of students' political experiences after high school graduation. Were high school students who worked in elections in high school more likely to be active and interested in politics later on than those who did not? We emailed the survey (through surveymonkey.com) to all Loyola Academy alumni from the graduating classes of 2004 through 2010, which asked about their post–high school involvement in politics and political science. They were asked whether they had been active in the political process in some way since high school graduation or had taken political science courses in college. The email list was from Loyola Academy's alumni office, 690 emails (excluding those returned as undeliverable) were sent out, and 104 responses (a 15.1% response) were received. For this study, we cross-tabulated the responses to the survey questions:

1. Did you serve as an election judge while at Loyola Academy?
2. Did you work in a political campaign while at Loyola Academy? Have you been involved in politics or worked in government since you attended Loyola Academy?
3. How have you been involved in politics or worked in government since you attended Loyola Academy?
4. How often do you check media for political news?
5. How do you now feel about getting involved in political activities?

We expected that high school students who had worked either as an election judge or campaign volunteer in high school were more likely to be involved later in politics.

Later Involvement in Politics

Of the 104 alumni who responded to the survey, 57% had taken political science while at Loyola, although the number of students who actually took political science courses is actually closer to 15% to 18% of the up to 500 students in any one graduation class. As Table 19-5 indicates,[32] a cross-tabulation of the responses to "Did you serve as an election judge while at Loyola Academy?" with "Have you been involved in politics or worked in government since you attended Loyola Academy?" showed that only 35 of the total 104 respondents became involved in politics after high school. Nonetheless, those who served as election judges while in high school were involved in politics at a much higher rate than those who did not serve in high school (46%, compared to 29%). The correlation coefficient is small (.196) but significant at the .05 level between serving as a judge in high school and later involvement in politics or government. There is an even stronger relationship between working

Table 19-5: High School Service Compared with Later Political Involvement Correlation: Serving as an Election Judge or Working in a Political Campaign in High School and Later Involvement in Politics or Government

	Served as Election Judge in High School	Worked in a Political Campaign in High School
Involvement in Politics or Government after High School (N=36)	45.7 (21)	73.9 (17)
Total (N=102)	100.0 (46)	100.0 (23)
Spearman's Rho	.191	.434[a]
Sig.	.056	.000

[a]Correlation is significant at the 0.01 level (2-tailed).

in a political campaign in high school and later political involvement. Table 19-5 shows that although fewer high school students worked in campaigns (N= 23) than served as judges (N= 46), the difference in involvement after high school between those who worked campaigns and those who did not is 50%, which is statistically significant at the .01 level (Pearson correlation coefficient= .436). This result affirms that high school students who worked either as an election judge or campaign volunteer in high school were more likely to be involved in politics later.

The 35 respondents who answered "Have you been involved in politics or worked in government since you attended Loyola Academy?" in the affirmative were then asked "How have you been involved in politics or government since you attended Loyola Academy?" Having been asked, to check all that applied, the choices given were:

- voted
- served as an election/poll judge
- volunteered in a political campaign
- worked as paid staff in a political campaign
- served as a government intern
- worked for the private sector in a job related to government or politics
- ran for public office
- worked in a paid government position

The data do not include the 69 alumni who said they were not active in politics. Figure 19-1 shows the breakdown of the responses given for those who served as election judges in high school, and Figure 19-2 shows the responses for those who had worked in campaigns in high school. Respondents who served as high school election judges were more involved in all activities mentioned than non–high school judges. Of the eight categories, two had no respondents: "worked as paid staff in a political campaign" and "ran for public office." Of the 35 respondents to

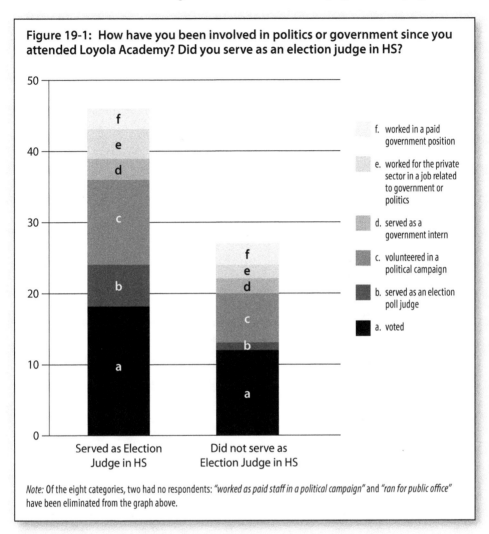

Figure 19-1: How have you been involved in politics or government since you attended Loyola Academy? Did you serve as an election judge in HS?

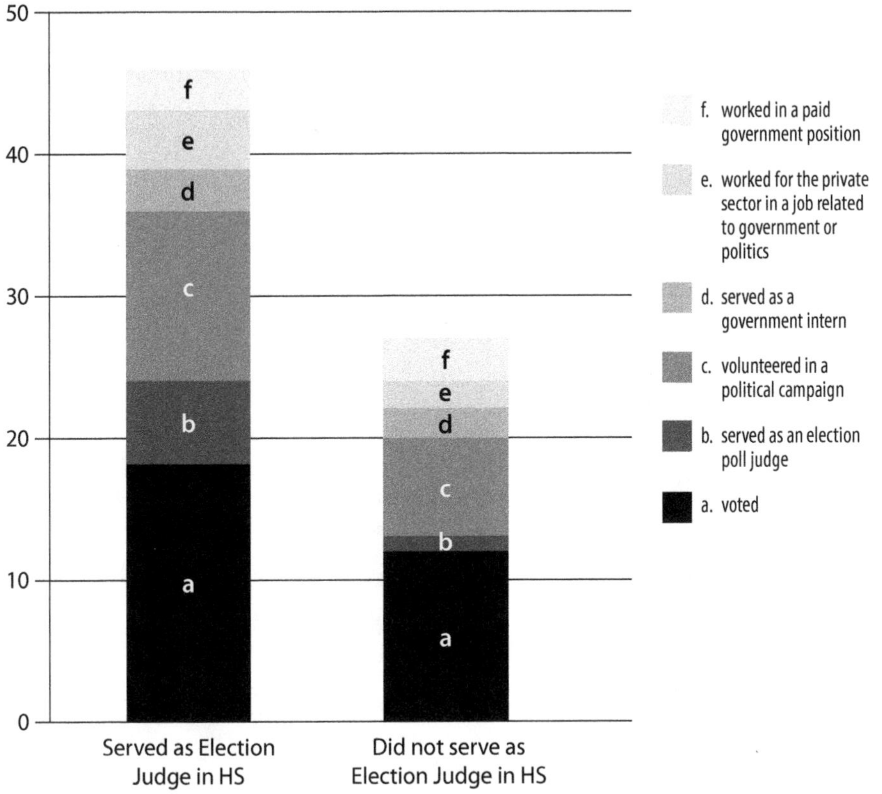

Note: Of the eight categories, two had no respondents: *"worked as paid staff in a political campaign"* and *"ran for public office"* have been eliminated from the graph above.

"How have you been involved in politics or government?" 20 had served as election judges, or 43% of the 46 former judges who responded, as opposed to 15 nonjudges (26% of 58 total nonjudges) who were active after high school. On the other hand, while there were only 23 respondents who had worked in political campaigns in high school, 17 (74%) answered positively to "Have you been involved in politics or government since you attended Loyola Academy?" and consequently recorded how they had been involved. Although fewer in number, the campaign workers were more involved in all but two categories: "voted" and "worked for the private sector in a job related to government or politics," as seen in Figure 19-1.

Were there any political activities significantly correlated with either of the high school activities? Table 19-6 shows a Spearman correlation of the responses to "How have you been involved in politics or government since you attended Loyola Academy?" and "Did you work in a political campaign when you attended Loyola Academy?" that indicates only one positive and significant correlation, not surprisingly, with volunteering later for a campaign. There is even a negative correlation between working for a campaign and having a private-sector job relating to

Figure 19-2: How have you been involved in politics or government since you attended Loyola Academy? Did you work in a political campaign in HS?

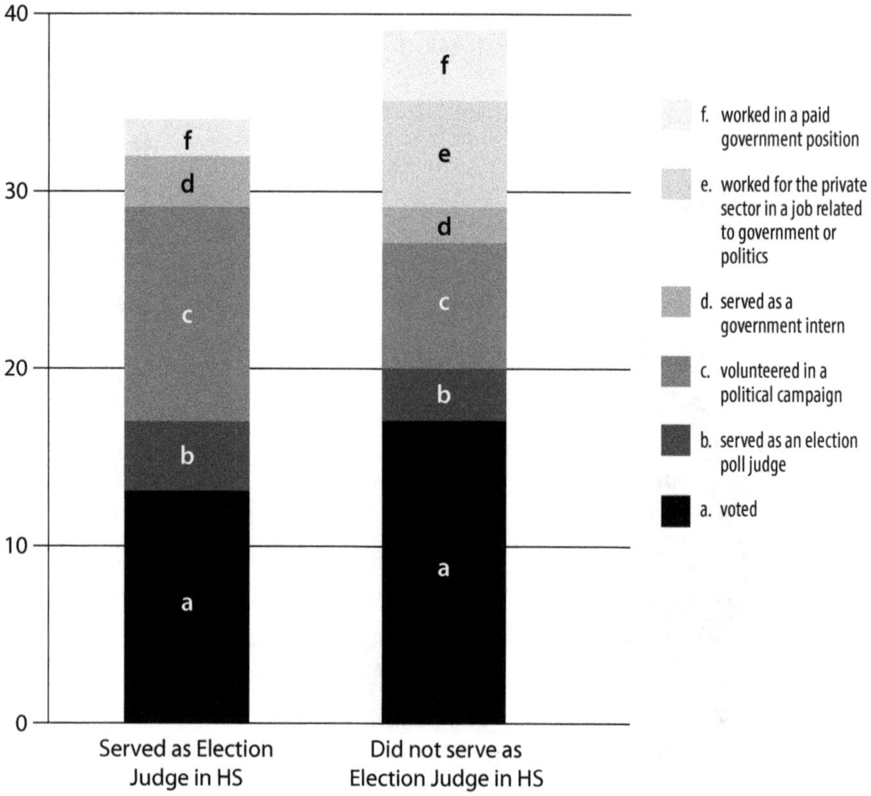

Note: Of the eight categories, two had no respondents: *"worked as paid staff in a political campaign"* and *"ran for public office"* have been eliminated from the graph above.

Table 19-6: Correlations of Serving as an Election Judge and Working in Political Campaigns in High School and Post–High School Involvement

	Voted after High School	Served as Election Judge after High School	Volunteered in a Campaign	Government Intern	Private-sector Job Involving Politics/ Government	Paid Government Position
Serve as an Election Judge in High School (Spearman's Rho)	.215	.273	.155	.046	.216	-.043
Work in Political Campaign in High School (Spearman's Rho)	-.201	.072	.394[a]	.150	-.363[a]	-.087
N	31	33	33	33	33	33

[a]Correlation is significant at the 0.05 level (2-tailed).

Table 19-7: Correlation between High School Political Involvement and Present Interest in Politics

	Serve as Election Judge in High School	Work in Political Campaign in High School
How Often Check Media for Political News (Spearman's Rho)	.263[a]	.110
Feelings Regarding Getting involved in Politics Now? (Spearman's Rho)	.219[b]	.224[b]
N	104	102

[a]Correlation is significant at the 0.01 level (2-tailed).
[b]Correlation is significant at the 0.05 level (2-tailed).

government. There were no significant correlations between "How have you been involved in politics or government since you attended Loyola Academy?" and "Did you serve as an election judge when you attended Loyola Academy?"

There are, however, correlations between working in elections in high school and current interest in politics. Findings in Table 19-7 show a significant correlation between checking the media for political news and having served as an election judge, but not having worked in a campaign in high school. However, there are weak but still significant correlations between a positive attitude toward getting involved in the political process and both types of high school election work.

Discussion

Enthusiasm for the electoral process was evident after the 2008 elections. From high school students' remarks and responses, it appeared that many students would remain politically active. Two students became interns in the offices of the public officials they had helped elect, and one student was offered a paid job in an alderman's campaign while still in high school. One student was hired by her victorious candidate to help run his campus campaign when she went to college in the fall.

There was less enthusiasm about the 2010 election. While 56% of the judges from the 2008 general election were very satisfied, only 41% evaluated their experiences at this level in 2010, reflecting the general downturn of enthusiasm found in off-year elections. Nonetheless, positive findings may only indicate that students are satisfied working in elections immediately after they are held. Whether the election service was meaningful in the long run is only evident by examining the results of the alumni study.

Although there were fewer alumni respondents who had been election workers in high school, a higher percentage of them said they were presently involved. Of the 104 respondents to the alumni survey, more than two-thirds of the respondents said that they had not been involved in politics in any way since high school. Yet while only 35 (34%) of all respondents said that they had been involved as adults, this was true of 74% of the 23 high school campaign workers, 46% of the 20 high school judges, and 50% (26) of the 52 respondents who served in either or both capacities in high school. Former high school campaign workers also indicated higher continued political interest than noncampaign workers. Although not statistically significant, a higher percentage of school election workers checked the media daily or more often, and a majority of former campaign workers also still felt positively about political involvement compared to non–high school election workers.

Serving as election workers in high school involved three socializing factors: involvement during an identity-forming age, peer involvement, and work in one's own community. The findings here seem to confirm that practical political experience in high school, if presented in tandem with classroom learning, can increase later political involvement.[33]

Turnout in recent elections also suggests that the youth vote can be mobilized. In 2008, voter turnout for voters 18–29 years of age was estimated at 51%. Yet in 2010, turnout for voters aged 18–29 was estimated only at 22.8%.[34] It was not clear which was a new normal level of youth involvement, the 2008 Obama high of 51% or the reversion to the lower level that appeared to reaffirm young voters' disengagement from politics. Yet in the 2012 election, voter turnout for youth reached more than 49%, nearly the 2008 level. Young voters comprised an estimated 19% of the total vote, and 58% of voters aged 18–29 were estimated to have voted in the battleground states. Since young voters favored Obama over Romney by 24% and their turnout was critical in the Obama victory,[35] CIRCLE estimated that 80 of the electoral votes from the battleground states depended upon voters 18–29 years of age.[36]

Further Research

This case study is only a beginning. In future work, we and other political scientists need to compare the experiences of election workers from other high schools, both in Illinois and in other states. Discovering what students liked or disliked about the election process will lead to improvements in promoting civic engagement. Examining student reactions to various types of campaign work will shed light on how to get adolescents to become involved even before they reach voting age. Since student election judge programs are fairly recent, it is still too early to assess their long-term effects on those who served. Nonetheless, comparing high school students' responses to those of college students in similar activities could increase understanding on developing long-term civic engagement at both educational levels.

The Influence of Civic Education on Electoral Engagement and Voting

20

By Diana Owen

There are a number of explanations for the increased youth electoral activation in 2008 and its subsequent decline in 2010. This study examines an underexplored piece of the puzzle of young people's electoral engagement—the preparation provided by civic education. It seeks to determine if people who had access to high-quality civic education programs, especially civics courses that incorporated active-learning elements, were more likely to participate in the 2008 presidential election than those who did not. I argue that civic education at the junior high and high school levels can convey the knowledge and skills necessary to encourage people to participate in elections throughout their lives. In addition, those whose civic education experiences include active-learning elements will be the most inclined to participate in elections.

It has become commonplace for scholars and political practitioners to lament young people's low levels of engagement in American election campaigns. Studies have documented declining voter turnout among young adults since the 1970s. In recent years, however, there have been some encouraging developments on the electoral front. Participation in presidential elections has increased in general, and turnout among young voters has been on the rise since the 2000 campaign. Fifty-one percent of 18–29-year-old voters cast a ballot in 2008, compared to 49% in 2004 and 43% in 2000.[1] As in 2004, the youth vote in 2012 was around 49%.[2]

Coinciding with the rise in turnout, youth engagement in campaign activities has increased in presidential elections, especially in 2008. Young people were energetic volunteers who provided candidates with corps of grassroots operatives. They were innovators who developed novel campaign strategies that employed new technologies, including social networking and video-sharing websites.[3] Despite these developments, however, the youth vote lags considerably behind turnout for citizens age 40 and older. Further, young people are more inclined to vote in presidential contests than in primary, midterm, or lower-level elections. For example, young voters were not enthusiastic participants in the 2010 midterm elections, as approximately 23% of eligible 18–29-year-olds voted in these midterm contests, compared to 41% of the general population.[4] Young voter turnout in 2010 also was down slightly from 25.5% in 2006 and about the same as in 2002, when 22% of 18–29 year olds went to the polls.[5] There are a number of explanations for the increased electoral activation in 2008, including the presence of a candidate who appealed to youth; a rise in young people's beliefs that they could influence the outcome of the campaign; enhanced outreach to youth by candidates, parties, and independent political organizations; and technological developments that contributed to a more open communications environment.[6]

This chapter examines another plausible piece of the puzzle of young people's electoral engagement—the preparation provided by civic education. A critical mass of younger citizens has gone through civic education programs prior to reaching voting age. All 50 states and the District of Columbia require that civics-related material be included in at least one course. Data from the survey conducted for this study indicate that approximately three-quarters of students have been exposed to civics material in their curriculum. However, the quality of civics instruction varies greatly across schools. Civic education can provide knowledge of how the system works, which forms the basis for the development of a sense of political efficacy and civic duty that facilitates participation.[7] In addition, civic skills conducive to electoral engagement can be developed through the civics curriculum.

As noted, despite the potential importance of civic education for producing engaged citizens, there are great disparities in access to civic education programs as well as large variations in curriculum quality. The number of people who have been exposed to a dedicated, high-quality civic education program is limited. Many receive their civic education incidentally as a small part of a class in a related discipline, like history.[8] Given this limitation, were people who had access to high-quality civic education programs, especially civics courses that incorporated active-learning elements, more likely to participate in the 2008 presidential election than those who did not?

This study addresses a larger group of Americans by exploring the following research questions: Does civic education at the precollege level influence electoral engagement and voting later in life? and What kinds of classroom instructional approaches are most conducive to creating citizens inclined to participate actively in elections? These questions are examined in relation to both traditional forms of campaign activity, such as working on a political campaign or attending a candidate's rally, as well as newer forms of campaign engagement associated with social media, such as social networking sites and video-sharing platforms to interact with the election. I argue that civic education at the junior high and high school levels can convey the knowledge and skills necessary to encourage people to participate in elections throughout their lives. People who take even a basic civics course are more likely than those who have no civic education to engage in campaigns. In addition, those whose civic education experience includes active-learning elements, such as participating in mock hearings and debates, using digital media for civic purposes, or including innovative instructional methods such as incorporating current events into lesson plans, will be the most inclined to take part in elections.

The chapter begins with a discussion of the literature examining the link between civic education and the development of participatory norms and behaviors. It then describes two survey data sets used for the empirical analysis as well as the methodology employed in the study. Next, I present the results of the hypothesis testing and data analysis. Finally, the chapter offers conclusions outlining the implications of this research for political scientists, policy makers, and educators.

Civic Education and Participatory Orientations

Civics instruction across the United States varies widely in its structure, content, and quality. Many schools incorporate civic education into social studies or American history courses rather than offering dedicated civics classes. Such courses may gloss over or be uneven in their coverage of voting and other forms of active political engagement. At the same time, some school-based programs that aim to improve civics instruction by going beyond standard lecture and textbook teaching methods alone have been implemented. Students in these programs learn about the constitutional and historical foundations of American government, the requirements of citizenship, and the structure and functions of the political system. They also become familiar with the skills needed for meaningful political and civic participation, such as speaking in public, participating in public hearings, contacting officials, meeting with community leaders about issues, and using media to engage the polity.

There has been a long-running debate over the priority that should be given to voting and campaign-related participation in classroom civic education versus imparting general knowledge about government and politics or focusing on community volunteerism. Some scholars contend that the civic education curriculum should have an overt focus on voting, with the goal of increasing turnout in elections.[9] Others believe that by encouraging intermediate civic traits, such as political knowledge, efficacy, and citizen duty, civic education is inherently promoting voting.[10] Just as scholars are divided, so is the scholarship. Some demonstrates that schools are an important agent of political socialization,[11] whereas other work indicates that schools play a more limited role.[12]

The Effectiveness of Civic Education

Scholars and practitioners long have contemplated whether civic education plays an important role in the development of civic attitudes, norms, values, and behaviors. A seminal study by Langton and Jennings traced the rise and implementation of high school civics courses in the United States dating back to 1915.[13] The study employed a national probability sample to evaluate the impact that high school American government and civics courses had on youth political orientations. The findings suggested that such coursework led to little, if any, increase in youth civic engagement or political participation after high school. This work, in conjunction with other studies that provided mixed support at best for the idea that schools influence the development of civic orientation or long-term gains in political knowledge,[14] contributed to the subsequent de-emphasis of civics in American public schools.

Other scholars, while noting some limitations of the extant curriculum, challenged these findings. Some have gone so far as to characterize the school as "the most important and effective instrument of political socialization in the United States."[15] More recent studies since the late 1980s support the contention that civic education contributes to the development of knowledge and norms that encourage political engagement.[16] These studies find that robust civics instruction can lead to increased levels of political knowledge and impart an understanding of the government and how it aids people in developing a sense of agency that encourages participation.[17]

As several chapters in this volume suggest, political engagement requires that people believe in their own ability to influence actual political happenings. A sense of political efficacy is derived not only through political knowledge, but also from other skills enforced through successful civic education programs. These skills, as mentioned earlier, include public speaking, debating skills, and an ability to work with people with differing points of view. Other advanced skills are the ability to define a problem, conduct background research, engage decision makers, evaluate public opinion, build coalitions and public support, and effectively use the media.[18] Such skills have been defined as "the communications and organizational abilities that allow citizens to use time and money effectively in political life."[19] As noted, increased political efficacy can lead to higher levels of political participation. Efficacy is an important determinant of political behavior, because without feelings of competency and a belief that one's actions are consequential, one has little incentive to participate in politics.[20]

Civic duty represents the responsibility people feel they have toward their government and society. While distinct from political efficacy, civic duty is closely related in that both concepts deal with the way in which individuals orient themselves within the broader political establishment. Studies consistently demonstrate that civic duty is an important predictor of political participation and voting.[21]

This link is especially evident when a direct connection is made in the classroom between the abstract concept of civic duty and actual engagement in politics, such as voting.[22] Research has shown that high school students who receive quality civic education are more inclined to develop a strong sense of responsibility to take part in political and civic affairs that persists after graduation.[23] A limited number of studies provide some evidence of a direct link between higher levels of civic education and increased voter turnout rates. For example, students with more education were much more likely to have voted in the 2000 presidential election than those with lower levels of education.[24] Another study found that high school students who complete a year of coursework in American government or civics are more likely to vote in an election following high school by a factor of three to six percentage points than students with no civic education.[25] The study discussed in this chapter supports the proposition that civic education is positively related to electoral engagement. Prior research in this vein examines earlier campaigns, but the empirical analysis here focuses on the 2008 presidential election.

Classroom Environment and Instructional Methods

Particular types of civic education and classroom instructional methods are especially conducive to making participatory citizens. Factors such as integrating current events into classroom curricula increase the likelihood of students' future political participation.[26] Current events, particularly when tailored to a student's interest or discussed in conjunction with an active classroom or community-based project,[27] are a key component of a course that can bolster civic knowledge and engagement by providing "nonduplicative civic knowledge," or new information not previously covered in earlier classes.[28] The 2005 California Survey of Civic Education reported that 61% of students in classes in which current events were regularly discussed said they were interested in politics, in contrast to 32% in classes in which current events discussions were not part of the curricula.

Other instructional tools can augment students' interest in politics. For example, Kahne and Middaugh's model for high-quality civic education is rooted in curricular support that goes beyond textbooks. They found that making classroom civics more personal and engaging (e.g., meeting civic role models, discussing local issues of relevance to the students) positively influenced high school students' commitment to civic participation. In addition, the study argues that an increase in these types of activities could help offset the civic opportunity gap created by differences in personal backgrounds and home environments, a finding replicated in crossnational studies.[29]

Finally, by participating in classroom-based political exercises, students develop more-positive views of government and the political system in general. A study of We the People: The Citizen and the Constitution (WTP),[30] developed by the Center for Civic Education, found that the program's participants develop stronger attachments to democratic attitudes and principles, as well as an enhanced sense of political interest and effectiveness.[31] Students who take part in Project Citizen, which integrates problem-solving, collaborative thinking, and crossdisciplinary approaches into the curriculum, emerge with a greater sense of their own agency as civic actors.[32] The program's alumni also are more inclined to register to vote and turn out than their peers.[33]

The study discussed in this chapter contributes to the civic education literature in a number of ways. First, it is a rare examination of the long-term implications of precollege civic education on political participation. It employs a unique national data set that accounts for various elements of respondents' civic education experience, including classroom environment, curriculum content, learning approach, and innovative teaching and learning elements. In addition, the study not only addresses the link between civic education and traditional forms of campaign engagement, it also takes into account newer aspects of electoral participation facilitated by digital technology.

Hypotheses

Previously presented research based on data from the two surveys employed in this study indicates that innovative approaches to civic education are related to higher levels of politicization. People whose civic education experience includes innovative curriculum elements are more likely to develop participatory norms and a continuing sense of civic duty than those with no civic education.[34] Similarly, civic education experience is linked to the use of social media for political engagement, as people who have taken part in a civic education program were more likely to engage in the 2008 campaign's digital platforms, such as Facebook and YouTube.[35] The study used in this chapter tests the following hypotheses related to voting and campaign involvement:

> H_1: The greater the amount and quality of precollege civic education, the more likely that people are to vote in presidential elections.
>
> H_2: The greater the amount and quality of precollege civic education, the more likely that people are to participate in campaign-related activities.

As should already be clear from the text, I hypothesize that taking a civics course of any kind in junior high and high school increases the likelihood that a person will participate in campaigns later in life. People who have no civic education are least likely to vote in a presidential election, whereas those who have taken part in a high-quality civic education program are most likely to turn out to vote. I hypothesize that civic education programs that incorporate such active instructional elements as discussing current events, participating in a mock trial or hearing and attending community meetings, are the most effective in promoting campaign engagement.

Data

This study employs data from two original surveys.[36] The Civic Education and Political Engagement Study (CEPES) examined the influence of civic training on the development of political orientation and citizenship skills. This study is unique in that it explored respondents' civic education experience through an extensive series of questions that took into account classroom civic education and participation in service-learning programs and extracurricular activities. Respondents evaluated their own civic education experience and reported their attitudes toward civics instruction in general. The survey included items related to political knowledge, political norms, attitudes, values, political participation, campaign activity, voting behavior, traditional media use, and new/social media use. The online survey was conducted by Knowledge Networks (KN) between May 14 and 28, 2010, and employed a national probability sample (n=1,228) drawn from KN's nationwide online panel.[37]

The same questionnaire with several additional items was administered to a sample of alumni of WTP. More than 30 million students have participated in We the People since 1987. The program's curriculum incorporates innovative instructional techniques, including a simulated congressional hearing in which students demonstrate their knowledge and understanding of constitutional principles before a panel of judges. The survey was administered online by the researchers to a sample of WTP alumni (n=1,002).[38]

Measures

Electoral Participation Variables

This study focuses on three aspects of electoral participation during the 2008 presidential election: 1) voting, 2) campaign participation, and 3) engagement via social media. Identical indicators were developed for the CEPES and the WTP alumni data sets. The voting measure is based upon respondents' self-reporting about whether they voted in the election or not.[39] Respondents ineligible to vote in 2008 either because they were not of voting age or were not American citizens were removed from the analysis. Self-reported turnout can be inflated, as people may give the socially responsible answer to a question. However, Berent, Krosnick, and Lupia, in addressing the registration and turnout measures in the American National Election Studies, found that "survey respondents' reports of their own registration and turnout behavior are more accurate than previously believed."[40] A partial explanation for this may be that survey respondents tend to turn out more in elections than people who choose not to participate in surveys. The voter-eligible turnout for 2008 was 62%, and 73% of the CEPES respondents indicated that they had voted. A similar measure of voter turnout was devised for voting in presidential elections prior to 2008.

The surveys included seven items that assessed respondents' participation in the campaign. These items include those typically found on surveys, such as the American National Election Studies, as well as a couple of additional items (e.g., item 7). They in no way represent all of the possible ways in which people can participate in elections—a limitation of most survey-based studies of electoral engagement. The indicators of campaign participation include:

1. volunteering for a candidate or political party
2. working for an organization that informed or mobilized voters
3. contributing money to a campaign or political party
4. wearing a campaign button or displaying a bumper sticker or yard sign
5. attending a campaign rally or meeting
6. calling in to a radio or television talk show
7. doing something on one's own to support or oppose a candidate

These items were combined to form an index of campaign participation that ranged from zero to seven (Cronbach's alpha=.688). This eight-point index was used in the OLS (ordinary least squares) regression analysis performed for the study. To facilitate the presentation of contingency table data used to illustrate the basic relationships, this index was collapsed to form a dichotomous measure meant to indicate whether a respondent had participated in any or none of these ways during the 2008 campaign.

Using social media to participate in the presidential contest increased in prominence in 2008. Seven indicators of using social media to engage with the campaign were included in the study:

1. used a social networking site, like Facebook, to engage with others during the campaign
2. watched online campaign videos, such as those on YouTube
3. followed a campaign via a blog
4. posted something related to the campaign on a blog, website, or video-sharing site
5. visited a candidate's website
6. used email to send information about the campaign to others
7. used Twitter to send or receive campaign information

These items were combined to form an eight-point index of social media engagement (Cronbach's alpha=.880). Again, a dichotomous measure was created that was meant to indicate whether a respondent had engaged with social media in any of these ways during the 2008 election or not for presentation of contingency table data.

Three indicators that tap participation through both traditional activities and social media were employed in the analysis. The first is an additive index that combines the traditional participation and the social media measures that ranges from zero to 16. For the second indicator, the dichotomous measures of campaign participation and social media engagement were combined to form a categorical measure of participation via traditional campaign activities and social media. This variable takes into account people who participated in the campaign through both traditional activities and social media, those who participated only in traditional ways, those who engaged solely through social media, and those who did not participate at all. In the general population, 15% of respondents participated in both types of activities, 14% took part in traditional activities only, 16% engaged only through social media, and 54% did not participate. Lastly, a dichotomous measure that tapped whether a respondent participated through either traditional activities or social media was constructed for use in contingency table analysis.

Civic Education Variables

A civic education index was constructed for the CEPES data as a basic indicator of the amount of civics instruction people received. This index consists of three categories: 1) people who had no civic education at all (24% of the sample), 2) those who took only a civics/social studies course (64% of the sample), and 3) individuals who took a civics/social studies course and participated in a civic education program (12% of the sample).[41] To compile these data, the survey asked respondents if they had taken a government, social studies, or civics class in junior high or high school.[42] Participants also indicated whether or not they had taken part in a civic education program that went beyond the basic government, social studies, or civics curriculum to incorporate such active and innovative learning features as field trips, interviews with civic leaders, debates, mock trials, hearings, and simulated elections. Survey respondents affirmed participation in approximately 35 different civic education programs. These programs differed in specific goals and instructional methods, but all involved some type of curriculum innovation. More than twice as many respondents to the CEPES conducted by KN participated in We the People[43] than in any other program. Additional programs included Kids Voting USA, Model Congress/Model United Nations, Street Law, Close Up, and Project Citizen. Students who participate in these programs can be predisposed to high achievement and strong civic attitudes. Some may self-select into a program or be encouraged to enroll by teachers and parents. However, others may be exposed to a program as a regular part of the curriculum.

The CEPES and WTP alumni surveys included items that tapped into the type of classroom civics instruction respondents received. These variables measured the extent to which the class experience included lecture, textbook-based learning, current events–based learning, classroom activities, and community-based activities. Each item was measured using a five-point indicator that ranged from never to always. A 15-point classroom instruction scale was constructed that used the current events–based learning, classroom activities, and community-based learning items (Cronbach's alpha=.799). A higher score on the civics classroom instruction scale indicated that a student experienced an interactive and engaging classroom setting.

The classroom environment indicator provided a general assessment of whether a student had primarily textbook- and lecture-based instruction or a more interactive learning experience. A more refined measure of students' experience with active learning also was developed that took into account specific classroom activities. Respondents were asked if they had ever taken part in a variety of activities in conjunction with their civics training. These were labeled "curricular activities," in that they were incorporated into or complimented the classroom curriculum directly, as opposed to extracurricular activities, which are typically not tied directly to classroom instruction. The 14 instructional activities included:

1. debates
2. a competition to test civic knowledge
3. mock trials
4. hearings
5. mock elections
6. delivering a speech
7. discussing current events

8. writing a letter to a government official
9. circulating a petition
10. attending a community meeting
11. meeting with government or community leaders
12. taking a field trip to a local, state, or federal government institution or historic site
13. community service
14. creating civics-related informational material, newsletters, videos, or websites

These dichotomous items were combined to form a civics curricular activities scale that ranged from 0 to 14.

Prior research indicates that extracurricular activities, including participation in clubs, service-learning, and volunteer opportunities, can be effective in encouraging political participation. These experiences expose people to new social networks and ideas and provide opportunities for learning interpersonal and leadership skills that can translate to the political realm.[44] The relationship of extracurriculars to politicization has been shown to differ across types of activities. Extracurricular activities more closely connected to political participation, such as serving on the student council, can predict future engagement to some extent.[45] Still, there are limits to the politicizing effects of extracurricular activities, especially as people with higher levels of self-efficacy, political interest, and leadership ability may be more likely to take part in extracurriculars than those who exhibit lower levels of these traits.[46]

The survey asked respondents if they had participated in 18 different types of extracurricular activities, each represented by a dichotomous variable. To test for the influence of extracurriculars on electoral engagement, I created four scales that represented specific categories of extracurricular activities—political, media-related, service, and sports/hobbies. The political activities scale (range 0 to 4) included participation in student government, debate team or mock trial, a political campaign, or political internship. The media-related extracurricular activities scale (range 0 to 4) consisted of participation in student newspaper, yearbook, radio or television station, and literary journal. A scale representing service extracurricular activities (range 0 to 4) took into account participation in a community-service organization, Boy or Girl Scouts, 4-H Club or other agricultural organization, and church or religious groups. The final scale (range 0 to 5) included participation in sports, hobby organizations, and other nonpolitical organizations, including cheerleading, band, choir, glee club, drama, and language clubs.

Civic Duty

A civic duty scale was constructed from four items that indicated that respondents felt that they have a responsibility to keep informed about public affairs, took part in government affairs, volunteered in the community, and served on a jury. The

16-point indicator was scored so that a high value equated with a strong sense of civic duty (Cronbach's alpha= .766). This attitudinal measure of civic duty is incorporated as a control variable in the analysis, as it is expected that people with a strong sense of duty are more inclined to vote and participate in elections.

FINDINGS

This study provided evidence to support the hypothesis that civic education is positively related to voting. As Table 20-1 shows, the greater the amount and quality of civic education, the more likely that people were to turn out to vote. "Quality" here refers to the amount of civic education respondents experienced, as well as the type of curriculum—ranging from no formal civic education to taking a civics course and participating in a civics program like We the People. Respondents who had no civic education were substantially less likely to report voting in 2008 and in prior presidential contests than those who had taken a civics course or participated in a civics program. There is a difference of more than 20 percentage points between those who had no civic education and those who had taken at least one civics or social studies course. Those who had gone through a civic education program were the most likely to cast a ballot. Eighty-eight percent of WTP alumni reported turning out in the 2008 presidential election, and 78% had turned out in previous electoral contests.

Taking age into account better specifies the relationship for young voters. Forty-eight percent of 18–29-year-olds who had no civic education voted in the 2008 presidential election, compared to 66% of those who had taken a civics or social studies course and 77% of those who had participated in a civic education program like We the People. Similar patterns are discerned for older age groups as well.

The analysis indicates a similar pattern that supports civic education's positive influence on voter participation. In keeping with the second hypothesis, the higher the level of civic education, the more likely people were to participate in the 2008 election. Sixty-two percent of those whose civics instruction included an innovative

Table 20-1: Voting and Civic Education Experience

	No Civic Education	Civics/Social Studies Only	Civics/Social Studies and Program	Total Sample	We the People Alumni
Voted in 2008 Election	55%	78%	83%	73%	88%
Voted in Previous Elections	48%	73%	78%	67%	78%

Notes:

χ^2 p≤.05 for Civic Education Index

Taking age into account better specifies the relationship for young voters. Forty-eight percent of 18–29-year-olds who had no civic education voted in the 2008 presidential election, compared to 66% of those who had taken a civics or social studies course and 77% of those who had participated in a civic education program like We the People. Similar patterns are discerned for older age groups as well.

Table 20-2: Campaign Participation and Civic Education Experience

	No Civic Education	Civics/Social Studies Only	Civics/Social Studies and Program	Total Sample	We the People Alumni
Traditional and Social Media Participation	7%	17%	24%	15%	53%
Traditional Participation Only	11%	14%	20%	14%	7%
Social Media Participation Only	12%	17%	19%	16%	21%
No Campaign Participation	70%	52%	38%	54%	19%

Note: χ^2 $p \leq .05$ for Civic Education Index

program engaged in the campaign either through traditional activities or social media, compared to 48% of those who took a civics or social studies course only and 30% of those who had no classroom civics instruction. Eighty-one percent of We the People alumni participated in the campaign in some way. Further, the level of engagement in the campaign increased with the quality of the civic education experience. As Table 20-2 illustrates, 24% of people exposed to a civics program took part in the campaign through both traditional activities and social media, as opposed to 17% of those who had only a civics or social studies class and 7% of those with no civic education. Fifty-three percent of alumni of WTP took part in the campaign through both traditional activities and social media, while another 21% engaged through social media alone and 7% participated in traditional ways.

The percentage of national survey respondents whose civic education experiences included active instructional elements is strikingly low. Participating in debates, discussing current events, and taking field trips to government and historical sites were mentioned most frequently by the CEPES survey participants (between 21% and 24%). Fewer than 20% of subjects reported participating in the majority of instructional activities. In addition, fewer than 10% of respondents had participated in a competition to test their civic knowledge, taken part in a hearing, written a letter to a public official, circulated or signed a petition, attended a community meeting, met a political leader, or prepared civic-related materials (see Table 20-3).

These findings strongly support the contention that high school civics curricula that incorporate active-learning instruction that develops civics skills will be more likely to produce citizens who will vote and actively take part in election campaigns. Table 20-3 shows the percentage of respondents to the CEPES who took part in 14 types of civics curricular activities and who voted and participated in the campaign. The combined campaign involvement measure that included both traditional and social media engagement was used in the analysis.[47] Across the board, people whose classroom civics experience incorporated active forms of instruction were more likely to vote than those who did not have these kinds of

Table 20-3: Civic Education and Political Engagement Study (KN)—Voting, Campaign Engagement, and Civics Curricular Activities

	Debate	Compete	Mock Trial	Hearing	Mock Election	Speech	Current Events	Letter	Petition	Attend Meeting	Meet Leaders	Field Trip	Community Service	Civic Material	Total Percentage/n
Voted	87%	88	85	68	89	85	88	89	87	90	88	88	91	93%	73% (905)
Engaged	85%	86	84	90	85	85	86	93	83	84	87	83	88	93%	46% (524)
Total	21%	5	12	2	12	18	24	9	5	8	5	24	7	1%	
χ^2 sign. voted engaged	.00 .00	n.s. n.s.	n.s. n.s.	n.s. n.s.	.00 .00	.03 .02	.00 .00	.01 .00	n.s. n.s.	.00 .00	n.s. .01.	.00 .00	.00 .00	.01 n.s.	

Table 20-4: We the People Alumni Survey—Voting, Campaign Engagement and Civics Curricular Activities

	Debate	Compete	Mock Trial	Hearing	Mock Election	Speech	Current Events	Letter	Petition	Attend Meeting	Meet Leaders	Field Trip	Community Service	Civic Material	n
Voted	92%	88	90	86	89	90	90	91	93	90	90	92	88	93%	88% (463)
Engaged	85%	86	91	89	87	86	85	86	93	89	87	83	88	94%	81% (539)
Total	88%	83	77	68	67	78	94	76	48	74	81	88	79	41%	
χ^2 sign. Voted Engaged	.00 .00	.00 .00	.00 .00	.00 .00	.00 .00	.00 .00	.00 .00	.00 .00	.00 .00	.00 .00	.00 .00	.00 .00	.00 .00	.00 .00	

experiences. For all but one item, 85% or more of those whose civic education included an instructional activity reported voting in the 2008 election. The findings were similar for campaign engagement. Eighty-four percent or more of respondents in each category of civics curricular activities participated in a campaign through traditional means, social media, or both. Ninety percent or more of those who took part in a simulated hearing, wrote a letter to a public official, or created civics materials engaged in the campaign.

One of the civics curricular measures—creating civics-related informational material, newsletters, videos, or websites—is particularly relevant for the use of social media in the campaign. Fewer people (1% of the CEPES sample) reported experience with this type of instructional activity than any other form. Although the number of cases in the category was small, this type of classroom activity may be relevant for preparing people to engage with social media during campaigns.

Findings for the WTP alumni sample appear in Table 20-4. Civics curricular activities are a regular component of the WTP curriculum. In contrast to the national sample, high percentages of respondents had engaged in almost all of the curricular activities. The smallest percentage was associated with creating civics-related media material and websites, likely because these are newer forms of instructional activity than, for example, taking part in a debate. Forty-one percent of WTP respondents created civics-related media as a part of their civic education experience. More than 90% of WTP alumni who created media materials and websites voted and engaged in the campaign.

An ordinary least squares regression analysis was run to further investigate the effects of classroom environment and curricular activities on campaign participation. The three dependent variables were the traditional campaign activity, social media engagement, and combined campaign engagement scales. Classroom factors represented by the classroom environment variable—the combined measure of the extent to which the respondents' civics instruction consisted of current events–based learning, classroom activities, and community-based activities—and the curricular activities index were included in the model. The four measures of extracurricular activities, the civic duty index, and demographic controls for age, sex, and race were incorporated into the analysis.[48] The classroom factors, extracurricular activities, civic duty measure, and demographic variables were treated as blocks of variables, and the R^2 for each block was assessed.[49]

As Table 20-5 demonstrates, the classroom factors were statistically significant predictors of traditional campaign activity, social media engagement, and combined campaign engagement. People whose civic education experience included active and innovative curricular experiences were more likely to take part in election campaigns. These factors explain more of the variance in each of the models than any of the other sets of variables, including extracurricular activities. The R^2 for the classroom factors block was higher than for any other block in each model. Classroom factors explained 16% of the variance in traditional campaign engagement, 7% for social media engagement, and 10% of combined engagement. The curricular activities measure was a strong and significant predictor of traditional

Table 20-5: OLS Regression Analysis of Traditional Campaign Activity, Social Media Engagement, and Combined Campaign Engagement on Classroom Factors and Extracurricular Activities

	Traditional Campaign Activity	*Social Media Engagement*	*Combined Campaign Engagement*
Classroom Factors			
Class Environment	-.003	.119[a]	.108[a]
Curricular Activities	.243[a]	.066[a]	.113[a]
R^2	.157	.071[a]	.101[a]
Extracurricular Activities			
Political	.270[a]	.084[b]	.138[a]
Service	.050[c]	.015	.028
Sports and Hobby	-.118[a]	-.037	-.061[c]
Media	.041	.013	.020
R^2	.076[a]	.006	.018[a]
Civic Duty	.175[a]	.202[a]	.224[a]
R^2	.031[a]	.018[a]	.027[a]
Demographics			
Age	.113[a]	-.215[a]	-.163[a]
Sex	-.045[c]	-.052[c]	-.059[b]
Black/African American	.023	-.056	.047
White	-.085[a]	-.110[a]	-.117[a]
R^2	.021[a]	.058[a]	.041[a]
Model R^2	.284[a]	.153[a]	.187[a]

Note:
a. $p \leq .01$
b. $p \leq .05$
c. $p \leq .10$

campaign activity, whereas class environment was not.[50] However, classroom environment was a stronger predictor of social media engagement than were curricular activities. Classroom environment indicated whether the instruction method focused generally on lecture, textbook-based learning, current events–based learning, or activities-based learning, whereas curricular activities encompassed a wide range of active learning innovations, such as classroom debates and simulated hearings. Both variables are statistically significant. The two classroom factors were significant predictors of combined campaign engagement, and the coefficients were of a similar magnitude.

Extracurricular activities explained less of the variance in campaign participation than did classroom factors. In fact, the R^2 for this block of variables was not significant for social media engagement and was very weak for combined campaign engagement. As one might expect, taking part in political forms of extracurricular activities, such as student government, debate team, and working on a campaign while in junior high or high school, was statistically significant in all three models and was the strongest individual predictor of traditional campaign activity. These activities were directly relevant for political engagement, and students predisposed toward politics may self-select into these extracurriculars. Participating in service-related extracurricular activities was positively related to traditional campaign activity, but this was not significant in the other two models. The relationship between sports and hobby-based extracurricular activities and all three measures of campaign activity was negative, and it was statistically significant for traditional and combined campaign engagement. Students may acquire some skills relevant for political engagement through these types of activities, such as cooperation and organizational skills and norms like political tolerance, but they may not make the connection to electoral participation.

Civic duty, as expected, was a statistically significant predictor in all three models. The relationship was strongest for the combined campaign engagement measure and weakest for traditional campaign activity. Age was the strongest predictor among the demographic controls, and it was statistically significant in all of the models. The direction of the relationship differed based on the type of campaign engagement. Age was the strongest predictor of social media engagement, as younger people were more likely than older individuals to take part in the 2008 presidential election in this way. However, older individuals were more inclined to participate in traditional ways. Sex was a weak predictor of engagement, with men slightly more inclined to participate than women. It is important to note, however, that women typically vote in elections at higher rates than men.[51] Generally speaking, race was not a strong predictor of campaign activity, which was surprising given the presence of an African American candidate in the race. The control for black/African American was not significant, and the coefficient for white was significant and negative.[52] The finding indicated that in the 2008 election, whites were less inclined to participate in campaign activities compared to members of other racial groups. Race alone, however, was not enough to predict campaign engagement; instead, the higher the education within each category of race, the more likely the participation in campaigns.

Conclusion

This study found that civic education matters in regard to voting and participation in election campaigns. Taking a course in social studies or civics in junior high or high school significantly increased the probability that a citizen would vote and engage in campaign-related activities. People whose civic education experience went beyond a standard course and included an innovative, active-learning program that facilitated the development of relevant sills for civic engagement, such as We the People, Kids Voting, or Close Up, were the most likely to participate in elections as adults.

Another finding was that classroom civics instruction is more important than extracurricular activities in promoting voting and electoral engagement. As the data indicate and prior research has shown,[53] the possible exception is the relationship of participation in politically related extracurricular activities, such as taking part in student government or working on a political campaign, to traditional campaign participation. However, students who engage in these kinds of extracurricular activities may be predisposed to politics. Nonetheless, the findings suggested that participation in politically and civically related extracurricular activities is a precursor to adult engagement for some people. Thus, it is prudent for schools to offer these opportunities for students, especially if such opportunities are linked directly to the civics curriculum.[54]

Engagement in campaigns through social media is a new and evolving phenomenon that warrants consideration by civic educators. This type of engagement can be meaningful, as when citizens participate in issue discussions on forums with others throughout the country or when they reach out to their peers to recruit volunteers for offline campaign activities. Social media use also can divert people from active engagement and encourage uncivil behavior.[55] Given that social media are now an entrenched element of the electoral process, civic educators may play a role in helping students develop skills for productive engagement. The majority of curriculum innovations reported by the CEPES and WTP alumni survey respondents are especially relevant for traditional forms of participation. The civics experience of few of the CEPES respondents included the creation of media-related materials, newsletters, videos, and websites. However, people whose civics instruction included these elements were highly inclined to participate in the campaign, especially through social media.

The findings of the study have implications for political scientists, policy makers, and educators. Researchers, including those whose work appears in this volume, have done much to advance the discipline's understanding of the ways in which civic education influences the development of participant attitudes, norms, and behaviors. Yet, many studies are from an era that predates the pervasive use of digital technologies that are becoming important conduits for political engagement. Further, research that examines the long-term implications of school-based civics curricula on political participation is limited. This study lays the foundation for further investigations into the specific types of civics instruction and curriculum innovations that best incline people to lifelong political and civic activation. It includes expanding knowledge of how new and emerging technological applications are a part of the civic life of the nation.

Policy makers should take seriously the findings of research, including this study, which indicate that civic education programs are successful in developing good citizens and support their development. Even as scholarship demonstrates the effectiveness of quality civic education, the future of many programs is in jeopardy as schools lack the resources to implement innovative civics curricula. The Education for Democracy Act, which funded civic education in the United States and emerging democracies that has benefitted millions of students, was cut from the federal budget in 2011. The federal emphasis of testing in reading and math has driven the curriculum away from educating citizens through interactive programs like Close Up and We the People. Such programs provide students, especially those who do not attend college, with the opportunity to debate, discuss current issues, study the Constitution, and present their ideas to others. As this research shows, these experiences can stimulate a commitment to electoral engagement after graduation.

The benefits of innovative civics curricula documented in this study are reinforced by interviews conducted with teachers and students associated with the We the People program in conjunction with this research project. A WTP teacher noted differences between WTP and AP American government:

> The big difference between, say, the AP government curriculum and the We the People curriculum is that AP government wants the students to know a lot of things and that's fine, but We the People requires the kids to actually consider the value in their thought and their opinion—to have critical thinking and informed thought.[56]

A WTP student alumna observed,

> Personally, I as a student have become really inspired to participate politically. Not only do I participate in a lot of online petitions ... but I've actually been campaigning in two national elections ... and I'll be continuing to do so this summer.[57]

The new media environment presents a challenge for civic education instructors who seek to teach students how to participate meaningfully in elections today. The findings presented here indicate that few classes integrate new media techniques for engaging in politics, but students who have this experience are very likely to take part in elections using digital technologies. If the 2010 midterm elections were any indication, campaign engagement through social media will increase and become more sophisticated over time. Candidates now embrace social media as both a supplement and an alternative to mainstream media, and citizens use new media to access the campaign. As social media has become an integral element of young people's daily lives, civic educators should consider ways of teaching responsible use of social media for political engagement.

SECTION III

Incorporating Civic Engagement into the Curriculum and Beyond

Introduction to Section III

Incorporating Civic Engagement into the Curriculum and Beyond

A person must constantly practice and build upon existing skills and knowledge to advance and achieve goals. Section Two provided excellent examples of single-course and single-experience options to facilitate students' development into effective citizens. This section promotes the view that single-course experiences are only part of a complete approach to civic engagement education. On their own, they are not enough to develop lifelong, civically engaged citizens. Instead, political scientists must create wider curricular and extracurricular programs that provide students with multiple learning opportunities by integrating civic engagement education throughout students' entire collegiate careers. To that end, the authors present four options: an interdisciplinary civic engagement minor, a connection of civic engagement courses within a political science major, the integration of civic engagement experiences into study abroad and internship experiences, and a study of the role of extracurricular organizations in fostering civic skills. While not an exhaustive selection of options, these chapters nonetheless present useful ideas for incorporating civic engagement into course and noncourse-based programs at colleges and universities.

Meinke begins with a review of civic engagement minors and certificate programs across several institutions. He then explains the creation of an innovative, interdisciplinary civic engagement minor, highlighting key hurdles in launching and maintaining such an endeavor. These programs often suffer from inconsistent involvement from overburdened faculty, lack of administrative buy-in, inconsistent or insufficient resources, and unavailability of credit space given existing major and graduation requirements. Meinke openly grapples with complex organizational and structural issues and sets forth important questions that anyone interested in pursuing this path should consider.

To succeed in creating an interdisciplinary minor, Meinke argues that the first step in overcoming these hurdles is building investment in the program across campus among faculty, staff, and administrators. In addition, he explains how the program's faculty created an interdisciplinary introductory course to provide students with the tools needed to succeed in the minor. This course also sets the foundation for the minor by teaching students that regardless of their majors, they need to understand and be able to navigate and work within a complex web of democratic rules and structures to effectively deal with the social, economic, and political problems that will confront them in their lives as citizens and civic leaders. While only in its first five years of existence, Meinke offers helpful suggestions for those interested in how such a program can be created and managed.

McHugh and Mayer take a slightly different approach by creating a ladder of civic engagement courses within the political science major. Using multiple methods at all levels of instruction, they present a variety of assignments and structures to determine which are effective at generating civic engagement skills, interest, and knowledge. They argue that integrating a sequence of experiences can better achieve the goals of civic engagement education. This sequence includes courses for majors and nonmajors, which allows students to interact with a group that has a wider variety of interests and concerns. McHugh and Mayer propose a linkage of courses within the major that stops short of a minor or concentration, but could be used as a template for departments whose faculty is committed to promoting civic education and engagement among students. As with all effective programs, this example relies on quality advising by faculty. This chapter could be particularly helpful for smaller departments that seek to promote civic engagement but may not be able to create more formal structures. By sharing these approaches, and building on one another's "experiments" with curriculum-based solutions, political science educators can, together, determine the most effective ways for departments and institutions of different types to move students toward civic engagement and leadership.

In agreement with McHugh and Mayer about how the problem of unconnected experiences leads to a loss of chances to deepen civic learning, McDonald explores the problem of a lack of integrative mechanisms in collegiate education. When faculty are not involved in all of a student's civic engagement experiences, this integration can be difficult for that student to manage alone. He argues that it is of utmost importance that students have opportunities to make sense of their civic engagement experiences, relate them to prior knowledge, and integrate them with course and program objectives to complete Kolb's cycle of learning.[1] After pushing educators to reconsider how students approach the learning process and use civic engagement experiences in their education, McDonald offers specific solutions for how teachers, advisers, and mentors can help students get more educational, developmental, and career value from civic engagement courses and programs. Critical reflection is a central component to his approach, which he explains as enriching and advancing traditional classroom learning.

Extracurricular experiences also can enhance traditional classroom learning. Strachan and Senter demonstrate that campus organizations are an underutilized option to promote civic engagement skills, provide civic engagement experiences, and build students' sense of efficacy. Administrators and faculty often pay scant attention to these organizations' civic engagement efforts, perhaps, as Strachan and Senter note, because they incorrectly assume that existing courses and miscellaneous activities are preparing students for active citizenship. Their research sheds doubt on this supposition and focuses on the importance of experiencing civic engagement in a variety of modes to inculcate active civic engagement as a value for today's youth.

To ignoring extracurricular organizations is to miss part of the youth picture, because students tend to be very social and their peers are of heightened importance as they enter into a formative identity period of life. Lack of inclusion of this area also ignores the historical role of voluntary associations in defining and pursuing broader collective goals, building community trust, and setting values and norms of behavior. To explore this additional piece of the citizenship puzzle, Strachan and Senter provide survey data of registered student organizations and their civic engagement activities. They argue that Greek organizations are particularly important because they socialize thousands of students across the entire country every year at every type of institution; they hold more, regular in-person meetings; their internal organizational structures mimic actual governing bodies; and they are a big source of community involvement. Thus, studying them may yield particularly fruitful information about increasing students' sense of civic efficacy and skill-building—information that can be used to encourage other student organizations and their faculty advisers to take a similar approach to the development of civic leaders. Though they acknowledge hindrances to using Greek organizations as an example and hope to include other types of student organizations in future work,

Strachan and Senter propose that Greek organizations may develop the leadership skills central to active civic engagement. In addition, their widespread presence on many college and university campuses allows for the development of multi-institutional research that can advance the goals of civic engagement education.

In sum, these chapters help uncover and examine assumptions about the place of civic engagement courses, experiences, and activities within a student's academic career. Integrating theoretical and empirical knowledge, interest in politics and the community, civic engagement skills, and actual lived experiences is the key to developing lifelong civically engaged citizens. Political science educators, among those most familiar with the needs of civil society and well-functioning democracies, should be leading efforts to transform all areas of campus life to promote civic engagement. We hope this section will begin a conversation about evidence-based research, teaching, and development of comprehensive civic engagement programs that are central to, rather than add-ons to, the collegiate curriculum and extracurricular experience.

Learning Objectives and Outcomes of an Interdisciplinary Minor in Civic Engagement

21

By Timothy Meinke

In Politics, *Aristotle starts with the assumption that political institutions, such as the state, are communities aimed at the highest good. According to his argument, it is only through engagement with this community that citizens can set forth and discuss notions of justice. If one agrees with these basic understandings of politics, then one goal of any political science program should be to encourage students across a campus to actively engage their communities. However, this goal often can be difficult to meet within a specific major, much less across an entire college campus. Through the use of a case study, this chapter explores the creation of a civic engagement minor program that is focused on community-based research and is open to students from a variety of disciplines.*

For as long as humans have pondered political questions, they have also thought about and discussed issues related to civic engagement. In his *Apology*, Socrates described and defended his intimate engagement with Athens, which he argued had been beneficial for the community at large. In *Politics*, Aristotle argued that it was only through engagement with the *polis* that humans could set forth and discuss notions of justice. Even at the start of academic political science around the end of the 19th century, the "founding fathers," as Stephen Leonard labeled them, were motivated by ideas of improving citizens through civic education.[1] The focus on improving civic engagement through education also has been a continuing theme throughout the history of the American Political Science Association (APSA). Hindy Schachter reported that APSA created four committees to study civic education in its first 36 years (1903–1939) of existence.[2] Most recently, the Task Force on Civic Education for the Next Century was created in 1996 because:

> Democracies, from nations to small communities, cannot survive and thrive without robust engagement in the political controversies (and the well-earned celebrations) that sustain them. Civic engagement in,

> and a personal sense of responsibility for, the health of our inescapably political life are the lifeblood of a liberal democracy.[3]

A similar sense of the matter has led many political scientists to develop and implement civic engagement pedagogies, beginning in the 1990s. An examination of the literature on these efforts, including a study of the papers presented on this subject at APSA's annual Teaching and Learning Conferences, reveals that much of the effort has come at the single-class level, as individual professors develop civic engagement assignments or classes. There has been growing interest in how political scientists can anchor this class-level approach in a larger academic framework, but little work has been done in applying these ideas programmatically. This concern leads to the central questions for this chapter: Can civic engagement principles be applied at the program level? If yes, what would such a civic engagement program look like?

To answer these questions, this chapter starts with a brief review of the literature on civic engagement efforts in political science, focusing on the criticisms of these efforts to highlight what could be improved by a programmatic approach. Next, the chapter presents a summary of some civic engagement programs currently in use at American colleges and universities. The chapter's primary focus is a case study of one of these efforts, the civic engagement minor at Lynchburg College in Lynchburg, Virginia. Detailed time-series data are unavailable given that the program has existed for only five years; a preliminary assessment of the effort, however, is presented and discussed. This assessment finds that the program has been successful in helping students understand the connection between their academic research skills and civic engagement, but it also finds that the program has not been successful in inspiring broad support for civic engagement across the whole campus.

The Study of Civic Engagement

In the statement of purpose for the 1996 APSA Task Force on Civic Education for the Next Century, Lief Carter and Jean Bethke Elshtain noted that "Americans, at this century's end seem indifferent, cynical, and perhaps afraid of politics. The evidence for the rise of political apathy and cynicism is convincing."[4] Political scientists have responded to this evidence in a variety of ways. Like good empiricists, they have studied governments' responses to these trends and found, for example, that "nine states require some study of American government, the Constitution, or civics for students enrolled in public institutions of higher education."[5] Other political scientists, such as Martin Wattenberg, have conducted comparative studies and concluded that the United States should adopt compulsory voting laws to ensure citizen engagement through voting.[6] The variety of responses is so broad that it also includes many scholars who either do not view these trends as worrisome or believe that responses to the problem have been ineffective.[7]

Most interesting for this book are those political scientists who have viewed these trends as problematic and have responded pedagogically. These pedagogical responses are also quite varied, but use of the service-learning method to increase students' limited knowledge about politics and a general sense of civic responsibility has received a great deal of attention, as several chapters in Section II of this volume demonstrate. These chapters are largely based upon the model of political participation developed by Verba, Schlozman, and Brady, who argued that civic participation by adults requires three "participatory factors": motivation, capacity and skills, and networks.[8] They effectively respond to previous findings that some earlier service-learning classes were neither developing the civic skills necessary for continued civic engagement throughout adult life nor requiring students to connect their academic skills to the service project.[9] While civic skills certainly include the ability to express opinions and work collectively, civic engagement education also must incorporate more specialized academic skills, such as discipline-based knowledge, as in the examples in Section II. If political science, biology, or other majors never realize that their specialized knowledge of the political system or stem cells can be used to engage their communities in a productive manner, then they will be less likely to be engaged as adults.

The same could be argued for Verba, Schlozman, and Brady's two other participatory factors. Students are more likely to be motivated to engage as adults if they make strong connections between their academic skills, which presumably they have some interest in using after graduation, and their active engagement in the community. On the development of networks, assume for this discussion that students make some excellent contacts in the field of nonprofit programs for the homeless through a political science service-learning class. It is doubtful that those contacts will develop into lifelong networks of engagement if the students are engineering or environmental science majors taking the class as an elective. Rather, it seems more likely that the networks students develop through the civic engagement experience will continue into adult life if they sense a strong connection between those networks and their professional interests and careers.

Strong contacts in a student's chosen field may not be enough to prompt lifelong civic engagement, however, without some knowledge of politics and the policy process. Therefore, the civic engagement experience should engage students with the community, reveal persistent community problems, require them to use their specialized academic skills in their engagement, help them to build networks of engagement, and teach them something about the political nature of civic engagement. Understandably, it is difficult for a single class to meet all of these goals, especially when the professor has other tasks to accomplish besides fostering civic engagement. Thus, this chapter suggests that it may be more productive to go beyond the single-course paradigm through the development and assessment of entire programs dedicated to civic engagement. After a brief summary of current efforts on the programmatic level, a case study of one such program, the civic engagement minor offered by the Political Science Department at Lynchburg College, a private liberal arts college in south-central Virginia with several professional and graduate programs, is discussed.

Current Civic Engagement Programs

No one seems to know for sure how many American colleges and universities have civic engagement programs, such as majors, minors, certificates, and transcript-recognized programs. For example, Butin found 48 institutions of higher education with majors and minors in community engagement, which includes majors and minors in civic engagement.[10] However, his list does not include some of the programs considered to be at the forefront of this movement, such as the civic engagement minor at the University of California, Los Angeles, or the Shepherd Program in the Interdisciplinary Study of Poverty at Washington and Lee University. It also does not include programs that other studies and reports have cited. For example, it does not include 12 of the 14 programs reported on by the Bonner Foundation in 2008 and listed in Table 21-1. Exactly how many such programs exist may never be known, but it is clear from even this brief analysis that there are more than a few, but not many. It seems as if civic engagement programs are an emerging trend, but it is too early to tell if they are a passing fad or a paradigm shift in pedagogy. The success or failure of current efforts likely will help to determine the answer to that question.

It is also difficult to conduct a simple count of programs because, as a discipline, those in political science have not agreed on exactly what constitutes "civic engagement." Answering the central questions of this chapter requires only some very broad criteria to provide the necessary focus. These civic engagement programs should highlight the political aspects of civic engagement, but also help students recognize the connection between their academic interests and community needs, require them to use and hone their specialized academic skills through their engagement, and help them develop networks that will encourage engagement with their communities long after graduation. All 14 of the civic engagement programs summarized in Table 21-1 meet these criteria. These are certainly not offered as a complete list of all of the civic engagement programs in American higher education today, but rather as solid examples that provide a variety of templates for institutions interested in implementing such a program.

One reason these 14 meet these criteria is because all received intellectual and financial assistance from the Corella and Bertram Bonner Foundation[11] in establishing their programs. In 2002, the Bonner Foundation received a grant from the US Department of Education's Fund for the Improvement of Postsecondary Education (FIPSE)[12] to support a program to help American colleges and universities develop civic engagement minors, certificates, or other academic programs. The institutions awarded assistance from this program were expected to meet certain criteria, but they were also given considerable freedom in designing their programmatic approach to civic engagement. These approaches are summarized in Table 21-1, but it first should be noted that the Bonner Foundation, in its own report on the project, found that these programs shared six characteristics:

> The academic initiatives distinguish themselves because they: provide intensive and long-term learning experiences, integrate academic

Table 21-1: Examples of Civic Engagement Programs

College or University	Type of Program	Requirements	Undergraduate Enrollment	Public/ Private	Liberal Arts?
Concord University	minor	19–31 credits: 4 courses, a full-time internship, and capstone class	1,950	Private	Y
Lynchburg College	minor	21 credits: 7 courses, 1 semester internship, and a community-based research project	2,200	Private	Y
Morehouse College	minor	24 credits: lead-in course, 5 core courses, public policy internship, elective courses, and capstone	3,000	Private	Y
Portland State University	minor	27 credits: lead-in course, 5 elective courses, 6 credits of community-based experience, and integrative seminar	16, 587	Public	N
St. Mary's College of California	minor	21+ credits: 7 courses with specific community-based service and engagement requirements	2,525	Private	Y
University California, Los Angeles	minor	1 lower- and 8 upper-division courses, 10 hours per week of service for 1 academic year and a public policy internship	16,000	Public	N
Colorado College	certificate	8–10 service hours/week over 2 years connected with work done in at least 5 courses	1,950	Private	Y
Mars Hill College	certificate	cocurricular transcript requires sequence of 6 semesters of weekly seminars and service	961	Private	Y
Rutgers University	certificate	19 credits: 6 courses and a 1 semester internship with a social action project for 10–12 hours/week	30,000	Public	N
University of Alaska, Anchorage	certificate	27 credits: includes classes in public policy and poverty or environmental sustainability, ethics, and 10 hours/week of community service	16,000	Public	N
Wagner College	certificate	6 courses, 270 hours of community service, and a portfolio demonstrating the connection between the student's service and academic courses	1,929	Private	Y
College of New Jersey	transcript	an interdisciplinary concentration that includes 9 courses and a 300-hour service requirement	5,910	Public	Y
Washington and Lee University	transcript	7 courses: 3 core requirements and 4 electives, a 300-hour internship with an antipoverty organization, and a capstone research paper	1,755	Private	Y
West Chester University	honors	9 courses, an additional interdisciplinary seminar, and a capstone project	9,400	Public	Y

Source: Civic Engagement at the Center (Hoy and Meisel 2008).

> and experiential learning, sequence increasing levels of challenge and complexity, connect to public policy and political processes, examine poverty, economic inequality, and social stratification, and incorporate global and international perspectives and experiences.[13]

These similarities are important, but Table 21-1 also reveals many different types of institutions experimenting with a variety of approaches. Perhaps most surprising is that civic engagement is not the exclusive domain of small liberal arts institutions. The institutions studied range in undergraduate enrollment from the 961 undergraduates enrolled at Mars Hill College to the 30,000 enrolled at Rutgers University. Six of the institutions are public, whereas eight are private. Though 10 consider themselves liberal arts colleges or universities, four of them, or almost 29%, do not self-classify in this way. These findings suggest that civic engagement programs could be developed in most institutions of higher education regardless of type or size.

As noted, Table 21-1 reveals a wide variety of programmatic approaches used by these institutions. Six have adopted minor programs; five have chosen to have students earn certificates; two provide transcript recognition for students who complete a concentration of courses; and one, West Chester University, used the six principles to shape its Honors program curriculum. While each program requires a student to make a multiyear commitment to the program and to engagement with the community, there is also a wide range in the number of credit hours and amount of service time required.

To fully answer the questions posed at the beginning of the chapter, a case study of one of these examples is the focus of the remaining pages. The minor program at Lynchburg College was chosen primarily for reasons of access. However, Lynchburg College was also a good choice because its enrollment, about 2,200 full-time undergraduate students, is close to that of the average-sized institution in the study. In addition, while it does classify itself as a liberal arts college, with 38 majors and 45 minors, it also has 13 preprofessional programs, which suggests that it could be a model to both liberal arts and more comprehensive institutions of higher education. Finally, the Political Science Department at Lynchburg College is the administrative and conceptual base for the civic engagement minor, which assures that it will have a strong political component and makes the case more interesting to political science educators.

The Civic Engagement Minor at Lynchburg College

This case study is limited by the fact that the Lynchburg College program has been in existence for only five years. As of the 2011–2012 academic year, one junior, two sophomores, and one freshman were enrolled in the civic engagement minor. Three seniors graduated from Lynchburg College with a minor in civic engagement in both the 2009 and 2010 graduating classes. The first graduate to receive the minor did so in 2008. Therefore, this case study is based upon the observations of only 11 students. On the other hand, a study of this size has virtues in that every document, every research project, and every student assignment and internship could be considered in reaching the conclusions. Student observations were collected through interviews with all of the students and each faculty and staff member involved in the program. The program was also observed through a careful reading of all related documents, especially the research projects and reflective essays each student was required to write for the capstone reflection class required of all minors.

The idea for a civic engagement minor at Lynchburg College (LC) began in January 2005 with a trip to the Bonner Foundation in Princeton, New Jersey, for a conference on best practices for creating certificate or minor programs in civic engagement. Subsequently, in July 2005, LC was awarded a FIPSE subgrant by the Bonner Foundation to develop a civic engagement minor. In little less than one year, the minor was drafted by a small steering committee that included one faculty member each from the Political Science, Nursing, and History Departments,[14] as well as the associate director for College and Community Partnerships at the Center for Community Development and Social Justice (CCDSJ). During the course of the year, the committee periodically sought feedback from students, administrators, staff, and interested faculty. Based upon those comments, it was decided that the Political Science Department in the School of Humanities and Social Sciences would become the home for the minor and be responsible for its evaluation. The Political Science Department was chosen for two primary reasons: first, the committee's belief that an understanding of politics is crucial for citizens to engage their communities in meaningful ways, and, second, the department was already promoting a number of cocurricular activities, such as student issue forums and experiential learning trips to Washington, DC, that could support and enhance the civic engagement minor. In addition, the members of the steering committee for the minor were retained as advisers and given the task of approving internships and research proposals submitted for the capstone research project. It was also hoped that the steering committee would help preserve the interdisciplinary spirit of the minor and ensure that the program had attachments across the campus rather than to only one department.

To encourage civic engagement beyond the college years by raising students' awareness of the connection between their academic skills and community needs, the committee also decided that the capstone project would require what some have labeled community-based research.[15] Community-based research uses the same methodologies as conventional research, but it is distinguished by five major characteristics. First, these research projects are generated by needs articulated by community partners who are actively engaged throughout the research process. Second, the research is conducted with and for, not on, members of a community. Third, the goal of this research is not just to produce gains in knowledge, but also to achieve positive social change and social justice. Fourth, the research promotes active engagement by students in their communities through the use of multiple skills learned in college such as research, communication, logic and argumentation, critical thinking, and discipline-specific skills. Finally, these projects are designed to promote long-term relationships between the academic institution and community partners.[16]

In April 2006 the LC faculty approved the civic engagement minor for inclusion in the 2006–2007 undergraduate catalogue. In an informational flyer sent to students at the beginning of the fall 2006 semester, the minor was described as follows:

> The new minor in civic engagement will help students to recognize and act on connections between their academic talents and specific needs in their communities. The final goal for the senior year is for students to engage a community partner in what is known as a community-based research project. . . . Along the way, students will take courses from a variety of disciplines on campus that will help them strengthen their research skills, build relationships with community partners, and challenge them to think more about important concepts such as community, justice, and citizenship. The minor has been designed to be open to students in all majors on campus.

Table 21-2: Requirements for the Civic Engagement Minor at Lynchburg College

This minor requires:	Credit Hours
Section 1 GS 220 Exploring Social Entrepreneurship and Leadership SOCI 209 Applied Sociology *OR* NRSG 310 (for nursing majors only) GS 307 Introduction to Civic Participation and Community-Based Research	 1 3 1
Section 2 Choose one course from: POLI 111 Quest for Justice I PHIL 204 Intro to Ethics	3
Section 3 Choose one course from: POLI 220 American Experience POLI 258 Local and State Government POLI 290 American Public Policy	3
Section 4 GS 415 Social Entrepreneurship Internship or any internship approved by the minor steering committee	3
Section 5 GS 311 Capstone CBR project or the student's major capstone course with thesis project approved by the minor steering committee GS 430 Putting Civic Engagement in Perspective	 3 1
Total Hours Required	18

Source: Lynchburg College Civic Engagement Minor Steering Committee.

Table 21-2 lists the 18 credit hours of classes required for completion of the minor. The first section in the table lists the three community-based research courses that each student was required to complete. The first course in the sequence, Exploring Social Entrepreneurship, is taught yearly by the associate director for College and Community Partnerships at the CCDSJ. The goal of the course is to introduce students to the personal and professional skills necessary for creating an organization that can effectively engage the community. It is similar to business entrepreneurship, except that its focus is on social change instead of economic activity. Topics include philanthropy, leadership, nonprofit fund-raising, and corporate social responsibility. Social entrepreneurs from the local community are invited to speak to the class several times during the semester. The second course, Applied Sociology, introduces students to a variety of research methods used in the study of social questions. The goal is to provide students with possible tools for their required capstone research projects during the senior year. This sociological research class was chosen because students are required to use a variety of research methods in a community-based research project assigned by the faculty at the beginning of the semester.[17] Lastly, Introduction to Civic Participation and Community-Based Research (CBR) introduces students to the principles of community-based research and requires them to design a CBR project that could be implemented as their capstone project.

The second and third sections of Table 21-2 list the courses designed to introduce students to the political dimensions of civic engagement. Both the Quest for Justice class offered by the Political Science Department and the Introduction to Ethics course taught by the Philosophy Department are designed to challenge students with some of the perennial questions underlying civic engagement, including "What is justice?" "What are the duties and responsibilities of citizens?" "What is the role of government?" and "What is ethical behavior when engaging the community?" Students also are required to take one of three American government offerings from the Political Science Department, listed in Section 3, which are designed to introduce them to the basic structures and policy-making processes of the governmental systems they will be engaging.

The fourth section is the requirement that all students complete a social entrepreneurship internship or the equivalent in their majors. The social entrepreneurship internship requires students to work with a nonprofit or governmental partner engaged with the community on an issue of interest to a student. Through this activity students are exposed to the needs of their community in a professional setting that gives them an opportunity to create networks that may be useful in assisting or promoting future engagement. The steering committee retained this flexibility to allow major-based internships in the hopes that these would encourage students to develop meaningful networks in their chosen field on issues they were motivated to address.

Finally, students are required to pursue and complete a community-based research project before they graduate. The goal is for students to experience collaborative, equitable partnerships with faculty and community members as they work together on research studies identified as needed by local community partners.

While students complete their community-based research projects they are also required to enroll in the Putting Civic Engagement into Perspective course, which provides an opportunity for students from different majors to come together and discuss their community-based research from a variety of perspectives. They reflect upon the coursework they have completed for the minor and how it has transformed their perspectives of their majors, democratic citizenship, and their own efficacy in engaging their communities.

A Case Study of the Lynchburg College Minor: What Were the Program's Goals?

This analysis of the civic engagement minor at Lynchburg College revealed that the program has five notable goals. First, the minor attempts to encourage civic engagement habits that will last beyond a student's time in college by seeking to develop the three participatory factors identified by Verba, Schlozman, and Brady.[18] They argued that adult civic engagement means that citizens have the desire to engage their communities, the ability to contribute something to their communities, and some connection to a network of like-minded engagers who encourage others to engage the community as well. This minor is built upon a belief that the best way to develop these participatory factors is to merge students' academic skills with actual community needs, so that student-citizens who see these connections will be more likely to engage civically throughout their adult lives. While the design of the minor was clearly based upon this model, the steering committee for the minor also added that it wanted students to develop a sense of the centrality of politics in civic engagement. So, the first goal was to encourage lifelong engagement by developing students' civic skills—desire, ability, networks, and a sense of the political—necessary for the engagement.

The second, related goal of the minor is to help students develop research skills, especially in the methods of community-based research previously described. Community-based research scholars criticize contemporary higher education's "inequitable and unresponsive relationship with the community."[19] To correct these problems, they suggest the community-based model of research. As previously discussed, this research begins with a relationship, an engagement, between a student and a community partner. In the Lynchburg College model, these relationships are facilitated through the CCDSJ. Through this relationship, the student and community partner come to an agreement on a research project that applies the student's skills to an identified community need. In discussions with other faculty and staff not on the committee, it was interesting to observe the number of ideas generated around a variety of majors. For example, colleagues in the Theater Department were excited by possibilities of having students use their theatrical skills to put on performances that called attention to a problem in their communities.

The hope of developing this kind of campuswide involvement is the third notable goal of the minor. While the Political Science Department is the programmatic home to the minor for the reasons already discussed, it was always a consideration of the steering committee to make the minor as accessible as possible to all disciplines on campus. As discussed in endnote 16, this concern led the committee to offer Nursing Research Methods as a possible substitute for the required Applied Sociology course in the hopes of attracting more nursing students. The consideration also led the committee to shape the catalogue structure in such a way that students could use their senior thesis projects, which many majors require, as the capstone project required by the minor (see Section 5 of Table 21-2). However, the committee realized that some students may be seeking additional skills beyond their majors that can be applied to their community situations. This concern led to the requirement that every student in the minor, except nurses, complete the Applied Sociology course, which provides a broad survey of methods and data collection techniques used in the study of sociological problems. The goal is to help students further develop the second participatory factor—the capacity, as Kirlin described it, "to contribute something to the effort."[20]

The desire for broad participation across the campus required building support for the minor from outside the academic programs. The committee at Lynchburg College was certainly aided by the award of the Bonner subgrant, but perhaps even more important was the contribution of the college's own CCDSJ. In 1999, the US Department of Housing and Urban Development and the Jesse Ball DuPont Fund awarded the CCDSJ grants to establish the Community Outreach Partnership Center (COPC), whose objectives have been carried out through research, consultation, outreach action projects, workshops, lectures, coursework, and a network of partnerships. Neighborhood revitalization and development projects are community driven to ensure their usefulness in and empowerment of neighborhoods and community-based organizations. This community-centered approach is consistent with the principles of community-based research. The goal is to use the center's activities over the last eight years to provide students with the community contacts they need to begin their research projects and build the networks that will remind them postgraduation of the importance of civic engagement to their lives and the well-being of their communities.

The final goal of the committee members was to be as practical and efficient as possible in the creation of this new academic program. They understood that while their primary goal was to go beyond the single-class paradigm, the necessary support or resources for a full civic engagement major did not exist. This limitation led to the practical compromise to create a minor instead of a major or certificate program. As already stated, the committee tried to build as much flexibility as possible into the overall requirements for the minor so as to attract students from the entire campus. The committee also tried to act efficiently by refraining from creating many new courses, but rather attempted to utilize courses already being taught at Lynchburg College. Only GS 307: Introduction to Civic Participation and Community-Based Research (CBR) and GS 430: Putting Civic Engagement into Perspective, which are both only one-credit courses, were new additions created by the committee and adopted by the faculty.[21] The rest of the requirements utilized preexisting classes.

A Case Study of the Lynchburg College Minor: Have These Goals Been Achieved?

The lack of data points makes sophisticated analysis impossible; however, one can make some initial observations based upon the results for each of the five goals described over the five years of the minor's existence to date. First, on the primary objective of promoting a lifetime of civic engagement by helping students develop the motivation, capacity, networks, and sense of politics needed for such engagement, the results are mixed. Every graduate of the minor reported continued engagement, and most had made career choices that make them professional engagers. However, there is reason to believe that the relationship between completing the minor and continuing engagement with the community is spurious because none of the students in the minor reported an increase in their desire to be civically engaged. This issue does not appear to be one of the flaws of the program because it is attributable to the high desire for civic engagement these students reported and demonstrated upon entering the program. It is doubtful that the minor is the cause for these graduates' continued engagement because they were predisposed to this behavior before entering the minor; in fact, it is a likely reason for their decision to take on the minor's requirements. If anything, the minor seems to give students, in the words of a special education major, "a greater appreciation for the 'engaged citizen'."[22] Students also reported increased awareness of specific problems, such as one international relations major who reported,

> Through my studies as a civic engagement minor I have noticed that there is a problem with drug rehabilitation programs in the Lynchburg, VA area.... Currently, a lack of treatment facilities and community jail diversion programs for drug users has trapped many individuals in a cycle of untreated drug abuse and criminal charges.

However, the minor has demonstrated no success at developing networks that continue to prod civic engagement after graduation, as only one of the graduates mentioned continued contact with the community contacts she made through her internship and CBR project. This result is perhaps not surprising given that none of the graduates have remained in Lynchburg, Virginia.

Most of the success with the first goal to date has come with developing the students' academic skills, helping them realize the usefulness of those skills in engaging the community, and increasing their awareness of the role of politics in civic engagement. Every student in the sample reported a sense of increased capacity for civic engagement and a greater appreciation for the connection between their academic skills and civic engagement. For example, a sociology student moved by the "alarming growth of the MS-13 gang, also known as 'Latin Kings,' in affluent northern Virginia neighborhoods," wrote a thesis in sociology that he also used as his civic engagement capstone project. In it, he argued "that postmodern and social bond theory, which provide more of a cultural and social process prospective" were the key to understanding this increase in youth crime. Every student also demonstrated an increased comfort level with research methods, especially community-based research. One student wrote, "I never really realized the importance of a good research question until I did this project." Another wrote simply, "I didn't know what community-based research was until I took [GS 307]." Finally, every student reported an increased awareness that, as a sociology major suggested, "To be civically engaged one must care about the politics of an issue." The very first graduate of the civic engagement minor wrote in her reflective essay that the minor had helped her to realize, "In order to make an impact on the civic life of any community, one must be familiar with its political processes and systems."

The minor has demonstrated more success in meeting the second goal. As stated, students reported increased levels of comfort with basic research methods and, specifically, community-based research, but the strongest evidence for this goal being met has come from the quality of many of their research projects. It appears that students, faculty, and staff all have become more comfortable in designing and implementing CBR projects. One quality project submitted by a political science major involved applying her social science research skills in a demographic study of the usage of a local food pantry and day shelter. Another project by an international relations major entailed a report for a local organic food organization on the supply of organic foods in the Lynchburg area based on a survey of local grocers. The three students enrolled in the capstone course for the 2011–2012 academic year developed strong ideas for their projects. For example, two of the students, both special education majors, worked with a local animal shelter and developed a report on best practices from throughout the country that may help the shelter deal with the city's large feral cat population. Perhaps most important for this study is the fact that the last six students who completed the minor or finished the capstone at the end of the 2011–2012 academic year chose to write a CBR report separate from the thesis required for each of their majors. This choice clearly demonstrates the students' motivation for civic engagement because it means one additional large research project for each of them before graduation. However, it also hints at the problems with the third goal revealed in the following discussion: a growing disconnect between the minor and other academic programs on campus.

The results for the third notable goal, which was to promote civic engagement across the campus, also have been mixed. On the one hand, the students completing the minor or due to complete their CBR project at the end of the 2011–2012 academic year came from a variety of disciplines: three from political science; two each from sociology, international relations, and special education; and one from biomedical science. For 10 students, this list seems to represent significant diversity in academic background, but upon further review it is notable that three of those majors—political science, international relations, and sociology—are from the School of Humanities and Social Sciences, which means that the minor has not attracted many students from either the natural sciences or the preprofessional programs, such as nursing.

After an initial period of support, the minor also has failed to sustain wide faculty or administrative involvement. There was initial support in the form of positive faculty votes and feedback, which included examples of community-based research projects that faculty had guided students through or hypothetical projects that could involve their majors. As mentioned, during one faculty meeting on the program, members of the Theater Department were excited by possibilities of having students use their theatrical skills to stage performances that called attention to a community problems. This enthusiasm peaked when the 2008–2009 academic year was named The Year of the Citizen at Lynchburg College, which meant that a variety of activities, classes, and guest speakers were arranged to promote a campuswide dialogue on the responsibilities of citizenship.

However, that initial enthusiasm has not evolved into sustained, involved support. This outcome is perhaps not surprising, given some simple facts that are true on most, if not all, campuses. Faculty have a variety of other important responsibilities, which makes it difficult for even a supportive faculty member to become a sustainably involved faculty member. Students at Lynchburg College have a large general education requirement, 51 hours out of the 124 needed for graduation, which, when combined with a major with large credit requirements such as nursing's 69, makes it difficult for even interested students to become civic engagement minors. Finally, it is rational for an administration to be reluctant to support a program that to date has demonstrated the ability to attract only three graduates a year out of a class of about 550 students, or around .5% of the yearly graduates from Lynchburg College.

One possible remedy currently being considered by the Steering Committee is to increase the number of courses that count for both a specific major and the civic engagement minor. The idea is that faculty would submit course syllabi with a civic engagement focus for consideration by the committee. Those deemed appropriate would then be added to the list of possible courses for the fulfillment of the minor. It also would be helpful if a funding source could be developed for faculty grants for submitting a civic engagement course design and providing further assistance if the course is added to the minor's requirements.

On the fourth goal, the desire to build support for the minor from outside the academic programs, there is strong evidence of success. The contribution of the college's Center for Community Development and Social Justice and its Community Outreach Partnership Center has been significant. The center's director teaches two of the required courses for the minor every year, and the contacts that the COPC has made with the community have been invaluable in helping the students find internships and community partners for their CBR projects. Most important for the minor is that the staff of the center, with the support of the Bonner Foundation, established a Bonner Leaders program at Lynchburg College two years before the creation of the minor. The program uses federal work-study funds and AmeriCorps Education Awards to create stipends for students who agree to complete 300 hours of service over a two-year period. This funding has been a significant development for the minor: six of the 11 students in this study were Bonner Leaders at Lynchburg College.

Normally, the type of academic program represented by the Bonner Leaders program exemplifies what Caryn McTighe Musil, in her analysis of civic education in American institutes of higher education, called the "helter-skelter approach to civic engagement" programs. Musil found, "A portion of community engagement is handled largely out of sight through formal institutional representatives. . . . All too often, civic engagement is not rooted in the very heart of the academy: its courses, its research, its faculty work."[23] There is not enough data for any firm conclusions, but it is possible the civic engagement minor is helping Lynchburg College overcome this "helter-skelter approach" to civic education by providing a strong connection between research and service for at least these few Bonner Leaders who also complete the minor.

At first glance, there is also strong evidence that the fifth goal was met by the steering committee for the minor. As has already been stated, the committee adopted a number of practical compromises, such as creating a minor instead of a major and only creating two new one-credit classes, which allowed the minor to win passage in only one year. However, that quick success seems to have built a foundation for future failure in that it required very little faculty or administration buy-in. So, again, faculty could be supportive and yet not involved, which may be a reason for the failures on goal three. It also appears obvious in hindsight that it was a mistake to only involve four people on the committee that created the minor. That structure was efficient for completing the task in a short period of time; however, it is now evident that it was unsuccessful in building an interest and investment in the minor across the campus that could be sustained over years. Finally, the success in building flexibility into the overall requirements for the minor has not resulted in many students graduating with the minor on their degree. As stated, only .5% of all Lynchburg College graduates are civic engagement minors. It may be that the lure of flexibility is offset by the required additional responsibility of completing a CBR project before graduation.

Conclusions

To return to the initial questions, it seems clear that civic engagement principles can be and have been applied in a variety of programs at a variety of institutions. To answer the second question with some depth, one such program was explored in detail. The civic engagement minor at Lynchburg College seeks to move beyond the one-course paradigm by creating a coherent, cohesive minor program that makes use of the many different resources the college has accumulated over the years. The ultimate goal for this minor is to prod and inspire, but also to equip students with the desires, skills, networks, and sense of politics they will require if they want to engage their communities in meaningful and productive ways in the future.

This five-year study of the minor revealed some success in meeting this goal, especially in developing community-based research skills and a greater awareness of politics, but it also highlighted some noticeable failures. The minor does not diminish students' desire to engage, but there are some good reasons to doubt if it is reaching all of its goals. Overall, it is clear that further study is required. Political science needs a comprehensive, comparative study of the different civic engagement programs being used across the country. Which are most successful, and what characteristics do they share? Even on assessments of single programs such as this one, political scientists need more data points, as well as better panel studies that contrast the experiences of students who complete the program's requirements compared with a control group of graduates who were not minors. Finally, to assess the community-based aspect of CBR, political science needs better data on the experiences of community partners. It would be especially helpful to know how useful the projects are and what long-term differences this engagement makes in the community.

There are also two possibly counterintuitive lessons for those who wish to undertake a similar endeavor at their institution of higher education. First, do not be in a rush to get the program added to the curriculum. It is worth the extra time necessary to build large faculty coalitions that are not only supportive but also invested in the program. Second, do not make practicality and efficiency top priorities. At least half of the requirements should be minor-specific classes because this structure will require commitment that someone be available to cover those offerings from both faculty and the administration. A final lesson that is obvious but that is often forgotten is that civic engagement is difficult academically, mentally, physically, and emotionally. It requires a real commitment of self and time. It will be, just as it always has been, a challenge to attract more student-citizens to such a task, but the reward, if successful, is a more complete polity.

The Different Types of Experiential Learning Offered in a Political Science Department: A Comparison of Four Courses

22

By Mary McHugh and Russell Mayer

Experiential learning is a well-established pedagogy in the teaching of political science. Part of its appeal lies in its potential to increase civic engagement in a generation of students who can be difficult to reach in general and have a distaste for politics in particular. This study examines how different types of experiential learning opportunities can be used to promote civic engagement pedagogical goals across a range of courses. Its multigoal, multimethod approach considers a variety of factors that affect the efficacy of different forms and applications of experiential learning for civic engagement. These effects are explored in the context of a single political science department's offering of a variety of experiential learning opportunities to majors and nonmajors at the introductory and advanced undergraduate levels.

Experiential learning is a well-established pedagogy in the teaching of political science.[1] Part of its appeal lies in its potential to increase civic engagement in a generation of students who can be difficult to reach in general and have a distaste for politics in particular. According to studies from the Center for Information and Research on Civic Learning and Engagement (CIRCLE)[2] and the Pew Research Center for the People and the Press,[3] despite the fact that there have been some modest gains in youth interest and participation in politics since the 2008 election cycle, political engagement among young people remains low relative to other age groups.

Students of this generation have come to expect an education that offers more than texts and lectures, and providing experiential learning opportunities to them both meets this demand and has well-known positive impacts on learning. Service-learning, so far the most studied component of the experiential learning umbrella, has been found to enhance students' civic engagement, academic engagement, interpersonal engagement, and their likelihood of degree completion.[4] A 2000 study by the Higher Education Research Institute shows that

> service participation shows significant positive effects on 11 outcome measures: academic performance (grade point average, writing skills, critical thinking skills), values (commitment to activism and promoting racial understanding), self-efficacy, leadership (leadership activities, self-rated leadership ability, interpersonal skills), choice of a service career, and plans to participate in service after college.[5]

Furthermore, this pedagogy, which requires active engagement by students, is a natural fit with the civic engagement agenda increasingly embraced by the discipline of political science,[6] institutions of higher learning, and society as a whole.[7]

Yet much of what is done when it comes to experiential learning is done in isolation and tends to focus on a single learning outcome (usually, increasing civic engagement) with a single type of activity (most frequently, some type of service-oriented, out-of-classroom experience).[8] This "standard" model has considerable value and is a relatively easily implemented first step that many in political science have taken. As Bringle and Hatcher state,

> Faculty who use service learning discover that it brings new life to the classroom, enhances performance on traditional measures of learning, increases student interest in the subject, teaches new problem solving skills, and makes teaching more enjoyable.[9]

However, the consideration of such factors as course content and structure, the type of experiential learning opportunity offered, the course level and type of student enrolled, incentives for participation, and how out-of-classroom experience and course content are linked opens the potential for demonstrating a much more significant and systematic positive effect of this exciting and important pedagogy. The multigoal, multimethod approach used in this study, therefore, considers a variety of factors that affect the efficacy of different forms and applications of experiential learning for increasing some necessary conditions for effective civic engagement, such as interest in politics, voter registration, actual voting, and work on political campaigns. These effects are explored in the context of a single political science department's offering of a variety of experiential learning opportunities to majors and nonmajors at the introductory and advanced undergraduate levels.

As part of a collegewide curricular revision that changed the standard undergraduate course from three to four credits, faculty at Merrimack College,[10] a small Catholic college located in the Northeast, were called upon to revise their courses in the fall of 2008 in ways that brought more depth to students' learning experiences. In response to this curricular change, a majority of those in the Political Science Department decided to add or enhance experiential learning as a component in their courses. This opportunity presented an opportunity to examine how different types of experiential learning opportunities could be used to promote different pedagogical goals, especially increased civic engagement, across a range of courses.

The student service-learning experience and its effects on a range of learning outcomes in four political science courses offered under the new, more in-depth curriculum were examined. As we, the researchers, were in the position of studying a naturally occurring event in quasi-experimental fashion, we made use of a range of quantitative and qualitative assessment measures already employed by the individual course instructors.[11] The lack of a common metric made comparison of effects across courses impossible; taken together, however, the effects of service-learning that were observed represent a range of interesting possibilities for the enhancement and expansion of experiential learning as part of civic engagement education.

Four Courses and Four Expectations

By way of context, a wide variety of experiential learning opportunities are available to students at the college at which this study was conducted. Undergraduates in the Schools of Liberal Arts, Science and Engineering, Education and Business, as well as students in the School of Advanced Studies, are typically presented with multiple experiential learning opportunities throughout their educational programs. About 450 of the college's 2,000 undergraduates engage in service-learning each year through the college's Service Learning Center, and numerous others participate in other forms of experiential learning, including internships, directed research, community service, study abroad, or cooperative education.

Four different experiential learning programs offered to undergraduates taking coursework in the Department of Political Science (within the School of Liberal Arts) were the focus of this study. Examining a range of experiential learning options with a single academic department had the advantage of controlling to some degree for the background and disposition of study subjects and the context in which effects were observed. The Political Science Department at Merrimack has long-established and well-known ties to the school's Service Learning Center, as well as a very popular internship program. The department has been among the college's early and enthusiastic adopters of the pedagogy of experiential learning. Furthermore, while not a specific major requirement, the department's focus on civic engagement dovetails nicely with the active, experiential, and community-based programs examined in this study.

For these reasons, most students in the department's courses view experiential learning opportunities as expected, or at least not unusual, components of their coursework. By and large, they are familiar with service-learning, its mechanics, the way it is supposed to fit into the curriculum, and even the educational philosophy that motivates it. Because of the relatively high and uniform comfort level with service-learning that students in this department (and the student body in general) have, two of the classical methodological concerns with the quasi-experimental design of this study were mitigated. First, testing effects were unlikely to occur, as these students were familiar with the pre- and posttest methodology used in places in this study to collect information. They were familiar with being probed and questioned about various experiential aspects of their academic lives. Second, there was little concern about the artificiality of the stimulus, the context, or some combination of these. If student attitudes and behaviors were affected by the experiential learning opportunities presented to them, it was likely to be a reaction to the particulars

Table 22-1: Experiential Learning Program Descriptions

Course	Course Content and Structure	Experiential Learning Opportunity
Current Issues in Politics and Government	A case-based course designed to expose nonmajors to current issues and theories in politics. Explicitly links a range of experiential learning options to a system of civic engagement points.	A range of civic engagement opportunities (e.g., service-learning experience, registering to vote, attending a lecture). Students were required to earn a certain number of civic engagement points and could earn extra credit with additional activities. Each activity required a short written reflection linking experiences to course materials.
Politics of the US	An introduction to the field designed for new majors. Service-learning was offered as an extra credit option.	An opportunity to earn extra credit by volunteering with a community organization, working in the public sector, and writing an end of semester short reflective paper.
Criminal Law	An upper-level elective for majors. Service-learning was assigned.	A required course component in which students volunteered with a community organization working in the criminal legal field and wrote a paper based on their experiences.
Directed Research[a]	A paid research experience for selected, academically talented majors who have completed the required methodology course. Students worked on a faculty-directed research project on youth homelessness.	A paid opportunity to work on all aspects of a research project (e.g., problem definition, design, data collection, analysis) under the supervision of a faculty member.

Note: [a]Not strictly a course, as students did not receive course credit for their participation in this directed research.

of the program in which they engaged rather than a more general response to the overall notion of doing experiential learning. Because the population of subjects was fairly familiar with experiential learning in general, observed effects were less likely to be attributable to the sheer novelty of the experiences. Indeed, this study presents a fairly conservative picture of the effects of these particular experiences on civic knowledge, skills, and attitudes, perhaps due to this institutional context.

The experiential programs examined in this study varied significantly in the student populations they target, the courses (both in terms of content and structure) to which they were linked, and the nature of the experiential learning opportunity to which student subjects were exposed. Consequently, the expected outcomes from each program were quite different. Table 22-1 describes each of the courses examined; Table 22-2 identifies the key differences in course levels and relations to the political science major, its incentives or requirements, and its components. The expected effects on student learning outcomes follow.

Because each experiential learning program offered in the department was different with respect to course level, students, course subject, incentive for participation, type of experience offered, and the way it was linked to course material, there were unique expectations for each in terms of which student attitudes were most likely to be affected by exposure to the experiential learning opportunity.

Table 22-2: Experiential Learning Program Components

Course	Course Level	Students	Course Subject	Incentive for Participation	Experience	How Linked to Course Material	Is Experience Linked to Course Content
Current Issues in Politics and Government	Introductory	Non-majors	US – General	Required and Extra Credit	Varies	Short Reflective Papers & Essays	Highly
Politics of the US	Introductory	Majors and Non-majors	US – General	Extra Credit	Service	Short End of Semester Reflective Paper	Somewhat
Criminal Law	Upper Level	Majors	Law	Required	Service	Required Course Paper	Highly
Directed Research[a]	Upper Level	Selected Majors	Policy	Paid	Research	None	Indirectly

Note: [a]Not strictly a course, as students did not receive course credit for their participation in this directed research.

Expected Outcome for Current Issues in Politics and Government Course: Substantial effects on sense of civic engagement, political efficacy, and civic duty. Of the four courses, this one linked the experiential components most clearly in the course syllabus and the course content. The experiences offered to students were all explicitly designed and presented as opportunities to enhance their civic engagement, a major course theme. In addition, because these nonmajors (see Table 22-3) were likely to start the course with relatively lower levels of engagement and efficacy, the potential for positive change created by these experiences was expected to be larger.

Expected Outcome for Politics of the US Course: Moderate effects on sense of civic engagement, political efficacy, and civic duty. Compared to the Current Issues course, the links between the experiential opportunities and major course themes were more tenuous. On average, the students in this course also started with a higher baseline level of interest and engagement in politics, and thus increases were expected to be less dramatic.

Expected Outcome for Criminal Law Course: Substantial effects on career and personal development. Because students selecting into this course were likely to have a strong, potentially preprofessional, interest in this field, the experiential learning component was likely to affect them more personally and developmentally. The service nature of this experience also was likely to translate into the area of personal development. Finally, because the experiential activities were required and formed the basis for a major course paper, effects were expected to be strong.

Table 22-3: Student Characteristics for POL 1000[a]

CLASS	%	MAJOR	%
FR	70%	Biology	4%
SO	17%	Business Administration	56%
JR	5%	Civil Engineering	1%
SR	8%	Communication Studies	5%
		Computer Science	1%
		Criminology	1%
		English	4%
		Fine Arts	4%
		Health Science	1%
		History	1%
		Mathematics	1%
		Philosophy	1%
		Political Science	4%
		Sociology	1%
		Sports Medicine	1%
		Undeclared Liberal Arts	12%

Note: [a] Some totals do not equal 100% due to rounding.

Expected Outcome for Directed Research Course: Moderate effects on orientation toward policy area and methodological/research skills. Explicit links to course material were weaker than in any of the other programs. Student exposure to a novel policy area (youth homelessness) and experience applying methodological/research skills to real-world problems were expected to affect student attitudes in these areas.

The diversity of courses, experiences, goals, and expectations was mirrored by the diversity of means of assessing outcomes that were applied to these four programs. For the Current Issues course, pre- and posttest surveys were administered in part to gauge student levels of the civic engagement both before and after their experiential activities. For the introductory Politics of the US course, students' reflective essays were examined and the instructor was interviewed to identify any gains in student understanding of course material attributable to the service-learning component of the course. For the Criminal Law class, an end-of-semester quantitative evaluation was administered to gauge student reactions to the out-of-class, experiential component of the course. For the directed research, the effects on students were gauged based on an open-ended, midproject, self-reflection completed by all students working on the project.[12]

Results

Results of the Current Issues and Politics Course (POL 1000). To determine how successful the class was in enhancing civic engagement, the instructor administered an anonymous pre- and posttest to the class of 77 students. The test asked the students about their voting habits, their interest in politics, their knowledge of politics, and their definitions of civic engagement and politics. Throughout the semester, the students were given random current-events quizzes and led discussions on newspaper articles of their choosing. Students also were required to participate in civic engagement activities. A point system rewarded students for their activities (e.g., a student gained 10 points for attending a lecture or donating blood). Students needed to reach a total of 60 points to receive an A for that part of their overall semester grade. Students also were allowed an opportunity to receive extra credit for participating in the service-learning program and writing a short reflective paper.

This class was created for nonpolitical science majors to fulfill one of the college's social science requirements. It was expected that most of the students would be freshmen. The class was taught for the first time in the fall 2008 semester, providing the opportunity to study this course from its beginning. As expected, more than 70% of the class were freshmen, and more than 50% were business majors, with very few social science majors.

In the pretest done on the first day of class, the students were asked demographic questions and questions about their voting habits, their experiential learning history, and their interest in and knowledge of politics (see Table 22-4).

Table 22-4: Prior Experiential Learning Activities of POL 1000 Students

Service-Learning	%	Directed Research	%
Y	8%	Y	3%
N	92%	N	97%
Study Abroad	**%**	**Internships**	**%**
Y	2%	Y	17%
N	98%	N	83%
Cooperative Education	**%**	**Student Campus Org**	**%**
Y	5%	Y	60%
N	95%	N	40%
Campus Ministry	**%**	**Leadership**	**%**
Y	16%	Y	32%
N	84%	N	68%

Table 22-5: Voting Habits of POL 1000 Students[a]

First Day of Class August 2008		*Last Day of Class December 2008*	
Old Enough to Vote	%	**Old Enough to Vote**	%
Yes	97%	Yes	100%
No	3%	No	0%
Registered to Vote	%	**Registered to Vote**	%
Yes	58%	Yes	81%
No	39%	No	19%
Not Yet	3%		
Registered with a Party	%	**Registered with a Party**	%
Yes	25%	Yes	32%
No	74%	No	68%
Not Yet	2%		
Worked on a Political Campaign	%	**Worked on a Political Campaign**	%
Yes	5%	Yes	3%
No	95%	No	97%
Have You Voted?	%	**Did You Vote in November?**	%
Yes	13%	Yes	69%
No	87%	No	31%

Note: [a]Some totals do not equal 100% due to rounding.

Students in the class did not have much background in experiential activities. As first-semester freshmen, those who had participated in these activities did so during their high school years. For most students, however, this class was potentially their first exposure to many of these types of experiential learning opportunities.

Looking at their voting history and habits, it is evident that most of the students had not been active in the electoral process thus far in their lives. As seen in Table 22-5, at the beginning of the semester, almost all of the students were old enough to vote, but 39% still had not registered. Since most were between the ages of 18 and 21, it was the first presidential election cycle in which they were old enough to vote. Those who were registered did not work on campaigns, join political parties, or even vote.

By the end of the semester, with the excitement created by the 2008 presidential campaign, it is not surprising (but still rewarding) to see that the number of students who registered to vote and who voted increased significantly. The number

Table 22-6: Change in Civic Engagement for POL 1000 Students[a]

First Day of Class, August 2008		*Last Day of Class, December 2008*	
Level of Interest in Politics	**%**	**Level of Interest in Politics**	**%**
Very High	4%	Very High	9%
High	11%	High	43%
Moderate	65%	Moderate	34%
Low	13%	Low	6%
Very Low/	5%	Very Low	7%
Not sure	2%	Not sure	0%
Liberal/ Conservative/ Moderate	**%**	**Liberal/ Conservative/ Moderate**	**%**
Liberal	24%	Liberal	43%
Moderate	32%	Moderate	29%
Moderate/Conservative	2%	Moderate/Conservative	1%
Conservative	28%	Conservative	19%
None	2%	None	1%
Don't know	12%	Don't know	6%

Note: [a] Some totals do not equal 100% due to rounding.

registered to a party or who worked on a campaign stayed the same. However, in looking at levels of civic engagement in Table 22-6, what is more interesting and significant is the positive change found in their levels of interest in politics and significant changes in their political ideologies.

Taken together, the students seemed to be more engaged in the political process and more interested. They also seemed to become more liberal as the course progressed. One reason might be the typical response that political scientists "make" their students more liberal. However, the effect of the Obama campaign and its appeal to a distinctly Democratic, liberal, prochoice, pro–gay marriage, pro–government health insurance youth vote cannot be discounted.[13]

In analyzing these results, one needs to consider which components of the class affected students becoming more engaged and interested in politics. The civic engagement points system[14] was instituted to force students to seek out experiential opportunities to accumulate points that would benefit their grade. Students were creative in suggesting activities, and, in some cases, negotiated with the instructor about which activities qualified. This exercise allowed the students to discuss these activities in a serious, academic manner. To gain points, students also needed to submit a reflective paragraph on how the activity fit the class. In some cases the assignment pushed, prompted, or impelled students to go to events they would otherwise not have attended, such as lectures or political rallies. More than 60% of the class reached the 60 points or higher level, and only 10% accumulated fewer than 30 points. Overall, students were able to find enough opportunities without much complaint.

Beyond these civic engagement points, students were encouraged to volunteer through the Stevens Service Learning Center[15] for a minimum of 12 hours in the semester to receive extra credit in the class. Only 10% of the class chose this option, but these students' reflective papers were able to make the connection between civic engagement and the learning goals of the class. For example, students who volunteered as after-school homework tutors at the Boys and Girls Club mentioned civic duty as part of their reflections on their experiences.

Some of the end-of-semester evaluations show that students seemed to enjoy the class and gained an understanding of the relevance and importance of current political events, one of the purposes of experiential learning activities and civic engagement education. The comments do not directly address the experiential components; however, one may speculate that if the assignments were not well received, the students would not have enjoyed the class as much.

As the civic engagement literature shows,[16] making a course more personal and more active gives students a better and more positive sense of what government

What did you like best about this course?

I liked how we were able to *work outside of class* and it was a good learning experience.

The interactive aspect allowed me to understand and listen to other peoples' opinions.

The forum environment encouraged us to express our unique views about the subject.

This course kept me very informed on *all that was going on in the world* and made me realize how important keeping up with *current events* is.

It was very interesting and always kept me entertained. I learned a lot about politics that I never knew. I loved talking about *current events.*

I liked the reality aspect of it. Everything that we learned can be *applied in someone's life almost daily.*

Politics is pretty boring, but you made it less boring.

I liked *civic engagement.*

Through this course, I've developed a *liking towards government.*

and politics are. Based upon this evidence from this course—taken from both the evaluation of the course and its experiential components—it seems that, designed properly, a course with an experiential learning component can play a role in helping nonpolitical science majors increase their interest in, appreciation for, and engagement with the world of politics.

Results of the Politics of the US Course (POL 1100). The Current Issues in Politics class had a specific goal of civic engagement; the Politics of the US course did not. However, in any introductory course in American government, the professor would be remiss if this theme was not at least minimally included in the course. At Merrimack, getting students involved in the surrounding community is not a difficult task because the Stevens Service Learning Center coordinates these efforts. It handles all the logistics of placements, transportation, and record keeping, and it keeps a list of agencies in need of workers and coordinates with students to ensure their placements match their preferences and the requirements of their classes. With the public policy themes inherent in the US survey course, instructors who include an experiential component in their courses could pick from almost any agency for student service-learning placements.

The instructor of the class examined is the most senior member of the department and has accepted the experiential learning pedagogy and encourages her students to get involved on an extra-credit basis. She wants students—many of whom have other time commitments that could prevent them for completing a required assignment—to have the option but not the requirement of participating. In part, this set-up gives her the ability to offer students who might be struggling in the class at midsemester a way to solidify their grades in a relevant manner.

This professor required that to earn extra credit, students had to work a minimum of 15 hours during the semester and write a reflective essay at the end of the semester that summarized their activities and their reactions to them. Unfortunately, only a handful of students took advantage of this opportunity. In reviewing their assessments of their service-learning assignments, the students agreed that their service-learning work made class material more meaningful, but they were divided on whether the experience increased their sense of social responsibility or improved their attitudes toward involvement or citizenship. In some ways, this result was not surprising, as students motivated to participate in service-learning by the lure of extra credit may be inclined to justify their experiences as academically relevant.

In addition to examining the student self-reflections, the instructor was interviewed. She was asked to identify any effects that experiential learning might have had in her class as a whole. She believed that the students who had direct political involvement "gained the most from their experience." More particularly, she commented that participation in these experiential learning activities allowed the students "to better understand politics, to correct simplistic or incorrect beliefs," and become "more nuanced in their approach towards government." She based most of her evaluations on class discussions and on her reading of the reflective essays, in which she discovered that her students were able to "realize the complexity of government and how difficult it is to make meaningful change." Thus, both instructor

TABLE 22-7: Evaluations of Service-Learning Experience Connections to Class Materials for POL 3150[a]	
How Were You Able to Incorporate Your Practical Learning at the Site with Your Academic Studies?	
Very Well	64%
Somewhat	21%
Not at All	14%
Was Service-Learning an Effective Way to Make Class Material More Meaningful?	
Yes	100%
Did Any of Your Classes' Assignments and/or Discussions Help You with Your Service-Learning Project?	
Yes	79%
No	21%

Note: [a]Some totals do not equal 100% due to rounding.

evaluations of students' class performances and students' self-reflections focused upon the academic gains from participation in service-learning activities. In sum, those who participated in service-learning seem to have increased their educational gains, though the limited participation in these programs also limited potential conclusions about this particular course. Nonetheless, it provides another option for students to connect multiple civic engagement experiences as they progress in their academic careers.

Results of the Criminal Law Course (POL 3150). In this class, students were required to do some sort of experiential learning activity. Most students did a service-learning assignment, in which they volunteered or interned for a minimum of 20 hours in at an organization related to criminal law. These included the district attorney's office, local police departments, the state police arson squad, a nearby house of corrections, and area law firms. Students enrolled in this class were predominantly political science majors who were either juniors or seniors.

When students were asked through a self-assessment questionnaire—required by the Stevens Service Learning Center and due at the end of the semester—about how well the assignment related to the class material, they responded positively. In the same questionnaire, when asked about the degree to which the service-learning experience required use of skills and transformed attitudes, the results were more mixed (see Tables 22-7 and 22-8).

This class, unlike the introductory course, did not explicitly stress the theme of civic engagement. Instead, the instructor emphasized to the students how important practical experience was in helping define their long-term career goals. This emphasis is evident in their responses. Nonetheless, students reported that

TABLE 22-8: Evaluations of Service-Learning Experience Attitudes and Skills for POL 3150[a]

Improved Attitude toward Community Involvement, Citizenship	
To a Great Extent	8%
To Some Extent	62%
To a Small Extent	15%
Not at All	15%

Development of Functional Skills	
To a Great Extent	8%
To Some Extent	62%
Not at All	31%

Enriched Classroom Learning	
To a Great Extent	23%
To a Small Extent	69%
Not at All	8%

Career Development	
To a Great Extent	31%
To Some Extent	31%
To a Small Extent	15%
Not at All	23%

Increased Sense of Social Responsibility	
To a Great Extent	8%
To a Small Extent	77%
Not at All	15%

Note: [a]Some totals do not equal 100% due to rounding.

their service-learning experiences had a modest effect on their attitudes toward citizenship and social responsibility. These results seem to indicate that upper-level majors might be realizing these values without an explicit or directed correlation to class content. Instead, it could be inherent to their choice of major.

Results of the Directed Study Experience. To gauge the effects on student learning in the directed research project on youth homelessness, students were asked at the midpoint in the project to write a brief, free-response essay reflection on their experiences working on the research project to date. They were prompted with the simple question, "What have you learned on this project?" and were asked to email the faculty supervising this project with their responses over the weekend. Six students were working on the project at that point, and all responded with statements that ranged from one to three paragraphs in length.

Analysis of these responses indicated that of the two areas identified as areas in which an impact on student attitudes was expected, only policy awareness was consistently reflected as an important item learned in this experience. Five of the six students referred to becoming more aware of the issues around homelessness, coming to understand the complexity of the issue, or discovering how agencies worked on this issue. On the other hand, only one of the students mentioned the application of data collection or research skills as a major lesson of this project. In addition, several students mentioned how this experience helped improve skills that were not explicitly research skills, but rather more generic life, civic engagement, and professional skills, such as collaboration, organization, working in groups, and group facilitation. Four of the six also mentioned personal growth in terms of awareness and compassion as important things they learned.

Self-reflection is only one way to measure transformation in attitudes, and it is possible that more objective measures would show that the expected improvement in methodological and research skills did in fact occur. It may be that students simply did not see this aspect of directed the research project as particularly important. In addition and in retrospect, the perceived benefits to students in terms of other skills and personal growth should not be particularly surprising, given both the complexity and scope of the research project and process, and the particular subject matter of the study. Finally, a larger number of participants will be needed in the future to better gauge the specific effects of this program.

Cumulative Civic Engagement?

The individual course results are interesting in and of themselves and suggest that the effects of experiential learning may, in fact, be greater and more diverse than has been traditionally assumed. On the one hand, looking at activities within a single political science department at one point in time limits the reach of conclusions, especially in the heightened political environment of the 2008 election. On the other hand, by considering the course-based results as a whole and speculating to some degree about how students might navigate multiple experiential learning opportunities over the course of their college careers, patterns emerge that suggest that experiential learning has a significant, unique, and perhaps even cumulative impact on students. Anecdotally, political science faculty have seen students building upon these activities to pursue other experiential learning opportunities (e.g., study abroad, internships). Further study is needed, and more longitudinal data must be collected to make any definitive claim, but they suggest some interesting developments.

Increasing academic and reflective demands on the student participants across courses and types of experiential learning opportunities were seen in this study. Students in the nonmajor class were introduced to key concepts and themes of civic engagement and could try out different forms of experiential learning, including service-learning, if they so choose. Since the course is designed for nonmajors, the goals of this class and thus the demands on the students could be that simple. Students in the Current Issues class went to lectures, wrote letters, gave blood, and did other volunteer activities. They reflected on all of these experiences through class readings and discussions. Students in the Politics of the US course are both majors and nonmajors. Most of these students had not taken the nonmajor class and were being introduced to the department for the first time. Since experiential learning was an optional assignment in this class, the students' reflective essays were required to be a little more analytical than the nonmajor class. The Criminal

Law class was a departmental elective with an intended population of majors and other upper-level students from related majors (sociology, criminology). The experiential learning activities in this class were required, and a paper discussing these activities was a significant component of the grade. Finally, the Directed Study Experience was open only to selected upper-level students who had the necessary maturity and skills to do community-based research and writing. Taken together, these four courses, laid out in this order, created a progressively higher level of learning at each step and allowed a political science major to go through a series of experiential learning courses if the student followed a certain path.

Adding experiential learning activities to other upper-level classes and possibly to the capstone seminar class[17] can create a unique and cumulative experience for students. Building out and integrating this sequence of experiences also has the potential to produce positive interaction effects of experiential learning that go beyond any individual, course-level effects observed. In part, the availability of opportunities to create such a ladder of experience may be due in the case of Merrimack College to the positions members of the Department of Political Science hold in the department and in other campus offices (service-learning director, chair of the department, assistant dean), but it is not the only reason. The dynamics of the department are quite collegial, and no one has been forced to adopt these components. The multiplicity of experiential learning opportunities can and has evolved organically in a similar fashion in Departments of Political Science across the country. Where members of a department have agreed on a set of learning goals, including promotion of civic engagement, and have recognized experiential learning as a way to achieve these goals, the integrated, programmatic level model of experiential learning suggested here can be replicated with similar encouraging results. As authors of the study, we encourage further adoption of this multilevel approach as part of the discipline's goals of increasing youth civic and political engagement. Finally, we welcome the development of multi-institutional studies to increase the evidentiary foundations of the most effective civic and political engagement educational programs.

Internships, Service-Learning, and Study Abroad: Helping Students Integrate Civic Engagement Learning across Multiple Experiences

23

By Michael K. McDonald

College students are increasingly participating in multiple civic engagement and experiential learning activities during their undergraduate careers. This trend toward multiple experiential learning, civic engagement activities raises a question that faculty advisers are and should be asking: How do we help students make sense of the various civic engagement experiences they have, both in and outside class? As existing scholarly research has few answers, this chapter attempts to fill that void by beginning a discussion around the question of how to help students make connections across experiences and integrate the whole of their experiential learning, civic engagement activities with the classroom curriculum. Pulling from several studies of integrating a single experience with classroom learning, this chapter draws four general lessons that can be applied to the enterprise of helping students integrate civic engagement learning across multiple experiences.

Experiential education has grown in popularity at American colleges and universities. Students and faculty are recognizing the educational value of experiential learning, and college departments and programs are increasingly offering academic credit for out-of-class learning opportunities.[1] In the field of political science, these experiential education activities often focus on civic and political engagement. The purpose of this chapter is to suggest that one important aspect of teaching civic engagement well is to help students integrate the learning that takes place across multiple experiences outside the classroom with the classroom curriculum.

A survey of colleges and universities belonging to Campus Compact, a coalition of colleges and universities focused on civic engagement, found that 712,000 students participated in service-learning programs in 2000, performing a total of 17 million hours of service. That figure was up from 688,000 in 1999, representing a one-year increase of 24,000 students.[2] In addition to the educational value of these experiences, students recognized their value in the competitive job market after graduation. As a result, more and more students are participating in internships, service-learning programs, study abroad, and other forms of experiential education.

Any number of in-class activities also can be considered experiential learning, but the focus here is on out-of-class experiential learning—particularly civic engagement–oriented internships, service-learning, and study abroad.

As an increasing number of students participate in civic engagement and experiential learning programs, another trend has developed for similar reasons. Students often engage in *multiple* experiences during their college careers.[3] The trend toward multiple experiential learning activities raises a question that faculty advisers are and should be asking: How do we help students make sense of and utilize the various civic engagement learning experiences they have, both in and outside class? Surely each experience contributes to their learning and development as citizens, but how can educators help them to integrate the learning they do at the internship site with learning taking place at a service-learning site? How can advisers help them to integrate what they learn through service-learning with what takes place while studying abroad? With so many disparate activities, what do students need to integrate and make connections across experiences and tie them all back to the curriculum and civic engagement learning? They can take full advantage of these opportunities and maximize their learning only by integrating their experiences with one another, the classroom, and their development as citizens.

Existing scholarly research says little about how to help students integrate learning across multiple experiential education activities. Several books and journal articles address the concept of integrating learning from experience with prior classroom knowledge, but for the most part the focus is on a single experience.[4] This chapter attempts to fill that void and begin a discussion around the question of how to help students make connections across experiences and integrate the whole of their experiential learning with the classroom curriculum and citizenship development.

To accomplish this goal, I begin with a review of some of the existing literature.[5] I focus on several studies concerning the integration of a single experience with classroom learning that offer particular insights into the challenges of integrating classroom learning with real-world civic engagement experiences, best practices for faculty and academic advisers, or some combination of these. From these studies, I draw out four general lessons that can be applied to the enterprise of helping students integrate learning across multiple experiences. These lessons will be discussed in greater detail later in this chapter, but they can be summarized as follows: *Lesson 1*: Integration Is More Difficult than We Think; *Lesson 2*: Reflection Is More Difficult than We Think; *Lesson 3:* Teach Students to Be Participant Observers; and *Lesson 4*: Embrace Professional/Career Development. The hope is that these lessons will provide important and practical advice to faculty and academic advisers seeking to help students make meaning of their experiential education, integrate the learning that takes place across multiple experiences, and build upon these to become civically engaged citizens.

Background on Experiential Learning

Concrete, real-world experience has been valued in the process of education at least since philosopher John Dewey articulated the concept of experiential education in the 1930s.[6] Dewey was concerned that students lacked the practical experience and knowledge necessary to fully understand and absorb, let alone apply, the concepts they were learning in the classroom. Abstract and theoretical concepts were lost on students who could not connect them to anything real and observable.[7] Along with the Progressive Educational Movement of the 1930s, Dewey called for a pragmatic education that linked knowledge with action. He wrote, "[T]here is an intimate and necessary relation between the processes of actual experience and education."[8]

Building upon Dewey's philosophy, education reform movements in the 1960s and 1970s attempted to connect classroom learning with the broader community. Since then, experiential education has been embraced by a diverse and growing collection of scholars. In the field of political science, experiential learning has become much more common.[9] In the classroom, simulations, negotiations, policy debates, case studies, and films have all become common teaching methods.[10] Outside the classroom, political science students are increasingly participating in internships or co-ops, service-learning projects, field research, and study abroad.[11]

A cursory review of the top political science journals reveals the fact that, among different types of experiential education, service-learning has received the most attention.[12] Barber and Battistoni were among the first to suggest that service to the community could provide important learning opportunities for students by contributing to their civic education and developing citizenship and openness to civic responsibility.[13] Since then, political scientists have connected service-learning with international relations concepts,[14] social capital,[15] political socialization,[16] and the development of democratic and civic values.[17] Delli Carpini and Keeter rightly conclude that the success of experiential learning is found in the integration of the experience with learning in the classroom, a key goal of civic engagement pedagogy as noted throughout this volume.[18] They note,

> Effective programs provide opportunities that are likely to lead students to both "bump into" and actively seek out information about politics that is relevant to their activities. At the same time, this specific information will be more easily learned, more likely retained, and more likely to be connected to broader kinds of political knowledge if the classroom curriculum is integrated with the service experience.[19]

The authors conclude that the key is to clarify the role that experiential learning plays in overall student learning and ask, "What does this experience contribute to the curriculum?"

Integrating Experience with Classroom Learning

This focus on integrating experience with classroom learning is common to most studies of experiential education, both within and outside the discipline of political science. Dewey recognized the need to connect experience with knowledge through reflection. In fact, he argued that reflective thinking was the key to making an experience educational.[20] By reflecting on an experience, individuals are able to connect the real world to theoretical concepts. Dewey emphasized the importance of reflecting not only on the details of the experience, but also on how one is affected by the experience.

The process of making the connection between experience and knowledge was more fully articulated by cognitive psychologist David Kolb.[21] Kolb posited a four-stage cycle of experiential learning during which a student moves from concrete experience to reflective observation, followed by abstract conceptualization and active experimentation. In moving from one stage to the next, the student makes sense of the experience and relates it to what he or she already knows. From the very beginning of the experiential education movement, the importance of integrating the experience with previous learning has been paramount.

Contemporary scholars have attempted to pin down the process of integrating experience with curriculum. For service-learning projects that are accompanied by a concurrent course, evidence suggests that learning is increased when reflective and integrative assignments link the activity to specific course objectives.[22] The same is true for internships.[23] Discussing internships for sociology students, Parilla and Hesser draw conclusions equally applicable in any discipline in regard to the integration of internships and academic learning. They suggest two ways in which internships can be structured to allow for integration. First, internships need to be situated within the overall curriculum rather than considered an appendage to it. This integration allows students to receive the necessary knowledge and skills that will allow them to be successful in an internship. Second, the internship must be structured to allow for constant connections between the job site and curriculum.[24]

When civic engagement projects do not run concurrently with a specific course, the process of integration is much harder. If a student is getting credit for the experience, often a series of workshops or an independent study accompanies the experience, during which reflection and integration can happen. However, many students participate in internships and service opportunities for which they cannot or choose not to receive credit. In those cases, very little supervision occurs at the institution of higher education, and the student is left to his or her own devices to make connections to classroom learning.[25]

However, the existing literature suggests that when this integration is successful there is a strong educational value for experiential learning. Internships are seen as a means to acquire not only professional job skills,[26] but also to experience the application of concepts and knowledge to real-world events.[27] Likewise, relevant service-learning projects can help students master complex concepts and put theory into practice.[28] In an often-cited experiment, Markus, Howard, and King randomly separated students in a large undergraduate political science course into two groups: one group was assigned to do a service-learning project alongside the course and the other group participated in traditional discussion sections.[29] The authors found that students doing service were more likely to say that they "performed up to their potential in the course," "learned to apply principles from this course to new situations," and "developed a set of overall values in this field." They also earned a higher grade on average than their peers who did not participate in service-learning.[30]

Along with increased interest in internships and service-learning, more and more students spend anywhere from one week to a full year studying abroad.[31] As study abroad has become more popular, scholars have paid increased attention to issues of program quality and curriculum integration.[32] At a minimum, curriculum integration involves ensuring that students can earn credit for the courses they take while abroad. Recent efforts in the study abroad community, however, focused on a richer integration of the experience abroad, with learning taking place at the home institution.[33]

Foreign language students make clear connections, as they are immersed in the language and culture they have been studying for several semesters. For other students, however, the integration of experience and learning is more complex. There has always been an expectation that studying in another country broadens students' personal experiences, familiarizes them with people and cultures different from their own, and helps them develop a certain level of global competence.[34] Colleges and universities are reaching out to disciplines and departments that have not traditionally been interested in study abroad to encourage new and creative approaches.[35] In addition, many institutions are trying to take the study abroad learning experience a step further, preparing students before they go abroad and communicating with them while they are abroad to help them make the connection between what they have been learning at their home institution and what they see and do abroad.[36]

What the existing literature makes clear is that it is important to integrate experience with classroom curriculum to ensure that the experience is educational. The remainder of this chapter examines several key insights that scholars have identified in their efforts to help students integrate a single experience with their classroom learning. Each of the four lessons that follows can be applied to the overarching goal of this chapter: to help students make connections across their multiple experiential learning activities and integrate these activities with the academic curriculum, thus fostering lifelong civically engaged citizens.

Lesson 1: Integration Is More Difficult than We Think

The idea that learning is contingent upon integration of the experience with the classroom is present in nearly all scholarship on experiential learning. Unfortunately, most of the literature stops there. There is too little discussion of *how* to go about integrating internships, service, and study abroad with classroom learning. Many authors seem to suggest that such integration is simple and easy to accomplish.

Peter Parilla and Susan Smith-Cullien, writing about criminal justice internships, draw attention to a few challenges to integration.[37] First, they note that many students are uninterested or even resistant to the idea of connecting their experiences with previous learning. The resistance is a result of a different set of priorities, the fact that integration is challenging to do, the reality that students see the relevance of work more easily than the relevance of academic knowledge, and the overwhelming nature of the experience itself. It is helpful to look at each factor in turn.

Students come to experiential learning activities, especially internships, with a different perspective than that of faculty. Students primarily view internships as a gateway to a career—an opportunity to build industry-specific knowledge, network with professionals, and, ultimately, get a job offer—and rightfully so. They also are encouraged by parents, friends, professors, and career advisers to think of internships in these terms. Parilla and Smith-Cullien argue that students' career focus is not necessarily a problem for the academic integrity of the experience. However, they suggest that this focus can become an issue:

> Problems arise when students become so deeply immersed in learning and doing the work at the site that they forget the academic goals of the internship. A major challenge for instructors is to keep students focused on these goals. They must ensure that students are not so fully caught up in the "new job" that they lose sight of the academic purpose of the internship—the analysis of the experience.[38]

As well as having a career focus, students often are resistant to integrating the new experiences with prior learning because it is a challenging intellectual endeavor. As Parilla and Smith-Cullien put it, "Students often resist what they find difficult."[39]

Additionally, a new experience such as an internship involves a great deal of new information and a new frame of reference as practitioner rather than student. Students frequently are more interested in assimilating the new information and experiences rather than revisiting previous classroom knowledge. At the same time, the new workplace information can seem much more relevant to students than abstract models and theories.[40]

Finally, the authors suggest that the experience at the internship site provides a powerful influence and professionalization that can be so complete that students lose their capacity to step back and critically assess the experience.[41] Students can become overwhelmed by their experiences, both in terms of the amount of time and effort they require and by a certain amount of culture shock that comes along with transitioning from the classroom to the workplace. Overwhelmed students become unable to step back and reflect on what they are doing and learning, and, as a result, they resist the more difficult integration step central to deep learning and lifelong engagement.

A second major problem, according to Parilla and Smith-Cullien, is that some students are simply unable to connect their experiences and prior learning. Writing about students doing service-learning while studying abroad, Nancy Wessel also notes student difficulty in integrating the experience with academic study.[42] There are two potential sources of difficulty. First, students have a tendency to forget content from other courses, especially those taken during the freshman or sophomore year.[43] Second, the process of integrating experiences and prior learning requires students to separate a particular event from everything they are experiencing and then relate that event to an abstract concept, which can be difficult to do, especially for a student already overwhelmed by the new experience.[44]

Educators can apply the same concepts to helping students integrate learning across multiple experiences. If integration is more difficult than faculty and advisers think, and if faculty and advisers passively let students make the connections on their own, students often will fail to make them. Thus, faculty must take an active role in encouraging, supporting, and providing opportunities for complex integration across experiences.

In working toward integration, faculty and advisers must be mindful of students' potential resistance to the process and the possibility that they will find it difficult to make connections. Overcoming resistance requires persuading students of the importance and value of integrating their experiences. There is undoubtedly both an educational and a professional value to reflective participation. The challenge is to convince students that it is worth the effort. In addition to convincing students of the value of integration, Parilla and Smith-Cullien suggest structuring assignments as to require integration.[45] For example, they suggest requiring journal entries that demonstrate an ability to connect the experience to prior learning.[46] Likewise, reflection papers or research papers at the end of a course could require proof of integration. For internships, a well-structured internship portfolio can force students to connect prior learning to the internship experience.[47] This is easy to do when students take a course concurrent with the experience, but that is not always the case. When forcing them to make connections is not an option, convincing them of the utility of doing so matters even more.

Overcoming the difficulty that some students have with integration is often a matter of giving them multiple opportunities to make connections. Journal reflections and integration papers are common tools, but there is also value in modeling the process of integration into conversations and discussions with students.[48] Some students find it easier to integrate experience with prior knowledge when interacting with their peers, especially those with similar or shared experiences. The key is not to assume that students will easily make connections, but instead to provide several opportunities and much encouragement to make the process easier.

One final note about the challenges of integration must be discussed. As Eyler and Giles state, it is important to clarify the type of learning likely to come from experiential education and to make sure that efforts and expectations are appropriate.[49] Applying learning models from cognitive researchers, Eyler and Giles note that, in addition to providing new factual knowledge, experiential education activities likely result in improvements in students' higher-order thinking skills and ability to apply knowledge to new situations.[50] These are two key parts of successful civic engagement. Thus, when working with students to integrate learning across experiences with the prior knowledge, educators should focus on application and synthesis rather than on new understandings of basic facts only.

Lesson 2: Reflection Is More Difficult than We Think

I noted earlier that scholars have long focused on structured reflection as the means to connect experience to prior knowledge. However, just as the process of integration is more difficult than faculty and advisers may think, so too is reflection. Asking students to think back over an experience will not, in and of itself, lead to integration.

Cognitive research states that learning involves the *construction* of knowledge. This construction is the process Kolb is describing—one of moving "from experience to thought and back again as learners construct and organize knowledge."[51] Eyler points out that educators have long embraced Kolb's model precisely because the continuous learning cycle it describes provides the necessary scaffolding for learning to take place.[52]

Kolb's model, illustrated in Figure 23-1, shows the process of integrating experience with classroom learning. It depicts a cycle of experiential learning wherein a student processes an activity through each stage in sequence, starting with the experience itself. Of course, before an experiential education activity begins, there likely will be an introduction or set of classes that introduce the student to theories and concepts to be tested, confirmed, or challenged during the out-of-class experience, but in terms of understanding how students learn through doing, it is helpful to examine Kolb's cycle. In the second stage, the student notes his or her reaction to the experience. As Collier and Williams put it, "[T]he initial observation and description of the service experience has now been transformed into something that is personally relevant through the intentional process of reflection."[53]

The third stage is really where integration happens, as the student incorporates abstract or theoretical concepts previously learned to "redescribe the service experience from a conceptual rather than descriptive perspective."[54] For this third stage to be successful, the student must have learned and understood these concepts

Figure 23-1: Kolb's Model

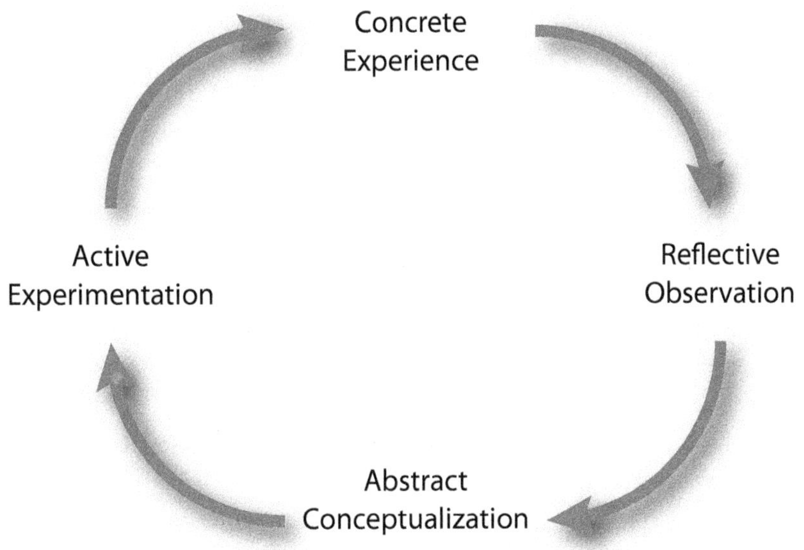

Source: Kolb, David A. *Experiential Learning*. Englewood Cliff, NJ: Prentice Hall, 1984.

at some previous point, either in the current semester or before. This may suggest that internships and service-learning will be most successfully integrated with classroom learning in the later years of a student's college education. Experiential education may indeed be useful for first- or second-year students, but faculty advisers should not expect the same level of integration with difficult classroom concepts. For this reason, it may be particularly helpful for students to get guidance from faculty later in their studies, after the abstract and theoretical concepts have been learned, to help them relate new experiential education activities back to earlier experiences. Finally, in stage four, the student applies the new understanding of concepts to different situations and begins the process anew.

To be sure, reflection is a necessary condition for integration. Without taking the time to reflect back upon an experience, a student could not possibly relate it to prior learning. However, reflection by itself is not a sufficient condition. In my experience working with students doing both internships and service-learning projects, many of them never get to stage three of Kolb's cycle. In journals and research papers, my students reexamine their experiences, but even when specifically instructed to link the experience to classroom knowledge, they often fail to make these connections.

Returning to Janet Eyler's study of reflection allows a better understanding of the issues involved.[55] Eyler attempts to identify ways to effectively use reflection in service-learning projects by drawing upon experiential learning theory, studies of situated cognition, problem-based inquiry, and adult cognitive development, as well as several key studies of effective reflection.[56] She notes that when it comes to "ill-structured" social problems, those with no clear and simple solutions, the ability to "identify, frame, and resolve these issues requires a fairly advanced level of cognitive development."[57] There is some evidence, she notes, that students participating in experiential education activities who connect their experiences with academic study through extensive reflection may develop this kind of advanced cognitive development. To achieve that goal, Eyler offers some prescriptions for good reflection that educators can apply both to the integration of a single experience to prior knowledge and to the overarching goal of integration across experiences.

A basic goal of experiential learning is to get students to challenge their preconceived assumptions. Eyler writes,

> One of the assumptions of experiential education is that students will be surprised by exposure to situations and information that conflicts with their assumptions about the world and that they will be challenged to explore further. The processes of cognitive development and deeper understanding of issues involve solving those conflicts through acquiring new information, assessing the validity of conflicting information, and restructuring the schema for organizing understanding. There is, however, much research that indicates that unless these assumptions are surfaced and explicitly addressed in the context of new information and experience, most people will simply hammer new information into old frameworks.[58]

Cognitive development theory thus offers several concrete recommendations for effective reflection and integration. First, educators need to surface underlying assumptions before the experiential learning activity even begins.[59] They need to show students, especially those operating at less-sophisticated levels of cognition, that the issues and problems they will encounter are ill-structured, and there will not always be easy answers or clear courses of action. This recognition of complication is particularly important for political science students, since the issues and problems of political science are almost always ill-structured and complex. Faculty interested in helping students uncover their underlying assumptions might consider directed writing assignments or journaling at the beginning of the experience. Another strategy I have used successfully is having older students who have already completed internships or service projects come back and speak with younger students beginning similar activities. The insights of their peers often help students examine their own assumptions in new and deeper ways.

The second recommendation shares a focus on preparing students before an experience. If they are going to be effective at integrating their experiences and their academic studies, they need to develop the habit of monitoring their own learning.[60] Learning contracts and goal setting are mentioned as effective tools for encouraging students to self-monitor their learning.[61] In short, it is not enough to tell them to reflect upon the experience and connect it to the classroom. They also must be encouraged to take responsibility for the process of learning while participating in the internship, service-learning project, or trip abroad.

Figure 23-2: One Student's Experiential Learning about International Development

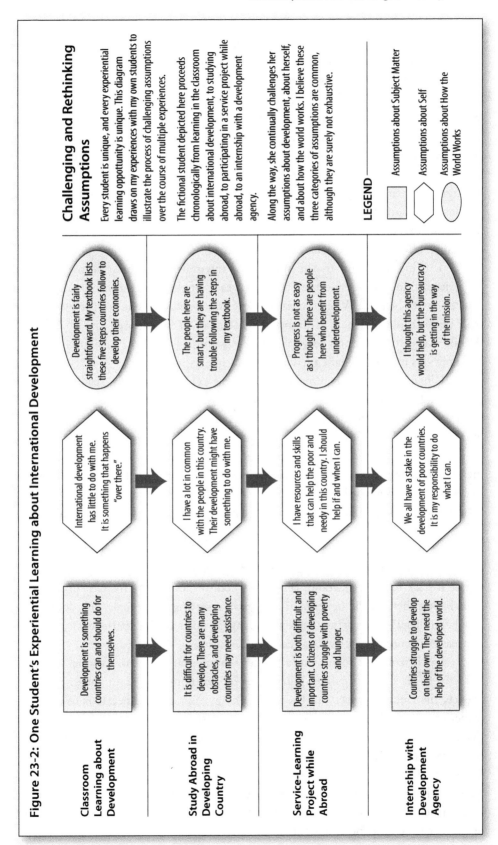

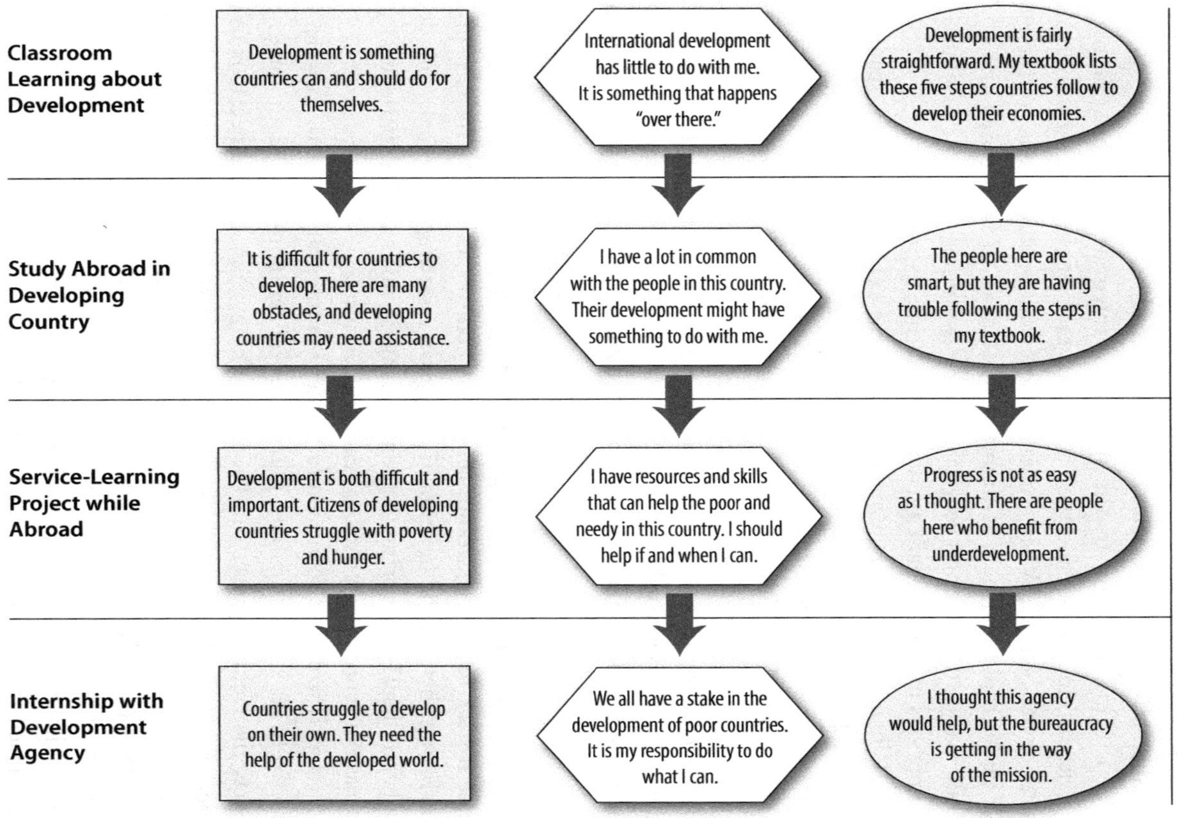

Classroom Learning about Development
Development is something countries can and should do for themselves.
International development has little to do with me. It is something that happens "over there."
Development is fairly straightforward. My textbook lists these five steps countries follow to develop their economies.
Study Abroad in Developing Country
It is difficult for countries to develop. There are many obstacles, and developing countries may need assistance.
I have a lot in common with the people in this country. Their development might have something to do with me.
The people here are smart, but they are having trouble following the steps in my textbook.
Service-Learning Project while Abroad
Development is both difficult and important. Citizens of developing countries struggle with poverty and hunger.
I have resources and skills that can help the poor and needy in this country. I should help if and when I can.
Progress is not as easy as I thought. There are people here who benefit from underdevelopment.
Internship with Development Agency
Countries struggle to develop on their own. They need the help of the developed world.
We all have a stake in the development of poor countries. It is my responsibility to do what I can.
I thought this agency would help, but the bureaucracy is getting in the way of the mission.

Challenging and Rethinking Assumptions

Every student is unique, and every experiential learning oppottunity is unique. This diagram draws on my experiences with my own students to illustrate the process of challenging assumptions over the course of multiple experiences.

The fictional student depicted here proceeds chronologically from learning in the classroom about international development, to studying abroad, to participating in a service project while abroad, to an internship with a development agency.

Along the way, she continually challenges her assumptions about development, about herself, and about how the world works. I believe these three categories of assumptions are common, although they are surely not exhaustive.

LEGEND

- Rectangle: Assumptions about Subject Matter
- Hexagon: Assumptions about Self
- Oval: Assumptions about How the World Works

A third recommendation is to make reflection a constant and ongoing process. Eyler notes, "The key to effective reflection during service is continuity; observations need to be continually processed, challenged, and connected with other information."[62] Faculty advisers need to encourage constant, guided reflection. For instance, requiring interns to submit a weekly journal entry and providing feedback and guidance for future reflection will encourage more integration than having students submit a single, longer journal at the end of an experience. There is also some evidence that students make connections more easily when reflecting upon their experiences in a group of peers. Verbally sharing their experiences and exchanging reactions and questions with other students provides an opportunity to reconsider assumptions and offers yet another outlet for reflection. This exchange can be arranged in a concurrent course or in a follow-up presentation, seminar, or workshop after their experiences have concluded.

Turning attention to the process of integrating learning across multiple experiences, in and outside the classroom, each of these recommendations about reflection are helpful. When students move from one experience to the next, there will be both old and new assumptions that need to be exposed and challenged. While every student and every experience is unique, Figure 23-2 illustrates how assumptions might be challenged across multiple experiences.

When instructors can make that process explicit and clear, students will be able to make connections between their experiences. They may have developed new assumptions traveling abroad that are now challenged in a service-learning project or at an internship. Teasing out these assumptions can make both experiences richer and increase the connection back to academic learning. Having students journal about their expectations and assumptions may help. Similarly, if students are meeting in a group to share their experiences, their peers may suggest underlying assumptions that a student has not yet considered. Regardless of what technique is used, the goal is to make uncovering and examining assumptions an explicit part of the process.

Likewise, if students are going to integrate learning across experiences and relate it back to the classroom, they must take responsibility for that process. By convincing them of the benefits of integrating, setting clear goals, and developing the habit of self-monitoring, students can again make both experiences richer and increase the connection back to academic learning.

Lastly, constant reflection facilitates the integration across experiences more effectively. As students submit journals or reflect more informally on a new experience, the faculty adviser can encourage integration and connections to previous experience and classroom learning. In many cases, the faculty member will not have been involved in the previous learning experience. This means that, unless the experience is part of a larger program, the faculty member will need to make an extra effort to learn about the student's previous experiences. It may be helpful to have the student write journal essays or a short reflection paper on what he or she learned in the previous experience to uncover the connections to the current experience and classroom content.

Lesson 3: Students Should Learn to Be Participant Observers

Recognizing that both reflection and integration are more difficult than one might think, educators can provide students with a valuable intellectual tool by following the advice of sociologist Wesley Miller.[63] In an effort to improve internship experiences and connect internships back to the mission of his liberal arts college, Miller advocates teaching students the methods of participant observation. The use of participant observation techniques, he argues, helps student interns integrate their experiences into the liberal arts curriculum.[64] Through a preinternship skills course, students can cover such topics as

> the epistemology of participant observation, analytical description, developing concepts and propositions based on observation, how to find patterns, recording and retrieving observations, and obstacles to interpreting and analyzing data (e.g. reactivity, selective observation).[65]

One clear benefit of teaching students to be participant-observers is to overcome the tendency discussed earlier of students losing their ability to step back and critically assess the experience. Trained in the techniques of participant observation, students will be more critical and aware of the socialization taking place in the internship or service-learning environment. They will be more likely to examine the workplace, and they will be in a better position to analyze the organization.

Teaching students to be participant-observers will help them to integrate a single experience with prior learning, but it will be even more effective in helping them integrate their learning across experiences. For example, imagine a student who learns about international development in the classroom, then travels abroad one summer with Oxfam International to help distribute food aid in Africa, and then interns with USAID the following semester. Each experience will certainly contribute to the student's learning. Possessing the skills of participant observation, however, will allow the student to make connections between the experiences and relate each back to the classroom, more fully understanding the organizational dynamics and challenges faced by Oxfam and USAID, thus taking a critical step in developing tools needed for successful civic engagement.[66]

Lesson 4: Faculty Should Embrace Professional/Career Development

I noted earlier that students often engage in experiential education, especially internships, for their potential career benefits. Students see these experiences as résumé boosters and ways to build skills and experiences that will be valuable in postgraduation job searches. Embracing those motivations and helping students see the professional development benefits of integrating experiences with classroom learning taps into students' natural motivations and broaden those motivations to include deeper learning.

Table 23-1: Transferable Skills Sought by Employers	
1.	Communication skills (verbal)
2.	Strong work ethic
3.	Teamwork skills
4.	Analytical skills
5.	Initiative
6.	Problem-solving skills
7.	Communication skills (written)
8.	Interpersonal skills
9.	Computer skills
10.	Flexibility/Adaptability

Source: Adapted from National Association of Colleges and Employers 2010.

In reality, experiential education does offer students valuable work-related skills and experiences.[67] The National Association of Colleges and Employers lists a set of transferable skills ranked highest by employers who hire recent college graduates (Table 23-1).[68] Many, if not all, of the skills listed are ones that students can obtain or strengthen through experiential education. In addition to building a valuable skill set, experiential education provides students with contacts and opportunities to network. It is quite common for internships and co-ops experiences to lead directly to job offers.

When working with students participating in these experiences, faculty should embrace the professional development aspect of experiential learning. Helping students make connections between the experience and future career aspirations may make them more willing to investigate connections between their experiences and classroom learning. In addition, connecting their experiences back to the classroom will improve their ability to market those experiences to employers. In cover letters and interviews, when students make connections between their internships or service-learning projects and their curricular learning, employers will better understand the educational value of the experience.

Conclusion

Political science professors increasingly have turned to out-of-class experiential, civic engagement activities as an important pedagogical tool. This chapter suggests that one important aspect of successfully teaching civic engagement and experiential learning is to help students integrate learning across multiple experiences and with what they are learning in the classroom. The existing literature offers little guidance in regard to how to go about achieving this goal. Several scholars have, however, offered important insights as to how to integrate a single experience with classroom learning, which can be applied to the process of integration across experiences. Future research is needed to determine what special challenges cross-experience integration creates and whether additional techniques can be employed by faculty advisers.

Student Organizations and Civic Education on Campus: The Greek System

24

By J. Cherie Strachan and Mary Scheuer Senter[1]

Given the prominent role of civil society in political socialization, this chapter—based upon a survey of student organization presidents on a Midwestern campus—explores whether student organizations function as the equivalent of collegiate civil society and whether they can supplement formal civic education efforts on campus. Findings indicate that traditional Greek organizations, while not the only organizations providing civic and political socialization, far outperform many other types of campus organizations in activities believed to cultivate members' civic identities, political skills, and political efficacy. They also cultivate bonding and social capital; yet other research shows that members of Greek organizations exhibit higher levels of both sexism and symbolic racism. The conclusion advocates more judicious use of political science literature to identify best practices for student groups to maximize their positive potential, given that they serve as the equivalent of campus civil society.

Colleges and universities are increasingly called upon to bolster students' civic and political engagement. Yet research in both political science and higher education suggests that college-level civic education and political science coursework are not consistently being taught in a way that successfully addresses such concerns. Given the prominent role of civil society in political socialization, this chapter—based upon an Internet survey of student organization presidents on a single campus—explores whether student organizations function as the equivalent of campus civil society and whether they can supplement formal civic education efforts on campus. Findings indicate that traditional Greek organizations far outperform many other types of campus organizations in activities believed to cultivate members' civic identities, political skills, and political efficacy. However, participation in Greek organizations is also associated with higher levels of both sexism and symbolic racism. The conclusion advocates more judicious use of political science literature to identify best practices for student groups.

Some critics argue that higher education currently fails to fulfill its civic mission.[2] Carol Geary Schneider, president of the Association of American Colleges and Universities (AACU), noted resistance to teaching democratic participation on college campuses.[3] Colleges and universities have embraced the service-learning method, but few explicitly attempt to teach students how to wield political influence.[4] Indeed, higher education scholars calling for reforms have expressed concern that administrators are paying superficial attention to cultivating good citizens—perhaps mistakenly assuming that required general education courses and volunteer community service work adequately prepare students to participate in public life.[5] Yet, more than half of college seniors report that college has had little or no effect on their plans to vote in the future.[6]

This civic education oversight is shared by faculty as changes in higher education have diminished their ability and motivation to focus on students' character development. Increasingly, professors have been socialized while in graduate school to prioritize research, and they face increasing demands to focus on research productivity even at institutions with heavy teaching loads. The inevitable result is less time to spend directly with students.[7] These trends, combined with colleges' reliance on part-time faculty and increasing class sizes, mean that "avenues to maintaining a sense of campus community and connecting faculty with students out of the classroom are increasingly limited."[8] Given these shifting priorities, professors give greater attention to the role of substantive coursework over other forms of interaction with students.

The limited effectiveness of these current approaches to civic education is highlighted by declining youth political participation since the 1970s, as explained in previous chapters. In short, formal civic education, focused on bolstering political knowledge in a classroom setting, seems to have worked well enough for prior generations of college students. It may not be enough, however, to stimulate political participation from current undergraduates. In response, an array of reformers has called for a renewed commitment to transforming college students into active citizens.[9]

Current Undergraduates

As previous chapters discuss and numerous sources indicate, youth participation in traditional political activities—including voting in elections, supporting political candidates, and following policy-making processes—has fallen dramatically. The authors of a 2002 project concluded that, at least in the realm of elections, the "generational chain of engagement has been broken" and that young people are "particularly uninvolved" both behaviorally and psychologically in explicit political activities. Despite increased youth voter turnout of 51% in 2008 and 49% in 2012, the plausibility of this concern is underscored by CIRCLE's ongoing assessment of the political engagement of young citizens (classified as individuals falling between the ages of 18 and 29). This assessment revealed that in 2010, 13% of young voters were "talkers," who took no action beyond discussion of issues; 13% were undermobilized registered voters, who failed to show up at the polls; and fully 23%

were civically alienated.[10] As the 2012 election approached, young voters were still characterized by waning political enthusiasm, as only 13% claimed to have given a lot of thought to the candidates in late 2011, a decline from 27% in late 2007.[11] The long-term trend of political disinterest, combined with waning interest post-2008, suggests that the spike in political interest in 2008 was contextual and difficult to maintain, especially in midterm and local elections or in presidential elections that lack either a charismatic candidate or a dramatic political issue.[12]

The one bright note in this new landscape is that members of the current generation are clearly not apathetic about broader social problems, but rather care quite deeply about such concerns.[13] Yet as other authors in this volume note, today's college students belong to a generation that largely rejects the political process as a way to solve problems. Surveys consistently indicate that students' preferred means of public participation include face-to-face volunteering and political consumerism in the form of both boycotting and "buy-cotting" products.[14] Optimists may be tempted to conclude that young people have simply found an alternative way to participate in politics and that increased participation in more traditional political outlets is either unnecessary or likely to occur in the near future.[15]

Yet such optimism may not be warranted, given young people's underlying definitions of good citizenship. The National Survey for Civic Engagement (NSCE)[16] reveals that, unlike older Americans, younger Americans have an apolitical and passive view of citizenship. When surveyed, 58% of those born after 1976 agreed that "simply being a good person" meets the criteria of good citizenship—compared to only 35% and 32% of the Baby Boomer generation (born between 1946 and 1964) and the Dutiful generation (born before 1946) respondents. This erosion of civic identity appears to have occurred over time and had a more dramatic effect on each successive generation. Hence, while members of other age cohorts (such as Generation X-ers, who were born between 1965 and 1976) also are more apolitical than their elders, differences between the oldest and youngest generations of voters provide the starkest contrast.

For example, during focus group discussions, no one from this younger group volunteered definitions of citizenship that included obligations to the broader community. In direct contrast to older focus group members, who explicitly associated citizenship with an obligation to participate, young people repeatedly endorsed the claim that choosing not to participate in politics is just as legitimate as deciding to become involved.[17] These attitudes appear to consistently characterize young citizens, as a 2006 poll revealed that 57% of 18- to 29-year-olds agreed with the claim that changing society is a choice, not an obligation or responsibility.[18] These findings suggest that the lack of civic identity among members of this generation[19] seems likely to suppress political participation well into the future.

Campus Civil Society as a Solution

Colleges and universities across the country have been called upon to rededicate themselves to the task of grooming students for not only civic, but also explicitly political leadership.[20] Summarizing the concerns over perceived inattention to the cultivation of such explicitly political engagement, former Harvard president Derek Bok exhorted professors to address the political needs of students. Bok (2006) left his call for action open, as he asked educators to do "whatever they can" to promote long-term political participation among students.[21]

Faculty will respond to these petitions with efforts to improve the activities over which they have the most control: curriculum requirements, substantive course content, and pedagogy.[22] Such endeavors have great potential to improve students' levels of political knowledge—which is certainly a welcome and valuable outcome.[23] Yet, if the underlying cause of low participation is a lack of civic identity, it seems unlikely that students will put such knowledge to good use and may even question its relevance if course-based knowledge is not integrated with actual experiences. As Peter Levine (2007) argues, no academic discipline sees the cultivation of good citizens as its primary purpose, especially as political science now emphasizes descriptive, empirical insights into political actors' behavior rather than normative assessments of good citizenship.[24] More important, classroom learning, even learning about political institutions and behavior in a political science class, is not the best predictor of long-term political participation throughout adulthood. This status is reserved for nonclassroom and extracurricular group activities—especially when the nature of these activities hones students' civic skills and identities.[25]

Despite a well-established correlation between nonclassroom activities and increased civic identity, as well as parallel findings in higher education research that documents the connection between campus life and students' future success, faculty has largely left concerns over the quality of campus life in the hands of administrators and staff.[26] Professors, however, especially political scientists familiar with the scholarly literature on associational life, should become more involved in efforts to assess and improve the impact of campus civil society on students' political development.[27]

Supplementing Students' Missing Experiences

Not only can this effort provide a welcome supplement to formal civic education, it also can compensate for a gap in students' political socialization. Some scholars believe that America's current college students have come of age during an era of declining associational life.[28] Skocpol (2003) takes this argument a step further. She argues that the large-scale, inclusive, federated organizations that historically played an essential role in cultivating good citizenship have been in a state of decline since the 1960s.[29] Rather than launching a broad-based organization, elites now raise funds to hire staff, pay lobbyists, and influence the media. Thus, the number of special interest groups has spiraled upward since the 1960s. Meanwhile, the number of broad-based organizations that actively involve citizens in decision making and coordinate their efforts across geographic boundaries (thus fostering civic identity, skills, and efficacy) has dwindled.

This transformation of American civil society has had a dramatic impact on the youngest generation of citizens. Indeed, CIRCLE's 2006 survey data indicate that young citizens, especially those who have not attended college, are "permanently missing some aspects of civic engagement—such as group membership—that were common thirty years ago."[30]

College students are still more likely to join groups than other Americans, but higher education research suggests that the types of groups they join are different than in the past, as broad-based student organizations have suffered a fate comparable to Skocpol's ideal groups.[31] A survey of student life deans conducted in 1998, for example, found that only 18% of college campuses belonged to a statewide student association focused on higher education policy. Only one in 12 had a student chapter of Public Interest Research Group (PIRG), an umbrella organization with a broad reform agenda and an institutional structure of federated chapters similar to that recommended in Skocpol's historical assessment of American voluntary associations.[32] Most of the deans surveyed reported that none of their student organizations was capable of mobilizing students across the entire campus. This claim encompassed student government associations, at a time when voting in campus elections and claiming interest in influencing campus governance declined to all-time lows.[33] It also extended to on-campus activities, as deans of students confirmed, "More people are doing things individually and in separate groups than campus wide."[34]

Given the potential importance of student organizations in cultivating good citizenship—as well as the possibility that these organizations are not living up to their full potential—the research presented in this chapter was undertaken to explore the types of organizational experiences provided on a typical college campus. It reflects a preliminary attempt to develop a systematic assessment of civil society on campus. Several ongoing national survey projects (most prominently those of the American Freshman and the National Survey of Student Engagement) rely on students' self-reports to assess the college student experience. None, however, systematically focuses on student organizations as the unit of analysis. The work discussed here represents a preliminary effort to remedy this gap in knowledge about the college experience.

Methods

In the 2009–2010 academic year, the campus of Central Michigan University (CMU) had 259 registered student organizations (RSOs)—ranging from traditional Greek organizations to special interest clubs, professional associations, and honor societies. CMU is a Midwestern public university located in rural central Michigan, with an enrollment of approximately 21,000 students on its main campus.

Given the need to develop a descriptive account of campus organizations' activities, the decision was made to administer a questionnaire to those most likely to possess this detailed information—the groups' current student presidents. Student presidents were preferred over faculty advisers, as faculty members do not always play an active role in the day-to-day activities of the organizations they sponsor. Staff members in the Office of Student Life were also ruled out as a reliable information source, as they collect and record only a minimal amount of required data about each group and its activities. Student presidents, on the other hand, are able to provide detailed information about their groups and members, because they are largely responsible for recruiting members and coordinating their activities.

To conduct the survey, email addresses for the 259 RSO presidents were obtained from the Office of Student Life, and a questionnaire was administered using the web survey software system SENSUS, available through the campus's Applied Social Science Research Center. After a series of reminders and a second wave of email for nonrespondents, 126 student presidents responded, yielding a response rate of 49%. The respondents reflected the full array of organizations on campus. Nonrespondents did not systematically represent any particular type or size of student group.[35] To the best of our knowledge, this data set is unique in providing detailed information from student leaders on a broad range of student groups and their organizational characteristics.

A preliminary review of the data indicated that some organizations were indeed undertaking activities likely to cultivate civic identity and promote political participation. Bivariate analyses were undertaken to determine whether these organizational characteristics were randomly distributed across campus groups or whether they could be attributed to a particular type of organization. Numerous potential causal variables were used in this preliminary assessment, including organizational type, organizational function, and membership demographics.

Particular attention was paid to both membership size and affiliation with a state or national organization—as the organizational traits of a large membership base and a federated structure have been praised by scholars of American civil society.[36] The number of members provided no insight into a student group's activities, although a federated structure was significantly correlated with a handful of organizational activities of interest. Presidents affiliated with a state or national organization, for example, were more likely than others to consult a constitution or by-laws and to rely on formal rules when making decisions, claim that their members shared core values, and believe that their members' volunteer efforts had a statewide or national impact.[37] In addition, the presidents of federated student groups were more apt to claim that they had sponsored or cosponsored a fund-raising event, distributed printed materials or brochures detailing the group's agenda and values, and purposefully recruited diverse members.[38]

Yet this pattern could not compete with the striking and consistent correlations between one particular type of student group—Greek organizations—and desirable organizational activities. A substantial majority (76%) of the Greek presidents on CMU's campus claimed affiliation with a national organization, and Greek organizations constituted slightly more than one-quarter (26%) of the campus groups with a federated structure. Consequently, including Greeks in the category of organizations with a national organization affiliation bolstered the explanatory power of this variable. However, when these fraternities and sororities were filtered out of this category, significant correlations between a federated structure and most of the organizational activities previously listed (consulting a constitution or by-laws, relying on formal rules, sharing core values, and sponsoring effective volunteer efforts) disappeared,[39] and only a handful (sponsoring a fund-raising event, distributing printed materials, and recruiting diverse members) remained.[40]

The relationship between traditional Greek organizations and desirable organizational activities does not mean that other student groups on CMU's campus are not engaged in similar activities. Yet the strength and consistency of this pattern, in combination with the fact that Greek organizations have the potential to socialize large numbers of students on CMU's campus and on many campuses across the country, justifies a closer look at the intersection of Greek life and campus civic engagement. Hence the remainder of this chapter reviews this pattern in greater detail.[41]

Frequency of Organizational Activities

To serve as a mechanism of political socialization, organizations must meet and undertake activities on a regular basis. Indeed, classic work on civil society suggests that average Americans used to attend organizational meetings and functions on a regular basis—with highly active citizens participating in weekly local meetings as well as serving as delegates at state and national conferences.[42] In the sample for the study discussed in this chapter, RSO presidents were asked about their members' conference involvement. All but one of the Greek presidents reported sending delegates to regional and national conferences, compared to only 57% of their non-Greek peers. Further, whereas both Greek and non-Greek delegates were equally likely to participate in conference discussions (75% and 72%, respectively), Greek delegates were more apt to help set organizational policies by participating in formal parliamentary proceedings (82% compared to 65%) and voting on proposed new policies (88% compared to 70%).[43]

RSO presidents also were asked to report how frequently their organizations engaged in a list of potential campus activities, with five answer categories ranging from a low of fewer than once per year (coded as a 1) to a high of once per week or more (coded as a 5). Many organizations reported holding meetings for the executive board and the full membership on a fairly regular basis. Once again, the Greek organizations met far more frequently. Weekly executive board meetings, for example, were reported by 84% of Greek presidents, but only 41% of non-Greek groups. Greeks were also far more apt to hold weekly meetings of the full membership (92% compared to 63%) and require members to vote on issues at these meetings at least once a month (82% compared to 60%).[44]

Further, presidents' responses indicated that Greek organizations not only hold more frequent meetings, but also undertake a wider and more frequent array of campus activities. Seventy-eight percent of Greek organizations, for example, reported holding educational, social, or fund-raising events at least four times each semester, compared to only 43% of non-Greek organizations. To sustain this level of activity, Greek presidents reported regularly turning tasks over to subcommittees, with 52% (compared to 25% of non-Greeks) claiming their organizations did so on a weekly basis.

Perhaps not surprisingly, the biggest gap between Greek and non-Greek organizations occurred in their likelihood of holding ceremonial events, with 84% of Greek organizations holding at least one such event each semester, compared to only 32% of non-Greek organizations. These types of activities are important because formal rituals provide organizational leaders with the opportunity to explicitly describe and celebrate a group's foundational values and agenda and serve as a powerful opportunity to socialize new members.[45] Interestingly, however, Greek organizations did not exceed other types of organizations in additional activities that provide explicit socialization opportunities, such as giving a speech or distributing written materials that explain a group's common values and agenda.

To summarize these patterns, mean scores on each of these items about frequency of organizational activities were compared. The independent sample t-test analyses, reported in Table 24-1, indicate that, aside from explicit attempts to explain organizational values in speeches and pamphlets, Greek organizations were, across the board, far more active than their non-Greek counterparts on campus.

Table 24-1: Frequency of Organizational Activities that Promote Civic Skills and Identities by Greek Status

	Greek	Non-Greek				
Activity	**M (SD)**	**M (SD)**	**Difference**	**t**	**P**	**N**
Membership Meeting	4.92 (.277)	4.44 (.854)	.477	2.75	.007[a]	25/97
Membership Votes	3.88 (1.09)	2.97 (1.10)	.911	3.70	.000[b]	25/96
E-Board Meeting	4.72 (.737)	4.05 (1.12)	.668	2.83	.006[a]	25/96
Active Subcommittees	4.24 (1.13)	3.42 (1.36)	.817	2.77	.007[a]	25/97
Sponsor Educational Event	3.16 (1.21)	2.65 (1.26)	.514	1.83	.069	25/96
Sponsor Social Event	3.32 (1.15)	2.30 (1.31)	1.02	3.56	.001[a]	25/97
Sponsor Fund-raising Event	3.08 (.881)	2.19 (1.13)	.898	3.62	.000[b]	24/97
Hold Ceremonial Event	3.28 (.737)	1.91 (.969)	1.37	6.60	.000[b]	25/97
Give Speech	2.88 (1.05)	2.53 (1.10)	.354	1.45	.150	25/97
Distribute Materials	3.04 (.978)	2.69 (1.06)	.349	1.49	.140	25/97

Notes:
[a] $p < .01$
[b] $p < .001$
Question: How frequently did your organization engage in each of the following activities?

RELIANCE ON DEMOCRATIC DECISION MAKING

Simply attending meetings and sponsoring events, however, is not enough to cultivate civic identity and hone civic and political skills. Scholars argue that internal organizational dynamics matter a great deal. Groups that mimic governmental bodies in their decision-making procedures are much more likely to cultivate civic identities and hone political skills. As a result, participation in youth organizations that require the full membership to participate in decision making, for example, 4-H clubs, have a greater impact on long-term adult political participation than those that turn such decisions over to an adult coach or mentor, such as athletic teams.[46]

RSO presidents, therefore, were asked to report how frequently different approaches to decision making were used, using five answer categories that ranged from a low of fewer than once per year (coded as a 1) to a high of once per week or more (coded as a 5). Once again, Greek organizations outperformed other types of organizations, as they relied more heavily upon activities associated with democratic decision making. Most Greek presidents reported that at least once per month important organizational decision making required: consulting the organization's constitution or by-laws (64% compared to 28% for non-Greeks); calling a full membership vote (84% compared to 48%); relying upon formal rules or parliamentary procedure (63% compared to 25%); and negotiating a compromise among members (68% compared to 41%). Table 24-2 reports the independent sample t-test analyses of the mean scores on these items, which support the claim that fraternity brothers and sorority sisters are indeed far more likely than their peers to learn important civic skills that will enable them to successfully undertake future political endeavors.

Table 24-2: Members' Involvement in Democratic Decision Making by Greek Status

	Greek	Non-Greek				
Activity	**M (SD)**	**M (SD)**	**Difference**	**T**	**P**	**N**
Consult Constitution	3.76 (1.20)	2.84 (1.14)	.925	3.57	.001[a]	25/97
Full Membership	4.24 (.830)	3.32 (1.24)	.910	3.47	.001[a]	25/97
Formal Rules	3.48 (1.78)	2.26 (1.42)	1.22	3.63	.000[b]	25/97
Negotiate Compromise	3.88 (1.20)	2.88 (1.45)	1.00	3.19	.002[a]	25/97

Notes:
[a] $p < .01$
[b] $p < .001$
Question: How frequently were decisions made in each of the following ways?

Perceptions of Organizational Influence

Scholars suspect that undertaking these types of activities not only builds civic skills, but also bolsters civic and political efficacy. When members learn that they can work together to accomplish shared agendas, they can easily envision undertaking civic and political endeavors in the future. Such efficacy is bolstered when organizational activities stretch across geographic boundaries, especially in a country with a large population and geographic scale. Knowing that group members are pursuing similar agendas across all 50 states or beyond or that members can unite to achieve national influence is empowering. Indeed, Skocpol (2003) emphasizes how important federated civic organizations were in America's past precisely because they helped members learn how to coordinate efforts and achieve results across the entire country.

Hence, RSO presidents were asked a series of questions intended to measure perceptions of their organization's influence. They were asked to assess whether their organization had attempted to influence policies on campus, in the local community, or at the state/national level, as well as whether their organization had attempted to influence social values or lifestyle choices on campus, in the local community, or at the state/national level. Answer categories for these questions ranged from a low of rarely or never (coded as 1) to a high of all the time (coded as 4).

Although Greek organizations were somewhat more likely to claim that they attempted to influence campus policies at least once in a while (65% compared to 42% for non-Greek organizations), presidents of both Greek and non-Greek groups overwhelmingly claimed that they rarely or never attempted to influence local community policies (83% and 75%, respectively). Greeks' lack of interest in local policy is somewhat surprising, as local zoning, noise, and parking ordinances affect members living in off-campus fraternity and sorority houses. Interestingly, both groups claimed more interest in influencing state and national policies at least once in a while—but the percentage of presidents making this claim was nearly identical (22% and 29%, respectively). Similarly, while a substantial number of presidents from both Greek and non-Greek groups claimed that their organizations attempted to influence social values and lifestyle choices on campus (64% and 57%, respectively), they also claimed that such efforts were never or rarely undertaken in the community (55% and 65%, respectively) or beyond (64% and 66%, respectively).[47]

Voluntary associations in the United States often are founded for reasons other than influencing either political decisions or cultural values, such as organizing recreational activities or bringing together people to pursue a shared hobby, yet the organizations that have historically served as the training ground for good citizenship have focused upon influencing broader collective decisions. Therefore, it is important that at least some voluntary associations are founded to further such agendas.[48] Organizations with these types of goals appear to be relatively uncommon on CMU's campus, as even highly active Greek presidents for the most part failed to recognize that the institutional resources at their disposal could be used to explicitly influence important political decisions and cultural values.

On the other hand, these student leaders are more cognizant of the impact of their organizations' volunteer activities. RSO presidents were also asked to assess the effect of their volunteer activities at the campus, community, and state/national level. Answer categories for these questions again ranged from a low of rarely or never (coded as 1) to a high of all the time (coded as 4). While all of the RSO presidents recognized the impact of their volunteer activities, Greek presidents claimed more impact at each level. For example, Greek presidents unanimously claimed that their volunteer activities affected the campus at least once in a while, compared to 74% of non-Greek presidents. Only one Greek president failed to claim a similar impact of volunteerism at the community level, which dropped the percentage to 95%, compared to 67% of non-Greek presidents. Most notably, a higher percentage of Greek presidents (77%) claimed that their volunteer activities were felt at the state/national level than the percentage of non-Greek presidents willing to make this claim about their impacts *on campus* (74%). In comparison, only 54% of non-Greek presidents claimed that their volunteer efforts had an impact beyond the local community. Table 24-3 reports the independent sample t-test analyses of the mean differences on these three items, which confirms that the scale of Greek volunteerism outpaces that of other campus organizations.

It may be that Greek leaders fail to recognize that the same organizational structure that enables them to accomplish substantial volunteer projects can facilitate more explicit political and social influence because they are members of an overtly apolitical generation. On the other hand, Greek members who have participated in such volunteer efforts presumably are far more likely to feel confident undertaking political and social influence campaigns in the future—if and when they choose to do so. Numerous fraternity websites, for example, recruit new members with the unsubstantiated claim that 76% of all members of Congress were members of a fraternity. If this claim is accurate, it would certainly support the hypothesis that Greek volunteer activities bolster political efficacy and likelihood of participation in politics.

Table 24-3: Presidents' Perceptions of Volunteer Activities by Greek Status

	Greek	Non-Greek				
Volunteering	**M (SD)**	**M (SD)**	**Difference**	**T**	**P**	**N**
Impacts University	2.82 (.664)	2.18 (.894)	.641	3.16	.002[b]	22/96
Impacts City	2.64 (.790)	2.07 (.954)	.563	2.57	.011[a]	22/96
Impacts State/Nation	2.18 (.894)	1.62 (.814)	.561	2.85	.005[b]	22/95

Notes:
[a]p < .05
[b]p < .01
Question: How frequently have members worked together on volunteer projects that affect society at the following levels?

The data set used in this study provides the opportunity to gauge in one additional way whether such collective efforts are likely. RSO presidents were asked to assess whether their members felt obligated to address broad social and political issues. Seventy-nine percent of Greek presidents either agreed or strongly agreed with this claim, compared to only 53% of non-Greek presidents. From this, it seems likely that Greek life not only hones civic skills, but also has the potential to cultivate the efficacy and identity known to bolster lifelong political participation.

Perceptions of Bridging and Bonding Social Capital

Finally, participation in associational life provides two types of beneficial outcomes, often labeled as bonding and bridging social capital. Bonding social capital provides members with a strong identity and the benefits of a close-knit community. Group members interact regularly, learn that they can trust and rely upon one another, and develop a set of shared values and norms. While bonding social capital is overwhelmingly beneficial to the members of such close-knit groups, political scientists often view it with suspicion, as it encourages the type of in-group prejudice and disdain for others that can undermine the compromise and negotiation needed to sustain liberal democracy, especially in a highly diverse country. Such concerns are ameliorated when civil society also produces bridging social capital, which occurs when members of a group are dissimilar or when different types of groups regularly interact with one another. Members of all of the groups learn to trust, respect, and cooperate with those whose values and circumstances are different from their own.[49]

Not surprisingly, given a recruitment process that highlights exclusivity and the purposeful cultivation of close-knit relationships among members, findings suggest that members of Greek organizations have high levels of bonding social capital. For example, RSO presidents were asked whether their organizations had core values that members are encouraged to share. Seventy-six percent of Greek presidents answered this question affirmatively, compared to 53% of non-Greek presidents.

Further, RSO presidents were asked to assess statements in regard to members having a tight bond with one another and if members feel obligated to help one another. Answer categories ranged from a high of strongly agree (coded as a 4) to a low of strongly disagree (coded as a 1). Greek presidents were especially apt to strongly agree with both these claims, with 75%—compared to 42% of non-Greek presidents—strongly agreeing that members had a tight bond, and 50%—compared to 26%—strongly agreeing that members were obligated to one another. An independent sample t-test of mean scores on these items, reported in Table 24-4, supports the claim that Greeks have higher levels of bonding social capital than other types of organizational members.

Greek organizations appear to excel at fostering bonding social capital; however, Greek organizations on CMU's campus will inevitably have difficulty bridging social capital through intergroup interactions simply because campus organizations at CMU are overwhelmingly homogeneous. Greek organizations are

Table 24-4: Presidents' Perceptions of Bridging and Bonding Social Capital by Greek Status

	Greek	Non-Greek				
	M (SD)	M (SD)	Difference	T	P	N
Bonding Activities						
Members Have Tight Bond	3.75 (.442)	3.26 (.714)	.490	3.20	.002[b]	24/96
Members Are Obligated to Help	3.42 (.654)	3.06 (.704)	.355	2.24	.027[a]	24/97
Bridging Activities						
Interact Regularly, Student Groups	3.33 (.702)	3.07 (.794)	.261	1.48	.143	24/97
Interact Regularly, Community Groups	2.79 (.721)	2.77 (.743)	.018	.110	.913	24/97

Notes:
[a]$p < .05$
[b]$p < .01$
Questions: Please indicate how strongly you agree or disagree with the following statements about your fellow members. Have a tight bond with each other. Feel obligated to help one another. Regularly interact with other student groups. Regularly interact with community groups off campus.

typically segregated by gender. So, it should come as no surprise that not a single Greek president (compared to 9% of non-Greek presidents) agreed that their organizational memberships were "very different" in terms of gender.

Further, Greek presidents across the board (compared to 6% of non-Greek presidents) also avoided the label "very different" to describe their memberships' racial and ethnic diversity. Moreover, similar numbers of Greek and non-Greek presidents labeled their organizational memberships as "mixed" (42% and 40%, respectively) and "pretty much the same" (58% and 54%, respectively) in terms of racial and ethnic diversity.[50]

These results correspond to a demographic analysis of campus organizations' membership undertaken with the assistance of the Office of Institutional Research. This analysis, based on individual-level student data collected by the university, indicated that 65% of CMU campus organizations were entirely homogeneous in terms of race/ethnicity in the 2009–2010 academic year, with 58% entirely composed of white students and 7% entirely composed of minority students. In addition, even organizations with "mixed" memberships were still overwhelmingly white. To some extent, this outcome is driven by low levels of diversity on campus, as the student body is approximately 90% white. It also occurs because recently conducted focus groups to assess the campus climate for diversity revealed that minority students still experience both micro-aggressions and overt racism on campus and in the community. Focus group discussions of these issues revealed that minority students purposefully seek out ethnic and race-based organizations as a way to carve out a safe and comfortable environment on a predominantly white campus located in a predominantly white, rural community.

On a somewhat promising note, both Greek (64%) and non-Greek presidents (70%) claimed that they would like more racial and ethnic diversity within their organizations. Further, Greek presidents supported this sentiment by affirming that they also would like more help attracting more members from diverse backgrounds (60% compared to 36%). These attitudes may bode well for efforts to more successfully integrate groups in the future. Such efforts must be initiated by campus personnel, however, as both Greek (92%) and non-Greek presidents (92%) overwhelmingly report that they do not explicitly recruit diverse members.[51]

To assess whether campus groups cultivate bridging social capital through intergroup interactions, RSO presidents were asked to assess statements claiming that their groups regularly interacted with other student groups on campus and with other groups in the community. Answer categories ranged from a high of strongly agree (coded as a 4) to a low of strongly disagree (coded as a 1). Respondents' answers suggested that their groups' levels of engagement with other groups are similar, as 42% of Greek presidents and 31% of non-Greek presidents strongly agreed that they regularly interacted with campus groups, whereas only 13% of Greek presidents and 16% of non-Greek presidents strongly agreed that they regularly interacted with community groups.[52] The independent sample t-test analyses of mean scores on these times are reported in Table 24-4 and show insignificant differences between Greek and non-Greek organizations.

Even though RSO presidents reported regularly interacting with other student groups, the amount of bridging social capital generated through such efforts is unclear because the question did not ask the respondents to report the specific types of groups or the specific types of cosponsored activities. Some cosponsored activities were obviously social events jointly undertaken by fraternities and sororities. Given the traditional orientation of most sororities, however, such interactions may actually reinforce negative stereotypes about women's roles in politics and public life.

Indeed, institutional structures on campus actually discourage regular interaction among diverse groups. CMU, for example, has four different Greek councils, each comprised of an executive board that governs all chapters underneath it. The National Pan-Hellenic Conference (NPC) represents traditional social sororities, whereas the National Pan-Hellenic Council (NPHC) serves multicultural sororities. Similarly, the Multicultural Greek Council (MGC) is largely comprised of African American fraternities, whereas the Inter-Fraternity Council (IFC) represents traditional social fraternities. In short, even within the Greek governing councils, organizations are segregated by race—a move initially intended to preserve minority students' autonomy, but which also undermines efforts to cultivate bridging social capital.

On a more positive note, Greek presidents report a whole host of activities that should bolster bridging social capital. Greek presidents are, for example, more likely than non-Greek presidents to report that their organizations: have a statement on diversity in their constitutions (96% compared to 65%), encourage members to interact with diverse others (79% compared to 56%), encourage members to participate in diversity training (57% compared to 23%), and require attendance at campus diversity events (70% compared to 31%). Clearly, these commitments reflect presidents' perceptions and may not reveal racial dynamics on campus. Critics may point out that Greek commitment to diversity goals may well reflect requirements imposed by their national charters rather than a genuine effort to promote racial and ethnic tolerance. Assessing the depth and impact of these self-reported behaviors, however, is beyond the scope of this project.

Greek organizations clearly provide members with ample benefits through bonding social capital. Further, these groups engage in activities that should facilitate bridging social capital. If college personnel, including faculty, made an effort to enhance the campus infrastructure and incentives, these groups could foster integrated group activities and increase collegiate bridging social capital.

Discussion

This project began with an open-ended effort to determine whether campus student groups can enhance formal civic education efforts on campus by compensating for an important missing experience in students' natural political socialization. Given pessimistic assessments of campus groups,[53] the finding that some organizations excel at cultivating the skills, identity, and efficacy associated with long-term political participation was reassuring.

Yet, given the reputation of Greek organizations, the finding that they are the campus groups so closely associated with many of these positive outcomes is also disconcerting. Greek organizations are regularly linked to troubling behavior across the country—including an example in 2010 when fraternity pledges at Yale yelled offensive chants threatening sexual assault in front of women's dormitories and the Women's Studies Center.[54]

Some argue that such incidents are isolated,[55] but fraternities have historically created a hostile climate for women on college campuses.[56] They still cultivate heightened levels of misogyny among members, who are also more likely than any other group on campus to commit rape, believe that women will protest but want to be forced to have sex, and believe that women enjoy physically rough sex.[57]

Fraternity membership is also associated with heightened hostility toward racial and ethnic minorities. A five-wave panel study at the University of California, Los Angeles, revealed that members of traditional Greek organizations, which are still largely all-white and may serve as white-ethnic enclaves on campus, not only increased their sense of ethnic victimization, but also their opposition to an ethnically diverse campus, their belief that ethnic organizations promote separatism, their opposition to interracial marriage, and their levels of symbolic racism.[58] After an in-depth study of diversity issues on his own campus, higher education scholar Greg Tanaka (2005) similarly concluded that participation in a Greek organization enhanced students' sense of community, but this community did not extend beyond their own ethnocentric groups. He surmises,

> It would not be too great a stretch to conclude that a tendency of homogeneous Greek organizations to reinforce homogeneous definitions of community could lead to a generation of national leaders who are unable to understand, empathize with, or collaborate with people of color years after leaving college.[59]

The findings described throughout this chapter and the research on the impact of fraternities on attitudes toward women and minorities present a dilemma: the campus equivalent of civil society appears to enhance the political influence of those who are also more likely to be sexist and racist. One prominent critic of fraternities argues that colleges and universities are responsible for the hostile campus climate caused by fraternities. Historian Nicholas Syrett (2011) claims, "If colleges support organizations promoting these attitudes, they tacitly condone them as well, encouraging men to believe there is a place for such beliefs on campus." The findings from this preliminary study of civil society and campus life extend this claim beyond campus. The unwillingness of colleges and universities to address this issue and their failure to provide comparable political socialization to large numbers of other students means that they are enabling men with these types of beliefs to wield undue influence in the political process long after they leave campus.

In response to such concerns, some advocate a wholesale ban on fraternities across all US colleges and universities.[60] Indeed, several primarily small, prestigious, liberal arts colleges have either never allowed the Greek system to flourish on their campuses or have subsequently banned them.[61] On the campuses where Greek life is absent or diminished, educators should be mindful of whether comparable opportunities for civic and political socialization are widely available to members of the student body. When thinking about how to structure alternatives, however, it must be acknowledged that homogenous groups are much better at producing the social trust, shared norms, and meaningful sanctions so intertwined with the cultivation of civic identity.[62] The dilemma becomes how to produce these collective goods while avoiding the ethnocentrism and intolerance also prone to tight-knit communities.

Banning fraternities and sororities is less common at public colleges and universities, perhaps because these institutions must be more sensitive to students' First Amendment rights of association. Public and private schools alike are reluctant to excise Greeks from campus life for additional reasons. Some administrators may secretly fear the lost revenue from tuition dollars and alumni donations, whereas others are concerned that banned fraternities will simply move off campus or go underground, where they will be subject to even less oversight.[63] Others are simply convinced that the positive contributions Greeks make to their campuses outweigh the negative consequences.[64] In a 2011 *New York Times* editorial justifying his decision not to ban fraternities and sororities, Cornell University president, David J. Skorton, wrote: "The Greek system is part of our university's history and culture, and we should maintain it because at its best, it can foster friendship, community service and leadership."[65]

It is far more common to eject a local Greek chapter in response to a specific scandalous incident or policy violation than it is to dismantle the Greek system on campus altogether. Doing so en masse would be a considerable undertaking, as Greek organizations are well-represented at institutions spread across the country. The North American Inter-Fraternity Council, for example, claims to represent 75 member organizations with 5,500 chapters and 350,000 members on 800+ campuses, whereas the National Pan-Hellenic Conference claims to represent 26 member organizations with 3,031 chapters and 285,543 members on 655 campuses.[66] These patterns led one scholar who studies fraternal organizations to conclude:

> It is thus unlikely that universities will ban these organizations altogether.... While perhaps unsatisfying, the most realistic path toward positive change is for university administrations to insist on playing a larger role in regulating these organizations, and to attempt to enlist members in change efforts.[67]

Overlooked in this proposed collaboration between fraternity members and administrators are professors. Yet professors, especially those familiar with the scholarly literature on civil society, should be at the forefront of endeavors to transform campus life. Unlike administrators, whose efforts will likely focus on pragmatic (and often reactive) attempts to suppress bad behavior, insight into the role associational life has played in American democracy should produce a more nuanced approach. Scholars can understand the need to undermine the damaging norms, attitudes, and behaviors produced by tight-knit fraternal organizations on campus, but can also be sensitive to the goal of preserving and strengthening their positive, civic by-products.

Faculty whose academic disciplines help them recognize the importance of students' civic and political engagement are more likely to be proactive on behalf of the entire student body, with its range of interests, not only on behalf of Greeks. These faculty are more apt to recommend campus civil society reforms that will provide equivalent civic engagement opportunities for all students on campus and not just those associated with the Greek system.

Lastly, faculty from the social sciences will be more sensitive to the inherent tension between administrative oversight, especially at a public institution, and campus groups' autonomy. After all, the benefits of civil society emerge because groups operate outside the realm of government control, as citizens learn how to deliberate to identify their shared agendas, and discover how to organize for collective action in pursuit of those agendas. Successful transformation of campus civil society requires the "democratization of academic culture."[68] In short, student groups must be encouraged to develop and pursue their own projects and cannot be perceived simply as a convenient labor force for expert (in this case, administrative or faculty) priorities. Youth associational life in high school is most effective at cultivating civic identity and long-term political participation when adults set aside control over the substance of decisions, but provide students with a deliberative infrastructure and facilitate its use.[69] Further, the history of American civil society indicates that members who participate in these types of organization will benefit, even if they are not directly responsible for launching and maintaining them.[70] Faculty members from the social sciences seem the most likely allies for sustaining this type of deliberative infrastructure on campus.

Campus civil society will be less than ideal if students are left to their own devices. Faculty and administrators must provide guidance in order for campus organizations to live up to their full potential, supplement formal civic education, and help to transform students into good citizens. In short, civil society on campus can and should be part of the solution as attempts are made to compensate for gaps in students' natural political socialization and fully support the liberal arts and citizenship missions of institutions of higher learning.

SECTION IV

Assessing Civic Engagement Objectives and Outcomes

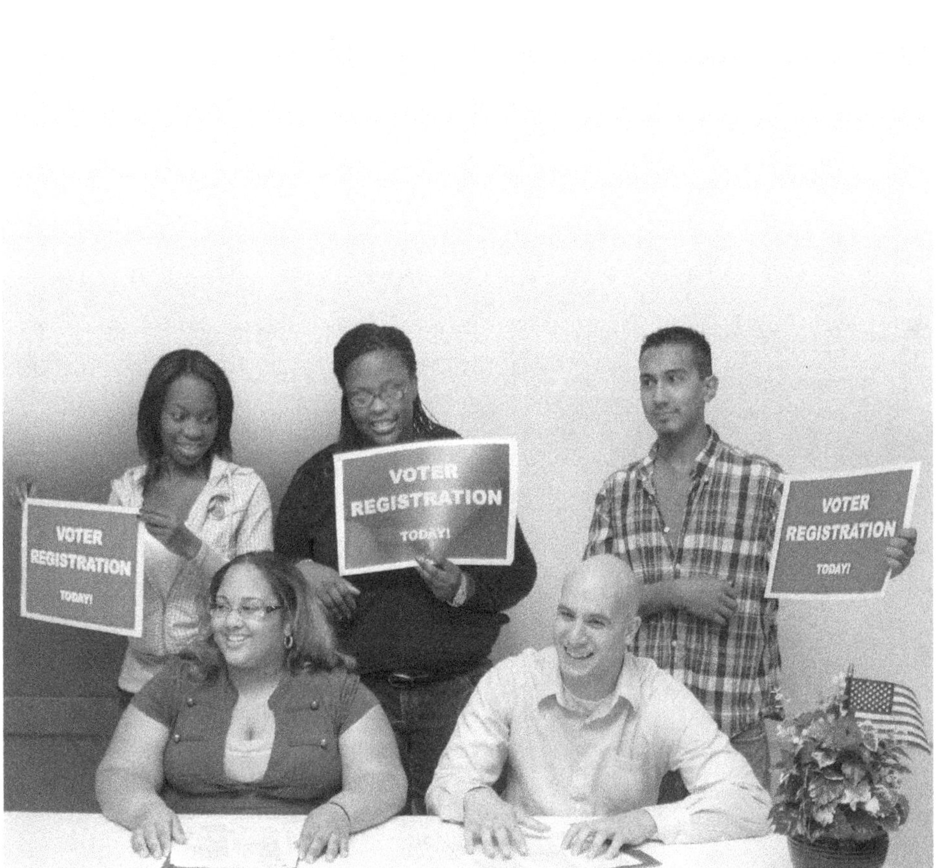

Introduction to Section IV

Assessing Civic Engagement Objectives and Outcomes

Section Four of *Teaching Civic Engagement: From Student to Active Citizen* provides helpful information about assessment designed to move political science educators forward *together* as teacher-scholars interested in developing civic and political leaders. The assessment toolkit provided in Chapter 25 describes a wide range of qualitative and quantitative options for assessment that range from simple headcounts to fully randomized multicampus field experiments, allowing readers to pick and choose an approach. It also sets forth a collection of assessment methods, based on educators' own learning, objectives, assessment needs, or research goals. Chapter 26 provides answers to some frequently asked questions about the assessment of student learning followed by an overview of (assessment) lessons learned and future directions for research highlighted in *Teaching Civic Engagement*. This chapter also includes an overview of the newly formed Consortium for Inter-Campus SoTL Research, along with a call for teacher-scholars throughout the discipline to join the consortium, pooling skills, knowledge, and resources to move civic education research forward. Finally, Chapter 27 provides an overview of assessment practices in the discipline, reviewing the assessment methods utilized in all civic education and engagement articles published in peer-reviewed political science journals in the 21st century.

Throughout this section, Bennion reviews the strengths and weaknesses of existing research and teaching on civic engagement education. In many cases, she uses chapters featured in *Teaching Civic Engagement* as examples. These chapters were selected because they provide some of the best existing models of civic engagement pedagogy across the discipline. However, the editors also acknowledge that this field is still developing in the discipline, and it is now time to consider

how political science educators can advance their pedagogical goals and refine their assessment methods. Thus, Section 4 highlights areas for improvement and calls for new and improved research. The editors hope that you will join us in our efforts to improve our collective knowledge of the best ways to educate and engage our students in the classroom, transforming them from students to active citizens and civic leaders for the future.

Assessing Civic and Political Engagement Activities: A Toolkit

25

By Elizabeth A. Bennion

This chapter is a how-to guide for assessing curricular and cocurricular activities designed to develop the knowledge, skills, and dispositions required for effective civic engagement. It describes relevant qualitative and quantitative measurement techniques and provides specific suggestions for assessing student learning and behavioral outcomes.

Institutions of higher education are facing increasing pressure to measure the impact of curricular and cocurricular activities. External accrediting agencies, such as the Higher Learning Commission, include "engagement" as a core component of re-accreditation efforts. As institutions and accrediting agencies make community involvement and citizenship development a core part of the mission of public higher education, it is important for colleges and universities to assess the effects of their efforts to foster the knowledge, skills, and dispositions required for active democratic citizenship.

Academics often view assessment as a burdensome external requirement, a time-consuming drain on resources, or an administrative or legislative excuse for enhanced control. Yet, there are many positive reasons why colleges and universities should actively encourage assessment of civic education programs and activities. There are also positive reasons for individual faculty and departments to pursue assessment opportunities. Impact assessment provides enhanced opportunities for evidence-based curricular and cocurricular programming, grant money, and donations, and increased cooperation from university, community, and legislative partners. Most important, assessment allows faculty to determine whether or not they are meeting their civic education goals as well as the effectiveness of their attempts to enhance students' civic knowledge, engagement, and orientation. Assessment also provides an opportunity to maximize the effectiveness of curricular and extracurricular programming, while aligning these activities with the larger missions of specific departments, colleges, and universities.

Further, assessment is a way to blend teaching and service with rigorous scholarship, because it provides an opportunity for scholarly presentations and publications. Too few schools actively encourage faculty to engage in the scholarship of teaching and the scholarship of application, even after the 1997 publication of Ernest Boyer's path-breaking call to action, *Scholarship Reconsidered: Priorities of the Professoriate*. Such scholarship gives faculty and staff an opportunity to inform their teaching and service, while also using teaching and service activities as fieldwork for innovative research projects that benefit themselves, their students, their universities, and their communities.

This chapter is a guide to assessing curricular and cocurricular activities designed to develop the knowledge, skills, and dispositions required for effective civic engagement. After reviewing preliminary steps that an educator should take in constructing a civic engagement course or activity, the text briefly describes relevant qualitative and quantitative measurement techniques and provides specific suggestions for assessing student learning and behavioral outcomes. This chapter is not intended to be a comprehensive guide to research methods. It is, instead, designed to help political science educators think about ways in which they can successfully assess civic engagement activities and pedagogy at the classroom, departmental, or campus level, thereby advancing understanding of the knowledge and skills students gain through specific approaches to civic education and engagement.[1]

Step 1: Select a Project

Civic education and participation can be promoted in a variety of ways. In the classroom, citizen action projects can be added to existing courses, and new engagement-based courses can be designed to allow students to practice hands-on civic and political engagement. Classes and political science clubs also can get involved in organizing campuswide engagement projects. As faculty and administrators select programs and activities to implement on their campus, they should think about the interests of their students, staff, and faculty as well as the resources at their disposal. While not all of the following apply to each case, they should consider:

- What kinds of events have been most popular in the past?
- Which campus units are already engaged in civic education and engagement activities?
- Are there enough students to sponsor a Rock the Vote concert?[2]
- Would local bands be willing to participate in a Vote Jam or Vote Slam party for free?[3]
- Is classroom-based voter registration feasible?[4]
- Are there enough student clubs to support registration tables across campus?

- Does someone on campus have the skills to design and edit a political weblog?[5]
- Does the campus or department have strong relationships with local radio stations or newspapers that would allow the creation of a regular voter education series?[6]
- Could such activities (festivals, registration drives, blogs, etc.) be incorporated into the curriculum?
- How might experiential learning activities with a civic engagement focus be incorporated into the political science major and existing courses?[7]

Faculty and administrators also should consider the full range of resources available, including partnerships among academic departments, student services, student clubs, and community organizations.

Faculty should explore these questions, and then start developing the goals that they hope to achieve by sponsoring a certain activity, taking into consideration:

- How will the selected activity (or series of activities) help faculty and students attain the previously mentioned goals or their corresponding learning objectives?
- How can the effectiveness of the program or activity in meeting these objectives be measured?

Once a project is selected, faculty should also select a series of research/assessment questions, such as:

- What will make this event or project a success?
- What criteria are being used to define success?
- How could this success be measured or documented?
- What learning outcomes are anticipated?
- How can these student learning outcomes be measured?
- How can assignments be constructed that not only fulfill traditional course learning outcomes, but also include ways to measure civic engagement learning or skill development?

A variety of methods can be used to assess short- and long-term learning, attitudinal changes, and behavioral outcomes. Pre- and postevent surveys, interviews, and focus groups are valuable tools for assessment. Because the purpose of civic education is to promote lifelong civic engagement and active citizenship, its effects may not be immediate. Longitudinal studies of alumni who participated in specific courses and projects are useful for assessing long-term impact.[8] Another long-term assessment mechanism involves a collegewide entrance and exit survey that can be compared with national surveys such as the National Survey of Student Engagement (NSSE) or the Higher Education Research Institute's (HERI) Coordinated Institutional Research Program (CIRP). Faculty should consider seeking approval for their assessment project from the institutional review board, which will allow faculty to present or publish their findings.[9]

Step 2: Select a Time Frame for Your Project

Repeated exposure to civic engagement messages and activities over a sustained period is the best way to produce long-term changes in students' attitudes and behaviors. Institutions can create a variety of one-time classroom or extracurricular activities designed to fit into a larger calendar of civic-oriented activities. Students' reactions to each event or assignment can be assessed through quantitative or qualitative instruments using postevent data collection or a pretest and posttest design. Similarly, student attitudes and learning outcomes in a single community-based learning course can be measured using a simple pretest and posttest design and employing surveys, interviews, and student reflection essays or focus groups at the beginning and the end of the course. Assignment rubrics and journal analysis can provide direct measures of student learning in civic engagement courses.[10] Alternatively, and perhaps most productively, institutions can create multisession or multiyear programs designed to immerse students in civic-oriented curricular and extracurricular events.[11]

A common freshman-year experience, a learning community, a lecture series, a civic engagement certificate, a leadership program, or a campus theme are some of the ways that colleges and universities have tried to increase connections among learners while building a coherent program focused on a common set of civic-oriented learning objectives. In such cases, longitudinal analysis is possible. A common freshman-year experience may be best assessed through a pretest and posttest of students before and after their freshman year.[12] A follow-up study of these students later in their college careers would help determine whether or not any changes observed were temporary or more enduring. A study of a coordinated, multiyear curricular infusion of civic content through general education requirements might be evaluated best through a panel study of specific students at the beginning of their academic careers and again as seniors or through a series analysis of a larger cohort of students. Student portfolios also can be used to analyze direct measures of student learning, incorporating assignments and reflections at various points in a student's academic career.

The nature of any civic education efforts as well as the nature of any assessment questions should determine the time frame for an assessment project. If the intent is to learn about reactions to a single activity or event, a short-term project is ideal. If the intent is to study changes in students' knowledge, attitudes, and behaviors over time, a longitudinal design is most appropriate. The same data collection techniques used in short-term assessment projects can be used in long-term projects, though controlling for intervening (extraneous confounding) factors may be more difficult in long-term studies of attitudinal and behavioral change. Either way, the gathering of short-term data may develop over several years into a long-term study as faculty observe the development and results of a project or course.

Step 3: Select a Research Method

Choosing a research method is central to the development of a good assessment project. Before selecting an assessment method, consider the question to be answered, the participants or phenomena to be studied, and the resources and data available. Also consider the faculty's ability to gather and analyze new data. Faculty should consider forming a learning community to review relevant literature and design a methodologically sound study that can be published as part of the growing body of research on civic education and student learning. The typical methodological choices are to use a quantitative, qualitative, or mixed-methods design. A qualitative design, such as a case study, uses qualitative data to create a narrative analysis. A quantitative design, such as a closed-ended survey, uses quantitative data to produce a statistical or numerical analysis. Alternatively, data may be collected in one form and converted to another form for analysis.[13] For example, open-ended reflection papers describing what students learned from a particular experience can be used to generate categories of responses. The papers can then be reread and coded to develop an analysis of the most frequent responses.[14] In addition, both types of data or analysis may be used to supplement one another. A quantitative analysis can provide actual numerical measurements of the effectiveness of voter education, registration, and mobilization efforts. Qualitative analysis can provide rich descriptions and interpretations of the activities from the perspective of the participants.

The purpose of the research, the type of data available, and the type of analysis desired should shape the research method. Specific quantitative objectives should be measured quantitatively. Broad research questions should be studied qualitatively. For example, the Scripps Howard Center for Civic Engagement at Northern Kentucky University (NKU) created a detailed list of specific quantitative objectives for its Step Up to the Plate: Be an Election Day Poll Worker program.[15] The objectives were to submit 150 student names to election officials, produce a 90% satisfaction rate among election administrators working with NKU students, and stimulate 70% of the student poll workers to indicate a willingness to be poll workers again in the future. Each of these objectives was detailed and specific, and easily measured through simple participant counts and surveys.

In contrast, Indiana University, Kokomo, sought to create a safe space to discuss election-related political controversies.[16] This objective is not quantifiable, but the achievement of this goal can be assessed by observing the flow of conversation at campus events or through focus groups that encourage people to talk about their feelings about the event. Even in such qualitative assessments, numbers can sometimes be helpful in assessing the event: the percentage of attendees who actually spoke in group discussions or the percentage of people answering "yes" in an anonymous survey asking whether or not they felt the event created a safe space to air diverse personal opinions could help determine whether or not most or all participants felt comfortable voicing their own questions and comments.

It is important to supplement overarching goals with specific learning objectives or research questions. Emporia State University sought to "develop a solid foundation" for participation in the democratic process and to "change the culture on campus" to be more actively engaged in the democratic process.[17] Such a broad set of goals and objectives is difficult to quantify; however, a variety of qualitative and quantitative indicators could be determined to help document the achievement of these broad goals. For example, faculty, staff, and students could work together to determine what would constitute a "solid foundation" for electoral participation, arriving at a list of knowledge, skills, and values required to pursue such activism. Instruments (surveys, interview questions, focus group themes, etc.) could then be designed to administer to students before and after the yearlong series of civic engagement events and activities. The changing campus culture could be measured using similar instruments, as well as content analysis of a campus weblog or official campus documents, including the institution's mission statement, bulletins, and promotional materials or some combination of these. Speeches by top administrators also could be examined to see how and how often they highlight civic and political engagement.

Each campus, each course, and each project has its own set of learning objectives. Good teaching requires instructors to set forth a variety of such objectives. If colleges and universities wish to provide students with the knowledge, skills, and dispositions required to become active members of the electorate, they must first decide what types of knowledge, skills, and dispositions such engaged citizenship requires. Once institutions know what it is they are seeking to teach, they can find both quantitative and qualitative ways to assess the effectiveness of their curricular and extracurricular civic education activities.

Quantitative Models

Three quantitative models are particularly appropriate for assessing the impact of campuswide efforts to register, educate, and mobilize voters. These methods include participant counts, surveys, and experiments.

Participant Counts. Participants in the American Political Science Association's (APSA) Teaching and Learning Conference civic engagement tracks have consistently argued that political science departments should work with others on campus to equip students with the combination of knowledge, skills, and attitudes required to lead civically engaged lives. Civic education and training for engagement can take place in the classroom or through extracurricular events. Campus events and activities are effective only if students actually participate in them. Participation is a necessary, though not a sufficient, requirement for transformation. As a first step toward measuring the effectiveness of campus activities, it is important to count and record the number of students participating in each civic engagement activity. Even a simple event count can provide an institution with important data. Such a count can be useful in generating and maintaining resources from departments, administrators, student government associations, and external funding agencies.

This type of participant count can be effective, particularly when assessing the impact of an on-campus voter registration drive. By counting completed registration forms, a campus can estimate the total number of students who registered. To test the effectiveness of different voter registration table locations and time frames, registration forms can be counted and recorded in each location per hour or per day. As the folks at Middle Tennessee State University discovered, it is important to coordinate efforts across campus.[18] The effectiveness of Rock the Vote, Vote Jam, and Vote Slam parties can be quickly calculated following the example of Western Kentucky University, which counted the total number of people attending each event and the total number of new and updated registration cards completed at each event.[19] This percentage yield can be compared to the registration rate (or numbers) at other events to help universities with long-term event planning.

This very basic form of assessment can be expanded to other types of civic engagement projects. For example, the extent of participation in Indiana University–Purdue University, Indianapolis's Democracy Plaza could be quickly assessed by counting the number of messages (in unique handwriting) posted on the outside permanent blackboards each week or each day.[20] (Of course, a content analysis of the entries would be required to assess the *quality* of the dialogue and nature of the ideas expressed in this open venue.)[21] Participation in an American Democracy Project weblog or interactive website[22] can be assessed by counting the number of contributors to the site each week. This number can even be disaggregated to compare rates of student, faculty, and community member postings. With proper software, readership levels also can be tracked by accessing the number of hits on the site and on particular pieces. This is the most basic form of assessment taking place at Indiana University, South Bend,[23] and the University of Wisconsin, River Falls,[24] and is easy to do.

Participant counts can provide information about the number of people attending events or contributing to a campus dialogue, but they tell little about who these people are, how they are responding to various events, or what they are learning. For many voter education events, supplementing a participant count with brief, self-administered participant surveys can help a campus better understand who is attending each event and how satisfied participants are with event quality. Surveys also can help provide an understanding of what participants hoped to gain from their participation in specific courses or events and whether or not they believe they have learned anything useful. By collecting such data through these surveys, a campus can assess the effectiveness of its efforts to expose students to new information about civic engagement and voting. In addition, survey data can be useful in developing a comprehensive plan for student education and engagement.

Closed-ended Surveys. Surveys can be used to gather data on students' knowledge, attitudes, opinions, and behavior. In closed-ended questions, respondents are asked to select their answer from among a list provided. The list of response categories provided should be both exhaustive and mutually exclusive.[25] In other words, the list should include all possible responses expected, and respondents should not feel compelled to select more than one—unless the evaluator specifically wants the respondent to check all that apply. Closed-ended questions provide uniformity of responses and are easily processed. In contrast, open-ended responses must be coded prior to data entry, and some respondents may give answers that are difficult to code or irrelevant to the assessment question.

Survey questionnaire items must be clear, precise, and unambiguous.[26] When designing a questionnaire, faculty must:

1. make items clear
2. avoid double-barreled questions
3. ensure respondents' competency to answer the questions asked
4. ask relevant questions
5. avoid biased terms
6. avoid negative terms
7. think carefully about question order

Double-barreled questions ask for a single answer to a combination of questions. For example, respondents might be asked to agree or disagree with the statement: "The United States should abolish the Electoral College and use a proportional representation (PR) system." Though some people might agree with this statement, others might wish to abolish the Electoral College yet reject the PR system as the best alternative. Moreover, some respondents may not understand the PR system well enough to answer the question. Similarly, asking about something respondents have never thought about before may generate "doorstep opinions"—opinions made up for the sake of the survey that fail to reflect any genuine underlying attitude. Providing a "don't know" or "haven't thought much about this" option helps limit the number of doorstep opinions a survey generates.

Specific words may carry negative connotations that skew results to questions about the public's support for specific policies. Similarly, stating that a particular public figure or political party supports or opposes a particular program may bias results by causing respondents to register their like or dislike for the individual or party rather than the policy or campaign proposal respondents are being asked to evaluate. Including negation in a "yes" or "no" question (e.g., "A candidate should *not* run negative ads." or "Candidates should be *prohibited* from running negative ads.") also can create misunderstandings among respondents.

Lastly, question order should be carefully considered for possible framing or cueing effects within the questionnaire. Asking respondents how important it is for citizens to vote in a democracy before asking them if they voted in the last election will almost certainly increase the amount of overreporting among people claiming to vote who did not, in fact, cast a ballot. Asking about a particular problem before asking respondents about the most important problems facing a city, state, or the nation will produce an unusually high number of respondents' demonstrating concern about the problem identified in earlier survey questions. Similarly, asking questions about the economy and then asking respondents whether or not they approve of the job the president is doing in office will bias results in ways that reflect citizens' attitudes toward the economy. It is a good idea to test different versions of a questionnaire with a small subset of the students before using it to officially assess student learning outcomes.

A good closed-ended survey item may take the form of a statement rather than a question. If a particular attitude or behavior can be summarized in a brief statement, respondents can be asked whether they agree or disagree with the statement using a Likert scale ranging from "strongly agree" to "strongly disagree" or from "frequently" to "never." If a single survey is administered after a class session, course, workshop, lecture, internship, field experience, or forum, students can be asked to report their own beliefs about whether or not these activities shaped their attitudes toward politics and their propensity to vote. They also can be asked specific factual questions about the voting process or local, state, and national government and politics or some combination of these. Ideally, students will be given pre- and postsurveys. In this case, students should complete a survey both before and after a specific event, course, semester, or series of activities.[27]

Pre- and posttest surveys are especially effective at measuring students' achievement of specific learning objectives in a particular course. Indeed, survey methodology can even be incorporated into a quasi-experiment to test the effectiveness of a new civic engagement module within an existing class. The pre- and postassessment surveys of Castleton State College of Vermont students provides an excellent example of this assessment design.[28] The surveys of 120 first-year students participating in the American Democracy Project (ADP) Learning Community were compared to the pre- and postsurveys of 94 non-ADP first-year students. By administering presemester surveys to both groups, evaluators could account for preexisting differences between the groups. This design allowed for a comparison of student attitudes before and after participating in the ADP Learning Community, as well as comparisons with the non-ADP group. The results suggested that learning communities can be a highly effective way of enhancing students' civic outlook and engagement.[29]

Longer-term studies measuring the cumulative effect of the college experience might even administer the pretest upon admission and the posttest upon graduation. Follow-up studies can be conducted with alumni five or 10 years after graduation. Longitudinal and panel studies are particularly appropriate because of the concern political scientists have about the lasting effects of students' college experiences. The pre-event survey establishes baseline data, whereas the postevent survey detects change in students' attitudes toward politics, including levels of knowledge, efficacy, and eagerness to participate in the democratic process. Data from a specific institution can be obtained through a survey designed by the institution or a national survey, such as the National Survey of Student Engagement (NSSE).[30] Campus results also can be compared to previous surveys at the same institution or to similar institutions regionally and nationally.[31]

Field Experiments. Surveys are often a very good source of data, but they rely upon students self-reporting their attitudes and behavior. A senior exit survey or interview might encounter problems caused by improper recollection or inaccurate reporting. This problem emerges particularly with voting behavior. In the

1990s, the gap between official voter turnout in presidential elections and reported turnout in the American National Election Studies (ANES) was more than 20 points.[32] While only half of all respondents actually voted, almost 75% of those surveyed reported doing so. Students who overreport voting also may overreport participation in election-oriented campus activities such as voter registration drives and candidate forums. If so, these estimates are biased because they overstate the effectiveness of campus efforts to register and mobilize voters. In addition, the relationship between the independent variable (i.e., voting) and the dependent variables (i.e., participation in a variety of campus-based activities) could be spurious. Both campus engagement and voting behavior could be caused by other variables not accounted for by the statistical model.

Randomized field experiments can overcome both problems by moving away from self-reported contact with voter education or mobilization campaigns and self-reported voter registration or turnout.[33] Students are assigned to particular "treatments," and their voting behavior is tracked through official voter files. Random assignment ensures that students in the control group will be similar to students in the treatment group(s) in terms of gender, age, race, ideology, partisanship, and other politically relevant characteristics. All external factors will affect both groups, allowing researchers to isolate the effects of the treatment. By randomly assigning students to a control group or a contact group, assessment teams can actually measure the effectiveness of specific efforts to educate, register, and mobilize voters. Results can be analyzed for a single institution[34] or across institutions[35] as long as a common protocol is followed.

New York State requires colleges and universities to mail every student a voter registration form. However, in other states, universities could mail voter registration forms to a randomly selected group of students and then check voter registration records to determine which of these students registered to vote.[36] Similarly, student volunteers could make get-out-the-vote calls to a randomly selected group of students. Researchers on campus could then match phone contact to actual voter turnout.[37] Any number of experiments could be designed on a college campus. Randomly selected students could be invited to attend particular events. These activities could be followed by surveys of both the contact and control groups or matched to voter records to determine the actual effect of such activities on voter turnout. Field experiments are superior to surveys for determining a cause-and-effect relationship. Students may canvass local neighborhoods in community-based field experiments, which would allow them to learn the impact of their own mobilization efforts, while also allowing for follow-up surveys that test changes in students' knowledge about and attitudes toward campaigns and elections.[38]

Despite these significant advantages, field experiments are limited in the number of variables they can examine simultaneously and are not always practical to administer. Researchers must consider the feasibility of randomizing the treatment and the availability of behavioral records, such as voter turnout records, course grades, and postcollege employment records, when designing such experiments. Large courses with multiple sections, civic education training modules, or educational opportunities, and educational institutions such as charter schools or magnet schools that use a lottery system to determine admission lend themselves well to randomized field experiments.[39]

Qualitative Models

Qualitative research is a method of data collection and analysis that is nonquantitative or not quantifiable.[40] The data are usually gathered using less-structured research instruments that utilize open-ended questions. Though the reliability of qualitative research results is much lower than that for the results calculated in quantitative research, qualitative research can take a more comprehensive look at the behaviors, attitudes, and motivations behind responses.

In a qualitative study, research questions rather than specific quantifiable objectives or hypotheses should be stated.[41] The researcher develops a central assessment question (or questions) and several associated questions. These questions are explored in open-ended surveys, interviews, and observations. Three qualitative techniques are particularly appropriate for assessing the impact of campuswide efforts to educate and engage students: open-ended survey questions, focus groups, and in-depth interviews.

Open-ended Survey Questions. Qualitative data provide detailed information about students' reactions to events. Closed-ended questions reduce the number of irrelevant responses, but they also may overlook some important responses that the evaluator did not anticipate. Open-ended questions allow respondents to interpret a question in their own way and to decide which facts and observations they deem most relevant. When designing an open-ended survey, the researcher must be very strategic and think carefully about how each question relates to the overall assessment questions and goals. However, the number of questions should be limited to avoid losing the respondents' attention and willingness to respond.

When constructing qualitative survey questions, ensure that the questions will solicit useful information. In other words, take care to compose questions that do not invite the respondent to answer simply "yes" or "no" or just provide a brief three- or four-word answer. By the same token, if questions are too broad, the responses may not provide the specific information needed to properly assess an event. For example, rather than asking if a student enjoyed attending a Debate Watch, ask what the student learned about the candidates through watching the debates. Instead of asking whether or not a student learned anything from a particular speaker, ask the student to list three specific things that he or she learned while listening to the speaker's presentation. In addition, the rules of question wording and placement discussed earlier for closed-ended surveys apply to open-ended questions.

Open-ended surveys can be self-administered based on a series of questions delivered by mail or email or conducted as phone interviews. For example, the Carnegie Foundation designed an open-ended phone interview for its Political Engagement Project (PEP). The project examined courses and programs that use various forms of experiential civic education at the college level, including service-learning, internships, semesters in Washington, DC, visiting speakers, simulations, collaborative social research project, and living/learning communities (see Chapter 4 for more details). The interview consisted of 24 open-ended survey questions that measured students' goals for the political engagement course, program, or experience; reactions to the course/program; perspective on the course/program pedagogies and experiences; perspectives on the course/program goals; assessment of the impact of the course/program; and responses to dealing with conflict. Because the survey was quite long, it made more sense to administer it as a phone interview than to rely on students to handwrite or type answers to all 24 questions. (In fact, many of the questions had several parts, resulting in a total of 35 potential questions.)

The PEP questionnaire was designed to allow students themselves to assess the impact of the experience. For example, students were asked:

- Did the experience change the way you think about what counts as politics or what it means to be politically involved?
- If so, how—what did you think before, and what do you think now?
- If not, what do these ideas mean to you?
- Is there anything important you learned in terms of your political knowledge or understanding of politics?
- If so, what and how did you learn it?
- Did your experiences in the course/program change your attitude toward politics—making you feel more of less connected with it, more optimistic or pessimistic that there is a way for you to connect, more confident of yourself and your ability to contribute?

As previously mentioned, such open-ended questions can be included in a written survey or administered via telephone or face-to-face interview. Open-ended surveys or interviews also can be supplemented by closed-ended surveys, as is the case with the Carnegie study.

In-depth Interviews. Interviewers typically talk with one respondent at a time when conducting in-depth interviews. An interview should be structured so that all respondents have a similar experience from the beginning to the end.[42] The questions do not have to be so strictly regimented that the general flow of conversation is interrupted, but a common theme or a common set of basic questions should exist for all participants. Some interviews are tightly structured (as in the example of the PEP Student Phone Interview Protocol); others, however, may be loosely structured, with a list of general questions or themes to discuss. A small number of loosely structured interviews can be used to generate research/assessment questions for future investigation. Such loosely structured interviews allow the most freedom for respondents to develop their own thoughts and follow their own thought processes, but they also run the risk of creating a long transcript that contains little information relevant to actual assessment questions. Some basic guidelines for interviews are as follows[43]:

1. Listen more, talk less.
2. Follow up on what participants say, and ask questions if you do not understand a response.
3. Avoid leading questions by asking open-ended questions instead.
4. Do not interrupt a respondent.
5. Keep participants focused and ask for concrete details.
6. Tolerate silence to give a participant time to think.
7. Do not be judgmental about participants' views or beliefs.
8. Do not debate with participants, simply record responses.

Data can be recorded by taking notes during the interview, writing up notes after an interview, or audio- or videotaping the interview for later transcription. The latter is usually the best and most accurate choice for interviews, though notes can still be taken to highlight key points made during the interview.

Focus Groups. Focus groups are group interviews that involve five to 10 people. The group interview is semistructured around a small set of themes of interest to the evaluator. The advice for single-person interviews applies to focus groups, but focus group facilitators must be particularly vigilant to strike a careful balance between keeping participants on track and allowing group dynamics to determine the flow of comments. This balance can be difficult as facilitators try to allow a natural rhythm and exchange of ideas while also ensuring that all participants are encouraged to share their views.

Focus groups have the advantage of efficiency in getting information from a number of people. The interactive group setting may stimulate new ideas and observations, while allowing evaluators to observe group dynamics. Notes can be taken during or immediately after a focus group, or the session can be videotaped for later review and transcription. The facilitator should keep the main research questions in mind and guide the discussion, making sure to touch upon relevant themes and questions. The discussion itself can be a learning experience for the participants as well as the evaluator. Events such as postfilm discussions lend themselves well to this approach because the group discussion is both part of the learning experience and part of the assessment process. Focus groups could be used to gather detailed information about a particular experience in a freshmen learning community or to ask students to consider both past and present reactions to similar events. In addition, focus groups can be useful in a mixed-methods study. The group can identify important themes and research questions for further (often quantitative) research.

Mixed-Methods Approaches

The ideal form of assessment for civic education and engagement outcomes includes a combination of quantitative and qualitative methods. This form of assessment is called a mixed-methods approach. A mixed-methods approach offers a range of perspectives on a program's processes and outcomes. Benefits of a mixed-method approach include:[44]

1. It increases the validity of findings by allowing an examination of the same event or learning experience in different ways.
2. It can result in better data collection instruments.
3. It promotes greater understanding of findings.
4. It offers something for everyone.

This process of looking at different data sources, called "triangulation," is the main advantage of the mixed-method approach.[45] For example, it is helpful to conduct focus groups to aid in the construction a questionnaire that will be distributed among a larger group of participants at a later date. Quantitative data can indicate the amount of change that occurred in student attitudes or behavior, whereas qualitative data can help provide an understanding of why change occurred. Both can be equally important. A focus group can lead to the construction of a closed-ended survey, which can be followed by in-depth interviewing to increase the validity and reliability of the research. In addition, various offices on campus, such as Student Affairs or Academic Affairs, may have different interests in the data. The chief academic officer(s) may be interested in hard facts and figures on the number of students reached by an initiative for university reports. In contrast, the chief student affairs officer(s) may be more interested in hearing what students say about a particular program in order to plan future campus programming. Using different methods of assessment allows the competing demands of different organizations to be met. More important, a mixed-methods approach provides the opportunity to continually build upon the strengths of each type of data collection and minimize the weaknesses of any single approach.[46]

Data also may be collected in one form and converted to another form for analysis. As explained earlier, open-ended reflection papers describing what students learned from a particular experience can be used to generate categories of responses for follow-up closed-ended surveys. Alternatively, the content analysis of student reflection papers, speeches, comments, or interview transcripts can be quantified to list the number of times students mentioned particular skills, values, behaviors, or beliefs. Content analysis of campus or local newspapers, radio stations, or television stations can include a quantitative analysis of the times specific words are mentioned or subjects are covered, or the number of media hits a specific program or activity generates, as well as a qualitative analysis of the nature and quality of the news coverage. Indeed, even some of these data can be quantified to reflect the balance of positive versus negative news stories, or the number of times faculty or administrators were interviewed as opposed to students.

Assessment Tips: Best Practices

As faculty design a course, event, or activity, they need to be sure to identify clear learning objectives and to consider how best to assess the effectiveness of their approach to educate and engage students. An assessment design should be part of the course design, rather than an afterthought. To maximize the ability to demonstrate learning, growth, and change, faculty should keep the following tips in mind:

- Use a pre-test/post-test design.
- Combine both indirect and direct measures of learning outcomes.
- Use a control group appropriate to the comparison group to allow the isolation of the effects of a specific intervention.
- Consider working with other instructors at an institution or across institutions to expand the sample size.
- Conduct a longitudinal analysis using follow-up surveys, calls, or focus groups to measure long-term learning outcomes.
- Use national surveys (e.g., GSS, NES, NSSE, HERI) to compare specific student groups to those at other institutions.

Such benchmarking need not be confined to large or long-term studies. One can compare one's own students, a department's students, or a single institution's students to students nationwide at any given point in time.

Large-scale, multicampus research projects should be developed to provide additional information about the effectiveness of a wide range of programs that achieve civic education goals. Political scientists are, perhaps, best positioned to do this kind of collaborative work. The questions that guide their discipline, their academic training, and their interest in an informed and engaged citizenry allow them to combine their teaching, research, and service commitments to produce important studies of interest to scholars, political practitioners, and university administrators. Using their disciplinary research tools to assess the effectiveness of civic education efforts is crucial to the success of this enterprise and the vitality of political science education in the 21st century.

Civic Engagement Research in Political Science Journals: An Overview of Assessment Techniques

26

By Elizabeth A. Bennion and Hannah M. Dill

The previous chapter presented an overview of assessment fundamentals, including a toolkit for assessing civic engagement courses and activities. This chapter takes a broader disciplinary perspective, providing a brief overview of civic education assessment efforts in political science. It provides a summary of civic education research published in disciplinary journals to determine the current state of the discipline and offers suggestions about how to move forward as a community of teacher-scholars interested in civic learning outcomes.

There are currently two political science journals that publish the scholarship of teaching and learning: *PS: Political Science & Politics* and the *Journal of Political Science Education*. Both publish articles by faculty teaching in (or across) various subfields within the discipline. The focus of some, but not all, of these articles is civic education and engagement efforts.

PS: Political Science & Politics

PS: Political Science & Politics—the peer-reviewed "journal of record" for the profession—was first published in 1968. The journal, which focuses on contemporary politics, teaching, and the discipline, first introduced a section on teaching, "The Political Science Teacher," in March 1991. This was renamed "The Teacher" in December 1991. A total of 246 articles have been published in "The Teacher" since 2000, with 8.9% of them focused on civic engagement, representing the work of 33 teacher-scholars. These articles include discussions of service-learning, civic engagement, political engagement, and civic skills (see Table 26-1).

To determine which articles focused on civic engagement and service-learning activities, each article published in "The Teacher" section of *PS: Political Science & Politics* was evaluated to determine if it focused on any of the subjects (e.g., civic engagement or service-learning) listed earlier. First, each title was checked to see if any of the key terms were mentioned. If so, this article was included in the "title" column of Table 26-1 for each term that appeared in the title. Next, the abstract of each remaining article was reviewed to see if any of the key terms (or related terms) appeared in the abstract. If the abstract included any of the key terms, it was recorded in the "abstract" row under each of the key terms in Table 26-1. If the abstract did not contain a discussion of any of the key terms, the article was either marked "inapplicable" or searched in full, depending upon whether the abstract included a discussion of matters relevant to civic education and engagement. To avoid double-counting, an article containing a discussion of a key term in the title was not counted again as including that term in the abstract and content. The same is true for articles that included each term in the abstract. If the subject is listed under "content," the term is only mentioned in the full text of the article, and not in the title or abstract. Indicating where the civic engagement terms were found in the text provides a clearer picture of the focus of each article and the centrality of specific civic engagement themes.

As Table 26-2 documents, half of the articles reported the results of classroom interventions on college campuses. Some of the interventions included students in

Table 26-1: *PS* Article Content

Subject Matter	Number of Articles	Percentage of Civic Engagement Articles (N = 22)
Civic Skill	1	4.5
Title	1	
Abstract	0	
Content	0	
Civic Engagement	13	59.1
Title	3	
Abstract	3	
Content	7	
Political Engagement	5	22.7
Title	3	
Abstract	0	
Content	2	
Political Skills	0	0
—	—	—
Service Learning	15	68.1
Title	7	
Abstract	4	
Content	4	

an international relations course working with a nongovernmental organization to provide welcome packages to refugee families, students in a citizenship and democracy course working on research with grassroots organizations to improve organizational structure and efficiency, and students in a government and political society course volunteering with local government service agencies. Interventions reported in the published articles took place in a single classroom or in multiple classrooms. Most describe the work of a single instructor; two projects incorporated multiple instructors.

Not all published work focused on classroom-based interventions or teaching strategies. Almost one-third of the articles presented theoretical pieces or meta-analysis of existing literature. Finally, several articles reported the effect of student activities outside the classroom or surveys measuring broader campus climates. For example, one article focused on a graduate and undergraduate student research team formed to organize and carry out a campuswide service-learning project. The project brought together community members, faculty, and students to renovate a campus building with sustainable features. Students also pursued collective and individual independent research projects that focused on sustainable methods, finding funding sources and creating programs on campus. Another study used surveys to gauge the effectiveness of a series of college student get-out-the-vote presentations on their high school audience members. Another reported the results of a survey of the student body at a mid-sized Midwestern campus, comparing campus results on the National Study of Student Engagement (NSSE) to national NSSE and CPS (Comparative Political Science) data. A final article surveyed political science professors about their views in regard to citizenship education.

Of the 11 articles that actually tested the effects of specific teaching techniques or classroom interventions, seven employed surveys to assess students'

Table 26-2: *PS* Intervention Type

Intervention	Number(22)	Percentage
No New Empirical Data (theoretical piece or meta-analysis)	7	31.8
Single Classroom Instructor	9	40.9
Single Instructor, Single Classroom	6	27.3
Single Instructor, Multiple Classrooms	1	
Single Instructor, Single Course, Different Students Studied over Time	2	
Multiple Classroom Instructors	2	9.1
Multiple Instructors, Multiple Classrooms, Single Campus	2	
Other	4	18.2
Out-of-class Student Engagement (e.g., service projects, high school presentations)	2	9.1
Survey-only (e.g., faculty/graduate assistant survey, student body survey)	2	9.1

Table 26-3: *PS* Assessment Methods

Assessment Methods	Number of Articles with Classroom Interventions	Number of Articles with Nonclassroom-Based Interventions	Percentage of Civic Engagement Articles (N=22)
Instructor Surveys	8	2	45.5
Post-, Open-Ended	0	1	
Post-, Closed-Ended	1	0	
Pre-, Post-, Closed-Ended	5	0	
Pre-, Post-, Mixed	2	1	
Course Evaluations	2	0	9.1
Postcourse, Open-Ended	2	0	
Reflections	5	1	27.3
Postintervention	1	0	
Pre-, Mid-, Postintervention	4	1	
Course Assignments	3	0	13.6
Postintervention Test Scores	1	0	
Pre-, Postintervention Written Work	1	0	
Pre-, Postintervention Written Work and Test Scores	1	0	
Interviews	0	1	4.5
Postintervention	0	1	
Other (interviews from agents at a service-learning agency)	1	0	4.5
No Assessment of New Intervention (8) (theoretical article, meta-analysis, analysis of national survey data study of student body)	NA	NA	36.4

perceived learning outcomes, five used student reflections expressed in papers or journals to assess student learning outcomes, and three used instructor-assigned tests or papers to provide direct measures of learning. Following best practices, most authors used both pre- and postcourse surveys to measure changes in students' knowledge and attitudes, whereas one relied solely on students' responses to postcourse surveys, including students' own perceptions of the impact of the course on their future attitudes and behavior. No interviews or focus groups were employed in published studies that reported the effects of classroom interventions. However, interviews were used to evaluate the learning outcomes of the graduate and undergraduate service-learning research team previously highlighted.

Table 26-4: Single versus Mixed Methods Approaches in *PS*

Assessment Methods	Number of Articles with Classroom Interventions	Number of Articles with Nonclassroom-Based Interventions	Percentage of Civic Engagement Articles (N=22)
Single Method	6	3	40.9
Instructor-Created Surveys	4	3	
Course Evaluations	1	0	
Student Reflections	1	0	
Mixed Methods	4	1	22.7
Survey, Student Reflections, Course Assignment, Agency Evaluations	1	0	
Survey, Student Reflections, Control	1	0	
Survey, Student Reflections, Course Assignment	1	0	
Course Evaluations, Student Reflections, Course Assignments	1	0	
Interviews, Reflections	0	1	
No Course/Campus Intervention Assessed (8)	NA	NA	36.4

Five Lessons Learned from the *PS* Review

Seven areas of weakness are evident based on this review of civic education and engagement articles published in *PS*. They are:

1. a lack of focus on political engagement and skill development
2. an overemphasis on single-classroom research
3. an overreliance on self-reported data
4. a scarcity of studies employing rigorous *qualitative* methods to better study students' own understandings of their experiences
5. an overreliance on single assessment methods
6. a paucity of research using explicit benchmarks or comparisons to national data
7. a lack of longitudinal studies that test what political scientists really want to know, that is, the long-term effect of their work, including the degree to which their students remain engaged throughout their lives

First, relatively few articles focused explicitly on the development of political engagement or skills, and only one focused specifically on the development of civic skills rather than a more general sense of engagement in public life (see Table 26-1).

This fact highlights a shortcoming of current work in the field. Political scientists promoting civic engagement often are encouraging the same type of engagement promoted in other disciplines, while avoiding an explicit focus on hands-on *political* skill development and experiences. As discussed in Chapter 1, there is no bright-line cut-off between political engagement and civic engagement, and, in fact, feminist theorists have criticized political science as a discipline for making the political work of women invisible by defining it as nonpolitical. At the same time, studies published since the 1990s show a tendency among many young people to reject politics in favor of (what they see as) less political forms of engagement, including volunteerism.[1] Many young people do not view politics as a way to solve problems or make a positive difference in their communities.[2]

Political scientists should continue to develop a collective understanding of the unique contributions of their discipline—and their responsibility to encourage students to develop attitudes, skills, and knowledge that prepare them for future political engagement and leadership. In fact, several of the projects highlighted earlier (e.g., working with an NGO or a local governmental agency) do seem designed to develop political skills, yet the instructors do not discuss the learning objectives of the course in these terms. Though this volume makes strides in this direction, it also highlights that political science as a discipline has yet to agree about what those skills are or to create a central repository of teaching ideas and assessment rubrics[3] to determine whether students are gaining such skills through their work with a specific department or university. Political scientists should work to move students "from community engagement to political engagement."[4]

Second, most classroom-based studies focus on a single instructor teaching a single course. Very few articles reported on collaborative projects among multiple instructors in multiple classrooms. None reported the results of multicampus pedagogical research. To move forward with the scholarship of civic engagement pedagogies, additional collaborative projects are needed that use standardized interventions and assessment instruments. A single instructor is often assessing students' work herself or himself, introducing potential bias. At a bare minimum, a rubric should be provided to at least two coders to measure intercoder reliability.

Another approach is to employ a standardized curriculum and assessment rubric for different instructors teaching the same course within the same institution. The multi-instructor, single-campus studies in *PS* did not use this level of standardization. Doing so could help determine whether learning outcomes for the course are consistent across instructors and classes. (Different interventions also could be tried in different sections of the course to test whether experiential learning, for example, affects student learning outcomes.) In addition, standardized rubrics could be used by professors teaching different courses within an institution. Recognizing that learning outcomes and program assessments are curricular, rather than course-specific, more systematic studies of programmatic learning outcomes are needed. Long-term civic learning relies upon multiple learning opportunities, as the chapters in Section 3 argue, rather than a single course or activity. Finally, such rubrics can also be used—along with a common intervention—by multiple professors at multiple institutions to determine whether the results of specific high-impact experiences and teaching practices are consistent and generalizable across instructors and institutions.

Third, most studies relied upon indirect rather than direct measures of student learning, especially in the form of student self-reports. Only four articles provided direct evidence of student learning, as measured by student work and supervisor evaluations.

Fourth, there is very little in-depth qualitative research on civic engagement pedagogy being published. This absence of literature may reflect an ongoing disciplinary bias toward quantitative (and survey) research, but more likely reflects the lack of rigorous qualitative and mixed-methods research being conducted. In our (unpublished) review of papers presented as part of the APSA's Teaching and Learning Conference civic engagement track, the authors of this chapter discovered many "show and tell" pieces that lacked quantitative data and conflated qualitative data with instructor impressions of a course or general student comments analyzed without respect to specific learning objectives or standardized rubrics. To move forward with the scholarship of "teaching and learning (SoTL) in the area of civic education and engagement, a mixed-methods approach that combines large-scale, multicampus quantitative research with in-depth interviews, focus groups, and rubric-guided analysis of student work and reflections is needed.

Fifth, too many studies were based on a single assessment method (see Table 26-4). As stated earlier, a greater variety of evidence would increase the ability of political scientists to measure student learning outcomes. Lee Shulman has called this the "union of insufficiencies."[5] Each assessment has deficiencies, but together they provide a more complete picture of student growth and achievement, and different assessment tools are better at measuring different learning objectives.[6] In addition, the use of different assessment techniques acknowledges the variety of prior knowledge, cultural experiences, and learning styles that students bring to the classroom. This is especially important when making claims about student learning using class assignments. Linda Suskie provides several examples in her "Common Sense Guide" to classroom assessment.[7] Poor writers who can easily visualize concepts will demonstrate knowledge of a complex concept if they can draw a diagram rather than write an explanation. Students from a culture that values collaboration may learn more from working with others than by studying alone. They may better demonstrate their understanding if they can work with others on a group presentation rather than make a solo presentation. Poor test takers who are very creative may better demonstrate their understanding if they can create a video rather than take a test.[8] The studies featured in *PS* were not yet using assessment mechanisms that cater to a full range of learning styles. Admittedly, reviewers for a peer-reviewed journal might quibble with the fact that an author used different assessment tools for different students, questioning the ability to provide a standardized rubric or scoring mechanism across different types of measures. Political scientists need to have this discussion within and across disciplines.

Sixth, and perhaps of greatest concern, is the fact that few studies actually answered the question that educators really care about. Time constraints, resource constraints, logistic concerns, and publication requirements all push educators toward "one-and-done" studies that overestimate the impact of a single course or intervention on a students' long-term political behavior. The ultimate goal of assessment is to provide comprehensive, long-term evidence of student achievement. In the case of civic education courses and curricula, the goal is to produce citizens equipped with the values, skills, and knowledge required to make a meaningful difference in their communities. To know whether this goal is being achieved, researchers need to know more about the long-term learning and accomplishments of graduates. What do they know, and what can they do at the end of the program? Finding out about their perceptions, attitudes, and skills five years after graduation, on the job, in graduate school, or throughout a student's life is difficult, but important to determining whether educators are achieving their overarching goal.

The Journal of Political Science Education

In recent years, the discipline's commitment to the scholarship of teaching and learning has grown, resulting in an annual Teaching and Learning Conference and a scholarly journal devoted exclusively to the publication of research on teaching and learning in political science. The advocacy efforts of faculty within the Political Science Education section of the APSA and the support of Executive Director Michael Brintnall moved these projects forward. The *Journal of Political Science Education* (*JPSE*) was first published in 2005. A total of 161 articles have been published in *JPSE* since 2005, with 23.6% of these focused on civic engagement. The articles represent the work of 63 teacher-scholars. They include discussions of service-learning, civic engagement, political engagement, and civic skills and political skills (see Table 26-5).

As was the case for the articles published in *PS*, most authors described their objective as promoting civic engagement through service-learning; however, a larger percentage of *JPSE* authors (45%) indicated that they were intentionally trying to foster explicitly political engagement. This number is encouraging, as is the explicit focus on civic and political skills in several *JPSE* articles.

Approximately two-thirds of the articles reported the results of classroom interventions on college campuses . Some of these interventions included students working on political campaigns, students in a research methods course conducting research for a community organization, and students preparing printed voting guides and fact checks for an online informational blog. Interventions took place in a single classroom or in multiple classrooms. As in the case of *PS*, most *JPSE* articles described the work of a single instructor, though several incorporated multiple instructors. *JPSE* has published more multicourse and multi-instructor research than *PS*. This number includes three articles that report the results of multicampus research projects, a research design which we the chapter authors would like to see more of in the future (see Table 26-6).

Table 26-5: *JPSE* Article Content

Subject Matter	Number of Articles	Percentage of Civic Engagement Articles (N = 38)
Civic Skill	4	10.5
Title	0	
Abstract	2	
Content	2	
Civic Engagement	25	65.8
Title	8	
Abstract	14	
Content	3	
Political Engagement	17	44.7
Title	3	
Abstract	5	
Contact	9	
Political Skills	5	13.2
Title	1	
Abstract	1	
Content	3	
Service Learning	24	63.2
Title	8	
Abstract	6	
Content	10	

As Table 26-6 shows, approximately 18.4% of the civic engagement articles published in the *JPSE* presented theoretical pieces of meta-analysis of existing literature. This number was lower than the approximately one-third of all civic engagement articles published in *PS*. This difference likely reflects the different missions of the journals. The original editorial board of the *JPSE* made it clear to potential authors that it was uninterested in "show and tell" pieces and would most favorably consider articles that provided details about a pedagogical innovation along with evidence that demonstrated the approach was successful in achieving those objectives. *JPSE* was designed as a scholarly journal featuring SoTL research designed to raise the profile and increase acceptance and recognition of the value of the scholarship of teaching and learning.

Table 26-6: *JPSE* Intervention Type

Intervention	Number	Percentage (N=38)
No Intervention Tested (theoretical piece or meta-analysis)	7	18.4
Single Classroom Instructor	16	42.1
Single Instructor, Single Classroom	7	
Single Instructor, Multiple Classrooms	3	
Single Instructor, Single Course, Studied over Time	4	
Single Instructor, Multiple Courses, Studied over Time	1	
Single Instructor, Panel Study, Same Students Studied over Time	1	
Multiple Classroom Instructors	9	23.7
Multiple Instructors, Multiple Classrooms, Single Campus, One point in Time	4	
Multiple Instructors, Multiple Classrooms, Single Campus, Different Students over Time	2	
Multiple Instructors, Multiple Classrooms, Multiple Campuses, One Point in Time	3	
Other	6	15.8
Out-of-classroom Student Engagement (e.g. service projects, high school presentations)	2	
Survey-only (e.g., faculty/graduate assistant survey, student body survey)	3	
Other (explain)	1	

Finally, several articles reported the effect of student activities outside the classroom or surveys administered to students or faculty across a campus. Unfortunately, only one of these studies compared survey results to national surveys, and none provided a longitudinal analysis of changes in student/alumni attitudes, knowledge, or reported behavior over time. On a positive note, three of the classroom effects studies included longitudinal components, studying the same students over time to determine whether there was a detectable long-term effect on patterns of engagement.

Of the 25 articles in Table 26-7 that tested the effects of specific teaching techniques or interventions in a classroom setting, 14 employed surveys to assess students' perceived learning outcomes; six used student reflections expressed in papers, questionnaires, or letters home to assess student learning outcomes; and eight used instructor-assigned papers to provide direct measures of learning (see Table 26-7). Compared to *PS*, these figures represented an increase in direct measures of assessment—though the number of studies employing direct measures was still quite low. More troubling is the fact that none of the authors explicitly compared precourse to postcourse work, or preintervention to postintervention student

Table 26-7: *JPSE* Assessment Methods

Subject Matter	Number of Articles with Classroom Interventions	Number of Articles with Nonclassroom-Based Interventions	Percentage of Total Civic Engagement Articles (N=38)
Instructor-Designed Surveys	14	5	50.0
Post, Closed-Ended	2	1	
Post Mixed	0	2	
Pre,- Post-, Closed-Ended	11	0	
Pre, Post, Mixed	1	0	
Multistate, Closed		2	
Outside Survey	1	0	2.6
National Survey Comparisons	1 (Harvard, NES)	0	
Course Evaluations	5	0	13.2
Postcourse, Open-Ended	1	0	
Postcourse, Closed-Ended	2	0	
Pre-, Postcourse, Closed-Ended	2	0	
Reflections	6	1	18.4
Postintervention	5	0	
Pre-, Mid-, Postintervention	1	1	
Course Assignments	8	0	21.1
Postintervention Written Work	8	0	
Interviews	3	0	7.9
Postintervention	1	0	
Pre-, Postintervention	2	0	
Focus Groups	1	1	5.3
Postintervention	1	1	
Other	1 (Syllabi/Textbooks)	1 (GPA)	5.3

work to support their contention that the course—or a specific component of the course—was responsible for students' performance.

Instructors were more likely to use a pre- and postintervention design when conducting indirect assessments of learning outcomes through the use of surveys. Following best practices, most authors used both pre- and postcourse surveys to measure changes in students' knowledge and attitudes; two, however, relied solely on students' responses to postcourse surveys, including students' own perceptions of the impact of the courses on their future attitudes and behavior. Authors publishing their

Table 26-8: Single versus Mixed-Methods Approaches in the *JPSE*

Assessment Methods	Number of Articles with Classroom Interventions	Number of Articles with Nonclassroom-Based Interventions	Percentage of Civic Engagement Articles (N=38)
Single Method	12	5	44.7
Instructor-Created Surveys	5	4	
Student Reflections	3	1	
Course Assignments	2	0	
Interviews	2	0	
Mixed Methods	13	1	36.8
Survey, Focus Group	1	0	
Survey, Course Evaluation	1	0	
Survey, Course Assignment	2	0	
Survey, Reflections	2	0	
Survey, Course Assignment, Interview	1	0	
Survey, Outside Survey	1	0	
Course Evaluation, Course Assignment	3	0	
Course Evaluation, Reflection	1	0	
Survey Text Book	1	0	
Survey, Focus Group, GPA	0	1	
No Course/Campus Intervention Assessed (7)	NA	NA	18.4

work in *JPSE* also were more likely than those publishing in *PS* to use focus groups and interviews to study students' own perceptions of their learning experiences.

Table 26-7 illustrates that while half of all civic education articles published in *JPSE* used instructor-designed surveys as a measurement instrument, almost as many (45%) used other assessment instruments. How many of these other approaches were used, following best practices, as one of several assessment tools? Table 26-8 provides a breakdown of single-method and multimethod studies of civic engagement published in *JPSE*.

Based upon the data presented here, it seems that the articles published in *JPSE* expand the total number of published studies focused on political engagement and skill development by studying multiple courses and instructors, providing direct evidence of learning outcomes, and utilizing nonsurvey-based methodologies such as interviews and focus groups to elicit student feedback about their learning experiences. Still more can be done to overcome each of these weaknesses in the literature. With one lone exception, the *JPSE* collection of articles did little to expand the range of studies that provide explicit benchmarks or comparisons to national data. Similarly, there is a lone exception to the general rule that political scientists are doing little to test long-term learning outcomes by studying the same students over time.

Conclusion

This chapter provides a comprehensive overview of assessment techniques used in studies of civic education and engagement published in peer-reviewed political science journals. On the one hand, it suggests progress within the discipline at moving beyond "show and tell" pieces that provide no empirical evidence to back up claims about student learning outcomes. On the other hand, the review of the literature highlights many areas for improvement as political scientists move forward with the scholarship of teaching civic and political engagement.

Moving Assessment Forward: Teaching Civic Engagement and Beyond

27

By Elizabeth A. Bennion

This chapter considers questions regarding assessment and discusses the ways that best practices can be used to move toward a fully rigorous, disciplinewide scholarship of civic engagement pedagogy. First, it answers a series of frequently asked questions.[1] *Second, it provides suggestions for improving civic engagement assessment in the discipline, including a discussion of the strengths and weaknesses of common approaches illustrated in* Teaching Civic Engagement. *Third, it provides a proposal to launch a disciplinewide discussion, generate testable hypotheses, and move the scholarship of teaching and learning forward.*

Classroom, program, campus, and intercampus assessment of civic learning outcomes will improve teaching and learning in the discipline, while serving as the basis for a robust line of scholarly inquiry for political scientists as researchers and educators. Building upon the toolkit provided in Chapter 25 and the overview of current assessment practices provided in Chapter 26, this chapter answers common questions about the assessment of student learning outcomes and explains how *Teaching Civic Engagement* readers can move the scholarship of civic engagement pedagogy forward.

What Is the Goal of Assessment, and Why Do It?

For educators, the ultimate goal of assessment is to improve student learning. According to Linda Suskie of the Middle States Commission on Higher Education, assessment is the ongoing process of: (1) establishing clear, measurable expected outcomes of student learning; (2) ensuring that students have sufficient opportunities to achieve those outcomes; (3) systematically gathering, analyzing, and interpreting evidence to determine how well students' learning matches the stated expectations; and (4) using the resulting information to improve student learning.[2]

For political science educators promoting civic education and engagement, the goal is to continually improve efforts to inform and engage students in civic and political affairs. If political scientists are working to help students develop the knowledge, skills, and dispositions required for a life of civic leadership, they need to know what works and why as well as what does not work to achieve this goal (and why). Assessment can document the effects of their work and continue to improve their ability to achieve pedagogical goals.

What Is the Difference between Student Evaluation and Assessment?

Assessment and evaluation have different goals. When faced with a "push" from the administration to build assessment into their courses and academic programs, many college educators push back by arguing that they already are doing assessment in all of their classes by evaluating student performance on a regular basis as part of the course design. What is the difference between such *evaluation* of student performance and course or program *assessment*? One way to conceptualize the difference is to consider the focus of the exercise. Evaluation focuses on grading student performance on an assignment or in a course, whereas assessment focuses on improving student performance the next time that one teaches the course, as Goldman and Zakel show in their research paper example.[3] An instructor may assign the paper to determine how well students can search and summarize a body of literature. Using a rubric, the instructor evaluates each paper and assigns a grade that reflects the level at which an individual student meets expectations. In this case, the instructor is comparing the work to a standard to determine a grade.

However, this same rubric can be used to assess the degree to which a specific learning objective (e.g., the ability to conduct a literature review) is being met in the course. The instructor can use the rubric to determine whether students, as a whole, are meeting, exceeding, or failing to meet specific learning objectives. When the instructor uses this information to change his or her teaching methods as a way to improve student performance, the instructor is carrying out an assessment. To summarize, evaluation is focused on making a judgment about the quality of a performance, work product, or demonstration of skills against a set of standards. In contrast, assessment is focused on measuring a performance, work product, or skill for the purpose of documenting strengths and growth and providing suggestions for improving future performance.

Assessment is about "intelligent efforts to improve instructional quality."[4] At the same time, classroom assessment focuses primary attention on observing and improving learning, rather than teaching. Classroom-based assessment should not be based on a one-size-fits-all rubric handed down by external actors or agencies. Rather, it should respect the academic freedom and professional judgment of the college faculty and incorporate the active participation of students to facilitate both student success and teaching effectiveness.[5] Ultimately, classroom assessment should be learner-centered, teacher-directed, mutually beneficial (to both student and teacher), ongoing, and rooted in good teaching practices.[6]

Why Aren't Grades Good Enough?

Course letter grades are insufficient for program or skill assessment because grades alone do not indicate exactly what students have and have not learned.[7] Course grades reflect students' overall performance in a single course. They are a composite of a student's achievement of course outcomes and do not necessarily indicate achievement of a specific learning objective. Grades reflect many things besides student mastery of course objectives, including effort, verbal ability, attendance, participation, and extra credit. When using student grades to assess student learning outcomes, one must match a specific item (or set of items) on an assignment to a specific learning objective.

From a program assessment standpoint, grades reflect the evaluation practices, policies, and criteria of individual instructors. Faculty teaching the same course may teach different materials, emphasize different learning objectives, and use different criteria for evaluating student achievement. When engaging in departmental assessment or conducting multicampus research, it is important to work with others to make appropriate choices and decisions about "what to assess, how to assess, and how to use the results."[8]

Although the composite course grades are insufficient for program assessment, students' grades that reflect a specific learning objective can be used for both course and program assessment.[9] For example, instructors can review student performance on specific items on a multiple-choice exam to test knowledge or recall of key facts. Instructors also can review student performance on an essay assignment to determine whether or not students have achieved a specific learning objective, such as formulating of a strong thesis statement or supporting claims with relevant evidence. The combined results of these instructor evaluations of students' work can serve as data for both course and program assessment. Such direct measures of learning are an important addition to more indirect measures, including student surveys.

What Is the Difference between Direct and Indirect Measures of Learning?

Ideally, an assessment plan includes both direct and indirect measures of student learning. Direct assessment acquires evidence about student learning and the learning environment, including exams, theses, research projects, dissertations, oral defenses, or portfolios scored using a rubric. Direct evidence of student learning is "tangible, visible, self-explanatory, and compelling evidence of exactly what students have and have not learned."[10] Sometimes student reflections provide direct measures of learning. Students' reflections on their values, attitudes, and beliefs are direct evidence of student learning, if developing such values is intended outcome of the program. For example, students' reflective journals about what it means to be a citizen and how they rate their own level of internal and external political efficacy might be an important measure of the degree to which a student has met attitudinal learning goals in a civic education course. To determine whether a particular course or curriculum contributed to these values, a pretest and posttest series of reflections on the same topics is needed.

Indirect evidence consists of "proxy signs that students are probably learning."[11] Institutional measures (e.g., retention rates, graduation rates, admissions rates into graduate programs, etc.) may provide indirect evidence of student learning. Indirect assessment is most often based upon evidence about how students feel about learning and their learning environment. It includes student reactions and self-reports about what they have learned. Measurement instruments include surveys, questionnaires, interviews, focus groups, and reflective essays, though each of these may be crafted to include direct as well as indirect measures of learning. Although direct evidence is more persuasive to the skeptical reader, indirect measures are more common in current SoTL research in political science. Both can be important when considering what students have learned (objectively) and what they (subjectively) believe they took away from a course. For example, students' belief that they gained a great deal of knowledge about politics could have long-term attitudinal and behavioral consequences, even if the students do not, in fact, know as much as they think they do.

Why Can't I Rely upon Student Feedback about What They Are Learning?

Students' reflections on their own learning tell what they *think* they learned, but do not provide direct evidence of learning. Postcourse surveys frequently ask students to reflect upon what they have learned in a course and how the course, or a particular civic engagement activity, will shape their future behavior. Studies of civic and political engagement often are based upon self-reported data about changes in students' attitudes, knowledge, and future behavior.[12] These responses, while suggestive and frequently encouraging, are not definitive, especially if they are based upon a postintervention survey alone, which requires students to compare a prior self to their "new and improved" self. Preintervention and postintervention comparison surveys that actually provide direct measures of students' political knowledge and standardized measures of their attitudes at each point in time are preferable to a survey that asks students to reflect upon whether or not their knowledge has grown and attitudes have changed.

Self-reports may be consistent with behavior when a self-report describes a set of behaviors that have occurred in the recent past. However, political science research suggests that respondents do not always accurately report their past political behavior. For example, people overreport voting and voting for the winning candidates. Furthermore, those who feel the greatest pressure to vote are the ones most likely to misrepresent their behavior when they fail to do so.[13] Among all nonvoters, the most likely to overreport casting a ballot are those who are more educated, partisan, and religious and those who have been contacted and asked to vote.[14] Self-reports may be even less consistent when the behavior has not yet occurred, because the report is based upon only an idea, or prediction, of how one will behave. People are not always good at predicting their own behavior.[15] This particular problem may be associated with students who have just completed a course (or program) designed to further civic and political engagement. They may feel pressured to report future engagement or feel temporarily motivated to engage, but may not follow up as life intervenes and the experience fades. Self-reports of future behavior represent aspirations rather than certainties; thus, they measure attitudes, not actual behavior.

What Is the Difference between Assessment and the Scholarship of Teaching and Learning?

Several scholars have noted that assessment differs from traditional research in both its purpose and nature.[16] Such scholars argue that traditional empirical research is conducted to test theories, whereas assessment is a form of action research designed to inform and improve one's own practice rather than make broad generalizations.[17] Peter Ewell suggests that assessment requires a craft-based approach rather than a scientific approach.[18] However, the four-step assessment cycle of establishing learning goals, providing learning opportunities, assessing student learning, and using the results is parallel to the four steps of action research: plan, act, observe, and reflect.[19]

According to Suskie, "[M]ost faculty and staff lack the time and resources required to design and conduct rigorous, replicable empirical research studies with impartial distance." [20] Yet, this condition does not preclude the possibility of rigorous classroom assessment research. As Suskie notes, assessment, like any other form of action research, "is disciplined and systematic and uses many of the methodologies of traditional research."[21] Assessment testing the effectiveness of classroom-, program-, and campus-based approaches to civic education and engagement provides the design and data needed for important scholarly research. Both classroom/program assessment and the scholarship of teaching and learning require clear goals, adequate preparation, appropriate methods, significant results, effective presentation, and reflective critique.[22]

SoTL scholars move beyond assessment designed to answer questions about their own courses, program, or university by attempting to answer larger questions about effective approaches to student learning. When scholars review relevant literature to determine a question that needs to be answered and then design a study to answer that question, they are engaged in research. SoTL scholars formulate hypotheses and test these hypotheses using empirical evidence. In sum, the scholarship of teaching and learning applies the recognized methodological tools of the discipline to questions of teaching and learning. This is as valuable to the discipline as inquiries into other phenomena.

Perhaps the major difference between course and program assessment and SoTL research is the purpose of the assessment. Course and program assessment are part of an ongoing systematic effort to understand and improve teaching and learning in specific courses or programs. They are a "perpetual work in progress."[23] SoTL research shares the ultimate goal of improving teaching and learning and, like all academic research, building upon previous work as a collective work in progress. Yet, the purpose of moving from course assessment to SoTL research is to share lessons learned with a broader audience. The goal is to build collective knowledge that will benefit faculty and students throughout the discipline.

Ultimately, SoTL research is trickier than most traditional disciplinary research, because complete standardization is impossible. First, as with most human subjects research, there are fluctuations in human performance that cannot be completely controlled.[24] For example, a student is sick or preoccupied on the day that he or she completes an assignment or takes a test. Multicourse/multi-instructor/multicampus projects introduce many additional variables that cannot be controlled to isolate the effect of a particular curricular innovation. Nonetheless, such efforts are worthwhile when testing hypotheses and claims about what works to engage students. Such multicourse, multicampus, and multi-instructor research helps determine which approaches work for which students, under which conditions, and in which contexts. Teacher-scholars participating in a multicourse/multicampus SoTL project should share a research protocol, set of learning objectives (or hypotheses), intervention protocol, and standard assessment rubric. Instructors also should provide information about other course content, context, and student demographics that might shape student performance related to specified learning objectives.

Moving Forward with the Scholarship of Civic Education and Engagement: Lessons from Teaching Civic Engagement

Teaching Civic Engagement: From Student to Active Citizen is designed to clarify vocabulary, summarize key literature, and introduce a broad range of approaches that political scientists can employ to promote civic education and engagement. The book, like any good assessment project, is a work in progress. Chapters represent a wide array of instructional strategies, disciplinary subfields, research questions, and assessment plans. The diversity of chapters included in the book provides a better understanding of the current approaches to civic engagement pedagogy and how the examples provided in the book may be used as a starting point for future scholarship. (A similar review of civic engagement articles published in peer-reviewed political science journals is the topic of the previous chapter.)

First, it is clear that several scholars are asking important questions and developing important theories that would profit from empirical study. Scholars have proposed interesting theories about how civic and political identity is formed (Gentry, Chapter 4) and the type of intellectual commitment required for long-term engagement (Harward and Shea, Chapter 2). These theoretical frameworks can be developed and empirically tested to further knowledge of the relationship among socialization, education, and long-term civic identity and engagement.

It is common knowledge among assessment experts that learning takes place over time both in and outside the classroom. Yet, relatively little is known about how students integrate multiple learning experiences during their college careers (McDonald, Chapter 23). Do extracurricular experiences, including internships and study abroad opportunities, really produce different learning outcomes than coursework? Does a specific combination of coursework, internships, and other types of experiential learning make a difference for students' long-term values and behavior? Do different types (or combinations) of experiences produce different results? What is the most effective way for students to integrate the knowledge and skills gained from multiple experiences? This is an ambitious research agenda, but one that political science can undertake as a discipline. Then it can be determined how colleges and universities can best take advantage of national programs, mandates, and grants to further civic education and engagement (Harris, Chapter 5). A multicampus study tracking different approaches using a common assessment rubric and metrics could help answer such questions. The Political Engagement Project provides a useful model of a multicampus research approach that employs both direct and indirect measures of student learning (see Beaumont, Chapter 3).

Second, it is clear that scholars who have designed worthwhile single-course and single-instructor studies nonetheless could benefit from multicourse and multi-instructor comparisons. Small courses make it difficult to generalize about the effectiveness of a particular instructional approach. A few students can change the results of a quantitative study in a small course (see, for example, Sanders, Chapter 14).

Third, it is clear that teacher-scholars hoping to build upon the work presented in *Teaching Civic Engagement* must think carefully about their assessment plans and research design *before* teaching a course or carrying out some other intervention. Both single-course and multicourse approaches to assessment must include both pretests and posttests if instructors wish to make claims about what students have learned through a particular activity or course. For example, one author featured in this book used a pretest survey with no posttest follow-up, whereas four others relied solely upon postcourse surveys. It is difficult to gauge student growth if the same instrument is not utilized both before and after the intervention being tested.

Fourth, instructors writing about multiple courses should consider whether the courses are actually comparable in terms of students' educational background, motivations, and learning objectives. Are students in McLauchlan's upper-level Practical Politics course really comparable to students in her required introductory-level American National Government course? If outcomes are different, can such differences be attributed to the differences in the hours of campaign work required (80 vs. 25) or to self-selection into a more rigorous upper-level course requiring a minimum of 80 hours of fieldwork? If there is little difference in student learning outcomes, is that because self-selection does not matter, or because introductory students had the benefit of working on high-profile presidential, gubernatorial, and US Senate campaigns versus lower-profile municipal-level races? Do the extreme variations in class size, composition, and learning objectives between the courses featured in McHugh and Mayer's departmental self-study allow for meaningful comparisons? These authors have helped researchers to ask these questions, a valuable contribution in itself, and this volume seeks to move the discipline forward to answer them.

Fifth, multicourse and program assessments need to be based upon predetermined, standardized rubrics. Not all courses need to have the same learning objectives, but all should fit within a predefined departmental framework—or curriculum map—so that they work collectively to meet (and are assessed according to) a single departmental assessment rubric. McHugh and Mayer present four interesting and important examples of experiential education within a single department. These work well as preliminary case studies, but they cannot be compared directly for effectiveness or divergent learning outcomes due to significant differences in the methods used to assess each course, ranging from pretest and posttest surveys to instructor reflections about what students had learned. Departmental curriculum mapping and assessment rubrics should be created to specify and assess predetermined learning objectives across the curriculum. Examples of classroom and program assessment instruments are available in *Assessment in Political Science.*[25]

Sixth, teacher-scholars engaging in civic education research should consider multiple assessment types and timings. McKinlay provides a strong example of triangulation, using multiple forms of assessment to support his claims about student learning outcomes in his innovative political theory course. His future work will include outside coders, allowing for an objective look at the data and tests of intercoder reliability. (For examples of studies employing multiple coders see McCartney, Chapter 17 and VanVechten and Chadha, Chapter 11.) Multiple assessment types should include direct evidence of student learning. Beaumont's multicampus study of the role of various student activities and teaching approaches in fostering political engagement demonstrates the benefits of this approach, collecting both direct and indirect evidence of student learning using quantitative and qualitative instruments. Direct evidence need not be limited to student papers, exams, and course portfolios. VanVechten and Chadha provide an innovative model for obtaining direct measurement of student learning outcomes—learning from others, building bridges across difference, and working through controversy with civility—rarely measured directly and systematically.

Finally, as noted at the beginning of the chapter, it is important that assessment measures match the learning objectives and content of each course. Assessment metrics should be designed before the course is offered, rather than after, so that expected learning outcomes can be articulated and an assessment rubric designed to match the expected outcomes in the course. For example, McCartney uses self-reported voting behavior as one measure of long-term political engagement, though the experiential learning students encountered had little to do with voting behavior (Chapter 17). Future iterations of her innovative work linking local action to global politics can provide better tests of ongoing political engagement. Multicampus collaborations will also help to overcome the "small N" problems of this, and much, SoTL research. Meanwhile, others should emulate her ongoing attempts to collect alumni data and follow students over time.[26] As seen in Chapter 26, very few studies in the discipline document the long-term effects of college experiences on students' civic and political behavior or identity.

Moving Forward Together: The Consortium for SoTL Research

Many professors engaged in civic education and engagement efforts in the classroom work at institutions where their primary responsibility is teaching. They lack access to multiple sections of large lecture courses to use when collecting quantitative data on student learning outcomes. They lack time or resources required to collect data beyond a single campus, or perhaps even a single classroom. Many innovative and thoughtful SoTL scholars face serious resource constraints. Systematic cross-campus data collection is valuable, but time-consuming. It requires a high level of infrastructure development, coordination, supervision, and communication.

The newly formed Inter-Campus Consortium for SoTL Research provides a structure for identifying, strengthening, and conducting promising SoTL projects.[27] Political scientists collecting assessment data on their own pedagogy and civic engagement efforts will collaborate with one another using the consortium's developed network and procedures. Consortium members will have the opportunity to participate in cross-campus research projects. Those who help collect data for a consortium-sponsored project will have access to the raw data collected from their own campus or regions, as well as a summary report of findings relevant to their campuses. They also will be eligible to submit an original project to the Advisory Board for peer review and possible selection as a consortium project.

By providing peer review, feedback, and a large pool of research subjects and locations, the consortium will enhance publication and grant opportunities for principal investigators, while providing valuable information and presentation opportunities to members about their own campuses and students. The consortium will help political scientists concerned with civic engagement pedagogy to meet their teaching, research, and service goals. It also will benefit the discipline as a whole by facilitating SoTL research with larger N and more diverse populations of subjects. High-quality, multicampus research will increase the number of significant research findings, enhance the external validity of SoTL research, and produce more generalizable knowledge. The results of this research will provide insight into best practices, with the potential to improve teaching effectiveness across the discipline.

CONCLUSION

Toward Civic and Political Engagement

Toward Civic and Political Engagement

By Dick Simpson

As Rick Battistoni writes in the Preface, teaching civics, civic and political engagement, and democratic citizenship by political scientists dates back to the 19th century and early 20th century. One could argue as well that it was a goal of political philosophers like Socrates millennia earlier. Since the end of the 20th century, political scientists have focused upon incorporating community service, service-learning, and community-based research into the missions and curricula of high schools, colleges, and universities. Rick Battistoni recounts that history. At this point in the 21st century, however, political scientists are now moving from requiring service-learning to teaching civic and political engagement. As authors from John Dewey to those of the Carnegie Foundation books have argued, political scientists now have to educate for democracy.

The editors of this book and the authors of its chapters assist this latest transformation by providing a theoretical framework and practical examples of effectively teaching lifelong engagement to students. Contributors review the state of our knowledge about what works and what does not in existing programs meant to encourage civic and political engagement. We provide examples of effective courses and programs in the full range of subfields, from urban studies and American politics to political philosophy, comparative politics, and international relations. We also supply quantitative and qualitative tools for assessing the effectiveness of these various initiatives.

The publication of *A Crucible Moment* by the Association of American Colleges and Universities (AACU) in 2012 provides a new momentum for teaching civic engagement.[1] AACU has featured the efforts of institutions to promote civic engagement in its *AACU News*, including, in the November 2012 issue, Governors State University's incorporation of civic engagement across its curriculum. In addition, the federal requirement that all colleges receiving federal funds must have programs celebrating Constitution Day on or around September 17, provides a kickoff every year for a more sustained civic and political engagement program on campuses.

Within the political science profession, many have worked since the early part of this century to build teaching and the scholarship of teaching. These efforts include the founding of a Political Science Education Section within the American Political Science Association (APSA), which now includes hundreds of members. A separate *Journal of Political Science Education* is thriving, and a major section of the APSA journal *PS* is devoted to articles on teaching and political science education. A separate APSA Teaching and Learning Committee guides teaching activities of APSA. An annual Teaching and Learning Conference—at which many of the chapters in this book were first presented as papers—offers opportunities to develop and refine pedagogical techniques and ideas. Now a book series on teaching and assessment, including this volume, is being published by APSA. Teaching and the scholarship of teaching are being fully recognized by the profession.

At the same time, there is a community of teachers and scholars coming together to support a coordinated effort to teach more effectively. This community is generally committed to using all the new techniques and technologies available. A number of members of this community are committed to improving the teaching of civic and political engagement to foster the creation of democratic citizens and political leaders. In short, you are not alone. There are many allies in the effort to teach civic and political engagement.

As Alison McCartney in the introductory chapter to this book points out, the time is now to incorporate the development of civically engaged citizens as a goal in the mission of institutions of higher learning. Curriculum should include, in addition to service-learning and civic education, the teaching of political engagement so that students participate in explicitly politically oriented activities that seek a direct impact upon political issues, systems, relations, and structures.

To aid in the process of accomplishing these goals, this book presents examples of effective civic and political engagement courses and methods from high schools and community colleges to elite research universities. Efforts from small liberal arts colleges to large public universities are surveyed. The message is simple—these techniques, when properly adapted, can be used in all educational institutions to teach democracy and train future political leaders.

In 2002, as Elizabeth Beaumont reports in Chapter 3, the Carnegie Foundation began a Political Engagement Project, which studied 21 courses and co-curricular programs throughout the country to determine how civic and political engagement can best be taught. In the extensive multiyear study that followed, the foundation researchers concluded that these 21 courses produced measurable and significant political learning, understanding, motivation, skills, and political efficacy. Equally important, they produced *no* change in party identity and ideology among the several thousand students taking these courses. In short, the researchers found that these were truly courses in political engagement, not political indoctrination. Students could be Democrat or Republican, liberal or conservative, or still discovering their political identities and still benefit from enhanced political learning, understanding, motivation, skills, and efficacy. As Beaumont indicates in Chapter 3, this goal can be achieved without political indoctrination.

Although these 21 courses employed standard methods like lectures and readings, five additional pedagogical strategies were used in various combinations by the instructors. It is important to stress that there were only *five* additional techniques employed, not a hundred different methods used to produce greater political engagement. As demonstrated in the preceding chapters, these same techniques are used to great effect by dozens of courses and civic engagement programs reported here. The techniques are:

1. Political discussion and deliberation
2. Political research and action projects
3. Invited speakers and the use of nonuniversity mentors
4. External placement as interns and workers
5. Structured reflection

Many courses discussed in this book use most of these same five techniques. For high schools, colleges, universities, or political science departments with a more extensive political engagement commitment, these techniques are employed in a sequence of courses to move students from apathy and disengagement to lifelong political engagement.

Some courses provided serious discussion and deliberation; others utilized invited guests speakers from the world of politics, government, civic groups, or community organizations. Still other courses used external placement or community-based research projects. Hopefully, many of these courses allowed for structured reflection both in oral and written forms by the students on what they have learned and how they have grown personally from their experiences.[2]

The goal, as Bobbi Gentry explains in Chapter 4, is to encourage students to form a strong political ego identity and pursue what the Carnegie Foundation identified as political learning, understanding, motivation, skills, and sense of efficacy. Along with the specific experience, these traits allow and encourage students to become permanently engaged as informed, participatory citizens and political leaders.

In this Conclusion, I first review my own experiences from more than 45 years teaching, in which I have sought to deepen students' political engagement. These experiences parallel many of those of the other authors. Then I draw out some of the main lessons to be learned from these experiences and an action agenda to move teaching of civic and political engagement forward.

Creating Political Leaders

In my own teaching, I utilize speakers; political research projects; a simulation called the National Student Issues Convention, discussed by Anthony Perry in Chapter 12; and external internships, with structured reflection class presentations and final papers like those discussed in Chapters 18 and 23. I also use film and video documentaries, many of which I have made professionally at the University of Illinois at

Chicago (UIC), to allow students to understand political events and government empathetically from the point of view of political and governmental actors.[3]

My goal is not to create "citizens" in the minimal sense of those who consume political media (newspaper, TV news programs, or blogs) and then passively vote. My explicit goal is to create political leaders. Judging from the number of my former students who have held elected office—from a US senator to a county commissioner to school board members and block club leaders—I have succeeded. One of my students was also a presidential candidate. And my former students have been Democrats and Republicans, liberals and conservatives.[4]

In the introductory American politics course I used to teach before becoming department head, I used the simplest of the techniques. Looking back, I still find the course to be very effective in introducing students to politics and government in ways that prepared them for fuller political engagement. Beyond the usual topics of American government structures and founding, I focused upon teaching political philosophy, political analysis, and political action in this course. I used dialectical methods to help students explore philosophy, analysis, and political strategy. This was not done in a small seminar, but rather in a course with between 100 and 450 students.

This course was coordinated through the use of a published workbook that provided day-by-day readings and assignment schedules along with study guides for the films and lectures and a series of exercises to develop specific skills.[5] I taught political philosophy in the course by assigning contradictory original works, such as the *Declaration of Independence*, *The Communist Manifesto*, and selections from *Reflections on the Revolution in France*, among more contemporary writings. This diversity of viewpoints forced students to decide for themselves what they believed, since they could not agree with all of the contradictory philosophers. I also made them analyze a political philosopher not read in the course in a short paper after completing an exercise in which students dissected a philosopher they did read and discuss.

Films and Volunteering

To teach political action, I use documentary films and volunteering in an election (or observing a government event, such as a city council meeting). The films allow students to empathetically participate in election campaigns, lobbying, protests, and even revolutions without the risk or cost of doing so. They help students see what it feels like to be politically involved and may inspire them to act in the future. This goes beyond what they learn analytically about different political strategies and how they have been and may be employed.

The advantages of student volunteering have been covered in Sections 2 and 3. Giving students extra credit for participating in a political campaign, serving as a poll watcher, or attending a government meeting for which they then write a short paper are more opportunities to provide political or governmental exposure with minimal personal or emotional risk. Betty O'Shaughnessy in Chapter 19 discusses the effect these options have even upon high school students.

Readings, Speakers, Action Research, and the National Student Issues Convention

My Chicago's Future course was selected for inclusion in the Carnegie Foundation study upon which Elizabeth Beaumont reports in Chapter 3. In this class, I use several techniques. Students are given readings on Chicago politics, such as my previous anthology, *Chicago's Future in a Time of Change*, which I have now replaced with my new coedited book, *Twenty-First Century Chicago*.[6] Over time I have published a number of books I have needed to teach courses my way. I also have made eight documentary films (now videos and DVDs web-streamed to students).[7] Many of my books and films are intended for a more general audience as well, but they allow me to show my students aspects of politics and government that they would not otherwise experience. One of the take-away lessons from my experience is that in designing one's own courses one may have to produce a number of one's own materials. Internet course delivery systems like Blackboard now make it much easier to distribute materials to a class in PowerPoint slides, audio lectures, movies, written exercises, and online discussion groups. These are no less labor-intensive to create. However, as more instructors teach political engagement classes, a commercial market for such materials will be produced, and materials will be able to be shared more effectively. Hopefully, teachers will find a number of examples in this book that can be easily adapted to their own courses while they are creating their own materials to use and share.

One reason why I personally have chosen to develop so many teaching materials and techniques is that I am not a great lecturer—I tend toward a monotone and to speak in formal teaching situations from detailed notes. This is despite the fact that I can give a great political speech on the campaign trail and am able to do good media interviews on camera or in front of a microphone. So I reserve lectures to provide a framework or elaboration of materials for students. I let books, films, speakers, direct experience, and discussion groups provide much of the course content.

For my Chicago's Future course, in addition to readings, overview lectures, and films, I bring 10–15 speakers to class a semester. Some are urban politics scholars, who talk about their latest research, but mainly I invite political and governmental officials and leaders from movements and civic organizations. These speakers are used to enhance students' political understanding and provide an account of real politics, a greater appreciation of diverse political roles, a deeper knowledge of political and policy process, and a greater appreciation of ethical issues. They also provide inspiration and help students develop stronger discussion, questioning, and deliberation skills.

For these goals to be achieved, the speakers have to be carefully selected and briefed on what is expected in their talks. It is not helpful to have them give their standard campaign or Kiwanis Club talk. Moreover, students have to be prepared with readings beforehand and given time in discussion afterward to reflect upon what they learned from the presentation. Another benefit of making people with political power consider the future of Chicago and handle thoughtful questions and suggestions from students is that they are forced to reflect upon the bigger picture in a way they do not often get to do in their positions of power. Students are actually participating in a real debate about the future of the metropolitan region in which they live.

Here are a few other guidelines for using speakers effectively:

1. *Ask:* Most faculty are surprised that "big name" speakers are easily convinced to come speak to university classes and lecture series. They often will do so without charge or for a modest honorarium if asked by the faculty member in a letter and a follow-up phone call.
2. *Organize for Optimal Impact:* It is best to organize speakers around a theme and ensure that different sides of the political spectrum and different points of view are represented. Think of the speaker series as a debate or dialogue over a topic. I frequently organize speakers on the future of Chicago around subtopics like "The Role of the City Council in the City's Future." A single speaker can have an impact on students, but a series of speakers with radically different viewpoints is more powerful and forces students to develop their own opinions. Of course, the campus community and the public should be invited to attend these talks, and they should ideally be covered by the media—especially the campus newspapers—to widen their impact. Media coverage also helps students understand how significant these presentations are, if TV cameras show up or students read an account of the presentation the following week in the campus newspaper.
3. *Realizing Their Potential Leadership Roles:* Beyond the information conveyed by the speakers, it is important for students to see that they can easily play the same public role as the speakers—they, too, can be public officials, scholars, and political leaders. Thus, it is important to invite minorities and women as well as white males to be speakers—younger leaders as well as senior officials. Speakers also should represent a range of institutions of higher learning—for example, public and private, large and small, two-year and four-year—so that students can relate to their experience.

At UIC, both the introductory American government students and the Chicago's Future students participate annually in the National Student Issues Convention, which is more fully described by Anthony Perry in Chapter 12. Students do not just study democracy during the half-day-long convention; they practice it as they work to create a consensus (or at least a majority) of their fellow students around an issue agenda of their common concerns, which candidates for public office and government officials then address directly. They learn deliberation, persuasion, and leadership in the process, but more than that, they gain a sense of efficacy. They learn that by joining together they can affect politics and government around the issues about which they feel most deeply. This convention provides an opportunity to learn by doing democracy, not by hearing a lecture or reading a book about it. Having politicians and public officials respond directly to the students' agenda of concerns is an eye-opening experience for many.

The Chicago's Future course ends with an action research project in which students study a single local government agency as if they were on the transition team advising a mayor, county board president, or village executive.[8] It is not a straightforward library research project like those done for other courses; rather, in this project, they must analyze government documents and interview government officials. Among other lessons they learn is that the so-called public information on the government to which they and their parents pay taxes is not easily decoded. If students can analyze a single government agency in this way, they can analyze any government agency to find out what they want or need to know. For their paper, students have to discover the legal basis of the agency, its funding and number of personnel over three years, its organization, method of delivering services, and forms of accountability. They end by evaluating how well the agency operates and what actions could be taken, based upon best practices in other cities, cost-benefit analysis, and public exposures in the media, to decrease waste and improve its effectiveness.

Internships and Structured Reflection

As Judithanne McLauchlan indicates in Chapter 18 and several other authors describe in their chapters, internships are an important component of political science programs. Many political science departments are satisfied to give students course credit if they find internships on their own and provide little guidance or structure for the experience. I believe this approach is inadequate to teach political engagement. At the University of Illinois at Chicago, internships are viewed as a capstone experience for those students who choose to use it. Double course credit is provided, as is help to ensure students select the best internship for themselves. Students are required to meet an hour a week in a seminar setting, read at least five books to provide a framework for their experiences, make group oral reports on those books to the entire class, and write a structured reflection paper. They also must receive an evaluation from their internship supervisor at the agency or organization at which they work for a minimum of 10 hours a week for 15 weeks.

Internships must allow students to attend government meetings, campaign strategy or training sessions, or community meetings so that they gain an overall understanding of these activities. That is, students cannot just be used as clerks at the agency or group where they work. The letter of agreement or contract at the beginning of an internship guarantees, or at least makes it more likely, that a student will have a substantive learning experience.

The internship placements vary widely and include political campaigns, government offices, civic groups, community organizations, and law offices, including public law offices like the State's Attorney. The requirement is that an internship must relate to government, politics, or the law. It is a chance for students to see what it is like to work in one of these fields and learn politics, government, or the law from the inside. The secrets to making internships at this level work are: 1) good placements, 2) ongoing classroom discussions and readings to deepen and enlarge the experience, and 3) reflections so that real learning occurs from the experience.[9] Other suggestions to maximize internships are given in various chapters of this book.

In the structured reflection paper that must be completed for each internship at the end of the semester, students reflect upon the books they have read (at least three of the five books are specific to the internship selected) and the experiences they had. For instance, if a student worked in a campaign, he or she might say that my book, *Winning Elections*, recommended that fund-raising should be done in a particular way or that the campaign should be organized in a specific way, but these aspects were not done that way in the particular campaign and the candidate lost.[10] Or students might note that the books on elections they read did not suggest using social media to reach voters, but their campaigns won because they employed these techniques.

Hopefully, students write about what they learn from their failed or winning campaigns. It is even more important that they reflect upon what they learned about themselves from their internship experiences and whether or not a career as a public official or a campaign consultant seems right for them. Some students take an internship with no prior political engagement experience, but the students who usually gain the most have already developed some political understanding, skills, motivation, and sense of personal and political efficacy from earlier classes and experiences.

Lessons for Teaching Political Engagement

This book has presented the experiences, assessments, and reflections of more than 30 fellow political scientists. Each has considered the state of teaching civic and political engagement today. One obvious use of this book is to provide a catalogue of best practices. Educators who want to make better use of speakers, simulations, volunteer opportunities, internships, or a variety of other teaching methods can find a how-to discussion of each. If one is teaching a public policy, political philosophy, or international relations course and wants to add a political engagement component, there are examples here to consider, adopt, or adapt.

Whether teaching at a high school like Betty O'Shaughnessy, a community college like Anthony Perry, or a research university like Diana Owen or Michael McDonald, educators can present the materials here to any principal, dean, or department head as evidence that there are legitimate, tested methods any school can adopt. The book also presents an entire section (Section 4, with chapters by coeditor Elizabeth Bennion) on how better assessment of these teaching techniques can be done in the future. The authors in this book also supply quantitative and qualitative data demonstrating that political engagement achieves important education goals. The literature that the authors review provides further arguments and support for civic, community, and political engagement as an effective pedagogy. Moreover, at the website developed with this book—www.apsanet.org/teachingcivicengagement—sample syllabi, course assignment instructions, and an extended bibliography on civic engagement are provided to further assist in course and program development.

There are additional lessons. First, there is more than one way to get to heaven. That is to say, there is no one right way to teach civic and political engagement. No party line that must be followed. Most of the methods that seem to work best are variations of the five methods identified by the Carnegie Foundation study, but there are many variations on their use.

Reading between the lines of the studies presented in this book and in the many papers presented at the APSA Teaching and Learning Conferences each year, the main secret of success seems to be the intentionality of the faculty member and careful course planning designed to teach civic and political engagement, democratic citizenship, and political leadership skills. Students learn in different ways, and faculty teach in various ways according to their personalities and teaching styles. Different methods work better for some students than others, but any of these techniques work if applied honestly and intentionally.

Second, efforts to teach political engagement should: 1) be grounded in the theoretical, psychological, political science literature; 2) be replicable in other classes at an educator's own and other schools; and 3) be rigorously assessed (preferably by standard measures and methods). Careful assessment allows educators to justify their courses to administrators, outside officials, certification agencies, parents, and government authorities. More important, such assessment allows educators to continually refine and improve the techniques employed.

Third, all goals of civic, community, and political engagement do not have to be and probably cannot be achieved in a single course. The chapters in Section 3 provide examples of how multiple courses and other campus programs can be used in a more comprehensive way to teach engagement. Different courses can achieve complementary goals. They can be grouped into a formal minor degree or a concentration and integrated across multiple experiences as suggested by Michael McDonald in Chapter 23.

Fourth, civic and political engagement experiences are not in competition with other education goals like developing analytical thinking. Rather, these techniques and goals are complementary. To learn civic and political engagement, students may begin with a volunteer or service-learning activity to be introduced to some sector of society such as the poor, as Michelle Lorenzini describes in Chapter 8. Later, they may encounter political and government officials as speakers in a class like my Chicago's Future class. They may become involved in a political campaign, as Arthur Sanders and Betty O'Shaughnessy describe in Chapters 14 and 19.

Additionally, students may become involved in student organizations, clubs, or simulations later in their campus careers, as described by Anthony Perry in Chapter 12, or in a study abroad program, as Michael McDonald describes in Chapter 23. They may be in internship programs during their senior year, like the ones described in a number of chapters, and write reflection papers about their experiences. At the same time as they are having these classroom experiences, they may be involved on their own initiative in extracurricular student protests, Facebook campaigns over sweatshop merchandise sold by the university, or in efforts in support for or opposition to university employee unions (see Strachan and Senter, Chapter 24). The lesson is that no one exercise nor any one course teaches civic engagement. Each educator plays a critical role in helping to create what the Carnegie Foundation calls "responsible citizen engagement."

Without question, campuses that formally undertake a full commitment to civic and political engagement are more likely to offer opportunities, create a campus climate conducive to the formation of future political leaders, and have the greatest possibility of succeeding in this mission. But each instructor teaches hundreds of students a year and thousands over their careers. If each provides an education for their students in democratic leadership, and if each succeeds in motivating even a portion of those they teach, they will have made an important contribution.

An Action Agenda

Authors of various chapters of this book offer a series of recommendations, which, taken together form an action agenda:

1. *Colleges and universities should educate for political participation.* The American Political Science Association should continue to support and foster the teaching of civic engagement through special tracks at the Teaching and Learning Conference, the publication of articles in its and related professional journals, and in the publication of books like this one.

2. *The federal government should expand its funding for such civic engagement courses and programs at colleges and universities, rather than contracting funding.*[11] As Jean Harris explains in Chapter 5, the federal government already requires colleges to provide a program each year on the US Constitution and give students voter registration information. It offers grants through the Help Americans Vote Act as well, but federal funding for teaching civic and political engagement is still woefully inadequate. Yet, the federal government has a real self-interest in stronger citizen participation and promoting the development of democratic leaders, if the republic is to endure.

3. *High schools, community colleges, four-year colleges, and universities should adopt teaching civic and political engagement as a goal in their mission statements.* To pursue this mission, they must promote and fund civic education and engagement classes and programs throughout their campuses.

4. *Assessment at the campus level is needed to determine how well universities are complying with the federal mandate* to offer students voter registration forms and how well educators are assisting students in getting registered to vote at their campus address as well as at their home address.[12] Campuses

should utilize techniques that have proven effective rather than merely seek to meet the legal mandate. More rigorous cross-institutional research, like that presented by Bennion and Nickerson in Chapter 13, can point the way forward in the quest to maximize the number of students who register and vote.

5. *Institutions of higher learning need to comply with the federal mandate for an education program pertaining to the US Constitution on September 17 of each year.* Currently, only a small number of campuses do. Constitution Day should be viewed as an opportunity to introduce students to issues of American government and recruit students for service-learning and civic education.[13]

6. *State and local governments should be encouraged to use students to assist in the administration of elections, especially as paid poll watchers and election judges.* Students have the computer skills many election judges do not, and the experience of working Election Day at a polling place is a nonthreatening way to introduce students to politics.[14] Courses should be designed to, at a minimum, encourage high school and college students to work as election judges or in political campaigns by providing clear opportunities and course credit for doing so.[15]

7. *Faculty should be encouraged to be politically engaged themselves*, model that engagement in the classroom, and bring real-world knowledge of politics and government into the class. This must be done without attempting to indoctrinate students with particular political views, but the content in this volume suggests that can be done without difficulty.[16]

8. *APSA should adopt a code of ethics similar to that of social workers, which recognizes the benefits of faculty civic engagement.*[17] The climate at many colleges discourages faculty political engagement as anti-intellectual or treats such involvement as a hobby like playing piano or basketball. Engaged faculty, however, serve as important role models for students. Making civic engagement as legitimate as research and teaching—a part of the expected professional activity—is an important change APSA should promote.

9. *Students should be encouraged to work with local governments, especially in smaller communities, to provide information on best practices.* These types of programs, as Jenkins explains in Chapter 7, are useful both to students, who learn more about politics and government, and to cash-strapped governments, which learn about better ways to deliver government services more effectively and cheaply. Providing opportunities for students to do similar work with nonprofit community and civic organizations is equally valuable.[18]

10. *It is the duty of political science faculty to provide students with the knowledge, skills, and tools to become informed advocates.*[19] It is also their job to help

students in their courses make the connection between community service and political engagement.[20]

11. *Civic and political engagement courses should be designed for cognitive* and *affective learning, along with effective service to the community.*[21] The goal of courses is not just to help students make a difference in the world now, but also to give them the knowledge and motivation to continue their involvement after graduation This means empowering students beyond their immediate impact on society.
12. *Civic education should be encouraged at the high school level, especially those courses which already use simulations or service-learning components.*[22] Many of the techniques in this book can be adapted to a high school curriculum. Thus, students who do not attend college or are unable to take civic and political engagement courses in college will have already been socialized to be active citizens. Those students who do go to college and take civic engagement courses will be starting at a higher level of skills, knowledge, and motivation in their advanced engagement efforts.
13. *More opportunities like Model UN, Mock Trial, Congressional Debate, and National Student Issues Conventions should be developed.* These programs encourage students from campuses across the country to collaborate in civic and political engagement initiatives.[23]
14. *Multiple courses should be created at the campus level with different goals to create distinctive learning opportunities and a ladder of experience in service-learning and civic and political engagement.* A single course cannot achieve all civic and political engagement goals, but a combination can develop the knowledge, skills, motivation, ego strength, and efficacy for serious engagement.[24] However, if there are multiple courses, there is a need to help students integrate learning across multiple civic and political engagement experiences.[25]
15. *Reflection is more difficult than often recognized, but it is essential to teaching political engagement.* Faculty need to help students constantly reflect upon what they are doing and the effects of their actions through oral class presentations, journal entries, peer discussions, and reflection papers.[26] Faculty should help students draw connections between practice and theory, between experience and academic concepts.
16. *If civic and political engagement is to receive recognition in the profession, gain support on campuses and at various levels of government, and become widely adopted in a more complete and integrated program, such as a minor degree and certificate programs, then it must be rigorously assessed by both qualitative and quantitative methods.*[27] Developing standardized questions and assessment methods must be a priority of APSA. The further development of a robust website on teaching and political engagement, including assessment techniques, will allow educators to continuously update best practices in teaching civic engagement.

Conclusion

It is hopeful that AACU, APSA, and other national educational organizations are making a priority of civic engagement and publishing works like *A Crucible Moment* and this book. This collection, written by teacher-scholars from high schools to research universities, has demonstrated that there are many successful efforts in teaching civic and political engagement. Teaching civics and training citizens and political leaders have been goals of the profession since at least the Progressives like John Dewey in the early 20th century. Low youth participation rates in politics and government show that encouraging more political engagement experiences is greatly needed. This volume provides practical suggestions as to how to get the job done—a how-to guide of best practices.

Included within these chapters are ever-better educational and psychological theories of how the process works best. The authors present qualitative and quantitative evidence of successful techniques and which assessment techniques best test various innovations. They also have developed an action agenda that is pragmatic and provides useful next steps forward.

For this action agenda to be adopted and teaching political engagement to become more common, however, there must be a renewed commitment from the discipline, from academia, and from the government. Individual faculty members have to be willing to do extra work to plan and coordinate these courses. Departments and universities must be willing to provide the required resources and faculty credit for teaching these courses. Faculty need time off to prepare them, recognition for undertaking them, and rewards in terms of promotion, raises, and tenure for those who do the extra work. At many schools, colleges, and universities, the rewards for publishing so outweigh the rewards for teaching that it requires a substantial and sometimes risky sacrifice on the part of faculty members to undertake these tasks.

Governments tend to reward high schools that teach the basics, such as reading, writing, and math rather than those that teach civic engagement, although many have adopted a passive service-learning requirement in recent years. State governments have drastically cut funding for state-supported public universities so that teaching political engagement often seems to be an unaffordable luxury. The federal government has promoted minor funding for some involvement of universities in student voter registration or a one-day program on the US Constitution, but there is no serious federal funding for teaching civic engagement or training the future political leaders of the country.

Nonetheless, the authors of this volume, the many participants in the civic engagement tracks at the APSA's Teaching and Learning Conferences, and thousands of political scientists throughout the country are resolved that the pace of the movement for change that began decades ago must be accelerated. We hope that the readers of this book will join us in this effort.

ENDNOTES

Online supplemental material is available on the *Teaching Civic Engagement* book website at http://www.apsanet.org/TeachingCivicEngagement.

PREFACE

1. Battistoni and Hudson 1997.
2. Bloustein 1999. See this work for an example of this perception.
3. National Society for Experiential Education 1990.
4. Liu 1996.
5. Harwood Group 1993, xii.
6. Boyte 1991, 765.
7. Campus Compact 1999, 3–4.
8. See Battistoni 2002; Jacoby and Associates 2009.
9. See Colby et al. 2007

CHAPTER 1

1. Dewey 1916. Used here is the 2009 edition, and the quote appears on page 79.
2. See, for example, Hutchins (1936) and *Education for Freedom* (1943).
3. Defined in note 4.
4. National Task Force on Civic Learning and Democratic Engagement 2012. Quotes appear on page 2. See also Sen. Bob Graham 2010.
5. Association of American Colleges and Universities 2004. This assessment was made after reviewing collegiate accreditation standards, educational associations' statements of best pedagogical practices, mission statements of colleges and universities, the statements of higher education administration and select faculty, and reports of qualities sought by employers.
6. Ostrom 1998, 756.
7. APSA Task Force on Civic Education in the 21st Century 1998, 636. While some side with Putnam (2000) and Skocpol (2003), who see a major decline in citizens' civic engagement, others see hope in Dalton's (2009) argument that it is more the mode than the amount of civic engagement that has changed in the United States. As the purpose here is not to arbitrate this debate, the authors of this volume agree with the task force's and Ostrom's calls for increased scholarly and pedagogical work in this area as a core part of higher education's overall mission and educating about politics.
8. There are many articulators of this idea. See, for example, Colby et al. 2003; Frantzich 2008; Levine 2007; Macedo et al. 2005; Putnam and Feldstein 2003; Zukin et al. 2006; Battistoni 2000, 614–616; Delli Carpini and Keeter 2000, 635–637; Hepburn, Niemi, and Chapman 2000, 617–622; Walker 2000, 646–649; Kirlin 2002, 571–575.
9. In just my survey of schools in the Colonial Academic Alliance, which includes 12 public and private colleges and universities of varying sizes, all had some, if not all, of these options. Civic engagement was not the rationale for this alliance's creation, and its membership mirrors an athletic conference. The other contributors to this volume and participants in the civic engagement tracks of the annual APSA Teaching and Learning Conference also represent a wide representation of higher education institutions that offer these options.
10. Data gathered from UCLA's Higher Education Research Institute's (HERI) annual surveys of 203,967 students from 270 colleges and universities in 2011; 271,441 students from 393 institutions in 2006; and

281,064 students from 421 institutions in 2001. See Pryor, DeAngelo, Blake, Hurtado, and Tran 2011; Pryor, Hurtado, Saenz, Korn, Santos, and Korn 2006; Sax, Lindholm, Astin, Korn, and Mahoney 2006.

11. For example, only 62.3% of undergraduates in 2009 were white, compared to 77.6% in 1990 and 82.6% in 1976; the number of students age 25 and older increased 43% between 2000 and 2009; and enrollment of women outpaced men, at 40% versus 35%, in 2009. See National Center for Education Statistics 2012. Meanwhile, for the 2007–2008 academic year, 77.2% of students at public four-year institutions received some form of financial aid (loans, grants, scholarships), and 86% of students at private, nonprofit, four-year institutions received aid. For the 2008–2009 academic year, the numbers rose, with 78.6% of students at public four-year institutions receiving aid, and 87.2% of student at private, nonprofit, four-year schools receiving aid. See Knapp, Kelly-Reid, and Ginder 2011. Butin (2010) reminds us that this trend started after World War II, but accelerated with the social movements of the 1960s and 1970s.
12. Newell 2001, 196–211. See also Saltmarsh and Zlotkowski 2011, 354–365.
13. See the chapters in Section 2 of this book and Pedelty 2001, 230–252.
14. President Barack Obama, January 24, 2012; see also President Barack Obama, January 27, 2012.
15. See, for example, "Higher Education Accreditation" 2004; recent discussions on the Gainful Employment rule at the US Department of Education, such as noted in Field 2011; Sen. Edward Kennedy 2012; President Barack Obama 2012.
16. As Fear and Sandmann (1995, 110) explain, "Given society's investment in higher education and its increasing calls for publically funded institutions of higher education to be accountable and responsive, it is imperative that universities take their public service function more seriously."
17. See the section on "Definitions and Parameters in Civic and Political Engagement Pedagogy" for a more complete discussion of definition and parameters of service-learning as well as civic and political engagement.
18. In addition to the works noted previously, see also Jacoby and Associates 2009; Colby et al. 2003; Battistoni and Hudson 1997; Eyler and Giles 1999; and the chapters in Sections 2 and 4 of this book.
19. Battistoni and Hudson 1997.
20. Leonard 1999, 749–754.
21. Cress 2005, 7–16.
22. This definition is inspired by and contains elements of those provided in the following works: Colby et al. 2003; Jacoby and Associates 2009; Levine 2007; London 2002; Macedo et al. 2005; Zukin et al. 2006; McCartney 2006, 113–128.
23. Worgs 2011, 89–116.
24. Others also discuss this distinction, such as Colby et al. 2003 and Levine 2007. Macedo et al. 2005 eschews a line between these two concepts, seeing them as inherently interrelated.
25. The phrase "Democracy is not a spectator sport," is widely attributed to Lotte E. Scharfman, a former president of the League of Women Voters.
26. Schachter 1998, 631–635.
27. Dewey 1916, 109ff; Cantor 1953.
28. Hativa 2000, as cited in Wilson, Pollock, and Hamann 2007, 131.
29. Colby et al.; numerous journal articles, including Smith and Boyer 1996, 690–694; Beaumont and Battistoni 2006, 241–247; Perry and Wilkenfeld 2006, 303–312; Oros 2007, 293–311; Janger 2003, 9–12; Baker 2003, 233–238; Bennion 2006, 205–227; McCartney 2006. See also the chapters in Sections 2 and 3 of this book, especially McHugh and Mayer on this point.
30. Bringle and Hatcher 1995, 112.
31. Ibid. See also the student-oriented service-learning guide created by Schoenfeld 2004.
32. Dicklitch 2003, 773.
33. See, for example, Colby et al. 2003; Battistoni and Hudson 1997; Beaumont and Battistoni 2006; Battistoni 2000; Hepburn, Niemi, and Chapman 2000; Delli Carpini and Keeter 2000; Kirlin 2002; Cress 2005; Perry and Wilkenfeld 2006; Janger 2003; Bennion 2006; McCartney 2006; Jacoby 2009; Smith, Nowacek, and Bernstein 2010.
34. Lisman 1998. See also Gugerty and Swezey 1996; Mendel-Reyes, 1997.
35. These concerns are more thoroughly explained in Colby et al. 2003, 263ff.
36. See also the bibliography for examples that the authors have built upon.
37. Macedo et al. 2005, 6.
38. Donahue 2011, 107.
39. Ibid., 107–109. While Donahue focuses specifically on service-learning, the authors in this volume argue that this advantage should be inherent to any properly designed civic engagement course or activity.
40. Beaumont, Colby, Ehrlich, and Torney-Purta 2006, 249–270. Note that Chapter 8 by Lorenzini comes the closest to having a set political perspective. However, her private, Catholic university has a particular, explicit mission of helping the poor that students are fully aware of when choosing to attend that school. We contend that seeking to help homeless people is not a partisan value, though the means through which these individuals should be helped is a more politically contested area.

41. For a discussion of these past efforts, see Schachter 1998, 631–635, and Farr 2004, 37–40.
42. Leonard 1999, 749–754, and "Making the Past into Prologue" 1999, 758–759.
43. Boyer 1996, 11–20.
44. Leonard 1999. See also Fear and Sandmann 1995.
45. Rimmerman 2011, 187–190; Battistoni and Beaumont 2006.
46. Ibid., 81–82. See also McHugh and Mayer, Chapter 21.
47. My thanks to Joyce Kaufman for this insight. See also Kaufman 2012.
48. See McHugh and Mayer 2012.
49. Colby, Beaumont, Ehrlich, and Corngold 2008, 47.

Chapter 2

1. Patterson 2003.
2. Riker 1982, 5.
3. Center for Information and Research on Civic Learning and Engagement (CIRCLE) 2002, 3; "Youth Voter Turnout Has Declined" 2002.
4. Ibid.
5. Higher Education Research Institute (HERI) 1999.
6. CIRCLE 2002 a and b.
7. Putnam 2001, 35.
8. Galston 2001, 217–34.
9. American National Election Studies. "ANES Guide to Public Opinion and Electoral Behavior." Accessed at www.umich.edu/~nes/index.htm.
10. *Time* 2008.
11. McDonald 2001.
12. Rock the Vote 2008.
13. Langer 2010.
14. Smith 2009.
15. CIRCLE press release, January 20, 2010.
16. McDonald 2010.
17. CIRCLE Fact Sheet, November 17, 2010.
18. Associated Press, September 26, 2012.
19. Ibid.
20. CIRCLE data on 2012 primary voter turnout. Several states were assessed and reported through a set of press releases. At http://www.civicyouth.org/tag/2012-election/.
21. CIRCLE press release 2012.
22. See Krehbiel 1998.
23. Typical negative campaigning is not what the authors of this chapter saw in the 2012 election. A survey by the Center for Political Participation from the fall of 2010 confirms this characterization of the current climate.
24. As suggested by Carter 1999.
25. Noonan 2010.
26. As cited in Libit 2009.
27. Freidman 2009.
28. Shea 2010a.
29. Eisner 2004.
30. Smith 2011.
31. Green and Gerber 2004.
32. Ibid 2004.
33. Ibid. 6.
34. Exley 2008.
35. Vargas 2008.
36. Gladwell 2010
37. Ibid. The first quote appears on page 6; the second on page 9.
38. Harward 2011.
39. Ibid.
40. Key 1964, 6–7.
41. Frantzich 1999, 6.
42. Shea 2010.
43. Colby et al. 2008.
44. Newman 1985, 35.
45. Sunstein 2001.

46. Comber 2008.
47. Shea 2010b.
48. Johnson et al. 1998, 2.
49. Shea 2010b.
50. Johnson, Johnson, and Holubec 1998, 28.
51. Shea 2010b.
52. McKeachie and Svinicki 2006, 4.
53. Shea 2010b, 13.
54. Bain and Zimmerman 2009.
55. Ibid.
56. Ibid., 10.
57. Miller 2009, 4.
58. Ibid.
59. Ibid., 7.
60. Ibid.
61. Ibid., 5.
62. Ibid., 8.
63. We thank an anonymous reviewer for making this very helpful suggestion.
64. Kuh 2008.
65. See Frank, Chapter 6.
66. Downs 1957.
67. Lopez et al. 2005.
68. Colby 2008.
69. Marks and Babcock 2010.
70. Lenhart 2010.
71. Konrath and O'Brian 2010.
72. As cited in Bryner 2010, 1.
73. Ibid.
74. Howe and Strauss 2007, 172.
75. Ibid., 174. After a short visit to Princeton University in 2001, *New York Times* columnist David Brooks noted, "The young men and women of America's future elite work their laptops to the bone, rarely questioning authority, and happily accepting their position at the top of the heap as part of the natural order of things."
76. Palmer 1993.

Chapter 3

1. National Task Force on Civic Learning and Democratic Engagement 2012.
2. Gutmann 1987, 287; Galston 2001; Barber 1992; Nussbaum 1997, 2010; Macedo 2000.
3. Fish 2004; Murphy 2004.
4. A description of the Political Engagement Project undertaken by the Carnegie Foundation for the Advancement of Teaching is available at www.carnegiefoundation.org/PEP. This chapter draws synthetically from several joint publications written collectively by members of our research team, including Anne Colby, Thomas Ehrlich, Joshua Corngold, and Judith Torney-Purta (Beaumont, Colby, Ehrlich, and Torney-Purta 2006; Colby, Beaumont, Ehrlich, and Corngold 2007), as well as from two single-authored works (Beaumont 2010, 2011). The initial Carnegie Foundation Political Engagement Project study was supported by Atlantic Philanthropies, the Carnegie Corporation, the Carnegie Foundation, CIRCLE, the Ford Foundation, the Hewlett Foundation, and the Surdna Foundation. Support for the research on political learning mechanisms and development of political efficacy was provided by a grant from the University of Minnesota and the McKnight Land-Grant Professorship.
5. See, for example, discussions of these challenges and concerns in Colby et al. 2007, Chapter 3, and Beaumont 2010.
6. See www.carnegiefoundation.org/PEP for short descriptions of the courses and programs involved in the research, copies of the full survey, and other research instruments used in the project.
7. Here and throughout, "pretest" "posttest" or "pre-post" indicates an initial survey administered at the beginning of each intervention and a follow-up survey administered at the end.
8. Astin 1993; Battistoni 2002; Kuh et al. 2005.
9. Colby et al. 2007.
10. We derived our scales through a two-stage process, first using exploratory factor analysis to create preliminary scales and then using confirmatory factor analysis to examine and further refine those scales. Cronbach's alphas for all scales were all above .64. Details on the scales and results showing pre- and postsurvey means, dependent variables, and significant gains from analysis of variance for specific outcomes are included in Colby et al. 2007. Additional information is available at www.carnegiefoundation.org/PEP.

11. Colby, Ehrlich, Beaumont, and Stephens, 2003; Youniss, McClellan and Yates, 1997; Flanagan and Sherrod 1998; Verba, Schlozman, and Brady 1995; Conover and Searing 2000.
12. Verba et al. 1995; Kirlin 2002; Torney-Purta 1997, 2002.
13. These included the Americorps/Corporation for National Service Assessment (see Aguirre International 2000); the Walt Whitman Center's Measuring Citizenship Project (see Barber, Smith, Ballou, Higgens, Dedrick, and Downing 1997); Rutgers' colleagues, the IEA international survey, and the Pew Foundations' Project 540.
14. For further discussion, see Beaumont et al. 2006 and Beaumont 2010.
15. Within subjects pre/post effect: n.s. Pillai's Trace $p = .964$; Paired sample t-tests conducted by group found no significant pre-post differences for either group). In addition, a chi-square test of independence indicated that students' party identifications did not differ markedly from pre- to posttest, $X^2(16, N=473) = 744$, $p<.001$). See Beaumont et al. 2006.
16. Colby et al. 2007, Chapter 3.
17. Junn 2004.
18. Beaumont 2011.
19. Beaumont 2010, 515.
20. Beaumont 2010, 2011; For a more thorough discussion of the different pedagogies, learning experiences, and activities used by faculty and program leaders in the study, see Colby et al. 2007.
21. Astin 1993; Dewey [1916] 1966; Tocqueville [1835] 1990.
22. Bandura 1997. See also Frank, Chapter 6.
23. Colby et al. 2007; Kirlin 2002; Verba, Schlozman, and Brady 1995.
24. Niemi and Junn 1998; Torney-Purta 2002.
25. Deutsch 1961; Piaget 1985/1975; Ulbig and Funk 1999.
26. Mutz 2002, 2006.
27. Huckfeldt, Johnson, and Sprague 2005; Morrell 2005.
28. Gurin, Nagda, and Lopez 2004.
29. See http://www.aascu.org/programs/adp/PEP/, n.d.

Chapter 4

1. CIRCLE 2012.
2. Kirby, Hoban, Barrios Marcelo, Gillerman, and Linkins 2008.
3. Ibid.
4. Gibson 2001; Zukin et al. 2006.
5. Such as Gibson 2001; Gimpel, Lay, and Schuknecht 2003; and Zukin et al. 2006.
6. Such as Bogard, Sheinheit, and Clarke 2008, 541–546; Converse and Niemi 1971; Highton and Wolfinger 2001, 202–209; and Plutzer 2002, 41–56.
7. Marcia 1991, 1980.
8. Gimpel et al. 2003; and Flanagan 2003, 257–261.
9. Gimpel et al. 2003.
10. Ibid.
11. Flanagan 2003.
12. Ibid.
13. Yates and Youniss 1996, 271–284.
14. Campbell et al. 1980.
15. Highton and Wolfinger 2001.
16. Plutzer 2002.
17. Ibid., 42.
18. Bogard et al. 2008.
19. Gibson 2001, 1.
20. Ibid., 10.
21. Ibid., 13.
22. Ibid.
23. Ibid., 50, 87.
24. Ibid., 87.
25. Marcia 1991.
26. Ibid., 529.
27. Marcia 1980.
28. Adams 1998.
29. Kroger 2007; Hoover, Marcia, and Parris 1997, 95–106.
30. Ross 2000.
31. Marcia 1991, 1980.

32. Kroger 2007.
33. Ibid.
34. My research involved a focus group study conducted with individuals between the ages of 18 and 24. A total of 18 participants were included in six focus groups. Participants were recruited from an advertisement on Craigslist. I conducted the original collection of the data in both note form and with a digital recorder as the participants answered questions. Participants consented to recording their voices and were informed of the audio recording in the study prior to arrival. Participants could choose at any time not to answer a question or end their participation. While a few participants chose not to answer questions, no participants dropped out of the study. The time of the focus group generally lasted between 45 minutes and an hour and a half for larger focus groups. A pilot was conducted prior to the formal focus groups to deal with awkward question wording and to capture an accurate time frame. Adjustments were made in the protocol and were given to the Institutional Review Board before the original data were collected.
35. Marcia 1980.
36. Marcia 1980; Kroger 2007.
37. Marcia 1991.
38. Yates and Youniss 1996, 279.
39. Settles 2004, 487–500.
40. Ibid.

Chapter 5

1. See, for example, Kirlin 2002, 571–575; Spiezio 2002, 14–21; Galston 2004, 263–266; Westheimer and Kahne 2004, 241–247; Ball 2005, 287–291; Dalton and Crosby 2008, 1–6.
2. Spiezio 2002, 14–21.
3. Colby, Beaumont, Ehrlich, and Corngold 2007.
4. Horowitz 2003. See also Chapter 1 by McCartney, and Chapter 3 by Beaumont.
5. For definitions of terms and further discussion of this point, see McCartney, Chapter 1.
6. The five learning outcomes on which the report claims there is consensus are strong analytic, communication, quantitative, and information skills; deep understanding and hands-on experience with the disciplines that explore the natural, social, and cultural realms; intercultural knowledge and collaborative problem-solving skills; civic, social, and personal responsibility; and integrative thinking and the ability to transfer knowledge from one setting to another. Association of American Colleges and Universities 2004.
7. Liberal Education and America's Promise (LEAP) 2012.
8. "Carnegie Selects Colleges and Universities for 2010 Community Engagement Classification" 2010.
9. Ibid.
10. Meacham and Gaff 2006.
11. Ibid.
12. National Center for Education Statistics 2009.
13. National Center for Education Statistics 2011.
14. California Community Colleges Chancellor's Office 2011.
15. APSA 1997, 744.
16. Dalton (2009) calls the traditional norms of American citizenship—voting, paying taxes, belonging to a political party—duty-based citizenship. His second type of citizenship, engaged citizenship, includes "participation, but in nonelectoral activities such as by buying products for political reasons and being active in civil society groups." The engaged citizen also includes "a concern for the opinion of others."
17. Ibid., 175–195.
18. SAVE is a national nonprofit organization, founded and run by students. Its mission is to increase youth voter turnout by removing access barriers and promoting stronger civic education. For more information, go to http://www.savevoting.org/Index.html.
19. The United States Student Association is the country's oldest and largest national student-led organization. Its mission is to develop current and future leaders and amplify the student voice at the local, state, and national levels by mobilizing grassroots power to win concrete victories on student issues. For more information, go to http://www.usstudents.org/.
20. Student PIRGs are independent, state-based student organizations that work to solve public interest problems related to the environment, consumer protection, and government reform. For more information, go to http://www.studentpirgs.org/.
21. Ibid. See also US Student Association at www.usstudents.org or http://www.presidentscommitment.org. Accessed August 12, 2009.
22. The signatories are Lee Pelton, president, Willamette University; Dr. Stephen G. Emerson, president, Haverford College; Nancy J. Vickers, president, Bryn Mawr College; Marvin Krislov, president, Oberlin College; S. Georgia Nugent, president, Kenyon College; Nancy L. Zimpher, president, University of Cincinnati; Dr. G.P. "Bud" Peterson, chancellor, University of Colorado, Boulder; M. Roy Wilson, MD, MS,

chancellor, University of Colorado, Denver; John J. Sbrega, PhD, President, Bristol Community College; Paul Pai, president, St. Louis Community College; and Dr. Marshall Drummond, chancellor, Los Angeles Community College District.

23. http://www.presidentscommitment.org. Accessed August 12, 2009.
24. Ibid.
25. Save Voting, accessed August 12, 2009.
26. "Your Vote, Your Voice" n.d.
27. Intercollegiate Studies Institute 2007. http://www.americancivicliteracy.org/report/major_findings_findg5.html.
28. Ibid. 2007.
29. Another status report on civic education in higher education would survey college core curriculums to determine how many civic education courses—political science, history, and economics—students are required to take. Ideally, institutions of higher education are assessing the quality of these courses.
30. APSA 2012.
31. Leonore Annenberg Institute for Civics of the Annenberg Public Policy Center at the University of Pennsylvania n.d.
32. Office of General Counsel 2012.
33. "Help America Vote College Program" 2002.
34. Ibid.
35. Farrell and Hoover 2004.
36. Student Voting Guide | Brennan Center for Justice n.d.
37. O'Loughlin and Unangst 2006.
38. Ibid., 13–14.
39. Ibid.
40. *Dunn v. Blumstein*, 405 US 330 (1972); Lipka 2008.
41. *Symm v. US*, 439 US 1105 (1979).
42. Schwab 2008.
43. Moscoso 2008.
44. Castle, Levy, and Peshkin 2009.
45. US Electoral Assistance Commission, n.d.
46. Emphasis has been added to remind the reader that courts have ruled that college students do have the right to register to vote using their school address.
47. US Electoral Assistance Commission.
48. Ibid.

Chapter 6

1. Colby et al. 2007, 4.
2. Lopez and Brown 2006.
3. Colby et al. 2007.
4. Keeter 2002, 12.
5. Furlong and Scheberle 2005.
6. Colby et al. 2003, 19.
7. Longo and Meyer 2006, 2–3.
8. Colby et al. 2003, xiii.
9. Ibid., 11.
10. Colby et al. 2007, 4.
11. Ibid., 18.
12. Ibid., 19–226.
13. Shea 2008, 4.
14. Mello and Davis 2007.
15. IEA Civic Education Study 2000.
16. Scorza 2007, 3.
17. Ibid, 17.
18. See the "Assessment/Evaluations" area of online supplement to the book, http://www.apsanet.org/TeachingCivicEngagement.
19. The Statistical Package for the Social Sciences (SPSS) version 16.0 was used to determine Pearson Chi-Square, degrees of freedom (df), and percent significance. For the purposes of this study, political engagement was defined as activities such as voting; participating in campaigns or political parties; contacting elected officials; running for office; being formally and informally involved in community decision making; making campaign contributions; participating in public forums; writing a politically oriented blog; participating in various forms of policy advocacy and lobbying, protesting, boycotting, etc.; and publicly displaying a political message. See also Chapter 1, McCartney.

20. Verba et al. 1995, 545.
21. Colby et al. 2007, 10.
22. The Politics of San Francisco 2011.
23. Colby et al. 2007, 147.
24. Simpson 2011.
25. Cain and Messitte 2008.
26. Verba et al. 1995.
27. Colby et al. 2007, 3.
28. Goff 2007.
29. Torney-Purta, quote, 2001, 2.
30. Longo 2005.
31. Colby et al. 2007.
32. Keeter 2002, 7.
33. Aquinas College 2008.
34. "Code of Ethics" 1996.
35. The "This Study" percentage reflects respondents who answered that they voted in "all" presidential elections since they were old enough to vote, the *Voice and Equality* percentage reflects eligible voter respondents who voted in the 1988 presidential election, the "Other Studies" percentage reflects eligible voter respondents who voted in the 2004 presidential election according to the US Census and all elections according to CIRCLE 2006, page 41.
36. The "This Study" percentage reflects respondents who answered "often" and "sometimes." Percentages from "Other Studies" are from Nelson, page 35.
37. The "This Study" percentage reflects respondents who answered "often" and "sometimes." Percentages from "Other Studies" are from Putnam, page 44.
38. The "This Study" percentage reflects respondents who answered "often" and "sometimes."
39. Percentages from "Other Studies" are from Putnam, page 41.
40. Percentages from "Other Studies" are from Putnam, page 43.
41. The "This Study" percentage reflects respondents who answered "often" and "sometimes."
42. Percentages from "Other Studies" are from Putnam, page 41.

Chapter 7

1. Astin, Vogelgesang, Ikeda, and Yee 2000. Eyler, Giles, Stenson, and Gray 2001.
2. Here, I refer to service-learning and community-based research under the more generic term of community-engaged projects, even though these are two distinct concepts. As Strand et al. (2003) note, community-based research is research conducted with and for, not on, members of a community and engages students alongside faculty and community members. There are a variety of definitions of service-learning, but commonalities across the definitions emphasize that these projects integrate service and classroom learning in a way that benefits both students and the community.
3. Ball 2005, 287–92.
4. Mann and Patrick 2000, 167.
5. Saltmarsh, Hartley, and Clayton 2009.
6. Ball 2005; Jenkins 2008, 357–369; Simpson 2010; Waggener 2006, 207–210; Walker 2000, 646–649.
7. Eyler et al. 2001.
8. Astin et al. 2000.
9. Ball 2005; Keen and Baldwin 2004, 384–294.
10. Eyler et al. 2001.
11. Ibid.
12. Saltmarsh, Hartley, and Clayton 2009. See McCartney, Chapter 1, for definitions of civic and political engagement and explanations of how they are distinct from volunteering or community service/participation.
13. Salmarsh, Hartley, and Clayton 2009. Perry and Katula 2001, 330–365.
14. Delli Carpini and Keeter 2000, 636.
15. Eyler and Giles 1997; Eyler, Giles, and Braxton 1997, 5–15; Giles and Eyler 1994, 327–39; Simpson 2010.
16. Ball 2005, 287.
17. Hunter and Brisbin 2000, 623–626.
18. Perry and Katula 2001.
19. Delli Carpini and Keeter 2000. Kirlin 2002, 571–575. For distinctions between terms here, again, see McCartney, Chapter 1.
20. Galston 2001, 217–34.
21. Galston 2001; Ball 2005.
22. Walker 2000, 649.
23. Waggener 2006, 207.

24. Ball 2005; Walker 2000.
25. Ibid.; Hunter and Brisbin 2000.
26. Walker 2000, 648.
27. Markus, Howard, and King 1993, 416.
28. Jenkins 2008, 359.
29. See http://www.norc.uchicago.edu/GSS+Website/.
30. Bardach 2009, 95.
31. Walker 2000, 649.
32. The University of Massachusetts, Dartmouth, is a regional state school located on the southern coast of Massachusetts. There are approximately 8,000 undergraduate students; the gender balance is the reverse of national trends as male students outnumber their female counterparts. Eighty-six percent of the students are white. Most come from Massachusetts, and the average high school GPA for incoming students is 3.1. The Political Science Department is fairly small, with nine full-time faculty and approximately 140 undergraduate majors; there is no graduate program in political science, although the campus is seeking to move to a doctoral-intensive Carnegie ranking.
33. These readings came from Gray and Hanson 2008.
34. The readings for these course meetings came from Pelissero 2003 and Stewart, Hedge, and Lester 2008.
35. Bardach 2009.
36. I serve on the town Finance Committee; this position enabled me to have direct access to town officials and gave me inside information on what projects were most needed. However, others who follow local politics should have been able to easily identify similar problems on which students could work. Even without insider knowledge, it would be easy to work with town officials to identify potential projects.
37. This was the initial set-up for the community-based research projects. However, I gave each team a good deal of latitude in dividing the work load among team members. While one team followed these initial guidelines, the other team did not, leading to some difficulties later described in further detail.
38. For the two questions about the syllabus (whether it clearly specifies policies and procedures and whether the professor adhered to the syllabus), the average rating across seven items was 1.04. As noted, the less optimal (1.4) ratings on the syllabus questions probably stem from the fact that I had to make changes to the syllabus and project based on changing availability of local government officials. Use of all student materials has been cleared by my institution's Internal Review Board.
39. Meredith 2009, 186–208.
40. While it would be useful to assess whether students had more knowledge about state and local government and politics as a result of this class as compared to other seminars, the variety of seminar offerings prevents such a comparison. There are no other faculty members in the department who offer seminars on state and local government or US public policy.

Chapter 8

1. Dalton 2008 is an exception.
2. In addition to the APSA Standing Committee on Civic Engagement and Education, the APSA Annual Teaching and Learning Conference includes programmatic tracks on civic engagement.
3. Colby et al. 2007; Lawry et al. 2006; Walker 2000.
4. Some universities might not adhere to this ethical call to action, but I believe the insights learned through this service-learning course have applicability for all institutions of higher education that seek to promote political engagement.
5. SLU offers more than 80 courses that directly integrate community service into academic content.
6. In recognition of the need to more closely integrate community service with academic learning and research, SLU established the Center for Service and Community Engagement in the fall of 2009.
7. For definitions of these terms, see McCartney, Chapter 1.
8. This course was initially offered in the fall of 2007 and taught by Fr. Richard Quirk. After this initial offering, I met with the instructor, administrators from Queen of Peace Center (QOPC), and students to evaluate the course. Based on these discussions and written course evaluations, I substantially revised the course content, research project, and service activities. The overall goal of the course revisions was to help students see more clearly the connections between their community service and political engagement. The course content is presented here in its revised form as taught by myself in the fall of 2008 and fall of 2009. This course is now offered annually at SLU with an enrollment of 15 to 20 students.
9. Galston 2003; Sax et al. 2003.
10. Longo and Meyer 2006.
11. Keeter et al. 2002; Putnam 2000; Teixeira 1992.
12. National Association of Secretaries 1999.
13. Pryor et al. 2007.
14. Hays 1998, 45.

15. Boyte 2004; Gibson 2001; Kellogg 2001. For further information and discussions of causes and connections to identity, see Beaumont, Chapter 3, and Gentry, Chapter 4.
16. In a national survey of college undergraduates, the Institute of Politics (2002) at Harvard University found that nearly 66% had volunteered recently in their community, and more than 40% volunteered at least a few times per month. See also Lopez 2004; Sax et al. 2003.
17. Sax 2000, 15.
18. Walker 2000, 647; Eliasoph (1998) argues that students see service as a replacement or more desirable alternative to political engagement.
19. Lawry et al. 2006, 29.
20. Lopez et al. 2006; Niemi and Hammer 2004.
21. Kiesa et al. 2007
22. Tisch 2008. For information on the 2010 and 2012 elections, see Harward and Shea, Chapter 2.
23. The millennial generation includes those born after 1985. Long et al. (2002) also report this finding in the *Wingspread Statement.*
24. Kiesa et al. 2007.
25. SLU students are involved not only in service in their local community, but also engage in community service around the globe. For example, one student organization, Students United for Africa (SUFA), raised more than $30,000 to build an elementary school in Ghana, and now is raising money to build a library for the community. Students from this organization have visited the village school and engaged in service in the local community. SLU also offers students the opportunity to participate in overseas service trips and enroll in international service-learning experiences in impoverished areas of the world.
26. Kiesa et al. 2007.
27. SLU student interview with a local news reporter, October 2007.
28. See Walker 2000.
29. The quotes in this section are drawn from the course proposal submitted by Nima Sheth and Amanda Ring-Rissler to the Political Science Department.
30. Kiesa et al. 2007.
31. Lawry et al. 2006; Walker 2000.
32. Barber and Battistoni 1993; Battistoni and Hudson 1997; Ehrlich 1999; Eyler and Giles 1999.
33. Faculty involved in the initial development of this course included Dr. Wynne Moskop, chair, Department of Political Science; Dr. Ellen Carnaghan, professor of political science; Fr. Richard Quirk, adjunct instructor of political science; Dr. Robert Cropf, chair, Department of Public Policy; Dr. Richard Colignon, chair, Department of Sociology and Criminal Justice; Dr. Mary Domahidy, associate professor in public policy; and myself. The two students who initiated this project were Nima Sheth and Amanda Ring-Rissler. Administrators from Queen of Peace Center involved in the development of the service learning component of the course included Connie Neumann, executive director; Azhar Hakim, director of operations; Will Hildebrandt, grant and quality manager; and Lara Pennington, grants and leadership associate.
34. Faculty members involved from the School of Social Work include Dr. Julie Birkenmaier, associate professor and director of field education, and Dr. Jami Curley, assistant professor.
35. As I am a member of QOPC's Community Board, I approached its executive director and director of operations to discuss potential areas of collaboration. We all agreed that this would be a mutually beneficial partnership and learning experience. The administrators were especially in agreement that it was key for the students to engage in collaborative research rather than just committing service hours to the organization.
36. Per QOPC's Annual Report, 80% of QOPC clients are homeless at admission, 90% have suffered trauma, 70% have co-occurring disorders, 51% are uninsured, and 49% are Medicaid clients.
37. QOPC provides services through four programs: Comprehensive Substance Abuse Treatment and Rehabilitation (CSTAR), Peace for Kids (a day care and child development center), St. Philippine Home (a transitional housing program serving women and their children), and Shelter Plus Care (permanent housing units that provide safe and affordable housing through rental assistance for homeless and disabled individuals and families).
38. SLU's campus is located in the city of St. Louis, in which 23.5% of the city's population lives below the poverty line, per 2008 US Census Bureau data.
39. Katz 1989.
40. The latter is particularly important in order for students to recognize that how different peoples define citizenship entails different responsibilities.
41. Students draw lots that assign them a high- (15%), middle- (35%), or low-income (50%) status based on global poverty figures. Each level then receives a corresponding meal based on income level. To view the toolkit, visit: http://actfast.oxfamamerica.org/uploads/OA-HBToolkit.pdf.
42. This was crucial to enable students to make the link between the course material and the research project.

43. The client interview was to be completed in the first section of the course, the provider interview in the second, and the stakeholder interview in the final section.
44. Shelter Plus Care is a HUD-funded rental assistance program. As a recipient of SPC vouchers, QOPC conducts hearings to screen clients ready to move to transitional housing and to ensure compliance with SPC regulations, which include continued case management.
45. The requirements for this course were an essay midterm exam (20%), three interviews for the research project (15%), class participation (10%), an essay final exam (20%), the final research project (30%), and course evaluation and reflection (5%). Student evaluations were collected anonymously with university approval.
46. Lara Pennington was one of the administrators from QOPC who oversaw the service-learning component of the course. At the time, she was an SLU graduate student in the School of Social Work completing her practicum at QOPC. After the completion of her practicum, she trained at the Rebecca Project in Washington, DC. Subsequently, she was hired full-time by QOPC as its community development associate responsible for coordinating the group's advocacy and public policy activities.
47. The agencies selected were Beyond Housing, Redevelopment Opportunities for Women (ROW), Catholic Charities Housing Resource Center (CCHRC), and the International Institute.
48. The national director of the Rebecca Project conducted the advocacy training sessions. This visit was funded by the VOICES Project at SLU.
49. *OneWorld* magazine 2006, 2.

Chapter 9

1. This class was intentionally designed to be very intensive in its service-learning requirements and is thus more demanding than other courses outlined in this volume and, potentially, in the words of an anonymous reviewer, "more suitable as training for students who aspire to be political leaders."
2. Many millennials find time to do volunteer work, and 85% of students prefer volunteerism to political participation. See statistics and quote in Harvard Institute of Politics Study 2000. For more information on youth voter turnout see Harward and Shea, Chapter 2, and Colby et al. 2007; Popkin and Dimock 1999; Niemi and Junn 1999; and Project Vote 2011.
3. Moely et al. 2002; Prentice 2007; Freyss 2006.
4. Prentice 2007.
5. Reinke 2003.
6. Parker-Gwin and Mabry 1998.
7. Galston 2001.
8. Hepburn et al. 2000, 618.
9. Myers-Lipton 1994.
10. Bradley 1997; Shumer and Belbas 1996.
11. The College of the Pacific—the liberal arts college within the comprehensive University of the Pacific—is a private school that enrolls a racially and ethnically diverse population of approximately 1,600 students, most of whom are undergraduates. The college is located in Stockton, one of California's largest cities, and the majority of students are California natives. Retrieved June 12, 2011, from the College of the Pacific website flyer: http://web.pacific.edu/Documents/school-college/COP%20Brochure.pdf.
12. Though the class is typically filled by political science majors, nonmajors who have declared a prelaw minor commonly take the course to partially fulfill their minor requirement. Other majors with a policy career bent, such as sociology majors, typically enroll as well.
13. All appendices are located in the online supplement to this book. See http://www.apsanet.org/TeachingCivicEngagement.
14. This significant time commitment seems to have limited the number of students who enrolled, at least anecdotally. At Pacific, more than 80% of students receive some form of financial aid to cover tuition and expenses. A substantial number of students also work at least part-time. Prior to the start of the semester, I emailed all enrolled students to set expectations about the significant time commitment that would be required. Approximately three students replied to indicate that extracurricular activities, work, or both would prevent them from participating that semester.
15. Being relatively new to Stockton at the time, I relied on a short list of nonprofit organizations that a senior colleague provided based on his experience and working relationships in the community. After briefly interviewing the short list of contacts, I decided to work with CPF based on several factors, most important of which were: 1) its proximity to campus; 2) CPF's willingness to accommodate student schedules and create four different service projects from which students could choose; and 3) a working relationship I had developed with one of the CPF officials with whom students would work. Despite being only three miles from campus, the short distance still provided a challenge for students without access to private transportation. Fortunately, student carpooling seemed to overcome transportation problems, as the university was unable to provide transportation to CPF for students. The selection of CPF was a blend of luck and opportunity.

16. Students signed consent forms prior to questioning, which gave them the right to opt out, and those were reviewed by the Institutional Review Board (IRB) for all responses included in this study.
17. Discussion prompts were posted online through Blackboard educational software. Students could view the prompts and respond to them in a semipublic (enrolled students only) setting. Students also could view each other's posts and were encouraged to respond.
18. The scale was adapted from Craig, Niemi, and Silver 1990.
19. It should be noted that only nine of the 14 students fully completed both the pre- and postsurvey. Students with missing data, for example, those who completed the pretest but not the posttest, were dropped from the analysis. Note that semester one was the service-learning course semester, whereas semesters two and three were the nonservice-learning semesters.
20. All but one or two students consistently submitted responses. While their responses were not anonymous, since they were receiving credit equivalent to class participation, I advised students that they would not be graded based on their approval or disapproval of the community partner. Rather, I told them that I wanted to see evidence that they were thinking critically about the questions, and were trying to link course concepts to real-life service.

Chapter 10

1. An earlier version of this chapter was published as Allen, Parker, and DeLorenzo 2012, 35–49.
2. Willis and Barlyn 2007, 21–31.
3. Ibid.
4. From 2006 to 2008, California State University, Chico, was named to the President's Higher Education Community Service Honor Roll for Excellence in General Community Service. Abowd 2006, 14–15; Learn and Serve America 2007.
5. The annual operational costs of CLIC are currently funded by the Department of Political Science at California State University, Chico; the university's student governing body; the local city government; and independent fund-raising efforts. CLIC's annual operating costs total approximately $70,000, depending upon annual funding grants. Annual rent is currently $24,000 for 1,384 square feet of dedicated space. The overhead cost for clerical staff, books, printing, mail, etc., is approximately $43,622. Because of CLIC's extensive size, four faculty each receive credit for one course per semester for their internship supervision work. One of these faculty members also serves as the department's legal studies internship coordinator and receives credit for one additional course over the span of an academic year to direct the overall administration of CLIC as well as any off-campus legal internships.
6. Pappas and Peaden 2004, 859–863.
7. Zucker and Zucker 2006, 93–110.
8. Willis and Barlyn 2007, 28.
9. Bureau of Labor Statistics 2010.
10. Ibid.
11. Ibid.
12. Ibid.
13. Willis and Baryln 2007, 23.
14. Ibid.
15. Before students can participate in a CLIC internship, they must first submit a detailed application listing their qualifications and program interests. Because of the popularity of CLIC internships, almost all available openings are filled by upper-division students. After submitting their applications, potential interns are interviewed by student program directors to assess whether they would be a good fit for particular programs based on the applicants' interests and the intern needs of each program. CLIC faculty have the final say about which applicants to accept as interns in their programs.
16. California Business and Professions Code 2010.
17. Escamilla 2006, 24–28.
18. Zucker and Zucker 2006, 95.
19. McCarthy 2007, 7.
20. Ibid.
21. During the 2009–2010 academic year, we asked CLIC clients to respond to a questionnaire concerning their experiences at CLIC. To get a better idea of the population the law clinic was serving, sociodemographic data were also collected from the respondents.
22. Robinson 2000, 605–612.
23. According to CSU, Chico, the Humans Subject Policy does not apply to our data because they are the "usual instructional testing and evaluation processes used to make judgments about student learning related to academic offerings of the University." Thus, full Internal Review Board clearance for all data used in this chapter has been received.

24. Both CLIC student program directors and administrative directors are selected through a competitive process as they work their way up the ladder. Each spring students submit applications for program and administrative director positions. All applicants then participate in interviews with the outgoing program and administrative directors and faculty. Based on their application and interview performance, new program and administrative directors are then chosen for the upcoming year.
25. Oros 2007, 293–311.
26. Trudeau 2005, 289–322.
27. Oros 2007.
28. Ehrlich 2000, Preface vii.

Chapter 11

1. The fall 2010 website represented the fifth iteration of a collaborative teaching project to develop a website to supplement American politics courses.
2. American politics or American government courses were included in this project principally because the content varies little across campuses, and similar issues and contemporary events are likely to be topics for discussion and analysis in each class. However, any number of classes that share topics could collaborate in a website project such as this; we have found that the medium is well-suited for humanities courses that include—but are not limited to—substantial discussion of current events. The website project was initiated in 2008 to coincide with the presidential election. Having found an open-source website platform that was then free (NING.com), Renée VanVechten recruited interested faculty from the APSA Political Science Education listserv, and three professors developed online activities and the site during fall 2008, re-creating the site in spring 2009 for their new classes. Over the next year, three more professors joined the project after hearing about it at the APSA Teaching and Learning Conference in 2009 and 2010. NING.com has since moved to a fee-based service, and one year of financial support was provided by two of the six participating institutions by mutual agreement and based on availability of funds.
3. For each semester from fall 2008 to fall 2010, a new website was created for each set of participating classes. The URL for fall 2010 was americanpoliticsfall2010.ning.com.
4. Jacoby and Associates 2009, 9. For definitions of civic engagement, see McCartney, Chapter 1. Using the words of Jacoby and Associates, who based their definitions on those by the Coalition for Civic Engagement and Leadership at the University of Maryland (2005), what we seek is that "Through civic engagement, individuals—as citizens of their communities, their nations, and the world—are empowered as agents of positive social change for a more democratic world."
5. For example, the Coalition for Civic Engagement and Leadership 2005.
6. We do not claim that every student who participates will learn the gamut of lessons represented in this list, nor do we anticipate that the website allows each to be equally or extremely well-developed. As with all educational exercises, what participants derive from assignments largely depends upon their own investments of time and energy. The academic website environment affords students the opportunity to learn civic lessons and develop and practice skills and sensibilities that constitute civic engagement. In this sense, it represents a hybridized space, one developed through compulsion (students participate as a class activity), but expands beyond it as students participate as inquiring citizens and individuals who are members of a larger national (and international) community. We have not measured whether these lessons stick beyond the semester in which they are practiced, yet we would expect that a personally transformative experience will change a person's thinking or approach to problem-solving in lasting ways.
7. Easton and Dennis 1965; Dudley and Gitelson 2003.
8. Campbell, Converse, Miller, and Stokes 1960.
9. Beaumont and Battistoni 2006.
10. Quoting Jacoby 2011; Bloom 1956; Bender 2003.
11. Pollock, Hamann, and Wilson 2005
12. Pollock and Wilson 2002.
13. Blount 2006.
14. Ibid. Quote appears on page 272.
15. Pollock, Hamann, and Wilson 2005, ref. to Cummings 1998.
16. Guttman 2000.
17. Avery and Hahn 2004.
18. Zuniga, Vasques-Scalera, Sevig, and Nagda 1997; Gurin, Nagda, and Lopez 2004; Strachan and Owens, forthcoming.
19. Pollock, Hamann, and Wilson 2005, 3.
20. See the course material and discussion questions available on the online supplement to this book. See http://www.apsanet.org/TeachingCivicEngagement.
21. The first two Town Hall meetings were scheduled prior to the start of the semester and were open to all students. In contrast to past semesters, when an average of 30 to 35 students took part, the first two live

chats included more than 95 students and were extremely difficult to manage, as most students' comments and questions overlapped. The final opportunity to participate in live chats occurred on one day late in the semester, during which three separate smaller chats were led by two professors. These were much more manageable, and each attracted 30 to 50 students apiece.

22. All courses except for UHD participated in the interview assignment. At UHD, students from the 90-person class interviewed each other.
23. In fall 2010, 19 students created a profile on the site but did not participate (they are included in the count of 328), and several more also contributed to the site and subsequently dropped the class (those individuals were excluded from the final count).
24. The same sets of students, however, did not complete the pre- and posttests (surveys). Because most professors encouraged but did not require their students to take the surveys, some students declined; in addition, others completed the first survey and subsequently dropped the class. Anonymity made it impossible to tell exactly who had taken both surveys.
25. Further details about the participating campuses can be found in the "Course Material" section in the online supplement to the book. See http://www.apsanet.org/TeachingCivicEngagement. The site contained privacy controls so that participants had to receive an invitation to join, and they could also be banned from the site for inappropriate behavior.
26. Two forums were begun and then restarted with a different title; these were combined. One thread only attracted 85 responses, probably because it duplicated the number of another one and because it came at the end of the semester after most students had met their website assignment quotas; this question was also excluded from the tally.
27. This number excludes a few that were intended to be a student profile (a required post for Discussion Question 1). The number of responses to student discussion forums was one to 41, and the modal response rate was eight.
28. Usage depended upon such factors as how many times they were required to post, but personal motivations also came into play. Each professor established a minimum number of required posts. These ranged from seven total (about one post every other week) to 24 (two posts every week). However, personal factors played a strong part in their website experiences, because many students did not meet the minimums set in their own classes. No professor awarded extra credit for extra posts. Further analysis revealed that those students required to post regularly tended to do so, and these classes also produced the highest number of "superusers"—students who far exceeded their requirements—and the fewest number of those who never used the site. In other words, there is a positive relationship between higher requirements (more frequent posts) and student behavior (number of posts, both in terms of consistency throughout the semester and the total number produced).
29. Jacoby and Associates 2009.
30. The task of coding the discussion questions was divided between the two authors (each assumed responsibility for coding an entire question). We developed our rubric first by together coding approximately 75 posts to one discussion question and samples from other discussion forums (not included in this analysis). Together, we then coded the first 25 posts of each discussion question used in this analysis. Next, we separately coded the remaining entries, continuing to compare notes to make certain we were applying the same criteria. We corrected discrepancies before analyzing the data. This process took about one week. To measure intercoder agreement, we selected a question not used in this analysis and separately coded the same 25 posts containing 162 statements, and found a high degree of agreement on our scoring of overall reflectiveness (.84, $p<.001$, Cohen's kappa), as well as the other variables used to determine the reflectiveness index.
31. All names have been changed to pseudonyms here and in every instance in which names are used.
32. As this post shows, students' misconceptions about current controversies often were apparent. Some of these misstatements went unremarked upon (such as the reference to killing a homosexual soldier; in this case, the soldier in question was heterosexual), but often a peer would call attention to these statements and correct them. Professors tried to provide basic facts about cases or events referenced in the discussion questions by addressing them in class, and by including links to relevant articles in the question prompts.
33. We also rated posts for negativity. We rated a response as "1" if the tone was strident, brash, and contained strong wording, and lots of CAPS or exclamation points. We tried to distinguish between a "passionate" post (in which the person had strong beliefs) and an angry one (possibly meant to insult or offend, expressing anger). A post received a "5" if it contained profanity, "yelling" at others, or strongly negative direct accusations, for example. In our reading of the posts throughout the site, we found only a few examples of a post or exchange that warranted a rating of "5." Most were in the 1–2 range. We estimate that about 15% of the posts were negative in tone, mostly on the lower end of a five-point scale.
34. This comment comes from the end-of-the-semester survey (December 2010) in response to the open-ended question: "What did you enjoy learning about most on the American Politics Project website?"
35. A large percentage (70.5%) agreed with the statement in the end-of-semester survey that they would have posted more if they had been "more interested in the topic"; however, 57.9% also agreed that they "posted as much as they wanted to."

36. The fact that a certain percentage of students volunteered these statements does not mean that others felt differently or that similar comments did not apply to them. Rather, based on verbal feedback and written communiqués, we believe many more students would have agreed that more of these outcomes were relevant to them, but we did not include a Likert scale to assess this panoply of outcomes.
37. A total of 149 students responded to this closed-ended question, posed on the end-of-semester survey.
38. Blount 2006; Jacoby and Associates 2009; Sloam 2010.
39. Pollock, Hamann, and Wilson 2005.
40. Levine and Cureton 1998.
41. Throughout the semester, the professors participating in the website project communicated with each other via conference calls, telephone, and email to work out student usage issues and administrative details. Email proved to be the most reliable form of communication, whereas conference calls were much harder to coordinate (one convened prior to the semester in July, and another occurred during September in anticipation of the second Town Hall meeting). Responsibility for posing the "Discussion Question of the Week" alternated regularly among the instructors. One professor assumed responsibility for coordinating the interview match-ups. Management of a site could be easily shared; however, administrative activities generally required one person to assume responsibility for coordinating activities among the professors. The site was hosted by a private company (NING) that began charging for services in July 2010; thus, the professors sought grants and funds through their universities to support the site. Ultimately, two located funds that covered the cost ($200 annually, per site). NING did (and continues to) offer free websites for educational use, but the number of participants was capped at 150, and no chat feature was available. Finally, to allow professors unfettered access to the survey data collected, one professor shouldered the cost of maintaining an account with Survey Monkey and others helped pay these costs (many universities have an account with a web-based survey company such as Survey Monkey, but access is normally limited to the faculty at that institution). Each website experience has taught the instructors new lessons about how to improve the experience, and the project continues to grow and unfold. We see great potential for international collaborations as well as interdisciplinary projects. Exercises that encourage dialogue and facilitate deliberation among students and educators can be incorporated into existing syllabi relatively easily, and activities can be tailored to fit individual instructors' preferences for learning outcomes and additional workload. Administrative responsibilities do generate additional work, but each professor in this project continues to find that the value and benefits of the website (both for their students and them) outweigh the administrative costs. For more information about joining this project or administering a new one, please contact the authors.
42. Galston 2003; Putnam 2000; Sax, Astin, Lindholm, Korn, and Mahoney 2003.

CHAPTER 12

1. Chickering and Gamson 1987. Ultimately, the studies are looking for engagement, not relevancy. The responses of students are positive because they have fun, but the research does not speak to the students finding these activities useful beyond learning the specific content knowledge. Also, the research provides little evidence that the students retain this knowledge over the long-term.
2. The agenda-setting model's success is documented in Perry and Wilkenfeld 2006. See also Colby, Beaumont, Ehrlich, and Corngold 2007; Smith 2003a.; and Chesney and Feinstein 1997.
3. Faculty can decide whether to participate in the convention only as a supplemental educational activity or to make other changes to courses that could include significant pedagogical modifications in which a course centers on the agenda-building activities. Content of the American government course can be directly linked to the agenda-building activities by having lectures and student discussions structured to focus on how the core American government lessons can link to an issue of student interest and the agenda-building process. The "Sample Projects" page in the "Course Material" area of the online supplement to this book includes a list of questions used to tie the agenda-championing activities to the traditional content found in American government courses. These questions have been used effectively in traditional classes during a lecture/discussion and/or for online discussion with hybrid or online courses. The "Discussion and Blog Prompts" page in the "Course Material" area of the online material includes: basic directions for students to write about an issue that they chose to champion. This area also includes: an assignment that asks students to build a strategic plan that illustrates how they could effectively promote their concern and to build a larger coalition of supporters beyond their class, with the ultimate goal of being able to impact the political agenda and a given legislative agenda. See http://www.apsanet.org/TeachingCivicEngagement.
4. Even though students may try to find or advocate solutions, they are encouraged not to dwell on any given solution, as this can destroy the capacity to build a coalition surrounding the concern. An example often given to explain this to students is the issue of health care. Since the early part of this century, most Americans, including political officials, agree that health care is a major concern that needs resolution. Yet, competition over solutions can destroy the potential agreement that the problem needs to be addressed. For the elected officials who formulate policy by looking at policy alternatives this is necessary, as they represent various constituencies; however, ordinary citizens do not have the position or the power to solve the issue. Rather, their role is to make sure the need is articulated to those who are formulating public policy.

5. Assigning various roles allows for more active participation during the group work.
6. Various methods of the agenda-setting model can be utilized, including very limited in-class preparation, and the focus can strictly be on the Student Political Issue Convention.
7. The initial issue being championed is not fully developed, and many students are not tied to a particular concern after their basic research. Rather, they are using these activities to participate in the discussion the next time the class meets.
8. Some are instructed, such as students who become the organizers of a convention; others figure this out on their own through the process. See the online website for this book for a brief description of the required essay for the class. It is required regardless of whether the student attends the convention, but it is a means of focusing attention on developing political voice. Therefore, the faculty who incorporate such activities into their courses can provide students with a better idea of how to proceed prior to the convention. Early-semester conventions often do not have this advantage, and faculty often use the convention as more of a kick-off for the essay activities as opposed to a midpoint of linking the student learning to the convention.
9. Depending on how a class is designed, the next phase can occur during the next class meeting or in a week or two. Faculty can design the debate around the issues to include formal lobbying. The lobbying time allowed requires more classroom time and should be built into the course. Courses that employ course management systems can have students continue the discussion online and significantly reduce the in-class time for this project.
10. Instructors can provide weekly questions that pertain to their issue discussion, development, and the chapter readings. The course material area in the online supplement provides examples of such questions. See http://www.apsanet.org/TeachingCivicEngagement.
11. Prior to voting on the number of issues on the class agenda, students should be told to look at the issues on the board. If there are 10 issues, then they need to determine how many issues they would not want to champion. That is, if there were five issues they would not wish to work to champion, then they should select at least five issues for the class agenda. This way, there are better odds that students will be able to work in a group on an issue they feel is important. Usually only a handful of students have locked in one or two issues that they have to champion; most are just starting to get engaged and take some level of ownership. Most classes with fewer than 30 students have only four or five issues that they wish to be on the agenda. By this point the students have learned the importance of working together collectively to champion and issue, and therefore, they seek to have large enough groups that have the opportunity to be successful as they attempt to impact the political agenda.
12. One key aspect of groups can be to have students develop issue-championing activities. Issue-championing activities are basically any activities that help build stronger support for the issue, thus helping to place the issue on the political agenda.
13. Providing the students with the concept of coalition building and the notion that starting with a class coalition often provides many more resources than individuals working alone from the beginning of a process gets students to collaborate.
14. Not only do smaller groups work more efficiently, smaller groups permit more students to participate directly. Larger groups with seven to 10 students can easily have students attempt to become free-riders, as the group can function without everyone participating. Therefore, even if many students want to work on the same topics, students should be encouraged to create smaller groups that are more manageable and can better hold members accountable. The smaller groups with the same or similar issues should coordinate their work. This system might not seem intuitive at first, but considering that one major justification of this project is to create a process that engages students, they need to be able to participate, be heard, and feel valued.
15. This assignment can be submitted electronically through a course management system.
16. The process described can continue beyond the convention, as the groups focus on their strategies for expanding their coalition and raising awareness beyond their class.
17. Invited elected officials are told both in their invitation letters and when they arrive to respond to the students' concerns in their speeches. Depending upon the number of officials and time restraints, the floor is opened to the students to ask more probing and specific questions. The plan for 2013 is to have a morning and an afternoon plenary session, with elected officials all on stage participating in town hall–style Q&A sessions.
18. These can be issues from the class agenda or they can be issues being discussed generally in class. This sourcing will depend upon if there are faculty who are incorporating the model throughout their courses or just coming to the convention with their students.
19. The keynote is best given at the opening session to kick off events and inspire students. However, depending on the elected official's schedule, some years the keynotes has been given to start the final plenary sessions.
20. Students receive class credit for developing and running a workshop. Some faculty require students to get 10% to 20% of their grade from "civic action activities." The Michigan Student Political Issues Convention has used student-led workshops, if there were enough faculty who incorporated the entire model

throughout their courses and when a convention is held late enough in the semester for students to develop presentations. When students develop and deliver workshops around their issue, they can receive credit for their formal class grade. When the convention is held early in a semester or the convention does not have faculty who integrate this approach throughout the semester, the workshops can be replaced with a series of speakers who focus on pertinent concerns. Other conventions have no workshops and may have faculty and community organizations lead discussions and highlight a series of public policy issues that may or may not make it onto the students' issue agenda.

21. When reserving conference space, make sure to reserve extra time for students to mingle with elected officials and other dignitaries after the formal convention has ended.
22. This is one example of voting caucus rules that have been used successfully. The voting rules are not hard and fast; however, they must be approved in the opening plenary session. Modification to the rules can and has been made in the opening session. Parliamentary procedure is used in both plenary sessions.
23. Assigned caucus rooms are placed in the programs. For a typical Michigan convention, 700 programs are printed. There are 30 programs, with a given caucus room listed on the program. Those running registration will only give programs with new voting caucus rooms after each room is filled. This ensures that there are enough people to conduct a vote in each voting caucus. The conventions at HFCC have ranged from 350 to 670 participants. The number of programs made will depend upon the expectation of attendance.
24. Faculty can give limited credit to students who volunteer for one of these positions.
25. A faculty person at a computer often acts as the tally person.
26. The convention chair has usually been a faculty member who helps organize and coordinate the convention. However, successful conventions also have been held with elected officials running the convention. A Michigan Circuit Court judge, a city council chair, and a county commissioner who had experience with the convention process have each participated as convention chairs on several occasions.
27. The number 7 is what has traditionally been accepted for state agendas. However, through parliamentary procedure, the number on the agenda can be modified by the students.
28. The conventions generally are three-quarters of a day, from 9:30 a.m. to 2:30 p.m. Wayne State held split-day events, which has not been done at HFCC. Students at HFCC are mostly enrolled in introductory American government courses, with smaller groups from upper-division courses—especially from other schools. Professor JP Faletta at St. Mary's College in Texas uses a combination of political science courses from introductory American government through senior-level courses. Students at HFCC from across the campus are invited to participate. Economics and history students whose professors work closely with the political science staff also frequently take part. Also, in the past, Wayne State had significant representation from biology and English courses. Most professors make participation optional, but it is marketed to students as a fun option for learning and participating. Students are registered and then complete the evaluations. The faculty usually have students write a report that describes the convention and relates it to their course.
29. Faculty at participating institutions determine the dates for the convention and the week to designate as National Student Political Issues Week.
30. Contact Anthony Perry at adperry1@hfcc.edu to get the most recent rules and procedures.
31. The student agenda-building process is organic, and therefore these are only suggestions.
32. Several of the fall conventions from 2004 to 2009 had faculty participating with their classes only. The classes developed a political agenda, and the results were submitted as part of the National Student Agenda.
33. *Educating for Democracy*, 10.
34. Niemi and Hanmer 2004.
35. Perry and Wilkenfeld 2006.
36. Independent research of the conventions was conducted by the Carnegie Foundation's Political Engagement Project. These results were published in Colby, Beaumont, Ehrlich, and Corngold 2007.

Chapter 13

1. Wolfinger and Rosenstone 1980.
2. Squire, Wolfinger, and Glass 1987.
3. Pultzer 2002; Bendor, Diermeier, and Ting 2003; Green and Shachar 2003; Fowler 2006.
4. Verba, Schlozman, and Brady 1995.
5. Wattenberg 2008.
6. Ibid. See also Chapter 2 (Haward and Shea) for an excellent discussion of the recent history of civic and electoral engagement among young people.
7. See Harris, Chapter 5, for more information about these requirements and hindrances to receiving voter registration information.
8. Colby et al. 2003.
9. Colby et al. 2007.
10. www.civicengagement.org/agingsociety/links/democracy_at_risk.pdf.

11. http://www.aascu.org/programs/ADP/.
12. For a summary of recent studies, see Gerber and Green 2004.
13. Green and Gerber 2000; Bennion 2005; Arceneaux and Nickerson 2010; Green and Karlan 2006; Nickerson 2006; Niven 2006.
14. Gerber, Green, and Larimer 2008.
15. Michelson 2005; Ramirez 2005; Frey and Suarez 2006.
16. Wong 2005; Gimpel, Shaw, and Cho 2006.
17. Trivedi 2005.
18. Nickerson 2008.
19. Pultzer 2002; Bendor, Diermeier, and Ting 2003; Green and Shachar 2003; Fowler 2006.
20. Bennion and Nickerson 2009, 2010, 2011; Mann 2011.
21. See Chapter 19 (Owen) for a discussion of the challenges of survey-based research on civic learning outcomes.
22. Arceneaux and Nickerson 2009.
23. Erikson 1981.
24. Falcone and Moss 2008.
25. Updating registration information is an important function, however. Many jurisdictions require that voters be registered at their current address to be eligible to vote. Furthermore, groups rely on the voter file, so updated information makes a voter more likely to be mobilized by campaigns and civic organizations.
26. Administration consent was not sufficient for Institutional Review Board (IRB) approval. As a result, it was necessary to secure IRB approval on more than 40 campuses—a significant bureaucratic hurdle.
27. A sample letter is included in the "Sample Projects" page in the "Course Materials" area of this book's online supplement. See http://www.apsanet.org/TeachingCivicEngagement.
28. A sample of the email text and the schedule for sending the emails is provided in Appendix the "Sample Projects" page of the "Course Materials" area of this book's online supplement. See http://www.apsanet.org/TeachingCivicEngagement.
29. Some schools sent fewer than three emails or used only one type of sender. Deviations from the protocol used in other schools are noted in the analysis.
30. Very few political science, psychology, and economics professors participated.
31. See the "Sample Projects" page in the "Course Materials" area of this book's online supplement. See http://www.apsanet.org/TeachingCivicEngagement
32. A few schools used only one type of presenter in the experiments. These schools are noted in the table reporting results.
33. Donner and Klar 2000; Arceneaux 2005; Green and Vavreck 2008.
34. The two samples with very low match rates could be due to a problem with the data provided by the school or the county. Since an identical matching algorithm was used for each school, the matching algorithm is unlikely to be the problem.
35. Nickerson 2007.
36. Bennion and Nickerson 2010.
37. Lupia and McCubbins 1998; Druckman 2001.
38. Kuklinski and Hurley 1994.

Chapter 14

1. Hoppe 2004; Swaner 2007; Boyte 2008.
2. Swaner 2007, 19.
3. Jacoby 1996; Eyler and Giles 1999.
4. There is also a school of thought in the civic engagement literature that ties such engagement to a feeling of giving back to the community (see Etzioni 1995). That is a worthy goal. My class, however, was not based on this perspective. Empowering citizens, not giving back to the community, was the goal of this experience.
5. Benson and Harkavy 2002, 362. According to the research, approaches such as this also can lead to personal development. (Eyler and Giles 1999; Pascarella and Terenzini 2005). Some arguments are made that it can even improve a student's mental health and overall well-being. Again, while such goals are worthy, they were beyond the scope of my concerns, nor did I try to assess whether such goals were achieved. (For a good overview of these broader issues as they relate to civic engagement, see Swaner 2007).
6. In 2003–2004 I was on sabbatical and did not teach the class. In 2000, I taught it as a summer class, timed so that the two party conventions met during the class.
7. Iowa is permitted to preceed New Hampshire, according to New Hampshire law, because it is a caucus in which no actual delegates to the nominating convention are chosen. The precinct caucuses, which receive all the attention in Iowa, are actually only the first stage of a four-stage process that leads to the selection of the actual convention delegation.
8. Similarly, in the 2004 contest, Sen. Joseph Lieberman rented an apartment in New Hampshire.

9. A student wishing to do an internship for credit in Drake University's Political Science Department completes an application with a member of the department that specifies the internship and the student's responsibilities, which should average between 10 and 20 hours per week; provides the contact information of the supervisor at the site; and steps out the writing assignments that will be done to demonstrate reflection on the internship and what it demonstrates about politics or government. The specific assignments vary depending upon both the internship and the department member who is the academic supervisor.
10. Students received separate grades for the internship experience and the class. This was done because I assumed, correctly as it turned out, that there would be students who would excel in their internships and think critically and reflectively about them, but who might not be able to achieve an "A" grade in the traditional portion of the class.
11. The syllabus and assignments for the class are available from the author.
12. Students received extra credit for participation in the forum. Three quarters of the class participated, even though most did not need the extra credit.
13. The university had its own broader Iowa Caucus Project designed to encourage student activity and involvement. Through that project, almost all of the candidates in both parties came to Drake to hold events, so there was plenty of activity on campus. A small class of students, none of whom was likely to be an undecided voter, did not meet the needs of the campaigns, however. The only guest speakers I was able to obtain were people with whom I had preexisting relationships. For example, the director of media relations in Iowa for Hilary Clinton's campaign was someone I had worked with a number of times in the past. He was willing to make time to come to class.
14. One of the students in the class was doing his internship with Drake's Iowa Caucus Project—this was set up long before the class began—and part of his responsibility was to see that these examples were posted to the Drake website. Permission was sought for two reasons. First, an open and frank dialogue in the blog was encouraged by keeping it accessible only to the class. Second, students should not violate the confidentiality of what was going on in the campaigns for which they were working. It was made it clear to students that there was no penalty for not giving permission, and, in fact, I as the instructor would not even know who the student in charge of posting had contacted and, therefore, I would not know who had asked that their blog entry not be posted to the public site.
15. Quite a few of the students—I do not have an exact number—had started working for the candidate of their choice over the summer (or even in the spring), long before this class began. Also, while this class was clearly not representative of the university's student body, it was typical of the upper-level politics classes that I teach in the department. The six-credit structure might indicate that these students were more interested in the practical side of politics than would be the case were only a traditional three-credit class on the nomination process offered, but it is not clear if this is true. In classes I teach on elections, a large percentage of students are involved as campaign volunteers. There also were a number of students who asked me if they could take the class without the additional three credits, not because they were not going to volunteer for campaigns, but because they did not have room in their schedules for the additional three credits. Those students were not allowed into the class, because of a concern it would create resentment among students that others in the class did not have to complete the internship assignments.
16. The difficulty recruiting guests to class referred to individuals coming to class to talk about various aspects of the campaign (for example, someone working on fund-raising discussing how money is raised, or a field coordinator discussing how to organize events). These talks offered no potential strategic gain for the campaigns, as by that time, all of the students were already working for someone. This initial visit was at a time when some of the students were still available. The purpose was to allow recruiting of potential volunteers, sweetened by the promise to distribute materials about the campaigns to a wider audience. Thus, the campaigns were very willing to send people to this particular class.
17. Use of all student data and comments has been cleared by Drake's Institutional Review Board.
18. In retrospect, I wish I had asked some more specific questions about the relationship of the internship experience to specific aspects of the class in the evaluation questionnaire. For example, I might have asked a series of questions about how the internship helped them better understand campaign finance or political advertising or voter behavior. This would have been particularly useful if some students did not answer "yes" to this question because they were thinking broadly about the class as a whole, but might have answered "yes" to a specific aspect of the class. Unfortunately, I did not do so. I only asked a broad question and asked students to elaborate. Use of all student information and comments was cleared by the Drake University Institutional Review Board.
19. The class started with *The Presidential Nominating Process* by Rhodes Cook. Students then read selected chapters from Steven Wayne's *Is This Any Way to Run a Democratic Election?* and *Red and Blue Nation*, volume I, edited by Pietro Nivola and David Brady, before reading the Lau and Redlawsk book. The other books read over the course of the semester were *Claiming the Mantle*, by Lawrence Butler; *Mediating the Vote*, by Michael Pfau, Brian Houston, and Shane Semmler; *Campaigns and Elections American Style*, by James Thurb-

er and Candice Nelson; and *The Internet Election*, by Andrew Williams and John Tedesco. Interested parties can contact me for a copy of the course syllabus.

20. Swaner 2007, 19.
21. Another 20% of the grade was for the quality of the writing, whereas the vast bulk of the grade came from their discussion of the Iowa caucus and its role in the nomination process.
22. See, for example, Fink 2003 for a discussion of the need to move away from "content" (telling students which connections are important and why they exist) to a more "learning-centered" approach (in which students develop an understanding of these connections on their own).
23. The Political Science Department could, for example, make sure there was a section of the introductory American politics class taught at the same time, ensuring a large number of potential volunteers and making it more likely that campaigns would send a representative.
24. The Iowa legislature is a part-time body that meets from mid-January until mid-April, which would fit nicely with Drake's spring semester.
25. Drake has just hired a service learning coordinator in an attempt to help with this concern.
26. See, for example, Mindich 2005; Macedo et al. 2005; Wattenberg 2007; and Sanders 2007. For a different perspective that emphasizes the ways in which young people are involved, see Dalton 2008 and Zukin et al. 2006.

Chapter 15

1. This chapter was originally presented at the 2008 American Political Science Association Conference on Teaching and Learning in San Jose, CA (February 2008). I wish to offer Lillian Lopez, my longtime colleague and friend, a wish of thanks for her generous feedback on early versions of this paper.
2. Putnam 2000; Macedo et al. 2005.
3. In addition to the information provided in Section 1 of this book, see also Bennett and Bennett 2001; Mann 1999.
4. Dalton 2008, 5.
5. Clearly, I have my doubts regarding a positive answer. I should disclose here that I hold some theoretical biases that I share from an approach to political theory with its roots in the work of Hannah Arendt. While it may represent an extreme form, I draw much inspiration from her analysis of the trial of one unthinking person. In *Eichmann in Jerusalem*, Arendt (1963) introduces a concept of thinking inherently tied to both the moral as well as the political realm. Many know Arendt's work for its Grecophile privileging of action (1998). I, too, find resources for inspiration here, but I am especially interested in bringing to view her overall concern with the dangers of thoughtlessness. I should also say that I am not prepared to offer only one account of "authentic" thinking as such.
6. Hunter and Brisbin 2000.
7. See Bracey 2005.
8. Arendt 1998, 50.
9. Gadamer 1976, 1989.
10. Arendt 1998, 49.
11. This literature is too voluminous to capture here. I am especially indebted to Derek Heater for two texts, *What Is Citizenship?* 1999 and *A Brief History of Citizenship* 2004. I have also been informed by Ronald Beiner's great collection of essays in *Theorizing Citizenship* 1995 and Richard Dagger's effort to bring together what he calls "republican liberalism" in *Civic Virtues: Rights, Citizenship, and Republican Liberalism* 1997.
12. Heater 1999, 2004.
13. Each time I taught this course, I conducted a preservice survey to gather some basic data about students' community service prior to this course. Rarely do I find evidence of active duty-based civic engagement (Dalton 2008).
14. Morningside is a comprehensive liberal arts college, with a full-time enrollment of 1,200 students. It is affiliated with the United Methodist Church. Most students come from within a 200-mile radius of Sioux City, especially from northwest Iowa, Nebraska, and South Dakota. The student body is primarily white, and many students are from rural communities in the region. Sioux City and the surrounding "Siouxland" region are diverse, especially with an increasing number of Hispanic, Asian, and Somali children in the local school districts.
15. For some general information about Morningside College, see http://www.morningside.edu/academics/research/factbook/MorningsideCollegeFastFacts.htm.
16. See the "Political Philosophy" page of the "Assessments/Evaluations" area of the online supplement to the book for a summary of the Morningside College Learning Outcomes and a brief summary of Morningside's General Education Program and graduation requirements. See http://www.apsanet.org/TeachingCivicEngagement
17. Nesteruk 2007.
18. See Berndt and Muse 2004.
19. Bloustein 1999.

20. Heater 2004.
21. See selection in Berndt and Muse 2004, 31.
22. See selection in Bloustein 1999.
23. Wenz 2007.
24. Ehrenreich 2002.
25. Keller 2005.
26. See the Iowa State Extension website for more information on the Poverty Simulation at http://www.extension.iastate.edu/news/2006/apr/122101.htm.
27. My colleagues in the Nursing School have found this to be a particularly useful exercise during the course of the school's curriculum. Most nursing students take a course in Community Health Nursing during their junior year, which relies heavily upon a service-learning component.
28. See the "Sample Projects" page in the "Course Materials" area of the online supplement to the book for the POLS 182: Citizenship Service Learning Experience assignment handout. See http://www.apsanet.org/TeachingCivicEngagement
29. See the Morningside College Service Learning Flag Assessment form on the "Political Philosophy" page of the Assessment/Evaluations area of the online supplement to the book. See http://www.apsanet.org/TeachingCivicEngagement. See http://www.apsanet.org/TeachingCivicEngagement.
30. All appendices are located in the online supplement to the book.
31. See the Morningside College Ethics and Personal Values Assessment form in the "Political Philosophy" page of the "Assessment/Evaluation" section located in the online supplement to this book. See http://www.apsanet.org/TeachingCivicEngagement
32. It is important to emphasize the importance of course-embedded assessments. Designing these assessments as part of the course pedagogy is somewhat time consuming, but, ultimately, aids and facilitates assessment of student learning. Furthermore, many of the other faculty in both Service Learning and Ethics and Personal Values courses meet regularly to discuss strategies for assessment as well as share data. Some validity testing of the assessment rubrics also have been provided in brown bag lunch meetings and some summer workshops.
33. Dalton 2008.

Chapter 16

1. See, for example, Fish 2008.
2. I thank an anonymous reviewer for this point.
3. There is much debate on what to call what students "do." At Franklin & Marshall College (F&M), the preference is to call it community-based learning rather than service-learning. The preference is community-based learning because service-learning sometimes has a negative connotation and is also sometimes perceived by many in academia as part of a liberal agenda. However, the term service-learning is more appropriate to this volume.
4. This is despite some ground-breaking earlier reports on the positive learning outcomes associated with service-learning. For example, see Eyler and Giles 1999; Eyler, Giles, Stenson, and Gray 2001. See McCartney, Chapter 1, for more discussion of this issue.
5. See, for example, Strage 2000, 5–13.
6. *US News & World Report* released a list of "10 College Classes That Impact the Outside World" on April 18, 2011. One of the courses selected was Human Rights–Human Wrongs, which is taught at F&M by Susan Dicklitch, professor of government and director of the Ware Institute for Civic Engagement. The article explains that these courses "allow undergraduate students to make a significant impact beyond the confines of their colleges, while honing skills that may one day be applicable to their careers." http://www.usnews.com/education/best-colleges/articles/2011/04/18/10-college-classes-that-impact-the-outside-world.
7. Bloom 1984.
8. For more examples, see Simpson 1972.
9. One of the team members acts as the detainee, and the other as his or her immigration attorney. I serve as the Immigration and Customs Enforcement (ICE) attorney, and my student assistant serves as the immigration judge.
10. The class blog is located at http://humanrights4all.blogspot.com. Students are expected to regularly post and comment on human rights issues in general, and often on asylum or immigration issues in particular that relate to what students are doing in the classroom and what they are doing with their detainees.
11. Although it is difficult to gather statistics on asylum seekers suffering from PTSD, a 2003 study by Physicians for Human Rights and the Bellevue/NYU Program for Survivors of Torture found that "significant symptoms of depression were present in 86% of the 70 detained asylum seekers, anxiety was present in 77% and PTSD in 50%." In *From Persecution to Prison: The Health Consequences of Detention for Asylum Seekers*, page 2.
12. Ramji-Nogales, Schoenholtz, and Schrag 2007, 341.

13. I am not an attorney, but an Africanist by professional training, and I serve as an expert witness on Cameroonian and Ugandan asylum claims. In the past, the class has worked exclusively with PIRC, but since 2010, students have expanded their partnership to include pro bono attorneys. It is important to note that students do not practice law, nor do they give legal advice to asylum seekers. Student work products are always checked and rechecked by the attorneys they are working with before it is submitted to immigration court.
14. York County Prison is located in York, Pennsylvania, approximately 20 miles from Franklin & Marshall College. It is a maximum-security county prison that rents out about 800 beds to the Department of Homeland Security to detain immigration detainees in the "removal process."
15. In the fall of 2011, HR-HW was taught as a two-course sequence offered simultaneously. Students enrolled in HR-HW, as well as a new course called Political Asylum Practicum. The course was co-taught with an immigration attorney who was able to provide even more professional instruction on legal writing and research, crucial to asylum cases. Students received two full course credits for the two courses. Because of the amount of work and dedication required of students to compile a compelling case and learn about the intricacies of asylum law and international human rights overall, it was important to reward them accordingly with a two-course credit.
16. To win asylum, asylum seekers have to prove that they have a well-founded fear of persecution, based upon one or more of the five enumerated grounds: political opinion, religion, ethnicity, race or nationality, and membership in a particular social group. The key nexus is that the government is the persecutor or cannot control the prosecutors. The granting of asylum, however, is discretionary in that it is up to the discretion of the immigration judge. The definition of asylum is based on the US Immigration Nationality Act (INA) but follows international law. Once asylum seekers win asylum, they acquire permanent residency and can naturalize to become US citizens. The formal definition of asylum is:

    > [A]ny person who is outside any country of such person's nationality. . . . And who is unable or unwilling to return to, and is unable or unwilling to avail himself or herself of the protection of that country because of persecution or a well-founded fear of persecution on account of race, religion, nationality, membership in a particular social group, or political opinion. 8 U.S.C. § 1101 (a) (42) (a); INA §101 (a) (42) (A).

17. The International standard is based on the UN Protocol Relating to the Status of Refugees, Article 1 (2).
18. Withholding of removal also offers relief from persecution, but the standard is higher—immigration detainees most prove that it is more likely than not that they will be persecuted on the basis of one of the five enumerated grounds. If they can prove that it is more likely than not that they will be persecuted, relief is mandatory. Although it is harder to win withholding of removal, the benefits are not as great. An immigration detainee's removal (deportation) order is withheld, but if country conditions change so that the detainee is no longer in danger of persecution, he or she can be removed from the United States. Similarly, detainees do not become permanent residents, and they cannot naturalize to become US citizens. Although this option is not as beneficial as asylum granted, it may be the only hope that the asylum seekers have to remain outside of their country.
19. Convention Against Torture relief is the least desirable form of relief because it is the hardest to win and provides the least amount of benefits. Because the United States signed the Convention Against Torture, the country is obligated by international law to defer the removal of anyone who can prove that they will be tortured by the state or by individuals working at the behest of the state.
20. I picked PIRC as the community partner because it was the only nonprofit organization working with detained asylum seekers in the York County Prison. The group agreed to vet cases and work with students on cases, providing training and legal oversight on the cases. The students would do the legwork on compiling evidence, and PIRC would provide legal representation in the courtroom for the asylum seekers.
21. Although students work on asylum, withholding of removal, and Convention Against Torture cases, for simplicity's sake, I will refer to the individuals as "detained immigrants." All these individuals share a common element in that they are seeking safe haven relief in the United States.
22. The fact that the students can log more than 150 hours in a semester on research on an asylum case makes it more feasible for a nonprofit legal organization or pro bono attorney to represent an otherwise unrepresented asylum seeker.
23. See, for example, Kolb and Kolb 2005.
24. A Memorandum of Understanding has been approved by the university, so that I may use anonymous student quotes.
25. The subjective basis for relief means that the detainee actually has a fear of returning to his or her country of origin. The objective basis for relief means that a reasonable person in the applicant's shoes would fear persecution.
26. Students are under the direct supervision of an attorney and only meet with an asylum seeker with an attorney present.
27. *INS v. Cardoza-Fonseca*, 480 US 421 (1987).
28. BIA test in *Matter of Mogharrabi*, 19 I & N Dec. 489 (BIA 1987); *INS v. Elias-Zacarias*, 112 US 812 (1992). This case set forth these criteria.

29. I spend a lot of time talking with each team and individual students to help them process their feelings. Another way I try to make sure that students do not become overwhelmed by their feelings is that I require that they submit their reflections on a weekly basis (electronically, via e-disk), so that I can monitor their emotional health. Students work with the school counseling services to make sure that they are not overwhelmed, and the team system and layers of support help keep them grounded.
30. There have been several instances in which immigration judges—during asylum seekers' individual merits hearings—have formally noted the impressive work that the Franklin & Marshall College students in the HR-HW class have done in compiling evidence for the evidentiary packet.
31. A legal memo details the strengths and weakness of a case along with relevant case law, whereas a legal brief is a persuasive argument focusing on the strengths of the case.
32. The six statutory bars to asylum are: firm resettlement, one-year filing deadline, commission of particularly serious crimes, persecution of others, danger to the security of United States, and commission of a serious nonpolitical crime outside the United States.
33. Torture is defined as

    any act which severe pain or suffering, whether physical or mental, is intentionally inflicted on a person for such purposes as obtaining from him or a third person information or a confession, punishing him for an act he or a third person has committed or is suspected of having committed, or intimidating or coercing him or a third person, or for any reason based on discrimination of any kind ... when such pain or suffering is inflicted by or at the instigation of or acquiescence of a public official or other person acting in official capacity (Convention Against Torture).
34. Post-2012, I will be unable to prescreen students for the class, because the "permission by the instructor" prerequisite has been removed from all senior seminar classes offered in the Government Department.
35. See Krathwohl, Bloom, and Masia 1973.
36. One student opined:

    I know that this is just a college course, but I literally feel like my whole life has been turned upside down. I have been pushed to every limit and tested in more ways than I thought that I would be ... I've spent hours printing out documents, typing up quotes and other documents, putting together the case, and mainly just stressing out about if I did a good enough job (Student "F", HR-HW 2006).
37. Another student in HR-HW got her entire family involved in helping her asylum seeker; see, for example, Goodwin n.d.
38. See Krathwohl et al.
39. See the article, Eric Schoeniger 2012.
40. Many of my students have gone on to law school to pursue human rights or immigration law, and several have pursued graduate studies in human rights, citing this class as the prime motivator.
41. Asylum seekers are not provided legal representation by the state—unlike criminal or civil law in which public defenders are provided without cost to the client.
42. As Trac Immigration shows, an important determining factor in the granting or denying of asylum is the presence or absence of legal representation. Those asylum seekers with a lawyer had a 64% denial rate, whereas those without a lawyer had a 93% denial rate. See http://trac.syr.edu/immigration/reports/159/.
43. The course in 2011 has since transformed into a two-course offering: Human Rights–Human Wrongs and Political Asylum Practicum. I now team-teach the class with an immigration attorney, and we partner with several pro bono attorneys as well as the community partner, PIRC. Given the amount of work expected of students, it was decided that it was unfair to reward students with an only one-course credit. The pre-2011 and post-2011 course syllabus are available in this book's online supplement.
44. As one former student of HR-HW wrote for her master's in human rights research paper,

    K and I were responsible for the daunting task of putting the documentation together for her asylum case. We poured through article after article, going through countless highlighters and pens, and logged many hours trying to find the right words, the strongest facts, and the correct testimonies of expert witnesses to guarantee that Isatu would be granted asylum, and set free. That task will always haunt me, yet at the same time will be something that I am most proud of. Her case and that class became my life. I could not help but feel that it could have been me, it should have been me, but because it wasn't, I had to do everything in my power and more, to help her (Student "H", HR-HW 2004).

CHAPTER 17

1. Dalton 2009; Colby et al. 2003; Frantzich 2008; Macedo et al. 2005.
2. Enrollment data obtained from Knapp, Kelly-Reid, and Ginder 2011. The table includes students from two- and four-year institutions. Data on the profession obtained from APSA, "Distribution of Subfields: Current APSA Members, Chart 1: A:3," accessed on February 2, 2012, at https://www.apsanet.org/imgtest/IA3.pdf. Note that the actual number of those teaching political science courses is almost certainly higher, as some prefer to only be members of other internationally focused associations.

3. Some courses are blends of international relations and comparative politics, such as a course that I teach on German politics and foreign policy.
4. Zivi 2007, 61.
5. Rios Millett McCartney 2006, 114.
6. See, for example, Friedman 1999.
7. See Ishiyama and Breuning 2006; Breuning 2005; Barber 2007; Ward 2007; Lantis 2011; Hudak, Sachleben, and Ward 2011.
8. One course, Diplomacy and World Affairs, at Occidental College, which I was only somewhat aware of soon after I created my own course, was briefly described in the appendix of Battistoni and Hudson's work. However, at the time of the book's publishing, this was offered as a history course. It is no longer offered, and I was never able to access a syllabus for what seemed like a path-breaking course.
9. I am currently compiling quantitative data gathered at the beginning and end of the classes as well.
10. McCartney 2006.
11. Earlier versions of this chapter were presented as "Connecting Civic Engagement and International Relations Pedagogy: An Effective Combination?" at the APSA Annual Meeting and Exhibition, Seattle, Washington, September 2011; "What Happens After Graduation? An Evaluation of the Impacts of Civic Engagement Courses on Post-College Practices" at the APSA Teaching and Learning Conference, Albuquerque, New Mexico, February 11–13, 2011, with other portions included in "Combining Civic Engagement and Traditional Research: A Second Option," APSA Teaching and Learning Conference, San Jose, California, February 21–24, 2008, and "Where Civic Engagement Is Forgotten: How We Can Practice What We Preach in International Relations," APSA Annual Meeting and Exhibition, Philadelphia, Pennsylvania, August 31–September 3, 2006. My thanks to my panel chairs and discussants at these conferences for their insightful comments, particularly Elizabeth Bennion and Mary McHugh.
12. The two coders were myself and a graduate assistant who had never taken the course or worked with me before. Intercoder reliability results are reported throughout this chapter.
13. McCartney 2006.
14. Towson University is located in Towson, Maryland, a suburb of Baltimore, and is the Baltimore County seat. It is the second-largest undergraduate institution in the University of Maryland system, with approximately 17,000 undergraduates. The student body is about two-thirds female and one-third male, with only about one-third of undergraduates coming from out of state. Tuition and fees for full-time, in-state students totaled $7,906 in 2012, and full-time, out-of-state student tuition and fees totaled $19,418. See www.towson.edu for more details. My thanks to the Towson University Faculty Development Grant program and the Office of the Dean of the College of Liberal Arts for their support of the development of these classes, this research, and the Model UN conference events. I also would like to thank the vice president for student affairs, Dr. Deb Moriarty, for her support through the creation of programs and funding streams to make these classes and the Model UN program a reality. Dr. Toni Marzotto and Dr. James Roberts, chairs of the Political Science Department, and Dr. Matthew Durington, director of the International Studies program, have made invaluable contributions to these courses and the Model UN program. Finally, the Political Science Department teaching assistants, Doug Woodruff, Britta Nelson, Brandy Jo Sykes, and Anneliese Johnson have added incalculable hours to these projects.
15. Tenth grade was chosen by BCPS because the curriculum in that year includes world history and political events. It also could follow-up on a ninth grade role-playing activity, Model Congress, run by BCPS.
16. Towson University, "Towson University Mission Statement," accessed on February 2, 2012, at http://www.towson.edu/main/abouttu/glance/mission.asp.
17. See Lisman 1998; Mendel-Reyes 1997; "Teaching/Theorizing/Practicing Democracy", 15–34; Gugerty and Swezey 1996.
18. McCartney 2006.
19. At this writing, schools have paid a modest fee of between $75 and $250 per school, regardless of number of participants, for breakfasts and snacks, and $75 per day for each substitute teacher. BCPS pays for bus transportation, which currently costs about $4,500. TU pays for all venue and materials costs, totaling approximately $2,000 (excluding staff costs, though I am not paid extra for my work with this event). In the last three years, two other school districts in Anne Arundel County and Charles County have sent delegations, and they pay for their own transportation as well as the school fee. Students pay only for an all-you-can-eat lunch buffet at a TU student cafeteria, which costs between $5 and $8.
20. See McCartney 2006.
21. A copy of the syllabus is available in the online supplement to this book.
22. As Omelicheva suggests, I provide students with evaluation criteria to increase the reliability and constructive results of peer assessments. Omelicheva 2005, 191–205.
23. A professor of secondary education comes to class to teach the students how to create an effective presentation and learning activity for a 10th grade audience. The students and I then provide both written and oral feedback on each presentation and activity to ensure quality and appropriate content.

24. Requirements for the class include an essay on civic engagement in a democracy; an essay evaluating the most important current activities of the UN; preparing for and working the UN Training Day; in-class research presentation; presentation for the community partner; a 20-page research paper; a five-page reflection paper; and class attendance and participation.
25. The first time the spring course was offered, I did not have this requirement for selection, and two students who were not really dedicated or had insufficient skills to pursue the advanced research required were allowed to take it. Given the suboptimal results in the quality of their research, contributions to the Model UN program, and conference participation, I have found the previous semester a useful indicator of success.
26. These students took the class before participation was limited to those who received a grade of B or higher. Their work was not of sufficient quality for conference presentation.
27. Note that four of these local-level presenters also were at a national or regional conference, giving them an additional chance to refine their oral presentation skills.
28. Just under two-thirds of these students took the three-credit option.
29. Of those who took the course for three credits, five were white males, nine were white females, and two were black females; two-credit students included two white males; and one-credit students included six white females and three white males.
30. The graduate students included one black female and one white female. I do not include them in these analyses as the class is directed toward undergraduates.
31. As students are graded on these essays, I admit that they may be trying to curry favor. They are prompted in the essay by three questions: 1) What did you get (personally and academically) out of the civic engagement experiences? 2) Are there any differences between your expectations of this class and what actually happened? Discuss. 3) What do you think overall about civic engagement and international relations? These questions are meant to give students wide latitude in their responses. I tell students that there are no "right" answers and that they are graded on their connections to and between class materials, class discussions, and class activities, as well as clarity of writing and level of reflection.
32. Lower numbers are for earlier years. A rating of good (or agree) was indicated by a numerical score of four out of five and a rating of excellent (or strongly agree) was scored a five out of five. The difference in noting good/agree or excellent/strongly agree is due to a change in phrasing of evaluations during this period.
33. Institutional Review Board approval was gained for use of all students comments, as long as the authors are not named. A full listing of all comments can be provided upon request.
34. While content coding is not an exact measure, myself and a graduate assistant independently went through these essays, and intercoder reliability is reported for all data used. The data on class assigned readings that are similar throughout all semesters were used as a control, and 100% intercoder reliability was found. Data are coded by paragraph, not by sentence.
35. The results of these surveys are incomplete due to an unfortunate loss of data and thus were not included.
36. Intercoder reliability was 99.5% in this category.
37. Intercoder reliability was 80.5% in this category.
38. This last category had lower rate of intercoder reliability at 64%. In the next round of data collection, more discussion between the two coders about this category will be required.
39. Intercoder reliability in this category was 75%.
40. Intercoder reliability was 96% in this category.
41. Intercoder reliability was 96% in this category.
42. For example, in the 2010 written evaluations, some variation of the word "challenging" appeared positively in five of 18 comments.
43. Putnam 2000; Putnam 2002; Bringle and Hatcher in Zlotkowski 1999.
44. Use of all survey data has been cleared by the Towson University Institutional Research Board.
45. Of the respondents, 18 were female and 7 were male, an appropriate gender distribution for the campus (see previous notes). Thirteen were political science majors, five were international studies majors, three were double majors in economics and political science, and one each majored in science, social science major, sociology, and double environmental science–political science. Eleven are pursuing or have master's degrees. On political affiliation, nine are Democrats, three are Republicans, four are libertarians, three are Greens, five have no affiliation, and one did not answer. If all former students had been included, the voting percentages most likely would be lower, as nonresponders also are less likely to have voted. Statistics of youth with college experience versus youth who have graduated were used, as some respondents were still in college. The statistics for those who have graduated were somewhat higher (64.7% in 2004; 41.0% in 2006; 71.9% in 2008; 37.4% in 2010), but my results are still higher. See CIRCLE, "Youth Voting: Quick Facts," accessed August 26, 2011, at http://www.civicyouth.org/quick-facts/youth-voting/#15. Note that college graduates always vote at higher levels than noncollege graduates or attendees.
46. At this writing, total costs for 2011–2012 are anticipated to total $14,320. BCPS Office of Social Studies is paying for $5,500 (bus transportation); BCPS schools are paying $2,750; non-BCPS schools are paying $2,825; and Towson University is paying $3,245. This cost equals about $72 per student for three days of activities.

Chapter 18

1. Portions of this chapter were presented at and further developed after conference presentations: "Teaching Political Science," Florida Political Science Association Annual Meeting, Florida Atlantic University, Jupiter, Florida, March 2011; "Incorporating Civic Education into the Curriculum," a presentation to university professors, English Teaching Resource Center, State Pedagogical University, Chisinau, Moldova, December 2010; "Political Campaign Internships and the Development of Leadership Skills," 10th International Conference on Experiential Learning, International Consortium for Experiential Learning, July 2006, Lancaster, England; "Incorporating Internships into Undergraduate Political Science Coursework," 2005; and "The Road to the White House: Teaching and Learning about US Presidential Campaigns through Civic Participation," 2004. Data from the American National Government course appeared in the article, "Learning Citizenship by Doing: Evaluating the Effects of a Required Political Campaign Internship in American Government," *Journal for Civic Commitment* 12 (January 2009).
2. Student internship paper, American National Government, Fall 2004. Students completed forms that approved use of all materials for research and publication.
3. Student internship paper, American National Government, Fall 2004.
4. Student internship paper, American National Government, Fall 2004.
5. Corporation for National and Community Service, "Civic Life in the US" available at http://civic.serve.gov/national.
6. Ibid.
7. Ibid. For more information on 2012 turnout, see Harward and Shea, Chapter 2.
8. *Florida Civic Health Index 2009*. Florida Joint Center for Citizenship and the National Conference on Citizenship.
9. The University of South Florida is a public institution that serves more than 47,000 students in Tampa, St. Petersburg, Sarasota-Manatee, and Lakeland, see http://www.usf.edu/About-USF/index.asp.
10. For more about this course, see http://www1.usfsp.edu/whitehouse/. Course materials, such as the syllabus, can be accessed and students' blogs about their campaign internships read, as well as links to radio and television pieces about the course.
11. Students also are required to keep a journal, write a paper, log their hours at their placement, and have their supervisor complete an evaluation. The POS 4941: Field Work course description in the USF Catalog is as follows: "opportunity for students to obtain practical experience as aides to agencies of government and political parties."
12. See McLaughlin 2005, 7–9. See also the course website, www.stpt.usf.edu/whitehouse, and this University Beat story about the course, http://www.youtube.com/watch?v=62aqUfZk29w.
13. In the event that students were unable to intern on one of the campaigns, they were permitted to substitute a research paper in lieu of the internship requirement. Very few students took the research paper option.
14. Student internship paper, American National Government, Fall 2006.
15. Please contact the author for a copy of the syllabus and the Field Work Packet for American National Government.
16. The Campaign Internship Job Fair also became an earned media event for the campus; it was covered by Bay News 9 (September 16, 2006) and the *St. Petersburg Times* (see "Homework for American Government Class Means Hitting the Hustings" by Donna Winchester, September 15, 2006).
17. Please contact the author for copies of these documents.
18. Student internship paper, American National Government, Fall 2006.
19. Student internship paper, American National Government, Fall 2006.
20. Student journal, American National Government, Fall 2004.
21. These events were covered, at different times, by ABC, NBC, WUSF, and the *Tampa Tribune*, in part because USFSP had a bipartisan group of youth voters. See, for example, Smith and Gedalius 2004, p. 1.
22. Please contact the author, jsm2@usfsp.edu, to discuss the ways in which this was achieved.
23. Please contact the author for a copy of the surveys. I also included a few questions from the Public-Release Questions from the 1988 NAEP Civics Assessment so that I could compare the data. See Niemi and Junn 1998, 164–181.
24. Note that my research design does not include a control group of students who took American National Government without the internship component. However, I have taught this class without the internship component many times, and I do offer general observations about the differences (from the instructor's point of view) in teaching this course with and without a campaign internship.
25. Herein lies an area for potential future research.
26. For one student that also included putting signs on his boat and anchoring it in Tampa Bay so it could be seen by drivers on the Howard Frankland Bridge during rush hour.
27. Student internship paper, American National Government, Fall 2004.
28. Student internship paper, American National Government, Fall 2004.
29. Student internship paper, American National Government, Fall 2006.

30. Student internship paper, American National Government, Fall 2004.
31. Student internship paper, American National Government, Fall 2004.
32. Student internship paper, American National Government, Fall 2004.
33. Student internship paper, American National Government, Fall 2004.
34. Student internship paper, American National Government, Fall 2004.
35. Student internship paper, American National Government, Fall 2006.
36. Student internship paper, American National Government, Fall 2006.
37. Student internship paper, American National Government, Fall 2006.
38. Student internship paper, American National Government, Fall 2006.
39. It may be the case that my enthusiasm and experience working on campaigns were important in working with students to capitalize on their internship opportunities by developing their knowledge, skills, and passion for political involvement. One student's evaluation noted:

    [The instructor] is very enthusiastic about what she does, and this makes the class more appealing. She has extensive experience in politics, and this shines through in her lectures. Her requirement of an internship on political campaign was wonderful—one of the best experiences I've had at the university.

40. As with the American National Government events, this drew media attention and was featured on WMNF 88.5 radio.
41. See, for example, the CIRCLE Fact Sheets about youth turnout and civic engagement in 2008 at www.civicyouth.org.
42. I created this "word cloud" using http://www.wordle.net/. As explained on its website, "Wordle is a toy for generating 'word clouds' from text that you provide. The clouds give greater prominence to words that appear more frequently in the source text. You can tweak your clouds with different fonts, layouts, and color schemes."
43. Hear more from students about what they learned as a result of their campaign internship in this WUSF 89.7 story about the course, http://www.youtube.com/watch?v=Kxd5vdOeBWU.
44. Student journal, American National Government, Fall 2004.
45. Student internship paper, American National Government, Fall 2004.

Chapter 19

1. CIRCLE 2010.
2. Levine 2006.
3. For instance, Chicago public schools dropped civics from their curriculum and now are seeking to add it back.
4. Putnam 2000, 402–403.
5. Macedo et al. 2005.
6. Levine 2006, 2–4.
7. Boryczka 2007; Klinkner and Mariani 2007; Meinke 2007; Mello and Davis.
8. Bernstein 2006; Hardt 2009; Meinke 2007; Mello and Davis 2007.
9. Islam, Munoz, and Crego 2010, 207.
10. Kolb 1984; Lowy and Hood 2004, 267–268; Metts 1995, 60.
11. Center for Collaborative Education. Accessed at http://www.ccebos.org/netsinits.html#atlas; Metts 1995, 89–91.
12. Marzano 1992, 130.
13. Marzano 2009, 8–9.
14. For instance, Blount (2006, 271–282) holds that students can learn about social systems, policy change, and leadership through a combination of academic study with experience, and that the value young people place on such informed experiences is significant in getting them involved. Longo, Drury, and Battistoni (2006) find that political competencies are best acquired through activities that recognize students' civic interests, provide guidance for practice, and allow students to voice their concerns. Likewise, Kirlin (2007, 30–32) argues that knowledge and interest in politics must go hand-in-hand and that practice is vital in developing civic skills. Levine 2007, 2, Macedo 2005, 152, 171; Metts 1995, 8, and others also see practical experience (such as political work) as an important learning tool; and young adulthood, Beaumont and Battistoni (2006, 241–247, 241–242) affirm, is a critical period for such political development.
15. Plutzer 2002, 54.
16. Stoker and Jennings 2004, 1–23.
17. In an earlier work, she finds few concrete ways for youth to develop political identity outside of election volunteer work, other than possibly applying skills learned in the community in election volunteer work. Gentry 2009, 19–21.
18. Macedo et al. 2005, 33.
19. Colby et al. 2007, 45–46.
20. Fine 2008.

21. Beaumont and Battistoni 2006, 242.
22. Jesuit-run high schools such as Loyola Academy emphasize student-centered learning as well as experiential learning, but with a spiritual dimension. Ralph Metts, S.J., adapted the spiritual exercises of St. Ignatius Loyola (used by Jesuits worldwide for prayer) to be used as a model for teaching and learning. In the IPP, teachers present a lesson (experience) in the context of a course, and students are then asked to reflect upon what they have learned and are encouraged to act upon or extend what they have learned later in their lives.
23. In the teaching of political engagement covered in this study, *context* consists of understanding a high school student's initial attitudes toward political involvement, *experience* is the actual election work, and *reflection* includes students' written reflections and survey responses. *Action* is political involvement later in life, and *evaluation* is the assessment of both initial student responses and evidence of later involvement. Metts 1995, 58, 81–104.
24. Commission on Research and Development 1994, 101–106; Marando 2011.
25. By the fall semester of 2006, students in both political science courses were required to either serve as election judges or work for political campaigns. Juniors could only work for political campaigns until the 2008 primary elections, when the state of Illinois allowed them to also serve as judges. Since 2008, all juniors enrolled either in Honors or advanced placement US history were given the opportunity to serve as election judges.
26. The Mikva Challenge 2011.
27. City of Chicago Board of Election Commissions, http://www.chicagoelections.com/page.php?id=176; Cook County Clerk, Elections, Suburban Cook County, http://www.cookcountyclerk.com/elections/studentinvolvement/zPages/default.aspx; Lake County Clerk, http://www.lakecountyil.gov/countyclerk/electionworkers/studentelectionjudgeprogram.htm.
28. These letters were copied and the originals returned to the students to use for later job or college references.
29. Orr n.d.
30. Magleby, Patterson, and Monson 2006.
31. Meirose 1994, 253–254.
32. I would like to thank Noah Kaplan for his most generous and helpful assistance with the statistics in my chapter.
33. The questions in the survey specifically named Loyola Academy, since all respondents were Loyola Academy graduates. "Loyola Academy" is sometimes simplified to "high school" in the tables.
34. Anecdotal evidence suggests that this proved true with some former Loyola students. In 2012, two alumni who had participated in the assignment in 2008 worked as campaign or field managers in successful Illinois state Senate campaigns, and recruited eight current Loyola students as volunteers. Another alumnus worked in the downtown Chicago Obama campaign office as paid staff. One former student worked for Obama both in his US Senate office and in the White House, where another alumnus is presently employed. This information is based only on personal contacts with these alums and does not include other students who may be active in politics.
35. "Younger Voters Were Racially Diverse" 2011.
36. CIRCLE 2012, "Updated Estimate: Youth Turnout was 50% in 2012", accessed November 2012"; CIRCLE 2012, "Youth Turnout: At Least 49%, 20-23 Million Under 30 Voted".
37. CIRCLE, "At Least 80 Electoral Votes Depended on Youth", accessed November 2012.

Chapter 20

1. Kirby and Kawashima-Ginsberg 2009. Sixty-two percent of eligible voters turned out in 2008, whereas 60% cast a ballot in 2004 (Michael McDonald, *United States Election Project*, http://elections.gmu.edu/voter_turnout.htm).
2. CIRCLE staff 2012.
3. Owen 2008, 2009.
4. Thee-Brenan 2010; CIRCLE staff 2010; McDonald 2010.
5. Lopez et al. 2007.
6. Kenski, Hardy, and Jamieson 2010; Owen 2008.
7. Delli Carpini and Keeter 1996.
8. Data from the national survey used in this study indicate that taking an advanced placement (AP) history course made no difference in whether a respondent had voted in the 2008 presidential election or not.
9. Niemi 2001.
10. Campbell 2006.
11. Hess and Torney 1967; Nie et al. 1996.
12. See Ehman 1980.
13. Langton and Jennings 1968.
14. Jennings and Niemi 1974; Connell 1972; Tedin 1974; Beck 1977; Ehman 1980; Jennings and Niemi 1981; Jennings 1996.

15. Hess and Torney 1967, 101.
16. Lambert et al. 1988; Niemi and Junn 1998; McDevitt and Chaffee 2000; Galston 2001; Meirick and Wackman 2004.
17. Torney, Oppenheim, and Farnen 1975; Delli Carpini and Keeter 1996; Niemi and Junn 1998; Tolo 1999.
18. Graham 2010.
19. Verba et al. 1995.
20. Easton and Dennis 1967; Abramson and Aldrich 1982.
21. Campbell 2006; Fieldhouse et al. 2007; Kelly 2008; Delshad 2009.
22. Potter 2005.
23. Campbell 2006; Owen and Soule 2010.
24. Dee 2003.
25. Bachner 2011.
26. Niemi and Junn 1998.
27. Youniss and Yates 1997.
28. Galston 2001.
29. Kahne and Middaugh 2002, 36–37. See also Ichilov 2007; Finkel and Smith 2011.
30. We the People: The Citizen and the Constitution is a civic education program that incorporates active learning elements into the curriculum, especially the use of simulated congressional hearings. More than 30,000 students and 90,000 teachers in the United States have been involved in the program since its founding in 1987. http://new.civiced.org/programs/wtp.
31. Brody 1994; Leming 1996.
32. Atherton 2000; Tolo 1998.
33. Soule and Nairne 2009; Eschrich 2010.
34. Owen and Soule 2010.
35. Owen et al. 2011.
36. The study was funded by the Center for Civic Education and was conducted by Diana Owen and a team of graduate student researchers at Georgetown University.
37. Knowledge Networks (KN) drew its sample from an online panel of respondents representative of 97% of American households. KN supplied technology to panel respondents who did not have Internet access. The survey respondents in this study were a random, representative sample of US households. The study had a sampling error of +/-3%. Information about the sampling techniques used by Knowledge Networks can be obtained from its website: http://www.knowledgenetworks.com/knpanel/index.html.
38. Participants for the WTP Alumni Survey were recruited through the WTP alumni network, WTP teachers, and WTP program coordinators. Respondents from 50 states and one American territory were represented in the sample. An attempt was made to recruit respondents who did not self-select into the WTP curriculum. Teachers and program coordinators reached out personally to students, and made special appeals to those who were not the top performers in the class, with some success. The sample is neither random nor representative of the general public; however, the WTP respondents were a valid sample of the WTP alumni population.
39. Since I did not have personal identifying information about the respondents, it was impossible to check these data against voter files.
40. Berent, Krosnick, and Lupia 2011, 5. They compared self-report voting measures from the 2008 American National Election Studies Panel to data painstakingly compiled from state voting records. They discovered problems with the typical methods used to validate voter turnout data in surveys, such as variations in the collection methods and quality of official voter turnout records by localities, as well as difficulties in matching survey respondents to voting records. This resulted in a "downward bias," as to the estimation of voter registration and turnout rates. Although there is some tendency to exaggerate turnout, the turnout rates among survey respondents are more accurate than has been assumed in the past, when estimates of overreporting were between 10 and 20 percentage points.
41. Six respondents participated in a civics program, but did not take a civics course. These respondents were eliminated from the analysis because there were too few of them to analyze.
42. The fact that respondents relied on recall of their civic education experience was a potential limitation of this study. To mitigate this pitfall, the instrument was subjected to rigorous pretesting of the items. The Georgetown University research team conducted an extensive survey and interview pretest on 288 subjects. A subsample of the survey respondents was interviewed to determine if these respondents had difficulty answering any of the questions. The interview subjects ranged from young people to octogenarians and included members of a senior citizens community in Florida. The subjects generally had little difficulty recalling their civics experience in some detail. A small number of items in which recall was sketchy, such as whether their high school civics course had been required or was an elective class, were eliminated from the study. The survey instrument was pretested further by Knowledge Networks on 50 subjects before the final version went into the field.

43. Seventy-five cases, or 14% of the sample of people who would have been eligible for the program since its inception in 1987.
44. Langton 1967; Verba et al. 1995; Owen 2000.
45. Gordon and Babchuk 1958; Ziblatt 1965; Beane et al. 1981; Beck and Jennings 1982; Olsen 1982; Ladewig and Thomas 1987; Putnam 1993; Youniss et al. 1997; Youniss and Yates 1998; Eccles and Barber 1999; Eccles et al. 2003.
46. Hanks and Ecklands 1978; Eyler 1982; Glanville 1999; Verba et al. 1995.
47. An analysis using the four-part campaign engagement measure (traditional and social media engagement, traditional participation only, social media engagement only, and no engagement) revealed similar findings and indicated that exposure to civics curricular activities was positively related to all forms of campaign engagement. A slightly higher percentage of people who engaged in both forms of campaign engagement was apparent across all categories of civics curricular activities.
48. A number of additional variables were included in the model, but were not statistically significant. These include an item that ascertained whether the respondent had an outstanding civics teacher and demographic controls for education and income. The education variable alone did not strongly predict campaign participation.
49. The correlation between the curricular activities and classroom environment measures is .367.
50. The bivariate correlation between traditional campaign participation and the civic activities scale is .367, compared to .160 for the classroom environment variable.
51. Center for American Women and Politics 2008.
52. Dummy variables were created for Hispanic Americans and Asian Americans to include them in the model. The coefficients were miniscule and nonsignificant. These groups are part of the omitted category in the final OLS regression models presented here.
53. See, for example, Eccles et al. 2003.
54. Youniss and Yates 1999.
55. Project for Excellence in Journalism 2012.
56. Personal interview with female student who participated in the We the People program at the high school level during the 2010–2011 academic year conducted by Rebecca Chalif, MA, research assistant, Georgetown University, on June 7, 2011.
57. Personal interview with We the People and AP American government teacher at the high school level during the 2010–2011 academic year conducted by Rebecca Chalif, MA, Research Assistant, Georgetown University, on June 20, 2011.

Section 3 Intro

1. Kolb 1984.

Chapter 21

1. Leonard 1999, 749.
2. Schachter 1998, 631.
3. Carter and Elshtain 1997, 745.
4. Ibid.
5. Kedrowski 2003, 226.
6. Wattenberg 2007.
7. As Leonard (1999, 749) suggested, "[T]he most significant obstacle to the revitalization of civic education in academic political science is that—sympathies notwithstanding—such efforts are likely to be considered by many, if not most, political scientists, as 'pure futility and waste.'"
8. Verba, Schlozman, and Brady 1995.
9. See, for example, Kirlin 2002; Hunter and Brisbin 2000.
10. Butin 2010.
11. For more information on the Bonner Foundation see http://www.bonner.org/.
12. For more information on Fund for the Improvement of Postsecondary Education (FIPSE) grants, see http://www2.ed.gov/about/offices/list/ope/fipse/index.html.
13. Hoy and Meisel 2008, 23.
14. There was no particular reason these three disciplines were chosen except that, in response to an email inquiry on interest in attending the January 2005 Bonner conference, one faculty member from each of those three disciplines both expressed interest and could attend on that snowy January weekend.
15. For example, Strand et al. 2003.
16. Ibid.
17. Nursing 310 can be substituted for this research requirement for two reasons: first, the course satisfies the goals of this section in that it teaches the basic research process by focusing on the methods used in nursing research. Second, the Nursing Department requires students to complete 69 credit hours for the major,

which, when added to the 51 hours of general education required of all students to graduate, leaves nursing majors with very little room in their schedule for minors, since students are only required to complete 124 credit hours overall to graduate. Based on the feedback received from the Nursing Department, the committee chose to include this substitution possibility based upon its goal to remain as open as possible to all disciplines on campus.

18. Verba, Schlozman, and Brady 1995.
19. Strand et al. 2003, 1.
20. Kirlin 572.
21. There is not much to report on the design of these courses, because they have always been taught as one-credit overloads by members of the steering committee for the minor. This goes to the criticism of the third and fifth goals in the analysis section of this chapter. If the reader has further interest in the nature of these two courses, they can find the syllabi on the companion website for this book.
22. All the quotes from students reported in this chapter were taken from the final reflective essays each student is required to write for the last assignment in GS 430: Putting Civic Engagement in Perspective, which is the reflective component of the capstone project.
23. Musil 2003, 4.

Chapter 22

1. We understand that experiential learning definitions vary, but for the purposes of this study we are using it as the umbrella term that encompasses several different parts of a students' education. Service-learning, community service, cooperative education, internships, directed research, and student leadership are common and familiar categories of experiential learning. Merrimack College describes experiential learning as something that engages students in a guided and facilitated process in which they construct new knowledge, skills, and values. Students participate in a purposeful experience, reflect upon their engagement and observations, conceptualize their experience in terms of their academic knowledge, integrate their learning into their academic and personal growth as members of the college community, and increase their civic engagement.
2. Kirby and Kawashima-Ginsberg 2009.
3. "Trends in Political Values" 2009.
4. Gallini and Moely 2003, 5–6.
5. Astin, Vogelgesang, Ikeda, and Yee 2000.
6. The *Journal of Political Science Education*, the APSA Political Science Education subgroup, and APSA's Teaching and Learning Conference show the increased attention given to the importance of civic engagement and pedagogy in the discipline of political science. For more specific examples, see the *Journal of Political Science Education* special issues (2006, 2010).
7. See McCartney, Chapter 1, and Beaumont, Chapter 3, for more discussion of this point.
8. See Campus Compact 2010; Huerta and Jozwiak 2008, 42–60; and Harlaub and Lancaster 2008, 377–393.
9. Bringle and Hatcher 1996, 222.
10. Merrimack College is a selective, independent college in the Catholic, Augustinian tradition, with 2,000 students representing 22 states and 20 countries. It is located in North Andover, Massachusetts, a suburb of Boston. The college is 80% residential, with slightly more females than males in attendance. The student body is predominantly middle- to upper-middle class. The college offers undergraduate degrees in the liberal arts, business, science and engineering, and education programs; it also offers master's programs in education and a range of certificate, licensure, and degree completion programs.
11. In one case, these measures were supplemented with a post-hoc assessment by the instructor of the impact of service learning on her students.
12. We acknowledge the limits of self-report data and the single institutional study. Please see Section 4 of this volume for ways to move forward in assessment.
13. Abramowitz 2001.
14. This was a component developed by Professor Patricia Siplon from St. Michael's College. She graciously allowed us to adopt it.
15. http://www.merrimack.edu/academics/EngagedLearning/ServiceLearning/Stevens/Pages/default.aspx.
16. See Astinand Sax 1993, 251–263; Eyler and Giles 1999; and "The Civic Mission of Schools" 2003.
17. Discussions have been taking place at both the departmental level and at the college about expanding experiential learning in a new general education curriculum to be launched in the near future.

Chapter 23

1. Eyler 2002, 520; Katula and Threnhauser 1999, 238–255. See also regular publications and press releases of the National Society for Experiential Education (NSEE), http://www.nsee.org. For one example of the trend in offering credit for experiential learning, see Sellnow and Oster 1997, 190–197. For a broader discussion of the trend toward experiential education—especially involving service-learning—within the field

of political science, see the September 2000 special symposium on service-learning in *PS: Political Science & Politics*.

2. Steffes 2004, 48.
3. During academic advising sessions, I often encouraged students to plan their career development paths to allow for multiple internships. For example, when my political science are students interested in competitive internships at the White House or State Department, I recommend participating in less-competitive internships as underclassmen so that they have the requisite knowledge and experience to be competitive candidates by their junior and senior years.

    One of the main points of this chapter is that this trend toward multiple experiences has received little attention in the literature on experiential and civic engagement education. In addition to anecdotal evidence from my own experience, some evidence exists to support the claim that students increasingly participate in multiple experiential education opportunities. See, for instance, Ducrot, Miller, and Goodman 2008, Article 6; Corbett and Kendall 1999, 66–76; Milstein and Krueger 1997, 100–116; Smith 2011, 205–222.
4. For a few prominent examples, see: Bryant, Schonemann, and Karpa 2011; Parilla and Smith-Cullien 1997, 225–241; Marcus, Howard, and King 1993, 410–419.
5. The literature on experiential education is vast, and a full review would be neither possible nor instructive.
6. Dewey 1938.
7. Katula and Threnhauser, 1999.
8. Dewey 1938, 7.
9. Statistics supporting this trend are difficult to come by, but Richard Battistoni noted in 2000 that service-learning in higher education had been increasing for more than a decade. Noting the leading role of political scientists, he said, "In many ways, political scientists have led the way in advancing the theory and practice of service learning, publishing one of the first volumes in the AAHE series on service learning in the disciplines."
10. Brock and Cameron 1999, 251–256; McCarthy and Anderson 2000, 279–294; McQuaid 1992, 532–534; Smith and Boyer 1994, 690–694.
11. Moon and Schokman 2000, 169–175; Marlin-Bennett 2002, 384–395.
12. Informal, qualitative review of the Top 10 political science journals from 1990–2011.
13. Barber and Battistoni 1993, 235–240.
14. Patterson 2000, 817–822.
15. Campbell 2000, 641–645.
16. Owen 2000, 639–640.
17. Hunter and Brisbin 2000, 623–626.
18. Delli Carpini and Keeter 2000, 635–637.
19. Ibid., 636.
20. Dewey 1933; Collier and Williams 2005, 83–147.
21. Kolb 1984.
22. Strange 2000, 5–13; Kendall 1990; Troppe 1995; Weigert 1998, 3–10.
23. Durham 1992, 35–52; Parilla and Hesser 1998, 310–329; Parilla and Smith-Cullien 1997.
24. Parilla and Hesser 1998.
25. Experiential education activities are not the only time students are left on their own to make connections to the classroom curriculum. The college experience is full of various opportunities to learn new things, and that learning process is up to the student. However, noncredit experiential education is distinct from these other opportunities in that it is often a university-sponsored activity—linked more formally with the university than are jobs, watching TV, or participating in social activities at which learning might take place. These civic engagement activities are things faculty and advisers help students set up precisely because they want them to learn something, but if students are not getting credit they are often left on their own to make meaning out of the experience. There needs to be an awareness of that fact and assistance provided to them integrate civic engagement activities with classroom learning.
26. Cantor 2011.
27. Marlin-Bennett 2002; Moon and Schokman 2000.
28. Breamer 1998, 557–561; Corbett and Kendall 1999, 66–76; Koulish 1998, 562–566.
29. Marcus, Howard, and King 1993.
30. Ibid. The group of students participating in service-learning was similar in most regards to the control group. Self-selection bias was avoided by informing students of the service project only after the start of the term. Additionally, postregistration comparisons of the group revealed no significant differences in terms of demography (sex, race, and year in school), personal attitudes and values regarding community service, or self-ratings of students' "desire to take this course." Likewise, the graduate students facilitating the different sections had comparable levels of teaching experience.
31. Insitute of International Education 2010.
32. Brewer and Cunningham 2009.

33. Ibid., 56–58.
34. Hopkins 1999, 36–42; Hunter, White, and Godbey 2006, 267–285.
35. Ruszczyk (coordinator, Education Abroad, University of Maryland) in discussion with the author, February 4, 2011.
36. Brewer and Cunningham 2009.
37. Parilla and Smith-Cullien 1997.
38. Ibid., 230.
39. Ibid.
40. Ibid.
41. Ibid.
42. Wessel 2007, 73–89.
43. Parilla and Smith-Cullien 1997.
44. Ibid.
45. Ibid.
46. Ibid., 232.
47. Portfolios are common in the arts and in the field of education, but they also have become more common in the last several years for students doing any kind of experiential learning. One excellent book on the topic is Zubizarreta and Seldin's *The Learning Portfolio* (2004). An informational PowerPoint from the University of Maryland Career Center and a one-page handout on portfolios that I use for political science students doing internships is available in the online supplement to the book. See http://www.apsanet.org/TeachingCivicEngagement.
48. Parilla and Smith-Cullien 1997.
49. Eyler and Giles 1999.
50. Ibid.; Strange 2000.
51. Eyler 2002, 520.
52. Ibid.
53. Collier and Williams 2005, 87.
54. Ibid.
55. Eyler 2002.
56. Batchelder and Root 1994, 341–356; Boss 1994, 183–198; Eyler and Giles 1999; Eyler and Halteman 1981, 27–34.
57. Eyler 2002, 521.
58. Ibid., 524.
59. Ibid.
60. Ibid.
61. Learning contracts are understood and used differently by different individuals, fields, and schools, but generally speaking, they are more formal documents consisting of learning objectives and other student requirements. For more information, see Anderson, Boud, and Sampson 2004. Additionally, examples of learning contracts and learning objectives are available in the online supplement to the book. See http://www.apsanet.org/TeachingCivicEngagement.
62. Eyler 2002, 526.
63. Miller 1990, 78–82.
64. Ibid.
65. Ibid., 80. Note: Miller is recommending a new idea, not reporting about a successful implementation of this kind of preinternship skills course. To my knowledge, no such preinternship course exists to teach new interns the methods of participant observation. As a result, I cannot offer a sample syllabus or textbook. The methods of participant observation are covered in some undergraduate-level qualitative methods courses and texts, but more research is needed on what methods of participant observation would best benefit students engaged in internships and other forms of experiential education, as well as what books and resources would be most helpful.
66. Referring back to Figure 23-2, the skills of participant observation will be helpful as students uncover and challenge underlying assumptions. Successfully challenging those assumptions through new observations and new understandings is likely to be a challenging endeavor. Making that process explicit and applying the methods of participant observation will make reflection a much richer experience.
67. Krysor and Pierce 2000, 25–31; Moon and Schokman 2000; Tillman, *Impact of Education Abroad on Career Development, Volume I*; Tillman, *Impact of Education Abroad on Career Development, Volume II*; Young and Baker 2004, 22–30.
68. *Job Outlook 2011*, 2010.

CHAPTER 24

1. We would like to thank our colleagues at Central Michigan University, for supporting this project with a Vision 2010 grant. We would also like to thank Monica Folske of the Center for Applied Research and

Rural Studies, for her considerable assistance with data collection for this project.
2. Levine 2007.
3. Schneider 2000, 98, 120.
4. Colby et al. 2003, 19.
5. Saltmarsh and Hartley 2011. See also Chapter 6 of Levine 2007.
6. Kuh and Umbach 2004.
7. Austin and Gamson 1983; Bowen and Schuster 1986; Kuh et al. 1991, 176–77.
8. Kuh et al. 1991, 177.
9. Boyer 1987; Colby et al. 2003; Carnegie Corporation of New York; Galston 2003; Ehrlich et al. 2000; Feith 2011; Levine 2007; Macedo et al. 2005; Shea and Green 2007; Wattenberg 2008; Youniss and Levine 2009.
10. CIRCLE 2011b.
11. PEW Research Center, 2011.
12. CIRCLE's comprehensive assessment of civic health in 2006, for example, indicated that "most young Americans are misinformed about important aspects of politics and current events." As a result, the "knowledge gap" between younger and older generations has steadily increased over time. CIRCLE 2006; Delli Carpini, and Keeter 1996; Galston 2001; Sax et al. 2003; Wattenberg 2008; Zukin et al. 2006, 83.
13. Robins and Grabow 2004; CIRCLE 2008.
14. Participation in these types of activities may have been triggered by mandatory community service requirements in high school, but the end result is that young people are often just as likely to participate in such activities as members of previous generations. Zukin et al. 2006, 86; CIRCLE 2006.
15. Dalton 2008.
16. Tufts University Tisch College of Citizenship and Public Service, "National Survey for Youth Civic Engagement," accessed on March 1, 2012, at http://activecitizen.tufts.edu/research-307/research-projects/the-national-survey-of-civic-and-political-engagement-of-young-people/.
17. Zukin et al. 2006, 99–100.
18. CIRCLE 2006.
19. For more on this point see Gentry, Chapter 4.
20. Boyer 1987; Colby et al. 2003; Colby et al. 2007; Ehrlich et al. 2000; Colby et al. 2003.
21. Bok 2006, 193.
22. Ibid., 53.
23. Niemi and Junn 2005.
24. Levine 2007, 112–113.
25. Verba, Schlozman, and Brady 1995; Youniss, McClelland, and Yates 1997.
26. Kuh et al. 1991, 176–177; Bok 2006, 53.
27. Strachan and Owens 2011.
28. Putnam 2000; Skocpol and Fiorina 1999.
29. Skocpol 2003.
30. CIRCLE 2006.
31. Levine and Cureton 1998.
32. Skocpol 2003. Note: Skocpol credits national policy entrepreneurs rather than local citizens within a particular community with establishing the federated infrastructure of her preferred voluntary associations. Similarly, the decision to launch and support PIRG chapters may not reflect the efforts of students on a particular campus. Yet, Skopol convincingly argues that participating actively in an organization with this type of organizational structure provides members with a better opportunity to cultivate civic identities, civic skills and political efficacy—even if they were not responsible for launching the organization themselves.
33. Levine and Cureton 1998, 54, 58.
34. As cited by Levine and Cureton 1998, 102.
35. Respondents were asked to identify the primary function of their student group. The first percentage reported for each category in the following list describes the sample, whereas the second percentage reported for each category describes the population of student groups on campus, according to CMU's student life website. Studies/Career: 37.3%, 37%; Social Issues: 14%, 14%; Sports: 13.4%, Not Reported; Social: 9.2%, 9.1%; Volunteer/Service: 7.6%, 9.5%; Religious: 7.1%, 6%; Culture/Ethnicity: 5%, 5.7%; Political: 3.4%, 2%.
36. Skopol 2003.
37. The mean scores and standard deviations (in parentheses) for local and federated student organizations (respectively) on these items, along with t-test results, were: Consult Constitution: 2.66 (1.20), 3.22 (1.17), $t(-2.61) = .01, p < .05$; Rely on Formal Rules: 2.13 (1.47), 2.74 (1.61), $t(-2.17) = .03, p < .05$; Share Core Values: 1.47 (.50), 1.64 (.48), $t(-1.94) = .05, p \leq .05$; and Statewide/National Volunteering: 1.49(.64), 1.86(.95), $t(-2.38) =.02, p < .05$.
38. The mean scores and standard deviations (in parentheses) for local and federated student organizations (respectively) on these items, along with t-test results, were: Sponsored Fund-raising Event: 2.62 (1.20),

3.06 (.96), $t(-2.26) = .03, p < .05$; Distributed Printed Materials: 2.42 (1.10), 2.93 (1.0), $t(-2.74) = .007$, $p < .01$; Recruited Diverse Members: 1.14 (.35), 1.04 (.20), $t(1.94) = .05, p \leq .05$.

39. The t-test analyses revealed that differences between local and federated student groups were no longer significant when controlling for Greek organizations. None of these t-scores were significant at the .05 level.
40. The mean scores and standard deviations (in parentheses) for local and federated student organizations (respectively) on these items, along with t-test results, were: Sponsored Fund-raising Event: 2.60 (1.20), 3.06 (1.0), $t(-2.02) = .04, p <.05$; Distributed Printed Materials: 2.40 (1.05), 2.93 (1.03), t (-2.50) = .01, p , .05; Recruited Diverse Members: 1.15 (.36); 1.04 (.19), $t(1.89) = .05, p \leq .05$.
41. Unless otherwise noted, chi square tests indicated that all of the percentage differences reported are significant at the .05 level.
42. Almond and Verba 1963; Schlesinger 1944; Skocpol 2003.
43. These percentage differences, however, were not significant at the .05 level.
44. The percentage difference with regard to full membership votes at least once per month was not significant at the .05 level.
45. Skocpol 2003.
46. Verba, Schlozman, and Brady 1995; Ladewig and Thomas 1987; Youniss, McLellan, and Yates 1997.
47. Only the first of these three percentage differences, with regard to campus policies, was significant at the .05 level.
48. Skocpol 2003. Indeed, this point is the key difference between Theda Skopol's work on American civil society and Robert Putnam's. Whereas Putnam is interested in the decline of all types of voluntary associations, Skopol is far more concerned about large-scale, federated organizations explicitly founded to influence cultural norms and political decisions.
49. Putnam 2000.
50. These percentage differences were not significant at the .05 level.
51. Of the percentage differences reported in this paragraph, only the difference reported for desiring assistance was significant at the .05 level.
52. These percentage differences were not significant at the .05 level.
53. Levine and Cureton 1998.
54. McMullen 2010.
55. Eberly 2011.
56. Syrett 2009, 2011.
57. Bleeker and Murnen 2005; Boeringer 1999; Foubert, Newberry, and Tatum 2007.
58. Sidanius, Levin, Van Lair, and Sears 2008.
59. Tanaka 2005, 112.
60. Flanagan 2011.
61. Examples of private colleges and universities that have banned fraternities and sororities include Alfred, Amherst, Bowdoin, Colby, Middlebury, and Williams. Others that still allow Greeks a presence on campus, but have eliminated or reduced the role of off-campus houses include Denison, Hamilton, Lawrence, and Union. Although falling short of an outright ban, in 2012 Princeton followed Yale, Cornell, and Colgate in prohibiting freshmen from participating in Rush activities. Cornell's president also pledged in 2012 to end the hazing that often accompanies Rush Week. In a reversal of these trends, however, in 2012 Swarthmore College, which had banned sororities since the 1930s, changed its policy in response to pressure from female students. Examples of private colleges at which the Greek system has never flourished include Bates, Bryn Mawr, Carleton, Claremont McKenna, Grinnell, Haverford, Pomona, Smith, Vassar, and Wellsley. See Bauer 2004; *Daily Princetonian* Editorial Board 2012; Gifford 2001; McMahon 2012; Skorton 2011; Snyder 2012.
62. Campbell 2006.
63. Armstrong 2011; New York Times 1994.
64. Eberly 2011.
65. Skorton 2011.
66. North American Inter-fraternity Council 2012; National Pan-Hellenic Conference 2011.
67. Armstrong 2011.
68. Saltmarsh and Hartley 2011.
69. Verba, Schlozman, and Brady 1995.
70. Skocpol 2003.

Chapter 25

1. An earlier version of this assessment toolkit was published as part of the American Association of State Colleges and Universities (AASCU) monograph, *Electoral Voices: Engaging College Students in Elections: An American Democracy Project Best Practices Guide*. The current version expands upon that toolkit, providing examples from the APSA monograph.

2. A discussion of Rock the Vote parties at the College of Staten Island and California Polytechnic State University, Pomona is included in *Electoral Voices*, Appendix 1. The entire monograph is available online: http://www.aascu.org/uploadedFiles/AASCU/Content/Home/AmericanDemocracyProject/voices.pdf.
3. Bloomsburg University of Pennsylvania's Vote Jam and Fort Hays State University's Vote Slam are profiled in *Electoral Voices*, Appendix 1.
4. See *Electoral Voices*, Appendix 1 (pages 97–99), for a discussion of Kennesaw State University's classroom-based voter registration strategy, including a class versus class competition to register voters outside the classroom. See also the discussion of Castleton State College of Vermont's First-Year Seminar Program that used learning communities to enhance students' commitment to civic engagement.
5. See *Electoral Voices*, Appendix 1 (pages 95–97), for a discussion of Indiana University South Bend's American Democracy Project interactive weblog.
6. *Electoral Voices*, Appendix 1 also includes a discussion of Indiana University, South Bend's American Democracy Project public radio series.
7. See McHugh and Russell (Chapter 21) for an example of four different ways to incorporate experiential civic learning into political science courses.
8. See Owen (Chapter 20) for an example of a survey designed to measure lasting outcomes of various forms of civic education.
9. See Bennion 2009, 4.
10. See McKinlay (Chapter 15), Dicklitch (Chapter 16), and Scourfield-McLauchlan (Chapter 18) for examples of learning outcomes assessed through student journals. See Lorenzini (Chapter 8), Sanders (Chapter 15), O'Shaughnessy (Chapter 19), and Meinke (Chapter 21) for examples of outcomes assessed by review of student papers and other coursework. In all cases, assessment can be strengthened by carefully tailoring the assignment and the evaluation rubric to match specific learning objectives.
11. See McDonald (Chapter 23) for a discussion of the importance of integrating learning across multiple experiences (e.g., internships, service learning courses, and study abroad).
12. See *Electoral Voices*, Appendix 1 (pages 83–85), for a discussion of Castleton State College of Vermont's First-Year Seminar Program, including a comprehensive assessment strategy.
13. See Tashakkori and Teddlie 1998, for a taxonomy of mixed methods models.
14. See Bennion 2006 for an example of this type of coding of student reflections on a required voter mobilization field experiment.
15. *Electoral Voices*, 105–107.
16. Ibid., 91–93.
17. Ibid., 87–89.
18. Ibid., 99–191.
19. Ibid., 124–125.
20. Ibid., 93–95.
21. VanVechten and Chadha (Chapter 11) take this next step, analyzing both the quantity and quality of posts to assess the success of their academic social networking project.
22. See, for example, Indiana University, South Bend's Democracy Blog. http://www.iusb.edu/~sbadp.
23. For details, see *Electoral Voices*, 95–97.
24. Ibid., 122–123.
25. Babbie 1990.
26. Ibid.
27. Recent attempts by political scientists to assess civic education outcomes are discussed at the end of the chapter, along with common shortcomings in the current literature.
28. For more details, see *Electoral Voices*, 83–85.
29. Ibid.
30. For information about the NSSE go to http://nsse.iub.edu/.
31. See, for example, the Bloomsburg University of Pennsylvania case study in *Electoral Voices*, 72–74.
32. Karp and Brockington 2005, 825–840.
33. Bennion 2008, 2009.
34. Bennion and Nickerson 2010.
35. See Gerber and Green 2000 for an excellent discussion of the power of randomized field experiments.
36. Multicampus field experiments conducted by Bennion and Nickerson (see Chapter 13) document the effectiveness of classroom-based voter registration, and the corresponding ineffectiveness of mail and email-based registration efforts.
37. See Green and Gerber 2004 for practical advice on designing a field experiment and helpful hints and online tools for analyzing experimental data.
38. See Bennion 2005, for an example of a successful student-led voter mobilization campaign. See Bennion 2006, for an evaluation of the effects of the experiment on the student canvassers.
39. Sometimes, courses are not randomly assigned, but rather offer a de facto quasi-experiment, differing pri-

marily or exclusively along the characteristics being studied. See, for example, Coleman and Mayer's September 2000 *PS: Political Science* article on student attitudes toward instructional technology.

40. Lofland and Lofland 1984.
41. Creswell 2003.
42. Gall, Borg, and Gall 1996.
43. Gay and Airasian 1992.
44. National Training and Technical Assistance Center 2006.
45. An excellent example of triangulation is the multimethod, cross-institutional, research design of the Political Engagement Project (see Chapter 3). PEP assessment combines pre-post student survey data with in-depth telephone interviews with students and faculty, students' performance on a targeted writing exercise, samples of students' work, and a faculty survey.
46. See Sylvester (Chapter 9) for another example of a study that combines precourse and postcourse surveys with student reflection papers, qualitative questionnaires, and longitudinal follow-up surveys.

Chapter 26

1. For a review of this literature see Longo and Meyer 2006.
2. Ibid.
3. See the online supplement to this book for examples.
4. Ball 2005.
5. Shulman 2004.
6. See Chapter 25 for a more detailed discussion of the virtues and limitations of various quantitative and qualitative research methods.
7. Suskie 2009.
8. Ibid., 39.

Chapter 27

1. Several of these questions were posed to the editors by the manuscript's anonymous reviewer.
2. Suskie 2009.
3. Goldman and Zakel 2009.
4. Skocpol 2009.
5. Angelo and Cross 1993.
6. Ibid.
7. Suskie 2009.
8. Ibid., 75.
9. Schreyer Institute 2012.
10. Suskie 2009, 20.
11. Ibid., 20.
12. See, for example, Bennion 2006.
13. Bernstein, Chada, and Montjoy 2001.
14. Ibid.
15. Ray 2009.
16. Upcraft and Schuh 2002.
17. Suskie 2009.
18. Ewell 2002.
19. Suskie 2009.
20. Ibid., 13.
21. Ibid.
22. Glassick, Huber, and Maeroff 1997, 23–24.
23. Suskie 2009, 50.
24. Ibid.
25. Deardorff, Hamann, and Ishiyama 2009.
26. In addition, scholars should continue to investigate the cumulative effects of civic education at the K-12 level, as Owens does in Chapter 20. A large-scale cooperative project between K-12 and college educators could move this innovative work forward, allowing researchers to collect accurate data about students' K-12 experiences mitigating against overreliance on subject recall.
27. To learn more about the Consortium or to join, go to http://is.gd/SoTL_Consortium or contact cofounders Elizabeth Bennion (ebennion@iusb.edu) and Cherie Strachan (strac1jc@cmich.edu).

Conclusion

1. The National Task Force on Civic Learning and Democratic Engagement2012 and "Governors State strives for Civic Engagement 2012.

2. The Carnegie Foundation for the Advancement of Teaching findings, empirical evidence, and recommendations for incorporating these techniques into class can be found in the book by Colby et al. 2007. Additional materials can be found at their website: http://www.carnegiefoundation.org/sites/default/files/elibrary/HTML/educating_for_democracy/docs/index.html.
3. Many of our films and video documentaries are web-streamed from http://www.uic.edu/depts/pols/ChicagoPolitics/cpef.htm. This web site includes study guides as well as the films. A film on the site called "Teaching Politics" details my teaching philosophy and shows footage from the techniques I use in class.
4. Among just a few examples, are former Democratic US senator and presidential candidate Carol Moseley Braun and former Republican Cook County commissioner Tony Peraica.
5. Simpson 1970. When copies were no longer available from Swallow/Ohio University Press in the 1990s, I published copies for my students through the publications department at UIC. The workbook is currently out of print, since I am no longer teaching the course.
6. Simpson1976–1993 and Simpson and Mixon 2012.
7. These films can be reviewed at http://www.uic.edu/depts/pols/ChicagoPolitics/cpef.htm.
8. This exercise is published in a general form in Simpson, Nowlan, and O'Shaunessey 2010.
9. One useful book I have all my students read is Reeher and Mariani 2002. This volume helps them understand how they should approach their internship and how to upgrade their work to a more demanding and rewarding experience within the organization.
10. Simpson 1996.
11. Paul Frank, Chapter 6.
12. Jean Harris, Chapter 5.
13. Ibid.
14. Ibid.
15. Betty O'Shaughnessy, Chapter 19.
16. Paul Frank, Chapter 6.
17. Ibid.
18. Shannon Jenkins, Chapter 7. See also Mahalley Allen et al., Chapter 10 and Michelle Lorenzini, Chapter 8
19. Michelle Lorenzini, Chapter 8.
20. Ibid.
21. Susan Dicklitch, Chapter 16.
22. Diana Owen, Chapter 20.
23. Anthony Perry, Chapter 12.
24. Mary McHugh and Russell Mayer, Chapter 22.
25. Michael McDonald, Chapter 23.
26. Ibid.
27. See Elizabeth Bennion, Chapter 25 for a discussion of various assessment techniques.

Bibliography

8 U.S.C. § 1101 (a) (42) (a); INA §101 (a) (42) (A).

Abowd, Mary. "The Power of Helping: CLIC Prepares Undergraduates to be Legal Advocates for the Poor." *Chico Statements* (2006): 14–15.

Abramowitz, Alan. "The Obama Generation." In *Rasmussen Reports*. May 1, 2001, accessed July 18, 2011. http://www.rasmussenreports.com/public_content/political_commentary/commentary_by_alan_i_abramowitz/the_obama_generation.

Abramson, Paul R., and John H. Aldrich. "The Decline of Electoral Participation in America." *American Political Science Review* 76, no. 3 (1982): 502–521.

Adams, Gerald R. *The Objective Measure of Ego Identity Status: A Reference Manual*. 1998. http://www.uoguelph.ca/~gadams/OMEIS_manual.pdf.

Almond, Gabriel A., and Sydney Verba. *The Civic Culture: Political Attitudes and Democracy in Five Nations*. Princeton: Princeton University Press, 1963.

American Association of State Colleges and Universities. *Electoral Voices: Engaging College Students in Elections*. N.p., September 2006. http://www.aascu.org/uploadedFiles/AASCU/Content/Home/AmericanDemocracyProject/voices.pdf.

American Association of State Colleges and Universities. Political Engagement Project (PEP). N.p., n.d. http://www.aascu.org/programs/adp/PEP/

American National Election Studies. "ANES Guide to Public Opinion and Electoral Behavior." Ann Arbor, MI: University of Michigan, Center for Political Studies, n.d. http://www.electionstudies.org/nesguide/nesguide.htm.

American Political Science Association. "Signup to Teach Constitution Day." Washington, DC, American Political Science Association, 2012. http://www.apsanet.org/content_20191.cfm.

American Political Science Association Task Force on Civic Education in the 21st Century. "Expanded Articulation Statement: A Call for Reactions and Contributions." *PS: Political Science & Politics* 29, no. 3 (1998): 636.

Anderson, Geoff, David Boud, and Jane Sampson. *Learning Contracts: A Practical Guide* London: Routledge Falmer, 2004.

Angelo, Thomas A., and K. Patricia Cross. *Classroom Assessment Techniques: A Handbook for College Teachers*. San Francisco: Jossey-Bass, 1993.

Ansolabehere, Stephen, and David M. Konisky. "The Introduction of Voter Registration and Its Effect on Turnout." *Political Analysis* 14 (2006):83–100.

Aquinas College. "Department of Political Science Faculty Directory." February 27, 2008. http://www.aquinas.edu/polisci/faculty.html.

Arceneaux, Kevin. "Negative and Positive Campaign Messages: Evidence from Two Field Experiments." *American Politics Research* 38, no. 1 (2010): 54–83.

———. "Using Cluster Randomized Field Experiments to Study Voting Behavior." *Annals of the American Academy of Political and Social Science* 601 (2005): 169–79.

Arceneaux, Kevin, and David W. Nickerson. "Who is Mobilized to Vote? A Re-Analysis of Seven Randomized Field Experiments." *The American Journal of Political Science* 53, no. 1 (2009): 1–16.

Arendt, Hannah. *The Human Condition*. 2nd ed. Chicago: University of Chicago Press, 1998.

Aristotle. *The Politics and The Constitution of Athens*, edited by Stephen Everson. Cambridge: Cambridge University Press, 1996.

Armstrong, E. A. "How Fraternities Dominate." *New York Times*. May 6, 2011. http://www.nytimes.com/roomfordebate/2011/05/05/frat-guys-gone-wild-whats-the-solution/the-threat-to-young-women

Association of American Colleges and Universities. Liberal Education and America's Promise (LEAP). n.p.: AAC&U, 2012, accessed on October 24, 2012. http://www.aacu.org/leap/.

———. *Taking Responsibility for the Quality of the Baccalaureate Degree*. Washington, DC: AAC&U, 2004.

Astin, Alexander W. *What Matters in College? Four Critical Years Revisited*. San Francisco: Jossey-Bass, 1993.

Astin, Alexander W., and Linda J. Sax. "How Undergraduates Are Affected by Service Participation." *The Journal of College Student Development* 39, no. 3 (1993): 251–63.

Astin, Alexander W., Lori J. Vogelgesang, Elaine K. Ikeda, and Jennifer A. Yee. *How Service Learning Affects Students*. Los Angeles: Higher Education Research Institute, 2000. Accessed on November 17, 2006. http://www.gseis.ucla.edu/heri/PDFs/HSLAS/HSLAS.PDF

Atherton, Herbert. "We the People... Project Citizen." In *Education for Civic Engagement in Democracy: Service Learning and Other Promising Practices*, edited by Sheilah Mann and John Patrick. Bloomington, IN: Indiana University Press, 2000.

Austin, A. E., and Z. F. Gamson. "Academic Workplace: New Demands, Heightened Tensions." In *ASHE-ERIC Higher Education Research Report, no 10*. Washington, DC: Association for the Study of Higher Education, 1983.

Avery, P. G., and C. L Hahn. "Diversity and US 14-year-olds' Knowledge, Attitudes and Experiences." *Educational Programs forImproving Intergroup Relations: Theory, Research and Practice*, edited by W. G. Stephan and W. P. Vogt, 195–210. New York: Teachers College Press, 2004.

Babbie, Earl R. *Survey Research Methods*. Belmont, CA: Wadsworth Publishing, 1990.

Babcock, Phil, and Mindy Marks. "Leisure College USA: The Decline in Student Study Time." *American Enterprise Institute for Public Policy Research* 7 (2010). http://www.econ.ucsb.edu/~babcock/LeisureCollege2.pdf

Bachner, Jennifer. "From Classroom to Voting Booth: The Effect of Civic Education on Turnout." Paper presented at the Annual Meeting of the Southern Political Science Association, New Orleans, 2011.

Bain, Ken, and James Zimmerman. "Understanding Great Teaching." *Peer Review* 11, no. 2 (2009): 9–12.

Baker, John R. "A Lesson 'In' Government: Connecting Theory and Practice in the Study of Municipal Government." *PS: Political Science & Politics* 36, no. 3 (2003): 233–38.

Ball, William J. "From Community Engagement to Political Engagement." *PS: Political Science & Politics* 39, no. 2 (2005): 287–91.

Bandura, Albert. *Self-efficacy: The Exercise of Control*. New York: Freeman, 1997.

Barber, Benjamin R. *An Aristocracy of Everyone: The Politics of Education and the Future of America*. New York: Oxford University Press, 1992.

Barber, Benjamin R., and Richard M. Battistoni. "A Season of Service: Introducing Service Learning into the Liberal Arts Curriculum." *PS: Political Science & Politics* (1993): 235–40.

Bardach, Eugene. *A Practical Guide for Policy Analysis: The Eightfold Path to More Effective Problem Solving*, 3rd edition. Washington, DC: CQ Press, 2009.

Batchelder, Thomas H., and Susan Root. "Effects of an Undergraduate Program to Integrate Academic Learning and Service: Cognitive, Prosocial Cognitive and Identity Outcomes." *Journal of Adolescence* 17 (1994): 341–56.

Battistoni, Richard M. *Civic Engagement Across the Curriculum: A Resource Book for Service Learning Faculty in All Disciplines*. Providence, RI: Campus Compact, 2002.

Battistoni, Richard M., and William E. Hudson, eds. *Experiencing Citizenship: Concepts and Models for Service-Learning in Political Science*. Washington, DC: American Association for Higher Education, 1997.

Bauer, M. D. "Small Liberal Arts Colleges, Fraternities and Antitrust: Rethinking Hamilton College." *Catholic University Law Review* 53 (2004): 347–412. http://www.law.stetson.edu/conferences/highered/archive/2005/LibArtsFratsAntitrust.pdf

Beane, James, John Turner, and David Jones. "Long-term Effects of Community Service Programs." *Curriculum Inquiry* 11 (1981): 143–55.

Beaumont, Elizabeth. "Political Agency and Empowerment: Pathways for Developing a Sense of Political Efficacy in Young Adults." In *Handbook of Research on Civic Engagement in Youth*, edited by L. Sherrod, J. Torney-Purta, and C. Flanagan, 515–51. Hoboken: Wiley, 2010.

———. "Promoting Political Agency, Addressing Political Inequality: A Multi-level Model of Political Efficacy." *Journal of Politics* 73, no. 1 (2011): 216–31.

Beaumont, Elizabeth, and Richard M. Battistoni. "Beyond Civics 101: Rethinking What We Mean by Civics Education." *Journal of Political Science Education* 2, no. 3 (2006): 241–47.

Beaumont, Elizabeth, Anne Colby, Thomas Ehrlich, and Judith Torney-Purta. "Promoting Political Competence and Engagement in College Students: An Empirical Study." *Journal of Political Science Education* 2, no. 3 (2006): 249–70.

Beck, Paul A., and M. Kent Jennings. "Pathways to Participation." *American Political Science Review* 76 (1982): 94–108

Beiner, Ronald. *Theorizing Citizenship*. Albany NY: SUNY Press, 1995.

Bendor, Jonathan, Daniel Diermeier, and Michael Ting. "A Behavioral Model of Turnout." *American Political Science Review* 97, no. 2 (2003): 261–80.

Bender, Tisha. *Discussion-Based Online Teaching to Enhance Student-Learning*. Sterling, VA: Stylus, 2003.
Bennett, Stephen Earl. "Young Americans' Indifference to Media Coverage of Public Affairs." *PS: Political Science & Politics* 31 (1998): 535–41.
Bennett, Stephen Earl, and Linda L.M. Bennett. "What Political Scientists Should know about the Survey of First-Year Students in 2000." *PS: Political Science & Politics* 34 (2001): 295–99.
Bennion, Elizabeth A. "Caught in the Ground Wars: Mobilizing Voters During a Competitive Congressional Campaign." In *The Science of Voter Mobilization*, edited by Donald P. Green and Alan S. Gerber, 123–41. *The Annals of the American Academy of Political and Social Science* 601 (2005)
———. "Civic Education and Citizen Engagement: Mobilizing Voters as a Required Field Experiment." *Journal of Political Science Education* 2, no. 3 (2006): 205–27.
———. "Getting Your Student Learning Survey Approved by the IRB: Three Simple Steps." *The Political Science Educator* 4 (2009).
Bennion, Elizabeth A., and David W. Nickerson. "The Best Way to Register Voters: Results from Randomized Field Experiments." Paper presented at the Annual Meeting of the Midwest Political Science Association, Chicago 2009.
———. "The Cost of Convenience: A Field Experiment Showing that Email Outreach Decreases Voter Registration." *Political Research Quarterly*, prepublished online September 24, 2010. DOI: *1065912910382304*.
———. "Do Online Voter Registration Systems Make a Difference? A Large Scale, Multi-Site Field Experiment." Paper presented at the APSA Annual Meeting, Chicago, April 2011.
Benson, L., and I. Harkavy. "Academically-based Community Service and University Assisted Community Schools as Complementary Approaches for Advancing, Learning, Teaching, Research and Service: The University of Pennsylvania as a Case Study in Progress." In *Learning to Serve: Promoting Civil Society Through Service Learning*, edited by M. Kenny, L. Simon, K. Kiley-Brabeck, and R. Lerner, 363–78. Norwell, MA: Kluwer Academic Publishers, 2002.
Berent, Matthew K., and Jon A. Krosnick. "The Quality of Government Records and Over-estimation of Registration and Turnout in Surveys: Lessons for the 2008 ANES Panel Study's Registration and Turnout Validation Exercises." Manuscript: Stanford University, 2011.
Bernstein, Jeffery I. "How Citizens Learn Political Skills." Paper presented at the APSA Annual Meeting, Philadelphia, August 2006.
Bernstein, Robert, Anita Chadha, and Robert Montjoy. "Overreporting Voting: Why It Happens and Why It Matters." *Public Opinion Quarterly*. 65 (2001): 22–44.
Bleeker, E. T., and S. K. Murnen. "Fraternity Membership, the Display of Degrading Sexual Images of Women, and Rape Myth Acceptance." *Sex Roles* 53, no. 7–8 (2005): 487–93.
Bloom, Benjamin S., J. T. Hastings, and G. F. Madaus. *Taxonomy of Educational Objectives: The Classification of Educational Goals, Handbook 1, Cognitive Domain*. New York: McCay, 1956.
Blount, Alma. "Critical Reflection for Public Life: How Reflective Practice Helps Students Become Politically Engaged." *Journal of Political Science Education* 2 (2006): 271–83.
Bloustein, Edward J. "Community Service: A New Requirement for the Educated Person." In *Education for Democracy*, edited by Benjamin Barber and Richard M. Battistoni, 490-93. Dubuque, IA: Kendall/Hunt Publishing Company, 1999.
Boeringer, S. B. "Associations of Rape Supportive Attitudes with Fraternities and Athletic Participation." *Violence Against Women* 5 (1999): 81–90.
Bogard, Cynthia, Ian Sheinheit, and Renee Clarke. "Information They Can Trust: Increasing Youth Voter Turnout at the University." *PS: Political Science & Politics* 41 (2008): 541–46.
Bok, D. *Our Underachieving Colleges*. Princeton, NJ: Princeton University Press, 2006.
Boryczka, Jocelyn M. "The Personal *Is* Political." Paper presented at the APSA Teaching and Learning Conference, Charlotte, NC, February 2007.
Boss, Judith A. "The Effect of Community Service Work on the Moral Development of College Ethics Students." *Journal of Moral Education* 23, no. 2 (1994): 183–98.
Bowen, H. R., and J. H. Schuster. *American Professors: A National Resource Imperiled*. New York: Oxford University Press, 1986.
Boyer, Ernest L. *College: The Undergraduate Experience in America*. Princeton, NJ: Carnegie Foundation for the Advancement of Teaching, 1987.
———. "The Scholarship of Engagement." *The Journal of Public Service and Outreach* 1, no. 1 (1996): 11–20.
Boyte, Harry. *The Citizen Solution*. St. Paul, MN: Minnesota Historical Society Press, 2008.
———."Community Service and Civic Education." *Phi Beta Kappan* n.p.: (1991).
———. *Everyday Politics: Reconnecting Citizens and Public Life*. Philadelphia: University of Pennsylvania, 2004.
Bracey, Earnest N. "The Philosophy of Phenomenology and the Study of Politics." *The Political Science Educator*. 10 (2008): 1011.
Bradley, L. Richard. "Evaluating Service-Learning: Toward a New Paradigm." In *Service-Learning: Applications from the Research*, edited by Alan S. Waterman. Mahwah, NJ: Lawrence Erlbaum, 1997.

Brady, K. P. "The Promises and Pitfalls of Social Networking Websites." *School Business Affairs*, 74, no. 9 (2007): 24–28.

Breamer, Glenn. "Service Learning: What's a Political Scientist Doing in Yonkers?" *PS: Political Science & Politics* 31, no. 3 (1998): 557-61

Brennan Center for Justice. "Student Voting Guide." N.p., n.d. http://www.brennancenter.org/content/pages/svg_state_write_ups

Breuning, Marijke. "The International Relations of APSA." *PS: Political Science & Politics* 38, no. 1 (2005): 15961.

Brewer, Elizabeth, and Kiran Cunningham. *Integrating Study Abroad into the Curriculum: Theory and Practice Across the Disciplines*. Sterling, VA: Stylus, 2009.

Bringle, Robert, and Julie Hatcher. "Implementing Service Learning in Higher Education." *Journal of Higher Education* 67, no. 2 (1996): 222.

———."A Service Learning Curriculum for Faculty." *Michigan Journal of Community Service Learning*, 2 (1995): 11222.

Brock, Kathy L., and Beverly J. Cameron. "Enlivening Political Science Courses with Kolb's Learning Preference Model." *PS: Political Science & Politics* 32, no. 2 (1999): 251–56.

Brody, Richard. "Secondary Education and Political Attitudes: Examining the Effects on Political Tolerance of the We the People . . . Curriculum." Calabasas, CA: Center for Civic Education, 1994.

Brooks, David. "The Organization Kid." *The Atlantic Monthly* (April 2001): 4–40.

Brown, Robert D., Robert A. Jackson, and Gerald C.Wright. "Registration, Turnout, and State Party Systems." *Political Research Quarterly* 52, no. 3 (1999): 463–79.

Brown, Robert D., and Justin Wedeking. "People Who Have Their Tickets But Do Not Use Them: 'Motor Voter,' Registration, and Turnout Revisited." *American Politics Research* 34 (2006): 479–504.

Bryant, J. Alison, Nicole Schonemann, and Doug Karpa. *Integrating Service-Learning Into the University Classroom*. Sudbury, MA: Jones and Bartlett, 2011.

Bryner, Jeanne. "Today's College Students Lack Empathy." LiveScience.Com. May 28, 2010.

Bureau of Labor Statistics, US Department of Labor. "Occupational Office Handbook, 2010–2011 Edition: Paralegals and Legal Assistants." N.p. November 5, 2010, http://www.bls.gov/oco/ocos114.htm.

Burnsed, Brian. "10 College Classes that Impact the Outside World." US News and World Report, April 18, 2011. http://www.usnews.com/education/best-colleges/articles/2011/04/18/10-college-classes-that-impact-the-outside-world.

Butin, Dan W. *Service-Learning in Theory and Practice: The Future of Community Engagement in Higher Education*. New York: Palgrave Macmillan, 2010.

Cain, Michael J.G., and Zach Messitte. "Maryland Professors at the Polls: A Pilot Project Encouraging Faculty (and Students) to Serve as Poll Workers in the 2006 Election." Paper presented at the APSA Teaching and Learning Conference, San Jose, CA, February 2008.

California Business and Professions Code. *West Annotated California Business and Professions Code*, sec. 6450. N.p.: West Group, 2010.

California Campaign for the Civic Mission of Schools. *Educating for Democracy: The California Survey of Civic Education*. New York: Constitutional Rights Foundation, 2005.

California Community Colleges Chancellor's Office. "Our Mission." Accessed June 14, 2011. http://strategicplan.cccco.edu/.

Campbell, Angus, Philip Converse, Warren Miller, and Donald Stokes. *The American Voter*. New York: John Wiley & Sons, Inc., 1960.

Campbell, Angus, Gerald Gurin, and Warren Miller. *The Voter Decides*. Evanston, IL: Row, Peterson and Company, 1954.

Campbell, David E. "Social Capital and Service Learning." *PS: Political Science & Politics* 33, no. 3 (2000): 641–45.

———. *Why We Vote*. Princeton: Princeton University Press, 2006.

Campus Compact. "Annual Membership Survey Results, 2010." 2010. http://www.compact.org/wp-content/uploads/2008/11/2010-Annual-Survey-Exec-Summary-4-8.pdf.

———. The Politics of San Francisco. 2011. http://www.compact.org/syllabi/political-science/the-politics-of-san-francisco/4004/.

———. *Presidents' Declaration on the Civic Responsibility of Higher Education*. Providence, RI: Campus Compact, 1999.

Cantor, Jeffrey A. "Experiential Learning in Higher Education: Linking Classroom and Community." ASHE-ERIC Higher Education Reports Series, 95–97. n.p. ASHE-ERIC, accessed February 5, 2011. http://www.ntlf.com/html/lib/bib/95-7dig.htm.

Cantor, Nathaniel. *The Teaching-Learning Process*. New York: Holt, Rinehart and Winston, 1953.

Carnegie Corporation of New York. *The Civic Mission of Schools*. New York: The Leonore Annenberg Institute for Civics of the Annenberg Public Policy Center at the University of Pennsylvania and the Campaign for the Civic Mission of Schools, 2003. www.civicmissionofschools.org

Carnegie Foundation. "Carnegie Selects Colleges and Universities for 2010 Community Engagement Classification." Accessed January 20, 2011. http://www.carnegiefoundation.org/newsroom/press-releases/carnegie-selects-colleges-and-universities-2010-community-engagement-classification

Carter, Lief H., and Jean Bethke Elshtain. "Task Force on Civic Education Statement of Purpose." *PS: Political Science & Politics* 30, no. 4 (1997): 745.

Carter, Stephen L. *Civility, Manners, Morals, and the Etiquette of Democracy.* New York: Harper Perennial, 1999.

Castle, Kim, Janice Levy and Michael Peshkin. "CIRCLE Working Paper #66: Local and Absentee Voter Registration Drives on a College Campus." CIRCLE. 2009.

Catholic University of America. "Office of General Counsel." *Summary of Federal Laws.* N.p., August 22, 2012. http://counsel.cua.edu/FEDLAW/voter.cfm

Center for American Women and Politics. "Gender Differences in Voter Turnout." Fact Sheet. New Brunswick, NJ: Eagleton Institute of Politics, Rutgers University, 2008, accessed on July 15, 2011. http://www.cawp.rutgers.edu/fast_facts/voters/documents/genderdiff.pdf

The Center for Information & Research on Civic Learning & Engagement (CIRCLE). "At Least 80 Electoral Votes Depended on Youth." Accessed November 2012. http://www.civicyouth.org/at-least-80-electoral-votes-depended-on-youth/

———. "Massachusetts Senate Election: Turnout Was Just 15%, Compared 57% for Older Americans." Press Release. 2009. http://www.civicyouth.org/massachusetts-senate-election-youth-turnout-was-just-15-compared-to-48-for-older-citizens-young-voters-favored-coakley/.

———. "Millennials Talk Politics: A Study of College Student Political Participation." N.p., 110 n.d. http://www.civicyouth.org/PopUps/CSTP.pdf

———. "Reweighted Exit Poll Data Suggests Youth Turnout May Have Reach 22.8%." *Fact Sheet.* 2010. http://www.civicyouth.org/reweighted-exit-poll-data-suggest-youth-turnout-may-have-reached-22-8/?cat_id=6.

———. *Understanding a Diverse Generation, Youth Civic Engagement in the United States.* 2011. http://www.civicyouth.org/wpcontent/uploads/2011/11/CIRCLE_cluster_report2010.pdf

———. "Updated Estimate: Youth Turnout was 50% in 2012; Youth Turnout in Battleground States 58%." Accessed November 2012. http://www.civicyouth.org/updated-estimate-50-of-youth-turnout-in-2012-youth-turnout-in-battleground-states-58/

———. "Youth Civic Engagement: Basic Facts and Trends." College Park, MD: University of Maryland, 2002. 3.

———. "Youth Turnout: At Least 49%, 20-23 Million Under 30 Voted." *CIRCLE Press Release.* Medford, MA: CIRCLE, Jonathan M. Tisch College of Citizenship and Public Service, Tufts University. Accessed November 17, 2012. http://www.civicyouth.org/youth-turnout-at-least-49-22-23-million-under-30-voted/.

———. "The Youth Vote in 2010: Final Estimates Based on Census Data." 2011. http://www.civicyouth.org//wp-content/uploads/2011/04/The-CPS-youth-vote-2010-FS-FINAL1.pdf

———. "Youth Voter Turnout Has Declined, by Any Measure." 2002. http://www.civicyouth.org/PopUps/v1.i.3.pdf.

———. "Youth Voter Turnout in Midterm Elections." v.714, October 2010. http://www.civicyouth.org/wp-content/uploads/2010/09/v7.i4_final.pdf.

———. "Youth Voting in the 2004 Election, CIRCLE Fact Sheet." 2005. Accessed February 17, 2005.

———. "The 2006 Civic and Political Health of the Nation." 2006. Accessed October 2006. http://www.civicyouth.org

Chesney, James, and Otto Feinstein. *Building Civic Literacy and Citizen Power.* New Jersey: Prentice Hall, 1997.

Chickering, A. "Strengthening Spirituality and Civic Engagement in Higher Education." *Journal of College and Character* 8, no. 1 (2006). Accessed February 8, 2008 http://www.collegevalues.org/pdfs/chickering%20remarks.pdf

Civic Youth. "Younger Voters Were Racially Diverse, Voted Democratic, and Approved of Barack Obama." *Around the Circle: Research and Practice.* January 2011. Accessed February 11, 2011. http://www.civicyouth.org/wp-content/uploads/2010/12/V8.i1_final.pdf

Coalition for Civic Engagement and Leadership (CCEL). "About Us: Definitions." University of Maryland. 2005. http://www.compact.org/initiatives/civic-engagement-at-research-universities/models-of-civic-engagement-initiatives-at-research-universities/civic-engagement-at-the-university-of-maryland/.

Colby, Anne, Elizabeth Beaumont, Thomas Ehrlich, and Josh Corngold. *Educating for Democracy: Preparing Undergraduates for Responsible Political Engagement.* San Francisco: Jossey-Bass, 2007.

Colby, Anne, Thomas Ehrlich, Elizabeth Beaumont, and Jason Stephens. *Educating Citizens: Preparing America's Undergraduates for Lives of Moral and Civic Responsibility.* San Francisco: Jossey-Bass and the Carnegie Foundation for Teaching, 2003.

Collier, Peter J., and Dilafruz R. Williams. "Reflection in Action: the Learning-Doing Relationship." In *Learning Through Serving: A Student Guidebook for Service-Learning Across the Disciplines*, edited by Christine M. Cress, Peter J. Collier, Vicki L. Reitenauer, and Associates, 83–147. Sterling, VA: Stylus, 2005.

Comber, Melissa. "Learning to Participate: The Effects of Civic Education on Racial/Ethnic Minorities." *National Political Science Review* 12 (2008).

Connell, R.W. "Political Socialization in the American Family: The Evidence Re-examined." *Public Opinion Quarterly* 1, no. 36 (1972): 323–33.
Conover, Pamela, and Donald Searing. "A Political Socialization Perspective." In *Rediscovering the Democratic Purposes of Education*, edited by L. M. McDonnell, P.M. Timpane, and R. Benjamin Lawrence, 91–124. Lawrence, KS: University Press of Kansas, 2000.
Converse, Philip, and Richard G. Niemi. "Non-voting Among Young Adults in the United States." In *Political Parties and Political Behavior*, edited by William J Crotty, Donald A. Freeman, and Douglas S. Gatlin. Boston, MA: Allyn & Bacon, 1971.
Corbett, Julia B., and April R. Kendall. "Evaluating Service Learning in the Communication Discipline." *Journalism and Mass Communication Educator* 53, no. 4 (1999): 66–76.
Craig, S. C., R. G. Niemi, and G. E. Silver. "Political Efficacy and Trust: A Report on the NES Pilot Study Items." *Political Behavior* 12 (1990): 289–314.
Cress, Christine M. "What is Service-Learning?" In *Learning Through Serving: A Student Guidebook for Service-Learning Across the Disciplines*, edited by Christine M. Cress, Peter J. Collier, Vicki L. Reitenauer and Associates, 7–16. N.p.: Stylus Publishing, 2005.
Creswell, John W. *Research Design: Qualitative, Quantitative, and Mixed Methods Approaches*. Thousand Oaks, CA: SAGE Publications, 2003.
Csajko, Karen, and Kara Lindaman. "Practice Makes Perfect: Engaging Student-Citizens in Politics Thought Theory and Practice." *Journal of Political Science Education* 7, no. 1 (2011): 65–78.
Cummings, Jack A. "Promoting Student Interaction in the Virtual College Classroom." Indiana Higher Education Telecommunication System, Faculty Paper, 1998. http://www.ihets.org/learntech/distance_ed/fdpapers/1998/52.html.
Dagger, Richard. *Civic Virtues: Rights, Citizenship, and Republican Liberalism*. New York: Oxford University Press, 1997.
Daily Princetonian Editorial Board. "Banning Greek Life." *Daily Princetonian*. March 20, 2012. http://www.dailyprincetonian.com/2012/03/30/30419/
Dalton, Jon and Pamela Crosby. "From Volunteering to Voting: Higher Education's Role in Preparing College Students for Political Engagement." *Journal of College & Character* 9, no. 4 (2008): 1–6.
Dalton, Russell J. *The Good Citizen: How a Younger Generation is Reshaping American Politics*. Reviseded.. Washington, DC: Congressional Quarterly Press, 2009.
Deardorff, M., K. Hamann, and J. Ishiyama. *Assessment in Political Science*. American Political Science Association: Washington, DC, 2009.
Dee, Thomas S. "Are there Civic Returns to Education?" CIRCLE Working Paper 8 (2003): 1–36.
Delli Carpini, Michael, and Scott Keeter. *What Americans Know About Politics and Why It Matters*. New Haven: Yale University Press, 1996.
———. "What Should be Learned Through Service Learning?" *PS: Political Science & Politics* 33, no. 3 (2000): 635–37.
Delshad, Ashlie. "Civic Duty and Voting: The Additive and Interactive Role of Election Specific Factors in American Presidential Elections 1972–1992." Paper presented at the Annual Meeting of the Southern Political Science Association, New Orleans, LA, January 2009.
Deutsch, Karl. "Social Mobilization and Political Development." *American Political Science Review* 55, no. 3 (1961): 493–514.
Dewey, John. *Democracy and Education: An Introduction to the Philosophy of Education*. New York: Free Press, 1966
———. *Experience and Education*. New York: Collier, 1938.
———. *How We Think. A Restatement of the Relation of Reflective Thinking to the Educative Process*. Boston: DC Health, 1933.
Dicklitch, Susan. "Real Service = Real Learning: Making Political Science Relevant Through Service-Learning." *PS: Political Science & Politics* 36, no. 3 (2003):773–76.
Donahue, David M. "Conflict as a Constructive Curricular Strategy." In *Democratic Dilemmas of Teaching Service-Learning: Curricular Strategies for Success*, edited by Christine M. Cress, David M. Donahue, and Associates, 101–9 Sterling, VA: Stylus Publishing, LLC, 2011.
Donner, Allan and Neil Klar. *Design and Analysis of Cluster Randomization Trials in Health Research*. New York: Arnold Publishers, 2000.
Downs, Anthony. *An Economic Theory of Democracy*. New York: Harper and Row, 1957.
Druckman James N. "On the Limits of Framing Effects: Who Can Frame." *Journal of Politics* 63 (2001): 1041–66.
Ducrot, J., S. Miller, and P. Goodman. "Learning Outcomes for a Business Information Systems Undergraduate Program." *Communications of the Association for Information Systems* 23 (2008).
Dudley, Robert, and Alan Gitelson. "Civic Education, Civic Engagement, and Youth Civic Development." *PS: Political Science & Politics* 36, no.2 (2003): 263–67.
Dunn v. Blumstein, 405 U.S. 330 (1972)
Durham III, Alexis M. "Observations on the Future of Criminal Justice Education: Legitimating the Discipline and Serving the General University Population." *Journal of Criminal Justice Education* 3 (1992): 35–52

Easton, David, and Jack Dennis. "The Child's Acquisition of Regime Norms: Political Efficacy." *American Political Science Review* 61, no. 1 (1967): 25–38.

Eberly, C. "Unfairly Singled Out." *New York Times*. May 5, 2011. http://www.nytimes.com/roomfordebate/2011/05/05/frat-guys-gone-wild-whats-the-solution/fraternities-are-unfairly-singled-out

Eccles, Jacquelynne S., and Bonnie L. Barber. "Student Council, Volunteering, Basketball, or Marching Band: What Kind of Extracurricular Involvement Matters?" *Journal of Adolescent Research* 14, no. 1 (1999): 10–43.

Eccles, Jacquelynne S., Bonnie L. Barber, Margaret Stone, and James Hunt. "Extracurricular Activities and Adolescent Development." *Journal of Social Issues* 59, no. 4 (2003): 865–89.

Ehman, Lee H. "The American School in the Political Socialization Process." *Review of Educational Research* 50 (1980): 99–119.

Ehrenreich, Barbara. *Nickel and Dimed: On (Not) Getting by in America*. New York: Henry Holt & Co., 2002.

Ehrlich, Thomas. "Civic Education: Lessons Learned." *PS: Political Science & Politics* 32, no. 2 (1999): 245–50.

———. ed. *Civic Responsibility and Higher Education*. Westport, CT: Greenwood Press, 2000.

Eisner, Jane. *Taking Back the Vote: Getting American Youth Involved in Our Democracy*. Boston: Beacon Press, 2004.

Eliasoph, Nina. *Avoiding Politics: How Americans Produce Apathy in Everyday Life*. Cambridge: Cambridge University Press, 1998.

Elshtain, Jean Bethke. "The Decline of Democratic Faith." In *Experiencing Citizenship: Concepts and Models for Service-Learning in the Classroom*, edited by Richard M. Battistoni and William E. Hudson. Washington, DC: American Association for Higher Education, 1997.

Erikson, Erik. *Identity: Youth and Crisis*. New York: W. W. Norton & Company, (1967) 1994.

Erikson, Robert S. "Why Do People Vote? Because They are Registered." *American Politics Quarterly* 9, no. 3 (1981): 259–76.

Escamilla, Mary. "Pro Bono? What's That?" *PreLaw* (2006): 24–28.

Eschrich, David. "We the People: The Citizen and the Constitution 2010 National Finalists' Knowledge of and Support for American Democratic Institutions and Processes." *Research Report*. Calabasas, CA: Center for Civic Education, 2010.

Etzioni, A. *New Communitarian Thinking: Persons, Virtues, Institutions and Communities*. Charlottesville, VA: University Press of Virginia, 1995.

Ewell, Peter T. "An Emerging Scholarship: A Brief History of Assessment." In *Building a Scholarship of Assessment*, edited by Trudy W. Banta & Associates. San Francisco: Jossey-Bass, 2002.

Exley, Zack. "The New Organizers: What's Really Behind Obama's Ground Game." *Huffington Post*, 2008.

Eyler, Janet. "Reflection: Linking Service and Learning – Linking Students and Communities." *Journal of Social Issues* 58, no. 3 (2002): 520.

Eyler, Janet, and Dwight E. Giles Jr. "The Importance of Program Quality in Service Learning." In *Service-Learning: Applications from Research*, edited by Alan S. Waterman. Mahwah, NJ: Lawrence Erlbaum, 1997.

———. *Where's the Learning in Service-Learning?* San Francisco: Jossey-Bass, 1999.

Eyler, Janet, Dwight E. Giles Jr., and John Braxton. "The Impact of Service-Learning on College Students." *Michigan Journal of Community Service Learning* 4 (1997): 5–15.

Eyler, Janet, Dwight E. Giles Jr., Christine M. Stenson, and Charlene J. Gray. *At A Glance: What We Know About the Effects of Service-Learning on College Students, Faculty, Institutions and Communities, 1993-2000: Third Edition*. N.p.: Corporation for National Service Learn and Serve America National Service Learning Clearinghouse. 2001. Accessed on March 14, 2008. http://www.servicelearning.org/filemanager/download/4192_AtAGlance.pdf.

Falcone, Michael, and Michael Moss. "Group's Tally of New Voters was Vastly Overstated." *New York Times* October 24, 2008, page A1.

Farr, James. "The Science of Politics – as Civic Education – Then and Now," *PS: Political Science & Politics* 37, no. 1 (2004): 37–40.

Farrell, Elisabeth, and Eric Hoover. "The Battle Over the Booth: Students Organize Challenges to Restrictive Voting Laws in an Effort to Increase Election Turnout." *The Chronicle of Higher Education*. September 17, 2004. Accessed December 27, 2008. http://chronicle.com/weekly/v51/i04/04a03201.htm.

Fear, Frank A., and Lorilee Sandmann. "Unpacking the Service Category: Reconceptualizing Service for the 21st Century." *Continuing Higher Education Review* 59 (1995): 110–122.

Feith, D., ed. *Teaching America, The Case for Civic Education*. Lanham, MD: R&L Education, 2011.

Field, Kelly. "Sen. Harkin Presses Education Dept. on Effectiveness of 'Gainful Employment' Rule." *Chronicle of Higher Education*. June 7, 2011. Accessed on January, 20 2012. http://chronicle.com/article/Sen-Harkin-Presses-Education/127786/

Fieldhouse, Edward, Mark Tranmer, and Andrew Russell. "Something About Young People or Something About Elections? Electoral Participation of Young People in Europe: Evidence from a Multilevel Analysis of the European Social Survey." *European Journal of Practical Research* 46, no. 6 (2007): 797–822.

Fine, Terri Susan. "Promoting Civic Engagement and the College Student Poll Worker Study: Who works the Polls on Election Day?" Paper presented at the APSA Teaching and Learning Conference, San Jose, CA, February 2008.

Fink, L. D. *Creating Significant Learning Experiences*. San Francisco: Jossey-Bass, 2003.
Finkel, Steven E., and Amy Erica Smith. "Civic Education, Political Discussion, and the Social Transmission of Democratic Knowledge and Values in a New Democracy: Kenya 2002." *American Journal of Political Science* 55, no. 2 (2011): 417–35.
Fish, Stanley. *Save the World On Your Own Time*. New York: Oxford University Press, 2008.
———. "Why We Built the Ivory Tower." *New York Times*. May 21, 2004
Flanagan, Constance. "Developmental Roots of Political Engagement." *PS: Political Science & Politics* 36, no. 2 (2003): 257–61.
———. "Shutter Fraternities for Young Women's Good." *The Wall Street Journal*. April 23, 2011. http://online.wsj.com/article/SB10001424052748704658704576275152354071470.html?mod=WSJ_hp_mostpop_read#articleTabs%3Darticle
Flanagan, Constance, and Lonnie R. Sherrod. "Youth Political Development: An Introduction." *Journal of Social Issues* 54, no. 3 (1998): 447–56.
Foubert, J. D., J. T. Newberry, and J. L. Tatum. "Behavior Differences Seven Months Later: Effects of a Rape Prevention Program on First Year Men who Join Fraternities." *NASPA Journal* 44 (2007): 728–49.
Fowler, James H. "Habitual Voting and Behavioral Turnout." *Journal of Politics* 68, no. 2 (2006): 335–44.
Frantzich, Stephen. *Citizen Democracy: Political Activists in a Cynical Age*. 3rd edition. Lanham: MD: Rowman and Littlefield, (1999) 2008.
Freidman, Thomas. "Where Did 'We' Go?" *New York Times*, September 29, 2009.
Frey, Valerie A., and Santiago Suarez. "¡Mobilización Efectiva de Votantes! Analyzing the Effects of Bilingual Mobilization and Notification of Bilingual Ballots on Latino Turnout." Unpublished Manuscript. Institution for Social and Policy Studies, Yale University. N.p., n.d.
Freyss, S. F. "Learning Political Engagement from the Experts: Advocacy Groups, Neighborhood Councils, and Constituency Service." *PS: Political Science & Politics* 39 (2006): 137–45.
Furlong, Scott R., and Denise Scheberle. "Exploring the Role of Political Science Courses in Civic Engagement." Paper presented at the Annual Conference of the Midwest Political Science Association, Chicago, IL, 2006.
Gadamer, Hans-Georg. "On the Scope and Function of Hermeneutical Reflection." In *Philosophical Hermeneutics*, translated by David E. Linge. Berkeley, CA: University of California Press, 1976.
———. *Truth and Method*. Translated by Joel Weinsheimer and Donald G. Marshall, 2nd ed. New York: Crossroad, 1989.
Gall, Meredith D., Walter R. Borg, and Joyce P. Gall. *Educational Research: an Introduction*. London: Longman, 1996.
Gallini, Sarah, and Barbara Moely. "Service-Learning and Engagement, Academic Challenge and Retention" *Michigan Journal of Community Service-Learning* (2003): 5–6.
Galston, William. "Civic Education and Political Participation." *Phi Delta Kappa* 85 (2003): 29–33.
———. "Civic Education and Political Participation." *PS: Political Science & Politics* 37, no. 2 (2004): 263–66.
———. "Political Knowledge, Political Engagement, and Civic Education." *Annual Review of Political Science* 4 (2001): 217–34.
Gay, Ir, and Peter Airasian. *Educational Research: Competencies for Analysis and Application*. Columbus, OH: Merrill Publishing, 1992.
Gentry, Bobbi. "Bridging Civic Engagement and Voting Behavior: A Theory of Political Identity." Paper presented at the APSA Teaching and Learning Conference, Baltimore, MD, February 2009.
Gerber, Alan S., and Donald P. Green. "The Effects of Canvassing, Direct Mail, and Telephone Contact on Voter Turnout: A Field Experiment." *American Political Science Review* 94, no. 3 (2000): 653–63.
———. *Get Out the Vote! How to Increase Voter Turnout*. Washington, DC: Brookings Institute Press, 2004.
Gerber, Alan S., Donald P. Green, and Christopher W. Larimer. "Social Pressure and Voter Turnout: Evidence from a Large-Scale Field Experiment." *American Political Science Review* 102, no. 1 (2008): 33–48.
Gerber, Alan S., Donald P. Green, and Ron Shachar. "Voting May Be Habit-Forming: Evidence From a Randomized Field Experiment." *American Journal of Political Science* 47, no. 3 (2003): 540–550.
Gibson, Cynthia. *From Inspiration to Participation: A Review of Perspective on Youth Civic Engagement*. N.p.: The Grantmaker Forum on Community and National Service, 2001.
Gifford, A. "Higher Ranked Colleges Lack Frats." *The Syracuse Post-Standard*. May 4, 2001. Sec A, 14.
Giles, Dwight E., and Janet Eyler. "The Impact of a College Community Service Laboratory on Students' Personal, Social, and Cognitive Outcomes." *Journal of Adolescence* 17 (1994): 327–39.
Gimpel, James G., Celeste Lay, and Jason E. Schuknecht. *Cultivating Democracy: Civic Environments and Political Socialization in America*. Washington, DC: Brookings Institution, 2003.
Gladwell, Malcolm. "Small Change: Why the Revolution Will Not be Tweeted." *The New Yorker*, October 4, 2010.
Glanville, Jonathan L. "Political Socialization or Selection? Adolescent Extracurricular Participation and Political Activity in Early Adulthood." *Social Science Quarterly* 80 (1999): 279–89.

Glassick, Charles E., Mary Taylor Huber, and Gene I. Maeroff. *Scholarship Assessed: Evaluation of the Professoriate.* San Francisco: Jossey-Bass, 1997.

Goff, Chris. "Teaching Political Engagement." *Free Exchange on Campus.* August 30, 2007. Accessed 2009. http://www.freeexchangeoncampus.org/index2.php?option=com_content&do_pdf=1&i=700

Goldman, G. K., and L. E. Zakel "Clarification of Assessment and Evaluation." *Assessment Update* 21, no. 3 (2009). Wiley InterScience. COI-10.1002/au.213. http://onlinelibrary.wiley.com/doi/10.1002/au.213/pdf#page=8.

Goodwin, Jan. "Broken Promises: Seeking Political Asylum in America." *Ladies Home Journal.* N.d. http://www.lhj.com/health/news/seeking-political-asylum-in-america/

Gordon, C. Wayne, and Nicholas Babchuk. "A Typology of Voluntary Associations." *American Sociological Review* 24 (1959): 22–29.

Graham, Senator Bob, and Chris Hand. *America The Owner's Manual: Making Government Work For You.* Washington DC: CQ Press, 2010.

Gray, Virginia, and Russell L. Hanson. eds. *Politics in the American States: A Comparative Analysis.* Ninth Edition. Washington, DC: CQ Press, 2008.

Green, Donald P., and Alan S. Gerber. "Do Phone Calls Increase Voter Turnout: An Update." *The Annals of the American Academy of Political and Social Science* 601: 66–84.

———. *Get Out the Vote: How to Increase Voter Turnout.* Washington, DC: Brookings Institution Press, 2004.

Grobow, R., and D. Robbins, eds. *What We Think: Young Voters Speak Out.* Bothel, WA: Book Publishers Network, 2004.

Gross, Neil, and Solon Simmons. "The Social and Political Views of American Professors." Working Paper, September 24, 2007.

Gugerty, Catherine R., and Erin D. Swezey. "Developing Campus-Community Partnerships." In *Service-learning in Higher Education: Concepts and Practices,* edited by Barbara Jacoby & Associates. San Francisco, CA: Jossey-Bass, 1996.

Gurin, Patricia, Biren A. Nagda, and Gretchen Lopez. "The Benefits of Diversity in Education for Democratic Citizenship."*Journal of Social Issues* 60, no. 1 (2004): 17–34.

Gutmann, Amy. *Democratic Education.* Princeton, NJ: Princeton University Press, 1987.

———. "Why Should Schools Care about Civic Education?" In *Rediscovering the Democratic Purposes of Education,* edited by L. McDonnell, P. M. Timpane, & R. Bejamin,73–90. Lawrence, KS: University Press of Kansas, 2000.

Halva-Neubauer, Glen A. "Public Affairs Internships: Coming of Age." In *Education for Citizenship,* edited by Grant Reeher and Joseph Cammarano. Lanham, MD: Rowman & Littlefield, 1997.

Hanks, Michael, and Bruce Eckland. "Adult Voluntary Associations." *Sociological Quarterly* 19 (1978): 481–90.

Hanmer, Michael J. *Discount Voting: Registration Reforms and Their Effects.* New York: Cambridge University Press, 2009.

Hardt, Jan. "Encouraging Student Political Engagement in Political Science Classes." Paper presented at the APSA Teaching and Learning Conference, Baltimore, MD, February 2009.

Harlaub, Stephen G., and Frank A. Lancaster. "Teacher Characteristics and Pedagogy in Political Science." *Journal of Political Science Education* 4, no. 4 (2008): 377–93.

Harward, Donald W. "Institutional Change Requires Student Involvement." *Bringing Theory to Practice Newsletter.* (2011) http://www.aacu.org/bringing_theory/newsletter/jan11/director.cfm.

Harwood Group. "College Students Talk Politics." (Dayton, OH: The Kettering Foundation, 1993).

Hays, Carol. "Alienation, Engagement, and the College Student." In *Engaging The Public: How Government and the Media Can Reinvigorate American Democracy,* edited by Thomas Johnson, Carol Hayes, and Scott Hays. Lanham, MD: Rowman & Littlefield, 1998.

Heater, Derek. *A Brief History of Citizenship.* New York: New York University Press, 2004.

———. *What is Citizenship?* Malden, MA: Blackwell Press, 1999.

Help America Vote College Program. "Help America Vote College Program Recipients." Washington, DC: United States Election Assistance Commission, 2002. http://www.eac.gov/payments_and_grants/help_america_vote_college_program_recipients.aspx#college_recipients_2010.

Hepburn, Mary A., Richard G. Niemi, and Chris Chapman. "Service Learning in College Political Science: Queries and Commentary." *PS: Political Science & Politics* 33, no. 3 (2000): 617–22.

Hess, Robert D., and Judith V. Torney. *The Development of Political Attitudes in Children.* Chicago: Aldine, 1967.

Higher Education Research Institute (HERI). "Most of the Nation's College Freshman Embrace the Internet as an Educational Tool, UCLA Study Finds." HERI Website. January 25, 1999. http://www.gseis.ucla.edu/heri/norms_pr_98.html.

———. "Press Release." University of California at Los Angeles. October 29, 2004. http://www.gseis.ucla.edu.

Highton, Benjamin. "Easy Registration and Voter Turnout." *Journal of Politics* 59, no. 2 (1997): 565–75.

Highton, Benjamin, and Raymond E. Wolfinger. "The First Seven Years of the Political Life Cycle." *American Journal of Political Science* 45, no. 1 (2001): 202–9.

Hopkins, Roy J. "Studying Abroad as a Form of Experiential Education." *Liberal Education* 85, no. 3 (1999): 36–42.

Hoppe, S. "A Synthesis of the Theoretical Stances." In *Service Learning: History, Theory and Issues*. Edited by B. Speck and S. Hoppe, 138–49. Westport, CT: Praeger, 2004.

Hoover, Kenneth, James E. Marcia, and Kristen Parris. *The Power of Identity: Politics in a New Key*. Chatham, New Jersey: Chatham House Publishers, Inc., 1997.

Horowitz, David. *Indoctrination U.: The Left's War Against Academic Freedom*. New York: Encounter Books, 2003.

Hovland, Kevin. *Shared Futures: Global Learning and Liberal Education*. Washington, DC: Association of American Colleges and Universities, 2006.

Howe, Neil, and William Strauss. *Millennials Go to College*. New York: Life Course Associates, 2007.

Hoy, Ariane, and Wayne Meisel. *Civic Engagement At The Center: Building Democracy Through Integrated and Cocurricular and Curricular Experiences*. Washington, DC: Association of American Colleges and Universities, 2008.

Huckfeldt, Robert, Paul E. Johnson, and John Sprague. *Political Disagreement*. New York: Cambridge University Press, 2005.

Hudak, Kristen, Mark Sachleben, and Deborah E. Ward. "2011 APSA Teaching and Learning Conference Track Summaries: Internationalizing the Curriculum I." *PS: Political Science & Politics* 44, no. 3 (2011): 660–62.

Huerta, Juan Carlos, and Joseph Jozwiak. "Developing Civic Engagement in General Education Political Science." *Journal of Political Science Education* 4, no. 1 (2008): 42–60.

Hunter, Bill, George P. White, and Galen C. Godbey, "What Does It Mean to Be Globally Competent?" *Journal of Studies in International Education* 10, no. 3 (2006): 267–85.

Hunter, Susan, and Richard A. Brisbin Jr. "The Impact of Service Learning on Democratic and Civic Values." *PS: Political Science & Politics* 33, no. 3 (2000): 623–26.

Hutchins, Robert Maynard. *Education for Freedom*. Baton Rouge, LA: Louisiana State University Press, 1943.

———. *The Higher Learning in America*. New Haven, CT: Yale University Press, 1936.

Ichilov, Orit. "Civic Knowledge of High School Students in Israel: Personal and Contextual Determinants." *Political Psychology* 28, no. 4 (2007): 417–40.

IEA Civic Education Study. "Teacher Questionnaire." 2000. http://www.wam.umd.edu/~jtpurta/Original%20 Documents/CivTQ.PDF.

INS v. Cardoza-Fonseca, 480 U.S. 421 (1987)

INS v. Elias-Zacarias, 112 U.S. 812 (1992).

Institute of International Education. "Campus Report Early Indication That Study Abroad is Rising," *Institute of International Education*. 2010. http://www.iie.org/en/Who-We-Are/News-and-Events/Press-Center/Press-Releases/2010/2010-11-15-Fall-2010-Study-Abroad-Snapshot-Survey.

Institute of Politics at Harvard University. "Attitudes Toward Political and Public Service: A National Survey of College Undergraduates." Cambridge, MA: Harvard University, 2002.

Intercollegiate Studies Institute. *Failing Our Schools, Failing America*. 2007. http://www.americancivicliteracy.org/report/major_findings_findg5.html.

Ishiyama, John, and Marijke Breuning. "How International Are Political Science Programs at Liberal Arts and Sciences Colleges and Universities in the Midwest?" *PS: Political Science & Politics* 39, no. 2 (2006): 327–33.

Islam, Frank, George Munoz and Ed Crego. *Renewing the American Dream: A Citizen's Guide for Restoring our Competitive Advantage*. IMC Publishing, 2010.

Jackson, Robert A., Robert D. Brown, and Gerald C. Wright. "Registration, Turnout, and the Electoral Representativeness of U.S. State Electorates." *American Politics Quarterly* 26 (1998): 259–87.

Jacoby, Barbara. "How to Deepen Learning through Critical Reflection." Recorded April 20, 2011. Magna Publications. http://www.magnapubs.com/catalog/how-to-deepen-learning-through-critical-reflection/.

———. "Service Learning in Today's Higher Education." In *Service-learning in Higher Education: Concepts and Practices*, edited by Barbara Jacoby and Associates, 3–25. San Francisco: Jossey-Bass, 1996.

Jacoby, Barbara and Associates. *Civic Engagement in Higher Education: Concepts and Practices*. San Francisco: Jossey-Bass, 2009.

Janger, Stephen. "Civic Education – A Close Up Look." *Extensions: A Journal of the Carl Albert Congressional Research and Studies Center* (2003): 9–12.

Jenkins, Shannon. "Sustainable Master Planning in Urban Politics and Policy: A Service Learning Project." *Journal of Political Science Education* 4 (2008): 357–69.

Jennings, M. Kent. "Political Knowledge Over Time and Across Generations." *Public Opinion Quarterly* 60, no. 2 (1996): 228–52.

Jennings, M. Kent, and Richard G. Niemi. *Generations and Politics*. Princeton: Princeton University Press, 1981.

———. *The Political Character of Adolescence*. Princeton: Princeton University Press, 1974.

Johnson, D., R. Johnson, and E. Holubec. *Cooperation in the Classroom*. Boston: Allyn and Bacon, 1998.

Johnson, D. W., ed. *Campaigning for President in 2008, New Voices and New Techniques*. New York: Routledge, 2009.

Junn, Jane. "Diversity, Immigration, and the Politics of Civic Education." *PS: Political Science & Politics* 37, no. 2 (2004): 253–555.

Kahne, Joseph, and Ellen Middaugh. "High Quality Civic Education: What Is It and Who Gets It?" *Social Education* 72, no. 1 (2008): 34–39.

Karp, Jeffrey A., and David Brockington. "Social Desirability and Response Validity: A Comparative Analysis of Overreporting Voter Turnout in Five Countries." *The Journal of Politics* 67, no. 3 (2005): 825–40.

Katula Richard A., and Elizabeth Threnhauser. "Experiential Education in the Undergraduate Curriculum." *Communication Education* 48 (1999): 238–55.

Katz, Michael. *The Undeserving Poor: From the War on Poverty to the War on Welfare.* New York: Pantheon Books, 1989.

Kaufman, Joyce P. "The Good News... and the Bad News." Paper presented at the APSA Teaching and Learning Conference, Washington DC, February 2012.

Kedrowski, Karen. "Civic Education by Mandate: A State-by-State Analysis." *PS: Political Science & Politics* 36 (2003): 225–27.

Keen, Cheryl, and Elizabeth Baldwin. "Students Promoting Economic Development and Environmental Sustainability." *International Journal of Sustainability in Higher Education* 5 (2004)

Keeter, Scott, et al. "Schooling and Civic Engagement in the U.S." delivered at the APSA Annual Meeting, August 2002, Boston, MA.

Keeter, Scott, Cliff Zukin, Molly Andolina, and Krista Jenkins. *The Civic and Political Health of the Nation: A Generational Portrait.* College Park, MD: Center for Information and Research on Civic Learning and Engagement (CIRCLE), 2002. http://www.civicyouth.org/research/products/Civic_Political_Health.pdf.

Keller, Bill. *Class Matters.* New York: Times Books, 2005.

Kellogg, Alex. "Looking Inward: Freshman Care Less About Politics and More About Money." *Chronicle of Higher Education* 47 (2001): A47–A50.

Kelly, Diann Cameron. "Civic Readiness: Preparing Toddlers and Young Children for Civic Education and Sustained Engagement." *National Civic Review* 234 (2008): 55–59.

Kendall, Jane C. *Combining Service and Learning: A Resource Book for Community and Public Service.* Raleigh, NC: National Society for Experiential Learning, 1990.

Kennedy, Edward M. "Kennedy Holds U.S. Senate Field Hearing in Boston on College Access and the Impact of the Credit Crunch on Student Loan Availability." US Senate Committee on Health, Education, Labor, and Pensions. March 17, 2008. Accessed on January 20, 2012. http://www.help.senate.gov/newsroom/press/release/?id=4a5f8ef0-9bed-48a4-a0a5-3ac0f6c2d6b0&groups=Chair.

Kenski, Kate, Bruce W. Hardy, and Kathleen Hall Jamieson. *The Obama Victory.* New York: Oxford University Press, 2010.

Key, V.O. *Politics, Parties, and Pressure Groups.* Cambridge, MA: Harvard University Press, 1964.

Kiesa, Abby, Alexander P. Orlowski, Peter Levine, Deborah Both, Emily Hoban Kirby, Mark Kirby, Karlo Barrios Marcelo, Joshua Gillerman, and Samantha Linkins. "The Youth Vote in the 2008 Primaries and Caucuses." CIRCLE Paper. http://www.civicyouth.org/PopUps/FactSheets/FS_08_primary_summary.pdf.

Kirby, Emily Hoban, and Kei Kawashima-Ginsberg. "The Youth Vote in 2008." Civic Youth, August 17, 2009. http://www.civicyouth.org/PopUps/FactSheets/FS_youth_Voting_2008_updated_6.22.pdf.

Kirlin, Mary Kittelson. "Civic Skill Building: The Missing Component in Service Programs?" *PS: Political Science & Politics* 31, no. 3 (2002): 571–75.

Klinkner, Philip, and Mack Mariani. "The Effect of a Campaign Internship on Political Efficacy, Trust and Responsiveness." Paper presented at the APSA Teaching and Learning Conference, Charlotte, NC, February 2007.

Knack, Stephen. "Does "Motor Voter" Work? Evidence from State-level Data." *Journal of Politics* 57, no. 3 (1995): 796–811.

———. "Election-day Registration: The Second Wave." *American Politics Quarterly* 29, no. 1 (2001): 65–78.

Knapp, Laura A., Janice E. Kelly-Reid, and Scott A. Ginder. *Enrollment in Post-Secondary Institutions, 2009; Graduation Rates 2003 & 2006; and Financial Statistics Fiscal Year 2009.* Washington, DC: National Center for Education Statistics. February 2011. Accessed on January 15, 2012. http://nces.ed.gov/pubs2011/2011230.pdf.

Kolb, Alice Y., and David A. Kolb. "Learning Styles and Learning Spaces: Enhancing Experiential learning in Higher Education." *Academy of Management Learning and Education* 4, no. 2 (2005).

Kolb, David A. *Experiential Learning.* Englewood Cliffs, NJ: Prentice-Hall, 1984.

Konrath, Sara, and Edward O'Brian. "Changes in Dispositional Empathy in American College Students Over Time: A Meta-Analysis." *Personality and Social Psychology Review* (2010).

Koulish, Robert. "Citizenship Service Learning: Becoming Citizens by Assisting Immigrants." *PS: Political Science & Politics* 31, no. 3 (1998).

Krathwohl, D. R., B. S. Bloom and B. B. Masia. *Axonomy of Educational Objectives: The Classification of Educational Goals Handbook II: Affective Domain.* New York: David McKay Co., Inc., 1973.

Krehbiel, Keith. *Pivotal Politics: A Theory of U.S. Lawmaking.* Chicago: Chicago University Press, 1998.
Kroger, Jane. *Identity Development: Adolescence through Adulthood.* Thousand Oaks, CA: Sage Publications, Inc., 2007.
Krysor, Darwin V., and Margaret Anne Pierce. "Does Intern/Co-op Experience Translate Into Career Progress and Satisfaction?" *Journal of Career Planning and Employment* 60, no. 2 (2000): 25–31.
Kuh, George D. *High Impact Educational Practices: What They Are, Who Has Access to Them, and Why They Matter.* Washington, DC: Association of American Colleges and Universities, 2008.
Kuh, George D., Jillian Kinzie, John H. Schuh, Elizabeth J. Whitt, and Associates. *Student Success in College: Creating Conditions that Matter* San Francisco: Jossey-Bass, 2005.
Kuh, George D., John H. Schuh, Elizabeth J. Whitt, R. Andreas, J. W. Lyons, C. C. Strange, L. E. Krehbiel, and K. A. MacKay. *Involving Colleges: Successful Approaches to Fostering Student Development Outside the Classroom.* San Francisco: Jossey-Bass, 1991.
Kuh, George D., and P. D. Umbach. "College and Character: Insights from the National Survey of Student Engagement." *New Directions for Institutional Research* 112(2004): 37–54.
Kuklinski, James H., and Norman L. Hurley. "On Hearing and Interpreting Political Messages: A Cautionary Tale of Citizen Cue-taking." *Journal of Politics* 56 (1994): 729–51.
Ladewig, Howard, and John K. Thomas. *Assessing the Impact of 4-H on Former Members.* College Station, TX: Texas Tech University, 1987.
Lambert, Ronald D., James Curtis, Barry Kay, and Steven Brown. "The Social Sources of Political Knowledge." *Canadian Journal of Political Science* 21 (1988): 359–74.
Langer, Gary. "Obama's No-Show: 29 Million." ABCNews.Com. November 3, 2010. http://blogs.abcnews.com/thenumbers/2010/11/obamas-no-shows-29-million.html
Langton, Kenneth P. "Peer Group and School and the Political Socialization Process." *The American Political Science Review* 61, no. 3 (1967): 751–58.
Langton, Kenneth P., and M. Kent Jennings. "Political Socialization and the High School Civics Curriculum in the United States." *American Political Science Review* 62, no. 3 (1968): 852– 67.
Lawless, Jennifer, and Richard Fox. *It Takes a Candidate: Why Women Don't Run for Office.* New York: Cambridge University Press, 2005.
Lawry, Steven, Daniel Laurison, and Jonathan VanAntwerpen. *Liberal Education and Civic Engagement: A Project of the Ford Foundation's Knowledge, Creativity, and Freedom Program.* 2006. http://www.fordfound.org/pdfs/impact/liberal_education_and_civic_engagement.pdf.
Learn and Serve America. "President's Higher Education Community Service Honor Roll Finalists for Excellence in General Community Service." March 26, 2007.
Lee, Jennifer. "Crucial Unpaid Internships Increasingly Separate the Haves from the Have Nots." *New York Times.* August 10, 2004.
Leming, Robert. "We the People...The Citizen and the Constitution." Calabasas, CA: The Center for Civic Education, 1996.
Lenhart, Amanda, Rich Ling, Scott Campbell, and Kristen Purcell. "Teens and Mobile Phones." Pew Internet and American Life Project, Pew Research Center. April 20, 2010.
Leonard, Stephen T. "Making the Past into Prologue: A Response to Professor Bennett." *PS: Political Science & Politics* 32, no. 4 (1999): 758–59.
———. "'Pure Futility and Waste:' Academic Political Science and Civic Education." *PS: Political Science & Politics* 32, no. 4 (1999): 749–54.
Levine, A., and J. S. Cureton. *When Hope and Fear Collide: A Portrait of Today's College Student.* San Francisco: Jossey-Bass, 1998.
Levine, Peter. *The Future of Democracy: Developing the Next Generation of American Citizens.* Boston: Tufts University Press, 2007.
Levine, P., and M. H. Lopez. "Youth Turnout Has Declined by Any Measure." College Park, MD: CIRCLE: The Center for Information and Research on Civic Learning and Engagement, University of Maryland. 2002. http://civicyouth.org/research/products/Measuring_Youth_Voter_Turnout.pdf
Libit, Daniel. "The Pros and Cons of Hissy Fits." *Politico*, October 1, 2009. Liberal Education and America's Promise (LEAP). N.p., 2012. Accessed on October 24, 2012. http://www.aacu.org/leap/
Lipka, Sara. "For Many Students, Electoral Enthusiasm Runs Up Against Barriers to Voting." *The Chronicle of Higher Education.* February 1, 2008. Accessed on December 27, 2008. http://chronicle.com/weekly/v54/i21/21a0210.htm
Lisman, C. David. *Toward A Civil Society: Civic Literacy and Service Learning.* Westport, CT: Bergin and Garvey, 1998.
Liu, G. "Origins, Evolution, and Progress: Reflections on the Community Service Movement in American Higher Education 1985–1995." In *Community Service in Higher Education.* Providence, RI: Providence College, 1996.
Lofland, John, and Lyn H. Lofland. *Analyzing Social Settings: A Guide to Qualitative Observation and Analysis.* Belmont, CA: Wadsworth Publishing, 1984.

London, Scott. *The Civic Mission of Higher Education: From Outreach to Engagement*. Washington, DC: Kettering Foundation, 2002.

Long, Sarah, John Salmarsh, and Kerrissa Heffernan. *The New Student Politics: The Wingspread Statement on Student Civic Engagement*. Campus Compact, 2002. http://www.cpn.org/topics/youth/highered/pdfs/New_Student_Politics.pdf

Longo, Nicholas. "Recognizing the Role of Community in Civic Education." (working paper, CIRCLE: The Center for Information and Research on Civic Learning and Engagement, College Park, MD, 2005.)

Longo, Nicholas, and Ross Meyer. "College Students and Politics: A Literature Review." (working paper 46, CIRCLE: The Center for Information and Research on Civic Learning and Engagement, College Park, MD, 2006.)

Lopez, Mark Hugo. 2004. "Volunteering Among Young People." College Park, MD: CIRCLE: The Center for Information and Research on Civic Learning and Engagement. 2004.

Lopez, Mark Hugo, and Benjamin Brown. "Civic Engagement Among 2-year and 4-year College Students." College Park, MD: CIRCLE: The Center for Information and Research on Civic Learning and Engagement. October 2006.

Lopez, Mark Hugo, Emily Kirby, Jared Sagoff, and Jason P. Kolaczkowski. "Electoral Engagement Among Non-College Attending Youth." CIRCLE Fact Sheet. July 2005. http://www.civicyouth.org/PopUps/FactSheets/FS_04_noncollege_vote.pdf

Lopez, Mark Hugo, Peter Levine, Deborah Both, Abby Kiesa, Emily Kirby, and Karlo Marcelo. *The 2006 Civic and Political Health of the Nation: A Detailed Look at How Youth Participate in Politics and Communities*. College Park, MD: CIRCLE: The Center for Information and Research on Civic Learning and Engagement. 2006. http://www.civicyouth.org/PopUps/2006_CPHS_Report_update.pdf

Lopez, Mark Hugo, and Karlo Barrios Marcelo. *Millennials Talk Politics: A Study of College Student Political Engagement*. College Park, MD: CIRCLE: The Center for Information and Research on Civic Learning and Engagement. http://www.civicyouth.org/PopUps/CSTP.pdf

Lorenzini, Michelle. "Beyond Civic Engagement to Informed Advocacy." In *Teaching Matters: Strategy and Tactics to Engage Students in the Study of American Politics*, edited by Dan Shea. New York: Longman, 2011.

Lowy, Alex and Phil Hood. *The Power of the 2x2 Matrix: Using the 2x2 Matrix to Solve Business Problems*. San Francisco, CA: Jossey-Bass, 2004.

Lupia, Arthur, and Matthew D. McCubbins. *The Democratic Dilemma: Can Citizens Learn What They Need to Know*. Cambridge: Cambridge University Press, 2008.

Macedo, Stephen. *Diversity and Distrust: Civic Education in a Multicultural Society*. Princeton, NJ: Princeton University Press, 2003.

Macedo, Stephen, Yvette Alex-Assensoh, Jeffrey M. Berry, Michael Brintnall, David E Campbell, Luis Ricardo Fraga, Archon Fung, William A. Galston, Christopher E. Karpowitz, Margaret Levi, Maria Levinson, Keena Lipstiz, Richard G. Niemi , Robert D. Putnam, Wendy M. Rahn, Rob Reich, Robert R. Rodgers, Todd Swanstrom, and Katherine Cramer Walsh. *Democracy at Risk: How Political Choices Undermine Citizen Participation and What We Can Do About It*. Washington, DC: Brookings Institution Press, 2005.

Magleby, David, Kelly D. Patterson, J. Quin Monson. "Evaluating the Quality of the Voting Experience: A Cross Panel Pilot Study of the November 7, 2006 Election in Franklin County, OH, Summit County, OH, and the State of Utah." *The Center for the Study of Elections and Democracy*. Provo, UT: Brigham Young University, 2006.

Mann, Christopher Baird. "Eliminating Registration Barriers: Large Scale Field Experiments on Lowering the Cost of Voter Registration." Paper presented at the APSA Annual Meeting, Chicago 2011.

Mann, Sheilah, and John J. Patrick. *Education for Civic Engagement in Democracy: Service Learning and Other Promising Practices*. Bloomington, IN: ERIC Clearinghouse for Social Studies/Social Science Education, 2000.

Marando, Gary. Interview and comments, May 2011.

Marcia, James E. "Identity and Self Development." In *Encyclopedia of Adolescence*, edited by Richard M Lerner, Anne C.Peterson, and Jeanne Brooks-Gunn. New York: Garland Publication, 1991.

———. "Identity in Adolescence." In *Handbook of Adolescent Psychology*, edited by Joseph Adelson. New York: Wiley Publications, 1980.

Markus, Gregory B., Jeffrey P. F. Howard, and David C. King. "Integrating Community Service and Classroom Instruction Enhances Learning: Results from an Experiment." *Educational Evaluation and Policy Analysis* 15 (1993): 416.

Marlin-Bennett, Renee. "Linking Experiential and Classroom Education: Lessons Learned from The American University – Amnesty International USA Summer Institute on Human Rights," *International Studies Perspectives* 3 (2002): 384–95.

Martinez, Michael D., and David Hill. "Did Motor Voter Work?" *American Politics Quarterly* 27 (1999): 296–315.

Marzano, Robert J. *Designing and Teaching Learning Goals and Strategies*. Bloomington, IN: Marzano Research Laboratory, 2009.

———. *A Different Kind of Classroom: Teaching with Dimensions of Learning*, Alexandria, VA: Association for Supervision and Curricular Development, 1992.

Massachusetts Department of Higher Education. "Mission of the Community Colleges." N.d. http://www.mass.edu/campuses/missioncc.asp

Matter of Mogharrabi, 19 I and N Dec. 489 (BIA 1987).

McCarthy, J. Patrick, and Liam Anderson. "Active Learning Techniques Versus Traditional Teaching Styles: Two Experiments from History and Political Science." *Innovative Higher Education* 24, no. 4 (2000): 279–94

McCarthy, Nancy. "$394 Million 'Justice Gap' Plagues Legal Services." *California Bar Journal* 7 (2007).

McCartney, Alison R. M. "Making the World Real: Using a Civic Engagement Course to Bring Home Our Global Connections." *Journal of Political Science Education* 2, no. 1 (2006): 113–28.

McDevitt, Michael, and Steven Chaffee. "Closing Gaps in Political Communication and Knowledge Effects of a School Intervention." *Communication Research* 27, no. 3 (2000): 259–92.

McDonald, Michael P. "Voter Turnout in the 2010 Midterm Election." *The Forum* 8 (2010).

———. "2010 General Election Turnout Rates." *United States Election Project*. Fairfax,VA: George Mason University, December 13, 2010. Accessed on January 27, 2011. http://elections.gmu.edu/Turnout_2010G.html.

McDonald, Michael P., and Samuel Popkin. "The Myth of the Vanishing Voter." *American Political Science Review* 95, no. 4 (2001): 963–74.

McHugh, Mary A., and Russell Mayer. "Do Lazy Students Learn Less From Service?" Paper presented at the APSA Teaching and Learning Conference, Washington, DC, February 2012.

McKeachie, Wilbert J., and Marilla Svinicki. *McKeachie's Teaching Tips: Strategies, Research, and Theory for College and University Teachers.* 12th ed. Independence, KY: Cengage Learning, 2006.

McMahon, M. "Greeks Adjust to Fall Rush Ban." *Yale Daily News*, September 10, 2012, http://www.yaledailynews.com/news/2012/sep/10/greeks-adjust-fall-rush-ban/

McMullan, Troy. "Prestigious Yale Fraternity Accused of Chants Offensive to Women." *ABC News*, October 19, 2010, http://abcnews.go.com/Health/US/yale-fraternity scrutiny-offensive-pledge-chants/story?id=11918602#.Twfn7dRVB9k

McQuaid, Kathleen. "The Use of Guided Simulations in the Introductory Level American Politics and State and Local Politics Courses." *PS: Political Science & Politics* 25 (1992): 532–4.

Meacham, Jack, and Jerry G. Gaff. "Learning Goals in Mission Statements: Implications for Educational Leadership." *Liberal Education* (Winter 2006). Accessed on December 27, 2008. http://www.aacu.org/liberaleducation/le-wi06/le-wi06_feature1.cfm.

Meinke, Tim. "Going Beyond One Class: Applying Civic Engagement Principles to an Entire Minor Program." Paper presented at the APSA Teaching and Learning Conference, Charlotte, NC, February 2007.

Meirick, Patrick C., and Daniel B. Wackman. "Kids Voting and Political Knowledge: Narrowing Gaps, Informing Votes." *Social Science Quarterly* 85, no. 5 (2004): 1161–77.

Meirose, Carl E., S. J., compiler. *Foundations*. Washington, DC: Jesuit Secondary Education Association, 1994.

Mello, Brian, and Angelique Davis. "Preaching to the Apathetic and Uninterested: Teaching Citizenship to Freshmen and Non-majors," Paper presented at the APSA Teaching and Learning Conference, Charlotte, NC, February 2007.

Mendel-Reyes, Meta. "Teaching=Theorizing=Practicing Democracy: An Activist's Perspective on Service-Learning in Political Science." *In Experiencing Citizenship: Concepts and Models for Service-Learning in the Classroom*, edited by Richard M. Battistoni and William E. Hudson. Washington, DC: American Association for Higher Education, 1997.

Meredith, Marc. "Persistence in Political Participation." *Quarterly Journal of Political Science* 4 (2009):186–208.

Metts, Ralph E., S. J. *Ignatius Knew*. Washington, D.C: Jesuit Secondary Education Association, 1995.

Michelson, Melissa R. "Meeting the Challenge of Latino Voter Mobilization." Edited by Donald P. Green and Alan S. Gerber. *The Annals of the American Academy of Political and Social Science* 601 (2005):123–41.

Miller, Ross. "Connecting Beliefs with Research on Effective Undergraduate Education." *Peer Review* 11, no. 2 (2009): 4–8.

Miller, Warren E., and J. Merrill Shanks. *The New American Voter*. Cambridge, MA: Harvard University Press, 1996.

Miller, Wesley. "Internships, the Liberal Arts, and Participant Observation," *Teaching Sociology* 18 (1990): 78–82.

Milstein, Mike M., and Jo Ann Krueger. "Improving Educational Administration Preparation Programs: What We Have Learned over the Past Decade." *Peabody Journal of Education* 72, no. 2 (1997): 100–116.

Mindich, D. *Tuned Out: Why Americans Under 40 Don't Follow the News*. New York: Oxford University Press, 2005.

Moely, B. E., M. McFarland, D. Miron, S. Mercer, V. Ilustre. "Changes in College Students' Attitudes and Intentions for Civic Involvement as a Function of Service Learning Experiences." *Michigan Journal of Community Service Learning* (2002): 18–26.

Moon, Jeremy, and Wykham Schokman. "Political Science Research Internships and Political Science Education." *Politics* 20, no. 3 (2000): 169–75

Morrell, Michael E. "Deliberation, Democratic Decision-Making and Internal Political Efficacy." *Political Behavior* 27, no. 1 (2005): 49–69.

Morton, Keith. "Issues Related to Integrating Service-Learning into the Curriculum." In *Service Learning in Higher Education: Concepts and Practices*, edited by Barbara Jacoby and Associates. San Francisco, CA: Jossey-Bass, 1996.

Moscoso, Eunice. "College Students Facing Barriers to Voting." *Marshall News Messenger*, 2008. Accessed on December 11, 2008. http://www.marshallnewsmessenger.com/hp/content/shared/news/stories/2008/10/VOT NG_COLLEGES05_1STLD_COX.html.

Murphy, James Bernard. "Against Civic Schooling." *Social Philosophy and Policy* 21, no. 1 (2004): 221–65.

Musil, Caryn McTighe. *Assessing Global Learning: Matching Good Intentions with Good Practice*. Washington, DC: Association of American Colleges and Universities, 2006.

———. Educating for Citizenship. *Peer Review: Emerging Trends and Key Debates in Undergraduate Education* 5 (2003): 4–8.

Mutz, Diana C. "Cross-Cutting Social Networks: Testing Democratic Theory in Practice." *American Political Science Review* 96, no. 2 (2002): 111–26.

———. *Hearing the Other Side: Deliberative Versus Participatory Democracy*. New York: Cambridge University Press, 2006.

Myers-Lipton, S. J. "The Effects of Service-Learning on College Students' Attitudes Toward Civic Responsibility, International Understanding, and Racial Prejudice." PhD diss., University of Colorado: Boulder, 1994.

National Association of Secretaries of State. *The New Millennium Project: American Youth Attitudes on Politics, Citizenship, Government, and Voting*. Washington, DC: National Association of Secretaries of State, 1999. http://nass.org/index.php?option=com_content&task=view&id=132&Itemid=298

National Association of Social Workers. "Code of Ethics." National Association of Social Workers, Section 6.04, 1996. http://www.socialworkers.org/pubs/code/code.asp.

National Center for Education Statistics (NCES). "Condition of Education: 2008." Accessed on January 11, 2009. http://nces.ed.gov/programs/coe/2008/tables.

———. "Condition of Education: 2010." Accessed on June 11, 2011. http://nces.ed.gov.programs/coe/tables/table-hep-2.asp.

———. "Fast Facts." Accessed on January 15, 2012. http://nces.ed.gov/fastfacts/display.asp?id=98.

———. "Trends in Nontraditional Student Enrollment." U.S. Department of Education, National Center for Education Statistics: September 23, 2004. www.nces.ed.gov/pubs/web/97578f.asp.

National Pan-Hellenic Conference. *National Pan-Hellenic Conference annual report, Advancing Sorority Together*. 2011. https://www.npcwomen.org/resources/pdf/Annual%20Report%202011.pdf.

National Society for Experiential Education. *Combining Service and Learning: A Resource Book for Community and Public Service*. Raleigh, NC: NSEE, 1990.

National Task Force on Civic Learning and Democratic Engagement. *A Crucible Moment: College Learning and Democracy's Future*. Washington, DC Association of American Colleges and Universities, 2012. Accessed on February 1, 2012. http://www.aacu.org/civic_learning/crucible/documents/crucible_508F.pdf.

Niemi, Richard G. "Trends in Political Science as They Relate to Pre-college Curriculum and Teaching." *Sea Change in Social Science Education*, edited by Charles White. Boulder, CO: Social Science Education Consortium, 2001.

Niemi, Richard G., and Michael Hanmer. *College Students in the 2004 Election*. College Park, MD: CIRCLE, 2004.

Niemi, Richard G., and Jane Junn. "Civic Education: What Makes Students Learn." New Haven, CT: Yale University Press, 1998.

Nelson, Candice. In *Financing the 2000 Election*, edited by David Magleby. Brookings Institution Press, 2002.

Nesteruk, Jeffrey. "Contributing to Our Student's Moral Lives." *Change* (2007): 52–53.

New York Times. "Fraternities Go Underground to Defy College Ban." August 29, 1994. http://www.nytimes.com/1994/08/29/us/fraternities-go-underground-to-defy-college-ban.html

Newell, William H. "Powerful Pedagogies" in *Reinventing Ourselves: Interdisciplinary Education, Collaborative Learning, and Experimentation in Higher Education*, edited by Barbara Leigh Smith and John McCann, 196–211. Boston, MA: Anker Publishing Company, 2001.

Newman, Frank. *Higher Education and the American Resurgence*. Foundation for the Advancement of Teaching. Princeton, NJ: Carnegie, 1985.

Nickerson, David W. "Does Email Boost Turnout?" *Quarterly Journal of Political Science* 2 (2007): 369–79.

———. "Is Voting Contagious? Evidence from Two Field Experiments." *American Political Science Review* 102 (2008): 49–57.

———. "Volunteer Phone Calls Can Increase Turnout: Evidence from Eight Field Experiments." *American Politics Research* 34 (2006): 271–92.

Nie, Norman H., Jane Junn, and Kenneth Stehlik-Barry. *Education and Democratic Citizenship*. Chicago, IL: University of Chicago Press, 1996.

Niven, David. "A Field Experiment on the Effects of Negative Campaign Mail on Voter Turnout in a Municipal Election." *Political Research Quarterly* 59, no. 2 (2006): 203–10.

Noonan, Peggy. "The Heat is On: We May Get Burned." *Wall Street Journal*, March 25, 2010.

North American Inter-fraternity Council. *About NIC.* 2012. http://www.nicindy.org/about/

Nussbaum, Martha. *Cultivating Humanity: A Classical Defense of Reform in Liberal Education.* Cambridge, MA: Harvard University Press, 1997.

———. *Not for Profit: Why Democracy Needs the Humanities.* Princeton, NJ: Princeton University Press, 2010.

Obama, Barack. "Remarks by the President in the State of the Union Address." Washington, DC January 24, 2012. Accessed on January 25, 2012. http://www.whitehouse.gov/the-press-office/2012/01/24/remarks-president-state-union-address

———. "Remarks by the President on College Affordability." University of Michigan: Ann Arbor, Michigan. January 27, 2012. Accessed on 28 January 2012 at http://www.whitehouse.gov/the-press-office/2012/01/27/remarks-president-college-affordability-ann-arbor-michigan.

Office of General Counsel of the Catholic University of America. "Summary of Federal Laws: Voter Registration Provisions in the Higher Education Amendments of 1998." August 22, 2012. http://counsel.cua.edu/FEDLAW/voter.cfm

O'Loughlin, Michael, and Correy Unangst. *Democracy and College Student Voting.* Third Edition. Salisbury, MD: The Institute for Public Affairs and Civic Engagement at Salisbury University, 2006: 13–14.

Olsen, Marvin E. *Participatory Pluralism: Political Participation and Influence in the United States and Sweden.* Chicago, IL: Burnham, 1982.

Omelicheva, Mariya Y. "Self and Peer Evaluation in Undergraduate Education: Structuring Conditions that Maximize its Promises and Minimize the Perils." *Journal of Political Science Education* 1, no. 2 (2005): 191–205.

OneWorld Magazine. Inaugural Issue 1, no. 1 (2006): 2.

Oros, Andrew. "Let's Debate: Active Learning Encourages Student Participation and Critical Thinking." *Journal of Political Science Education* 3, no. 3 (2007): 293–311.

Orr, David. "Cook County Clerk Election Judge Manual, Suburban Cook County." N.p., n.d. http://www.cookcountyclerk.com/elections/DocumentLibrary/2011%20Judge%20Manual_Final.pdf

O'Shaughnessy, Elizabeth. "Getting High School Students Involved as Illinois Election Judges at Loyola Academy: A Case Study on Civic Engagement." Paper presented at the Midwest Political Science Conference, April 2009.

Ostrom, Elinor. "Civic Education for the Next Century: A Task Force to Initiate Professional Action." *PS: Political Science & Politics* 29, no. 4 (1998): 756.

Owen, Diana. "Election Media and Youth Political Engagement." *Journal of Social Science Education* 78, no. 2 (2008): 14–25.

———. "Media in the 2008 Election: 21st Century Campaign, Same Old Story." In *The Year of Obama*, edited by Larry J. Sabato, 187–204. New York: Longman, 2009.

———. "Service Learning and Political Socialization." *PS: Political Science & Politics* 33, no. 3 (2000): 638–40.

Owen, Diana, and Suzanne Soule. "Civic Education and the Development of Participatory Norms." Paper presented at the APSA Annual Meeting, Washington, DC, September 2010.

Owen, Diana, Suzanne Soule, Jennifer Nairne, Rebecca Chalif, Michael Davidson, and Katherine House. "Civic Education and Social Media Use." *Electronic Media and Politics* 1, no. 1 (2011): 1–23.

Owen-Smith, P. "What is Cognitive-Affective Learning?" *Journal of Cognitive Affective Learning* 1, no. 1 (2004): 11. Retrieved February 8, 2008. https://www.jcal.emory.edu//viewarticle.ph?id=31&layout=html

Palmer, Parker J. *To Know as We are Known: Education as a Spiritual Journey.* New York: Harper Collins, 1993.

Pappas, Christine, and Charles Peaden. "Running for Your Grade: A Six-Week Senatorial Campaign Simulation." *PS: Political Science & Politics* 37, no. 4 (2004): 859–63.

Parilla, Peter F., and Garry W. Hesser. "Internships and the Sociological Perspective: Applying Principles of Experiential Learning." *Teaching Sociology* 26 (1998): 310–29.

Parilla, Peter F., and Susan L. Smith-Cullien. "Criminal Justice Internships: Integrating the Academic with the Experiential." *Journal of Criminal Justice Education* 8, no. 2 (1997): 225–41.

Parker-Gwin, R., and J. B. Mabry. "Service Learning as Pedagogy and Civic Education: Comparing Outcomes for Three Models." *Teaching Sociology* 26, no. 4 (1998) 276–91.

Pascarella, E., and P. Terenzini. *How College Affects Students: A Third Decade of Research.* Volume 2. San Francisco: Jossey-Bass, 2005.

Patterson, Amy S. "It's a Small World: Incorporating Service Learning into International Relations Courses." *PS: Political Science & Politics* 33 (2000).

Patterson, Thomas. *The Vanishing Voter: Public Involvement in the Age of Uncertainty.* Cambridge, MA: Alfred A. Knopf Publishers, 2002.

Pedelty, Mark. "Jenny's Painting: Multiple Forms of Communication in the Classroom." In *Reinventing Ourselves: Interdisciplinary Education, Collaborative Learning, and Experimentation in Higher Education*, edited by Barbara Leigh Smith and John McCann, 230–52. Boston, MA: Anker Publishing Company, 2001.

Pelissero, John P, ed. *Cities, Politics and Policy: A Comparative Analysis.* Washington, DC: CQ Press, 2003.

Perry, Anthony D., and Britt S. Wilkenfeld. "Using an Agenda Setting Model to Help Students Develop and Exercise Participatory Skills and Values." *Journal of Political Science Education* 2, no. 3 (2006): 303–12.

Perry, James L., and Michael C. Katula. "Does Service Affect Citizenship?" *Administration and Society* 33 (2001): 330–65.

PEW Research Center., *The Generation Gap and the 2012 Election: Angry Silents, Disengaged Millennials.* Washington DC: PEW Research Center, 2011. http://www.people-press.org/files/legacy-pdf/11-3-11%20 Generations%20Release.pdf

———. "Trends in Political Values and Core Attitudes: 1987–2009." Pew Research Center for the People and the Press, May 21, 2009. http://people-press.org/reports/pdf/517.pdf.

Physicians for Human Rights and the Bellevue/NYU Program for Survivors of Torture. *From Persecution to Prison: The Health Consequences of Detention for Asylum Seekers.* 2003. http://www.survivorsoftorture.org/files/pdf/perstoprison2003.pdf

Piaget, Jean. *The Equilibrium of Cognitive Structures: The Central Problem of Intellectual Development.* Chicago: University of Chicago Press (1975) 1985.

Plato and Aristophanes. *Four Texts on Socrates.* Translated by Thomas G. West and Grace Starry West. Ithaca, NY: Cornell Press (1984) 1998.

Plutzer, E. "Becoming a Habitual Voter: Inertia, Resources, and Growth in Young Adulthood." *American Political Science Review* 96, no. 1 (2002): 41–56.

Pollock, Philip H., Kerstin Hamann, and Bruce M. Wilson. "Teaching and Learning Online: Assessing the Effect of Gender Context on Active Learning." *Journal of Political Science Education* 1, no. 1 (2005): 1–16.

Pollock, Philip H., and Bruce W. Wilson. "Evaluating the Impact of Internet Teaching: Preliminary Evidence from American National Government Classes." *PS: Political Science & Politics* 35, no. 3 (2002): 561–566.

Popkin S. L., and M. A. Dimock. "Political Knowledge and Citizen Competence." In *Citizen Competence and Democratic Institutions*, edited by S.L Elkin and K.E. Soltan. University Park, PA: The Pennsylvania State University Press, 1999.

Potter, Lee Ann. "Documents and Civic Duties," *Social Education* 67, no. 7 (2004): 385–91.

Prentice, M. "Service Learning and Civic Engagement." *Academic Questions* 20 (2007): 135–45.

Project Vote. Accessed on February 19, 2011. http://www.projectvote.org/youth-voting-.html.

Pryor, John, L. DeAngelo, L. P. Blake, S. Hurtado, and S. Tran. *The American Freshman: National Norms for Fall 2011.* Los Angeles: Higher Education Research Institute, 2011. http://heri.ucla.edu/ PDFs/pubs/TFS/Norms/Monographs/TheAmericanFreshman2011.pdf

Pryor, John, Sylvia Hurtado, Victor Saenz, Jose Louis Santos, and William Korn. *The American Freshman: Forty Year Trends.* Los Angeles: Higher Education Research Institute, UCLA, 2007. http://www.gseis.ucla.edu/heri/PDFs/06CIRPFS_Norms_Narrative.pdf

Putnam, Robert. *Bowling Alone: The Collapse and Revival of American Community.* New York: Simon and Schuster, 2002.

———, ed. *Democracies in Flux: The Evolution of Social Capital in Contemporary Society.* Oxford: Oxford University Press, 2002.

———. *Making Democracy Work.* Princeton: Princeton University Press, 1993.

Putnam, Robert, Lewis M. Feldstein, and Don Cohen. *Better Together: Restoring the American Community.* New York: Simon and Schuster, 2003.

Ramirez, Ricardo. "Giving Voice to Latino Voters: A Field Experiment on the Effectiveness of a National Nonpartisan Mobilization Effort." *The Science of Voter Mobilization* (2005).

Ramji-Nogales, Jaya, Andrew I. Schoenholtz, and Philip G. Schrag, "Refugee Roulette: Disparities in Asylum Adjudication." *Stanford Law Review* 60, no. 295 (2007).

Ray, William J. *Methods Toward a Science of Behavior and Experience.* Belmont, CA: Wadsworth, 2009.

Redlawsk, David P., and Nora Wilson. "Local Political Involvement and Service Learning." Paper presented at the APSA Teaching and Learning Conference, Washington, DC, February 2006.

Reeher, Grant, and Mack Mariani. *The Insider' Guide to Political Internships.* Boulder, CO: Westview, 2002.

Riker, William H. *Liberalism Against Populism.* Prospect Heights, IL: Waveland, 1982.

Rimmerman, Craig. "Service-Learning and Public Policy." In *Service-Learning in the Liberal Arts: How and Why It Works*, edited by Craig A. Rimmerman, 71–83. Lanham, MD: Lexington Publishers, 2011.

———. "Service-Learning Lessons." In *Service-Learning in the Liberal Arts: How and Why It Works*, edited by Craig A. Rimmerman, 187–190. Lanham, MD: Lexington Publishers, 2011.

Robinson, Tony. "Service Learning as Justice Advocacy: Can Political Scientists do Politics?" *PS: Political Science & Politics* 33, no. 3 (2000): 605–12.

Rock the Vote. 2008. "Who Are Young Voters?" *Rock the Vote Website.* http://www.rockthevote.org/about/about-young-voters/who-are-young-voters/.

Rosenstone, Steven J., and Raymond E. Wolfinger. "The Effect of Registration Laws on Voter Turnout." *American Political Science Review* 72, no. 1 (1978): 22–45.

Ross, Marc Howard. "The Relevance of Culture for the Study of Political Psychology." In *Political Psychology: Cultural and Cross-cultural Foundations*, edited by Stanley A. Renshon and John Duckitt. New York: New York University Press, 2000.

Ruszczyk, Lauren (Coordinator, Education Abroad, University of Maryland) in discussion with Michael K. McDonald, February 4, 2011.

Saltmarsh, John, Matt Hartley, and Patti Clayton. *Democratic Engagement White Paper.* Boston, MA: New England Resources Center for Higher Education, 2009.

Saltmarsh, John, and Edward Zlotkowski, eds. "Conclusion: Looking Back, Looking Ahead, A Dialogue." *Higher Education and Democracy: Essay on Service-Learning and Civic Engagement*. Philadelphia, PA: Temple University Press, 2011. 354–65.

Sandel, Michael J. *Justice: What's the Right Thing To Do?* New York: Farrar, Strauss, and Giroux, 2009.

Sanders, A. *Losing Control: Presidential Elections and the Decline of Democracy*. New York: Peter Lang, 2007.

Sax, Linda. "Citizenship Development and the American College Spirit." In *Civic Responsibility and Higher Education*, edited by Thomas Ehrlich. Westport, CT: Greenwood Press, 2000.

Sax, Linda, Alexander Astin, Jennifer Lindholm, William Korn, Victor Saenz, and Kit Mahoney. *The American Freshman: National Norms for Fall 2003*. Los Angeles: Higher Education Research Institute, UCLA, 2003.

———. *The American Freshman: National Norms for Fall 2006*. Los Angeles: Higher Education Research Institute, UCLA, 2006. http://heri.ucla.edu/PDFs/pubs/TFS/Norms/Monographs/TheAmericanFreshman2001.pdf

Schachter, Hindy Lauer. "Civic Education: Three Early American Political Science Association Committees and Their Relevance for Our Times." *PS: Political Science & Politics* 31, no. 3 (1998): 631–5.

Schlesinger, A. M. "Biography of a Nation of Joiners." *The American Historical Review* 50, no. 1 (1944): 1–25.

Schneider, C. G. "Educational Missions and Civic Responsibility: Toward the Engaged Academy." In *Civic Responsibility and Higher Education*, edited by Thomas Ehrlich, 98–122. Phoenix, AZ: The American Council on Education and Oryx Press, 2004.

Schoenfeld, Robert Max. *Service-Learning Guide and Journal: Higher Education Edition*. Seattle, WA: Service Learning Higher Ed, 2004.

Schoeniger, Eric. "Change Agents: The Transformative Effects of Community-Based Learning." *Franklin and Marshall Magazine* (2012).

Schreyer Institute. "Assessment of Student Learning." *Online Newsletter, Penn State University*. 2012. http://www.assess.psu.edu/faq.

Schwab, Nikki. "Confusing Voter Registration Laws Could Affect Presidential Election." *US News and World Report*. September 24, 2008. Accessed December 11, 2008. http://www.usnes.com/articles/news/campaign-2008/2008/09/24/confusing-voterregistration-laws-could-affect-presidential-election.html.

Scorza, Jason. "Social Entrepreneurship and Undergraduate Learning: Challenges and Opportunities for Political Science." Prepared for the APSA Annual Meeting, Chicago, IL, 2007.

Sellnow, Timothy L., and Laura K. Oster. "The Frequency, Form, and Perceived Benefits of Service Learning in Speech Communication Departments." *Journal of the Association for Communication Administrations* 3 (1997): 190–7.

Settles, Isis H. "When Multiple Identities Interfere: The Role of Identity Centrality." *Personality and Social Psychology Bulletin* 30, no. 4 (2004): 487–500.

Shea, Daniel M. "Introduction: Democracy's Midwife." In *Teaching Matters: Engaging Students in the Study of American Government*, edited by Daniel M. Shea, 1–16. Upper Saddle River, NJ: Pearson, 2010b.

———. "Nastiness, Name-Calling and Negativity: The Allegheny College Survey of Civility and Compromise in American Politics." Center for Political Participation (2010a). http://sites.allegheny.edu/civility/.

Shea, Daniel M., and J. C. Green, eds. *Fountain of Youth, Strategies and Tactics for Mobilizing America's Young Voters*. Lanham, MD: Rowman and Littlefield, 2007.

Shea, Daniel M., J. C. Green, and C. E. Smith. *Living Democracy*. Englewood, NJ: Prentice Hall, 2007.

Shea, Daniel M., J. C. Strachan, and M. R. Wolf. "Local Party Viability, Goals and Objectives in the Information Age." In *The Parties Respond: Changes in American Parties and Campaigns*, 5th Edition, edited by M. Brewer and L.S. Maisel. Boulder, CO: Westview Press, 2012.

Sherrod, L. R., J. Torney-Purta, and C. Flanagan. *Handbook of Research on Civic Engagement in Youth*. Hoboken, NJ: John Wiley and Sons, 2010.

Shipler, David. *The Working Poor: Invisible in America*. New York: Knopf, 2004.

Shumer, R., and B. Belbas. "What We Know About Service Learning." *Education and Urban Society* 28 (1996): 208–23.

Sidanius, J., S. Levin, C. Van Laar, and D.O. Sears. *The Diversity Challenge: Social Identity and Intergroup Relations on the College Campus*. New York: Russell Sage, 2008.

Simpson, Dick. *Chicago's Future in a Time of Change*. Champaign, IL: Stipes, (1976) 1993.

———. "Teaching Political Engagement." Paper presented at the APSA Teaching and Learning Conference, Philadelphia, PA. February 2010.

———. *Who Rules? Introduction to the Study of Politics*. Chicago: Swallow Press, 1970.

———. *Winning Elections: A Handbook in Participatory Politics*. New York: Pearson Longman, 1996.

Simpson, Dick and Constance A. Mixon. *Twenty-First Century Chicago*. San Diego: Cognella, 2012.

Simpson, Dick, James Nowlan, and Elizabeth O'Shaunessey. *Struggle for Power in Cities and States*. New York: Pearson Longman, 2010.

Simpson E. J. *The Classification of Educational Objectives in the Psychomotor Domain*. Washington, DC: Gryphon House, 1972.

Skocpol, Theda. *Diminished Democracy: From Membership to Management in American Civic Life*. Norman, OK: University of Oklahoma Press, 2003.

———. "Foreward." In *Assessment in Political Science*, edited by Michelle D. Deardorff, Kerstin Hamman, and John Ishiyama. Washington, DC: American Political Science Association, 2009.

Skocpol, Theda, and M. P. Fiorina, eds. *Civic Engagement in American Democracy*. New York: Sage, 1998.

Skorton, D.J. "A Pledge to End Fraternity Hazing." *New York Times*. August 23, 2011. http://www.nytimes.com/2011/08/24/opinion/a-pledge-to-end-fraternity-hazing.html

Sloam, James. "Introduction: Youth, Citizenship, and Political Science Education: Questions for the Discipline." *Journal of Political Science Education* 6, no. 1 (2010): 325–335.

Smith, Ben. "Dem Campaigns Embrace New Software" *Politico*. June 21, 2011. http://www.politico.com/news/stories/0611/57443.html

Smith, Charles. "X-Generation or X-Institutions: Experience, Performance, Motivation and the Potential for Effective Civic Education in Schools." Unpublished doctoral thesis. Detroit: Wayne State University, 2011.

Smith, Denise Dwight. "Experiential Learning, Service-Learning, and Career Development," in *Facilitating the Career Development of Students in Transition*. Edited by Paul A. Gore. Columbia, SC: University of South Carolina, National Resource Center for the First Year Experience and Students in Transition, 2011. 205–22.

Smith, Elizabeth S. "Using the Experimental Method to Assess the Efficacy of a Service Learning Approach to American Government." Paper presented at the APSA Teaching and Learning Conference, Washington, DC, February 2005.

Smith, Elizabeth T., and Mark A. Boyer. "Designing In-class Simulations." *PS: Political Science & Politics* 29, no. 4 (1996): 690–4.

Smith, Heather. "Young Voters Ignored in 2009 Election." Rock the Vote Press Release, November 4, 2009. http://www.rockthevote.com/young-voters-ignored-in-2009.html

Smith, Michael B., Rebecca S. Nowacek, and Jeffrey L. Bernstein, eds. *Citizenship Across the Curriculum: Scholarship of Teaching and Learning*. Indianapolis, IN: Indiana University Press, 2010.

Snyder, S. "Reversing an old ban on sororities at Swarthmore." *Philadelphia Inquirer*. March 25, 2012. http://0www.lexisnexis.com.catalog.lib.cmich.edu/hottopics/lnacademic/?verb=sf&sfi=AC01NBSimplSrch

Soule, Suzanne, and Jennifer Nairne. "Youth Turnout in the 2008 Presidential Election: Delving Deeper with Data from the We the People Alumni Network." Presented at the Annual Meeting of the Midwest Political Science Association, Chicago, IL, April 2009.

Spiezio, K. Edward. "Pedagogy and Political (Dis)engagement." *Liberal Education* 88, no. 4 (2002): 14–21.

Squire, Peverill, Raymond E. Wolfinger, and David P. Glass. "Residential Mobility and Voter Turnout." *American Political Science Review* 81, no. 1 (1987):45–65.

Steffes, Jeanne. "Creating Powerful Learning Environments Beyond the Classroom." *Change: The Magazine of Higher Learning* 36, no. 3 (2004): 48.

Stevens Learning Center at Merrimack College. "About." Stevens Learning Center, Merrimack College. http://www.merrimack.edu/academics/EngagedLearning/ServiceLearning/Stevens/Pages/default.aspx

Stewart, Joseph, David M. Hedge, and James P. Lester. *Public Policy: An Evolutionary Approach*, 3rd edition. Boston: Thomson Higher Education, 2008.

Stoker, Laura, and Kent Jennings. "Social Trust and Civic Engagement across Time and Generations." *Annual Review of Political Science* 7 (2004): 1–23.

Strachan, J. C., and C. T. Owens. "Learning Civic Norms Outside of the Classroom: Diversity and Campus Associational Life." *Journal of Political Science Education* 7, no. 4 (2011): 464–82.

Strand, Kerry, Sam Marullo, Nick Cutforth, Randy Stoecker, and Patrick Donohue. *Community-based Research and Higher Education: Practices and Principles*. San Francisco: Jossey-Bass, 2003.

Strange, Amy A. "Service-Learning: Enhancing Student Learning Outcomes in a College-Level Lecture Course." *Michigan Journal of Community Service Learning* (Fall 2000): 5–13.

Student PIRGs. "About." N.d. http://www.studentpirgs.org/.

Survey of Civility and Compromise in American Politics." Center for Political Participation http://sites.allegheny.edu/civility/

Suskie, Linda. *Assessing Student Learning: A Common Sense Guide*. Second Edition. San Francisco: Jossey-Bass, 2009.

Sustein, Cass. "Boycott the Daily Me!" *Time*. June 4, 2001.

Swaner, L. "Linking Engaged Learning, Student Mental Health and Well-Being, and Civic Development: A Review of the Literature." *Liberal Education* 3, no. 1 (2007): 16–25.

Sylvester, D. E. "Fostering Student Leadership in Tackling Community-Based Problems (Brief Report)." *Journal of Cognitive Affective Learning* (2008).

———. "Service-Learning as a Vehicle for Promoting Student Political Efficacy." Special Issue on "Service-Learning for Political Participation." *Journal for Civic Commitment* 14 (2010).

Symm v. U.S., 439 U.S. 1105 (1979).

Syrett, N. *The Company He Keeps: A History of White College Fraternities.* Chapel Hill: The University of North Carolina Press, 2009.

———. "Schools are Culpable." *New York Times*. May 6, 2011. http://www.nytimes.com/roomfordebate/2011/05/05/frat-guys-gone-wild-whats-the-solution/colleges-condone-fraternities-sexist-behavior

Tanaka, G. *The Intercultural Campus: Transcending Culture and Power in American Higher Education.* New York: Peter Lang, 2005.

"Task Force to Set Agenda for Civic Education Program." *PS: Political Science & Politics* 30, no. 4 (1997): 744.

Tedin, Kent L. "The Influence of Parents on the Political Attitudes of Adolescents." *American Political Science Review* 68 (1974): 1579–92.

Teixeira, Ruy. *The Disappearing American Voter.* Washington, DC: The Brookings Institute, 1992.

Thee-Brenan, Megan. "Obama's Youthful Voters More Likely to Skip Midterms." *The New York Times*, August 10, 2010. http://www.nytimes.com/2010/08/11/us/politics/11poll.html (accessed September 23, 2010).

Tillman, Martin. *Impact of Education Abroad on Career Development*, Volume I. Stanford, CA: American Institute for Foreign Study. http://www.goaifs.com/advisors/pdf/Impact_of_Education_AbroadI.pdf.

Timpone, Richard J. "Structure, Behavior, and Voter Turnout in the United States." *American Political Science Review* 92, no. 1 (1998): 145–58.

Tisch, Jonathan. "Turnout by Education, Race and Gender and Other 2008 Youth Voting Statistics." College Park, MD: CIRCLE, 2008. http://www.civicyouth.org/PopUps/FactSheets/FS_08_exit_polls.pdf

Tobin, Gary, and Aryeh K. Weinberg. *A Profile of American College Faculty: Political Beliefs and Behavior.* San Francisco, CA: Institute for Jewish and Community Research, 2006.

Tocqueville, Alexis de. *Democracy in America.* Translated by Henry Reeve. Revised by Frances Bowen and Phillips Bradley. New York: Vintage Classics, (1835) 1990.

Tolo, Kenneth W. "An Assessment of We the People...Project Citizen: Promoting Citizenship in Classrooms and Communities." Austin, TX: Lyndon B. Johnson School of Public Affairs at the University of Texas, 1998.

———. *The Civic Education of American Youth: From State Policies to School District Practices.* Austin, TX: Lyndon B. Johnson School of Public Affairs, University of Texas, 1999.

Torney-Purta, Judith. "Review Essay: Links and Missing Links between Education, Political Knowledge, and Citizenship." *American Journal of Education* 105, no. 4 (1997): 446–57.

———. "The School's Role in Developing Civic Engagement: A Study of Adolescents in Twenty-Eight Countries." *Applied Developmental Science* 6, no. 4 (2012): 203.

Trivedi, Neema. "The Effect of Identity-Based GOTV Direct Mail Appeals on the Turnout of Indian Americans." The Science of Voter Mobilization. Special Editors Donald P. Green and Alan S. Gerber. *The Annals of the American Academy of Political and Social Science* 601 (2005):115–22.

Troppe, Marie. *Connecting Cognition and Action: Evaluation of Student Performance in Service Learning Courses.* Providence, RI: Campus Compact, 1995.

Tufts University Tisch College of Citizenship and Public Service. "National Survey for Youth Civic Engagement." Accessed on March 1, 2012. http://activecitizen.tufts.edu/research-307/research

Ulbig, Stacy G., and Carolyn L. Funk. "Conflict Avoidance and Political Participation." *Political Behavior* 21, no. 3 (1999): 265.

United States Census. "US Voter Turnout Up in 2004, Census Bureau Reports." May 26, 2005.

United States Election Assistance Commission. "Compendium of State Poll Worker Requirements." August 2007. http://www.eac.gov/assets/1/Page/A%20Compendium%20of%20State%20Poll%20Worker%20Requirements.pdf

———. "Help America Vote College Program Recipients." Help America Vote College Program Recipients. N.p., n.d. http://www.eac.gov/payments_and_grants/help_america_vote_college_program_recipients.aspx#college_recipients_2010

United States Senate Committee on Health, Education, Labor and Pensions. "Higher Education Accreditation: How Can the System Better Ensure Quality and Accountability?" 108th Congress, second session, February 26, 2004. Accessed on January 10, 2012. http://frwebgate.access.gpo.gov/cgi-bin/getdoc.cgi?dbname=108_senate_hearings&docid=92-438

University of Illinois at Chicago Department of Political Science. "Chicago Political Encyclopedia of Film." 2009. http://www.uic.edu/depts/pols/ChicagoPolitics/cpef.htm

Upcraft, M. Lee, and John H. Schuh. "Assessment vs. Research: Why We Should Care About the Difference." *About Campus* 7 (March–April 2002): 16–20.

US Students. "About." N.d. http://www.usstudents.org/.

Vargas, Jose Antonio. "Obama Raised Half a Billion Online." *Washington Post Online*, November 20, 2008.

Verba, Sidney, and Norman H. Nie. *Participation in America: Political Democracy and Social Equality*. New York: Harper and Row, 1972.

Verba, Sidney, Norman H. Nie, and Jae-On Kim. *Participation and Political Equality*. New York: Cambridge University Press, 1978.

Verba, Sidney, Kay Lehman Schlozman, and Henry E. Brady. *Voice and Equality: Civic Volunteerism in American Politics*. Cambridge, MA: Harvard University Press, 1995.

Waggener, Tamara Ann. "Citizenship and Service Learning." *Academic Exchange Quarterly* 10 (2006): 207–10.

Wahlke, John C. "Liberal Learning and the Political Science Major: A Report to the Profession." *PS: Political Science & Politics* 24, no. 1 (1991): 48–60.

Walker, Tobi. "The Service/Politics Split: Rethinking Service to Teach Political Engagement." *PS: Political Science & Politics* 33 (2000): 646–49.

Ward, Deborah E. "Internationalizing the American Politics Curriculum." *PS: Political Science & Politics* 40, no. 1 (2007): 110–2.

Wattenberg, Martin P. *Is Voting For Young People*. Second Edition. New York: Pearson/Longman, 2007.

Weigert, Kathleen M. "Academic Service Learning: Its Meaning and Relevance." *New Directions for Teaching and Learning* 73 (1998): 3–10.

Wenz, Peter. *Political Philosophy in Moral Conflict*. Boston, MA: McGraw-Hill, 2007.

Wessel, Nancy. "Integrating Service Learning Into the Study Abroad Program: US Sociology Students in Mexico." *Journal of Studies in International Education* 11, no. 1 (2007): 73–89.

West, Ellis. "Some Proposed Guidelines for Advocacy in the Classroom." *PS: Political Science & Politics* 31, no. 4 (1998).

Westheimer, Joe, and Joseph Kahne. "Educating the 'Good' Citizen: Political Choices and Pedagogical Goals." *PS: Political Science & Politics* 37, no. 2 (2004): 241–47.

Willis, Clint, and Suzanne Barlyn. "Bringing the Law to Life: NYU's Clinical Program Helps Students Change the World – One Case at a Time." *The Law School: The Magazine of the New York University School of Law* (2007): 21–31.

Wilson, Bruce M., Philip H. Pollock, and Kerstin Hamann. "Does Active-Learning Enhance Learner Outcomes? Evidence from Discussion Participation in Online Classes." *Journal of Political Science Education* 3, no. 2 (2007): 131–42.

Wolfinger, Raymond E., and Jonathan Hoffman. "Registering and Voting with Motor Voter." *PS: Political Science & Politics* 34 (2001): 85–92.

Wolfinger, Raymond E., and Steven J. Rosenstone. *Who Votes?* New Haven: Yale University Press, 1980.

Wong, Janelle S. "Mobilizing Asian American Voters: A Field Experiment." *The Science of Voter Mobilization*, edited by Donald P. Green and Alan S. Gerber, 102–14. *The Annals of the American Academy of Political and Social Science* 601 (2005).

Worgs, Donn. "Public Education and the Coproduction of Public Education." In *Public Engagement for Public Education: Joining Forces to Revitalize and Equalize Schools*, edited by Marion Orr and John Rogers, 89–116. Stanford, CA: Stanford University Press, 2011.

Yates, Miranda, and James Youniss. "Community Service and Political-Moral Identity in Adolescents." *Journal of Research on Adolescence* 6, no. 3 (1996): 271–84.

Yoder, Amy E. "Barriers to Ego Identity Status Formation: A Contextual Qualification of Marcia's Identity Status Paradigm." *Journal of Adolescence* 23, no. 1 (2000): 95–106.

Young, Darlene S., and Robert E. Baker, "Linking Classroom Theory to Professional Practice." *Journal of Physical Education Recreation and Dance* 75, no. 1 (2004): 22–30.

Youniss, James, and P. Levine, eds. *Engaging Young People in Civic Life*. Nashville, TN: Vanderbilt University Press, 2009.

Youniss, James, and Miranda Yates. *Community Service and Social Responsibility in Youth*. Chicago: University of Chicago Press, 1997.

Youniss, James, James McClellan, and Miranda Yates. "What We Know about Engendering Civic Identity." *American Behavioural Scientist* 40 (1997): 620–31.

Your Vote, Your Voice. "Your Vote, Your Voice." N.d. http://www.yourvoteyourvoice.org/index.php?colleges&elections/

Ziblatt, David. "High School Extracurricular Activities and Political Socialization." *Annals of the American Academy of Political and Social Science* 361 (1965): 20–31.

Zivi, Karen D. "Examining Pedagogy in the Service-Learning Classroom: Reflections on Integrating Service-Learning Into the Curriculum." In *Experiencing Citizenship: Concepts and Models for Service-Learning in Political Science*, edited by Richard M. Battistoni and William E. Hudson. Washington, DC: American Association for Higher Education, 1997.

Zlotkowski, Edward. "Pedagogy and Engagement." In *Colleges and Universities as Citizens*, edited by Robert G. Bringle, Richard Games, and Edward A. Malloy. Boston: Allyn and Bacon, 1999.

Zubizarreta, John, and Peter Seldin. *The Learning Portfolio: Reflective Practice for Improving Student Learning*. San Francisco: Jossey-Bass, 2004.

Zucker, Kiren Dosanjh, and Bruce Zucker. "Including Undergraduate Students in Service Learning Legal Clinics." *Guild Practitioner* 63, no. 2 (2006): 93–110.

Zukin, Cliff, Scott Keeter, Molly Andolina, Krista Jenkins, and Michael X. Delli Carpini. *A New Engagement: Political Participation, Civic Life, and the Changing American Citizen.* Oxford: Oxford University Press, 2006.

Zuniga, X., C. Vasques-Scalera, T. D. Sevig, and B. A. Nagda. "Exploring and Bridging Race/ethnic Differences: Developing Intergroup Diaglogue Competencies in a Co-learning Environment." Paper presented at the American Educational Research Association Meeting, Chicago, IL, 1997.

About the Authors

Mahalley D. Allen (PhD, University of Kansas) is associate professor of political science at California State University, Chico. Her research and teaching interests include judicial politics, constitutional law, and public policy. Allen has published articles in numerous journals, including *American Review of Politics, Harvard International Journal of Press and Politics, Policy Studies Journal, Political Research Quarterly*, and *State Politics and Policy Quarterly*.

Richard Battistoni (PhD, Rutgers University) is professor and chair of political science and professor of public and community service studies at Providence College. From 1994 to 2000, he served as the founding director of the Feinstein Institute for Public Service at Providence College, the first degree-granting program that combines community service with the curriculum. Battistoni also has developed and directed service-learning efforts at Rutgers and Baylor Universities. His extensive publications on civic engagement include *Education for Democracy* (with Benjamin Barber), *Civic Engagement Across the Curriculum: A Resource Book for Faculty in all Disciplines*, and *Experiencing Citizenship: Concepts and Models for Service Learning in Political Science* (with William Hudson).

Elizabeth Beaumont (PhD, Stanford University) is assistant professor of political science at the University of Minnesota, Twin Cities. Her research focuses on political theory, public law, and political socialization, particularly democratic theory and political engagement and constitutional theory and development. Beaumont was a research scholar at the Carnegie Foundation for the Advancement of Teaching, where she coauthored two books based upon her Carnegie research: *Educating for Democracy: Preparing Undergraduates for Responsible Political Engagement* and *Educating Citizens: Preparing America's Undergraduates for Lives of Moral and Civic Responsibility*. Her newest book, *The Civic Constitution* (Oxford University Press, forthcoming 2013) focuses on the role of civic ideals, discourses, and struggles during several crucial eras of constitutional formation and change.

Elizabeth A. Bennion (PhD, University of Wisconsin, Madison) is an award-winning professor in the Department of Political Science at Indiana University, South Bend. She teaches courses in American politics, with an emphasis on political behavior and engagement. Bennion's favorite research strategy is to use randomized field experiments to test the effectiveness of real-world interventions in promoting civic engagement. As campus director of the American Democracy Project, she organizes and moderates frequent candidate debates and issue forums, in addition to hosting a weekly live-televised political news show. She has presented and published numerous articles on civic engagement pedagogy.

Michael Brintnall (PhD, Massachusetts Institute of Technology) is executive director of the American Political Science Association. He formerly directed the National Association of Schools of Public Affairs and Administration and held several other positions, including vice president for academic affairs at Mount Vernon College and director of the Economic Development Program Evaluation Office at the US Department of Housing and Urban Development. Brintnall also held faculty appointments in political science at Brown University and Mount Vernon College. Research and public policy interests include urban public policy and development, nonprofit organizations and new models of public governance, and international roles of scholarly associations in civil society and development. He is a founding member of the InterAmerican Network for Public Administration Education.

Sivan Chaban (MA, University for Peace) graduated from Towson University's Honors College with a BA in international relations after completing a thesis paper on the involvement of the United Nations High Commissioner for Refugees with Kurdish refugees during the First Gulf War. Chaban also participated in the University for Peace's Model United Nations Conference, at which she won the award for Best Strategist on the Human Rights Council as the delegate of the Russian Federation. Her current research focuses on the ways in which international law and a human rights-based approach can effectively address and eventually prevent the AIDS crisis among displaced populations in Africa.

Anita Chadha (PhD, Auburn University) is associate professor at the University of Houston, Downtown. Her teaching interests include American government, political participation and democracy, public policy, public administration, and organizational theory. Chadha's research agenda focuses on the use of technology in the classroom, patterns of voting (overreporting of voting), legislative term limits, and the functions and workloads of state legislative fiscal offices. Her articles have appeared in *American Politics Quarterly*, *Journal of Public Affairs and Issues*, *Public Opinion Quarterly*, and *State and Local Government Review*.

Teodora C. DeLorenzo (JD, New College of California) is professor of political science at California State University, Chico. Her research and teaching interests include legal research and writing, clinical and internship experiences, and civil rights and liberties. In 2012, DeLorenzo coauthored "Civic Engagement in the Community: Undergraduate Clinical Legal Education," published in the *Journal of Political Science Education*.

Susan Dicklitch (PhD, University of Toronto) is professor of government, associate dean of the college, and director of the Ware Institute for Civic Engagement at Franklin & Marshall College in Lancaster, Pennsylvania. Her work focuses on human rights, political asylum, democratic transitions and civil society in Africa. Dicklitch has served as an expert witness in more than eighty political asylum cases in US Immigration Court. She is the author of *The Elusive Promise of NGOs in Africa: Lessons from Uganda*, and several scholarly articles on human rights and civic engagement pedagogy.

Paul E. Frank (PhD, Boston University) has spent much of his life engaged in politics. He served as an assistant to former presidential candidate Michael Dukakis and ran as a candidate in the 2004 election for Roseville City Council. Frank also has worked in the California State Assembly and Senate, on several local campaigns, and for a nonprofit health care organization as a government relations representative. He currently sits on several local boards and commissions. Frank has been teaching American government, international relations, and California politics at Sacramento City College since 1996.

Bobbi Gentry (PhD, City University of New York Graduate Center) is assistant professor and chair of political science at Millikin University, where she teaches courses in American politics, media and politics, and American politics and film. Research interests include youth participation in both the civic arena and elections and pedagogical questions about encouraging student engagement through writing. Gentry has presented her work at several conferences, including the APSA's Teaching and Learning Conference.

Jean Wahl Harris (PhD, State University of New York, Binghamton) currently serves as professor and chair of the Political Science Department and a faculty associate of the Women's Studies Program at the University of Scranton. Her research interests include women as political actors, the gendered effect of public policies, and civic engagement. Harris was the recipient of the University of Scranton's John L. Earl III award for service to the university, faculty, and community. She is coauthor of *American Democracy Now.*

Brian M. Harward (PhD, University of Georgia) is associate professor of political science and director of the Center for Political Participation at Allegheny College. He teaches constitutional law, judicial process, and philosophy of law, among other courses in American politics. Harward's research interests include campaigns and elections, poverty law, participation in the US Senate, congressional oversight, and executive power. Along with books and articles published about these subjects, including the forthcoming *Presidential Campaigns Decoded* (ABC-CLIO, 2013), Harward also has published several articles related to teaching and liberal education, including "The Disorienting Dilemma: The Senior Capstone as a Transformative Experience" in *Liberal Education.*

Shannon Jenkins (PhD, Loyola University, Chicago) is associate professor of political science at the University of Massachusetts, Dartmouth, specializing in US state politics, women and politics, and public policy. Her research focuses upon decision making in state legislatures, particularly the role of political organizations and gender in shaping outputs in these institutions, and the impact of specific pedagogical practices on student learning outcomes in political science courses. Jenkins's research has appeared in the *Journal of Political Science Education*, *Legislative Studies Quarterly*, *Political Research Quarterly*, *PS: Political Science & Politics*, *State Politics and Policy Quarterly*, and *Social Science Quarterly.*

Michelle Lorenzini (PhD, Washington University) is assistant professor of political science at Saint Louis University. Her research interests include the politics of financial development in East and Southeast Asia, trade dependence and the socialization of trade risk, and the scholarship of teaching and learning related to civic engagement. She teaches courses in international and comparative political economy. Lorenzini is director of the Atlas Program, which seeks to increase awareness of global issues to promote discussion and action.

Elizabeth Matto (PhD, George Washington University) is assistant research professor at the Eagleton Institute of Politics at Rutgers University and director of the Institute's Youth Political Participation Program (YPPP). She leads research as well as educational and public service efforts designed to celebrate and support the political learning of high school and college students and civic action among young adults—including those holding and running for office. Matto's current research project is "The Classroom-Kitchen Table Connection: The Effects of Political Discussion on Youth Knowledge and Efficacy."

Russell Mayer (PhD, University of Michigan) is associate professor of political science and vice provost at Merrimack College. His scholarship aims to understand the reasons why young people participate in politics and promote teaching pedagogies that foster greater civic engagement among students. Mayer's work also focuses on the methods of assessing the impact of these pedagogies. He has published several articles that consider alternative approaches to promoting civic engagement in such journals as the *Journal of Political Science Education*.

Alison Rios Millett McCartney (PhD, University of Virginia) is associate professor of political science at Towson University and former director of the International Studies program. Her research and teaching interests include German politics and foreign policy, Polish politics and foreign policy, the European Union, civic engagement, and the scholarship of teaching and learning. In addition to publishing several articles, her forthcoming book, *A New Germany in a New Europe*, will be published by Lexington Books. She has received several awards for her civic engagement work, including the Maryland-DC Campus Compact Service-Learning Scholarship Award and the University System of Maryland Regents Award for Mentoring.

Michael K. McDonald is a doctoral candidate in the Department of Government and Politics at the University of Maryland, College Park. His current research focuses on the impact of strengthening intellectual property rights on social outcomes in the developing world. Additional research and teaching interests include international political economy, American trade and foreign policy, international and economic development, international public health, and the scholarship of teaching and learning. McDonald presented papers on civic engagement and service-learning at the 2011 and 2012 APSA Teaching and Learning Conferences.

Mary McHugh (MA, Boston College) is director of the Stevens Service Learning Center and an adjunct faculty member in the Political Science Department at Merrimack College. She teaches a variety of classes on US politics and American political institutions. Research interests include examining how experiential learning affects and enhances students learning. McHugh is a regular presenter at the APSA Teaching and Learning Conference.

Patrick F. McKinlay (PhD, University of Notre Dame) is a professor in the Political Science Department at Morningside College. His teaching and research interests include European history, political thought, US politics, international relations, citizenship, and political economy. He has presented his work at the APSA Teaching and Learning Conference, in addition to other national and regional conferences.

Judithanne Scourfield McLauchlan (PhD, Rutgers University) is associate professor of political science and the founding director of the Center for Civic Engagement at the University of South Florida, St. Petersburg, where she teaches courses in American politics and public law. Her latest book, *Congressional Participation as Amicus Curiae before the US Supreme Court*, explores how members of Congress attempt to influence Supreme Court decision making in specific cases. She has worked for the US Supreme Court, the US Senate Judiciary Committee, the US Department of Justice, and the White House, in addition to managing statewide operations for several presidential campaigns. McLauchlan was awarded her university's highest teaching award, the Chancellor's Award for Excellence in Teaching, and was a Fulbright Scholar to Moldova in 2010 and 2012.

TIMOTHY MEINKE (PhD, University of Maryland, College Park) is currently chair of the Political Science and International Relations Departments at Lynchburg College and was a member of the committee that designed that college's civic engagement minor in 2005–2006. Research interests include welfare politics, promoting civic engagement among undergraduates, and using studies of genocide to understand evil and politics. He has presented papers on the relationship between power and policy at the American Political Science Association annual conferences and the 2008 Midwestern Political Science Association and is currently working on answering questions about politics during the US. Civil War. Meinke is a past chair of the APSA Teaching and Learning Conference.

DAVID W. NICKERSON (PhD, Yale University) is associate professor of political science at the University of Notre Dame. Nickerson's research uses experiments to study how organizations mobilize individuals to register, vote, volunteer, and donate. He has published numerous articles in journals such as *American Journal of Political Science*, *American Political Science Review*, *Political Research Quarterly*, and *Public Opinion Quarterly*. Nickerson was a post-doc research fellow at both Yale and Princeton Universities.

BETTY O'SHAUGHNESSY (PhD, University of Illinois, Chicago) is presently adjunct professor at the University of Illinois, Chicago and also teaches political science and US history at Loyola Academy. She is coauthor of *The Struggle for Power and Influence in Cities and States*, with Dick Simpson and James Nowlan

DIANA OWEN (PhD, University of Wisconsin, Madison) is associate professor of political science and director of American Studies at Georgetown University, where she also cofounded the Communication, Culture, and Technology graduate program. She is the author of *Media Messages in American Presidential Elections*, *New Media and American Politics* (with Richard Davis) and *American Government and Politics in the Information Age* (with David Paletz and Timothy Cook), and editor of *The Internet and Politics: Citizens, Voters, and Activists* (with Sarah Oates and Rachel Gibson) and *Making a Difference: The Internet and Elections in Comparative Perspective* (with Richard Davis, Stephen Ward, and David Taras). Her current research projects focus on the intersection of civic education and political engagement with digital media in American politics and elections.

SALLY A. PARKER (JD, University of Pacific, McGeorge School of Law) is assistant professor of political science at California State University, Chico. Her research and teaching interests include legal studies, administrative law, and civic engagement. Parker began teaching in 2006 after practicing as a civil litigation attorney focused on workers' rights.

ANTHONY PERRY (PhD, Wayne State University, Detroit) is associate dean of Social Science at Henry Ford Community College, where he also teaches political science. Perry introduced the Student Political Issues Convention to Henry Ford Community College in 2004. He developed and facilitated a similar student convention (previously known as the Urban Agenda) with the late Professor Otto Feinstein at Wayne State University. Perry is directing a newly created Democracy Institute at Henry Ford Community College to promote public service, political engagement, and political and public policy knowledge among college students and the greater community.

Arthur Sanders (PhD, Harvard University) is the Ellis and Nelle Levitt Distinguished Professor of Politics and associate provost for curriculum and assessment at Drake University, where he has been a member of the faculty since 1990. His research focuses on citizen politics in the United States, including examinations of public opinion, the impact of mass media, and campaign finance. In 2007, Sanders published his most recent book, *Losing Control: Presidential Elections and the Decline of Democracy.*

Mary Scheuer Senter (PhD, University of Michigan) is professor of sociology and director of the Center for Applied Research and Rural Studies (CARRS) at Central Michigan University. Through CARRS, she has been involved with more than 100 projects for community organizations, governmental units, and campus offices. Her current work focuses on diversity issues within higher education. She is a member of the American Sociological Association's Department Resource Group and is working with Roberta Spalter-Roth, director of the ASA's Department of Research and Development, on a longitudinal study of sociology majors graduating in 2012.

Daniel M. Shea (PhD, State University of New York, Albany) is professor of government and director of the Goldfarb Center for Public Affairs and Civic Engagement at Colby College. His research and teaching interests include campaigns and elections, civility in politics, the dynamics of the party system, the politics of media, and grassroots political activism. Shea has written numerous articles and authored or edited 19 books, including *Can We Talk? The Rise of Rude, Nasty, Stubborn Politics*, and *Let's Vote! The Essentials of the American Electoral Process* in 2012.

Dick Simpson (PhD, Indiana University) is professor at the University of Illinois, Chicago (UIC) and former head of the Department of Political Science. Simpson is a specialist in city politics, elections, African politics, and teaching political engagement. He is the author of numerous books and more than 100 professional journal articles, documentary films, and newspaper op-ed columns. Simpson has won many teaching awards, including the UIC Silver Circle and UIC Excellence in Teaching Award and was cochair of the committee that created the APSA Excellence in Teaching Award.

J. Cherie Strachan (PhD, University at Albany) is director of the Women and Gender Studies Program and professor of political science at Central Michigan University. She is the author of *High-Tech Grassroots: The Professionalization of Local Elections*, as well as numerous articles and book chapters. Her recent publications focus on the role of civility in a democratic society and college-level civic education interventions intended to enhance students' civic skills and identities. Strachan's applied research, which focuses on facilitating student-led deliberative discussions sessions and enhancing campus civil society, has resulted in an affiliation with the Kettering Foundation.

Dari E. Sylvester (PhD, Stony Brook University) is associate professor in the Department of Political Science and director of Research at the Jacoby Center for Public Service and Civic Leadership, University of the Pacific. Sylvester has earned numerous teaching-oriented awards, including the 2008 Hoefer Prize for Leadership in Experiential Learning for outstanding achievements in both teaching and scholarship and the 2010 American Political Science Association's Sosa-Riddell Award for the Mentoring of Undergraduate Latino/a Students. Her published works in the scholarship of teaching and learning include a 2010 article in the *Journal for Civic Commitment* and a chapter in the 2011 text *Democratic Dilemmas of Teaching Service-Learning: Curricular Strategies for Success* (edited by Christine M. Cress and David M. Donahue).

RENÉE BUKOVCHIK VANVECHTEN (PhD, University of California, Irvine) is associate professor at the University of Redlands. Van Vechten's research and teaching interests include American politics, with particular focus on legislative processes in California and at the national level, and the scholarship of teaching and learning. In 2008 she received the Rowman and Littlefield Award for Innovative Teaching in Political Science for a simulation she developed to teach congressional processes and the Innovative Teaching award at the University of Redlands. She is author of *California Politics: A Primer, 2nd Edition* and a forthcoming book published by CQ Press, *The Logic of California Politics.*

INDEX

Printed in the USA
CPSIA information can be obtained
at www.ICGtesting.com
LVHW080430230923
758653LV00013B/1560

9 781878 147400